DANIEL M. SMITH
University of Colorado

The American Diplomatic Experience

HOUGHTON MIFFLIN COMPANY • Boston
New York   Atlanta   Geneva, Ill.   Dallas   Palo Alto

Printed in the U.S.A.

Library of Congress Catalog Card Number: 73-175171

ISBN: 0-395-12569-3

Preface

My purpose in writing this history of American foreign relations was to embody essential facts and interpretations within a volume brief enough to permit classroom use of additional assigned readings. The number of excellent monographs and special studies available in relatively inexpensive paperback form is so large, and the possibilities for instructional use correspondingly so attractive, that a short general account seemed to meet a need. I have endeavored to strike a balance between the essential facts and the latest scholarly interpretations without hesitating to indicate my own personal views. The traditional introductory chapter on the machinery of diplomacy has been omitted, but this necessary information is incorporated into Chapter 2 and throughout the text. The Additional Readings at the end of each chapter are intended not as comprehensive bibliographies but as selective guides for further study. To a large extent they also serve as an acknowledgement of my indebtedness to the scholarly work of other historians.

Daniel M. Smith

Contents

The American Diplomatic Experience

Benjamin Franklin at the French court

1

THE DIPLOMACY
OF REVOLUTION

1. COLONIAL STRIFE AND FRENCH INTERESTS

American independence emerged from a major realignment of European power. French aid and ultimate alliance contributed significantly to the triumph of the patriot cause. Moreover, the Americans were able to take advantage of the general hostility and estrangement that Great Britain faced in the Old World.

The protracted Anglo-French duel for supremacy in North America provided the backdrop of the American Revolution. Between 1688 and 1763, France and England fought each other in four major wars: War of the League of Augsburg (1688–1697); War of the Spanish Succession (1701–1713); War of the Austrian Succession (1740–1748); and the Seven Years' War (1756–1763). Although the causes of these wars were usually confined to Europe, they inevitably affected the colonial world. Colonies became both the *tools* and the *stakes* in these conflicts. The colonial map of North America eventually was drastically altered by these great conflicts. By the Treaty of Utrecht in 1713, England gained Acadia (Nova Scotia), Newfoundland, and Hudson's Bay from France, and obtained title to Gibraltar from Spain. The Seven Years' War, hailed by English colonials such as Benjamin Franklin as a great national war for empire, virtually eliminated France from North America. In the Treaty of Paris in 1763, France ceded Canada and Louisiana east of the Mississippi River to Great Britain; Spain lost the Floridas, acquiring New Orleans and the remainder of Louisiana west of the Mississippi in compensation from her French ally. The British Empire seemed at the pinnacle of its wealth and power. Yet forces were already at work for its dissolution. The expulsion of France from North America not only embittered Anglo-French relations, it opened the road to the American Revolution by freeing the

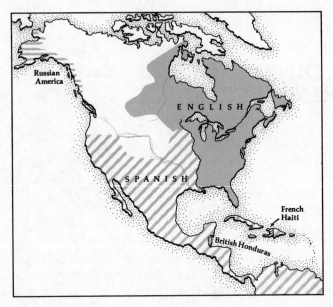

North America in 1763

English mainland colonies of the French menace along their borders. After 1763, English colonists felt less constrained than before to press issues of local self-government and of taxation, even to the point of an open rupture with the British crown.

After the peace of 1763, French leaders felt deeply humiliated by British victories and British arrogance and longed for France's erstwhile pre-eminency on the continent. British diplomats reflected their nation's newly won status by insisting upon precedence at foreign courts, adding to French woes. It was not surprising, therefore, that many Frenchmen plotted another war of revenge and redress against hated Britain. The Duc de Choiseul, the French Foreign Minister, began military and diplomatic preparations even as the Seven Years' War was drawing to an end.

Fully aware of the dangers of another round with the British, Choiseul observed hopefully the unrest in the English colonies on the mainland of North America. The colonial disputes with the British government seemed to offer a promising prospect of diverting Great Britain's attention from Europe and thereby weakening her power. The situation also presented the possibility of a golden opportunity for France to strike directly at the British. As Choiseul wrote his royal master, Louis XV:

England is the declared enemy of your power . . . and she will be so always. Many ages must elapse before a durable peace can be established with this state, which looks forward to the supremacy in the four quarters of the globe. Only the revolution which will some day occur in America . . . will put England back to the state of weakness in which Europe will have no more to fear of her.

Choiseul feared that, unless checked, the British empire would expand to embrace all of western North America and would menace Spain's position in the Caribbean and in South America. In an effort to prevent this he strengthened the French Family Compact alliance with Spain and dispatched a naval officer to North America to survey the situation at first hand.

Meanwhile, the London authorities belatedly tightened the colonial machinery. They enacted new measures to prevent the lack of colonial support in the recent war from recurring, to regulate western settlement and avoid arousing Indian outbreaks, and to provide for the defense of North America. The Proclamation Line of 1763 barred settlers from moving westward across the Appalachians, trying to divert them to Canada or to Florida. Objections by colonial and English land specu- lators, however, doomed that policy. In addition, the Quebec Act of 1774 incorporated the trans-Appalachian area into predominantly Catholic Canada, providing a new grievance to the mainland colonies, which were overwhelmingly Protestant. The Stamp Tax, levied in 1766 to raise some of the revenue to cover defensive and administrative costs, aroused enough colonial resistance to force its repeal. The British rekindled colonial discontent soon thereafter by passing the Townshend Duty Act of 1767. Agitation and economic boycotts against British goods and merchants obtained its repeal by 1770. During these recurrent crises— which the colonials saw as involving local self-government—colonial unity and a nascent sense of nationalism began to be forged. The Tea Act of 1773, followed by renewed colonial resistance and "tea parties," and the so-called Intolerable Acts of Parliament in 1774, culminated in the calling of the First Continental Congress and the beginning of armed resistance at Lexington and Concord in 1775.

In Versailles caution ruled as the colonial crisis unfolded. Hopes for revenge mingled with fears of arousing British hostility or adverse colonial reactions to French intermeddling. Besides, each colonial crisis seemed to approach the point of open warfare and then subside after further British retreats and concessions. Choiseul lost office in 1770, partly because his cautious sovereign feared his aggressive schemes against Britain. In 1774, when Louis XVI came to the throne, the Count de Vergennes took charge of French foreign affairs. Although actually indecisive and sometimes rash, Vergennes was widely regarded as the epitome of a successful diplomat, supposedly energetic, icily reserved, and unimpulsive. He resolved to preserve the Family Compact with Spain, to retain Austria as an ally, and to seek an eventual war with England but only at the most opportune time. The outbreak of armed clashes between Britain and her American colonies in 1775 seemed to bring that moment nearer.

On September 10, 1775, the Continental Congress created a nine-member Secret Committee of Correspondence charged with "corresponding with our friends in Great Britain, Ireland and other parts of the world." Headed by Benjamin Franklin, the committee sought to obtain arms and munitions from abroad for the patriot armies. Achard de Bonvouloir, a French secret agent sent to America in the disguise of a merchant from Antwerp, contacted Franklin and other members of the Committee through a bookseller in Philadelphia. The Committee members convinced the agent of patriot determination to continue the struggle against England. Bonvouloir reported to Vergennes that the rebel leaders soon would assert American independence.

Should France aid the patriots? The French Ambassador in London advised that the hour of France's great opportunity had come. So, too, did that swashbuckler and adventurer, Caron de Beaumarchais. Beaumarchais had acquired fame first as a watchmaker, designing one so small that it could be worn as a ring by Madame de Pompadour, royal mistress of Louis XV, and then as a successful playwright (*Barber of Seville,* among other plays). In London on a secret mission to recover some stolen documents, Beaumarchais met Arthur Lee, a colonial agent for Massachusetts, and was readily persuaded that the war in America offered France the long-sought opportunity for revenge and redress. In close contact with Vergennes, Beaumarchais urged that the rebels be given secret aid to stir trouble but to avoid a premature break with Britain. Other influential Frenchmen also were advocating a similar course.

Vergennes at last concluded the time had come to act. He was convinced the war would continue for some time, but felt that French unpreparedness and the lack of rebel military success precluded more than secret military aid. Finally, Vergennes concluded that an independent America would be no threat to France, since the new nation would probably be exhausted by the war and, moreover, might well consist of several separate republics. He summed up the advantage to France of American independence:

First, it will diminish the power of England, and increase in proportion that of France. Second, it will cause irreparable loss to English trade, while it will considerably extend ours. Third, it presents to us as very probable the recovery of a part of the possessions which the English have taken from us in America, such as the fisheries of Newfoundland. . . . We do not speak of Canada.

To have mentioned Canada, of course, might well have reduced colonial ardor by reviving the old fear of France. Louis XVI reluctantly capitulated to his minister's advice and agreed to expend one million livres in a program of secret military aid. Spain provided similar funds, and military supplies were soon being funneled to the Americans through Beaumarchais' "private company," Roderigue Hortalés et Cie.

The momentous decision to provide secret aid was made nearly two months before the Americans formally proclaimed their independence in July, 1776, and before Silas Deane of Connecticut, agent for the Secret Committee of Correspondence, had arrived in France to seek aid. Deane came disguised as a French-speaking merchant and he utilized secret ink in his correspondence, but his ruse did not long prevent British agents from ascertaining his mission. Deane signed a contract with Beaumarchais, and vital military supplies soon were flowing to America. Approximately 90 percent of the munitions used by the Americans during the next two years came from this source. Although French interest in the American Revolution in part reflected the sympathies of French liberals in the Age of Enlightenment, the primary motive of the French crown obviously was national self-interest.

2. RECOGNITION AND ALLIANCE

On July 2, 1776, the Continental Congress declared American independence and two days later approved the Declaration of Independence. That step reflected both the tendency of the revolution to evolve beyond a mere redress of grievances and an awareness of the need for foreign sympathy and aid. A special committee was appointed to frame a model treaty for the establishment of diplomatic and commercial relations with other states. The "Plan of 1776" or model treaty was largely the work of John Adams. It provided for treaties of amity and commerce, and incorporated liberal concepts of neutral rights, based on the assumption that the new nation, an exporter of foodstuffs and raw materials, would normally be neutral during Europe's wars and therefore would benefit from an international system designed to protect commerce from belligerent interferences. There were three principal provisions: "free ships, free goods" or the immunity from seizure of nonmilitary goods, even enemy owned, when carried under a neutral flag; a narrow definition of contraband goods subject to belligerent seizure (foodstuffs and naval stores were excluded); and the right of a neutral to trade with the belligerents.

The Congress discussed but rejected a formal military alliance with France. Such a connection with one of the most powerful European states would involve obvious dangers to a weak and newly established United States. Moreover, reflecting widespread mercantilist concepts, Congress believed that to deprive England of America's commerce and shift it to France would be enough of an inducement for French recognition. Congress instructed its representatives merely to promise if recognition of the American republic should involve France in war with

Britain, the United States would refrain from aiding France's enemies and would promise not to conclude a separate peace without six months' advance notice. Neither territorial concessions nor military cooperation were provided. A series of military reverses in America and the urgent advice of Franklin were ultimately necessary to convince Congress that a higher price would have to be paid for French entry into the war.

Benjamin Franklin and Arthur Lee joined Silas Deane on the American mission in Europe. Franklin overshadowed his inexperienced colleagues; then seventy years of age, he had had many years of quasi-diplomatic experience as a colonial agent in London. Moreover his publishing enterprises and his scientific inventions and writings had brought him worldwide fame as a philosopher of the Age of Enlightenment. Witty and charming, suave and tactful, this Republican savant was welcomed into the salons of the French intelligentsia and aristocracy. Acutely aware of the force of public opinion, Franklin appeared in the simple attire of an American, and he carefully cultivated the French court. An astute propagandist, Franklin also concocted fake Indian atrocities and other alleged news stories designed to embarrass the British cause at home and abroad. Attesting to his fame and his skills, the British government was deeply disturbed by his arrival in France. Anxious not to provoke a premature showdown, however, London officially ignored Franklin's mission and in other ways overlooked or minimized French secret aid and collaboration with the rebels.

Even Franklin's diplomacy could not obtain diplomatic recognition while the war news from America was so discouraging. An attempt to invade Canada failed, and patriot arms suffered a series of defeats in 1776 and 1777. In 1777, the British launched an offensive designed to crush the rebellion by cutting the United States in two. In a pincers movement, Sir William Howe's large New York-based force was to march up the Hudson River to Albany and there meet the army of General John Burgoyne, "Gentleman Johnny," which was to drive down from Canada. Instead, Howe turned south to capture the rebel capital at Philadelphia, leaving Burgoyne to meet disaster at the Battle of Saratoga. Surrounded by the newly reinforced and invigorated Americans, Burgoyne surrendered his entire army on October 17, 1777.

Saratoga has been viewed as one of the most decisive battles of the war in terms of psychological and diplomatic effects. While perhaps an exaggerated interpretation—Britain after all was not ruined militarily by the reverse, and France already was so deeply involved in the American cause that disentanglement would have been most difficult—the victory at Saratoga enormously enheartened the patriots and dramatically revealed to Europe that the rebels could defeat a veteran British army in the field. The Lord North ministry in London recognized its significance and tried to end the war by conciliation before France became openly involved. While a mission was sent to America to offer restoration of local autonomy, a return to the status quo of 1763, a secret agent, Paul Wentworth, was dispatched to Paris to promise Franklin and Deane generous treatment if the Americans would abandon independence and return to the empire.

Franklin made no attempt to conceal Wentworth's overtures. Instead, he skillfully played upon French fears that the breach between colonies and mother country might be speedily healed, leaving France to face a reunited and ill-disposed British empire. Despite the reluctance on the part of his Spanish ally to act, Vergennes, in late 1777, promised diplomatic recognition if the Americans would continue to resist the British. After weeks of close negotiations, on February 6, 1778, France signed two epochal treaties with the United States. The first, a Treaty of Amity and Commerce, recognized American independence and placed commerce on a most-favored-nation basis, meaning that any trade concessions made by one signatory to another state would automatically be extended to the other signatory. The second, a secret Treaty of Alliance, provided that: in case France became involved in war with England, the United States and France would fight until American independence had been assured; neither power, without the consent of the other, would make a separate peace with the common enemy; and each guaranteed forever the possessions of the other in the Americas. To prevent a revival of former fears of the "French menace" in America, France renounced claims to Canada and Louisiana, and acknowledged the right of the United States to conquer and annex those areas if she saw fit.

The Continental Congress quickly approved the French treaties in early May, 1778, after only two days of debate. Both sides probably fully understood the implications of the mutual territorial guarantee "forever." The French government obviously intended to keep the new nation permanently and closely attached to France. On this side, the treaties greatly stimulated the expansionist hopes of the Americans (Canada, Florida, and the West Indies beckoned), and French aid was expected in helping to expel Britain from the Western Hemisphere. American patriots responded enthusiastically when France formally entered the war against Great Britain. France's magnanimity and generosity were widely praised, especially since she had demanded neither territory nor commercial concessions as the price of recognition and alliance. The old Francophobia perhaps did not entirely disappear, but a new era of friendship and cooperation seemed at hand.

3. BRITAIN FACES A HOSTILE EUROPE

Spain reacted ambivalently to the American Revolution. It shared with its French ally the view that the revolt would weaken haughty Britain and ought to be encouraged. Yet, while thirsting for revenge, the Spanish government had no love for republicanism and feared the example of colonial rebellion might spread to Spanish America. In addition, Spain was afraid independent English colonies might be more aggressive and expansionist once freed of restraints from the mother country. Still, if Spain were to have an opportunity for revenge and the recovery of lost territory, the American rebellion could not be allowed to subside too soon. Therefore, the Spanish government had joined France in providing some secret military aid to the rebels, at first through Beaumarchais' firm and later through Gardoqui and Company. But Spain was most unenthusiastic about recognizing American independence and resisted Vergennes' entreaties for joint action after the news of Saratoga.

The Count de Floridablanca, Foreign Minister for Charles III, professed to be hurt when France acted without Spain in recognizing the Americans. In addition to disliking rebels and fearing their example, Floridablanca was aware of British strength. He ignored, therefore, advice from his Ambassador in Paris, the Count de Aranda, that it would be to Spain's advantage to recognize the American Republic and to negotiate a favorable boundary settlement with it while the war was still under way. Yet Spain wanted to recover Florida from Britain and above all Gibraltar, which it had lost in 1704. Floridablanca eagerly maneuvered to persuade or coerce Great Britain into paying a steep price for continued Spanish neutrality. As he wrote, "They [the English] must know that what we do not get by negotiation we know how to get with a club." But the club was not that frightening; the British government, despite its desire to keep Spain out of the war, was unwilling to yield Gibraltar.

Despairing of success through negotiations, Spain prepared to enter the war. Early in 1779, she presented an ultimatum proposing Spanish mediation of the dispute and in effect conceding de facto recognition to the Americans, but with boundaries based upon the existing war map *(uti possedetus)* that would have left large areas of the United States in British hands. Even before London could reject the offer, Spain had signed the secret Treaty of Aranjuez with France on April 12, 1779. Under its terms Spain would enter the war in alliance with France if Britain rejected mediation, and, thereafter, they both would fight until Spain recovered Gibraltar. At Spain's insistence the treaty made no reference to American independence. In her eagerness to bring Spain into the conflict, France had made concessions that were inconsistent with the terms and spirit of its alliance with the United States. In 1778 France and America had pledged to make joint war until the independence of the United States was secured, yet Aranjuez not only failed to make any reference to that goal but pledged France—and therefore in effect the United States, without its knowledge or consent—to wage war until Spain had regained Gibraltar. When the implications became clear later on, the Americans learned an early lesson about the entangling possibilities of European alliances. Nevertheless, by June of 1779 Spain was at war with Great Britain.

Overjoyed at so promising a development and confident that the Spanish government was prepared to recognize the United States and to extend military aid, the Continental Congress sent John Jay to Spain to negotiate the desired arrangements. Despite Jay's talents, it was a mission of futility. A descendant of an old and wealthy New York family of French-Dutch origins, Jay had been educated at King's College (later renamed Columbia) and had acquired some diplomatic experience as secretary to a royal boundary commission named to settle a dispute between the colonies of New York and New Jersey. Accompanied by his attractive and ambitious wife, Jay journeyed to Spain and there sought the peripatetic court of Charles III (almost constantly on the move due to the King's passion for hunting). After surviving rough roads, flea-bitten inns, and gouging landlords on his way inland, Jay arrived at the court to discover that Floridablanca was not very interested in negotiations. The Spanish government saw little reason to extend aid to the upstart republic and was most reluctant to recognize it until Great Britain should do the same. In fact, Spain still hoped to blackmail England into concessions and even then was involved in secret diplomacy with London. Thus, the American envoy was not officially received. Jay was further embarrassed by debts coming due, incurred by an overeager Congress in anticipation of funds it confidently expected Spain to provide. Except for a small loan to cover those drafts, Jay could obtain nothing from Floridablanca. Not even the offer of a favorable boundary settlement, waiving American claims to navigate the Mississippi River, could move the Spanish court. Jay finally left for Paris in disgust. There he learned that Spain desired to remove the United States from the Mississippi line and that France would support Spanish aims when and if Spain should recognize the American republic. Although Spain proved a grievous disappointment to the Americans, her war with Britain was of some benefit in isolating that power.

And British isolation in the war was becoming a serious factor, but not because the European countries had any great liking for rebels and republics. Except for France, the rest of Europe waited for Great Britain to recognize the United States before they would make any move in that direction. European liberals were sympathetic to the American cause, but they were few in number and had little influence upon their governments. Most of the European states were monarchical and were repelled by the thought of abetting revolutionaries anywhere. Yet British power and British arrogance had stored up a residue of ill will on the continent. Moreover, the efforts of the Royal Navy to interfere with neutral commerce involving France and America threatened the trade of a number of European states. France and the Americans had developed an extensive commerce in arms and naval stores with the Dutch. British attempts to suppress that traffic led to clashes and ultimately, by 1780, to an Anglo-Netherlands war. Even so, it was not until 1782 that the Netherlands recognized the United States and signed a treaty of amity and commerce.

British interferences with neutral trade aroused growing resentment on the continent. Frederick the Great of Prussia had observed England's mounting troubles with great interest, but had preserved a careful neutrality. His refusal to permit Britain to employ Prussian mercenaries, however, caused the Americans to misread his purposes as sympathetic to their cause. Similarly they also misinterpreted the actions of Catherine the Great of Russia, who in 1780 organized a so-called League of Armed Neutrality, composed of Russia, Prussia, Denmark-Norway, Sweden, and three other powers, to oppose British highhandedness on the seas. The Empress Catherine certainly had no fondness for the Americans, and the armed league—an "armed nullity" in her own words—was simply intended to protect Russian commercial interests and to win prestige for herself as a mediator in the war. An overjoyed Congress sent Francis Dana to Russia to seek recognition and to offer to join the armed league, but he could make no progress at all. In fact, Russia did not recognize the United States until 1809, a failure that indicated not hostility but remoteness and indifference.

4. A GENEROUS PEACE

By 1781, Britain stood alone against a hostile world. A war to suppress rebellious colonies had spread to include France, Spain, and the Netherlands, while a League of Armed Neutrals increased England's isolation. Ill tidings from the battlefields of America were to complete her sense of dangerous encirclement.

In 1779, responding to peace moves under way in Europe, Congress appointed John Adams as truce negotiator and drafted instructions for his guidance. He was to ask Britain to recognize fully American independence and to grant generous boundaries along the Great Lakes, the Mississippi, and the 31st parallel. The highly desirable category included fishing rights off Newfoundland, the cession of Canada, a commercial treaty, and war damages. Europe seethed with talk of peace as Austria and Russia sought prestige as peacemakers and Spain continued to maneuver for Gibraltar. These European schemes would have proved unfortunate for the United States, since they called for a settlement based on the existing war map. Even within the French government, opposition mounted against continuation of the war. The Finance Minister, Jacques Necker, urged peace as imperative in view of the depressed state of French finances. Fortunately for Vergennes, still intent on victory, and for the United States, George III adamantly spurned any talk of peace that would concede any form of American independence or that would allow foreigners to meddle in an internal British problem.

Nevertheless, Vergennes could not be certain that a half-loaf settlement might not become necessary. To prepare the Americans for less than they hoped, and to free himself of Adams whom he disliked, the French minister intimated to Congress that it would be wise to recall Adams and to draw up new peace terms, or to leave the problem to him alone if necessary. Adams, an able patriot lawyer from Massachusetts, was a proud and often tactless diplomat who spoke openly not of French generosity to America but of America's advantages to France. Franklin once remarked of Adams that he was an honest and often a great man, but that sometimes he was "positively mad." (In turn, Franklin's colleagues often unfairly criticized him for blandness and love of ease.) Already rather open attempts to influence American politics had undermined the position of Conrad Alexandre Gerard, France's first minister to the United States, and had split Congress into Gallic and anti-Gallic factions. Gerard's successor, the Chevalier de la Luzerne, was more tactful but he too used social influence, propaganda, and even bribery to create a pro-French group in the Congress subservient to French influence and French diplomatic aims. What France sought was a relatively weak United States closely tied to French policy. For that reason, and also because of ties with Spain, French diplomats discouraged American schemes for Canada and territorial claims along the Mississippi. Congress, however, did not recall Adams but enlarged the peace commission to five—Adams, Franklin, Jay, Henry Laurens of South Carolina (captured by the British), and Thomas Jefferson (who never arrived). The commissioners were instructed to take no action without the knowledge and concurrence of the French government.

Suddenly the diplomatic scene rapidly improved for the American cause. A combined army of American and French troops, aided by a French fleet commanded by Admiral François de Grasse, laid siege to the army of Lord Cornwallis at Yorktown and compelled its surrender on October 19, 1781. The surrender was decisive not in a military but in a psychological sense. Lord North reportedly staggered upon receipt of the news and exclaimed, "Oh God! It is all over!" Even the stubborn George III, who dreaded being recorded as the first modern British monarch to end his reign with less territory than when he had begun, gradually came to see that the war must be ended. Britain seemed encircled by enemies, the public debt was mounting, taxes were rising, and a growing mood of war weariness gripped the people. Early in 1782 the North ministry fell, replaced by one under Lord Rockingham. The new ministry was committed to a restoration of peace, but divided over whether to grant independence or to try to repair the empire.

Lord Shelburne, the minister responsible for colonies, sent a wealthy

Scottish merchant, Richard Oswald, to open talks with the Americans in Paris. Franklin informed Oswald that independence with generous boundaries would be necessary. In the advisable category, he included indemnities, free trade, and the cession of Canada. The wily old statesman hinted that Canada in British hands would compel the United States to retain firmly its alliance with France, while Canada's cession presumably would weaken those ties.

Shelburne was soon reconciled to granting independence but wanted to hold off extending recognition until after a treaty had been negotiated. Jay, who had joined Franklin as the negotiations began and in effect took charge due to the latter's gout, at first insisted upon prior recognition of independence. He soon became justifiably suspicious that Vergennes was delaying negotiations pending the outcome of an attempt to capture Gibraltar. Moreover, he was alarmed at indications that the devious Frenchman, via secret contacts in London, was trying to protect Spain's interests by restricting American boundaries along the Appalachians. Jay decided to abandon his insistence on prior recognition and to enter secretly into direct negotiations with the British. Adams, joining Jay in the exchanges, thoroughly agreed with the latter's suspicions; Franklin acquiesced after some protestation. Congress's injunction to work in close harmony with Vergennes was thus pushed aside, and a preliminary treaty of peace with Great Britain was signed on November 30, 1782.

The peace terms Britain granted on the whole were most generous. Undoubtedly British leaders hoped to drive a wedge into the Franco-American alliance, as well as to heal the wounds of the war. They recognized the independence of the United States and fixed its boundaries along the line of the St. Lawrence–Great Lakes system, the Mississippi River, and the 31st parallel to the south (a secret article placed the southern boundary at the 32°28″ line if Britain retained the Floridas). These were notable concessions, since the United States had not conquered the southwestern territory and only controlled part of the northwest. Both powers were to enjoy navigation of the Mississippi from its source to its outlet. American citizens were granted the "liberty" to fish off Newfoundland and Canada. The greatest difficulties were encountered over payment of prewar colonial debts to British creditors, and over treatment of the Loyalists in America who had supported the cause of the crown. Passions ran high against the Loyalists, thousands of whom had fled during the war, and the American negotiators were extremely reluctant to concede their return and their recovery of confiscated property. Finally it was agreed that British creditors should meet "no lawful impediment" in recovering their debts, and that persecutions of the Loyalists should cease while Congress would recommend to the states the restoration of their property.

The United States in 1783

The preliminary peace did not go into effect until definitive treaties were signed between Britain and her other opponents on September 3, 1783. Technically, the United States had not violated the provision of the Franco-American alliance against a separate peace, although the spirit obviously had been strained. Vergennes displayed some resentment at the actions of his ally and shock at British generosity. The English, he remarked, "buy the peace more than they make it." He apparently feared that both French and Spanish diplomacy had been weakened. Franklin handled his vexation skillfully, cautioning Vergennes that Britain must not know the alliance had been disturbed. Franklin even obtained more funds from the straitened French treasury. Vergennes no doubt soon perceived the utility of the separate Anglo-American peace in persuading Spain to accept an end to the war without the recovery of Gibraltar.

For all the costs of the war, France gained little beyond prestige. Additional gains in terms of enduring Franco-American ties might have resulted, had it not been for Vergennes' devious diplomacy, for after all France generously had given the Americans nearly $2 million and had loaned them over $6 million. Spain, too, gained little, recovering the Floridas but facing a dynamic new nation along the Mississippi. Although many in Great Britain had predicted loss of the mainland colonies would doom the empire and would end British wealth and prosperity, in fact Britain was to learn some lessons from the revolution and was soon to build an even larger empire. The United States was the main beneficiary of this world war. It obtained its independence and acquired a domain into which to grow, its future expansion blocked only by a weak and declining Spanish power to the south and to the west.

Additional Reading

Excellent accounts of the colonial background of the Revolutionary War are by Max Savelle, *The Origins of American Diplomacy: The International History of Anglo-America, 1492–1763* (1967) and Richard W. Van Alstyne, *The Rising American Empire* (1960). For the diplomacy of the Revolution, see Van Alstyne, *Empire and Independence: The International History of the American Revolution* (1965). *The Peacemakers: The Great Powers and American Independence* (1965) by Richard B. Morris is particularly revealing about the intrigue and chicanery American representatives faced upon their baptism in Old World diplomacy. Also useful is *The Age of the Democratic Revolution: A Political History of Europe and America, 1760–1800* (1959) by R. R. Palmer. William C. Stinchcombe, *The American Revolution and the French Alliance* (1969) probes the implementation of the alliance and its effect upon American thought and politics. In *To The Farewell Address: Ideas of Early American Foreign Policy* (1961) Felix Gilbert analyzes the impact of European thought and politics upon American attitudes and policies during and after the Revolution. These studies largely supplant the older accounts by Samuel Flagg Bemis, *The Diplomacy of the American Revolution* (1935) and E. S. Corwin, *French Policy and the American Alliance of 1778* (1916). Several excellent studies exist on the principal American diplomats and peace negotiators: Gerald Stourzh, *Benjamin Franklin and American Foreign Policy* (1954); and the older biography by Carl Van Doren, *Benjamin Franklin* (1938); Page Smith, *John Adams* (1962), Vol. I and Gilbert Chinard, *Honest John Adams* (1933); and Frank Monaghan, *John Jay* (1935) and Richard B. Morris, *John Jay, the Nation and the Court* (1967). Isabel de Madariaga, *Britain, Russia, and the Armed Neutrality of 1780* (1962) and M. L. Brown, Jr., ed., *American Independence through Prussian Eyes* (1959) examine these aspects of the war. On the western territories see P. C. Phillips, *The West in the Diplomacy of the American Revolution* (1913); T. P. Abernathy, *Western Lands and the American Revolution* (1937); and N. V. Russell, *The British Regime in Michigan and the Old Northwest, 1760–1796* (1939).

John Jay

2

REDEEMING THE
NATIONAL PATRIMONY,
1783–1795

1. THE TRIALS OF INDEPENDENCE

The United States under the Articles of Confederation (1781), a loose union of 13 self-willed states, faced seemingly insuperable difficulties in commanding respect abroad and allegiance at home. Lacking adequate revenue and military forces, unable to enforce its will at home or abroad, the Confederation government was regarded in Europe with a mixture of hostility and contempt. John Adams, sent to England as minister in 1785, was coldly received by the British authorities and found himself unable, during his three-year stay, to engage in any serious negotiations. Contemptuously, Britain refused to name a minister to the United States. In disgust, Adams finally abandoned his post in 1788; not until 1791 did the British at last send a diplomatic representative to America.

It was too much to expect, therefore, that during these years any progress could be made at persuading Great Britain to evacuate American territory along the northern frontier or to negotiate a satisfactory commercial arrangement. Spain proved hardly more cooperative in regard to the adjustment of similar issues, and even relations with France were disturbed by the inability of the bankrupt Confederation Congress to begin repayment of the wartime debt of 35,000,000 livres. Thomas Jefferson, successor to Franklin as minister to France, noted that the American diplomats in Europe were the lowest and most obscure members of the diplomatic tribe, an excellent school in humility for the representatives of the upstart republic. As John Adams observed from London, "They [the European powers] will be pleased to see us weakened, and our growth a little retarded. It behooves the United

States, then, to knit themselves together in the bonds of affection and mutual confidence. . . ."

In all probability the fledgling United States would have experienced great difficulty in international relations whatever its form of government. America was simply too weak to obtain satisfactory settlements from the great European powers; success was not to be scored until the vicissitudes of Old World politics were to offer golden opportunities to astute American diplomats. Even so, the obvious weaknesses of the Confederation surely contributed to the problems of diplomacy. Lacking taxing power, the Confederation Congress had to rely for revenue either upon borrowing or upon requisitions to the states, which often failed to comply; it could not regulate commerce, nor could it draft troops; and it lacked courts in which to enforce its will. Its inability to protect and encourage commerce abroad was one of the principal reasons for the call for a stronger form of government in the mid-1780's. The new frame of government established under the Federal Constitution, devised in 1787 and inaugurated in 1789, greatly enlarged the executive and legislative powers of the central government and gave it new tools with which to conduct foreign relations.

Under the new federal charter, still in effect today, the national government was given exclusive authority over foreign relations. The states of the union retained no independent role, although in fact they sometimes might exercise local powers in ways that could affect foreign affairs. Although the foreign relations power was divided between the President and Congress, such imposing powers were entrusted to the chief executive that he obviously gained the initiative in shaping and administering foreign policy. The new Constitution gave the President control over the treaty-making process, although it stipulated that the finished product had to be sent to the Senate for approval by a two-thirds majority; it made him commander-in-chief of the armed forces and chief executive officer of the nation, sworn to uphold the laws of the land and to protect the national interest; it vested in him alone the power to receive foreign ministers, thus giving him control over the recognition process and making him the only official channel for diplomatic communications; and by virtue of his position and his constitutional duty to report on the state of the union, the President gained the initiative in the formulation of new policies. Use of executive agreements, although not binding upon subsequent administrations, have freed chief executives to a large degree from the necessity of submitting treaties to the Senate, as has the use of executive agents and informal emissaries abroad. Powers vested in the Senate included approving treaties and presidential appointments, and sharing with the House of Representatives control over appropriations, general legislation, the war-declaring power, and the impeachment process. Both houses also in effect were given the right to launch investigations or to adopt legally nonbinding resolutions. Thus, although the executive took control of an imposing set of powers over foreign relations, Congress retained sufficient authority to harass the President or even to create a virtual deadlock between the two branches of government, as acrimonious debates over the Versailles Treaty in 1919–1920 and Southeast Asian policy in the 1960's and 1970's have revealed.

2. BOUNDARIES AND TRADE

Both the United States and Great Britain failed to live up to the terms of the 1783 peace; the violations of the former primarily reflected the weaknesses of its central government, while those of the latter resulted from a more deliberate policy. The treaty had specified creditors should encounter no lawful impediments in recovering prewar debts, yet during and after the Revolutionary War a number of American state governments enacted measures confiscating debts to English creditors and blocking their legal recovery. Maryland and Virginia, for example, prohibited use of their courts for such purposes, and other states required British creditors to post bond covering counterclaims before they could sue for payment. The Confederation Congress, unable to do more than recommend to the states observance of the treaty, could not compel compliance. The peace treaty also declared that there should be no further prosecutions or confiscations of the property of individuals who had remained loyal to the Crown during the Revolutionary War; that Congress should recommend to the states the restitution of property confiscated from those Loyalists who had not borne arms; and that exiles should be permitted to return and try to regain their possessions. There had been extensive wartime property seizures, and an estimated 100,000 Loyalists had fled from the country. Congress made the recommendations as agreed but to little avail. Returning Loyalists met serious resistance in their efforts and some even encountered prosecution or physical violence.

Great Britain was in no way blameless either. Contrary to treaty provisions, British troops carried away slaves and other property when they evacuated such cities as New York. Far more serious, however, was the issue of the Northwest posts. The British peace negotiators had failed to appreciate the importance of the northwest territory—especially posts along the Great Lakes–St. Lawrence River system—to the Indian tribes in the area which professed loyalty to the Crown and to the fur trading interests operating in the region. A sudden withdrawal might enrage the Indians, to the harm of British Canada, and might be costly to the fur traders. Therefore, despite the treaty requirement for evacuation with all due speed, on April 8, 1784, the day before the 1783 peace was formally ratified, the British government secretly ordered continued occupation of seven posts on American soil—Dutchman's Point and Point-au-Fer on

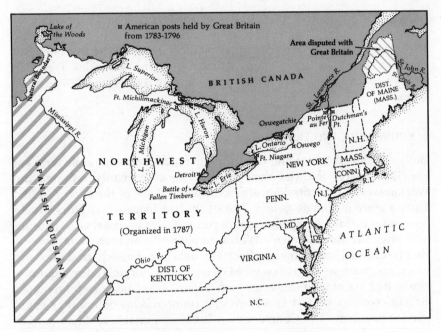

The Northeastern Boundary of the United States, 1783–1794

Lake Champlain; Oswegatchie on the St. Lawrence River; Oswego on Lake Ontario; Niagara, Detroit, and Michilimackinac, which dominated the portages between the other lakes. For 12 years after the signing of the peace treaty the British flag flew over American territory and British officials controlled American commerce on the Great Lakes. At first the British merely meant to delay evacuation until their fur traders and Indian officials could adjust to the situation, but they soon made a deliberate decision to remain in order to exploit American weaknesses and the confidently anticipated disintegration of the Union. Thus, American violations of the treaty merely provided an excuse for Britain's noncompliance. While retaining the posts, British authorities hoped to repair the mistake of 1783 by creating an Indian buffer state in the Northwest.

The result was mounting American dissatisfaction. In addition to the issue of the posts, Americans had good reason to suspect British officials were supplying arms to the Indians living in the northwest territory and were encouraging them to resist American authority and the influx of pioneer settlers. Armed with British weapons, these Indians repulsed a punitive expedition led by General Josiah Harmar in 1790, and the following year almost annihilated a large force commanded by Arthur St. Clair. The Indians and their English patrons seemed on the verge of expelling the Americans entirely from this vast and attractive area.

Moreover, exploiting the discontent of American frontiersmen with a central government unable or unwilling to respond to their needs, British officials encouraged separatist sentiment. In Vermont, local unhappiness caused a group including Ethan Allen to negotiate special commercial arrangements with Canada and even to talk of political union with that country. A British Privy Council report of 1790 listed six areas along the American frontier as possibilites for separatism. It was not surprising, therefore, that the United States government under both the Articles of Confederation and the Federal Constitution regarded the removal of British forces from the northwest posts as vitally necessary to redeem the national inheritance and to preserve the Union.

Still another major grievance involved the lack of a commercial treaty with Great Britain. Somewhat belatedly, many Americans were beginning to appreciate the advantages they had formerly enjoyed as citizens of the British Empire. At first it was hoped that the bulk of American trade could be shifted from England to France, America's benefactor and ally in the recent war. Although France shared that hope and made a number of concessions at the expense of its mercantilist regulations (but not all that Americans had wanted), it proved impossible to reorient the bulk of American commerce. Commercial treaties with Sweden, Prussia, and the Netherlands were similarly unavailing. The simple reality was that Americans had become too accustomed to British manufactured goods, depended upon British credit, and found a ready market for their raw materials and foodstuffs within the British system. Regardless of political separation, commerce continued to flow substantially in the old colonial channels. In 1790, for example, slightly under one-half of all American exports went to Great Britain and 90 percent of the imports came from that country.

It was doubly galling, therefore, when Britain refused to grant the United States a satisfactory commercial treaty opening the empire to American commerce. Powerful British shipping interests and Loyalist refugees from America objected strongly to more liberal treatment of American trade. Mercantilist concepts provided still another barrier. Why should England retreat from the old Navigation System under which she presumably had waxed rich and strong? Spokesmen such as Lord Sheffield argued that it must be retained as vital to the nation's future especially since Britain already dominated the American market. Many Americans felt that despite nominal independence their country was being treated like a colony. American raw materials and food products, but not American manufactures, were allowed to enter the British home islands aboard American vessels, but Canada and the West Indian colonies were closed to American ships. One of the major influences behind the adoption of the new constitution in 1787–89 was the hope that a stronger government could force or persuade Great Britain to adopt a more generous trade policy.

Another commercial grievance arose in 1793 at the outbreak of the Wars of the French Revolution (discussed in Chapter 3). At war with revolutionary France, England issued an Order-in-Council in that year forbidding neutral ships from transporting foodstuffs to France and its West Indian possessions. Invoking its unilateral Rule of War of 1756, that trade not open in peacetime could not be opened in wartime (although the United States had enjoyed some trade with the French colonies in peacetime), the Royal Navy began to seize American vessels trading with the enemy. From the American viewpoint these interferences and seizures violated a neutral's rights under international law and practice to trade freely with belligerents in all but military goods, except in the case of a valid blockade, which did not exist then.

Even before this crisis, a disagreement over foreign policy had begun to develop within President Washington's administration. Assuming office in 1789 as the first chief executive under the Federal Constitution, President George Washington had appointed Thomas Jefferson Secretary of State and Alexander Hamilton head of the Treasury Department. Jefferson already had achieved world fame as the author of the Declaration of Independence and Virginia's statute of religious freedom. Truly a man of unequaled genius—an architect, a natural historian, and a philosopher of liberalism and democracy—Jefferson had served as wartime governor of Virginia and then as postwar minister to France. Although only 32 years of age when he assumed the Treasury post, Hamilton of New York was highly regarded in financial circles. Of illegitimate birth and highly ambitious, Hamilton was soon to become Washington's chief counselor and a sort of unofficial prime minister meddling in the affairs of other executive departments. Division along party lines soon emerged as the agrarian interests, represented by Jefferson in the Cabinet and by James Madison of Virginia in the Congress, became alienated by Hamilton's fiscal policies favoring the commercial and financial classes and seeking to strengthen the central government at the expense of the states. Foreign policy issues undoubtedly played a major part in the growing factionalism. Jefferson and Madison looked upon Great Britain as implacably hostile to the United States, and they wanted the nation to remain oriented toward its ally, France. America had to stand up for its rights and free itself of British economic dominance they believed. As early as the First Congress, Madison introduced a measure for discriminatory tonnage duties against British ships entering American ports, both to compel England to accept a satisfactory commercial arrangement and to divert American trade to France and other continental European countries. Madison and Jefferson saw France as the counterpoise to overweening British power, and their interests and sympathies were increased by the French Revolution that indicated America's ally was following a similar course of republican development.

Hamilton, on the other hand, seems to have been motivated by a sentimental and philosophical preference for Great Britain. He and his supporters, soon to be known as Federalists, were alarmed by the anarchy and revolution in France and were apprehensive of the doctrines of popular democracy at home, symbolized by the Jeffersonian Republicans. On more practical grounds, Hamilton realistically recognized that America was closely tied economically to Britain and could only suffer from a trade war. Interferences with commerce would deal the American economy—dependent upon the tariff for revenue—a heavy blow and would impair the nation's credit. Hamilton was almost desperate in his eagerness to avoid any serious confrontation with England but he feared a ruinous war might result over a number of issues—the northwest posts, commercial questions, issues of neutral rights, or the French alliance. He successfully defeated attempts of economic coercion or of diplomatic pressure against Great Britain, interfering with Jefferson's conduct of diplomacy and on several occasions undercutting the Virginian. He secretly informed the first British Minister, George Hammond, who arrived at the capital in 1791, that Jefferson did not really represent the administration's views on such issues as the posts, trade, and neutral rights. Hamilton's meddling and obviously great influence over President Washington finally caused Jefferson to resign his position in 1793 and return to Monticello temporarily while political lines hardened.

Prior to his resignation, Jefferson had drawn up a long report to Congress on grievances against Great Britain. The report touched off a furor in Congress and throughout the nation, heightened by recent British seizures of about 250 American vessels trading with France. Patriotic passions ran dangerously high, and the Hamiltonians were filled with dread that the country was on the verge of a ruinous war. Early in 1794 Congress passed a measure imposing a 30-day embargo against the entry of foreign ships into American ports. The embargo, obviously aimed at Great Britain, was extended for another month and Congress passed measures to strengthen the national defense. A nonintercourse act against Britain was blocked in the evenly divided Senate only by the casting vote of Vice President John Adams. War talk was rife and angry Jeffersonians attacked administration supporters as "Monocrats" and British lackeys.

3. JAY'S TREATY

Fortunately for peace, events favored the Hamiltonian Federalists. Angry at American failures to compel England to respect neutral rights, revolutionary France began to seize American ships trading with England. The British government, not desiring war though not inclined to make many concessions, eased its trade interferences. Taking advantage of these developments, President Washington decided to send a special envoy to London to try to negotiate a settlement. Hamilton apparently wanted the mission, but his opponents objected and it was entrusted to John Jay, Chief Justice of the United States Supreme Court.

Jay, although an experienced and able diplomat, was known to be pro-British and a Federalist in sympathies. The Jeffersonians consequently opposed his nomination but could not prevent his confirmation by the Senate. As a result of their opposition, however, Washington dropped the previous practice of consulting the Senate in framing diplomatic instructions, and instead himself, with Hamilton's advice, drew up the papers for Jay. The envoy was directed to settle the outstanding issues with Britain and if possible to obtain a commercial treaty. Indulging once more his penchant for personal diplomacy, Hamilton undercut Jay's already rather weak position by informing the British minister that the United States would not join a new league of armed neutrals then taking shape in Europe. Any attempt to play on that possibility would probably have been unsuccessful anyhow, since the British government was convinced the armed league was a nullity and would have resented any effort by Jay to capitalize on it, thereby wrecking the negotiations and consequently insuring war. Yet Hamilton's unorthodox backstage diplomacy was highly improper.

Arriving in London, where he was well received, Jay found it necessary to ignore most of his instructions in order to get a treaty that was even partly acceptable. The British preferred peace and were prepared to give up the northwest posts, but not to make many other concessions. Jay faced the painful choice of either accepting a half-loaf or of leaving with no treaty at all and probable war. Therefore he signed what became known as Jay's Treaty on November 14, 1794. By its terms Great Britain pledged evacuation of the northwest posts (completed in 1796), granted American ships access to India, and regularized commerce with the British Isles. As for American desires to traffic directly with the British West Indies, the British threw them merely a sop: American ships of seventy tons or less could trade directly with those colonies provided that the United States did not subsequently reship tropical products such as sugar. The Senate was to delete that "concession" as too restrictive and costly. Jay in effect had to renounce freedom of the seas: he acquiesced in Britain's "right" to seize French property aboard American ships, to confiscate foodstuffs intended for the enemy as long as compensation was made, and to treat naval stores as contraband. Nothing was said about British impressment of American seamen from the decks of American ships, nor about the American version of neutral rights. A notable feature, however, provided for commissions to clarify the northeastern boundary and to settle the issues of colonial debts and recent ship seizures.

News of the treaty's terms set off a great deal of controversy in America. The Jeffersonians attacked Jay's handiwork as a craven surrender to hated Albion, an abandonment of American rights, and a betrayal of the nation's obligations to France by in effect denying that country access to American markets. Moreover, although the Jay Treaty provided that its terms were not intended to set aside other treaties to which either country was a party, it seemed contrary in spirit and even in letter to America's obligation to France respecting neutral rights and privateering. The French government, in fact, asserted that Jay's Treaty amounted to an Anglo-American alliance. Even Hamilton was not entirely pleased, although he defended the treaty as preferable to a war that might follow. Jay was widely denounced and burned in effigy, putting a blight on his presidential ambitions. Yet the Federalists closed ranks and managed to obtain Senate approval of the treaty by the bare two-thirds margin of 20 to 10. Subsequently, despite Jeffersonian opposition and French denunciations, the House of Representatives appropriated the funds necessary to implement the terms of the treaty.

Jay deserved better from his critics. Despite its defects, his treaty at least removed the British from the northwest posts and began to regularize Anglo-American commerce. Removing the British from the posts, preceded by the victory of General "Mad Anthony" Wayne over the northwest Indians at Fallen Timbers in 1794, ended separatist intrigue along the northern frontier. The treaty thereby settled enough grievances to postpone war with Great Britain for almost two decades, valuable time for the United States to gain territory, wealth, and population. If war in 1812 had its perils, as events amply demonstrated, surely it would have been even more dangerous in the mid-1790's.

4. INDIANS AND INTRIGUE IN THE OLD SOUTHWEST

The 1783 treaty of peace also left boundary problems along the new nation's southern frontier. Generously ceding what it no longer possessed, Great Britain had granted its rebellious offspring a southern boundary along the 31st parallel westward to the Mississippi River, and the right to navigate that great waterway from its source to its outlet in the Gulf of Mexico. Spain controlled both banks of the lower Mississippi and naturally contested the American claim to navigation. In addition, owing to its military operations in the Mississippi during the Revolutionary War, the Spanish government claimed jurisdiction over both banks of the Mississippi above the 31st parallel as far north as the Ohio and Tennessee Rivers. From the viewpoint both of international practice and actual possession and control, Spain's case was stronger than that of the Americans. Moreover, Spanish authorities feared that if the Americans were permitted to use the river an influx of settlers into the sparsely inhabited Spanish domains might result in their eventual loss. To prevent this from happening Spain turned to diplomacy, western separatist intrigue, and the use of Indian tribes as buffers.

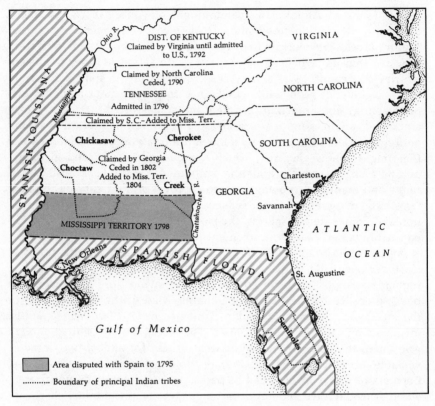

The Southern Boundary of the United States, 1783–1795

In 1784, Spain closed the Mississippi to American use, hoping to discourage the flow of settlers across the Appalachian Mountains into the lands drained by that great river and its tributaries. At the same time, since only a few hundred Spanish soldiers defended all of Louisiana, Spain sought to persuade the United States to sign a treaty abandoning navigational claims in exchange for commercial privileges with the Spanish peninsula. Don Diego de Gardoqui, exuding charm and with a liberal expense account, came to America as minister in 1785 to promote these ends. At that time John Jay was the Confederation's Secretary of Foreign Affairs, and Gardoqui judged him a vain and ambitious man who could be easily handled. Gardoqui dispensed lavish gifts to important personages—Washington received a jackass from the Spanish king—entertained extensively, and apparently made "loans" to some congressmen. Gardoqui offered Jay a treaty that would permit American ships to trade with the Spanish homeland and the Canary Islands, plus a mutual territorial guarantee and a 30-year alliance, in return for which the United States would have to renounce its navigational claims and agree to a compromise on the southern boundary with Florida. Since Congress objected to the proposed terms, Jay framed a counterproposal whereby the United States would obtain commercial privileges with Spain and temporarily suspend, for 25 or 30 years, its claim to the Mississippi; America would give up nothing permanently nor would it yield anything it then possessed, and it would maintain the option of reopening the issues later in accordance with its growing interests and power. In the interval, American commerce would stand to benefit. Realistic though he sought to be, Jay's proposal aroused the fierce opposition of western settlers, land speculators, and those southern states that had territorial claims in the disputed area. Commerce with Spain meant little to them, while navigational rights were vital to the growth of the southwest. Unable to obtain the two-thirds support in Congress necessary for approval of a treaty under the Articles of Confederation, Jay had to abandon his efforts.

Spanish authorities realized even a treaty would not necessarily provide security for Louisiana; an open field could not be locked up. American settlers already were moving west of the mountains in growing numbers. To exploit these settlers' resentment of the weak Confederation government's neglect of their interest, Spanish officials embarked on separatist intrigues to entice them toward dependence upon Spain. Several frontier leaders, such as John Sevier and James Robertson, briefly flirted with the "Spanish Conspiracy." The most notorious, James Wilkinson of Kentucky, a young and unscrupulous Revolutionary War officer, compiled a long record of intrigue and plotting. Wilkinson journeyed to New Orleans and persuaded the Governor of Louisiana to open the Mississippi to certain favored individuals and thereby demonstrate to western settlers that only Spain could satisfy their most pressing economic problem—the need to use the river to ship their goods to market. Given a Spanish pension, Wilkinson returned upriver to promote his conspiracy. Ultimately all efforts such as his failed. The settlers remained patriotic, even if discontented, American citizens, and progress toward statehood plus the promise of a stronger central government under the Federal Constitution doomed the projects of the conspirators.

The Spanish used Indian intrigue as the third weapon in their defensive arsenal. Five powerful and populous Indian tribes dwelt within the disputed territory or in nearby Florida: Creeks, Chickasaws, Cherokees, Choctaws, and the Seminoles in Florida. Utilizing gifts of arms and supplies, and exploiting Indian resentments and fears of encroaching white settlers, Spain tried to weld the tribes into a grand confederacy capable of blocking further American expansion westward. The half-breed Creek chief, Alexander McGillivray, who had fought on the Tory side in the American Revolution and was personally embittered at his treatment by the patriots, proved a useful tool. Known as the "Emperor of the Creeks" and primarily oriented toward Spain, McGillivray was not above accepting sizable pensions and military ranks from both sides, until his death in 1793. Federal Indian agents—James Seagrove of Georgia was the first assigned to the Creeks—tried to counter Spanish influence and to win Indian allegiance to the United States by dispensing gifts or bribes and by exercising personal influence sometimes at the risk of their lives. Indian diplomacy and the growing military strength of the United States, demonstrated by General "Mad Anthony" Wayne in the northwest in 1793–1794, helped check Spanish designs and also preserved an uneasy peace along the frontiers of the white settlements.

Fearful of an explosion if some concessions were not made to the westerners, Spain in 1788 permitted Americans to float goods downstream to New Orleans subject to a 15 percent customs duty and to reexport from that port for an additional 6 percent charge. These concessions did not wholly mollify the westerners who wanted to import and export via the river free of charge. Understandably, in 1789 western sentiment welcomed the coming of a stronger American government that hopefully could solve the problem.

5. PINCKNEY'S TREATY

Thomas Jefferson assumed his post as Secretary of State in 1790 convinced that sooner or later European distresses would facilitate American diplomatic successes. Eventually conflict between Great Britain and Spain enabled the United States to extract advantageous settlements from each power, but not until after Jefferson had left office at the end of 1793. Great Britain, preoccupied with its war with revolutionary France, signed Jay's Treaty in 1794 because English trade with America was extensive and profitable, the fur traders had moved their operations northward into Canada, and new relations had been worked out with the northwest Indians. War with the United States was both unnecessary and undesirable. A roughly similar development largely explains the Spanish-American settlement the following year.

By 1795, Spain realized that separatist conspiracies and Indian intrigues had failed, that the United States was growing in power, and that the frontier settlers were becoming more dangerous. Moreover, in the previous year, Spain had abandoned its alliance with Britain and made peace with revolutionary France. Soon, in fact, Spain was to become an ally and then a puppet of France. The young chief minister, Manuel de Godoy (the favorite of Spain's dissolute Queen), who directed affairs for Spain's corrupt and inefficient monarchy, feared an angry Great Britain might punish its faithless ally. He particularly was apprehensive that the Jay Treaty might contain a secret clause for an Anglo-American attack against Spain in the Western Hemisphere. Prudence, therefore, seemed to require concession to the Americans.

On October 27, 1795, the new United States Minister, Thomas Pinckney, signed the Treaty of San Lorenzo with Spain. The treaty recognized American rights to navigate the Mississippi, provided that American goods could be deposited free of duty at New Orleans for reshipment abroad (a three-year grant subject to renewal), fixed the boundary along the 31st parallel, and included a promise by both Spain and the United States not to incite Indian attacks against each other. Other clauses pledged adherence to a liberal concept of neutral rights. Although the Americans failed to obtain commercial access to Spain's West Indian colonies, the Treaty of San Lorenzo, or Pinckney's Treaty as it was generally called, was one of the most popular in American diplomatic annals. The Senate granted its approval by a unanimous vote in early 1796.

Jay's Treaty and Pinckney's Treaty were significant landmarks in the history of the new nation. Aided by European difficulties, a youthful United States surmounted its weaknesses and without war redeemed the promise of empire contained in the 1783 peace treaty. National unity and progress had received an immense stimulus.

Additional Reading

Two good recent studies of Washingtonian foreign policy are by Alexander De Conde, *Entangling Alliance: Politics and Diplomacy under George Washington* (1958) and Paul A. Varg, *Foreign Policies of the Founding Fathers* (1963). De Conde's account emphasizes Hamilton's influence on Washington's policies and depicts Jefferson as far more realistic than usually portrayed. See also an article by A. H. Bowman, "Jefferson, Hamilton and American Foreign Policy," *Political Science Quarterly*, LXXI (1956), 18–41. Varg's study, although acknowledging that Hamilton advocated a supplicant position toward Great Britain, sees the Hamiltonians as the realists and Jefferson and Madison as the idealists in foreign policy. Favorable to England is C. R. Ritcheson, *Aftermath of Revolution: British Policy toward the United States 1783–1795* (1969). J. P. Boyd, *Number 7: Alexander Hamilton's Secret Attempts to Control American Foreign Policy* (1964) details Hamilton's highly improper undercutting of Jefferson's diplomacy. Also see Helene J. Looze, *Alexander Hamilton and the British Orientation of American Foreign Policy* (1969). The older classic studies on the two key negotiations of this era are by Samuel Flagg Bemis, *Jay's Treaty: A Study in Commerce and Diplomacy* (1923, rev. ed. 1962) and *Pinckney's Treaty: America's Advantage from Europe's Distress, 1783–1800* (1926, rev. ed. 1960). A. L. Burt, *The United States, Great Britain and British North America* (1940) concludes that any attempt at threatening to join an armed neutrality in 1794 would have failed disastrously. See also

Bradford Perkins, *The First Rapprochement: England and the United States, 1795–1805* (1955). Arthur P. Whitaker, *The Spanish-American Frontier, 1783–1795* (1927) takes issue with Bemis about the effect of the Jay Treaty on the Pinckney Treaty. John C. Miller, *Alexander Hamilton* (1959) and *The Federalist Era, 1789–1801* (1960) treats the impact of foreign policy on the formation of political parties, as do Joseph Charles, "The Jay Treaty: The Origins of the American Party System," *William and Mary Quarterly*, XII (1955), 581–630 and J. A. Combs, *The Jay Treaty: Political Battleground of the Founding Fathers* (1970). For Jefferson, consult Dumas Malone, *Jefferson and the Ordeal of Liberty* (1962); Lawrence S. Kaplan, *Jefferson and France* (1967); and Merrill D. Peterson, "Thomas Jefferson and Commercial Policy, 1783–1793," *William and Mary Quarterly*, XXII (1965), 584–610. On Jay, see Frank Monaghan, *John Jay* (1935). General accounts of this period are found in Merrill Jensen, *The New Nation: A History of the United States during the Confederation, 1781–1789* (1950); Arthur B. Darling, *Our Rising Empire, 1763–1803* (1940); and R. W. Van Alstyne, *The Rising American Empire* (1960).

Celebrating the purchase of Louisiana

3

TROUBLED RELATIONS WITH FRANCE, 1793–1803

1. THE FRENCH REVOLUTION AND AMERICAN NEUTRALITY

The United States rejoiced at the tidings of the French Revolution in 1789. Americans hailed the abolition of feudalism and the creation of a constitutional monarchy as notable advances in the progress of human freedom. France seemed to be following the path of the American Revolution. Soon, however, a number of Americans, especially more conservative citizens, became appalled as the revolution plunged into a bloody Reign of Terror. Jeffersonians continued to applaud the revolutionary cause or to apologize for its excesses, but Federalists condemned the guillotining of the deposed Louis XVI and deplored the anarchy they saw enveloping most of France. By 1793 the new revolutionary republic was at war with most of the conservative and monarchical states of Europe, including Great Britain. Attitudes toward the French Revolution thus played a major role in the formation of political parties in the United States. Federalists were all the more inclined toward friendship with Great Britain, now visualized as the defender of constitutionalism and order against the virus of revolutionary anarchy and destruction, while Jeffersonian Republicans saw parallels between their own efforts for greater democracy at home and the epic struggle under way in France.

The French Revolution posed several dilemmas for the Washington administration. In 1793 the French Republic sent Citizen Edmond Genêt as its first minister to the United States. Should America receive the minister of a revolutionary government execrated by almost all the powers of Europe and by many conservatively inclined Americans as well? Was the alliance of 1778 still valid, and what reply should the government give if revolutionary France tried to invoke it? Hamilton advised Washington that the alliance was no longer valid, having been concluded with a defunct government. Gratitude, he held, had no place in international relations, and France had aided America in the Revolutionary War for purely self-interested reasons. Jefferson argued more persuasively that treaties were concluded between nations and remained in effect regardless of changes in government. He pointed out that France had not yet invoked the mutual defense clause of the alliance and if she did, the United States would be justified in basing its response upon considerations of its own interests, including the state of its military preparedness. In short, he suggested the United States could find some way of remaining at peace without denouncing the treaty. As for Citizen Genêt, Jefferson believed he should be received, for the people of each nation had the right to a government of their own choice and Genêt represented such a government. Jefferson thereby formulated the practical policy, long followed by the United States, of recognizing governments regardless of their nature, as long as they exercised de facto control with the consent of their own peoples. Washington agreed and subsequently received Genêt. France, fortunately, never invoked the alliance, apparently because she realized America's weakness and hoped for a friendly nonbelligerency.

Jefferson was overruled on the question of a formal proclamation of neutrality. In his opinion, an announcement of neutrality was unwise because it would restrict the government's freedom of action and would preclude possible bargaining with an anxious Britain. Moreover, in contrast to Hamilton, Jefferson preferred the American position or attitude to be more pro-French than pro-British. President Washington nevertheless chose to issue a proclamation on April 22, 1793 omitting the word "neutrality," and the government enacted legislation in 1794 to enforce his prohibition against partisan activities on American soil or by American citizens. Jefferson subsequently complained that the British government had requested no reassurances from the United States, despite its alliance with France, because all it could ask had already been freely given.

When the youthful and indiscreet French minister arrived in the United States, he assumed Americans would show gratitude for past French aid. Genêt's enthusiastic reception upon landing at Charleston and his virtually triumphal overland journey through the Jeffersonian back country to the federal capital at Philadelphia contrasted sharply with his cold and formal reception by President Washington. But even before presenting his credentials, Genêt had disregarded Washington's proclamation of neutrality by commissioning privateers to prey upon English commerce and by planning with certain Americans armed raids against Spanish territory. Subsequently he ignored repeated warnings against sending out "French" privateers from American ports. His uninhibited deeds and words even embarrassed many of his Jeffersonian admirers. Finally an exasperated Washington demanded his recall. A new faction was in power in France and, rather than return home to face possible arrest and execution, the unabashed Genêt sought asylum in the United States and married an American girl.

Paris reciprocated by forcing the recall of the American minister to France, Gouverneur Morris. Scarcely any more restrained than Genêt, Morris had made himself objectionable by outspoken hostility to the French Revolution and by his efforts on behalf of the royalists. In contrast, his successor, James Monroe, showed such open sympathy for the revolutionary regime that President Washington recalled him in disgrace in 1796. Meanwhile the Jay Treaty had provoked intense condemnation in France as allegedly contrary to the 1778 Franco-American treaties and as virtually an Anglo-American alliance. The French reaction reflected a growing disappointment that the United States was pursuing a strict definition of neutrality rather than one inclined in favor of its ally France. Consequently French diplomats in America first attempted to use propaganda and intrigue to prevent approval of the Jay Treaty, and then rather openly intervened in the 1796 presidential election, hoping to ensure Jefferson's victory over Adams.

Weary of the burdens of office and the stings and abuses of party politics, Washington decided not to seek a third term in the presidency. At first he planned to announce his decision in a valedictory address, using a draft prepared by Madison in 1792, adding to it a further warning of the dangers of factionalism. Hamilton objected to Madison's draft, which had praised republicanism and therefore might appear as pro-Jeffersonian and pro-French. Hamilton completely redrafted a message for the retiring chief executive, and advised that he time its publication to embarrass the administration's opposition. There can be little doubt that Hamilton sought to use the valedictory to weaken the Jeffersonians and to undercut ties with republican France. Washington's motives, though probably unconsciously tinged with politics, had the nobler aim of impressing upon the American people advice against excessive partisanship and foreign entanglement.

Washington's Farewell Address, released through a Philadelphia Federalist newspaper on September 17, 1796, warned against emotional attachments to foreign countries and "the insidious wiles of foreign influence." In regard to foreign alliances, it should be America's "true policy to steer clear of permanent alliances . . . ," while trusting to temporary alliances for emergencies. In the political climate of the times, Washington clearly was warning against such permanent and troublesome alliances as the French tie, and his remarks were construed as criticisms of the Jeffersonian Republicans. Subsequent generations of Americans saw only enduring wisdom in his words but distorted his warnings against foreign meddling in America and against permanent alliances as an isolationist proclamation against any kind of foreign political connections.

During the election of 1796 Federalists and Republicans hurled charges of slavish pro-British and pro-French sentiments at each other. The French minister, Pierre Auguste Adet, openly electioneered for Jefferson and predicted a Franco-American war if John Adams and the Federalists won. Finally Adet announced he was suspending his ministerial functions because of the Jay Treaty. Although Federalists condemned such blatant foreign interference in an American election and appealed to American patriotism, Adet's labors apparently did help Jefferson's cause in Pennsylvania and other areas. When the results came in, Adams won the presidency by a margin of only three electoral votes, while Jefferson received the vice-presidency.

2. A SNUB FROM PARIS

When John Adams relieved George Washington of the burdens of office in 1797, he inherited a growing crisis with France. Jefferson's defeat dashed French hopes that the United States could be brought back to full allegiance to its old ally. Even before Adams could assume his new duties, France had launched a limited sea war against the New World republic. Claiming the right to retaliate for America's failure to compel Britain to observe American rights as a neutral, the French government began sending raiders to seize American ships. In 1795 alone, they took an estimated 316 vessels; in 1796, a French privateer fired on one ship, and another tortured by thumbscrews the captain of the *Cincinnatus* of Baltimore in an unsuccessful attempt to persuade him to declare his cargo English so it could be confiscated. The French government refused to receive Charles C. Pinckney as minister replacing James Monroe. Then early in 1797, a French decree proclaimed that American merchantmen carrying enemy goods of any kind would be subject to seizure and that Americans found serving aboard English ships would be treated as pirates.

Unlike Hamilton or Jefferson, President Adams felt no emotional or intellectual attachment to either the British or the French cause. In many ways, Adams was unsuited for leadership in an era of growing democracy—he was reserved and aloof in bearing, thin-skinned and sensitive to criticism, and found politics discomforting and unpalatable. Yet he was also a strong-willed man of great intellectual power with complete devotion to the national good as he saw it. Although determined to free his administration from Hamilton's influence and control, Adams unwisely retained in his cabinet several holdovers from Washington's administration who were Hamilton's men. These officials maintained frequent contact with the former head of the Treasury and slyly urged Hamiltonian policies upon Adams.

Adams hoped to approach foreign affairs from the viewpoint of strictly American, rather than pro-British or pro-French, interests. He did not view France's complaints as valid nor her retaliations as justified, yet he hoped to avoid war with that republic. Adams sought what a later age would term a "bipartisan" foreign policy by attempting a peaceful settlement with France, since the Jeffersonian Republicans obviously favored peace; Hamilton then concurred because he hoped to free America through negotiations from the entangling alliance of 1778. Vice President Jefferson, in view of his office, declined to lead the commission Adams planned to send to France, but was willing to cooperate with the chief executive. Ignoring opposition from more partisan Federalists, Adams named a Republican, Elbridge Gerry, to join Federalists John Marshall and Charles C. Pinckney in negotiating a settlement with the French.

In France, although a number of informed individuals deplored the drift toward hostilities with America, the corrupt and arrogant five-man Directory clearly inclined toward a hard line. Its Foreign Minister was the clever and able but often unscrupulous Charles Maurice de Talleyrand, a member of the old nobility and onetime Bishop in the Roman Catholic Church. Talleyrand, with an amazing instinct for survival and an apparently insatiable desire to regain the family fortune lost in the revolution, directed foreign affairs not only for the Directory but also for the Napoleonic regime and the Bourbon restoration. He had spent several years in exile in the United States prior to assuming his post under the Directory, but his experiences left him hostile toward the Federalist administration and filled him with contempt for what he regarded as a spineless and crassly materialistic nation.

The Directory did not want war with the United States in 1797, but it was convinced that America should be humiliated and taught a lesson. Therefore, Talleyrand followed a policy of nearly interminable delay and procrastination in diplomatic exchanges, while French seizures of American vessels continued. He saw no great danger, in a badly miscalculated view of the situation, that full-scale war would ensue since the United States was too weak and cowardly. He calculated that delaying tactics would discredit Adams and facilitate a Jeffersonian victory in 1800, thereby restoring the United States to its proper allegiance to France. Moreover, Talleyrand needed time to advance his plan for recovering Louisiana from Spain and rebuilding the French empire in the New World.

Working as the corrupt agent of the Directory, Talleyrand established a regular practice of demanding bribes or "sweeteners" as the price for serious diplomatic negotiations. For example, when France granted Portugal a peace in 1797, the excommunicated ex-Bishop obtained a bribe of eight million francs that he shared with the Directory and justified on the grounds that Portugal had prospered in the wartime trade by preying upon commerce while brave Frenchmen bled for liberty. Adams's commissioners inevitably encountered similar demands. In any case, the French authorities were not prepared to offer much in the way of acceptable terms. The American envoys had instructions to obtain a new treaty to supplant the alliance of 1778, either scrapping or sharply modifying it, and to secure financial compensation for the damages suffered by American commerce. In exchange, the United States would grant France privileges similar to those extended Britain by Jay's Treaty—that is, an abandonment of the liberal definition of neutral rights. Talleyrand refused to receive the three commissioners officially and through private intermediaries demanded a "loan" to France and a "douceur" to the Directory and himself. Subsequently, Talleyrand's go-between revealed the loan would amount to approximately $12 million (to be arranged by purchase of depreciated Dutch securities at face value), plus a bribe of a quarter-million dollars.

The three envoys apparently were less shocked by the demands than by the sums requested. In any case, they felt a loan would violate neutrality principles, and they were unwilling to pay a bribe until negotiations proved successful. Yet as one of the intermediaries told them, *"You must pay money, you must pay a great deal of money."* Pinckney responded, "It is no, no; not a sixpence"; an answer popularized in America as "Millions for defense but not a penny for tribute." The anxious bribe-seekers even utilized female wiles to cajole the envoys and that old benefactor of America, Beaumarchais, lent his talents to the scheme. But all was to no avail. Marshall and Pinckney finally abandoned the mission as hopeless, but Gerry, fearful of war, remained until summarily recalled by Adams.

3. THE QUASI-WAR

As reports arrived of the mission's failure, President Adams seriously considered requesting Congress to declare war. Instead, aware of the pro-French Republican opposition's strength, Adams settled on an intermediate course between full war and peace—to wage quasi or limited and undeclared war at sea until public opinion hardened enough to demand all-out hostilities. Republicans furiously opposed Adams's request to Congress for enlargement of the armed forces. They accused the administration of needlessly forcing war with the country's old ally. France, Adams's opponents claimed, had legitimate complaints about America's recent policies, and they accused Adams of trying to align the nation on the English side. Suspecting an administration plot to conceal France's readiness for peace, opposition spokesmen demanded to see the envoys' reports. Adams deftly entrapped the Republicans by releasing the documents. The reports of Marshall, Pinckney, and Gerry, referring to the bribery attempts by Talleyrand's agents—Mr. "X", Mr. "Y", and

Mr. "Z"— aroused the nation to a fury and deeply embarrassed Jefferson and his supporters.

War fever swept the country in the spring of 1798. Tricolor cockades or badges, previously popular as a sign of sympathy toward the French Revolution, fell into disfavor. Black cockades, similar to those worn by patriots during the American Revolution, were sported by administration supporters, and Federalist youths clashed with Jeffersonians in the streets. Federalist newspapers sounded the tocsin for a war to defend the national honor, and Adams briefly won something like genuine popularity with his countrymen. Not adverse to spurring the war fever, Adams told one cheering crowd, "The finger of destiny writes on the wall the word: War." War was the only alternative to submission to France, he declared, and further efforts at negotiations would be both futile and disgraceful.

As popular excitement mounted, it took an ugly turn. Prominent Republicans, including Vice President Jefferson, were closely watched. Ministers denounced from their pulpits atheistic revolutionary France, and some warned that secret groups were working for a similar bloody upheaval in America. Rumors circulated of French invasions and plots to incite a slave insurrection in the South. Americans apparently have long had a tendency to believe in conspiratorial "devil theory" versions of history, and naturally the French Revolution seemed to conservatives both here and in Europe as a universal menace to property and stability. A nativist reaction against radical aliens in America ensued, and a witch-hunt was launched to silence or to drive out dissidents and opponents. The 1798 Alien and Sedition Acts and the Naturalization Act revealed the superpatriotism and national paranoia of the time. Dangerous aliens could be arrested and deported by presidential orders; persons conspiring to oppose governmental measures or uttering or publishing "any false, scandalous and malicious writing" against the government, Congress, or President, were liable to heavy fines and imprisonment; and residence requirements for naturalization of aliens were increased from five to fourteen years. When a Quaker pacifist, George Logan, on his own sounded France on the prospects for peace, the Federalist-dominated Congress adopted the Logan Act in 1799 to punish unauthorized diplomacy by private persons.

In this climate, Congress passed a series of measures supporting a limited naval war with France: it denounced the 1778 alliance as invalid; established a separate Navy Department; appropriated funds for warship construction; and authorized a Provisional Army of 50,000 men. George Washington was called out of retirement to assume command of the army. Congress embargoed trade with France, barred French ships from American ports (except in distress), and permitted the American Navy and armed privateers to seize armed French vessels on the high seas. American ships drove French "picaroons" or small privateers, which had brazenly operated against American shipping off the coasts of the United States and within sight of land, into their West Indian lairs, and the American Navy safely convoyed American ships trading in the Caribbean Sea. Yet, while these exploits aroused national pride, especially when the U.S.S. *Constellation* captured the French frigate *L'Insurgente,* Adams recognized the extent of Republican opposition in the Congress and the division within the country. Therefore he did not request a formal declaration of war, and ordered unarmed French ships not to be molested. Time was needed for war passions to promote greater unanimity.

4. RAPPROCHEMENT WITH GREAT BRITAIN

Jay's Treaty had cleared the way for improved relations with England. The exchange of new envoys, Federalist Rufus King to the Court of St. James, and Robert Liston, a kindly and able Scotsman, to the United States, facilitated the beginning of a better era. King got along well with the British upper class and Liston established similarly warm relations with Federalist leaders in this country. Cultural ties remained close with the former mother country, and commerce flourished as Britain relaxed its interference with American trade. Impressment—the seizure of alleged British subjects from the decks of American ships for service in the Royal Navy—did not cease, but the British exercised greater care to avoid abuses, and citizens who had been wrongly impressed were often released upon the presentation of evidence by the State Department. In the *Polly* case (1800), a British prize court relaxed previous efforts to halt American commerce with enemy colonies, accepting the device of "broken voyages," whereby enemy goods landed in America and subsequently re-exported were not subject to seizure under the Rule of War of 1756. In effect, Americans were able to carry on a lucrative trade with France, Spain, and their overseas possessions with little or no British interference. Exports from the United States rose sharply, from $20 million in 1792 to $94 million in 1801, about half of which represented the re-export of foreign goods. Further contributing to improved Anglo-American relations, Britain fed capital into American investments, principally government securities. The United States provided Britain with large quantities of foodstuffs and raw materials, and in return absorbed English manufactures. One historian has described the connection as the "Atlantic Economy," with an underdeveloped United States supplying raw materials and receiving badly needed capital, skilled labor, and industrial techniques from the world's foremost manufacturing country.

But international "friendships" are more often founded on negative factors, in this case the existence of a mutual enemy or threat, revolutionary France. Great Britain, at war with France, naturally welcomed the breakdown of the old Franco-American alliance. Britons hailed Washington's Farewell Address, with its anti-French undertones and its advice against entangling alliances, as wise and statesmanlike. They interpreted Adams's victory over Jefferson in the 1796 race as an encouraging sign that the United States would continue friendly policies toward Britain. King George III praised the noble conduct of Adams's envoys in the XYZ episode, and Britain looked forward to a new ally as the undeclared Franco-American war at sea began.

Britishers were greatly impressed with American resolve and naval prowess in the conflict with France. The United States was allowed to purchase naval guns and equipment in England, and some cannon and powder were even given for harbor defense in what can be called the first "lend-lease" program. American and British naval units cooperated in operations against French raiders and exchanged information about French activities and plots. Speculation arose that the United States would even buy or "borrow" British warships, but Adams and Congress relied instead upon naval construction in the United States. The American Navy expanded to 45 assorted vessels, and the government commissioned 365 privateers; they captured a total of 85 French prizes.

Anglo-American cooperation extended to Saint Domingue in the Caribbean, once France's richest sugar-producing colony. A Negro slave insurrection led by ex-slave Toussaint L'Ouverture, "the Black Napoleon of the Antilles," had swept French power from the island. Swallowing their horror of a Black republic, Britain and the United States successfully sought to weaken France and to exploit the island's trade while persuading L'Ouverture not to try to export revolutionary ideas to the slaves in the American South and the British Caribbean colonies. L'Ouverture cooperated out of necessity although, until Napoleon's attempt at reconquest, he formally professed loyalty to France.

So close was the Anglo-American accord that some Americans spoke of the advisability of a formal alliance with Great Britain. Adams was not favorably inclined, however, reasoning that an alliance would be an unwise and unnecessary entanglement, since even if America formally declared war against France, Britain of necessity would have to cooperate closely with the United States despite the absence of a treaty of alliance. Moreover, he knew that Anglophobia had not disappeared in America; an alliance would be highly unpopular with large numbers of citizens, especially Jeffersonian Republicans, and would promote greater disunity within the country. Even so, some of his opponents wildly charged Adams with plotting alliance and even a marriage tie with the British royal family to establish monarchy in the United States.

5. ADAMS CHOOSES PEACE

Personal and political factors rapidly cooled President Adams's ardor for a full-fledged war with France. Republicans opposed additional war measures and, as reports arrived that France apparently wanted peace, the war fever among other citizens quickly waned. Moreover, Adams felt deeply humiliated when George Washington forced him to accept Hamilton as second in command of the Provisional Army; the ambitious Hamilton, entitled by seniority only to a lesser rank, had persuaded Washington to threaten resignation unless he got his way. Hamilton eagerly sought an opportunity for martial glory. He was attracted by schemes to conquer Louisiana and Florida, and looked favorably upon proposals for joint Anglo-American operations against Spanish-French rule in the Caribbean and northern South America on behalf of Latin American rebels. Adams, on the other hand, believed that hostilities against the enemy should be confined to the high seas.

By 1799, the French Directory and Talleyrand had also lost enthusiasm for the quasi-war. They never wanted a large conflict and now began to fear an Anglo-American alliance, which would frustrate Talleyrand's plans for the retrocession of Louisiana. Various Frenchmen warned that the Directory's course since 1797 had been most unwise and if maintained could only work to harm France. When Napoleon Bonaparte overthrew the Directory in 1799 and established his dictatorship as First Consul, Talleyrand convinced him that peace with the United States had to be restored. He also persuaded the military dictator to adopt his scheme for recovering Louisiana from Spain, and using it as a granary for sugar from Saint Domingue after suppressing the slave insurrection. Even before Napoleon's coup, William Vans Murray, America's minister in the Netherlands, had been told the French government sought peace and was ready to negotiate courteously and seriously if Adams would send a new mission to Paris.

Placing the national welfare above personal and party considerations, President Adams seized the opportunity for peace. Although he knew that more extreme Federalists passionately preferred war and that he risked a serious division within his own party—a split that in fact helped defeat his bid for re-election in 1800—Adams early in 1799 ignored his Cabinet and Federalist leaders and appointed Murray, Oliver Ellsworth, the Chief Justice of the United States Supreme Court, and W. R. Davie of North Carolina, to negotiate with France. Furious infighting within Federalist ranks resulted, and Adams eventually had to dismiss both Secretary of State Timothy Pickering and Secretary of War James McHenry for disloyalty to him and obstructionism of the peace effort. Adams thereby presented a rare example of patriotic statesmanship, sacrificing his political future for the sake of the nation's true interests.

By the time Ellsworth and Davie joined Murray in Europe, Napoleon had become First Consul and politely received the envoys. Obviously this was not to be a repeat of 1797. To emphasize the changed climate, Napoleon observed George Washington's death, late in 1799, by decreeing ten days of mourning in the French army and ordering other observances in honor of France's late colleague in arms. Joseph Bonaparte, Napoleon's brother, officially headed the French delegation in the protracted negotiations that continued for seven months. The delay, in part the result of Napoleon's absence on military campaigns in Italy and in part due to Talleyrand's illness, also reflected conflicting French and American desires. Adams's envoys sought a new treaty that would terminate the 1778 alliance. They also asked compensation for French seizures of American ships and cargoes since 1793. Napoleon, however, still hoped to keep the United States allied to France and offered compensation for spoliation claims only if the 1778 alliance remained valid. A new armed league of neutrals was forming on the continent, in which he hoped to involve the United States either directly or by implication. French diplomacy thus sought to disrupt the Anglo-American rapprochement and to use America as a tool in the struggle against Britain.

Napoleon finally offered a compromise. Since his war with Great Britain was coming to an end, at least temporarily, he offered a settlement based on abandoning the 1778 treaties and the damage claims. The American commissioners accepted the compromise, agreeing to postpone negotiations both on the question of the 1778 alliance and the spoliation claims, and consented to sign an accord restoring normal relations. The Convention of Môrtefontaine, usually referred to as the Convention of 1800, accordingly was signed on October 1, 1800. The Convention in theory was simply a modus vivendi, suspending the issues of alliance and claims for subsequent adjustment while ending the quasi-war and reiterating the doctrine of liberal neutral rights first acknowledged in 1778. The Convention reached the Senate after the results of the 1800 presidential race revealed Adams had narrowly lost his bid for re-election. Owing to opposition from the more partisan Federalists, the Senate first rejected the treaty, but public pressures led to its approval on February 3, 1801, with the deletion of the clause providing for future negotiations about the status of the 1778 treaty. France accepted and so, in effect, the United States abandoned its claim for indemnity in exchange for the termination of the 1778 alliance. French maritime decrees were repealed and the quasi-war was over. Unknowingly, by choosing peace rather than war in 1799–1800, Adams opened the way for one of the greatest real estate deals in history.

6. THE PURCHASE OF LOUISIANA

On the same day the Convention of 1800 was signed, Napoleon secretly concluded the Treaty of San Ildefonso with Spain for the retrocession of Louisiana. The Spanish government had for some time looked upon that sparsely settled and vast territory, which it had acquired from France in 1763, as an expensive "white elephant." It was costly to administer, paid few taxes, and was vulnerable to American frontier pressures. Talleyrand assured the weak Spanish monarch, Charles IV, that Louisiana in French hands would be "a wall of brass forever impenetrable to the combined efforts of England and America." Appealing to the ambitions of that monarch and his dissolute Queen, Napoleon also promised to create an Italian kingdom for their son-in-law and daughter. Subsequently, since Spain delayed, France promised never to transfer the province to a third power, and the deal was reaffirmed in 1802. In the interval, Napoleon signed a preliminary peace with Great Britain at Amiens in 1802, smoothing the way for the new colonial venture. The French did not actually take possession of Louisiana until December, 1803, 20 days before the Americans took it over. The Spanish crown was doubly duped, for Napoleon also violated his promise of an Italian kingdom.

Rumors of the retrocession aroused great alarm in the United States, especially in the western states vitally interested in the use of the Mississippi River. The alarm increased when Spanish officials in 1802 suspended the right of free deposit at New Orleans. The suspension, assumed mistakenly to be at Napoleon's orders, clearly violated the terms of Pinckney's Treaty of 1795. Diplomatic pressure brought its revocation. The prospect of mighty France replacing weak Spain as their neighbor to the west disturbed Americans. Surely that would frustrate prospects of western expansion and boded ill for the future security of the United States.

President Jefferson shared the popular distress. Pro-French though he still undoubtedly was, he could not contemplate the retrocession with equanimity. Although he apparently never took the possibility of an alliance with Great Britain very seriously, he did toy with the idea and used it to put diplomatic pressure on Napoleon. Jefferson wrote Minister Robert Livingston in Paris that Louisiana in French hands would make France in effect "our natural and habitual enemy" and would compel us to "marry ourselves to the British fleet and nation." He also utilized other channels to convey his concern and the possibility of a defensive alliance with England. Finally, Jefferson obtained a $2 million appropriation from Congress and dispatched James Monroe to France to offer up to $10 million for New Orleans and the Floridas. As a last resort, if this failed and if Napoleon closed the river to American navigation, Monroe had orders to proceed to London to discuss an Anglo-American alliance.

To his great surprise, Monroe discovered that Napoleon was willing to sell all of Louisiana (but not the Floridas since he did not possess them) for a total of $25 million. That dazzling opportunity opened up for several reasons: the Negro rebellion in Saint Domingue had proved too costly to subdue, and without the sugar isle Louisiana lost much of its value; war was about to resume in Europe, which would leave Louisiana vulnerable to British sea power; sale to the United States would in effect drive a wedge between that republic and Great Britain, or at least make their collaboration less likely; and, finally, Napoleon needed money for his

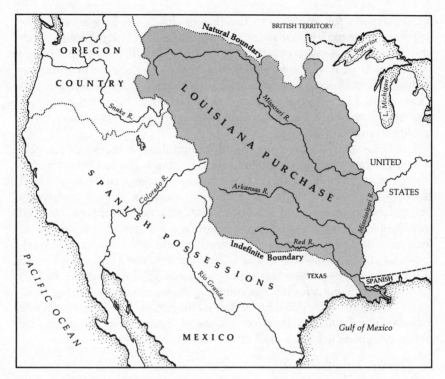

The Louisiana Purchase, 1803

European ventures. Monroe and Livingston swallowed their hesitation about such an unauthorized bargain, and after some haggling that reduced the French asking price from $25 million to $15 million, they signed the purchase treaty on April 30, 1803. The United States acquired title to a vast domain of 828,000 square miles of land for about three cents per acre. In addition to the money and to America's assumption of its citizens' claims against France for seizing their ships, the United States promised citizenship to the inhabitants of Louisiana, and by implication eventual statehood in the Union in accordance with constitutional procedures. The purchase agreement did not define the boundaries of the new acquisition, other than what they had been under French and Spanish domination. As Talleyrand remarked to the American envoys, "You have made a noble bargain for yourselves, and I suppose you will make the most of it."

The absence of specific constitutional provisions for the acquisition of territory troubled President Jefferson, who would have preferred to await adoption of a Constitutional amendment for that purpose. Time would not permit, however, so he manfully brushed aside his legalistic scruples and accepted the bargain. Federalists, recently critical of Jefferson's administration for inactivity in the face of the crisis, now attacked the purchase as unconstitutional and a colossal waste of federal funds. Their shift had less to do with principle and more to do with politics and fear of the creation of new states which might weaken the role of the older states in the Union. Most Americans enthusiastically hailed the purchase. Called into special session, the Senate voted overwhelmingly for the treaty, and both houses of Congress approved the necessary funds for the transaction.

The Louisiana Purchase had manifold significance: it averted possible war with France and entanglement with England; it more than doubled the national domain and greatly encouraged western settlement; it placated the western states and ended separatist dangers; it removed a major foreign threat from America's borders and thereby encouraged isolationism; it established a precedent for the future acquisition of territories and peoples; and it enormously stimulated American nationalism and enlarged the role of the federal government. It also embroiled the United States in new territorial controversies, for Jefferson and his successors advanced highly questionable claims that in acquiring Louisiana the United States also had obtained title to much of Texas and West Florida. The Louisiana Purchase serves as a monument to a rational policy of expediency on behalf of the national interest.

Additional Reading

The most recent study of the Franco-American conflict is *The Quasi-War: The Politics and Diplomacy of the Undeclared War with France, 1797–1801* (1966) by Alexander De Conde. On the Farewell Address, see his previously cited work, *Entangling Alliance* (1958), and his "Washington's Farewell, the French Alliance, and the Election of 1796," *Mississippi Valley Historical Review,* XLIII (1957), 641–658. Felix Gilbert, *To the Farewell Address* (1961) examines the history of the concepts of the address. R. L. Ketcham, "France and American Politics, 1763–1793," *Political Science Quarterly,* LXXVIII (1963), 198–223, analyzes the domestic impact of the French connection. The Adams era is covered by John C. Miller in both *Alexander Hamilton: Portrait in Paradox* (1959) and *The Federalist Era* (1960); Stephen G. Kurtz, *The Presidency of John Adams* (1957); and Page Smith, *John Adams* (2 vols., 1962). Also see the older biography by Gilbert Chinard, *Honest John Adams* (1933). Paul A. Varg, *Foreign Policies of the Founding Fathers* (1963) is useful for this period, as are G. W. Allen, *Our Naval War with France* (1909) and S. F. Bemis, *The American Secretaries of State and Their Diplomacy* (1927), Vol. III. L. M. Sears, *George Washington and the French Revolution* (1960) and E. F. Kramer, "Some New Light on the XYZ Affair: Elbridge Gerry's Reasons for Opposing War with France," *New England Quarter-*

ly, XXIX (1956), 509–513, explore aspects of Franco-American relations. For the Convention of 1800, see Peter P. Hill, *William Vans Murray, Federalist Diplomat* (1971). Two excellent multivolume studies are being written on Jefferson and his Secretary of State: Dumas Malone, *Jefferson and the Ordeal of Liberty* (1962) and *Jefferson the President: First Term, 1801–1805* (1970); and Irving Brant, *James Madison: Secretary of State, 1800–1809* (1953). Lawrence S. Kaplan, *Jefferson and France* (1967) analyzes Jefferson's attachment to France. For Louisiana, see E. Wilson Lyon, *Louisiana in French Diplomacy, 1759–1804* (1934) and A. P. Whitaker, *The Mississippi Question, 1795–1803* (1934). Bradford Perkins examines relations with England in *The First Rapprochement* (1955), cited in the previous chapter.

Impressment of American seamen from the Chesapeake

4

THE TRIALS
OF NEUTRALITY,
1793–1812

1. LIBERAL NEUTRAL RIGHTS

The "lessons" of the years 1793–1812 in American history might be entitled how the United States government failed to relate policy to available power. A cycle of wars convulsed the Old World, set off by the French Revolution and continued by the schemes of Napoleon Bonaparte to build a new Roman empire in the West. A comparatively weak United States, interested in exporting foodstuffs and raw materials to Europe and its colonies, unavoidably was trapped between the two mighty antagonists of these wars—Great Britain, the mistress of the seas, and France, the most powerful military force on the continent. Instead of prudently retreating in the face of the blows these two belligerents aimed at each other, Presidents Jefferson and Madison attempted a spirited defense of America's neutral rights. They thereby drifted into an unwanted war for which the country was almost totally unprepared.

The harsh truth is that no body of generally accepted neutral rights existed in 1793. Small navy powers with substantial commercial interests had long contended that as neutrals they had a right to continue trading freely with other neutrals and even with the belligerents during a war, except in contraband goods directly related to military use. They held that lists of contraband goods should be severely limited, that belligerent blockades of enemy coasts should be actually effective in order to be legal, and that enemy-owned goods aboard neutral vessels should be immune from confiscation, as "free ships make free goods." Great naval powers such as England, on the other hand, naturally sought to control neutral commerce and to strike hard at the economy of an opponent. In their hands contraband lists tended to expand to include foodstuffs and naval stores, normally considered civilian goods, and other materials capable of either civilian or military use. The *"consolato del mare"* or so-called law of the sea, made enemy goods subject to seizure even if carried under a neutral flag. In the unilaterally proclaimed "Rule of War of 1756," England prohibited neutral trade in wartime that was not open in times of peace. By this proclamation she intended to prevent an opponent from opening its colonies to neutrals in order to compensate for its own naval weaknesses. In practice, belligerents also frequently announced "paper blockades" that could not be effectively enforced, to frighten neutrals and to justify random interference with their commerce.

Almost from its birth, the United States had endorsed a liberal doctrine of neutral rights. The Founding Fathers foresaw that the interests of the new nation would best be served by a policy of trade and neutrality. Therefore they emphasized liberal neutral rights in the model treaty Plan of 1776. Subsequently commercial treaties concluded with France (1778 and 1800), the Netherlands (1782), Sweden (1783), Prussia (1785), and Spain (1795) included liberal provisions for neutral commerce. This policy reflected both American self-interest and American principles—an idealistic internationalist view of a world knit together by peaceful commerce, where power diplomacy would be supplanted by commercial relations. Unfortunately for the young republic, however, while other powers acknowledged those principles, Great Britain did not.

2. IN THE BELLIGERENT VISE

The United States escaped relatively unscathed during the first phase of the Wars of the French Revolution and Napoleon, from 1793 to the Peace of Amiens in 1801. In the rapprochement following the Jay Treaty, Great Britain tolerated a large amount of American trade with the enemy. France proved less amenable, to be sure, but lacked naval power, while the United States struck back effectively at French raiders during the Quasi–War. In the second phase of the wars, however, beginning in 1803, America was much less fortunate. Great Britain now found her very existence at stake in the long struggle against the greatest conqueror of modern times. Napoleon triumphed on the continent and for a period even threatened to invade England. Timely naval victories, especially at Trafalgar in 1805, spared Britain that test but left her isolated from the rest of Europe. Under those circumstances the British government showed less inclination than earlier to make concessions to American trade. Soon both great antagonists felt compelled to strike at each other by indirect means that inevitably affected the neutrals.

Napoleon was convinced that England, which he contemptuously described as a "nation of shopkeepers," could be forced to her knees by economic warfare. Appealing to widespread Anglophobia in Europe, he proclaimed that this "modern Carthage," a ruthless and selfish mercantile power, must be destroyed and the continent freed of its economic enslavement. His "Continental System" would achieve that liberation by closing French-controlled Europe to English goods and ships. In the Berlin Decree of late 1806, Napoleon proclaimed a blockade of the British Isles, although he obviously lacked the navy to enforce it, and thereby closed the continent to British ships and wares. Britain retaliated in 1807 with a series of Orders in Council blockading all French-held Europe and forbidding neutral traffic with the area unless neutral vessels first stopped at a British port and purchased a license to trade with the enemy. Napoleon countered with the Milan Decree of December, 1807, which stated that neutral ships observing British regulations or submitting to a British search would be seized if they ventured into continental ports. Hapless neutrals such as the United States were caught in a vise, doomed if their shipping complied with the orders of either of the belligerents and obviously unable to comply with both.

Even prior to that cycle of retaliation and counterretaliation, American commerce had suffered increasing British interferences. France and Spain had opened their colonies to neutral trade, attempting to offset their naval weaknesses by using neutrals to circumvent the British blockade. American shippers eagerly exploited these new opportunities, until Britain invoked the Rule of '56 to prohibit the traffic. American traders sought to escape the Rule via so-called "broken voyages," whereby they would take goods of enemy origin to an American port, unload them, pay duties on them, and then re-export them as "Americanized" products. Britain winked at that traffic during the first phase of the European conflict, as the *Polly* decision in 1800 indicated, but after 1803 British authorities were no longer so lenient. Influential Englishmen, especially those connected with the shipping interests, viewed broken voyages as mere subterfuges that undercut the war effort against France and enriched greedy neutrals at Britain's expense. And the device was becoming more farcical, since American ships often merely pretended to land enemy goods in America and to pay duties, most of which were refunded in drawbacks, before exporting the cargoes to French-held Europe or to the enemy colonies. The re-export trade was very profitable for America, amounting in 1806 to $60 million of a total foreign commerce worth $138 million. In the *Essex* case in 1805, a British prize court gave notice that ships involved in such broken voyages would be regarded as engaged in one continuous trip between two blockaded enemy ports and thus subject to seizure.

Some Britons urged even more drastic enforcement of the blockade. Sir James Stephen, close to influential British political leaders, published a pamphlet in 1805 entitled "War in Disguise; Or, the Frauds of the Neutral Flags." Stephen argued that evasions of the blockade were enriching the neutrals and benefiting the enemy. He called for more stringent enforcement, even though it might bring war with the neutral states. In his opinion, however, the United States would not fight. Moreover, he expressed the hope that many Americans would appreciate that England was defending the cause of constitutionalism and liberty not only for herself but for all the world. The licensing system and the tighter blockades adopted in 1806 and 1807 reflected the views of Stephen and others.

3. AN ABORTIVE TREATY

It might have been wiser if the leaders of a nation hopeful for continued peace had bent before the policies of the Old World powers, but President Jefferson and his Secretary of State, James Madison, were determined to defend vigorously American rights and interests. Most Federalists favored adjustment to Britain's maritime system. In their view, the United States should draw closer to England, the last bulwark against the great tyrant Napoleon. Jeffersonian Republicans, on the other hand, disliked Britain almost as intensely as Federalists hated revolutionary and imperial France. As zealous defenders of American sovereignty and honor, they felt confident Britain would survive Napoleon and they welcomed British embarrassments in Europe as favorable to a firm defense of America's rights.

In view of his determination to press the English hard, Jefferson probably should have supplemented his economic policies with greater military and naval preparedness. Diplomacy unsupported by power, then as later, merely served to arouse contempt abroad. Jefferson's failure in this area reflected both his political philosophy and his pacifist inclinations. A fervent believer in the power of reason, he had long feared standing armies and navies as not only costly but dangerous to liberty and popular government. Moreover, his administration entered office determined to reduce the national debt inherited from the Federalists. Aided by Secretary of the Treasury Albert Gallatin, Jefferson launched a sweeping curtailment in federal taxes and expenditures. The budget-shearers found an attractive target in the naval establishment inherited from Adams; they sold or laid up naval warships and halted construction. The frugal President even thought of removing all warships from the water and inexpensively dry-docking them near the capital city for possible future use! He also considered a scheme to substitute for sea going warships a few hundred small gunboats that could be manned in times of emergency by volunteer militia, thus defending America's ports at a very low cost. The War of 1812 painfully revealed the inadequacy of that device. The oceangoing navy was saved from what looked like certain extinction only by the Tripolitan War of 1801–1805, when Jefferson dispatched warships to the Mediterranean to discipline the piratical North African states that were preying upon American ships. Although the operation obtained some success, these piratical forays were not permanently ended until Commodore Stephen Decatur's naval actions in 1815.

Jefferson responded to belligerent challenges by using the threat of economic coercion, unstrengthened by naval or military preparations. He remembered colonial boycotts against British goods and believed that similar measures would compel belligerents to respect American rights. Unfortunately he failed to appreciate the national tempers of Britain and France. The mood in Great Britain increasingly leaned toward a desperate struggle for survival. Britons regarded their country as defending neutrals from the rapacious imperialism of Napoleon, yet an ungrateful United States chose that moment of supreme peril to weaken the very sea power that shielded it. Moreover, British leaders were simply too preoccupied with the struggle in Europe to spare much time or sensitivity for the Americans. As for Napoleon, he too had little respect for what he regarded as a weak, materialistic, and craven United States. Probably his wisest course, as suggested by his advisers, would have been to treat American commerce generously, and by freely opening the European market to American trade he would have increased the probabilities of an Anglo-American clash. Instead that despot cynically and brazenly interfered with American trade. Between 1807 and 1812, in fact, he seized and condemned more American ships and entire cargoes than the English did: 468 to 389. Napoleon was determined to bludgeon America, rather than to cajole it, into serving the Continental System.

Yet Great Britain with its control of the seas remained the most serious offender against American interests. Although Anglo-American trade was increasing and each country was the other's best customer, British shippers and their government seemed only concerned with commercial rivalry and growing American prosperity. After 1803, the Royal Navy seized or detained hundreds of American vessels. Some estimates indicate that from 1805 to 1808 the British seized or detained at least one American merchantman every other day, although many were subsequently released; the rate declined after 1808 only because of greater caution by American shippers and because of the effects of the embargo. Adding gall to injury, the British government permitted her ships and exporters to carry on the kind of trade with Napoleonic Europe that was prohibited to Americans. The Royal Navy often enforced the blockade not off the European coast but off the American shore. Seizures sometimes occurred within actual sight of land. British warships also abused American hospitality, anchoring in American harbors to observe the loading and sailing of ships for subsequent seizure. In 1804, H.M.S. *Leander* lay off the harbor of New York for a prolonged period and on one occasion opened fire on an American ship, killing a member of its crew.

British warships frequently halted every ship departing from New York City, and several dozen ships at a time might be compelled to lie at anchor awaiting search.

Impressment of seamen was also becoming a particularly irritating issue. The Royal Navy, noted for its harsh discipline and miserable pay, long had relied upon involuntary service to fill its ranks. The need for impressment naturally became greater during wartime. Yet many English tars left or deserted the British merchant and naval service for the American merchant marine where wages were higher and personal danger less. In searching American vessels for contraband, British boarding parties regularly lined up the crews and removed British seamen for impressment into the Royal Navy. It was not always easy to distinguish between American and British nationals, and if a Royal Navy commander was short of hands he might not take excessive care. Moreover, Great Britain did not recognize naturalization but observed the principle of indelible citizenship—once a Briton always a Briton. The ease with which a British deserter could acquire fraudulent citizenship papers in any American port made the problem more acute. The British government brushed aside American contentions that a ship flying the United States flag was an extension of the national territory and therefore immune from impressment, although the British usually released bonafide American seamen from impressment after presentation of satisfactory evidence. Nevertheless, prior to 1812 the British impressed at least 8,000 American seamen, many of whom served long years or even died in the British naval service. Impressment probably became the most grievous single affront to American principles and national honor.

For a brief time in 1806, Anglo-American relations showed some sign of improving significantly. Unfortunately, Jefferson spurned the opportunity by his insistence upon greater concessions. Congress enacted a weak nonimportation act in 1806, but postponed its enforcement pending negotiations with England. A new ministry in London replaced haughty Anthony Merry as minister to the United States with the young David Erskine and his American wife. William Pinkney joined James Monroe in London with instructions to obtain the end of impressment and a more generous treatment of the re-export trade, in exchange for repeal of the nonimportation act. During the following lengthy discussions, the two envoys found the British negotiators willing to make important concessions regarding neutral trade with Europe but not to renounce impressment. The Americans offered to prohibit British deserters from sailing under the American flag, but without success. The Admiralty viewed impressment as vital, and it seriously questioned American enforcement of any ban against deserters or any promises to turn them over to the British government. Convinced that Britain would curtail impressment in practice, though retaining it in theory, and eager to obtain some relief for American commerce, Monroe and Pinkney decided to ignore their instructions and to conclude an agreement.

The Monroe-Pinkney Treaty was signed on December 31, 1806. Its provisions exempted foodstuffs from the contraband category, permitted trade with the nonblockaded ports of Europe, and recognized with some limitations the device of "broken voyages." In effect, Britain displayed readiness to return to the generous policy of the *Polly* decision of 1800. In exchange, the United States promised to rescind nonimportation and to prohibit enactment of further embargoes for the next ten years. In view of Napoleon's recent Berlin Decree, the American envoys accepted a British reservation of freedom of action if France enforced that decree or if the United States failed to resist it.

When the treaty arrived in Washington, Erskine enthusiastically rushed it to the State Department. To his surprise, neither Madison nor Jefferson displayed any pleasure. Both viewed the pact as woefully inadequate. Madison told the disappointed minister that the failure to end impressment and the conditional nature of the commercial concessions made it very unlikely that the Senate would approve it. The President apparently thought a little more pressure would secure the whole, but as it turned out, he seriously misjudged the British temper. Yet his spurning of a possible reconciliation unquestionably reflected the sentiments of large numbers of his fellow citizens on the issue of impressment.

4. EMBARGO: A WEAPON THAT FAILED

America and England moved closer to the brink of hostilities after the rejection of the Monroe-Pinkney Treaty. The British government struck back at the Berlin Decree with the Orders in Council. A new Tory ministry, with the caustic but able George Canning in the Foreign Office, pledged vigorous prosecution of the war. Canning soon earned himself the not entirely deserved reputation as America's "implacable and rancorous enemy," in the words of John Quincy Adams.

In this less favorable climate, the *Chesapeake* affair could not have been more ill-timed. British officers were incensed when they learned that some deserters from their navy had enlisted aboard the American warship *Chesapeake,* and with the knowledge of its commander, Commodore James Barron. On June 22, 1807, H.M.S. *Leopard* hailed the *Chesapeake* at a distance of about ten miles from the American coast and demanded that the ship submit to a search. Correctly refusing to comply with such a flagrant violation of sovereignty—even Great Britain recognized warships as immune to searches—Barron had to strike his colors after three broadsides hit his unprepared ship, killing three of his crew and wounding 18 others. The British then removed the deserters from the *Chesapeake*'s shattered decks. One turned out to be a British subject and was duly hanged at Halifax; the other three were bona fide American citizens, two of whom the British released nearly five years later, after the furnishing of proof, and the third died in prison in the interval.

The *Chesapeake-Leopard* incident inflamed America from one end of the country to the other. Federalists raged at the British "man-stealers" and "murderers." Erskine warned his government that "the indignation of the People . . . has been excited to the most violent extent. . . ." Jefferson could easily have obtained a war vote in Congress. He delayed so long in acting, however, that popular passions began to cool. Instead of summoning Congress to declare war, the President closed American ports to British warships, and demanded from London an apology, reparations, and cessation of impressment. The British government was ready to apologize for the *Chesapeake* outrage, but not to retreat on impressment. Negotiations therefore failed. Once more Jefferson asked for all and ended with nothing.

The administration turned to more stringent economic coercion. Jefferson signed the Embargo Act into law in December, 1807. It prohibited American ships from entering all foreign ports, while supplementary legislation banned land traffic with Canada. Jefferson still relied upon economic pressure to succeed where diplomacy had failed. He wrote the Governor of Virginia, "Let us see whether having taught so many other useful lessons to Europe, we may not add that of showing them that there are peaceable means of repressing injustice, by making it to the interest of the aggressors to do what is just."

The Embargo Act was ostensibly not directed at any one foreign power but was merely a measure to protect United States shipping. In fact, of course, it was aimed squarely at Great Britain. Jefferson hoped it would achieve a quick success; if not, he apparently resolved upon war. Instead, his continued caution and hesitation converted a temporary measure into a more or less permanent policy of economic coercion. Failure to launch military preparations and the subsequent turning from one economic measure to another aroused increasing contempt in France and Great Britain. Napoleon welcomed embargoes and nonimportation acts as adjuncts to his Continental System. That, however, did not induce him to treat American trade any more generously. The Embargo hurt Britain. Grain prices rose in the British Isles while the exportation of manufactured goods to America declined. Some British exports, nevertheless, continued to get in under the Embargo, while cotton imports from the United States, vital to the textile industry, had been sufficiently large in 1807 to cushion the effect of the ban. Moreover, Napoleon's attempt to place his brother Joseph upon the Spanish throne stirred rebellion in Spain's colonies and opened their markets to British trade. The Embargo inflicted losses upon Britain, but it could not compel its capitulation.

The Embargo in many ways caused the United States more distress than its intended target: American ports from New England to New

Orleans were clogged with idle ships; thousands of seamen were unemployed; and commercial firms were forced to close their doors. Soup kitchens fed those out of work. Manufactured goods were scarce and expensive. Agricultural areas across the nation also suffered as foreign markets were closed, with resulting gluts of farm products and falling prices.

So many complaints flowed into Washington that Jefferson drafted a form reply to defend his policy. The baneful effects of the Embargo were especially acute in maritime New England—the Federalist stronghold that had opposed the measure from its inception. The agricultural South and West, although more willing to support the ban on patriotic and partisan grounds, were also injured. The administration soon found itself fighting a losing battle to enforce an increasingly unpopular prohibition. Ships legally engaged in the coastal trade often encountered convenient bad weather and sought refuge in West Indian or Canadian harbors, where they of course engaged in trade. Some vessels even claimed to have been blown off course across the Atlantic to European ports. An enormous illicit traffic sprang up that defied suppression. Despite his fame as a libertarian, Jefferson created virtually a police state to enforce the Embargo. Laws authorized the seizure of suspected goods and ships, required governmental permission to load cargoes aboard vessels, and forced craft involved in coastal trade to post bond against violations of the Embargo. Sympathetic juries, particularly in New England, frequently failed to convict accused violators regardless of the evidence.

The Embargo had all the disadvantages of war without its sense of national purpose and patriotism. Inability to enforce it undermined the federal government's authority at home and exposed its impotence to all the world. Discontent mounted and the Federalist party began to revive. The intensity of opposition to the Embargo shocked Jefferson. He began to fear that the country was on the verge of civil war. Moreover, he was deeply disappointed by the Embargo's failure to force England to retreat. He had greatly miscalculated both America's willingness to endure self-inflicted injuries and the coercive effects of the ban upon the belligerents. Whatever the Embargo's effects in stimulating domestic manufacturing and some belated liberalization of the British maritime system, it must be viewed as essentially a failure.

5. THE ERSKINE AGREEMENT

As a weary Jefferson transferred the presidency to James Madison, popular outcry forced repeal of the Embargo. The Nonintercourse Act of 1809 replaced it, restoring commerce with all the world except Great Britain and France. If either of those two offenders should repeal its decrees, the President was empowered to restore trade with that country. A weak measure, it aroused more British contempt; on the other hand, it pleased Napoleon in terms of his Continental System. The new act, like its predecessor, was also very difficult to enforce. Ships trading with neutral Europe found it only too easy to enter forbidden ports under one pretext or another.

James Madison, the fourth President of the United States, was a brilliant political philosopher justly famed for his role in framing the Federal Constitution. Yet, he has usually been viewed as one of the nation's weakest chief executives. Short in stature, shy and retiring, reflective rather than decisive, he was not an outstanding administrator or public leader. His inaugural address, delivered in a nervous and low tone and filled with dull platitudes, characterized the administration that followed. Federalist opponents, foreign observers, and even some of his fellow Republicans, derisively dismissed him as an irresolute and timid political cipher. Several recent studies have partially rescued his reputation, depicting him as a stronger leader than previously recognized. It would be difficult, nevertheless, to describe him as an outstanding chief executive.

In many ways the weaknesses of the Madison administration merely reflected the weaknesses of the United States as a world power. Madison intended to continue Jefferson's economic warfare only for a short time; if England did not relent, he planned to ease the country into a war necessary to defend its interests and to vindicate its honor. Unfortunately, because of his own defects of leadership and his failure to prepare the United States for possible war, Madison like Jefferson bogged down in the morass of economic coercion.

For a short time in 1809, Anglo-American relations once again appeared to take a turn for the better. Erskine's reports of American readiness to deal effectively with British deserters, plus the undesirable effects of the Embargo and the Nonintercourse Act upon the British economy, brought about a more favorable attitude in London. Canning instructed Erskine to negotiate a treaty revoking the Orders in Council, provided that the United States would agree to repeal all commercial restrictions aimed at Britain, to accept the Rule of '56, and to consent to the Royal Navy capturing American vessels violating nonintercourse with France. Erskine soon realized that insistence upon the latter two demands would prevent an agreement. Erskine decided to ignore those points in an effort to conclude an adjustment before the two countries drifted closer to war. The negotiations resulted in the Erskine Agreement, signed in April, 1809, in which the American government promised to renew commerce with Britain in exchange for the lifting of the Orders in Council. Americans cheered news of the agreement. Hundreds of heavily laden ships rushed across the Atlantic as Madison proclaimed nonintercourse only against France. A new era seemed at hand when other vexing issues, including impressment, might be solved.

But Canning angrily repudiated the Agreement and recalled Erskine in disgrace. Dominant opinion in England expressed unwillingness to allow any breach in the blockade as the price for America's goodwill. An embarrassed Madison had to reimpose nonintercourse with Great Britain, and so the last promising opportunity for an Anglo-American rapprochement passed.

Canning aggravated American feelings when he sent Francis James Jackson to replace Erskine. Widely known as "Copenhagen" Jackson for his role in the brutal attack upon the Danish fleet and capital city, the new Minister was arrogant, tactless, and contemptuous of most Americans. He arrived with an entourage of eighteen servants and a haughty Prussian baroness as wife. In heated exchanges with the Secretary of State, Jackson charged that the American government had known about Erskine's instructions and persuaded him to violate them. At one stage the Minister in effect called the President a liar when Madison denied the accusations. The State Department broke off discussions with Jackson and finally, in a step warmly approved by Congress, requested his recall. Instead of promptly complying, the Foreign Office allowed Jackson to stay in the United States for the remainder of the year for which he had been paid. The discredited Minister spent the time propagandizing against the Madison administration and being entertained lavishly by Federalist partisans. Nearly two years passed before London sent a replacement.

6. DRIFTING TO WAR

The unpopular Nonintercourse Act was allowed to expire while the administration tried to replace it with Macon's Bill No. 1, a measure permitting importation of British and French goods but keeping American ports closed to the ships of those two countries. Congress instead enacted Macon's Bill No. 2 in 1810, a weak attempt at negative economic coercion or blackmail. The act restored commerce with the two great antagonists, but provided if either France or Britain repealed its objectionable acts, the President could reimpose nonintercourse on the other until it too complied.

Madison regarded the new measure as dishonorable since, in effect, it allowed Britain to control American commerce. He found a welcome escape in Napoleon's attempt to exploit the measure. In August, 1810, the Duc de Cadore, Napoleon's Foreign Minister, announced the Emperor had revoked the Berlin and Milan Decrees conditional upon a British repeal of its Orders, or American action to "cause their rights to be respected by the English." Far from being hoodwinked by Napoleon, as many historians have assumed, Madison was fully aware of the dubious nature of the French repeal. Yet he decided to accept the Cadore letter at face value, in order to compel the British to retreat. If that failed, he would end what he regarded as an intolerable situation by going to war with England. He wrote his Attorney General that Napoleon's action at least offered hope of extricating the United States from "a mortifying peace" or from the necessity of war with *both* belligerents.

The American government, therefore, pretended to find the French repeal satisfactory in order to concentrate on the principal offender against its rights, Great Britain. On November 2, 1810, Madison issued a proclamation acknowledging Napoleon's retraction of his decrees and imposing nonintercourse against Britain until its government should repeal the Orders in Council. The implications were clear: Britain either had to retreat or face the probability of war.

Events moved inexorably toward a final break. Pinkney, the American Minister in London, abandoned his post in despair over negotiations. The new British envoy to the United States, Augustus J. Foster, discovered that, while the State Department accepted his offer of reparations for the *Chesapeake* affair, the settlement had come too late to be of much significance in improving relations. Moreover, American pride had already been satisfied when the frigate *President* in May, 1810, clashed with the lighter British warship *Little Belt* and inflicted heavy damages on the latter. Foster failed to make any progress on other issues owing to the inflexibility of his instructions. Britain agreed to repeal the Orders only when assured that Napoleon had actually retracted his decrees and that the continent was not only reopened to neutral commerce but to British goods as well.

Federalists and other critics, bitterly opposed to Madison's course, called the 12th Congress, elected in 1810–1811, the "War Hawk" Congress, branding its members reckless and expansionist warmongerers. According to most historians, a disgusted electorate sent to Congress younger and more daring representatives filled with zeal for a showdown with Great Britain. During the debates in the new Congress, when Canada was frequently mentioned as a target, Virginia's disgruntled John Randolph of Roanoke ridiculed what he called "one eternal monotonous tone—Canada! Canada! Canada!" as like the call of the whippoorwill. He charged that land hunger, not defense of the national interests and honor, was the real motive for war. Recent studies, however, reveal that the issue of war or peace had played only a minor role in the elections, and that the number of new members in the 12th Congress was not significantly larger than in the previous one. Even the term "War Hawk," applied to such young and ardently nationalist congressmen as Henry Clay of Kentucky, elected Speaker of the House, John C. Calhoun of South Carolina, and Felix Grundy of Tennessee, no longer seems appropriate. These men and others having similar views demonstrated no real eagerness for hostilities. They simply were tired of humiliating half-measures and affronts to the nation's honor, and could perceive no course other than war to end an intolerable situation. Gradually their fellow Republicans came to agree with them; Jeffersonian pacifism and economic coercion no longer seemed adequate to defend the nation's interests.

Madison provided little guidance to the new Congress, although he and Secretary of State James Monroe essentially concurred with the so-called War Hawks. Madison's failure to lead reflected not only his personal timidity and his belief that war-making was the responsibility of Congress, but also his desperate hope that the prospect of hostilities might yet wring concessions from Great Britain. Congress, therefore, drifted by stages into a declaration of war. It passed a weak army bill, but not one to enlarge the navy, and did not approve a recommended tax increase until after war had been declared. In April, 1812, Congress adopted a 90-day embargo to prepare American shipping for hostilities. At last, on June 1, the President sent his "war message" to Congress. He reviewed the long record of grievances against England—impressment, violations of territorial waters and illegal seizures of ships, the Orders in Council, and alleged British instigation of Indian outrages in the Northwest. Yet his message did not explicitly recommend a declaration of war, leaving that question to Congress alone.

Congress spent two weeks in impassioned debate before it passed a resolution for war. Although the West and South most strongly favored war, and the northeastern states, especially New England, most strongly opposed it, divisions largely reflected party rather than sectional lines. The vote in the House for war was 79 in favor to 49 opposed. All the Federalist members voted against war, joined by some Republican defectors, while 90 percent of the Republicans in the House supported the war resolution. The vote in the Senate was much closer, 19 votes for war to 13 against. A proposal to include France failed by only four votes.

The British Minister received notification on June 18, 1812, that a state of war existed between the United States and Great Britain. Ironically, even then the British government was retreating on the Orders in Council. A serious economic depression in England at last persuaded the ministry that it was unwise to sacrifice the American market. The government acted slowly, however, and encountered further delay when a fanatic assassinated Prime Minister Spencer Perceval in the lobby of the House of Commons. The ministry did not complete withdrawal of the Orders in Council until June 23, five days after the American declaration of war (not yet known in London). Contrary to British expectations, when Madison learned of the repeal he refused to suspend the state of war. Impressment still remained unresolved, and the British repeal reserved the right to reimpose the Orders if future French or American actions seemed to necessitate it.

Whatever the subsequent debate about the wisdom of the war, it was not a hasty decision and it came only after repeated efforts for a peaceful settlement. Despite numerous injuries at the hands of France, the American government went to war against England only, preferring one opponent at a time and rightly viewing the mistress of the seas as the most serious malefactor. America had suffered most from the Royal Navy's suppression of its commerce. Psychologically, too, Britain still seemed to regard America as a colony, controlling its commerce and economy, treating its representatives with condescension, and impressing its seamen. Many Americans also believed British officials had instigated recent Indian outrages in the Northwest, in hopes of preventing American growth and prosperity. When General William Henry Harrison defeated the northwest Indians at Tippecanoe in November, 1811, he found newly made British arms on the field beside the fallen Indian warriors. Many citizens viewed war as essential to defending the nation's honor and to reaffirming its independence and sovereignty. Some western advocates of war in 1811–1812 did in truth express land hunger for Canada, as well as the desire to eliminate the Indian menace by expelling their British masters from North America. The primary motive even in the western states, however, was not agrarian cupidity. The entire country, not just a section, suffered from the British blockade and writhed at British affronts to American honor. Canada became the direct target for American military actions because of its proximity; at least there the enemy was accessible to American power.

Madison hoped to use France to offset American unpreparedness. He entertained no thought of allying with Napoleon, of course, for the latter had also injured American interests. Madison felt that as long as Napoleon reigned on the continent, Britain would be too preoccupied to spare much attention to the minor war in North America. After compelling Britain to accept a reasonable settlement, the United States could then concentrate upon France, he decided. That strategy had much to commend it, but unfortunately Napoleon's power even then was on the wane. The invasion of Russia that ultimately destroyed the Grand Army and set the stage for Napoleon's abdication coincided with the beginning of the War of 1812.

Additional Reading

A useful guide to the literature on the causes of the War of 1812 is by W. H. Goodman, "The Origins of the War of 1812: A Survey of Changing Interpretations," *Mississippi Valley Historical Review*, XXVIII (1941), 171–186. Older but useful interpretations include: A. T. Mahan, *Sea Power in its Relations to the War of 1812* (1905); Julius W. Pratt, *The Expansionists of 1812* (1925); and A. L. Burt, *The United States, Great Britain, and British North America* (1940). Bradford Perkins, *Prologue to War* (1961) emphasizes the role of national honor. So too do works by Reginald Horsman, *The Causes of the War of 1812* (1962); Roger Brown, *The Republic in Peril: 1812* (1964); and Norman K. Risjord, "1812:

Conservatives, War Hawks, and the Nation's Honor," *William and Mary Quarterly*, XVIII (1961), 196–210. P. C. T. White, *A Nation on Trial: America and the War of 1812* (1965) agrees. *The War of 1812* (1965) by Harry L. Coles is largely devoted to the war itself but has an excellent brief account of its causes. Lawrence S. Kaplan examines the role of France in American diplomacy: *Jefferson and France* (1967); "Jefferson, the Napoleonic Wars, and the Balance of Power, " *William and Mary Quarterly*, XIV (1957), 196–217; and "France and Madison's Decision for War, 1812," *Mississippi Valley Historical Review*, L (1964), 652–671. On impressment, see J. F. Zimmerman, *Impressment of American Seamen* (1925) and Anthony Steel, "Impressment in the Monroe-Pinkney Negotiations, 1806–1807," *American Historical Review*, LVII (1952), 352–369. L. M. Sears, *Jefferson and the Embargo* (1927) and E. F. Heckscher, *The Continental System* (1922) examine economic warfare. On the two leading American statesmen of the period consult Dumas Malone's *Jefferson the President: First Term, 1801–1805* (1970) and Irving Brant's multivolume biography, *James Madison: Secretary of State, 1807–1809* (1953), *The President, 1809–1812* (1956), and *Commander in Chief* (1961). Brant vigorously defends Madison against his detractors in these volumes and also in his "Madison and the War of 1812," *Virginia Magazine of History and Biography*, LXXIV (1966), 51–67.

Signing of the Treaty of Ghent

5

WAR AND PEACE
WITH BRITAIN,
1812–1818

1. A DEFENSIVE WAR

The War of 1812, although not one of America's more illustrious military ventures, psychologically became a second war for independence. The nation fought to vindicate its honor, to obtain respect for its rights, and to defend its seamen and its trade on the high seas. In short, it struggled to compel Great Britain and in a sense all Europe to recognize the independence of the United States. It was a defensive war, although the need to strike the enemy at his most vulnerable point required that America invade and conquer Canada. Despite the failure of that incredibly mishandled effort, and the fact that by 1814 the United States stood beleaguered on all sides, America obtained her basic object. By the war's end, Europe's leaders, and especially the British, could no longer avoid acknowledging that the United States was a fully sovereign nation entitled to the same considerations as the long-established states of the Old World.

Incredible bungling, incompetence, cowardice, and missed opportunities initially characterized the war on land since the United States was almost totally unprepared for hostilities. When Congress declared war, the standing army numbered little more than 7,000 men, facing about 4,000 British regulars in Canada. Yet, in comparison to Canada with a population of approximately one-half million, the United States boasted over six million inhabitants and should have been able to field between 200,000 and 300,000 armed men. Congress authorized enlarging the regular army to 50,000 men and recruiting 50,000 12-month volunteers. Mustering more than about 35,000 men in the national forces at any one time proved impossible, however. For all the patriotic flag waving, obviously large numbers of citizens either opposed the war or felt apathetic toward it. The state militia numbered far more than the national army, but on the whole they, like the regulars, were poorly trained and unreliable for lengthy campaigns. The army's commanding officers in 1812 were equally unprepared, inexperienced in handling large bodies of men, and often more adept at the arts of politics than of war.

Confusion and inefficiency in the field matched the same in the executive departments in Washington. Despite unquestioned brilliance as a political theorist, President Madison fell short as an inspiring or effective wartime leader. His temperament did not suit the presidency of a sprawling and far from united republic. The President neither led Congress nor mobilized public opinion, nor did he display the administrative talents required in a time of crisis. Mediocrity characterized the cabinet with the exception of Secretary of State James Monroe, and the War, Navy, and Treasury departments lacked administrative machinery for a far-flung war. On the other hand, Madison did reveal certain strengths and virtues. Repeated defeats did not dishearten him, and he remained tolerant of a strident opposition that sometimes verged on treason. In contrast to 1798–1799, no domestic witch hunts nor repressive legislation occurred, and the divisions caused by the war could be more readily repaired after the struggle ended.

Congress did little to help the executive. The very session that declared war in 1813 adjourned without legislating the necessary taxes. Subsequent taxes proved insufficient, so the government raised most funds by that time-honored inflationary device of the printing press—borrowing in the form of Treasury notes and bonds. The First Bank of the United States had expired in 1811, and no central mechanism existed to handle the Treasury's needs and state banks proved inadequate. Moreover, New England bankers, holding most of the nation's specie, refused to cooperate in purchasing federal notes—apparently some New Englanders preferred instead to buy English securities. Yet somehow the nation staggered through the war and ultimately obtained better leadership both in the army and in the executive departments in Washington. Unfortunately by then earlier opportunities for military gains had vanished, and the United States found itself almost everywhere on the defensive.

Despite the fact that basic American strategy against Canada was defective, with greater determination and skill the Americans probably could have attained more success. The most promising approach would have been to concentrate American forces in an assault on Montreal. The fall of that city would have cut the St. Lawrence–Great Lakes water life line of upper Canada, thereby dooming most of British North America in one blow. President Madison favored that strategy, but circumstances demanded a nearly fatal dispersion of forces. American troops were scattered along a vast northern frontier where communication and transportation through unsettled wilderness areas were painfully slow. New England declined to allow its well-trained militia to be called into federal service. Making the best of a bad situation, the administration shifted to a strategy of using local forces in diversionary attacks along the river-lakes line with, hopefully, the main force still to be directed at Montreal.

A series of fiascoes resulted. British officials initially had little hope of successfully defending Canada and resigned themselves to regaining its possession at the eventual peace conference. They were much too pessimistic. On the far western end of the front, Governor William Hull of Michigan Territory marched into Detroit, losing his baggage and confidential papers to the British on the way, and briefly invaded Canada. General Isaac Brock, Governor of Upper Canada and a tireless, courageous, and skillfull military commander, rallied his Indian allies, led by the great chief Tecumseh. Brock waged a masterful campaign of propaganda and maneuver that forced Hull back into Detroit, where Brock persuaded him to surrender on August 16. Hull was later courtmartialed and sentenced to hang for cowardice, but Madison pardoned him because of his distinguished record in the Revolutionary War. After the fall of Detroit, Brock hastily moved to the Niagara front to meet the next threat to his sparsely populated province. There he faced the inexperienced General Stephen Van Rensselaer, commanding a force of regulars and militia. Van Rensselaer attacked Queenston, Canada, and won initial successes during which the valorous Brock was killed. When the New York militia refused to cross the international boundary to aid the regulars, however, British counterattacks overwhelmed the Americans and drove the remnants back across the frontier. On the eastern front, the regular army's senior Major General, Henry Dearborn, advanced so hesitantly against Montreal that his so-called offensive never really got underway. By end of the year, the Americans not only had failed totally in the expected easy conquest of Canada, but had lost national territory and faced the serious threat of British control of the lakes system.

The Americans fared better in 1813. Oliver Hazard Perry defeated the British ships at Put-in-Bay on September 10, and won naval control of Lake Erie. William Henry Harrison recaptured Detroit and temporarily occupied Canadian soil, defeating the enemy at the Battle of the Thames on October 5, 1813, at which Tecumseh was slain. In the Southwest, General Andrew Jackson led an expedition against the Creek Indians, allies of Spain and Britain, and decisively defeated them at Horseshoe Bend in March, 1814. But these were essentially defensive victories and fell far short of the bright hopes of 1812.

The war at sea, although more creditable to American honor, succeeded hardly any more than that on land. When hostilities began, the United States had a small but competent navy of seven frigates and nine lesser craft, plus approximately 170 gunboats scattered along the coasts.

A British grand fleet of 600 warships, including 130 ships of the line (battleships) and 116 frigates opposed them. Despite the requirements of the war in Europe, Britain assigned about 100 ships to the waters around the United States. In the early months of the war, Americans won some spectacular single ship victories, in one of which the *Constitution* captured the British frigate *Guerriere*. A shocked London *Times* exclaimed, "Never before in the history of the world did an English frigate strike to an American." Additional Yankee successes aroused growing concern, especially since the well-built, well-commanded American ships showed greater superiority than the English vessels they challenged. Adopting tactics of avoiding single ship contests, Britain soon exploited her vast sea power to drive the Americans off the high seas. The United States also had commissioned 500 privateers or privately owned armed ships, which captured some 1,300 prizes and drove English insurance rates sky-high. But all these accomplishments were hardly more than annoying pinpricks to mighty Britain. By 1814 the Royal Navy controlled American waters, had almost completely eliminated American commerce, and had clamped a tight blockade on the ports and coasts of the United States. American foreign trade nearly vanished and tax revenues fell off with the dearth of imports. Because the nation was forced to depend on inadequate land transportation, commodities glutted some areas while severe shortages existed elsewhere. Moreover, command of the seas enabled the British to ravage the American coasts and to undertake military operations wherever they chose.

2. DIPLOMACY IN THE MIDST OF WAR

Peace overtures began almost as soon as the United States declared war. Foster, the departing British Minister, urged Madison and Monroe to suspend hostilities until Britain could respond with possible concessions, but they declined. Madison feared that suspending hostilities so quickly would abort the growing war spirit, and he had little faith that Britain would be conciliatory. Subsequently, as noted before, he learned that the noxious Orders in Council indeed were being repealed, but he still feared the English government might restore them at some future time unless the two nations had concluded some sort of binding settlement. Moreover, he insisted on cessation of impressment and the release of American seamen from British service.

Great Britain did not want war. At first London thought that repeal of the Orders would quickly restore peace. Sir George Prevost at Halifax, Governor-in-chief of Upper and Lower Canada, proposed a truce to General Dearborn, but Madison refused to permit it. In London, the American *chargé*, Jonathan Russell, received instructions to demand not only repeal of the Orders but an end to impressment. In exchange, the United States offered to enact laws barring British subjects from employment in the American navy or merchant marine. Lord Castlereagh, who had taken charge of the Foreign Office in 1812, rejected the offer. As he remarked to Russell, "no administration could expect to remain in power that should consent to renounce the right of impressment, or to suspend the practice. . . ." Unwilling to retreat further, Britain reluctantly accepted war and soon engaged in it much too vigorously for the comfort of the Americans.

During these abortive exchanges, Czar Alexander of Russia launched a peace bid of his own. He offered to mediate the Anglo-American war because it would disrupt Russo-American trade and divert Britain from the primary task of defeating Napoleon. John Quincy Adams, the American Minister at St. Petersburg, transmitted the offer, which reached Washington in the spring of 1813. By that time, Madison was eager for negotiations. He promptly appointed Albert Gallatin, the esteemed Secretary of the Treasury, and James Bayard, a very able Federalist from Delaware, to join Adams in negotiations under Russian auspices. The President later added Jonathan Russell and Henry Clay— the Kentucky "War Hawk" and Speaker of the House of Representatives—to the peace commission, making it an able if incongruous group. Clay personified the young Westerner, fond of whiskey, cards, and the ladies, and his late hours often scandalized Adams, a severely self-disciplined and hard-working man. Gallatin, smooth and tactful, in fact represented the administration and managed to keep peace among his self-willed colleagues.

After arriving in Russia, the American envoys cooled their heels before they finally learned that Great Britain had declined the Czar's offer. Realizing that Russia would probably support the American position on neutral rights, the British government objected to the presence of a third party in any peace negotiations with the United States. Instead, Britain offered to enter into direct exchange with the Americans. Belatedly learning of that offer, the Americans left Russia for Ghent in the Lowlands, where the negotiations took place.

3. 1814: A YEAR OF PERIL

The British resolved to try their fortunes at war prior to concluding a peace. Castlereagh, who had offered direct talks largely to evade Russian mediation, indicated no haste to open the negotiations. By 1814, the tide of war in Europe had turned strongly in England's favor. Napoleon was defeated and forced to retire to Elba, thereby freeing Britain to concentrate on America. Moreover, British opinion had hardened toward the United States. Had not that ungrateful republic, insensitive to ties of blood and history, turned on England in the hour of its greatest danger? Many Britishers viewed their nation as having fought Napoleonic imperialism on behalf of all free countries, including the United States.

Instead of understanding Britain's role and tolerating temporary irritants, the United States had, in effect, allied with the bloody tyrant. Such treachery demanded punishment. Britain wanted to teach the Americans a painful lesson lest they again assault the mother country while she fought a war for survival. Moreover, chastisement offered an attractive opportunity to eliminate or curb a commercial and industrial rival before it grew too strong.

Transporting veteran troops from the continent to the New World, Great Britain planned a massive invasion via Lake Champlain to cut off New York and New England from the rest of the Union. She planned a second large-scale attack at New Orleans to seal the vast Mississippi Valley, to dishearten the western inhabitants, and perhaps to reestablish Spanish rule in Louisiana under British protection. Britain intended to use coastal raids and amphibious operation in Chesapeake Bay to distract attention from the major blows and to undermine American morale. Madison's administration, the British believed, might well be overthrown in the aftermath of dismaying defeats, thus strengthening immeasurably Britain's position at the peace table.

General Prevost cautiously led a veteran army of 15,000 men southward along Lake Champlain, convinced that he must have naval control of the lake. But Thomas Macdonough, who skillfully maneuvered the American fleet at Plattsburg Bay, denied Prevost that control and he withdrew his disgusted forces into Canada. General Robert Ross and Admiral Sir George Cockburn operated with impunity in Chesapeake Bay, capturing and burning Washington after routing the American defenders. Entering the capital city close on the heels of the fleeing President and the First Lady, the British helped themselves to a hastily abandoned presidential banquet and set fire to the White House, the Capitol, and other public buildings before they withdrew to their waiting ships. The Americans, however, repulsed a subsequent assault on Baltimore, then the fourth largest city in the United States.

In the South, Sir Edward Pakenham, the Duke of Wellington's brother-in-law, attacked New Orleans with an army of 8,000 veterans. Advancing through difficult terrain and grossly underestimating the fighting qualities and leadership of General Andrew Jackson's forces, Pakenham delivered a frontal assault on the well-prepared American lines on January 8, 1815. Pakenham was killed and his men fell back before murderous fire. The British forces suffered 2,100 casualties, including 700 dead, while Jackson's men emerged with only 21 casualties.

News of Jackson's glorious victory reached Washington at about the same time as envoys from the Hartford Convention. Reflecting the mounting unhappiness of many New Englanders with the war, and fears of British invasion, a group of opponents of "Mr. Madison's War"—

including representatives from Connecticut, Rhode Island, and Massachusetts—convened in Hartford in December, 1814, at the invitation of the Massachusetts General Court. Calling itself moderate rather than die-hard Federalist secessionist, the convention requested amending the Federal Constitution to require a two-thirds vote by each House of Congress to admit new states, to declare war except in case of invasion, or to levy an embargo. The request implied a threat of secession if the federal government refused to adopt these and other demands designed to protect New England's minority position in the Union. The tremendous upsurge of patriotism aroused by Jackson's victory, and news of a peace treaty from Ghent, made the Hartford proposals seem so ridiculous that the convention envoys hastily departed from the capital. The Battle of New Orleans, fought a few days after the signing of the Peace of Ghent but before the news reached America, has been seen by many historians as an anticlimatic victory. Recent studies, however, indicate that it was far more than merely a fillip to national pride. If Pakenham had won instead, Britain might have refused to ratify the peace treaty and might have demanded reopening the negotiations with territorial gains in view.

4. THE PEACE OF CHRISTMAS EVE

While war continued in America, the peace negotiators finally met at Ghent. The British delegation led by Lord Gambier, a short-tempered naval officer, included young Henry Goulburn of the Colonial Office, and Dr. William Adams, a legal expert. Although the Britishers were less able than their American counterparts, it should be kept in mind that Britain's chief attention was focused on Europe and the forthcoming Congress of Vienna. Moreover, Gambier and especially Goulburn had more ability than usually assumed, and Ghent was close enough to London to enable the ministry to control the exchanges.

Monroe initially instructed the American commissioners to insist upon renunciation of impressment as the sine qua non or absolute prerequisite of peace, and to seek acknowledgment of the American version of neutral rights. Early in 1814, he added other terms and directed the envoys to try to obtain the cession of Canada as the best guaranty of future Anglo-American tranquility. Subsequently, under the ominous clouds of Napoleon's fall and a hardening of British public temper, Gallatin persuaded Madison to abandon the impressment issue. The Americans at Ghent, though on the defensive, thereafter had the clear advantage of knowing precisely what the United States would accept as a minimum: a peace restoring the prewar status quo.

As the negotiations got under way on August 8, 1814, British opinion demanded nothing less than humiliation of the foe. One London journal asked for a "Peace such as America *deserves*, and British *generosity* may bestow . . . upon . . . a faithless, unprincipled, and corrupt Government." The ministry, on the other hand, aware that a prolonged war would be costly, adopted a more flexible attitude. It hoped, however, that British victories in America would compel the Madison administration to accept territorial losses. When he presented the British terms to the American envoys, Goulburn exceeded his instructions and demanded as a sine qua non the creation of an Indian buffer state between Canada and the United States, carved out of the Northwest territory. Britain also refused to restore fishing liberties off Newfoundland without an equivalent concession, and demanded that the United States cede territory along the prewar boundary in Maine, New York, and the Lake Superior area, and that the American republic alone agree not to maintain warships on the Great Lakes. Absolutely refusing to consider such terms, the American commission drew up a masterly refutation intended to appeal to public opinion in Europe and the United States. Hoping to apply pressure on London, the commissioners then prepared to leave for home. Anxious not to end the negotiations, and still confident of victories in America, the British ministry gradually modified its terms and eventually proposed a peace based on the *uti possedetus* or the territory held by each side at the war's end. The Americans countered by insisting upon the prewar status quo and once more packed to leave Ghent. Previously depressed by reports of the burning of Washington, John Quincy Adams and his colleagues took heart when news of Macdonough's victory at Plattsburg Bay and the collapse of Prevost's invasion arrived. Meanwhile, the British raid on Washington and news of Britain's demands at Ghent strengthened American resolve to continue the war. Even Federalists admitted the unacceptability of the British conditions.

These events in America made it clear to London that additional and costly military efforts would be necessary before extensive territorial gains could be obtained. Wellington, whom the ministry wanted to take command of the war in the New World, advised that he could not promise success unless naval control of the lakes could be secured. In the present circumstance, he viewed his government's demands for territory as without justification: "You can get no territory; indeed, the state of your military operations, however creditable, does not entitle you to demand any." At the same time the ministry also viewed with dismay signs of serious cleavages among the victorious allies at Vienna, where Russia revealed disturbing ambitions for a Polish kingdom. In Goulburn's own words, Britain needed to save itself "the embarrassment which an American war would cause . . . as regarded her free action in European affairs. . . ." Moreover, the heavily burdened British taxpayer, weary after twenty years of nearly continuous warfare, was losing enthusiasm for prosecuting the war against the United States. The British ministry realistically decided to conclude peace based on the American proposals.

Signed on December 24, 1814, the Peace of Christmas Eve formally recognized that neither side had won the war. All the heroism and valor, the bloody and costly sacrifices of both belligerents, seemed in vain as the treaty simply restored the status quo ante bellum. Each side agreed to return such small slices of the other's territory as it had managed to occupy during the war. Great Britain abandoned hopes for an Indian buffer and territorial gains. For its part, having gone to war in defense of neutral rights, the United States accepted a treaty that completely ignored impressment and maritime seizures. The issues causing hostilities remained unsettled. Thus the American diplomats, often over praised for their labors at Ghent, only managed to avoid losses for the United States. Yet they merited recognition for their courage in the face of adversity and for their persistence in continuing negotiations until events made peace possible.

Though many in England, and on the continent, viewed the Treaty of Ghent as a defeat for British diplomacy, Napoleon's return from Elba quickly diverted attention from America. In the United States, Jackson's victory at New Orleans happily preceded by about ten days the tidings that peace had been concluded at Ghent and led to the flattering if erroneous belief that America had defeated mighty England and then had generously granted her peace. At last the United States succeeded in compelling the mother country to admit fully the independence of her former colony. Wartime blunders and defeats, opposition to war, and threats to the Union were all forgotten in the general rejoicing at the coming of peace. Sectionalism and partisanship faded into the background as the country experienced a great upsurge of patriotic sentiment and unity. Even President Madison achieved something close to national popularity. The Senate quickly approved the treaty and Madison exchanged ratifications with Great Britain. The Federalist party soon died away, and the "Era of Good Feelings" commenced.

Ghent obviously failed to achieve either indemnity for past wrongs at Britain's hands or security against their repetition in the future, and clearly, Jefferson and Madison had thrust an unprepared and disunited country into a perilous war, which yielded rather meager results. Nevertheless, all turned out well. The war succeeded in eliminating the Indian menace in both the Northwest and the Southwest and in removing barriers to expansion of settlement. England was now closer than ever before to thinking of the United States as an equal in the community of states, and not merely as a former colony. Time also revealed that Ghent closed one period of American history and opened another. Europe was not to experience another general war until 1914, ample time to free the United States from serious foreign threats and to enable it to concentrate upon its own internal development and expansion.

5. AFTERMATH OF GHENT

To many Americans at the time, Ghent seemed merely a temporary truce before another round of war would be necessary to compel England to recognize America's rights. The peace treaty, after all, failed signally to remove the underlying causes of conflict. Yet the postwar years brought several Anglo-American agreements that greatly improved relations between the two countries and established a permanent foundation of peace.

An improved attitude on the part of statesmen on both sides of the Atlantic contributed greatly to the new era. Foreign Secretary Castlereagh began to cultivate friendlier relations with the United States on the basis of equality and mutual respect. Of course, economic and diplomatic realism, not sentiment, motivated his change in attitude. When he sent a new representative to Washington, Charles Bagot, Castlereagh instructed him to avoid involvement in America's domestic politics and to smooth over any diplomatic problems that might arise. The tactful and amiable Minister succeeded so well that he achieved the distinction of being the only diplomat in Washington who escaped a serious clash with John Quincy Adams, President Monroe's able but testy Secretary of State. Adams apparently never warmed to the new atmosphere and received Castlereagh's overtures with some distrust and caution. President Monroe, on the other hand, responded much more positively and welcomed the detente.

One of the problems left unresolved at Ghent was the threat of a naval arms race on the Great Lakes. Aware of the strategic importance of the lakes, during the war both sides had begun to construct warships on a large scale. Congress, however, was anxious to reduce taxes and the public debt, and soon retrenched on expenditures after the war and called a halt to American construction. Fearing that Britain planned to maintain its existing forces and to build new warships, Washington proposed an agreement to limit drastically naval armaments on the lakes. After some delay, the British government acquiesced. The English people were weary of war and taxes, and Parliament was unenthusiastic about new defense burdens. Apparently the ministry realized that a costly naval arms race ultimately had to be won by the United States, in view of its advantages in proximity and resources. Accordingly, it also recognized that Canada's security depended less on arms than on the continuation of good Anglo-American relations. The Rush-Bagot Agreement in April, 1817 sharply restricted naval armaments on the lakes; each side pledged to maintain no more than four small armed vessels in the lakes system,

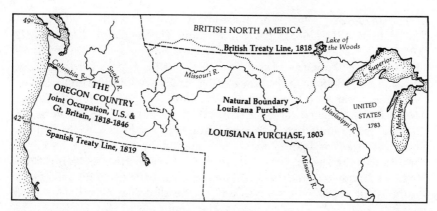

The Convention Line of 1818 with Great Britain

but the pact omitted any mention of land fortifications. The agreement, therefore, while favorable to the United States, did not appear of any major significance at the time. Only after the passage of many years and new crises did the agreement assume importance as a major international advance toward disarmament and a peaceful "unguarded" frontier.

The peace negotiators in 1814 had been unable to agree on more than a temporary commercial treaty to replace the arrangement made by Jay in 1794. Several other issues also remained unsettled after the 1814 treaty and both sides recognized that these problems could endanger Anglo-American relations if left unresolved for a long period of time. Monroe sent Albert Gallatin to join the Minister, Richard Rush, in London for negotiations on these questions. The resultant Convention of 1818 renewed the 1815 commercial treaty (but failed to open the British West Indies to American trade), restored in a somewhat restricted form American fishing rights off Newfoundland and Labrador, and extended the boundary between Canada and the United States westward from the Lake of the Woods along the 49th parallel to the Rocky Mountains. Since neither country yet felt any acute concern about the Oregon territory on the Pacific northwest coast, the convention provided for it to be open for the next ten years to citizens of both countries without prejudice to the claims of either power.

These postwar adjustments relieved the major strains on Anglo-American relations that might have endangered the recently established peace. They also enabled Secretary of State Adams to concentrate on solving the Florida question with Spain.

Additional Reading

The most thoroughly researched account of the war and postwar years is by Bradford Perkins, *Castlereagh and Adams: England and the United*

States, 1812–1823 (1964). For the military aspects, see Harry C. Coles, *The War of 1812* (1965); J. M. Hitsman, *The Incredible War of 1812* (1965); P. P. Mason, ed., *After Tippecanoe: Some Aspects of the War of 1812* (1963); E. F. Beirne, *The War of 1812* (1949); and A. T. Mahan, *Sea Power in its Relations to the War of 1812* (1905). Wilbur Devereux Jones, "A British View of the War of 1812 and the Peace Negotiations," *Mississippi Valley Historical Review*, XLV (1958), 481–487, points out that the war essentially took on the features of a sideshow to the British. That was true for France also, as explained by Lawrence S. Kaplan, "France and the War of 1812," *Journal of American History*, LVII (1970), 36–47. *A Nation on Trial: America and the War of 1812* (1965) by P. C. T. White is an excellent brief account of the diplomacy of the war and peacemaking. Still useful are the older studies by F. A. Updyke, *The Diplomacy of the War of 1812* (1915) and A. L. Burt, *The United States, Great Britain, and British North America* (1940). A popular account of the peace negotiations is by Fred L. Engelman, *The Peace of Christmas Eve* (1962). On Madison, see the older critical evaluation by Henry Adams, *History of the United States during the Administrations of Jefferson and Madison* (1891), Vol. IX and Irving Brant's much more favorable *James Madison: Commander in Chief, 1812–1836* (1961). On the American peace commissioners see S. F. Bemis, *John Quincy Adams and the Foundations of American Foreign Policy* (1949); Raymond Walters, Jr., *Albert Gallatin: Jeffersonian Financier and Diplomat* (1957); Bernard Mayo, *Henry Clay: Spokesman of the New West* (1937); and Clement Eaton, *Henry Clay and the Art of American Politics* (1957). Canadian-American relations are examined by J. M. Callahan, *American Foreign Policy in Canadian Relations* (1937); E. W. McInnis, *The Unguarded Frontier* (1942); Hugh L. Keenleyside and G. S. Brown, *Canada and the United States* (rev. ed., 1952); and C. P. Stacey, "The Myth of the Unguarded Frontier, 1815–1871," *American Historical Review*, LVI (1950), 1–18.

John Quincy Adams

6

FLORIDA, LATIN AMERICA, AND THE MONROE DOCTRINE, 1815–1826

1. EXPANSION INTO THE FLORIDAS

America has exhibited expansionist tendencies since its earliest colonial origins. After independence the country's leaders began to visualize the United States as heir to the empires of Europe. With a dynamic economy, and freed from the embroilments of the Old World, the young nation could hope to enlarge its economic and political system and to expand its influence over most of the Western Hemisphere. The War of 1812 demonstrated the need for greater economic independence from Europe, and its apparently victorious end enormously stimulated American nationalism. Ardently nationalist spokesmen such as Henry Clay soon began championing not merely a new era of national economic measures at home but the extension of an "American System" to all the New World. This exuberant mood, short-lived though it was, manifested itself in territorial expansion into Florida, in recognition of the independence of Latin American states emerging from Old World rule, and in promulgation of the Monroe Doctrine—the classic statement asserting the common identity of the hemisphere and divorcing it from Europe.

American leaders had long been conscious of the strategic and economic importance of the Floridas. That peninsula and its panhandle dominated coastal routes between the Atlantic and the Gulf of Mexico, and controlled the outlets of several rivers draining the southwestern United States. If the Floridas fell into the hands of a power stronger than Spain, the United States feared they would be like a pistol pointed at it, especially threatening the outlet of the Mississippi River. In 1803 Jefferson had attempted to remove that threat by purchasing New Orleans and West Florida. Instead his agents brought home from Paris one of the greatest real estate contracts in all history, the treaty for the purchase of Louisiana. Swallowing his scruples, Jefferson quickly tried to exploit its ill-defined boundaries by interpreting it to include much of Texas and West Florida to the Perdido River. Under Spanish rule Louisiana had never included any of Florida, although after regaining title to Florida in 1783 Spain placed the administration of West Florida under the governor of New Orleans. Despite the weakness of American claims, Jefferson confidently predicted that "in good time" all the Floridas would pass to the United States.

Spain proved more stubborn than he had expected. Neither diplomatic blandishments nor threats of force could move Madrid. Congress in 1804 authorized the executive to extend customs controls to Mobile, but Spain protested such bold aggression and Jefferson drew back. Instead, in his message to Congress in 1805, he tried to browbeat the Spanish into compliance, referring to strained relations and the possible necessity of raising 300,000 troops to defend the nation's interests. He then obtained a secret appropriation of $2 million with which he hoped to buy the area. Though efforts to bribe Napoleon into forcing Madrid's consent seemed promising for a while, the great tyrant's decision in 1808 to seat his brother Joseph on the Spanish throne ended that scheme. Napoleon thereafter took more interest in preserving Spain's empire as an extension of his own than in bartering parts of it to the United States.

Fearful that France or Great Britain might seize the Floridas for their own, Congress in 1811 adopted a secret "no transfer" resolution, which stated that transferal of any part of the Floridas into other hands would be contrary to American interests. In the previous year, American settlers around Baton Rouge in West Florida had staged a revolution against Spanish rule with the encouragement of the Madison administration. President Madison promptly extended American jurisdiction over West Florida to the Pearl River. In 1813, during the war with England, the American army had occupied Mobile. West Florida thus passed bloodlessly and by stages into American control. Spain could only feebly protest what many in Europe regarded as virtual highway robbery.

The same type of revolutionary technique was also attempted in East Florida. Madison in 1812 used the former governor of Georgia, George Mathews, to try to obtain possession of the coveted eastern half by encouraging or instigating a revolution among its inhabitants and by engineering a request for incorporation into the United States. Aware that East Florida posed a more delicate problem than West Florida, the President cautioned Mathews to "hide your hand and mine" in the venture. Mathews indiscreetly employed American armed forces to support the revolution, which came to an ignominious end when the Spanish repulsed an attack at St. Augustine. An embarrassed Madison recalled his overzealous agent, although American forces continued to occupy parts of East Florida until the end of the war with Great Britain.

The Floridas, 1803–1819

2. THE TRANS-CONTINENTAL TREATY OF 1819

Spain's grasp on Florida continued to weaken after 1815. Ferdinand VII reoccupied his throne, only to face liberal opposition at home and revolution in the Americas. East Florida was fast becoming an intolerable nuisance to the United States. A haven for runaway slaves, it swarmed with a variety of cutthroats and adventurers who supplied the Seminole Indians with arms and incited pillaging raids across the border into the United States. Spain obviously could not preserve order and failed to fulfill the provisions of the Pinckney Treaty for controlling its Indians.

John Quincy Adams, appointed Secretary of State by President Monroe in 1817, speeded the Spanish departure from Florida. The new Secretary was a highly disciplined and enormously intelligent man with a vast experience in foreign affairs. Born in Massachusetts in 1767, his parents, the great patriot statesman John Adams and his brilliant and self-educated wife, Abigail, imbued him with ambition, exacting morality, and dedicated patriotism. At age 11 he accompanied his father across a storm-tossed and British-controlled Atlantic to a diplomatic mission in Europe. Young Adams profited greatly from his unusual educational opportunities, observing firsthand the protocol and diplomacy of the French court, and conversing with many of the principal public figures of the day. In 1780, Adams went to Russia as secretary to Francis Dana on the latter's futile mission to obtain recognition and aid. From these experiences Adams learned much about diplomacy, modern history, and languages. Returning to advanced standing at Harvard, Adams graduated with high honors and began to study law. His legal career quickly ended when President Washington appointed him Minister to the Netherlands. Subsequently he held the same position in Prussia, prior to being recalled in 1801 by his proud father, the retiring President, who did not want to ask Jefferson to retain his son at his post. After a term in the United States Senate, when he broke with his Massachusetts Federalist backers over the embargo issue, Adams returned to diplomacy in 1809 as Minister to Czarist Russia. He also played an important part in the peace negotiations at Ghent, before heading the American Legation in Great Britain.

John Quincy Adams was nearly 50 years old when he took charge of the State Department in 1817. A lonely figure, short, thickset, and with a massive bald head, Adams practiced severe self-discipline. Throughout his long life he adhered to a rigid regime of early rising, study and exercise, and faithful reading of the Scriptures, often in French or German to polish his mastery of those languages. A fervent patriot and advocate of national expansion, as early as 1796 he wrote that the American system would "infallibly triumph over the European system," and in 1811 he defined the United States as "a nation, coextensive with the North American continent. . . ." The mission of the United States, he believed, was to civilize all North America and by example to help eradicate European colonialism from the entire hemisphere. His wealth of diplomatic experience and his notable achievements as Secretary of State rank him foremost among the occupants of that office. Adams established an excellent working relationship with President Monroe, who also boasted much diplomatic experience, in which each recognized the proper function of the other. As Jefferson observed from his retreat at Monticello, the two seemed ideally suited for each other, with Adams' acute intelligence balanced by Monroe's maturity of judgment.

The revolutionary movements surging across Spain's empire in America complicated the new Secretary's negotiations with the Spanish Minister, Luis de Onís, over Florida. The Spanish government understandably resented American aid and sympathy to the rebels and anxiously tried to prevent diplomatic recognition of the revolutionary governments. Adams and Monroe played upon Madrid's apprehensions in order to hasten Spain's inevitable retreat from Florida. Onís proposed a settlement fixing the western boundary of the Louisiana Purchase close to the Mississippi River, while Adams demanded cession of East Florida and about one-half of Texas. Meanwhile events continued to reveal Spain's inability to preserve order in Florida. Indians from Florida attacked American surveyors marking the border, and filibusters or near-pirates operating from Amelia Island caused Monroe to order its occupation despite Spain's theoretical sovereignty.

Jackson's famous raid into Florida in 1818 dealt the final blow to Spanish pride and pretensions in that province. Washington sent General Andrew Jackson to pacify the border and authorized him to pursue Indian raiders into Florida if necessary, but not to attack any Spanish forts or garrisons. The hero of New Orleans saw a good opportunity to evict Spain entirely from Florida and to seize it as indemnity for Indian outrages. "The whole of East Florida [should be] seized . . . and this can be done without implicating the Government," he wrote. "Let it be signified to me through any channel . . . that the possession of the Floridas would be desirable . . . and in sixty days it will be accomplished." Monroe later denied he had signalled Jackson to act, but he probably knew of his impetuous general's plans and failed to curb him. Believing he had the administration's blessing, Jackson with 3,000 troops invaded East Florida in March, 1818 and rapidly overran the province. He seized the Spanish fort at St. Marks, defeated the Seminoles, captured Pensacola, and deposed the Spanish governor. Jackson also captured two English subjects—Alexander Arbuthnot, an elderly Scots trader, and Lieutenant Robert Ambrister, on suspension from the British Marines— who were tried by a military court for inciting the Indians. Arbuthnot was hanged from the deck of his own ship, and Ambrister was executed by firing squad in accordance with military courtesy.

News of Jackson's foray aroused a furor in Europe and the United States. The drumhead trial and execution of two Englishmen naturally irritated the British government, but its anger subsided when it received evidence of the men's complicity. Spain sharply protested the flagrant violation of its sovereignty and demanded restoration of Florida, payment of an indemnity, and punishment of General Jackson. The Madrid government failed to obtain support from Great Britain, however, for Foreign Secretary Castlereagh, more concerned with the European political situation than Florida, continued his rapprochement with the United States. In fact, Castlereagh earlier had advised Spain to cede Florida in exchange for a favorable western boundary. Jackson's political opponents in the United States called loudly for his reprimand and introduced a censure resolution in Congress. Most of Monroe's cabinet agreed with the critics, but Adams vigorously defended the general's actions as within the scope of his instructions and amply justified by Spain's misrule in Florida. Since his latest exploits had made Jackson even more a great national hero, especially in the Indian-hating and anti-Catholic western states, President Monroe, following Adams's advice, decided to restore Florida to Spain but to forego punishing the general. A note to Onís defended Jackson's raid, in light of Spain's inability to control the area, as fully justified "By the ordinary laws and usages of nations. . . ." In a further strongly phrased communication, designed largely for its effect upon European and American public opinion, Adams called Spain to account for its misrule in Florida and warned that she must either maintain order or cede the province to the United States.

Capitulating to the inevitable, Onís renewed negotiations. In the treaty he concluded with Adams, the United States exchanged its paper claims to Texas for the cession of East Florida and agreed to pay its citizens' claims against Spain to the extent of $5 million. Exploiting the

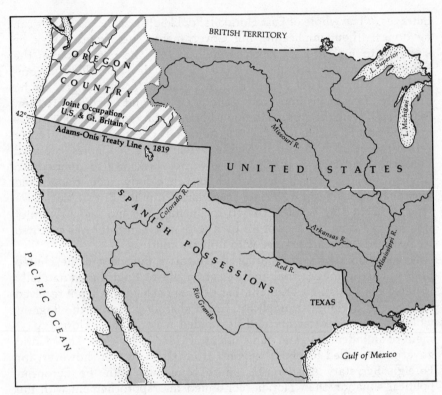

The Transcontinental Treaty of 1819

opportunity, Adams proposed and won a definite boundary line between Spanish possessions and the Louisiana territory across the continent to the Pacific Ocean, running along the Sabine, Red, and Arkansas rivers to the 42nd parallel and the sea. The United States thereby gained whatever title to the Oregon territory Spain possessed.

The Adams-Onís or Trans-Continental Treaty was signed on February 22, 1819. Congress speedily granted its approval, for most Americans were pleased with its terms and Texas had not yet become an object of popular interest. Adams felt justifiably proud of his role in securing this epochal treaty and advancing America's borders across the continent. "It was," he recorded, "perhaps, the most important day of my life." Lest he be swept with a false pride, however, the devout patriot hastened to attribute the great diplomatic victory to "the work of an intelligent and all-embracing Cause." Spain stalled final ratification of the treaty for two years in the vain hope of obtaining Washington's pledge not to recognize the independence of its former colonies in Latin America. Patience and pressure finally prevailed, and in 1821 the two countries exchanged ratifications.

3. RECOGNITION OF LATIN AMERICA

Napoleon's seizure of the Spanish throne in 1808 inadvertently "shook the tree of liberty" in the Americas. A nationalist revolt in Spain and her colonies against the hated French overlords established juntas or councils that claimed to rule in the name of Ferdinand VII, heir to the deposed Charles IV. In America the movement veered toward complete independence, especially after the collapse of the Napoleonic empire enabled Ferdinand to assume the throne as a divine-right absolute monarch. Accumulated resentments against years of economic exploitation, political misrule, and social condescension by the mother country exploded in a wave of revolutions that by the early 1820's had destroyed most of Spain's once vast empire.

Americans knew little about Spanish America until the Wars of the French Revolution and Napoleon relaxed Spain's mercantilist system and opened the colonies to neutral commerce. American traders eagerly entered these markets and often served, intentionally or not, as propagandists for revolution and independence. President Jefferson and his fellow citizens observed with great pleasure the anti-French and pro-independence developments in Spain and its colonies. In his so-called Large Policy of 1808, Jefferson envisaged a New World, freed of its shackles to the Old, within which the United States would greatly expand its commercial and political influence. His immediate interests, however, centered on the possible acquisition of Florida and Cuba.

Yet the Large Policy remained unfulfilled. Both Jefferson and Madison of necessity concentrated their attention upon Great Britain and the controversy over neutral commerce. The Embargo and the War of 1812 precluded American ships from exploiting the newly opened markets, while British trade with the area flourished. The Madison administration did send consuls and agents to Latin America to promote commerce and report upon local conditions. The United States also unofficially received rebel emissaries and recognized the belligerent rights of the rebels. Despite the sympathies of Madison and Secretary of State Monroe for the cause of Latin American independence, however, official policy remained one of neutrality and watchful waiting.

The Monroe administration continued that cautious policy. Although the second great revolutionary current that swept Latin America after Napoleon reaped more success than the earlier wave, compelling reasons still demanded caution: the success of the independence movements remained in doubt for some years and stable de facto governments emerged slowly; delicate negotiations with Spain were underway over Florida; and the United States feared that the conservative coalition directing Europe's destinies after 1815 might react to precipitous American action by intervening on Spain's behalf. Yet American neutrality operated in favor of the Latin American revolutionaries. Rebel vessels entered the ports of the United States and rebel agents purchased war materials there, sometimes with the rather clear connivance of the federal government. Most Americans sympathized with the revolutionary cause, seeing it as following America's own example of casting off Old World monarchical rule. Henry Clay was one of the most ardent advocates of Latin American independence. The Kentuckian repeatedly urged immediate diplomatic recognition of the revolutionary regimes, and the extension of an "American System" to embrace all the Western Hemisphere and set it apart from Europe.

Secretary of State Adams did not share Clay's enthusiasm. He had never showed much interest in Spanish America and lacked a sympathetic appreciation of its culture and institutions. In his cold and detached view, he did not identify the cause of Latin America with America's own revolutionary past, and he greatly doubted the ability of the people of the region to achieve democracy as well as independence. He tended to agree with the opinion of his distinguished father, John Adams, who observed to him in 1818: "They will be independent, no doubt, but will they be free? General Ignorance can never be free, and the Roman Religion is incompatible with a free government." Although John Quincy Adams later expressed greater enthusiasm about Latin America's freedom, he advised President Monroe to delay recognition until stable governments had been founded and until all reasonable prospects of Spanish reconquest had vanished. Adams thus built on the practical de facto recognition policy developed by Jefferson in 1793.

By the end of 1821 events at last seemed to favor recognition. Striking patriot victories over Spanish arms revealed the hopelessness of Spain's efforts to subdue the independence movements. Buenos Aires (Argentina), Colombia, Venezuela, Chile, and Mexico had achieved independence, and Brazil separated from Portugal in 1822. The Florida roadblock also had been removed by then. Moreover, the United States felt growing concern over Latin America's resentment of Washington's inaction and over the possibilities of European intervention. On March 8, 1822, President Monroe sent to Congress a message recommending recognition of Argentina (the United Provinces of the Rio de la Plata), Colombia, Chile, Peru, and Mexico. Although some months elapsed before ministers were appointed to these new states, the decision to recognize them was a daring step. Spain was still trying to suppress the revolts and protested Monroe's action sharply, while conservative Europe also responded unfavorably. Great Britain, a rival of the United States for trade and influence in Latin America, reluctantly followed Washington's lead in 1824. Although some historians have debated which of the two nations rendered the most aid to the cause of Latin American independence, it seems clear that neither did very much and that Latin America essentially won its freedom by its own unaided efforts.

4. CANNING FLIRTS WITH WASHINGTON

In 1815, the great powers of Europe, fresh from their final triumph over Napoleon, joined in a Quadruple Alliance to preserve the peace and stability of conservative and monarchical Europe. The alliance of Great Britain, Austria, Prussia, and Russia permitted a rehabilitated France to join in 1818. Americans often confused the European coalition with the Holy Alliance, the name of Czar Alexander's vague scheme for a league of Christian rulers and states. Under the guidance of the Austrian Chancellor, Prince Metternich, the allies met in a series of congresses called to uphold legitimacy and to suppress liberalism and revolution. Austrian troops quelled a liberal movement in Italy, and France intervened in Spain in 1823 to restore Ferdinand VII to absolute rule. Rumors spread that another congress soon would convene to authorize France or Russia to aid Spain in America. Americans anxiously observed these events in Europe, fearful that the reactionary allies might turn their attentions to Latin America, or even to the United States, that worldwide symbol of successful revolution and republicanism.

The policies of its continental allies also disturbed Great Britain. Liberal Britons objected to the interventions, while the conservatively inclined government was distressed at actions that threatened to interfere with markets and to upset the distribution of power. Officials in London feared that the restoration of the Spanish mercantilist system would endanger British trade with Latin America, but at the same time they realized that Spain unaided could not suppress the rebellions against its rule.

Although many Americans viewed Foreign Secretary Canning, Castlereagh's successor, as a caustic Yankeephobe, he sought to continue his predecessor's policy of cultivating friendlier relations with the United States. When the American Minister, Richard Rush, called in mid-August, 1823, to congratulate him upon his recent declaration to Paris opposing any French designs on the former Spanish colonies, Canning began a "flirtation" with Washington. How would the United States respond, he asked Rush, to a proposal for cooperation against possible European intervention in Latin America? Canning suggested that a joint Anglo-American statement might make the following points:

1. We conceive the recovery of the colonies by Spain to be hopeless.
2. We conceive the question of the recognition of them, as independent states, to be one of time and circumstances.
3. We are, however, by no means disposed to throw any impediment in the way of an arrangement between them and the mother country by amicable negotiations.
4. We aim not at the possession of any portion of them ourselves.
5. We could not see any portion of them transferred to any other power with indifference.

Canning thus sought an Anglo-American entente to offset France and its conservative allies. A joint declaration, he hoped, would check French schemes and preclude the calling of a congress to consider Latin America. Moreover, since Canning viewed with apprehension American designs on Cuba, a self-denying statement such as this would also serve to tie Washington's hands.

The news of Canning's overture reached Washington in early October, 1823. Although flattering, in view of Canning's past snubs and condescending attitude, it was not entirely unheralded. On several occasions since 1815 the American government had approached the Foreign Office on the possibilities of cooperation in extending diplomatic recognition to the Latin American republics. When Czar Alexander of Russia issued an edict in 1821 prohibiting foreign vessels from intruding within 100 Italian miles (one Italian mile equals 6085.2 feet) of the coasts of Russian America north of the 51st parallel, Secretary of State Adams sharply protested such an attempt to claim sovereignty over part of Oregon. He informed the Russian Minister that "we should contest the right of Russia to *any* territorial establishment on this continent, and that we should assume distinctly the principle that the American continents are no longer subjects for any new European colonial establishments." The Secretary informed London of his views and suggested cooperation in defending both powers' claims in Oregon. The Monroe administration thus was predisposed to some type of Anglo-American concert when it learned of Canning's conversations with Rush.

The prospects of European intervention deeply disturbed Monroe and most of his advisers. According to Adams, who reacted much more calmly to the reported dangers, the President was "alarmed far beyond anything that I could have conceived possible," while Secretary of War John C. Calhoun was "perfectly moonstruck" in his apprehensions. Monroe inclined toward accepting Canning's proposal. He consulted the two retired Republican statesmen, Jefferson and Madison, both of whom advised collaboration with Britain. Jefferson described the issue as the most momentous question to face the nation since Independence. But Adams objected to a joint declaration. In his view the danger of actual intervention was overrated, and he suspected Canning's primary purpose was to bar the United States from acquiring Cuba or other territory in Latin America in the future. As he remarked to his cabinet colleagues, while the American government did not intend to seize Texas or Cuba, the inhabitants of those provinces might someday request incorporation into the United States. Moreover, he preferred independent action as a warning to Europe: "It would be more candid, as well as more dignified, to avow our principles explicitly to Russia and France, than to come in as a cock-boat in the wake of the British man-of-war."

Adams's arguments for a unilateral declaration to the Old World apparently persuaded Monroe. He chose to make the announcement, however, in a message to Congress rather than in diplomatic notes to the powers concerned. His first draft of the message included a fervent declaration on behalf of the causes of liberalism in Europe, condemning French intervention in Spain and endorsing Greek independence from the Ottoman Empire. Adams convinced him to tone down his comments, pointing out the advantages of taking a stand squarely against European intervention in the New World while disclaiming any intention of intervening in the affairs of the Old. Adams also answered his colleagues' fears that the allied powers would view Monroe's message as virtually a declaration of war. Intervention was not probable, he argued, but if it did occur, both America's honor and considerations of self-defense would leave no choice but to resist. The United States, he believed, could not permit Britain to get sole credit for defending Latin America.

5. THE MESSAGE

On December 2, 1823, Monroe sent his annual message to Congress. The pronouncements that were to become famed as the Monroe Doctrine were embodied in two widely separated parts of the document. Monroe enumerated three main principles in regard to foreign policy: noncolonization, the "two-spheres" concept, and nonintervention. Of these the first and second reflected Adams' advice, but Monroe's primary concern rested with the last, which he viewed as most immediately important. After referring to negotiations with Russia about the southern boundary of Russian America, in the first part of the message, the President advanced the principle that "the American continents, by the free and independent condition which they have assumed and maintain, are henceforth not to be conceived as subjects for future colonization by any European powers." A novel pronouncement without status in international law and practice, this precept ultimately became one of the most often invoked dictums of the Monroe Doctrine. In the second section of the message, Monroe stated his "strong hope" for the success of the Greeks, but he followed that expression of liberal sympathies with a declaration of abstention from Europe and an enunciation of the concept of two spheres:

In the wars of the European powers in matters relating to themselves we have never taken any part, nor does it comport with our policy so to do. . . . With the movements in this hemisphere we are of necessity more immediately connected. . . . The political system of the allied powers is essentially different in this respect from that of America. . . . We owe it, therefore, to candor . . . to declare that we should consider any attempt on their part to extend their system to any portion of this hemisphere as dangerous to our peace and safety.

The New and Old Worlds, in other words, were spheres apart; by

implication, Monroe seemed to be reserving the Western Hemisphere
for republicanism, although in subsequent messages he retreated from
that claim.

Monroe then uttered his famous prohibition of armed intervention by
outside powers for purposes of controlling a state in the New World. The
United States would not interfere with any existing European colonies
within this hemisphere, he declared, but it would regard any attempt by
the European powers (other than Spain) to oppress or to control the
newly independent states in Latin America "as the manifestation of an
unfriendly disposition toward the United States." Reiterating the concept of two spheres, the President reassured the world that it was the
policy of the United States neither to intervene in the internal affairs of
Europe nor to condone attempts by the European allies to extend their
political systems to the Americas.

The genius of Monroe's message rested not in its uniqueness but in its
pithy statement of firmly held American convictions about relations with
the Old World. The conception of the New World as distinct from Europe
by virtue of its geography, economy, culture, and special interests of its
own, originated in the early colonial period and to some extent was
shared by the more educated inhabitants of Latin America. It followed
logically that the New World should remain aloof from and reject
meddling by the Old World. Earlier American policies of neutrality and
nonentanglement put forth during the Washington and Jefferson administrations already expressed these concepts; Monroe restated them
now for all the Americas.

American self-interests as well as ideals underlay Monroe's pronouncement in 1823. In a negative sense, his message reflected concern
with the security of the United States, deemed to be endangered by any
European armed intervention on Spain's behalf or by any transfer to a
European power of Spanish colonial territory in the New World. The
prohibitions against intervention or further colonization were directed
primarily at France and Russia, the two powers thought most likely to
attempt to suppress the revolutions in Latin America or to acquire new
territories in the Western Hemisphere. But the prohibition also included
Great Britain as a target, because of its suspected designs upon Cuba.
The anti-British motive should not be exaggerated, however, for clearly
Monroe and even Adams viewed the message as a stopgap measure to
warn the European allies and to hold the line against them, pending
further developments. If intervention became more imminent or actually
occurred, the Monroe administration intended to cooperate with Great
Britain in resisting it. Despite their mutual suspicions, the two English-
speaking powers obviously had a common interest in preventing European intervention or new acquisitions of territory in Latin America.
Moreover, Britain alone possessed the naval power requisite to a
successful opposition. In a positive sense, Monroe's pronouncement not

only expressed ideological sympathy with the Latin American revolutions but served as a manifesto for an American System in the entire hemisphere, within which the United States could flourish by exercising economic and political leadership.

6. SIGNIFICANCE OF THE MESSAGE

Monroe's message had very little immediate impact. Most Americans cheered their President's remarks as hurling defiance at the crowned despots of the Old World. Yet few apparently really expected hostilities to ensue, and no measures were taken to prepare the country for a possible war. Within a short time the excitement died down and the message was almost forgotten. Nearly two decades elapsed before the President's words were revived and, with some extensions, christened the Monroe Doctrine.

Europeans in general either ignored Monroe's message or treated it with contempt. Some liberals responded favorably, hailing the American President's declaration as a bugle blast for freedom, but they constituted a minority nearly everywhere on the continent. Conservative opinion tended either to dismiss the message as arrogant bluster, unworthy of much comment, or to see it as a dangerous fulmination on behalf of republicanism and an impermissible attempt to separate the New World from the ancient centers of Western Christendom and civilization. But whatever the alarm professed by some conservatives, none of the major powers on the continent took any official notice of the President's remarks. They thought of the United States as too weak and the declaration as too obviously an empty bluff to dignify it with a protest.

Although Monroe could not have been certain in 1823, historians have concluded that very little danger existed of any but diplomatic intervention by the allies on Spain's behalf in the New World. The French government never seriously considered any large-scale armed venture in Latin America, and confined its intervention schemes to the possibility of seating European princes upon American thrones, a plan the Spanish king adamantly opposed. The Russian czar, Alexander I, thought primarily in terms of trying to reconcile Spain and her colonies through mediation, and, in fact, he assumed a friendly attitude toward the United States. Prussia and Austria, the other two great powers on the continent, defended Spain's theoretical sovereignty over its rebellious colonies but were not disposed to provide her with any practical aid.

In the British Isles, conservatives as well as liberals initially approved Monroe's verbal defiance of the "Holy Alliance." Their reactions, of course, focused upon the American President's nonintervention dictum, while they generally tended to ignore the noncolonization statement. The *Times* of London praised Monroe's bold warning as "plain speaking" and "just speaking." Canning, however, was less pleased. Annoyed at the rejection of his overture for a joint statement, he viewed the message as cheap trickery intended to steal a march upon Great Britain in Latin America and to pose before the world in heroic garb. He warned Rush that Britain would not recognize the noncolonization principle, for it regarded unsettled areas of the New World as still open to colonizing ventures. On the other hand, he hoped Monroe's unilateral declaration would strengthen Britain's efforts to prevent the calling of a congress on Latin America.

Canning's irritation at Monroe's statement to Congress and the world was understandable. In October, 1823, nearly two months before the issuance of the message, the Foreign Secretary had tired of awaiting Washington's response to his overture and had acted quietly to block any French plans for intervention. He requested and on October 9 obtained French disavowals of any intention to intervene by armed force in Latin America or of any design upon Spanish colonial territories in what became known as the Polignac Memorandum. Canning, therefore, and not President Monroe, defused the threat of intervention. After Monroe's message to Congress, Canning countered what he regarded as an unfair American maneuver by making the Polignac Memorandum widely known in Latin America.

Apparently the majority of Latin American leaders had never seriously worried about the dangers of intervention. If it occurred, most Latin Americans looked to British power for protection, and not the words of the American President. Moreover, some monarchist and conservative elements among the liberators in Latin America disliked Monroe's implication that the New World was reserved for republicanism. Some liberals, conversely, especially in Chile and Colombia, welcomed the President's statement and anticipated closer relations with the United States. The United States soon dashed their hopes. In 1824, the Colombian representative inquired of Adams what practical steps the government contemplated to give force to Monroe's warning to Europe—a defensive alliance, in other words. Adams replied that the danger of intervention seemed to have passed but that, in any event, only Congress could authorize defensive commitments. If a threat should develop, he admitted the United States would act forcibly but only in cooperation with some other great friendly power, meaning Great Britain. Brazilian and Mexican overtures received similar answers, making it quite clear to more thoughtful Latin Americans that the Doctrine was a unilateral policy declaration, to be enforced only at such times and places as the interests and power of the United States demanded. In short, it was a self-centered policy, and the American people and government were unwilling at that time to assume any definite obligations to protect Latin America.

The fiasco of the Panama Congress in 1826 underscored the United States' reluctance to become involved with its southern neighbors. After receiving an invitation to a general conference of Latin American states at Panama, the Senate, plagued by political infighting and isolationist objections, so delayed confirmation of the two American delegates that one died before he could leave for Panama, and the other arrived so late that the congress had convened and adjourned before he got there.

For all its immediate futility, Monroe's self-defense pronouncement of 1823 eventually became immensely important. Its explicit formulation of American ideals and interests outlined a program on which the United States would base future action when it had grown sufficiently powerful and interested to apply the Doctrine, at first only in North America but eventually in the entire hemisphere.

Additional Reading

The role of John Quincy Adams in the settlement of the Florida question, recognition of Latin American independence, and formulation of the Monroe Doctrine is examined by Samuel Flagg Bemis, *John Quincy Adams and the Foundations of American Foreign Policy* (1949). Also see his *The Latin American Policy of the United States* (1943). For earlier diplomacy, see Clifford L. Egan, "The United States, France, and West Florida, 1803–1808," *Florida Historical Quarterly*, XLVII (1969), 227–252. Walter LaFeber has edited a useful volume on Adams's contributions, *John Quincy Adams and American Continental Empire* (1965). *The United States and the Independence of Latin America 1800–1830* (1941) by Arthur P. Whitaker concentrates on Latin America but also contains a brief treatment of the Florida issue. Also see C. C. Griffin, *The United States and the Disruption of the Spanish Empire, 1810–1822* (1937). For more detailed examination of the 1819 treaty, the following are valuable: P. C. Brooks, *Diplomacy and the Borderlands: The Adams-Onís Treaty of 1819* (1939); H. B. Fuller, *The Purchase of Florida* (1906); and Isaac J. Cox, *The West Florida Controversy, 1798–1813* (1918). A previously cited study, *Expansionists of 1812* (1925) by Julius W. Pratt, has an excellent account of Mathew's venture in East Florida. For Jackson's raid, see Marquis James, *Andrew Jackson, The Border Captain* (1933) and Bradford Perkins, *Castlereagh and Adams: England and the United States, 1812–1823* (1964). Three valuable studies on the British role in Latin America include: J. Fred Rippy, *Rivalry of the United States and Great Britain over Latin America, 1808–1830* (1929); C. K. Webster, ed., *Britain and the Independence of Latin America, 1812–1830* (2 vols., 1938); and William Kaufmann, *British Policy and the Independence of Latin America, 1804–1828* (1951). The classic study of the origins of Monroe's famed message is by Dexter Perkins, *The Monroe Doctrine, 1823–1826* (1927); also see his briefer *A History of the Monroe Doctrine* (1941; rev., 1955). E. H. Tatum, Jr., *The United States and Europe, 1815–1823* (1936) stresses the inclusion of Great Britain among Monroe's targets, while Gale W. McGee, "The Monroe Doctrine—A Stopgap Measure," *Mississippi Valley Historical Review*, XXXVIII (1951), 233–250, points out the administration's continued readiness to cooperate with Canning. William Appleman Williams, "The Age of Mercantilism: An Interpretation of the American Political Economy, 1763 to 1828," *William and Mary Quarterly*, XV (1958), 419–437, suggests the Monroe Doctrine proclaimed an American System for the Western Hemisphere. J. A. Logan, Jr., *No Transfer* (1961) examines the relationship of that principle to the Monroe Doctrine. Among the useful articles on the Doctrine are T. R. Schellenberg, "Jeffersonian Origins of the Monroe Doctrine," *Hispanic American Historical Review*, XIV (1934), 1–32; W. S. Robertson, "The Monroe Doctrine Abroad in 1823–1824," *American Political Science Review*, VI (1912), 546–563, and "South America and the Monroe Doctrine, 1824–1828," *Political Science Quarterly*, XXX (1915), 82–105; and I. C. Nichols, Jr., "The Russian Ukase and the Monroe Doctrine: A Re-evaluation," *Pacific Historical Review*, XXXVI (1967), 13–26.

ENGLAND

AMERICA

The Oregon boundary dispute

7

ANGLOPHOBIA AND DIPLOMACY IN THE 1840's

1. STRAINS AND CLASHES IN ANGLO-AMERICAN RELATIONS

A common language, as George Bernard Shaw once observed, may divide two peoples rather than unite them. In the years between independence and the Civil War, many strands connected the United States with the mother country; history, law, language, cultural similarities, and economics bound together the two peoples. An "Atlantic economy" had developed during the colonial era and continued to operate after 1783. In a very real sense, the United States occupied the position of an underdeveloped country, hungry for capital and skills. Trade, though relatively less important to the United States because of its vast and expanding internal market, than to a primarily commercial country such as Britain, flourished between the two countries as much after 1783 as during the colonial days. In the years 1821 to 1850, for example, the United States purchased about 40 percent of all its imports, largely manufactured goods, from the British and sold to them between 35 and 50 percent of its total exports, mostly agricultural products of which raw cotton comprised the bulk. Conversely, the United States was Britain's best customer. The migration of British investment capital, skilled labor, and technology overseas was also vitally important for a country such as the United States, rich in undeveloped resources. British firms sent commercial agents to America, banks established branches here, and financiers invested capital, estimated to have totalled $125 million by 1837, in federal, state, and local bonds and in trade, agriculture, and transportation. By 1860, nearly 600,000 British-born immigrants lived within the United States, some of whom brought with them highly desirable skills and technology. The controversies and animosities that loomed so large in the history of the period reflected misunderstandings and nationalistic tensions rather than conflicts of basic interests between England and America. Precisely because of their mutual interests and connections, it seemed, tempers flared on both sides of the Atlantic and differences frequently became exaggerated.

Originating in colonial clashes and the Revolutionary War, a tradition of hostility to Britain and Britons had developed in the United States. The controversies that finally culminated in the War of 1812 nurtured this sentiment of animosity, suspicion, and distrust. Indications of British snobbery and condescension toward America and its society, and of course the age-old resentment of the debtor toward the creditor, deeply rankled many Americans.

Even after the post-Ghent diplomatic adjustments, old controversies remained and new ones arose. Since its independence, the United States had sought full rights to trade with the British West Indies. Still clinging to mercantilist doctrines and under pressure from its own shipping interests, the British government had refused to open the Caribbean colonies under terms satisfactory to the Americans. Economic retaliation adopted by Congress after 1815, and the desire of West Indian planters to import American foodstuffs for their slave work force, caused Parliament in 1822 to open certain West Indian ports to direct American trade. Encouraged by that development but irked by remaining restrictions, President John Quincy Adams imposed a retaliatory tariff on West Indian goods entering the United States aboard British vessels. Adams demanded free trade as a right, not a privilege, but he badly misjudged the British temper. London withdrew all the concessions previously offered pending repeal of the discriminatory tariff. The deadlock was not broken until Andrew Jackson succeeded Adams as President and in effect offered to accept whatever trading privileges Britain would offer. Therefore, in 1830, the British ministry restored direct trade to Americans, subject to such duties as it should deem advisable.

The Canadian Rebellion of 1837 provided a new irritant. That short-lived uprising aroused vast interest and sympathy in the United States. Canadians, many Americans fondly believed, were about to follow their example in casting off Old World monarchical shackles, and surely would soon seek incorporation into the glorious American Union. They felt keenly disappointed, therefore, when the rebel leader, William Lyon Mackenzie, and his followers were forced to abandon their "capital" in Toronto and fled to tiny Canadian-owned Navy Island in the Niagara River. Unfurling his republican flag on Navy Island, Mackenzie enlisted a number of American volunteers into his rebel "army" and received a measure of support from so-called sporting "Hunters' Lodges" that sprang up along the American side of the border. The government proclaimed American neutrality and tried to prevent raids across the border, but local sentiment and negligent officials hampered the carrying out of its policies. Loyal Canadians deeply resented these raids and loudly condemned United States authorities. In that inflamed setting, a party of Canadian soldiers crossed to the American side of the Niagara River in December, 1837, seized the American ship *Caroline* that had been supplying the rebels, and set it afire and adrift in the river. One American sailor died in the scuffle. A great outcry arose throughout the United States at these violations of territory and life, amply provoked though they appeared to most Canadians. Fortunately for peace, President Martin Van Buren managed to calm excited citizens living along the border.

2. A WAR OF PEN AND INK

The British traveler contributed greatly to the swelling tide of Anglophobia in the United States. America had long piqued the curiosity of Europeans. Prior to the late 1820's, businessmen comprised the largest number of English observers coming to the United States, and their written accounts usually reflected favorably on life in the New World republic. Beginning in the 1820's and 1830's, however, a veritable flood of British travelers came over to tour America and observe its life and institutions. Many returned home to write of their experiences. Two hundred and thirty travel books about North America were published between 1830 and 1860, in addition to numerous newspaper and periodical accounts and commentaries. Most of these later travelers were upper-class and Tory in social position and outlook—a kaleidoscopic array of authors, journalists, scientists, clergymen, military officers on leave, noble sportsmen, actors, artists, and lecturers. Whatever their acknowledged purpose, almost all seemingly came to observe, to criticize, and to write a profitable book about their experiences.

Most of the visitors came predisposed to finding fault. Conservative in politics and distressed by a growing popular demand at home for parliamentary reform, the travelers usually viewed democracy with deep abhorrence and with determination to expose the shortcomings of the vaunted New World republic. Thomas Brothers, for instance, admitted his chief purpose in coming to America was to write a book demonstrating that a democracy could have "as much oppression, poverty, and wretchedness as any other form of government." Another source of bias derived from the unfortunate effects of the Panic of 1837. Large amounts of British capital invested in the securities of American states and municipalities suffered under the impact of the Panic since six states, one territory, and a number of municipalities either defaulted on their obligations or repudiated them outright. The victimized English bondholders understandably reacted bitterly and tended to regard all America as a nation of thieves and swindlers. Moreover, the migration of skilled laborers to the United States disturbed British manufacturers since it depleted the work force of the homeland and facilitated the growth of competitive industry overseas. They hoped exposure of the "truth" about America might discourage that exodus. (In the 1960's, Europeans raised similar outcries about the "brain drain" of scientists and engineers, attracted to the United States by higher salaries and better living conditions.)

The lack of copyright protection for foreign books in America also greatly agitated English literary circles and publishers. American publishers often reprinted valuable books, such as those by Charles Dickens, without permission of the authors or payment of any royalties. Repeated protests and appeals proved unavailing until 1891, when Congress belatedly enacted a measure protecting foreign copyrights. Not surprisingly, touring authors who themselves had been the victims of literary piracy often took a jaundiced view of life in the United States.

Finally, the very vastness of America and the limited time available to most visitors made a balanced view very difficult. A few weeks or even months hardly afforded sufficient time for a searching inquiry, especially in view of primitive transportation facilities and the rawness of newly opened frontier areas. Alexis de Tocqueville was an exception. Sent in 1831 by the French government to survey the American penal system, de Tocqueville spent ten months touring the country observing closely all facets of American life. After his visit he wrote an unusually perceptive account, *Democracy in America,* still valued for its penetrating insights. Unfortunately, most of the British travel books fell lamentably short of the standards set by de Tocqueville.

A brief examination of a few of the numerous British travelers and their books indicates their nature and effects. Captain Basil Hall, an urbane and witty but caustic high Tory, published his popular *Travels in North America* in 1829. Hall filled his three volumes with hostile comments on American travel facilities, democratic practices, boasting, and abuse of the English language. Frances Trollope was perhaps the most infamous, in American eyes, of all the travel authors. An intelligent but sharp-tongued woman, she came over to rescue her family's declining fortunes but failed in a commercial venture in Cincinnati. She returned home to recoup in her two-volume *Domestic Manners of the Americans* (1832), published just as agitation for parliamentary reform reached a crescendo. English conservatives hailed Mrs. Trollope's book as an accurate and badly needed exposé of the defects and dangers of democracy. Mrs. Trollope with more venom than insight excoriated American morality, religion, society, and politics, finding extremely little to praise in any area. As she observed of the Americans, "I do not like them. I do not like their principles, I do not like their manners, I do not like their opinions. . . ." But Americans took revenge, subjecting her to unmerciful satire in the press and on the stage. One of the more favorably inclined visitors, Harriet Martineau, portrayed a reasonably balanced view of American life and promise in her *Society in America*

(1837), despite the fact she, like most foreigners, felt deeply pained by the existence of slavery in a land supposedly dedicated to human rights and freedom.

Barely thirty at the time, the most famous of all the literary travelers, Charles Dickens, came to the United States in the early 1840's to recuperate from an illness. Widely known for his popular novels, Dickens was hailed as one who surely would probe beneath the surface crudities of American life to perceive the underlying spirit and promise. Although resolved to avoid the mistakes of his predecessors, Dickens failed to maintain a completely balanced view. Worn out by adulation and the rigors of American travel, and appalled by slavery, the unrestrained journalism of the day, and the turbulence and violence of American life and politics, Dickens penned some highly critical comments in his *American Notes* (1842). His novel, *Martin Chuzzlewit,* even more unrestrained than *American Notes,* aroused the ire of American clergymen and editors who railed against what they regarded as gross caricaturing, and the novel was publicly burned. As Thomas Carlyle gleefully commented, *Chuzzlewit* had all America fizzing like one giant soda bottle. Dickens himself subsequently acknowledged regret at some of his less temperate statements.

Culturally still dependent upon the mother country, Americans reacted with hurt and resentment to these critics. Distorted though they usually were, the criticisms contained enough truth to be painful to a people striving for national development and respect. The English literary quarterlies, such as the *Quarterly Review* and *Blackwood's Magazine,* further exacerbated these wounded feelings by their reviews of the travel books and their articles on America that sometimes surpassed even the vitriol of Mrs. Trollope. As one early review article concluded, "No man valuing genuine freedom or possessing real sentiments of humanity could for a moment tolerate the idea of passing his days in a country where such brutalizing scenes [slavery] are perpetually before his eyes."

Americans anxious to refute the critics quickly launched counterattacks concentrating upon the squalor and defects of life in mother England. The *North American Review* played a leading role in these skirmishes, while literary figures such as Washington Irving and James Fenimore Cooper took up pen in their country's defense. The literary "Battle of the Quarterlies" raged across the Atlantic and contributed to the difficulties of adjusting diplomatic problems. One American writer, Timothy Flint, semiseriously described a "war of frock and petticoat" that might grow out of such literary volleys. Fortunately calmer counsels prevailed in both countries, and the 1840's, despite the literary strains, witnessed the signing of two notable Anglo-American treaties. By the early 1850's, the war of the quarterlies began to subside, as a new type of British traveler—middle-class reformers more sympathetic to American democracy—began to arrive in this country.

3. THE NORTHEASTERN BOUNDARY DISPUTE

The imprecisions of the Peace Treaty of 1783 spawned serious boundary disputes between British Canada and the United States. The peace-makers had specified the northern boundary of the United States should run from the Bay of Fundy up the St. Croix River to the highlands, thence to the source of the Connecticut River, and down that stream to the 45th parallel and the St. Lawrence River. Unfortunately, they used a map defective in details for sketching the boundaries, and did not attach a copy to the formal treaty. Subsequently, explorers found not one but two St. Croix rivers, and a mixed commission provided by the Jay Treaty in 1798 fixed the present stream as the proper one. Surveying the remainder of the boundary proved impossible, however, since no agreement existed defining what constituted the highlands, and since the Connecticut River turned out to have three distinct sources. Overlapping claims involved some 12,000 square miles. The Americans advocated a line north from the St. Croix to the St. John's River, while the British declared the proper line lay to the south along the Penobscot, which would give them a greatly desired all-weather military road. In addition to the northeastern tangle, another difference developed over the correct boundary line between Lake Superior and the Lake of the Woods.

The Treaty of Ghent had provided for another attempt to establish the boundary by commission and if that failed, as it did, it provided for submission of the problem to arbitration by a third power. John Quincy Adams suggested a compromise in 1822, but political pressures from the states most vitally concerned—Maine and Massachusetts—and Anglophobe sentiment throughout the country, prevented action. All else failing, both countries agreed to arbitration, and under a special agreement reached in 1827, they submitted the issue to the King of the Netherlands. In 1831, that monarch rendered an essentially political rather than judicial (based on the merits of the claims) decision, which virtually divided the disputed territory between the two claimants. Britain, nevertheless, was willing to accept the award. President Jackson felt similarly, but for political reasons he submitted the award to the Senate without a recommendation. That body advised rejection on the grounds that the arbitrator had not given a judicial decision.

Violence flared in the disputed territory a few years later. Rival lumberjacks and land agents from New Brunswick and Maine clashed in 1838–1839 in what became known as the "Aroostook War." Attempts by Maine residents to evict the New Brunswick "intruders" resulted in the capture of fifty Americans. Authorities on both sides of the border mobilized the militia, while Congress appropriated $10 million and authorized the President to raise troops for Maine's defense. A surge of patriotic temper and outrage swept the United States, and one group of Ohio citizens urged the government to press all grievances against Great Britain to "the last extremity." The leaders on both sides, however, preferred to avoid war and established a truce in 1839. Yet the situation remained potentially explosive. Further contributing to the unease, in 1841 a Canadian named Alexander McLeod was tried for murder in New York as one of the raiders in the earlier destruction of the *Caroline.* The British government lodged strong protests and war seemed probable but, fortunately for all concerned, McLeod had an alibi and the court acquitted him. In the same year, the British in turn outraged many Americans by freeing the slaves aboard a coastal ship, the *Creole,* which rebellious blacks had seized and sailed into Nassau.

4. THE WEBSTER-ASHBURTON TREATY

Events even then were working toward a compromise. In Great Britain, the Whig ministry, with the sometimes bellicose Lord Palmerston as Foreign Secretary, fell from power. A more conciliatory Tory ministry headed by Sir Robert Peel as Prime Minister took over, and Lord Aberdeen replaced Palmerston, who had refused an apology over the *Caroline* and had adopted a threatening attitude during McLeod's trial, in the Foreign Office. Aberdeen hoped to avoid a war over "a few miles more or less of a miserable pine swamp." Daniel Webster, Secretary of State under Presidents William Henry Harrison and John Tyler, held similar pacifist views. An able lawyer and a brilliant orator at the peak of his illustrious political career, the "Godlike Daniel," moved alike by ambition and a desire for patriotic service, determined to achieve a peaceful settlement. Thoroughly familiar with the details of the dispute and an Anglophile, Webster knew intimately a number of influential Englishmen.

Taking the initiative, Webster informed London that the administration wished to seek a compromise. Peel and Aberdeen quickly responded and happily selected the elderly Lord Ashburton (Alexander Baring) as a special envoy to the United States. Married to an American woman, the noble lord long advocated Anglo-American friendship. Webster, who had known him before, welcomed Ashburton, and the two dispensed with formalities in their negotiations.

Webster and Ashburton readily agreed to ignore the confusion of claims and counterclaims and to divide the contested area. The United States received nearly 7,000 square miles to Britain's 5,000 square miles, which included the coveted military route. Ashburton also accepted the inaccurately surveyed boundary line along the 45th parallel, which favored the Americans and contained a fort at Rouses Point, and he yielded some 6,500 square miles between Lake Superior and the Lake of the Woods. Other arrangements included a treaty for the mutual extradition of accused criminals, Anglo-American naval cooperation to suppress the international traffic in slaves, and an apology of sorts for the *Caroline* incident.

The two statesmen arrived at an acceptable and mutually advantageous

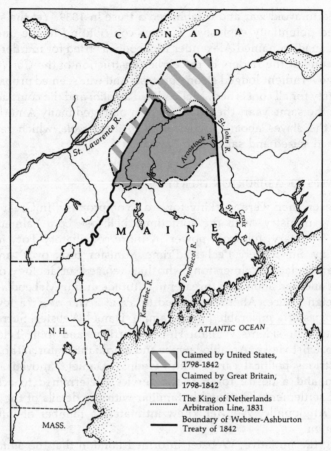

Claimed by United States, 1798-1842
Claimed by Great Britain, 1798-1842
The King of Netherlands Arbitration Line, 1831
Boundary of Webster-Ashburton Treaty of 1842

The Northeastern Boundary Dispute and Settlement of 1842

compromise. Ashburton had yielded in an area of strategic importance for Canada's defense and communications. Perhaps he would have conceded more if the Duke of Wellington, a member of the Tory cabinet who was greatly concerned about Canada's security, had not pressured him so much. Even so, the treaty encountered bitter criticism from Palmerston and the Whig opposition.

Maine and Massachusetts presented the chief stumbling blocks to the compromise. Both states had claims in the disputed area and regarded any boundary short of their desires as a cession of American territory. In a vulnerable political position—his own Whig party had disowned President Tyler—Webster made every effort to win the assent of the leaders of those two states. It was known that Benjamin Franklin, during the peace negotiations at Paris, had marked the boundaries of the United States on a map "with a strong red line." Professor Jared Sparks of

Harvard, who had done archival research in France, had seen a map that might have been Franklin's and he reproduced it from memory for Webster. The Sparks "red line" map favored the extreme British claims, and Webster secretly showed it to the commissioners of Maine and Massachusetts to overcome their resistance to the compromise. The two states finally yielded, consoled by the payment of $150,000 to each in compensation for its claims.

The Webster-Ashburton Treaty still had to face the Senate. Webster launched a carefully planned propaganda campaign in the press to convince his countrymen that he had struck the most advantageous agreement possible, and that they had a choice of his treaty or none at all and possible war. He readily persuaded the Whigs, who represented commercial interests that stood to suffer grievously if hostilities ensued. The Democrats likewise agreed, their attention distracted by the tariff issue and the congressional elections upcoming in 1842. The treaty, whose terms had not been revealed to the public, went before the Senate along with Sparks' map. Persuaded that Webster had obtained more than the nation warranted and aware of the dangers of war, the Senate granted approval by a vote of 39 to 9. After the Senate acted, Webster released his correspondence with Ashburton to the public in a manner designed to exaggerate the British concessions.

Authentic copies of the maps used by the peacemakers in the 1780's later turned up in England and America. Contrary to Sparks' version, these supported the extreme American territorial claims. Webster, therefore, has been accused of being a better propagandist than a diplomat in surrendering land rightfully belonging to the United States. Yet, cartographic evidence per se had not really interested him. He had realistically sought the most satisfactory compromise possible under the circumstances. To have asked for more in 1842, as he argued, would have jeopardized any possibility of settling this explosive issue. The Webster-Ashburton Treaty terminated an era of accumulating grievances and opened the way for steady improvement in Anglo-American relations.

5. OREGON

The Oregon territory claimed by the two English-speaking powers embraced a vast empire, rich in furs, timber, arable land, and rugged scenery. It comprised nearly a half-million square miles, lying between 54°40" north latitude and the 42nd parallel, and east to the Rocky Mountains. Four countries had staked claims to it, but Spain ceded her rights to the United States in the 1819 Adams-Onís Treaty, and Russia withdrew north of the 54°40" line in separate treaties concluded with the Americans and the British in 1824 and 1825 respectively.

The two remaining rivals based their claims on discovery and on settlement. The British had the better of both arguments. A vague claim

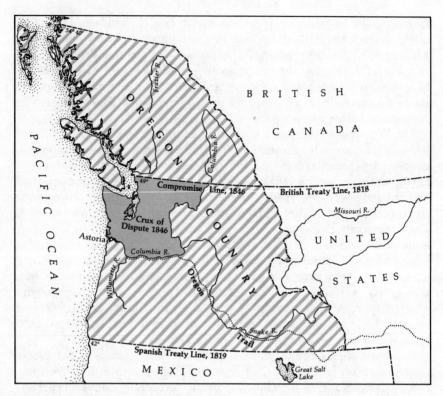

The Oregon Question

to discovery went back to the voyage of Sir Francis Drake in the late 16th century, followed by more substantial claims based on the explorations of Captain James Cook in 1778, Captain George Vancouver in 1792, and overland expeditions by fur trappers and traders of the North West Company. American claims rested primarily upon Captain Robert Grey, a New England trader who had named the Columbia River in 1792. The undefined western limits of the Louisiana Purchase, and the official expedition of Lewis and Clark in 1805 supported the American case.

In 1811, John Jacob Astor's Pacific Fur Company established a post named Astoria on the south bank near the mouth of the Columbia. Sold to the British-owned North West Company to escape capture during the War of 1812, the post theoretically returned to American sovereignty under the terms of the Treaty of Ghent. In 1821, the North West Company merged with the influential Hudson's Bay Company. Officials of the enlarged company were determined to hold the lands north of the Columbia and they viewed the river as a vital communications route for their fur operations. By then the disputed area had narrowed to the region between the Columbia and the 51st parallel, with America's title to the south and Britain's to the north virtually conceded by each government. The Hudson's Bay Company provided the concrete basis for Britain's claim; it sought to strengthen its position by abandoning Astoria on the south bank of the river, and moving its headquarters inland to Fort Vancouver on the north bank, opposite the present city of Portland. Its fur trappers ranged far inland in order to forestall American trappers, and firmly discouraged intrusions into the company's domain. Fearful that this would not suffice, the British founded the Puget Sound Agricultural Company to promote farm settlements around Puget Sound, but its success was minimal.

Prior to the 1840's, the attractions of Oregon had received good publicity in the United States, and a trickle of settlers began to enter the area. Hall Joseph Kelley, a Massachusetts teacher, devoted years to promoting the settlement of Oregon. As early as the 1820's, Kelley began to correspond with members of Congress about its advantages and urged governmental support of settlements. Though he failed to achieve a settlement or to obtain congressional support, Kelley succeeded as a propagandist. One person he influenced, Nathaniel J. Wyeth, twice journeyed to Oregon and helped blaze what became known as the Oregon Trail. Methodist and Congregational missionaries also established several missions in Oregon. They were not particularly successful in converting the Indians and trappers, but they did help publicize the attractions of this vast territory.

Substantial American settlement did not occur until the "Oregon Fever" of 1843–1844. The influx resulted from several factors: economic depression in the United States, attraction of rich free land in Oregon, love of adventure, and patriotic desire to make good the national title to the Pacific northwest. Oregon's American population increased from less than 500 in 1841 to around 6,000 by 1846. Most of these pioneers settled south of the Columbia in the Willamette Valley, because of the area's fertility and uncertainty about the national title to the territory to the north. As a result, officials of Hudson's Bay Company, fearful of clashes with the turbulent and independent frontiersmen, moved their headquarters north to Vancouver Island in 1845. In so doing, the company removed the one concrete British interest from the disputed area—the land between the Columbia and Puget Sound.

6. POLITICS, DIPLOMACY AND THE OREGON TREATY

The Convention of 1818 had provided joint access to Oregon for citizens of Great Britain and the United States for ten years. The first crisis sprang from American domestic politics in the early 1820's. Apparently anxious to refute political charges that he had betrayed or surrendered the nation's claims to Texas in the 1819 treaty with Spain, and to prevent a repetition of that in Oregon, Secretary of State John Quincy Adams pressed American claims to the Pacific coast as far north as the 51st parallel. Supported by the anxious Hudson's Bay Company, in 1825 Foreign Secretary Canning proposed a boundary running west from the Rocky Mountains to the Columbia, and down that river to the sea. When he became president, Adams sent Albert Gallatin to London to press America's case for more. An ardent imperialist and not overly fond of Adams and the Americans, Canning by that time inclined toward not even conceding the Columbia line. The ministry overruled him and offered Gallatin the Columbia, plus the isolated Olympic Peninsula, in order to satisfy American desires for harbors within the Strait of Juan de Fuca. Realizing that time and fecundity were on America's side, Gallatin rejected the offer. Then, in 1827 both countries agreed to extend indefinitely the 1818 provision for joint access, subject to termination by either power.

The Oregon question should have been settled during the friendly negotiations between Webster and Ashburton in 1842, but neither man then viewed the issue as urgent. Moreover, when he left London for America, Ashburton's instructions on Oregon reverted to Canning's 1825 offer of the Columbia only. When the issue came up, Webster naturally could not accept less than Gallatin had rejected in 1826. Clearly indicating the primary importance the United States attached to obtaining a good harbor on the Pacific coast, Webster offered to accept the Columbia if Britain would persuade Mexico to cede San Francisco Bay and northern California to the United States. Webster's tripartite scheme never materialized. That same year Navy Lieutenant Charles Wilkes reported that navigation of the Columbia River was made hazardous by a bar at its mouth, strengthening America's desire for a harbor within the Strait of Juan de Fuca.

The great migration of settlers to the Pacific northwest in the mid-1840's caused expansionists to demand acquisition of the "whole of Oregon." In 1844 the Democratic presidential nominee, James K. Polk of Tennessee, ran on a platform designed to appeal to expansionists, calling for "the re-occupation of Oregon and the re-annexation of Texas." Although Polk emphasized Texas during the campaign, after his election he felt committed to obtain as much of Oregon as possible. Polk's inaugural address asserted that America's title to Oregon was "clear and unquestionable," presumably meaning the entire area, and led to excited talk of a possible war. Lord Aberdeen, Britain's pacific Foreign Secretary, dreaded hostilities but nevertheless wrote his Minister in Washington, "We are perfectly determined to yield nothing to force or menace. . . ." The London *Times* complained of "that ill-regulated, overbearing, and aggressive spirit of American democracy." Privately, however, Polk was willing to settle for less than all Oregon. He apparently intended his verbal threat merely to persuade Great Britain to accept a settlement satisfactory to the United States. Unfortunately, British Minister Richard

Pakenham, without consulting London, rejected Polk's compromise offer of an extension of the boundary along the 49th parallel to the sea.

Polk angrily withdrew the offer and in ringing terms declared to Congress the irrefutability of America's title to all of Oregon. He obtained from a most fearful and reluctant Congress authorization to give the required year's notice terminating the treaty of joint access. The President believed that a show of firmness was the wisest way to deal successfully with the British. As he commented to a member of Congress, "The only way to treat John Bull was to look him straight in the eye. . . ." Expansionists and most Democrats hailed the President's bellicose stand, but Whigs, Southerners dependent upon cotton sales to Britain, and financial and commercial circles were anxious to avoid a course that might well lead to war. Moreover, the country wavered on the verge of hostilities with Mexico over Texas, and many felt that one war at a time was more than enough. Consequently, growing sentiment within the United States favored peace and compromise on Oregon, while similar forces within Great Britain also called for a peaceful adjustment.

Heretofore Lord Aberdeen had met difficulty in trying to persuade his cabinet colleagues of the necessity to abandon the Columbia River line, but the sharpening crisis at last cleared the way. Moreover, the leader of the opposition party concurred, despite Lord Palmerston's earlier opposition. Therefore, when Polk indicated to London that he expected a friendly settlement, the Tory ministry offered a division along the 49th parallel to the Pacific, with Vancouver Island remaining British, and Hudson's Bay Company retaining free navigation of the Columbia and control of its property south of the boundary. Maneuvering carefully to avoid a personal retreat and to disarm the extremists, Polk requested the Senate's opinion of the British proposal. The Senate advised acceptance by a heavy margin, and the treaty was signed in June, 1846, and quickly ratified.

In accepting the 49th parallel, Polk obviously had given up nothing to which the United States had a valid claim. In the past the American government had repeatedly offered to accept that line, only to encounter British resistance. By the Oregon Treaty, Polk at last obtained for his country a share in the magnificent waterway within the Strait of Juan de Fuca. With the acquisition of San Francisco as the result of the Mexican War, the United States gained two of the best harbors on the entire Pacific Coast.

What motivated Britain's "surrender" in Oregon? Clearly it held stronger title to the region north of the Columbia by virtue of actual occupation and settlement than the United States did. Some historians have found the answer in the Irish potato famine of 1845 and the presumed need for large imports of American wheat. In fact, the famine was not as serious in 1845 as later, and in any case Great Britain had access to other foreign sources of wheat. Far more important was the Peel-Aberdeen ministry's eventual decision that a few thousand or more square miles of virtually uninhabited territory in the Pacific northwest did not merit a war with the United States. It was now known that the Columbia was not particularly valuable for navigation nor essential for the fur operations of the Hudson's Bay Company. In addition, many in Britain viewed as reasonable the American desire for a harbor in the Oregon territory, and deemed good commercial relations with the United States too valuable to jeopardize. Finally, an attitude of "little Englandism" began spreading in Great Britain; a belief that colonies were costly burdens, and that Britain's future lay not in acquiring more territory but in repealing restrictive mercantilist laws—the "Corn Laws"—and relying upon free trade with all the world. The Tory ministry carefully prepared the British public for retreat in Oregon and managed to establish a party truce with the opposition Whigs while peacefully resolving the issue with the United States.

Additional Reading

The best general treatment of Anglo-American relations in the period through 1846 is by Frank Thistlewaite, *America and the Atlantic Community: Anglo-American Aspects, 1790–1850* (1959). H. C. Allen gives a briefer account in *Conflict and Concord: The Anglo-American Relationship Since 1783* (1959). On travelers and the war of the quarterlies, see Jane Mesick, *The English Traveller in America, 1785–1835* (1922); Max Berger, *The British Traveller in America, 1836–1860* (1943); and M. F. Brighfield, "America and the Americans, 1840–1860, As Depicted in English Novels of the Period," *American Literature,* XXI (1959), 309–324. *John Quincy Adams and the Foundations of American Foreign Policy* (1950) and *John Quincy Adams and the Union* (1956) by Samuel Flagg Bemis provide good accounts of Adams's role in the boundary and trading disputes with Great Britain. A. B. Corey, *The Crisis of 1830–1843 in Canadian-American Relations* (1941) is the best single study of the northeastern boundary controversy. For other aspects of the Webster-Ashburton negotiations see: R. N. Current, "Webster's Propaganda and the Ashburton Treaty," *Mississippi Valley Historical Review,* XXXIV (1947), 187–200; Thomas Le Duc, "The Maine Frontier and the Northeastern Boundary Controversy," *American Historical Review,* LIII (1947), 30–41, and his "The Webster-Ashburton Treaty and the Minnesota Iron Ranges," *Journal of American History,* LI (1964), 476–481; and Wilbur D. Jones, "Lord Ashburton and the Maine Boundary Negotiation," *Mississippi Valley Historical Review,* XL (1953), 477–490, and his *Lord Aberdeen and the Americas* (1958). C. M. Fuess, *Daniel Webster* (2 vols., 1930); O. P. Chitwood, *John Tyler: Champion of the Old*

South (1939); and J. S. Reeves, *American Diplomacy under Tyler and Polk* (1907) are older but still useful studies. The role of fur traders in Oregon is briefly examined by J. S. Galbraith, *The Hudson's Bay Company as an Imperial Factor, 1821–1869* (1958). Frederick Merk, the leading scholar on Oregon, sums up his principal conclusions in *The Oregon Question* (1967). Also see Merk's *Manifest Destiny and Mission in American History* (1963) and *The Monroe Doctrine and American Expansionism, 1843–1849* (1966). *Winning Oregon* (1938), by Melvin C. Jacobs, emphasizes the role of pioneer farmers in the final solution, while Norman A. Graebner, *Empire on the Pacific* (1955), sees the desire for good commercial harbors as the key to the 1846 treaty. On the 1844 election and Polk's diplomacy the most recent study is by Charles G. Sellers, *James K. Polk, Continentalist, 1843–1846* (1966). Also see E. A. Miles, "'Fifty-Four Forty or Fight'—An American Political Legend," *Mississippi Valley Historical Review*, XLIV (1957), 291–309. P. S. Klein, *President James Buchanan* (1962), examines Buchanan's overrated role in the Oregon negotiations. A. K. Weinberg, *Manifest Destiny* (1935), analyzes the expansionist psychology in the Oregon controversy. Briefer treatments of the period are by R. W. Van Alystyne, *The Rising American Empire* (1960) and W. H. Goetzmann, *When the Eagle Screamed* (1966).

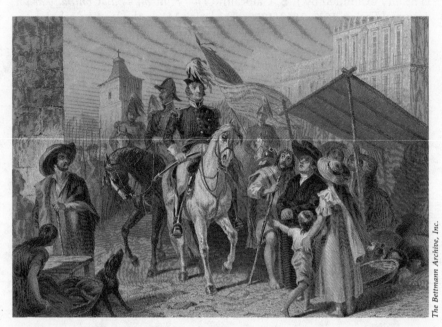

General Scott entering Mexico City

8

MANIFEST DESTINY
AND THE MEXICAN WAR

1. THE SPIRIT OF MANIFEST DESTINY

A fervent expansionist spirit gripped Americans in the 1840's and 1850's. Although some spoke confidently of a United States coextensive with the northern half of the Western Hemisphere (the true "continentalists" for whom the term "Manifest Destiny" probably should be reserved), most Americans limited their interests to a few desirable areas along the periphery of the United States, primarily Texas and the Pacific coast.

By their very nature, most of the English colonies along the Atlantic seaboard had expansionist leanings. After Independence, that expansionist trend turned toward areas adjacent to the United States. Geographer Jedediah Morse confidently predicted in 1789 that the center of empire would shift from Europe to the New World; the unsurpassed merits and energies of the Americans, he wrote, destined them to people and to rule most of North America. Others, such as Thomas Jefferson, saw limits to the future growth of the United States. In his view, geography and the representative political system of the American republic set definite natural limitations on its expansion, confining it within the boundaries of the Louisiana Purchase and the Rocky Mountains. Distances were too great and communications too slow for the Union to extend beyond those limits. When Americans did settle Oregon, as Jefferson expected, they would establish a sister republic to the United States. In the flush of nationalism following the War of 1812, expansionism again aimed toward a specific area, Florida. John Quincy Adams and a few others, such as John C. Calhoun, advocated continental expansion, but President Monroe remained Jeffersonian in his belief that American settlers would people North America and would found similar republics.

After relative quiescence in the 1820's and 1830's, expansionism reached an apogee in the 1840's. By then the actual flow of pioneers into Texas, Oregon, and California had aroused great popular interest in the acquisition of those areas. Moreover, the impressive growth of American agriculture, commerce, and manufacturing directed the nation's attention toward the need to expand domestic and foreign markets. Cheap or free land enticed farmers, feeling the effects of the depression years following the Panic of 1837, to move into Oregon and California. Merchants took particular interest in acquiring good harbors on the Pacific coast to facilitate penetration of the Asian markets. Technological advances such as the steamship, the railroad, and the telegraph, were beginning to annihilate distances and to make more conceivable a Union stretching from ocean to ocean. In the reform atmosphere of the period, expansionism assumed the status of yet another crusading humanitarian movement that would increase economic and social opportunities for American citizens and would benefit benighted foreigners by associating them with a more advanced people. Politics also played a part as Democrats sought to mobilize expansionist sentiment against their opposition, the Whigs. Yet probably most Americans in the 1840's and '50's favored only limited expansion into desirable nearby areas. Only a minority seriously advocated incorporation of all North America, and possibly Central America as well, into the United States.

John L. O'Sullivan, editor of the *Democratic Review,* a literary journal, and of the *New York Morning News,* seems to have coined the timely phrase "Manifest Destiny." A brilliant man and often enraptured by some lofty scheme, O'Sullivan had important connections in the Democratic Party and gradually became the chief philosopher of continental expansionism. He first used the term "Manifest Destiny" in an editorial in the *Democratic Review* in July, 1845, to justify the annexation of Texas. In another editorial later that year in the *New York Morning News,* O'Sullivan rationalized the American claim to Oregon:

Our claim is strongest. That claim is by the right of our manifest destiny to overspread and to possess the whole of the continent which Providence has given us for the development of the great experiment of liberty and federative self-government entrusted to us.

"Manifest Destiny" quickly captured the popular mood and became an often used slogan to justify expansionism both in its more limited and in its continental aspects. A happy invention, it implied divine purpose and sanction behind the inevitable destiny of the United States to expand over all North America. In addition to the argument of natural growth, the ideology of Manifest Destiny included several other important concepts: geographical predestination or the expansion to natural boundaries or limits; political gravitation or the magnetic attraction of the United States to peripheral territories and peoples; beneficent use of the soil whereby sturdy Americans would use the bounties of nature as Providence intended and for the benefit of the entire world; the natural right to security, by ridding the nation of threats along its borders, and by obtaining access to strategic outlets such as the mouth of the Mississippi River or the magnificent harbors on the Pacific Coast; and the concept of democratic mission or the duty of Americans as modern Israelites, possessing the world's most advanced political system, to carry the word of liberty and self-government to the world's benighted, either by example as most Americans believed, or by expansion as some advocated. In Jefferson's words, the United States was an "empire for liberty." Incorporation into the American union would regenerate backward peoples such as the Mexicans. Of course, self-interest underlay Manifest Destiny—the land hunger of restless pioneers and settlers for the offerings of Texas, Oregon, California, and other territories, and the desire of commercial interests for harbors on the Pacific to tap the markets of the Orient. But loftier motives also played a part—nationalism and the sense of democratic mission. Exuberant patriotism, revealed in the quest for an American art and literature freed of dependence upon Europe, the founding of numerous historical societies, and the publication of patriotic histories and textbooks, characterized the era. The annual July 4th celebration had become a sort of national "religious" holiday. O'Sullivan aptly expressed this exuberant but devout mood as early as 1838:

The far reaching, the boundless future will be the era of American greatness . . . the nation of many nations is destined to manifest to mankind the excellence of divine principles; to establish on earth the noblest temper ever dedicated to the worship of the Most High—the Sacred and the True. Its floor shall be a hemisphere— . . . and, its congregation a Union of many Republics. . . .

2. THE TEXAS REVOLUTION

Some historians, apologetic for the imperialism of the United States in the 1840's, have depicted Texas and California as international derelicts—sparsely populated and poorly governed centers of intrigue and turmoil, and the objects of foreign attention—finally sheltered within the American union. Americans desired both and finally acquired Texas without armed conflict and California by force. In both cases, the American government professed concern about foreign intrigue and designs on the two provinces, so the political security element operated strongly in its policies. In reality, however, agricultural expansionism and nationalism motivated the desire to annex Texas, and commercial expansionism underlay the push for California.

From 1803 to 1819 the United States maintained a weak claim to Texas, based upon a dubious interpretation of the Louisiana Purchase. In those days Texas did not hold much interest for the United States or for Spain except as a buffer zone against Yankee intrusions. In 1820 the area had a population of only 4,000 people and a few military posts. However, a few frontiersmen and politicians, such as Senator Thomas Hart Benton of Missouri, felt disappointed when the United States surrendered its claim to Texas in the Adams-Onís Treaty of 1819.

Yet the peopling of Texas with Americans inevitably resulted from the steady western flow of trappers, traders, and pioneer farmers. Moses Austin inaugurated the first substantial American emigration into Texas in late 1820. He secured permission from the Spanish authorities to bring in 300 families. After his death, his son Stephen Austin obtained a renewal of the grant in 1823 from the newly independent Mexico. Mexican authorities hoped by liberal land grants to entice immigrants who would become loyal citizens of Mexico and adhere to the Roman Catholic faith. Other impresarios also brought colonies of settlers to Texas, which formed part of the province of Texas-Coahuila. Most of these emigrants were American Protestants from the southern states, although only a few owned Negro slaves. By the early 1830's Texas had a population of approximately 30,000 American settlers and several thousand slaves.

Alarmed at the large influx of American settlers and an abortive uprising in Texas, the Mexican government began to fear its ultimate loss to the United States. Consequently an 1830 law barred further immigration from the United States, prohibited the additional importation of slaves, tightened the requirement for the profession of the Catholic faith by all citizens, and increased the Mexican military establishment in Texas. The law proved almost impossible to enforce. Immigrants continued to enter from the United States, slaves still were imported, and the customs laws were flouted, while friction increased between the American settlers and the Mexican military authorities.

American residents tried to obtain separate statehood for Texas within the Mexican federal system but failed. The new Mexican dictator, Antonio Lopez de Santa Anna, alarmed the inhabitants by suppressing federalism and centralizing authority over the states. Santa Anna sent more troops into Texas and issued orders for the strict enforcement of the customs laws. American settlers rebelled in the second half of 1835 and established a provisional government. When Santa Anna invaded Texas with a large army in 1836 and massacred the small American garrison at the Alamo, the enraged Americans declared the independence of Texas on March 2. Subsequently the Texan army commanded by Sam Houston defeated the Mexican forces at San Jacinto and captured the Mexican President. Santa Anna was released two months later after pledging to withdraw all Mexican troops from Texas and to help obtain recognition of its independence. Although the

Mexican Congress rejected that agreement, obtained under obvious duress, Texas in fact had succeeded in its bid for freedom. The Texans immediately sent commissioners to Washington to seek recognition, aid, and annexation.

On several occasions prior to the Texas Revolution, the government had attempted unsuccessfully to "rectify" the border established by the 1819 treaty to include a substantial part of Texas within the United States. President Jackson, a westerner and an ardent nationalist, long had wished to correct what he and others regarded as the mistake of 1819. In 1829 he appointed Anthony Butler as Minister to Mexico and authorized him to offer $5 million for a boundary west of the Nueces River. Butler remained in Mexico City for six years of intrigue, threats, and schemes to bribe high Mexican officials into compliance. Although Jackson wrote "What a scamp" on one of Butler's letters outlining his efforts at bribery, he apparently did not object to such questionable tactics. The outraged Mexican government finally demanded Butler's recall.

After the Texas Revolution, however, President Jackson's behavior became scrupulously correct. He invoked the neutrality laws, but enforcing them proved impossible because of the strong sympathies of many Americans for the rebel cause, and the difficulty of policing the long border between Mexico and the United States. Mexicans understandably resented the flow of volunteers and war materials across the border into Texas, and felt that the revolution could never have succeeded without such unneutral help from the Americans. Agents of Texas openly recruited volunteers in the United States, promising liberal land grants as well as opportunities for glory. Some of these militant emigrants left for Texas in organized groups with bands playing and flags flying. Mexico had a legitimate grievance against the United States government, regardless of its apparently sincere efforts to observe neutrality.

Several reasons governed Jackson's prudent course. At first he could not be certain of rebel success. Moreover, he wanted to avoid embarrassing his successor to the presidency, Martin Van Buren, who might otherwise face a Democratic Party split over the sharpening slavery issue. Jackson did not extend diplomatic recognition to the new republic until March 3, 1837, when the revolution had obviously succeeded and sentiment in Congress favored the step. Jackson avoided annexation, however, because he feared both war with Mexico, and opposition within the United States to the expansion of slavery. The growing abhorrence of the slave system caused even an ardent expansionist such as John Quincy Adams to oppose annexation. Van Buren adhered to Jackson's policy. Consequently the Texas Republic, under President Houston, withdrew its offer of annexation and began to seek foreign recognition of its independence. Houston thereby cleverly played upon American fears of the British and the French taking an active interest in preserving an independent Texas and exploiting it commercially. France recognized Texas in 1839, and Britain in 1840; the Netherlands and Belgium followed. For nearly nine years prior to its incorporation into the United States, Texas enjoyed recognition as an independent state by the leading powers and commercial countries of Europe.

3. TEXAS ENTERS THE UNION

The issue of Texas remained quiescent until President Tyler revived it in 1843. Disowned by the leaders of his own Whig Party, Tyler, a southerner and a nationalist, was eager to achieve fame and to rehabilitate his own political cause by annexing Texas. The President and his two Secretaries of State, Abel P. Upshur, who served until killed in 1844 by an explosion aboard the warship *Princeton,* and his successor, John C. Calhoun, professed fear of a British plot in Texas. The abolitionist movement was very active in Great Britain, and at the World's Anti-Slavery Convention that met in London in mid-1843 delegates enthusiastically discussed the possibilities of abolishing slavery in Texas. Tyler and his advisers were convinced that Britain and France hoped to restrain the further expansion of the United States, wanted to obtain an assured access to the raw cotton resources and the low-tariff market of Texas, and attempted to frustrate annexation by arranging a Mexican-Texas settlement based upon the continued independence of the latter. According to reports arriving in Washington, Foreign Secretary Lord Aberdeen, eager to end slavery in Texas, planned to persuade Texan authorities by offering them diplomatic support and a large loan to adopt compensated emancipation. If that happened, it would have isolated the southern states and their peculiar institution. Although they used these rumors and fears to overcome domestic opposition to annexation, Tyler and probably Polk felt genuinely apprehensive of what they viewed as a threat to the nation's security. Former President Jackson added his voice to the advocates of speedy annexation, defending it as necessary to counter British schemes to convert Texas into a satellite state. Texan authorities, eager to quicken the pace of incorporation, played successfully upon such fears.

Upshur began negotiations for annexation in October of 1843. Apparently he and Tyler hoped to neutralize domestic opposition from the Whigs and the abolitionists by associating Texas with the issue of Oregon and emphasizing the alleged European threat to America's vital interests in both areas. Calhoun, Upshur's successor as Secretary of State, continued those efforts but in a less tactful manner. A fiery southerner, Calhoun was determined to complete annexation and to defend the southern slave system against its critics at home and abroad. Obviously Britain and France hoped Texas would remain independent, and the British would have preferred to see the end of slavery there, but neither country plotted or conspired against the United States. In a note to Washington in late 1843, Britain's Foreign Secretary Lord Aberdeen attempted to explain his Texas policy as not unfriendly toward the United States. Unfortunately, Aberdeen added an ill-chosen phrase that his government was "constantly exerting herself to promote the general abolition of slavery throughout the world." In a reply to the British minister in Washington, Sir Richard Pakenham, Calhoun sounded a clarion call in defense of slavery and the annexation of Texas. The institution of slavery, he argued, benefited both the master and his human chattel, and the peace and prosperity of the Union depended upon its maintenance. It followed logically, therefore, that annexation of Texas was vital to the security of the United States.

On April 22, 1844, a treaty for the annexation of Texas went before the Senate. President Tyler warned in his accompanying message that, if the treaty failed to receive approval, Texas would seek closer ties with foreign states, and the United States would end up nearly surrounded by European possessions. To assuage antislavery sentiment in the northern states, Robert J. Walker, a Pennsylvanian residing in Mississippi, published a pamphlet in which he argued that Texas was the last remaining area suitable for the expansion of slavery. Thereafter, having reached its natural limits, the system was doomed to ultimate extinction because of the soil exhaustion resulting from its one-crop economy. Walker's arguments apparently had little effect in convincing or silencing northern opponents of annexation. Calhoun's note to Pakenham appeared in the press, and its intemperate defense of slavery gave added fuel to the abolitionist cause and to more moderate opponents of the expansion of slavery. The year 1844 was also a presidential election year, and the Texas issue could not be divorced from politics. Democrat Martin Van Buren and Whig Henry Clay, the leading candidates for nomination, tried to defuse the issue by stating their opposition to annexation at the present time. When the treaty came to a vote in the Senate on June 8, therefore, 35 nays to 16 yeas defeated it; all Whig Senators except one, plus seven Democrats, voted against annexation.

Van Buren paid a heavy political price for his stand on Texas. Clay obtained the Whig nomination as expected, but a revolt by southerners and their northern expansionist allies gave the Democratic nomination to James K. Polk of Tennessee. Polk's platform, designed to appeal to nationalist sentiment in both the North and the South, called for "the reoccupation of Oregon and the reannexation of Texas at the earliest practicable period. . . ." Tyler had gained renomination by a rump group of supporters but withdrew from the race in order to strengthen the pro-annexation forces. A third group—the Liberty Party—also entered the campaign and adamantly opposed any extension of slavery. Texas became the main foreign policy issue. When the results came in, Polk had won a narrow victory, receiving 50.7 percent of the popular vote and

170 electoral votes to Clay's 105. The Liberty Party vote clearly damaged Clay in such crucial states as New York. Yet Polk's election represented more of a triumph for the expansionists across the nation than merely a southern victory. He had run a particularly good race in the western section of the country where expansionism was popular.

Lame-duck President Tyler interpreted the outcome of the election as a mandate for expansionism. Therefore he recommended to Congress that Texas be annexed by a joint resolution. Since a resolution required only a simple majority in each house, Tyler hoped to sidestep the roadblock of a two-thirds majority for approval of a treaty in the Senate. Even so the outcome was close. The joint resolution passed the House early in 1845 by a vote of 120 to 98, and the Senate by 27 to 25. Tyler signed it into law on March 1, three days before his term ended. The resolution provided two alternative methods of annexation: immediate incorporation when Texas should accept the terms, or the appointment of a commission to negotiate annexation. Advocates of the latter looked to gain time to reconcile Mexico to annexation and thereby to avoid a probable war.

Although as President-elect, Polk had indicated his support of the second alternative, after his inauguration he adhered to Tyler's course of seeking immediate annexation. By the terms of the resolution, Texas, upon the adoption of a popularly-endorsed constitution, would gain admission as a state in the Union. It would retain possession of its public lands and would assume the burden of its own public debt. Estimates put the latter at a total of $7 to $12 million, so Texan authorities toyed with the idea of British-French intercession for Mexican recognition to use as a bargaining point with Washington. Under British and French pressure, Mexico reluctantly agreed to recognize the independence of Texas if it would not seek annexation to the United States. That realistic step came too late. By then Polk's emissaries had promised Texas concessions after annexation, and a referendum revealed that the overwhelming majority of Texans favored prompt union with the United States. On December 29, 1845, President Polk signed the act admitting Texas as a state in the American Union. The "derelict" at last had found shelter.

4. WESTWARD TO CALIFORNIA

California far more than Texas was a "derelict" on the international scene. Founded by the Franciscans in the 18th century, California contained a sparse population and was remote from the center of Spanish power in Mexico. Under Mexican rule, California became increasingly restless and unruly. Mexico maintained a rather tenuous hold on the distant province, and repeated if somewhat halfhearted revolts broke out against the incompetent and corrupt officials sent to govern California. Turbulent and feebly defended, California, like a prize, awaited any strong and expansionist power that sought her.

American interests in California developed from essentially commercial origins. New England merchants took sea otter off the California coast and shipped the pelts to a thriving market in China. As the sea otter became nearly extinct, American whalers began to frequent California waters and to use the harbors at Monterey and San Francisco for supplies and ship repairs. New Englanders also came to California to purchase hides and tallow, used in the leather and candle industries in the United States. Agents of American firms penetrated the interior of the province and some became permanent residents. Overland trappers, such as Jedediah Smith in 1826 and the Patties in 1828, also eventually entered California in search of beaver. A number of these American traders and trappers married into native California families, absorbed the local culture, and rose to prominent positions in the economic life of the province.

These contacts greatly whetted American interest in California. Enthusiastic travelers brought back glowing accounts of California's climate and soil, a veritable Eden awaiting the vigorous Yankee to realize its full potential. As Richard Henry Dana exclaimed in his *Two Years Before The Mast* (1840), an account of life on a hide and tallow ship, "In the hands of an enterprising people, what a country this might be!" The Western Emigration Society, founded to encourage settlement in California, extolled the land as "a perfect paradise, a perpetual spring." Stimulated by such glowing reports, and driven by economic hardships after the Panic of 1837, a considerable exodus of American settlers left for California in the early 1840's. By 1846, they comprised perhaps 800 to 900 of California's total population of about 8,000 people. Not surprisingly, Mexican officials began to display concern at the influx, fearing California might become another Florida or Texas.

The Jackson administration expressed the first official American interest in acquiring California. Commercial motives obviously governed this move, for the influx of American farmers did not begin until nearly a decade later. An expanding commerce with China and other Asian nations required good ports on the Pacific coast. Schemes for a transcontinental railroad with its western terminus at San Francisco Bay also strengthened the desire for a Pacific frontage. Commercial interest, therefore, and not the vague sentiment of Manifest Destiny, explained the thrust to the Pacific. As early as 1835, President Jackson authorized Anthony Butler to offer the Mexican government $3.5 million for California north of the 38th parallel, including the splendid harbor at San Francisco Bay. The Mexican authorities did not see fit to accept the offer. Interest in California continued to grow during the Van Buren and Tyler administrations. As noted before, Secretary of State Webster during his negotiations with Ashburton had toyed with a scheme involving Oregon and California. An ominous sign of American intentions occurred in 1842, when Commodore Thomas Ap Catesby Jones of the U.S. Navy, under the mistaken impression that war had broken out between Mexico and the United States, seized Monterey, California, and hoisted the American flag before discovering his mistake and sailing away.

When Polk took the oath of office in 1845, near anarchy existed in California. Influential native Californians and American residents plotted to throw off the Mexican yoke and to seek independence or annexation to the United States. An ardent expansionist, Polk desired California essentially for commercial reasons. Moreover, British and French interests in the province alarmed him. France had established a consulate in Monterey, and the Hudson's Bay Company had erected a trading post in San Francisco and sought large land grants from the Mexican authorities. From a variety of sources Polk heard greatly exaggerated reports about British activities to frustrate American designs on California. Actually the British government, as distinguished from some of its more zealous citizens, had no intention of becoming seriously embroiled with the United States over California. The area was remote and this was the era of "Little Englandism." Both Britain and France hoped that Mexico would retain California, but they were not prepared to risk war with the United States to ensure that end.

Alarmed at rumors of Anglo-French designs, Polk resolved to acquire California by peaceful means. The first method he tried—purchasing the territory from Mexico—failed. In 1845 he sent John Slidell to Mexico City with instructions to offer $15 to $20 million, $40 million if required, for the purchase of New Mexico and California. The Mexican government refused even to discuss such a real estate transaction with Slidell. The second method in effect was to encourage a California revolution and request for annexation. Thomas O. Larkin, the American consul in California, was instructed to observe closely British and French penetrations into the province and to explain to local leaders that the United States had no desire to expand except as the inhabitants of territories along its borders voluntarily requested it. Larkin interpreted his orders as meaning to encourage a local insurrection along the lines of the Texas model, with annexation to follow. Meanwhile, if war should come between Mexico and the United States, the American Navy received instructions to seize San Francisco Bay to forestall possible moves by Great Britain or France.

John C. Frémont and the outbreak of war with Mexico ruined Larkin's plans for a peaceful acquisition. An official explorer for the American Army, and the son-in-law of Missouri's influential Senator Thomas Hart Benton, the dashing Captain Frémont entered California with a small party in 1845 and remained until local authorities ordered him to withdraw. Frémont's arrogant behavior enraged native Californians and wrecked Larkin's patient work. Subsequently, Frémont reentered California and aided the American settlers who had launched the "Bear Flag" revolt on June 10, 1846. Before the revolt could go much further, news arrived of the outbreak of the Mexican-American War. California was to become American not by purchase nor by annexation but by conquest.

5. WAR WITH MEXICO

The Mexican government refused to recognize the annexation of Texas and withdrew its minister from Washington in March, 1845. Subsequently, when it became clear that the Texans would accept the offer of annexation, Mexican President José Joaquin Herrera recommended to the Mexican Congress that it declare war upon the United States. The official reaction from Washington decried Mexico's behavior as unrealistic and aggressive. Texas after all had been independent for nine years and had been recognized diplomatically by the world's major commercial powers. Moreover, as many Americans knew, the Mexican government verged on bankruptcy, unable to obtain credit abroad or to pay its debts, and faced political turmoil and revolution at home. Why then should it make such an issue over a long-lost territory? Most Americans lacked the sensitivity to comprehend Mexico's feelings of outraged nationalism and endangered security. The gulf between the two peoples and cultures was too great to permit much understanding by either side.

Texas was not the only irritant in Mexican-American relations. Years of wrangling diplomacy went into persuading the Mexican government to reaffirm the boundaries of the Adams-Onís Treaty and then actually to survey the boundary. Not until 1831 did obtaining a commercial treaty with that government become possible. Mexico's frequent revolutions and civil disorders had resulted in considerable property damages and some losses of life to American and other resident foreigners; in fact, 22 Americans were summarily executed in 1835 for alleged involvement in an abortive revolution. President Jackson became so exasperated with Mexican unwillingness to pay damage claims that he spoke of possible war to compel redress. Finally, in 1839, the two countries concluded a treaty for arbitration; subsequently, Mexico accepted an award of over $2 million in compensation to American claimants, to be paid in regular installments. Mexico made only three payments before defaulting because of a virtually empty treasury. Not only Americans but Europeans, too, viewed Mexico as a turbulent and unstable country unable to live up to its international obligations and fully deserving chastisement. Thus France in 1838 waged the so-called Pastry War to press the claims of its nationals against the Mexican government.

Upon taking office, President Polk regarded the Texas annexation issue as settled. The question of the Texas-Mexican boundary, however, remained unclear. Texas very dubiously claimed its boundary extended to the Rio Grande River, and had forced such a "treaty" upon Santa Anna while he was in captivity. In Mexico's view, if it recognized the loss of Texas, which it did not, then the Nueces River formed the proper

Texas, 1836–1846

boundary line. The Nueces had marked the boundary of the Texas area while it still belonged to Mexico, and no Texan settlements existed beyond that river. Although many in the United States questioned the claim to the Rio Grande, and the annexation resolution by Congress had not specified a boundary, Polk unhesitatingly accepted the Texas version. Also resolved to acquire California, Polk used the strategy of pressing the Rio Grande claim vigorously and then combining it with the debts issue to obtain the Pacific Coast province from the weak and bankrupt Mexican government. He ordered General Zachary Taylor, commander of American forces in the Southwest, into Texas in 1845 and in January, 1846 directed him to march his army from the Neuces to the Rio Grande. Texans and most Democrats heartily approved Taylor's move to the disputed river line, but the opposition Whigs criticized it as provocative. Meanwhile, believing that the new regime in power in Mexico was ready to reach an agreement, Polk decided to send John Slidell of Louisiana to Mexico City.

Slidell was a known expansionist, whose appointment offended Mexican officials and reaffirmed American intentions. Moreover, Polk had received information that Mexico would only accept a commissioner to negotiate about Texas. Yet he appointed Slidell as a regular minister and instructed him to negotiate on wider issues than Texas, believing the time opportune to increase pressures on Mexico City. Polk authorized Slidell to offer to assume American claims against Mexico in exchange for consent to a boundary along the Rio Grande. In addition the United States would pay $5 million for the inclusion of New Mexico and up to $25 million for California. The absolute minimum for a settlement, however, remained acceptance of the Rio Grande boundary.

When Slidell arrived in Mexico City in late 1845, the Herrera government had collapsed and one under General Mariano Paredes had replaced it. The new regime refused to receive Slidell on the grounds that he came as a regular minister rather than as a special commissioner. The objection was not merely legalistic, for Mexico felt it had suffered a grievous injury over Texas that had to be repaired before the resumption of ordinary diplomatic intercourse. Probably no Mexican government could have long survived the rage of its own countrymen if it had entered into negotiations with the American envoy.

When Slidell returned to Washington, he advised the President that only force could obtain a settlement. Polk's thoughts had increasingly turned in that direction. While Slidell was still in Mexico, the President had informed the Cabinet that he would ask Congress to authorize forcible measures if the mission failed. The administration now decided upon war. News of a clash between Taylor's forces and the Mexicans along the Rio Grande on April 25, 1846, arrived fortuitously and enabled the President to request a declaration of war on the grounds that Mexico was the aggressor. As he phrased it in his War Message to Congress on May 11, "after repeated menaces, Mexico has passed the boundary of the United States, has invaded our territory and shed American blood upon the American soil." Despite American forbearance and repeated attempts at conciliation, Polk declared, war existed and by the act of Mexico.

Patriotic fervor swept the United States. This outburst of outraged nationalism even temporarily silenced Polk's Whig critics in Congress. Those who wanted to debate the issue or examine the documents submitted along with the President's message were muzzled by the Democratic leaders, who insisted upon an immediate vote. The House of Representatives adopted a resolution for war after a half-hour's consideration, by a vote of 174 to 14, with 35 abstentions; the Senate concurred on the following day by a margin of 40 to 2. On May 13, 1846, when Polk signed the resolution, the United States was formally at war with Mexico.

Historians have waged a spirited debate over the causes of the War with Mexico. One group, reflecting wartime northern criticism of the conflict as deliberately provoked to expand slavery—"slaveholders' conspiracy"—arraigned the Polk administration for forcing war upon a weak and chaotic Mexico. That view generally prevailed until after World War I, when several historians shifted the responsibility from America and Polk to Mexico. According to this school, Mexico brought the war upon itself by its internal turbulence and its unrealistic pride. Most historians today take a more balanced view. War in 1846 was almost unavoidable. A United States in the full flush of nationalism and expansionism, conscious of its own rapidly growing wealth and power, observed with mounting contempt and exasperation a Mexico that was chronically bankrupt and revolution prone, unable either to fulfill its international obligations or to defend its peripheral territories, and yet unwilling to reconcile itself to its losses. Mexican public opinion can best be described as an explosive mixture of fear and patriotic belligerency. Years of observing the Yankees expanding into territories along their borders had convinced many thoughtful Mexicans that any compromise on Texas would merely ensure further American aggression and the loss of California, New Mexico, and perhaps other areas. An editorial by one Mexico City newspaper, *El Tiempo,* aptly expressed that view:

The war which we fight today is not solely for the defense of our honor or a part of our territory; it is a war of independence, a national war, because on its outcome depends our existence.

Fear of the Yankee colossus curiously mixed with a patriotic conviction that Mexico could easily defeat its grasping neighbor. The Mexican army appeared larger than that of the United States on paper, and Mexicans thought of Americans as crass materialists who had revealed their cowardly colors in the War of 1812. Moreover, many Mexicans believed that distance and the prospective support of Great Britain and France would rescue them from any attempted invasion.

And what role did President Polk play? Recent studies reveal that he was not a warmonger, but it cannot be said that he was strongly oriented toward peace. Polk was a narrow patriot and an expansionist. Yet he did not go to war merely to seize territory. He reasonably could hope eventually to acquire California and the intervening area by "peaceful" means, although when the war began he acted with dispatch to seize what he and other Americans had long desired. Polk decided upon war with Mexico, it seems, because his patience in trying to deal with that country was exhausted. Of course, the perspective from Mexico City differed radically from that of Washington. Simple judgments of guilt and innocence, therefore, seem inappropriate as explanations for so complex an event as the Mexican War. Both sides shared the responsibility for the outbreak of hostilities, though perhaps the United States deserved greater blame in view of its size, maturity, and expansionist appetites.

6. A WAR OF CONQUEST

The Mexican War fell far short of universal popularity in the United States. Although most Americans initially responded patriotically to the call to arms, opposition increased as the war continued. Comparable in many ways to the Vietnam War in the 1960's, the war with Mexico came to seem immoral to a growing number of Americans. Moreover, as victory followed victory, American armies penetrated deeper into Mexico with apparently no peace in sight. Members of the small peace movement, which intermixed with abolitionism, reacted to the Mexican War with disappointment and dismay. They viewed all war as uncivilized and unchristian; this particular war seemed to them a naked struggle for conquest and a means of extending the southern system of human bondage. The great Unitarian leader William Ellery Channing declared that if he were to fight, justice would require that he serve on the side of Mexico. Henry Thoreau, advocate of passive civil disobedience, went to jail briefly rather than pay a Massachusetts state poll tax that might help support the war. A workers' convention in New England resolved that its members would not take up arms to sustain southern slaveocrats in exploiting fellow human beings. And in 1847, the Massachusetts legislature passed a resolution condemning the war as a "war of conquest" and "against freedom, against humanity, against justice, against the Union. . . ."

The Whig Party, joined by some northern Democrats, provided a mounting but not particularly effective opposition to the war. Polk failed to arouse popular support and to silence critics. Whigs branded the conflict "Mr. Polk's War," and Illinois Congressman Abraham Lincoln asked on what precise spot of American territory Mexico had spilled American blood. Critics denounced the war as an executive usurpation of Congress' power to make war, since Polk allegedly had provoked it deliberately by ordering Taylor's army into the disputed territory. Yet while damning the war, Whig congressmen felt compelled to vote for military appropriations so as not to let down "our boys in service." The war was spawning a growing moral revolt in the northeastern and northwestern sections of the country that affected the Democratic as well as the Whig party. Opponents to the expansion of slavery backed the Wilmot Proviso, an appropriation bill amendment to prohibit slavery in any territory acquired from Mexico. Although never passed, the struggle over the proviso polarized northern versus southern opinion, helped create a new third party in the 1848 elections (the Free Soil Party), and pointed the way toward eventual secession and civil war. The Mexican War was truly a "dose of arsenic" for American politics and the American Union.

The military aspects of the war were eminently satisfactory. The vast power of the United States quickly made itself felt against Mexico, despite the smallness and unreadiness of the American army when the war began. The army easily overran New Mexico and California, but Mexico proved more difficult. Bluff old General Taylor, despite his excessive caution and lack of military skill, won victories at Palo Alto and Resaca de la Palma and captured Monterrey in northern Mexico. Relations between the victorious general and the cold and aloof President soon became severely strained, in part because Taylor, a Whig, not unwillingly listened to the calls coming his way for the presidential nomination in 1848. By his own choice Polk was a one-term chief executive, but he took politics seriously and the situation pained him greatly. Moreover, Polk soon decided to strike at the heart of Mexico in order to compel the enemy to make peace on terms satisfactory to the United States. He ordered Taylor onto the defensive and sent another Whig general, Winfield Scott, to invade Mexico. Since he could not find any Democratic commanding generals, he at least hoped to play one Whig military hero off against the other. "Old Fuss and Feathers" Scott and his small army (around 14,000 men) landed at Veracruz in March, 1847 and marched inland some 260 miles to the heart of Mexico. Mexico City fell on September 14, 1847. Scott's military skill and the bravery of his outnumbered army enormously impressed both the American public and European observers. The navy had fewer opportunities for glory than the army but it too acquitted itself well.

Scott, like Taylor, believed with some justification that the President harassed his operations unnecessarily. Scott was extremely irritated when Polk dispatched Nicholas P. Trist, chief clerk of the State Department, as a special commissioner to accompany the invading army in order to negotiate peace when and if he found a Mexican government sufficiently realistic to talk. The general soon found the chief clerk more congenial than he had expected, however, and the two cooperated effectively to terminate the war.

On the day the United States declared war, Polk's cabinet had met to consider the dangers of European intervention on Mexico's behalf. Anxious to forestall any outside interference, the Secretary of State, James Buchanan, advised a public statement that the war was for defense, not for the conquest of territory. The President refused, asserting that while defensive motives governed America's actions, the nation was entitled to California and other areas as an indemnity for past claims and the costs of a war that had been forced upon it. Polk preferred to risk a broadening of hostilities rather than to tie his hands by a public disavowal of territorial gains. Great Britain and France viewed the war as aggressive, but neither power cared to intervene militarily to aid Mexico. After all, Mexico had been turbulent and its government unrealistic, but more importantly, the United States was too powerful to be challenged lightly.

Polk initially had desired only New Mexico and upper California, but as the war continued and Scott penetrated more deeply into the heartland of Mexico, Polk began to stiffen his terms to include lower California and parts of northern Mexico. A movement for "All Mexico" began to emerge in the United States. Ardent Manifest Destinarians, such as John L. O'Sullivan, at first had held that territories should come into the Union only voluntarily. As the war continued, however, they swallowed their aversions and contemplated absorbing all of Mexico by conquest, either in stages or in one gulp. Polk apparently preferred to do it in stages. Trist subscribed to a more idealistic version of continentalism and hoped to absorb Mexico by conciliation and persuasion rather than by conquest. A very able if pretentious diplomat, he tried unsuccessfully to work for peace through Santa Anna, whom the United States had permitted to return to Mexico. Even after the loss of its capital, the Mexican government merely offered to settle for the Nueces boundary and actually requested reparations. Polk remarked that Mexico behaved as if it were the victor. Consequently, and because of displeasure at Trist's conciliatory methods, Polk ordered the envoy back to the United States.

Trist defied his recall and continued his anxious quest for a negotiated peace before American forces occupied the entire country. The British chargé in Mexico shared his fears and aided him in his efforts. Success finally came with the signing of the Treaty of Guadalupe Hidalgo on February 2, 1848. The terms provided for the Rio Grande boundary and the cession of New Mexico and upper California. The United States agreed to pay Mexico $15 million, and to assume the claims of its citizens against the Mexican government.

This treaty by a discredited agent enraged Polk, for it fell far short of his expanded war aims. He had little choice, however, but to overcome his resentment and to submit the treaty to the Senate. By that time the All Mexico movement clearly did not command the support of most Americans. Its greatest appeal centered in the large cities of the Northeast and the Northwest, and even there it probably influenced only a minority. Southerners took a lukewarm attitude toward the All Mexico program, fearing the incorporation of eight million Mexicans of an alien culture and mixed races into the Union, and realizing that slavery probably would not prove economically feasible in most of that territory. Whigs, many northern Democrats, and abolitionists, strongly opposed annexation of all Mexico. Aware of the increasing opposition to the war, which threatened to hurt his own political party, Polk realized that it would be difficult to defend rejection of a treaty which conformed substantially to his initial directives to Trist. He therefore submitted Trist's treaty to the Senate with a recommendation for approval.

The Senate consented to the Treaty of Guadalupe Hidalgo on March 10, 1848, by a vote of 38 to 14. For his statesmanlike efforts, Trist

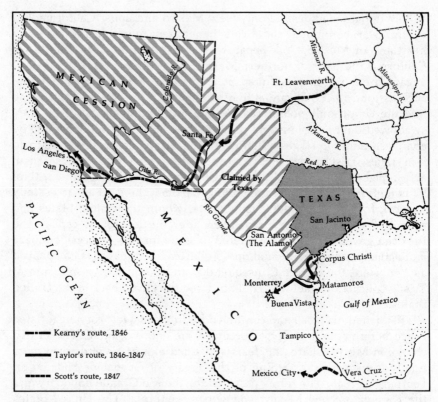

The Mexican Cession, 1848

was dismissed from office and denied back pay; not until 25 years later did Congress rectify that wrong. The end of the war brought a general feeling of relief across America, although the debate over slavery in the newly acquired territories continued until temporarily resolved by the Compromise of 1850. So ended a war that had greatly enlarged the domain of the United States, at a small cost in lives and money (13,000 deaths, more by disease than bullets, and nearly $90 million), but at an incalculably greater cost politically and morally. The final slice of Mexican territory came in the Gadsen Purchase of 1853, when the United States paid Mexico $10 million for an area now part of New Mexico and Arizona desired for the purpose of a possible transcontinental railroad route.

Additional Reading

Two works are indispensable for the study of American territorial imperialism: Albert K. Weinberg, *Manifest Destiny: A Study of Nation-*

alist *Expansionism in American History* (1935), which examines closely the ideology of expansionism; and Frederick Merk, *Manifest Destiny and Mission in American History* (1963), which depicts continentalism as an aberration of the true American spirit. Merk's *The Monroe Doctrine and American Expansionism, 1843–1849* (1966) suggests that national security considerations were deliberately used to rationalize expansionism. Norman A. Graebner has edited a valuable anthology on expansionism, *Manifest Destiny* (1968). Also see Richard W. Van Alstyne, *The Rising American Empire* (1960) and Charles Vevier, "American Continentalism: An Idea of Expansion, 1845–1910," *American Historical Review,* LXV (1960), 323–335. On the Texas issue, basic studies include: Justin H. Smith, *The Annexation of Texas* (1911); Stanley Siegel, *A Political History of the Texas Republic, 1836–1845* (1956); and W. C. Binkley, *The Texas Revolution* (1952). Also see K. J. Brauer, "The Massachusetts State Texas Committee: A Last Stand Against the Annexation of Texas," *Journal of American History,* LI (1964), 214–231. The British and French roles are examined by E. D. Adams, *British Interests and Activities in Texas, 1838–1846* (1910); W. D. Jones, *Lord Aberdeen and the Americas* (1958); and Henry Blumenthal, *A Reappraisal of Franco-American Relations, 1830–1871* (1959). The commercial thrust to California is emphasized by Norman A. Graebner, *Empire on the Pacific* (1955). On California, consult G. M. Brooke, Jr., "The Vest Pocket War of Commodore Jones," *Pacific Historical Review,* XXXI (1962), 217–233; J. A. Hawgood, "The Pattern of Yankee Infiltration in Mexican Alta California, 1821–1846," *Pacific Historical Review,* XXVII (1958), 27–37; and F. A. Knapp, Jr., "The Mexican Fear of Manifest Destiny in California," *Essays in Mexican History* (1958), 192–208, edited by T. E. Cotner and C. E. Castañeda. Excellent accounts of the American penetration of Texas and California are found in Ray Allen Billington, *Westward Expansion, A History of the American Frontier* (1949) and *The Far Western Frontier, 1830–1860* (1956). Older controversial interpretations of the causes of the Mexican War appear in Herman Von Holst, *The Constitutional and Political History of the United States* (1881), Vol. III and James Ford Rhodes, *History of the United States from the Compromise of 1850* (1902), Vol. I, both of which criticize the United States and emphasize the role of southern expansionism; versus Justin H. Smith, *The War with Mexico* (1919, 2 vols.) and S. F. Bemis, *The Latin American Policy of the United States* (1943), which attribute the responsibility primarily to Mexico. Glenn W. Price, *Origins of the War with Mexico: The Polk-Stockton Intrigue* (1967) reaffirms the older thesis that Polk conspired to provoke war. In addition to the studies cited above by Graebner and Merk, see Charles G. Sellers, *James K. Polk: Continentalist, 1843–1846* (1966), which depicts Polk as following a very aggressive diplomacy. The historiography of the causes of the war are examined by P. T. Harstad and R. W. Resh, "The Causes of the Mexican War: A Note on Changing

Interpretations," *Arizona and the West,* VI (1964), 289–302, and by Ramón Ruiz, ed., *The Mexican War: Was It Manifest Destiny?* (1963). An excellent brief account of the war and its diplomacy is by Otis A. Singletary, *The Mexican War* (1960). Also see the shorter sketch by William H. Goetzmann, *When the Eagle Screamed: The Romantic Horizon in American Diplomacy, 1800–1860* (1966). An older but still useful account is *The Movement for the Acquisition of All Mexico, 1846–1848* (1936), by J. D. P. Fuller. The divisive effects of the war are examined in a recent volume by Samuel Eliot Morison, Frederick Merk, and Frank Friedel, *Dissent in Three American Wars* (1970).

Commodore Perry at Yokohama

9

EXPANSIONIST AMERICA, 1849–1860

1. "YOUNG AMERICA"

The Mexican War gave a tremendous stimulus to American nationalism. Unlike 1812, the United States demonstrated great determination and fighting prowess. It was not simply Mexico's defeat—that had been expected—but it was the sweeping nature of the victory that impressed both Americans and Europeans with the strength of the North American republic. Veritably, it seemed to many Americans that they had made the eagle scream and the buffalo bellow.

The Young America movement represented an idealized expression of the nationalism and sense of mission stimulated by the war. Most Americans were convinced that democratic republicanism was the wave of the future. They sympathized deeply with the liberal revolutionary currents that agitated Europe in 1848. The tide seemed to roll irresistibly over France, Italy, the Germanies, and Hungary, but unfortunately only to recede in failure within a few months.

The collapse of the bourgeois monarchy of Louis Philippe in France and the emergence of the Second Republic pleased most Americans. Unfortunately for republicanism, however, the French elected as their President Louis Napoleon Bonaparte, a nephew of the great Napoleon, and he soon made himself dictator. By 1853 he had assumed the title of Napoleon III and had proclaimed the Second Empire. Americans were dismayed and some even talked of aiding revolutionists to overthrow monarchy and autocratic rule everywhere. Most of the press in the United States regarded Napoleon III unfavorably, and relations between the two governments, while formally correct, distinctly lacked cordiality.

The Hungarian revolution also aroused great enthusiasm in America, only to bring disappointment. Casting off Austrian Hapsburg rule, Louis Kossuth and fellow liberals proclaimed an independent Hungarian republic in 1849. Within a few months Austrian forces, aided by over a hundred thousand Russian troops, restored imperial authority and drove Kossuth into exile. Prior to Kossuth's fall, the State Department had ordered A. D. Mann to Hungary to determine if conditions warranted recognition of the republican regime. Although the revolt collapsed before Mann arrived, the Austrian Minister in Washington, Chevalier Hülsemann, vigorously protested against such meddling. Daniel Webster, once again head of the State Department, penned a spread-eagle reply that delighted most of his fellow citizens. Patriotically if irrelevantly, Webster declared that compared to the United States Hapsburg possessions seemed in contrast merely "a patch on the earth's surface." When Kossuth came to America in 1851 he received a hero's welcome: clubs were organized in his behalf, balls were given, and mass meetings cheered his remarks. President Millard Fillmore invited him to dinner and Congress held a banquet in his honor. Yet for all his hopes, Kossuth failed to obtain meaningful support for his revolutionary cause.

The Young America movement in this country resembled the "Young Italy" and other liberal nationalist movements in Europe. By 1852, Young America had become a distinct political group. George N. Sanders of Kentucky, a volatile Democrat and one of the group's most active spokesmen, believed that the spread of republicanism in Europe, and throughout the world, would promote the prosperity as well as the happiness of all. He and others thought the United States ought to enlarge its markets and grow in strength, and by its influence inspire universal liberty and republicanism. The election of Democrat Franklin Pierce as President in 1852 appeared at home and abroad as a triumph for Young America. His election apparently alarmed several European powers, who professed fear that under Pierce the United States might embark upon a policy of active interference in the Old World in behalf of revolutionary movements. Yet the American people and their government were far too practical to do more than cheer republicanism abroad. Sympathy cost America little, but it would not risk serious involvement in European politics.

2. ISTHMIAN DIPLOMACY

The history of Anglo-American relations in Central America revolves around the question of an isthmian interoceanic canal, in which both nations took a vital interest. Great Britain had possessions in Belize (British Honduras), a protectorate over the Mosquito Indians, and extensive commercial interests in the Caribbean Sea and the Pacific. The United States, with an extensive coastline on the Pacific Ocean, found the markets of East Asia increasingly attractive. All the ingredients for a keen rivalry existed—territory, commerce, and security.

American power and influence spread into Central America during the Polk administration, at the high noon of Manifest Destiny. Apart from sheer expansionism and love of adventure, Central America attracted Americans because of their growing awareness of the need for an interoceanic canal somewhere in the isthmus. Discovery of gold in California set off a rush of prospectors and settlers in 1848 and 1849. Three routes connected the west coast with the eastern part of the United States: a long and arduous overland journey by horse or wagon; an equally trying journey by sea around Cape Horn at the tip of South America; or a voyage to Nicaragua or Panama, transit across the isthmus, and embarkation on another vessel to complete the trip to the California gold fields. Americans operated both transit routes across the isthmus and had formulated plans for the construction of a ship canal.

In 1846 the United States concluded one of its most amazing treaties. The Republic of New Granada (later Colombia), which owned Panama, feared Great Britain might extend its control from the Mosquito Shore southward to Panama. To forestall that possibility, the United States chargé, Benjamin A. Bidlack, signed the New Granada or Bidlack Treaty in 1846. By its terms, the United States guaranteed the sovereignty of New Granada over Panama and the maintenance of the transit in exchange for "free and open transit" across the isthmus. Despite fears of entanglement, the Senate approved the treaty in 1848. Subsequently, in 1850, American entrepreneurs began construction of a railroad across Panama, while Cornelius Vanderbilt undertook the Nicaraguan transit.

President Polk sent an agent to Central America to counter British influence in Nicaragua. The agent negotiated an unauthorized treaty with that republic giving the United States exclusive control of the canal route and guaranteeing Nicaraguan sovereignty. Another American envoy signed a treaty with Honduras to acquire Tigre Island in the Gulf of Fonseca for the defense of a Nicaraguan canal. Already alarmed by the Bidlack Treaty, British officials in Central America temporarily seized Tigre Island in October, 1849. Both London and Washington viewed the rivalry more calmly than their representatives in Central America. The United States had not ratified the treaties with Nicaragua and Honduras, and Britain evacuated Tigre Island.

The restraint of both governments indicated that neither wanted to risk war over unilateral control of an isthmian waterway. The United States, even under the expansionist-minded Polk, merely wanted to prevent a British monopoly of the isthmus. President Zachary Taylor, Polk's Whig successor, and Secretary of State John M. Clayton sympathized with Whig commercial interests that stood to suffer if hostilities with Britain broke out. Since the British ministry was also pacifically inclined, negotiations began in Washington for a compromise.

The talks resulted in the signing of the Clayton-Bulwer Treaty on

April 19, 1850. Great Britain and the United States pledged neither to seek exclusive control of the canal routes nor to fortify them, neither to colonize nor to exercise dominion over any part of Central America, and they guaranteed the neutrality of any canal that should be built. The Senate approved the treaty without any great difficulty. Subsequently, when Britain's continued presence in Belize and the Mosquito Shore became an issue, Democratic and other critics charged that the treaty violated the Monroe Doctrine and represented a defeat for the United States. Some historians have agreed with this interpretation and view the Clayton-Bulwer Treaty as contrary to the long-term interests of the United States in the exclusive control of any interoceanic canal. Yet judged in the context of the times, American diplomacy had won a limited victory through the Clayton-Bulwer Treaty. Its terms blocked further British expansion in Central America and admitted the United States to a sort of partnership in an area where Great Britain had long shown predominance.

Implementing the Clayton-Bulwer Treaty proved more difficult than its negotiation. For nearly a decade the pact seemed stillborn. Secretary Clayton, in a subsequent exchange of notes, accepted the British interpretation that the pact's self-denying provisions did not apply to British Honduras and its dependencies. Clayton's successors, however, adopted a contrary view. When Britain proclaimed a crown colony over the Honduran Bay Islands in 1852 and retained the Mosquito protectorate, many Americans denounced those actions as violations of the treaty and the Monroe Doctrine. Relations became even more strained when in 1854 an irate mob attacked the American Minister at Greytown on the Mosquito Shore. The captain of the American warship *Cyane* demanded an apology and reparations from the citizens of Greytown. When they failed to comply, he trained his guns on the town and brutally demolished it. Fortunately no lives were lost, although British and other foreign-owned property was destroyed. Washington brushed aside a sharp British protest. Not surprisingly, negotiations to clarify the Clayton-Bulwer Treaty broke down completely.

Moreover, the filibustering, or irregular military activities of the American William Walker and his assortment of adventurers and cutthroats greatly disturbed Britain. After an abortive effort to occupy lower California, Walker and his men seized control of Nicaragua in 1855. Many Americans, including the Democratic administration of Franklin Pierce, looked with sympathy on this "civilizing" venture. Walker's fall in 1857, however, removed that barrier to an Anglo-American understanding. In 1859–1860, Britain recognized Nicaraguan sovereignty over the Mosquito Shore and abandoned the Bay Islands to Honduras. This satisfied Washington and at last the Clayton-Bulwer Treaty succeeded in neutralizing Central America.

3. CUBA

Cuba, the "Pearl of the Antilles," had long stood as a prize eagerly sought by most of the great powers. Rich in sugar and molasses, the island became a frequent target for Spain's enemies. After the successful revolt of the mainland colonies, Cuba, the "Ever-Faithful Isle," along with Puerto Rico and a few lesser isles, alone remained of Spain's once vast empire in the Americas. Yet Cubans were restless under Spain's unenlightened rule and threatened to revolt. During the turbulent 1820's and the following decade, large numbers of Spanish troops were stationed in Cuba to suppress revolution and overcome dissent. Madrid had learned little from the loss of its mainland colonies and continued the same policies of abuse and neglect in Cuba.

Thoughtful Americans very early realized the strategic importance of Cuba. Located a few hundred miles off the southern coast of the United States, that island dominated the main trade routes into the Caribbean Sea and the Gulf of Mexico. In the hands of a strong power, Cuba could menace the security of the United States, as the missile crisis with Soviet Russia dramatized in 1962. From the time of the Jefferson administration, standard American policy opposed Cuba's transfer to any power stronger than Spain. Americans saw the sugar isle as a ripening apple that eventually would fall into the grasp of the United States, but until that happy moment arrived they were content to see it remain in the hands of a declining Spain. In fact, American leaders also opposed Cuban independence, which might result in the establishment of a Black republic similar to the bloody example of Haiti in the 1790's, or might open the way for British or French domination. Thus Americans cheered the independence movement in the rest of Latin America but looked with disfavor upon the possibilities of Cuban independence or the liberation of the island by Mexico or Colombia.

Economics also focused American attention upon Cuba. During the American Revolution, Spain had temporarily opened the island to American trade. After the Peace of 1783, Americans naturally wanted to expand that commerce, while Spain attempted to restore the old closed mercantilist system. Then during the long wars of the French Revolution and Napoleon, Spain again had to open the island to outside trade. In 1818, Spain finally abandoned most of the mercantilist system and opened Cuba to foreign commerce but imposed heavy import duties. American trade with Cuba flourished despite those restrictions, and by the 1850's Cuba ranked third in importance in the foreign trade of the United States.

Slavery added another factor to America's interest in Cuba. By the 1850's an estimated 450,000 Negro slaves labored in Cuba's sugar cane fields. Many southerners, therefore, favored annexation in order to

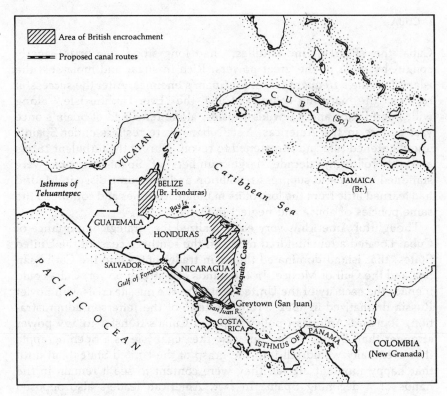

The Caribbean and Central America in the 1850's

increase the domestic supply of slaves. They also feared that a slave insurrection in Cuba might ignite a similar upheaval in the United States. They even suspected Great Britain of trying to persuade Spain to free the slaves in Cuba, thereby psychologically isolating the southern slave states. After the Compromise of 1850 temporarily ended the sharp sectional conflict over the Mexican Cession, many frustrated southerners saw hope for their minority position within the Union only by annexing Cuba to create new slave states.

The restiveness of the Creoles or Spanish-descended element in Cuba encouraged American aspirations. In 1822 some Cubans had looked to the United States for aid against Spain and talked of independence or annexation. Although they took no action, Americans became alarmed at the possibility that either France or Great Britain might acquire the island. When Foreign Secretary Canning in 1825 proposed a tripartite agreement by France, Britain, and the United States guaranteeing Spain's sovereignty over Cuba, Washington declined such a self-denying entanglement. After the Mexican War whetted America's expansionist appetite and focused attention on an isthmian canal, interest in Cuba revived. President Polk offered Spain as much as a $100 million for the island, only to get an indignant rejection. In the words of one of that government's ministers, Spain "would prefer seeing it sunk in the Ocean" rather than transfer Cuba to any other power.

A number of Cuban slave owners and businessmen preferred United States annexation to continued rule by Spain. A sizable Cuban exile group plus the sons of many Cuban Creoles, who had received their educations in the United States where they learned democratic ideals, came to favor annexation; an alarmed Spain put a stop to such dangerous educational ventures in 1849. On the other hand, other Creoles, including Narciso López, apparently preferred independence to annexation, though they hoped for aid from the United States.

Born in Venezuela and later an official in Cuba, López fled to the United States when authorities discovered his revolutionary plotting. There he recruited an assorted lot of adventurers, but federal officials halted a raid from New York in 1849. Moving his headquarters to New Orleans, López received aid and sympathy from friendly southerners and enlisted a number of Mexican War veterans in his "army." Ostensibly bound for California, his red-shirted force of around 750 men landed in Cuba in 1850. The local populace failed to rally to the side of the invaders, however, and López beat a hasty retreat back to the United States. Undaunted, he made a third and final attempt in 1851. Plans for an internal uprising to coincide with the landing of the liberators went awry when the Spanish authorities detected the plot and adopted drastic countermeasures. They quickly captured López and his men. His second-in-command, W. L. Crittenden, son of the Attorney General of the United States, and 49 other Americans were summarily executed by firing squad. A more ceremonious fate awaited López, who was slowly garroted before a large crowd in Havana. News of the executions inflamed the American South. A mob in New Orleans, a hotbed of filibustering activity, destroyed the Spanish consulate and Spanish-owned property. Subsequently, when Spain pardoned the remaining American prisoners, Congress appropriated $25,000 in compensation for the Spanish property destroyed in the riot.

Spain looked hopefully to Britain and France to help protect Cuba against the United States. Both of those powers, with extensive Caribbean possessions and interests of their own, also seriously feared American expansionism. Neither, however, cared to challenge the United States directly. Therefore, in 1852, the British and French governments once again proposed to the United States a tripartite treaty to assure continued Spanish sovereignty over Cuba. President Fillmore refused on the grounds of America's traditional policy of avoiding entangling treaties. Moreover, Cuba held too much importance to the United States for such a sweeping self-denying pledge.

Efforts to acquire Cuba continued. President Pierce proclaimed in his inaugural address in 1853 no "timid forebodings of evil from Cuba" would restrain him. He used the banker August Belmont to make another purchase offer but the attempt failed. Apparently Pierce approved the plans of John N. Quitman, a former Governor of Mississippi and an ardent expansionist, for a filibustering raid on Cuba to coincide with an expected native revolt. Timely Spanish arrests in 1855 prevented those plans from materializing. Pierce also sent a hotheaded expansionist, Pierre Soulé of Louisiana, as Minister to Spain. Soulé tried to exploit the 1854 Spanish seizure in Cuban waters of an American vessel, the *Black Warrior,* to force Spain either to sell Cuba or lose it in a war. Madrid bypassed him and arranged an amicable settlement with Washington, releasing the ship and compensating its owners for the seizure.

The Pierce administration feared that war for the expansion of slavery would split the Democratic Party, but still hoped that Cuba could be acquired. Pierce authorized Soulé to offer up to $130 million for the island. If that failed, he was instructed to examine the possibility of detaching Cuba from Spain by other means, in other words by encouraging a revolution in the island. Following instructions, Soulé in October, 1854 conferred at Ostend and Aix-la-Chapelle with the American ministers to Britain and France, James Buchanan and John Y. Mason. The three ministers recommended that their government should try to purchase Cuba and, that failing, seize the island if continued Spanish possession presented too great a danger to the United States. Their so-called Ostend Manifesto became known publicly in a garbled version and aroused sharp criticism in America and Europe as blatantly expansionist and proslavery. The administration beat a hasty retreat and ignored the advice of the three envoys. Yet James Buchanan, winner of the presidential race in 1856, continued the prosouthern policy toward the Cuban question. As late as 1860, both sections of the divided Democratic Party still advocated acquisition of Cuba.

These annexationist schemes had failed basically because of two underlying factors: the sectional controversy over the expansion of slavery, and the opposition of Great Britain and France to a change in Cuba's status. Mutual rivalries and suspicions among the three major powers helped maintain a precarious status quo in the Caribbean.

4. THE LURE OF THE PACIFIC

The lure of trade and souls in need of saving drew Americans to East Asia. The vast Pacific area, and above all the teeming populations of China and Japan, offered tempting prospects for profitable commerce and for spreading the Gospel. Although diplomacy lagged behind these interests and often vacillated in a series of fits and starts, certain basic tendencies eventually emerged in American foreign policy. Cooperation with other western powers, above all with Great Britain, was recognized as necessary to obtain treaties with Oriental states and to insure their observance. American policy also gradually reflected the open door principle—an insistence upon commercial equality for all foreigners, and a preference for the maintenance of the territorial integrity and independence of Asian states as most favorable to the interests of the United States—in relations with East Asia.

Americans entered China on the coattails of the English. Direct trade began in 1784 when the *Empress of China,* a former Revolutionary War privateer, sailed from New York to Canton bearing a cargo of raw cotton, lead, fur, and ginseng (a root alleged to restore virility that was much in demand in China), to exchange for Chinese silks, spices, and chinaware. The trade soon flourished and in 1786 the merchant Samuel Shaw became America's first consul in Canton. Canton was the only Chinese port opened to westerners. The proud Celestial Kingdom, regarding all foreigners as crude barbarians, subjected these aliens to irksome restrictions. Nevertheless trade grew brisk and profitable. Much to the disgust of the assertive English merchants, their American rivals accepted the status quo without serious protest. Finding suitable goods to exchange for Chinese wares posed the major difficulty. Ships engaged in the trade scoured the Pacific in their search, thereby explaining early contacts with California, the northwest coast of North America, Hawaii, and other places. A Boston firm, Bryan, Sturgis and Company, took furs from the Pacific coast of America to China via Hawaii, where they obtained sandalwood. Such activities eventually helped bring about the extremely significant Pacific mapping and exploring expedition of Lieutenant Charles Wilkes of the United States Navy in 1838–1841. The chief items of American exports to China consisted of furs, cotton textiles, metals, and silver, while Chinese tea, silks, dishes, and camphor comprised the bulk of the imports. Americans also became involved in the importation of opium into China, though the English controlled the bulk of that nefarious traffic. By the 1840's, American traders were Britain's chief rivals in China. The flourishing commerce entailed more than mere trade; a two-way cultural exchange was inseparable from the flow of material goods.

Evangelism accounted for the second major American interest in China. The American Board of Commissioners for Foreign Missions sent David Abeel and Elijah Bridgman as the first missionaries to Canton in 1830. Eager to convert China's hundreds of millions, missionaries learned Chinese, translated (often poorly) Christian scriptures and tracts into Chinese, and founded missions, hospitals, and schools. In contrast to American merchants, who were content with the toehold they had in China, missionaries pushed for treaties with the Manchu government to compel removal of the ban against Christianity and to open new areas to the Gospel. They frequently urged "gunboat" diplomacy against the weakening imperial regime and quickly called for their government's support whenever they encountered obstacles from local Chinese authorities. Despite their zeal, they made very little progress in converting the mass of Chinese. Christianity represented not merely an alien religion to the Chinese but a western challenge to the very fabric of Chinese society and culture. As an American diplomat perceptively observed, "For a Chinaman to accept Christianity involves so complete a surrender of all that belongs to his education, his theory of government, and society, his views of nature, his ancestral worship, his domestic relations, and his modes of life, that it is a wonder that a convert is made." One Chinese official, Prince Kung, summed up the attitude of many of his countrymen when he remarked to a westerner, "Take away your opium and your missionaries, and you will be welcome." Yet while the soul-savers failed in their primary task, both in China and in Japan, they acted as a progressive force for the modernization of the Orient, introducing western ideas and technology along with their Biblical messages. They also helped interpret East Asia to the occidental world, moulding American opinions and exercising an incalculable influence upon our foreign policy.

Unlike the American traders, the British objected to the limited contacts permitted by the Chinese government. Clashes resulted in the outbreak of the misnamed Opium War in 1839, actually fought over the much larger issue of regularizing economic and diplomatic relations with a government that viewed all westerners as inferiors and barbarians. Americans preserved neutrality, but afterwards, as occurred with subsequent Anglo-Chinese conflicts, they reaped the benefits won by English arms. The Anglo-Chinese Treaty of Nanking in 1842 opened five Chinese ports to trade. Although China extended similar privileges to American merchants, Washington decided that the time had arrived for diplomatic negotiations. President Tyler sent Caleb Cushing, backed by a squadron of naval warships, to China where he overcame Chinese reluctance by a threat of force and concluded the Treaty of Wanghia in 1844.

The Cushing Treaty obtained privileges similar to those granted the British, but it was so carefully drafted that other countries used it as a model. The treaty opened Canton, Amoy, Foochow, Ningpo, and Shanghai to American trade, permitted alien residents to bring their families and to establish schools, hospitals, and churches, and granted extraterritoriality or the right of Americans accused of crime to be tried under American law before American consular courts. It also included a most-favored-nation clause that assured Americans of any privileges they might extend to other foreigners.

In the years after Wanghia, America's China policy became indistinct and unarticulated. The distance between China and Washington prevented consistent involvement and our interests remained primarily commercial and religious rather than political. Yet gradually the American government settled on what later became known as the open door policy—that American interests would fare best if China preserved its independence and extended equal privileges to all foreigners. During the bloody Taiping Rebellion (1850–1864), with its quasi-Christian overtones, Commissioner Humphrey Marshall warned of the danger of Chinese dismemberment by Britain and Russia. The United States declined to participate in the Anglo-French wars against China in 1857–58 and 1860, although again it shared the benefits won by others at gunpoint. The Treaty of Tientsin, concluded by the United States and the other western powers in 1858 after the first Anglo-French War, opened additional ports to trade, regularized tariff duties, and provided for the establishment of direct diplomatic relations at the hitherto forbidden imperial capital at Peking. After the second round of the Anglo-French War in 1860, when the English and the French occupied Peking and burned the Emperor's summer palace, the United States again shared in concessions extorted from the helpless empire. In contrast to the European powers, however, America's "hitchhiking" imperialism rested entirely on commercial and religious motivations. Despite the plans and pleas of a handful of Americans interested in acquiring coaling stations and ports, Washington showed no interest in obtaining territory in China or elsewhere in the far Pacific.

Relations with China after the Anglo-French wars remained quiet until the 1880's. The first American Minister to reside in Peking, Anson Burlingame, arrived there in 1861. He greatly advanced the policy of cooperating with the European powers to ensure China's observance of the treaties, while opposing the Empire's dismemberment and avoiding threats of force. After his resignation, he accompanied a Chinese diplomatic mission to the West and while in Washington helped negotiate the so-called Burlingame Treaty of 1868. Among other provisions the treaty permitted entry into the United States of Chinese workers or coolies, then desired for construction of the transcontinental railroads. Within a few years the Chinese population in the United States increased substantially, numbering about 75,000 by 1880. The influx triggered a nativist reaction, particularly in California, and resulted in demands for exclusion of the Chinese, allegedly unassimilable aliens dangerous to American society and economy. Anti-Chinese agitation, riots, and even lynchings resulted in the suspension of Chinese immigration by law in 1882 and 1892, leaving a legacy of ill will and humiliation in China.

The 1840's and '50's, the high tide of Manifest Destiny, saw more Americans than before looking westward to the Pacific as the future seat of empire and trade. As mentioned earlier, the desire to exploit the fabulous markets of China underlay much of American interest in acquiring ports in California and Oregon. This also marked the era of the fast and graceful Yankee clipper ships, especially designed for Far Eastern trade. With vast clouds of canvas borne by towering masts, the clipper ship was a marvel in naval design and reduced the average time for a round trip to China from 14 months to six months. As a result, American shipping briefly captured much of the East Asian carrying trade previously dominated by the British, and pressed Britain hard in the Atlantic as well. For these reasons, Americans took greater interest in Asia at midcentury than at any other time until the closing years of the 19th century.

Hawaii also attracted Americans, first as whalers and China-traders and then as missionaries, the first arriving in 1820 to convert the native monarchs and to graft the New England Calvinist conscience and Sabbatarianism on the easygoing population. American merchants and sugar plantation owners gradually dominated the economy of Hawaii, making it an adjunct of the United States. Although the American government disavowed any desire to acquire Hawaii, it feared British and French designs on the islands. A treaty of annexation was negotiated in 1854, but President Pierce withdrew it because of British protests and a provision for immediate statehood. Hawaii nevertheless remained closely tied economically to the United States and within its political sphere.

The opening of Japan to the West was inevitable in this expansionist climate. America took the lead, moved once again by commercial and religious drives. Japan had lived in self-imposed isolation since 1638, expelling foreign traders and missionaries and permitting only Chinese and Dutch traders limited access at Nagasaki. As trade flourished with China in the 19th century, American shippers sought coaling stations in Japan and became interested in the Japanese market itself. Missionaries also grew anxious to harvest souls there, and they urged an official expedition, using force if necessary, to break open the gates of Japan. Eventually these groups persuaded Washington to act. After the failure of less imposing attempts in 1846 and 1849, Commodore Matthew Perry led a powerful naval squadron for the task. With four black steamships belching smoke and guns cleared for action, Perry's squadron entered Yedo (Tokyo) Bay on July 3, 1853. Perry admirably combined firmness with tact. He delivered a letter from the President of the United States to the Emperor of Japan and announced that he would return the following spring for a reply.

Perry's display of force aroused great debate within Japan. One group advocated resistance, while others, aware of China's fate in the Opium War, realized that they retained no option except to comply with the western demands for relations. Also at that time Japanese feudalism under the shogunate—traditional name for the hereditary military dictatorship in Japan—was beginning to break down. Perry's visit coincided with these developments and speeded them up. The Shogun finally decided to accept the inevitable, so when the Commodore returned in 1854, they negotiated and signed the Perry Treaty. Its terms provided for the return of shipwrecked sailors, permitted trade at the remote ports of

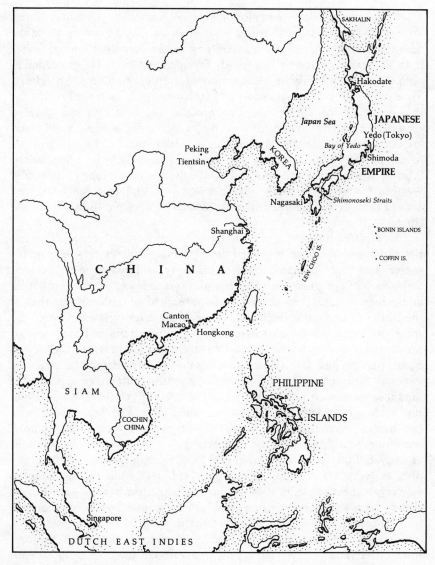

East Asia in the 1850's

Shimoda and Hakodate, and included a most-favored-nation clause. Although the Perry Treaty fell far short of American expectations, it at least cracked Japan's closed door. Other powers hastened to conclude similar agreements. Perry also had established bases at Okinawa and in the Bonin Islands, but Washington declined to annex them. The United States sought an empire of trade, not colonies, in the far Pacific.

The first American consul in Japan, Townshend Harris, arrived in

1856. Persevering despite personal isolation and native hostility, Harris argued to Japanese authorities that they would be wiser to make additional concessions to a friendly and nonimperialistic United States than to await coercion by the greedy European powers. He succeeded in obtaining a new treaty in 1858, a model for others to follow. The Harris Treaty opened other Japanese ports to foreign commerce, provided for the residence of aliens and the practice of their religion, granted American citizens extraterritorial rights, adopted a fixed tariff, and included a most favored nation clause. Other powers followed in his footsteps. The United States had assumed leadership in a benevolent type of western imperialism and established itself as Japan's foremost western friend. As a result, the first Japanese diplomatic mission sent abroad came to the United States in 1860 to exchange ratifications of the treaty.

The western impact disrupted Japanese mores, values, and institutions. Many Japanese regarded foreigners as desecrators of Japan's sacred soil and attributed natural disasters and, with better reason, diseases to their presence. The economy underwent a severe inflation and a loss of gold. Antiforeign elements rallied to the Emperor against the Shogun, and antiforeign riots and civil disorders ensued. One of the rebellious nobles fired on foreign ships in the Straits of Shimonoseki, provoking a joint western armed retaliation in 1864 in which the United States participated. In 1866, the western powers forced upon Japan a very unequal tariff treaty, which along with extraterritoriality remained a Japanese grievance until removed in the late 19th century. Meanwhile, the Meiji Restoration overthrew the shogunate and Japan adopted a constitution that nominally made the Emperor supreme. Restrictions were removed against missionary activity in 1873. American missionaries predominated in the evangelical field, though here as in China they only converted a fraction of the populace. As Japan rapidly adopted western technology and at least outwardly modernized its government and society, the American image of Japan changed from condescension to admiration. Americans proudly regarded Japan as their protégé, a nation they sponsored and introduced to modern civilization. Therefore, the United States was first to express readiness to abandon extraterritoriality and the fixed tariff treaty. America influenced Japan greatly, especially in the fields of business, agriculture, and education. But time revealed that Japan retained strong feudal elements and was even more influenced by the example of European imperialism than by the more peaceful example of the United States.

Additional Reading

American reactions to the liberal revolutions in Europe are examined by Merle Curti, "Young America," *American Historical Review,* XXXII

(1926), 34–55 and "Austria and the United States, 1848–1852," *Smith College Studies In History*, XI (1926), No. 3; A. J. May, *Contemporary American Opinion of the Mid-Century Revolutions in Central Europe* (1927); and in two previously cited works, Frederick Merk, *Manifest Destiny and Mission in American History* (1963), and Henry Blumenthal, *A Reappraisal of Franco-American Relations, 1830–1871* (1959). The older standard study of Anglo-American rivalry in Central America is by Mary Wilhelmine Williams, *Anglo-American Isthmian Diplomacy, 1815–1915* (1916). Richard W. Van Alstyne, in "The Central American Policy of Lord Palmerston, 1846–1848," *Hispanic American Historical Review*, XVI (1936), 339–359, "British Diplomacy and the Clayton-Bulwer Treaty, 1850–1860," *Journal of Modern History*, XI (1939), 149–183, and *The Rising American Empire* (1960), views the Clayton-Bulwer Treaty as a defeat for the Monroe Doctrine. Dexter Perkins, in *The Monroe Doctrine, 1826–1867* (1933), sees it as a victory for Monroeism. Also see Frederick Merk, *The Monroe Doctrine and American Expansionism* (1966). Other studies of British diplomacy in Central America are by Kenneth Bourne, "The Clayton-Bulwer Treaty and the Decline of British Opposition to the Territorial Expansion of the United States, 1857–1860," *Journal of Modern History*, XXXIII (1961), 287–291; Thomas L. Karnes, *The Failure of Union: Central America, 1824–1960* (1961); and Mario Rodríguez, *A Palmerstonian Diplomat in Central America: Frederick Chatfield, Esq.* (1964). The best account of William Walker's career is in *Filibusters and Financiers* (1916) by W. O. Scroggs, but the popularized version by A. H. Carr, *The World and William Walker* (1963) is also interesting. R. A. Courtemanche has written an interesting account of Britain's reaction to the filibusters—"The Royal Navy and the End of Walker," *The Historian*, XXX (1968), 350–365. The standard accounts of American policy in Cuba are by Basil Rauch, *American Interests in Cuba, 1848–1855* (1948) and A. A. Ettinger, *The Mission to Spain of Pierre Soulé, 1853–1855* (1932). On the filibusters, see R. G. Caldwell, *The López Expeditions to Cuba, 1848–1851* (1915). Biographies that bear in part on American policy toward Cuba are by T. D. Spencer, *The Victor and the Spoils: A Life of William L. Marcy* (1959) and P. S. Klein, *President James Buchanan* (1962). See too J. A. Logan, *No Transfer* (1961). P. S. Foner, *A History of Cuba and Its Relations with the United States* (1962), Vol. I, and the shorter but highly interpretive account by Lester D. Langley, *The Cuban Policy of the United States* (1968) are useful general surveys of American interests in Cuba. General surveys of American policy in the Pacific and East Asia are by Tyler Dennett, *Americans in Eastern Asia* (1922); Foster Rhea Dulles, *America in the Pacific* (1932), and *China and America* (1946); and John K. Fairbank, *Trade and Diplomacy on the China Coast* (1953, 1964), and *The United States and China* (1948). Earl Swisher, *China's Management of the American Barbarians* (1953) is a classic account on that subject. The origins of the American China myth are analyzed by William L. Neumann, "Determinism, Destiny, and Myth in the American Image of China," in G. L. Anderson, ed., *Issues and Conflict* (1959) and Paul A. Varg, *Missionaries, Chinese, and Diplomats* (1958). Te-kong Tong's *United States Diplomacy in China, 1844–1860* (1964) is a well-researched recent study. On the opening of Japan, see Arthur Walworth, *Black Ships off Japan: the Story of Commodore Perry's Expedition* (1946) and S. E. Morison, *"Old Bruin": Commodore Matthew C. Perry, 1794–1858* (1967). Payson J. Treat, *Diplomatic Relations between the United States and Japan, 1853–1895* (2 vols., 1932) is the standard account. Broad interpretive surveys are by E. O. Reischauer, *The United States and Japan* (rev. ed., 1957); William L. Neumann, *America Encounters Japan: From Perry to MacArthur* (1963); and F. R. Dulles, *Yankees and Samurai: America's Role in the Emergence of Modern Japan, 1791–1900* (1965).

The Merrimack *(left) versus the* Monitor *(right)*

10

THE DIPLOMACY
OF THE CIVIL WAR

1. CONFEDERATE HOPES AND ILLUSIONS

The long-predicted dissolution of the Federal Union came in the aftermath of Abraham Lincoln's victory in the presidential election of 1860. Accumulated grievances and fears convinced southern whites that their section could no longer remain secure within the old union. Ultimately eleven southern states adopted ordinances of secession and joined in a new compact, the Confederate States of America. Jefferson Davis of Mississippi, an able and distinguished political leader, was chosen as President of the Confederacy.

Davis had serious weaknesses as chief executive of a new and revolutionary state: he was outwardly reserved and even cold in manner; approached his duties too leisurely; often bogged down in petty details; and failed to appreciate early enough the crucial importance of foreign policy. But he favorably impressed European observers accustomed to cruder American politicians. One English visitor, W. H. Russell of the *Times* (London), wrote of Davis after an interview, "Wonder to relate, he does not chew [tobacco], and is neat and clean-looking, with hair trimmed, and boots brushed." He eventually obtained a very able Secretary of State, Judah P. Benjamin, an English-Jewish immigrant from the West Indies who had come to the South prior to secession. He and Davis became close friends and the President loyally defended him against his numerous critics. Benjamin reacted as many of those southerners who could not adjust to defeat, and after the collapse of the Confederacy he journeyed to England where he established a successful legal career as a Queen's Counsel.

The capital of the new republic, after a brief period in Montgomery, Alabama, was moved to Richmond, Virginia, in order to be near the center of the war in the East. Secessionists believed they were following the example of those patriots who in 1776 had broken the shackles of George III's tyrannical rule. Unfortunately for the South, optimism and self-righteousness too frequently substituted for the more sober thought and realistic planning that the situation required. Contemptuous of the supposed crass commercialism and racial hodgepodge of the northern states, many southerners confidently expected the North to accept secession or at the most to put up only a token effort to preserve the old union. They thought a few victories by southern arms surely would sober the North and would demonstrate the South's unconquerable resolve for independence. They confidently expected Europe to recognize promptly the new republic. The European upper classes' preference for the southern gentility as opposed to the more plebian society and manners of the North, the trading attractions of the low tariff South, and above all the power of King Cotton, they assumed, would leave the European powers no other choice. As one confident southern politician wrote early in 1861, "Great Britain, France, and Russia will acknowledge us at once in the family of nations." Southern leaders thought of recognition as right and inevitable, instead of viewing it as a goal requiring careful analysis and planning to obtain. Southerners at all levels of authority and responsibility failed to foresee the desperate struggle before them and to appreciate the fact that, as in 1776–1778, foreign aid would be vital. Consequently the Confederacy neglected at the outset to define clear and realistic goals and to adopt the most effective means of achieving them.

The South placed most of its hopes on the power of King Cotton. Daniel Christy of Ohio had published a book in 1855, *Cotton is King,* which touched off much discussion in the United States and in Europe about the industrialized world's dependence upon the raw cotton of the South. The cotton textile industry was regarded as the veritable lynchpin of modern industry. Great Britain, the world's leading industrial and commercial nation, had a vast cotton textile industry that annually consumed nearly three million bales of cotton; France had a smaller industry that involved nearly a million people; and of course the northern states of the United States also had an extensive cotton textile industry. British efforts to develop alternative sources of cotton in Egypt and India had collapsed, so the industrial world in 1860 still overwhelmingly depended upon the southern supply.

Southerners understandably concluded that the modern world could not long endure without their cotton. All the South needed to do, many presumed, was to proclaim its independence and to await diplomatic recognition by the major European states. If the North tried to interfere with the export of cotton to Europe, sheer economic necessity would compel Great Britain and France to intervene to reopen the source of supply and to end a war disrupting their prosperity. To quicken intervention, the Confederacy quietly embargoed cotton exports in 1861, curtailed cotton planting, and burned some cotton to increase the scarcity. Very little cotton moved to Europe from southern ports in 1861–1862, although the Union blockade had not yet actually taken effect.

Yet King Cotton diplomacy failed. Unfortunately for the South, the years 1858 and 1859 had yielded bumper crops of cotton, much of it stored in European warehouses. Moreover, since the market for cotton goods had recently declined, textile manufacturers, merchants, and speculators welcomed an apparent cotton famine in order to drive up their prices. Consequently Europe did not feel the full effects of the southern embargo until late 1862 and 1863, too late for it to achieve the hoped-for results. By then, the North had demonstrated its determination to prevent secession, and initial southern military victories gave way to a far less clear situation on the battlefields. The principal European powers prudently decided to await further developments in the war before recognizing the South or challenging the blockade. Large numbers of English factory workers had in fact been laid off as the cotton shortage worsened, but most of them were voteless and in any case relief measures were adopted for them. Also by 1863 the supply of cotton from other sources had begun to increase. In addition, much southern cotton again began to flow to Europe, either licensed by the Union government for export from occupied southern areas or illegally exported by collusive southern and northern profiteers. Desperately in need of funds from Europe to finance war purchases, Confederate authorities themselves shipped some cotton abroad. Yet even if King Cotton had reaped the full economic effects hoped for by the South, it probably still would not have won European recognition and intervention. The major European powers had national interests of their own to weigh carefully and these probably would have precluded entanglement in the American Civil War. It was romantic and naive for southerners to expect the great powers of Europe to rush to their rescue, even if they were economically pinched or emotionally sympathetic.

2. UNION AND CONFEDERATE DIPLOMACY

Union diplomacy tried to deny the South all external aid and comfort while Union armies suppressed secession on the battlefields. President Lincoln selected an able politician, William H. Seward of New York, to direct the State Department. At first, Seward seemed too brash and rash for his responsibilities. He apparently assumed, as did many others in America and abroad, that the roughhewn Lincoln was unfit for his duties and would gratefully leave the actual governing to Seward. In one of his first acts, Seward proposed a vigorous foreign policy to end European meddling in the Western Hemisphere, and advocated war with Spain and France if those two states continued their machinations in the Caribbean (Spain was in the process of reannexing Santo Domingo). Apparently he underestimated the seriousness of the rebellion and hoped to discourage Europe from any interference in the American Civil War. Lincoln ignored his proposal and soon made it clear to the Secretary of State that he intended to assume his full responsibilities as chief executive. Thereafter the two men worked smoothly and effectively as a team. Lincoln chose Charles Francis Adams, son of John Quincy Adams and a very able lawyer and diplomat, for the crucial London post. Although never sure in the early years that he might not have to pack his bags and hastily leave England, as war threatened between the two countries, Adams's tireless diplomacy contributed immensely to keeping Britain neutral.

To discourage foreign intermeddling and to pursue Lincoln's theory of the indissolubility of the Union, the State Department denied the existence of a civil war within the United States. Seward explained it as merely a local armed rebellion or sedition that federal authorities were engaged in suppressing, of no real interest to foreign nations. Unfortunately, the Union government sought to cut off the South from access to the European markets it sorely needed for the goods and arms that its own economy could not produce in sufficient quantity. Lincoln, in April, 1861, proclaimed a blockade of southern ports and coasts, warning neutral vessels not to try to enter the blockade zone under pain of capture and confiscation. A blockade was clearly recognized as a means of waging international war and could hardly be explained as a device to suppress a local rebellion or conspiracy. Probably Lincoln would have better accomplished the same end by merely closing the customs houses in southern ports and hence the ports themselves. In any case, other evidence clearly indicated, euphemisms aside, that North America faced a large-scale war. Therefore, the British government in May, 1861 issued a declaration of neutrality, followed by France and other states.

The British declaration of neutrality in effect recognized the belligerent rights of the Confederacy and extended to its warships and men the same privileges in British ports as accorded to the established Union government. Naturally this news greatly cheered the South, which expected full diplomatic recognition to follow. For the same reasons, it outraged the North. The recognition of belligerency seemed a most unfriendly act, particularly since London had acted just as Charles Francis Adams arrived in England. Seward angrily warned Britain and the continent: "Foreign intervention would oblige us to treat those who should yield it as allies of the insurrectionary party and to carry on the war against them as enemies. . . ." The British Foreign Secretary, Lord John Russell, offered the explanation that Great Britain had merely recognized a factual situation, but this did not satisfy the Secretary of State. General sentiment now recognizes that Britain sooner or later would have been compelled to issue such a proclamation, in order to warn its citizens of the dangers of trading with or visiting North America and in order to activate its neutrality statutes. At least she acted early in the war before initial southern military victories plunged the North into an even more sullen and angry mood.

The *Trent* affair revealed the potential explosiveness of Anglo-American relations. It also demonstrated Seward's skill in handling both foreign crises and American public opinion. The Confederate government had decided to send regular would-be ministers to England and France, and appointed two distinguished southerners, James M. Mason and John Slidell, respectively, to London and Paris. The two envoys made their way through the still porous blockade to Havana where they took passage on the British mail steamer *Trent* sailing for England in November, 1861. Captain Charles Wilkes of the U.S.S. *San Jacinto,* acting on his own authority, halted the *Trent* on the high seas, boarded the vessel, and forcibly removed the two envoys and their secretaries. The *San Jacinto* then triumphantly bore the political captives to the United States. Wilkes' feat elated the northerners, depressed by recent news from the battlefields, who hailed it as a signal victory over both the South and "perfidious" Britain. The dashing Wilkes became a popular hero; even members of Lincoln's cabinet, including the secretary of the navy, acclaimed the seizure. Seward and the President, however, soon realized that Wilkes' action did not differ greatly from the detested old British practice of impressment. Henry Adams, son of the American minister in Great Britain, could hardly believe the news of the seizure; "Good God," he wrote his brother in America, "what's got into you all? What do you mean by deserting now the great principles of our fathers, by returning to the vomit of that dog Great Britain?"

News of the seizure caused a wave of anger to sweep over England. It represented a challenge to British rights and British honor. *Punch* expressed the national mood in a cartoon depicting a fatherly John Bull rebuking a smaller but brash Yankee, "You do what's right, my son, or I'll blow you out of the water." Prime Minister Palmerston remarked angrily to a meeting of the cabinet, "You may stand for this but damned if I will!" War preparations began as the ministry decided to present an ultimatum to the American government. Fortunately the dying Prince Consort, Albert, managed to blunt the tone of the note before it was presented, and the sudden breakdown of the newly laid Atlantic Cable permitted enough time between exchanges for soberer counsels to make themselves heard on both sides of the ocean. Even so, the British minister had instructions to request his passports if within seven days the Union government did not comply with the demand for release of Mason and Slidell. Lincoln and Seward found themselves caught between British demands and the predictable anger of the northern public if they released the southerners. After lengthy cabinet discussions, they decided to release the two envoys. Seward managed to gloss the bitter pill by expressing satisfaction that Great Britain at last had acknowledged American principles against impressment. Public tempers swiftly cooled in both countries as one of the most acute foreign crises of the war subsided.

3. EUROPEAN OPINION AND THE CIVIL WAR

Southerners had confidently assumed in 1861 that Great Britain would favor their cause. In fact much prosouthern sympathy, although often exaggerated, and even more anti-Yankee sentiment abounded in Britain. The Russian ambassador in London perceptively analyzed those sentiments in 1861:

The English Government, at the bottom of its heart, desires the separation of North America into two republics, which will watch each other jealously and counterbalance one the other. Then England . . . would have nothing to fear from either; for she would dominate them, restraining them by their rival ambitions.

Many conservatively inclined Englishmen rejoiced when the violent breakup of the American Union demonstrated the fatal flaws of popular democracy. *Blackwood's Magazine* clearly expressed that upper class point of view: "It is precisely because we do *not* share the admiration of America for her own institutions and political tendencies that we do not see in the impending change [secession] an event altogether to be deplored." Some members of the English gentry probably also felt an affinity with their southern counterparts. Many observers sensed that the North was not fighting in behalf of human freedom, but only to force a reluctant South to return to a union that it detested. Not surprisingly, therefore, most major British newspapers in 1861, and throughout the war, took prosouthern or strictly neutral stances.

Confederate propagandists eagerly seized upon these sentiments and attitudes. Henry Hotze, a young southern journalist of Swiss origins, had charge of southern propaganda in Great Britain. An able journalist, he decided that Union publicists in England had erred on the side of brashness. He adopted instead a more cautious and quieter campaign aimed at influencing the British upper classes. He purchased a journal, *The Index,* and through its columns and the friendly British press Hotze fed a stream of carefully prepared articles and news releases. These emphasized the themes of the South's resolute determination for independence and its military strength, while portraying the North as guilty of military brutalities and atrocities on southern soil. They also emphasized the common economic interests between the South and Great Britain. A number of prominent Britishers, including merchants, manufacturers, and shipbuilders, endorsed the Confederate cause and urged British recognition of the South.

Confederate propaganda, however, faced an almost insurmountable problem—the existence of slavery in the South. Even ardent prosouthern sympathizers could only deplore that system. Yet initially slavery did not become an overriding issue in the war. The Lincoln administration repeatedly emphasized that its primary purpose simply lay in preservation of the union. Many English liberals found that attitude difficult to understand and inclined toward criticism of the North's efforts to keep the South in the Union by the bayonet. Yet liberals and radical reformers such as John Bright and Richard Cobden early concluded that the underlying issue in the Civil War, of crucial importance to Britons as well as Americans, involved the future of democracy and human freedom. Lincoln finally strengthened that group's convictions when on January 1, 1863 he issued the Emancipation Proclamation freeing slaves in the rebellious states. The proclamation probably immediately affected only those liberals in Britain and on the continent who already sympathized with the North, but the long-term results proved much larger. A desperate South finally acknowledged the proclamation's importance when, late in the war, it offered to abolish slavery in exchange for diplomatic recognition of the Confederacy. It should be kept in mind, however, that neither sentiment nor morality but rational calculations of their own national interests shaped the policies of the major European powers toward the war.

The British ministry clearly held prosouthern feelings to a degree, but that fact has often been exaggerated. Lord Palmerston, the Prime Minister, felt mildly inclined toward the South, and Chancellor of the Exchequer William E. Gladstone publicly praised the southern leaders and urged recognition of the Confederacy. Lord Russell, the foreign secretary, remained much more neutral. His caution helped to offset Palmerston's hostility toward the North and to keep the British government from hasty or unwise actions. The ministry did debate seriously in 1862 whether or not the time had come to recognize southern independence. The Confederacy showed impressive organization, and its armies in the east had inflicted notable defeats upon Union forces. As Palmerston wrote Russell after Second Bull Run, "The Federals . . . got a very complete smashing . . . even Washington or Baltimore may fall into the hands of the Confederates." Russell agreed that the time had come for possible recognition of the South. The editor of the *Times* of London expressed the general view: "The time is approaching when Europe will have to think seriously of its relations to the two belligerents. . . . That North and South must now choose between separation and ruin, material and political, is the opinion of nearly everyone who, looking impartially and from a distance on the conflict, sees what is hidden from the frenzied eyes of the Northern politicians." But before they could act, news arrived that northern armies had checked General Robert E. Lee's forces at Antietam on September 17. The British government prudently decided to await further developments on the

American battlefields. As Russell subsequently told Parliament, recent events indicated the possibility of a complete northern victory, and the North could justly regard Britain's recognition of the South as an "unfriendly act." Union triumphs at Gettysburg and Vicksburg in mid-1863 precluded all possibility of British intervention.

Palmerston and Russell based their decision to avoid premature recognition of the Confederacy or attempted mediation on hardheaded calculations of British interests rather than on sentiment. Sober reflection revealed that Britain's economic relations with the industrialized North far outweighed those with the rural South, cotton notwithstanding. The Union was England's best customer, providing a large market for British goods and attracting large amounts of British capital as investments in railroads, land, and securities. It also exported large quantities of foodstuffs and raw materials to the British Isles. The war had greatly stimulated trade between the two countries. While the Confederacy purchased war supplies in Great Britain, the Union bought even larger quantities of arms and war materials in England and on the continent. British officials also recognized that the Yankees held a hostage in Canada. The British Minister at Washington, Lord Lyons, and anxious officials in Canada repeatedly warned London that Canada would be highly vulnerable to northern attack in case of an Anglo-American war. Seward had given ample indications on that score. He also cautioned the British that the United States would repay in kind any unneutral act in some future war involving Great Britain and not America. Finally, British leaders understood a harsh fact that most southerners ignored—recognition would antagonize the North but in itself would not break northern determination to force the South back into the Union. Only actual armed intervention by Britain and other interested European states would help the South to make good its bid for independence—too high a price for trying to hasten the end of the conflict.

Britain's failure to recognize the independence of the Confederacy or to challenge the Union blockade bitterly disappointed the southerners. The recognition of belligerency in 1861 and the ability of Confederate agents to exploit loopholes in British law to build commerce raiders in British shipyards had cheered them. Such English-built cruisers as the *Florida* and the *Alabama* inflicted great damage upon Union commerce and created panic in northern shipping circles (see Chapter 11). The South also expected to build first-class ironclads in Britain, capable of directly challenging Union blockade squadrons, until Adams's protests caused the British ministry to seize those craft. These few marks of British benevolence fell far short of southern expectations. As the war dragged on and decisive aid was not forthcoming, hope turned to rancor in the South. The disappointed Slidell described Britain's attitude toward the South as "a tortuous, selfish, and time-serving policy." President Davis complained bitterly to the Confederate Congress about the failure of Europe to challenge the blockade, and both he and Secretary Benjamin privately accused Great Britain and France of duplicity toward the South. British consulates in the South under the control of the British Legation in Washington also wounded southern pride. Moreover British consuls often clashed with Confederate authorities over the conscription of British residents in the South. The consul at Richmond was expelled for particularly officious meddling. Finally, southern anger and disappointment exploded in a "diplomatic break" with Great Britain. In October, 1863, the South ousted all British consular officials on the grounds of intolerable "encroachment on the sovereignty of the Confederate States." The break perhaps gave the best indication of the essentially evenhanded nature of British neutrality by late 1863. Ironically, the Civil War ended with both sections of the United States embittered at Great Britain, the North because of British aid to the South, and the South because it had not received enough British aid.

The French on the other hand merely wanted to see the American Civil War ended as soon as possible, mainly because of the economic distress to the cotton textile industry brought about by the war. Many Frenchmen, however, recalled the old traditional friendship with the United States and opposed any unfriendly moves by their government. In addition, liberals and workers also disliked slavery and tended to identify their efforts for greater freedom and a return to republicanism in France with the cause of the Union. On the other hand, Emperor Napoleon III and his court obviously sympathized with the South and repeatedly toyed with the idea of recognizing the South and mediating the war. As a low tariff area and a cotton producer, an independent South could offer many advantages to France. Above all, Napoleon's schemes in Mexico, where he sought to place Maximilian on a puppet throne, depended to a large degree upon a divided United States unable to enforce the Monroe Doctrine (see Chapter 11). Confederate propaganda under Henry Hotze was also active in France and helped to give the French press a prosouthern tone.

Napoleon received the Confederate envoy Slidell warmly if unofficially in 1862. He and members of his government openly displayed prosouthern attitudes and led Slidell to expect French diplomatic recognition and intervention in the war. But Napoleon dared not act without British cooperation, which was not forthcoming. In November, 1862, after the Confederate victory in the bloody battle at Fredericksburg, Napoleon's government proposed that Great Britain and Russia join France in urging a six months' truce in the war and lifting of the blockade. The South would have welcomed such a move, as the British knew, but the North would have spurned it bitterly. Consequently both Britain and Russia declined to act. Then in the spring of 1863, Napoleon on his own proposed to Washington that representatives of North and South meet on neutral ground to discuss a settlement. Seward courteously but firmly rejected the suggestions, and Congress adopted a resolution denouncing mediation as an unwarranted foreign interference. Napoleon also had wanted to challenge the blockade but without British cooperation he dared not do more than lodge protests at Union violations of neutral rights. For a time, Napoleon also permitted Confederate agents to purchase and build warships in France. Southern military reverses in the second half of 1863 and in 1864, however, caused him to stop delivery of the vessels. Not even southern promises of cotton and a free hand in Mexico could move that suddenly cautious ruler. As the war ended, southern disappointment and anger focused against France almost as much as against England.

Although poles apart ideologically from the great North American republic, Czarist Russia gained the reputation during the Civil War as the Union's best friend. The Russian government firmly rejected all proposals for European mediation or intervention in the war and did not harbor southern agents or activities on her soil. When two Russian fleets visited San Francisco and New York City in 1863, officers and crews received a warm welcome with lavish displays of American gratitude and friendship. The visit of the fleets was widely interpreted as a sign of Russia's friendship for America and a stern warning to Great Britain and France not to intervene on the side of the South. Subsequently scholars learned that in fact Russia had feared war with the Anglo-French bloc over the Polish question and merely wanted to get the fleets to sea before they could be bottled up in the Baltic and Black Seas. Russia's official policy, however, unquestionably favored the Union, reflecting not sentiment but Russia's interests in a strong United States able to offset British power.

Spain, after some ambivalence, also pursued a course of careful neutrality in the war. A divided United States might enhance both Cuba's safety and Spain's efforts to reannex Santo Domingo, the Spanish reasoned, but they had no assurances that an independent South, no longer restrained by the North, might not be highly aggressive and expansionist. Seward cleverly played upon that danger, and Madrid decided to spurn southern overtures for recognition in exchange for a guarantee on Cuba. The other governments of Europe, whatever the sympathies of their ruling classes, also practiced a careful neutrality. The Union cause was particularly popular among the middle classes of the German states, because of the immigration of many Germans to America in the past, and the tendency of German liberals to identify their own hopes for German unification and democracy with the struggle of the North.

4. THE BLOCKADE

By 1861 the United States had established itself as the foremost defender of neutral rights. It had gone to war in 1812 in defense of those rights against British transgressions. After 1815, in an era of general peace and free trade, even Great Britain mellowed in its assertion of belligerent rights. In 1856, therefore, Britain joined the other maritime powers in signing the Declaration of Paris, which asserted that free ships made free goods, narrowly defined contraband goods subject to seizure, and interpreted a legal blockade as an effective one. But the United States declined to sign the Declaration because it prohibited privateering, which America still regarded as one of its principle defensive weapons in case of war against a strong naval power. When the Confederacy threatened to flood the seas with privateers preying upon northern commerce, however, the Union government belatedly tried to adhere to the Declaration. Seward obviously hoped thereby to bar southern privateering. Britain objected to such opportunism, and the effort to outlaw southern privateers failed. Since most foreign ports were closed to their prizes, however, only a few privateers actually put to sea. The South instead relied upon regular warships as commerce raiders.

It came as a surprise, therefore, when the Union government in effect abandoned liberal neutral rights during the Civil War. In the unaccustomed role of a great sea power, the United States used its navy to the utmost to cut off the South from the markets and war resources of Europe. Yet to enforce the blockade that Lincoln proclaimed in April, 1861, the Union Navy had only forty steam and fifty sail vessels, some of which were not immediately available. A crash program of naval construction increased the fleet to 79 steam and 81 sail warships by the end of the year; ultimately, by the end of the war, the fleet had grown to nearly 700 vessels. Not all of these were efficient or formidable war craft, but they sufficed against a foe who had far less. Obviously the Union blockade in 1861 was only a "paper blockade"; the same type which the United States had condemned vigorously when Great Britain and France used it during the Napoleonic wars. Even if in 1861 the navy had stationed all the warships off the southern coasts, some 3,500 miles long, with numerous ports, bays, and inlets, it would have amounted to a ratio of only one ship for each 66 miles of coast line. The ratio gradually improved in succeeding years, until by 1865 theoretically one ship could patrol each six miles of blockaded coast. A large number of vessels continued to enter or leave southern ports until almost the end of the war; 56 clearing Charleston, South Carolina, in the first half of 1863 despite the blockade. The Confederacy argued that the blockade never really succeeded, and some scholars have agreed. The evidence indicates, however, that most of these vessels entering or leaving the South were small, fast blockade-runners which carried very little cargo and had to await favorable weather or other conditions to slip into or out of ports. Certainly by 1863 the blockade proved reasonably effective and became progressively more so in succeeding years. The shrillness of southern complaints about Europe's acceptance of the blockade amply attested to its eventual effectiveness.

The Union Navy relied primarily upon so-called flying squadrons roaming the principal sea routes to cut off the South. Blockade-runners were small, fast, and difficult to intercept immediately off the southern coasts. They usually slipped out of the South, picked up a cargo in a neutral port in the British Bermudas or in the Caribbean, and then awaited a favorable opportunity to reenter the South. Union warships found it easier and more effective to seize those neutral vessels carrying war supplies from Europe to a neutral port in the Caribbean, for subsequent reshipment through the blockade into the South. Unfortunately, the Union could only justify such seizures under the old British concept of continuous voyage or ultimate destination, against which America had often protested in the past. In addition to such long-range enforcement of the blockade, with seizures taking place hundreds or even thousands of miles away from the blockaded coasts of the South, Union warships frequently hovered off neutral ports in the Caribbean or lay in wait barely outside the three-mile limit for ships suspected of trading with the Confederacy. Union commanders sometimes entered within the three-mile limit or even within neutral harbors to make their captures. They even in effect blockaded Matamoros, Mexico in order to intercept goods intended for overland transportation into the South. Ultimately the Supreme Court upheld most of these seizures on the grounds that the ships and goods were in fact involved in one continuous journey with the ultimate destination being the blockaded South.

These Union naval practices naturally aroused intense anger in Great Britain, especially among commercial and shipping interests involved in trade with the South. Rear Admiral Wilkes's squadron seemed particularly obnoxious in British eyes. On one occasion, 40 Liverpool shipowners complained to the ministry that Wilkes had virtually blockaded the port of Nassau in the British Bahamas. Union warships often entered and left neutral harbors without requesting the customary permission, and they sometimes fired upon or chased suspected blockade-runners or neutral supply vessels within neutral waters. One of Wilkes's more zealous commanders pursued a suspected British vessel, the *Blanche,* into Havana harbor and, ignoring the Spanish flag that local officials had raised over the *Blanche* to protect it, proceeded to board and fire the ship. Although Wilkes disavowed the deed, it seemed to foreign observers only too typical of arrogant Yankee behavior.

The reversal of America's historic role during the Civil War reveals a basic fact of international life: national survival necessarily outweighs mere considerations of ideals and principle. The action of overzealous and inexperienced naval officers, most of whom had only recently volunteered for the service, explains part of the difficulty in 1861–1865. Even so, officially sanctioned departures from America's past practices indicated only too clearly the expediential nature of so-called international law and morality.

Although the British government did protest specific abuses by American naval officers, it accepted various northern extensions of past British practices, such as the application of the doctrine of continuous voyage. Above all, Great Britain did not challenge the legality of the Union blockade, even when it was most porous. Apart from the desire to avoid a costly war with the Union, the British ministry was well aware that the United States was setting a number of precedents that might be of great advantage to England in case of a future war where America remained neutral. Palmerston reminded Parliament that no nation took more interest than Great Britain in preserving belligerent rights at sea to the utmost degree possible. And the *Times* pointed out to its readers, "a blockade is by far the most formidable weapon of offence we possess. Surely we ought not to be overready to blunt its edge. . . ?" British forbearance paid handsome dividends in World War I when a neutral United States found its protests against the British blockade weakened by the precedents set by the Union Navy in the Civil War.

5. COLLAPSE OF THE CONFEDERACY

After four years of heroism and almost unbelievable sacrifice, a still defiant South succumbed to the hammer blows of an equally determined North. Superior manpower, industry, and finance at last drove the South to its knees in April, 1865. Conceived in illusions and self-deceptions, the Confederacy expired in an atmosphere of despair intermingled with wild hopes and rumors of a last-minute rescue by Great Britain or France. Almost to the very end, reports circulated in the South that England and the North had gone to war or that Napoleon was landing troops to save the South and smash the blockade. Union diplomacy, buttressed by essential military victories and naval power, had succeeded in preventing the South from obtaining any substantial foreign support and encouragement. But essentially Europe's hardheaded awareness of where its own true interests lay, rather than skillful diplomacy, should receive credit for this accomplishment.

Additional Reading

The best general study of Confederate diplomacy is still F. L. Owsley's *King Cotton Diplomacy,* first published in 1931 and revised in 1967.

Charles C. Cullop, *Confederate Propaganda in Europe, 1861–1865* (1969) praises the work of Henry Hotze. An excellent article by Henry Blumenthal, "Confederate Diplomacy: Popular Notions and International Realities," *Journal of Southern History,* XXXII (1966), 151–171, examines the reasons for the disappointment of southern hopes for foreign recognition and intervention. For Union diplomacy, see G. G. Van Deusen, *William Henry Seward* (1967), which depicts Seward as an able and far-visioned statesman of American expansion; James G. Randall, *Lincoln the President* (4 vols., 1945–55); and Richard N. Current, *Mr. Lincoln* (1957). A popularized study is by Jay Monaghan, *Diplomat in Carpet Slippers* (1945). Also valuable is M. B. Duberman's study, *Charles Francis Adams* (1961). A perceptive account by Norman Graebner, "Northern Diplomacy and European Neutrality," in David Donald, ed., *Why the North Won the Civil War* (1960), 55–78, stresses the role of realism in shaping British and French policy. F. L. Owsley, "America and the Freedom of the Seas, 1861–1865," in Avery Craven, ed., *Essays in Honor of William E. Dodd* (1935), 194–256, examines the fate of liberal neutral rights during the war, as does James P. Baxter in two articles, "The British Government and Neutral Rights, 1861–1865," *American Historical Review,* XXXIV (1928), 9–29, and "Some British Opinions as to Neutral Rights, 1861–1865," *American Journal of International Law,* XXIII (1929), 517–537. Ludwell H. Johnson, "Commerce Between Northeastern Ports and the Confederacy, 1861–1865," *Journal of American History,* LIV (1967), 30–42, reveals how that old American habit, trading with the enemy, continued during the Civil War. The role of Europe in the Civil War is covered in two older studies, E. D. Adams, *Great Britain and the American Civil War* (2 vols., 1925) and D. Jordan and E. J. Pratt, *Europe and the American Civil War* (1931). For France, these should be supplemented with a recent study by Lynn M. Case and W. F. Spencer, *The United States and France: Civil War Diplomacy* (1970) and Henry Blumenthal's stimulating interpretive study, *A Reappraisal of Franco-American Relations, 1830–1871* (1959). An article by Wilbur D. Jones, "The British Conservatives and the American Civil War," *American Historical Review,* LVIII (1953), 527–543, reveals that the pronorthern, wing of that party was predominant throughout the war. Joseph M. Hernon, Jr., "British Sympathies in the American Civil War: A Reconsideration," *Journal of Southern History,* XXXIII (1967), 356–367, finds much anti-U.S. sentiment among the English working classes. Also see W. D. Jones, *The Confederate Rams at Birkenhead* (1961). On the role of Canada, the best works are by R. W. Winks, *Canada and the United States: The Civil War Years* (1960) and Kenneth Bourne, *Britain and the Balance of Power in North America, 1815–1908* (1967). Philip Van Doren Stern, *When the Guns Roared: World Aspects of the American Civil War* (1965) is a popular account of the impact of the Civil War abroad.

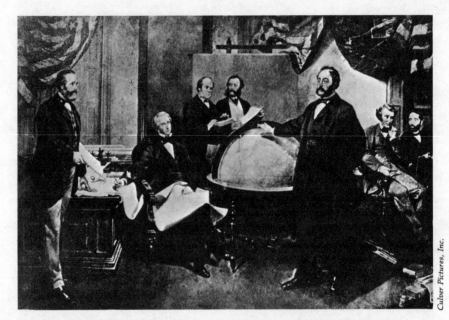

Russian Minister Baron de Stoeckel stands in front of the large globe while Secretary of State William Seward (seated left) points with his pen, as though asking the Russian to sign the Alaska Purchase Agreement

11

AFTER 1865:
AN UNCERTAIN DIRECTION

1. CHALLENGES TO THE MONROE DOCTRINE

For nearly two decades after 1823, President Monroe's famous policy statement lay fallow. Most Americans simply forgot it and as a nation overlooked European violations of the noncolonization, nonintervention, and two-spheres dictums. Great Britain, for example, seized the Argentine-claimed Falkland Islands in 1833, exercised a protectorate over Nicaragua's Mosquito Shore, and briefly blockaded Cartagena, Colombia. France tried to extend the boundaries of French Guiana at Brazil's expense, and waged the so-called Pastry War with Mexico in 1838–1839 over the nonpayment of claims and debts. Both Spain and France devised schemes to establish monarchy in Mexico. These episodes, however, occurred in areas as yet remote to the interests of the United States, and at a time when the development of the territory and resources they already possessed absorbed the energies of the American people.

A change in attitude occurred in the 1840's and with it a rediscovery and broadening of Monroe's declaration. Americans were in an exuberant expansionist mood, proud of their nation's progress and power and interested in the acquisition of new territory. They could no longer overlook European "meddling" in the New World, at least when it seemed to affect areas of direct interest to the United States.

President Tyler began the revival when he professed alarm at Anglo-French diplomatic interferences in the Texas question. In his annual message in 1842, Tyler warned against outside intrusions: "Carefully abstaining from all interference in questions exclusively referring themselves to the political interests of Europe, we may be permitted to hope an equal exemption from the interference of European Governments in what relates to the States of the American Continent." Although he did not refer to Monroe's policy by name, Tyler did restate some of its principles.

James K. Polk also responded with great alarm to Anglo-French activities in North America. He misinterpreted a statement about Texas by the French Prime Minister, François Guizot, to mean an advocation of a European-style balance of power in the Western Hemisphere. Polk used his annual message to Congress in 1845 to make a trenchant restatement of Monroeism: "In the existing circumstances of the world the present is deemed a proper occasion to reiterate and reaffirm the principle avowed by Mr. Monroe. . . ." Balance of power concepts, he declared, "cannot be permitted to have any application on the North American continent, and especially to the United States. We must ever maintain that people of this continent alone have a right to decide their own destiny." Polk in effect extended the scope of the Monroe Doctrine to prohibit not only European armed intervention but even diplomatic intervention and to oppose the transfer of any territory in the Americas, voluntarily or not, to a European power. To forestall a plan by Creoles in Yucatan for annexation to Great Britain, Polk prepared to use armed intervention to help suppress a race war between the white elite and the Indian masses in that province. Fortunately the civil war subsided before force became necessary.

Polk's restatement of Monroe's principles was generally regarded in Europe as a gratuitous facade for American imperialism. Democrats hailed his words and condemned any form of European meddling in this hemisphere, but Whigs and conservative "realists" such as John C. Calhoun feared that the United States would become dangerously overcommitted as the guardian of the entire Western Hemisphere. Calhoun, a participant in the events of 1823, declared that Monroe had directed his words against one specific threat and therefore they were inapplicable to later developments. In his view, a principle laid down in 1823 did not bind the United States to resist every incident of European intervention in this hemisphere, and it should act only when events clearly imperiled its own interests. The majority of Americans, however, tended to endorse Polk's enlarged concept of the Doctrine. Polk's contributions to Monroeism are second in importance only to the original pronouncement of 1823. In the years after Polk, the Doctrine became a fixed policy, almost a sacrosanct dogma, in American foreign policy and public opinion.

The Monroe Doctrine even won a measure of recognition in Europe during the decade of the 1860's. Naturally, the great European powers did not recognize the Doctrine as having legal international status, as many Americans did, but they began to appreciate that the United States took the policy seriously and increasingly had the power to enforce it. Two challenges to Monroeism, at least as Polk had defined it, occurred during the American Civil War. The first involved the Dominican

Republic, a poverty-ridden turbulent country troubled by growing strife between its Negro and mulatto masses and the ruling white or Creole elite. Seeking protection against their own lower classes, the Creoles in 1861 obtained reannexation to Spain. This greatly disturbed Secretary of State Seward, and when warning Spain of American distress at reannexation, he invoked the Monroe Doctrine. The Spanish government declined to acknowledge its pertinence and inquired how the vaunted North American democracy could deny the Dominicans the right of self-determination. Since the American Civil War was then raging, Seward could do no more to prevent the union. By 1865, facing a costly Dominican revolution caused in large part by its own mistakes, Spain decided to abandon annexation. The primary reason, of course, was not Seward's opposition but the realities of Dominican problems. The United States, therefore, could not validly interpret the withdrawal as a victory for the Monroe Doctrine. In another incident, however, Spain did acknowledge the existence of the Doctrine. In 1864, in retaliation for the mistreatment of Spanish workers in Peru, Spain occupied several small Peruvian islands. An American protest brought reassurances that the action was only temporary and that it in no way violated Monroe's famous declaration.

French schemes in Mexico more seriously challenged Monroeism. A number of conservative Mexicans had long viewed monarchy as the only reliable solution for Mexico's chronic political turbulence. Benito Juárez reinforced their convictions when he triumphed over the conservatives and began to institute reforms highly distasteful to the landed aristocracy and church hierarchy. Napoleon III of France, obsessed with grandiose dreams of a revival of French power and prestige, responded to the entreaties of the Mexican monarchists. An opportunity for intervention presented itself when Juárez defaulted on payments due foreign creditors. Britain, France, and Spain agreed in 1861 to a tripartite armed intervention to compel payment of Mexico's foreign obligations. When it became apparent that France's interest went beyond mere debts, Britain withdrew from the venture; Spain subsequently also recalled its forces. France alone continued the intervention and by mid-1863 its troops had occupied Mexico City. In the following year, after a farcical plebiscite, the French army installed the Archduke Maximilian of Austria as Emperor of Mexico. Juárez rallied Mexican patriotism to his side and continued resistance. It seemed obvious that only French arms enabled Maximilian and his wife Carlota to cling precariously to the ancient throne of Moctezuma.

Although the American public condemned French intervention as a violation of the Monroe Doctrine, President Lincoln and Secretary Seward dealt cautiously with the issue. The Civil War in America hardly permitted risking an armed clash with a great European power, already inclined to favor the cause of the southern Confederacy. Moreover,

Seward undoubtedly remembered the rebuff he had received from Spain in the Santo Domingo affair. The United States declined to recognize Maximilian, however, professing neutrality toward the struggle and continuing relations with the Juárez government.

After the Civil War ended in Union victory, American sentiment became even more hostile to the French venture. Supported by a reunified country and a veteran army, Seward began to apply diplomatic pressure to compel French withdrawal. He stepped up his policy of "pin pricks," refraining from invoking the Monroe Doctrine by name but making it abundantly clear that American principles and interests opposed the maintenance by a European power of a monarchical regime in Mexico. Obviously the victorious Union now found itself in a position to apply force if necessary to expel the French. Napoleon announced early in 1866 that his troops would leave, and by 1867 completed the withdrawal. Maximilian's empire promptly collapsed, and the Juárez forces captured and executed him. A number of factors explain Napoleon's retreat: costly military operations in Mexico plus continued Mexican resistance, mounting criticism within France plus the growing unpopularity of the Napoleonic regime, and the menace of Prussian power in Europe. Clearly the United States' opposition acted as one factor in his decision, thereby vindicating the principles, if not the name, of the Monroe Doctrine.

2. A RESURGENCE OF MANIFEST DESTINY?

Territorial expansion, except for the Gadsden Purchase, had halted during the 1850's. Sectional controversy and the Civil War diverted American attention from further acquisitions of territory, while they resorted to the costly process of democracy by the bayonet. After 1865 reconstruction and internal economic growth preoccupied Americans too much for them to take any great interest in schemes for enlarging the national domain. Moreover, Congress under Radical Republican control was determined to reduce the power of the executive under President Andrew Johnson, after the strong wartime administration of Lincoln, and to control reconstruction policy in the South. Congressional opposition to Johnson's expansionist schemes reflected to a large degree political partisanship and a challenge to executive leadership. Finally, some Americans had even earlier begun to oppose expansionism on ideological grounds; acquisitions of areas beyond the continental United States, inhabited by mixed races and presumably unsuitable for eventual statehood, represented costly imperialism alien to America's democratic concepts. Postwar expansionism, therefore, indicated less a response to the popular temper than the result of the plans and hopes of a few Americans in key positions of authority.

William H. Seward, who continued to serve after Lincoln's assassination, remained an ardent expansionist. After some early blunders, Seward had developed into one of the nation's outstanding secretaries of state, skilled in diplomacy and with a statesmanlike grasp of the national interest. A disciple of Manifest Destiny, he had reluctantly concluded prior to 1861 that expansionism had to be opposed as long as it served the southern slavocrats, but after 1865 a purged America could resume its historic course, spreading its commerce and its values across the globe. Seward believed that the reunified United States could exert great economic and political influence in Latin America and Canada. He felt the country needed naval bases in the Caribbean to protect the isthmian routes and to check European interferences, and he believed Mexico and Central America would probably eventually enter the American Union. Seward intended to prepare Hawaii for annexation by strengthening its economic ties with the United States, and he foresaw an eventual contact and rivalry with Russia in the western Pacific. In China and Japan, Seward worked to promote America's economic interests by the open door principles. Apart from his visions of an expanding empire of commerce and influence, Seward apparently also hoped that a vigorous foreign policy would strengthen the Johnson administration, then under furious Radical Republican attack.

Accompanied by his son, Seward early in 1866 embarked on a cruise of the Caribbean. Ostensibly traveling for reasons of health, he carefully observed suitable sites for naval bases and coaling stations. The Civil War had demonstrated the desirability of American naval bases to prevent European interferences and to protect the isthmian transit routes. The Danish West Indies or Virgin Islands seemed a particularly attractive possibility. Denmark desired to rid itself of a possession that offered few economic compensations. After months of haggling over a price, Seward and the Danish minister signed a purchase treaty in 1867 for $7.5 million. The inhabitants of the Virgin Islands approved annexation in two plebiscites and the Danish Parliament ratified the sale. Congress, however, proved more resistant, and the treaty failed to win much support among the American people. Despite the arguments and pleas of the administration and the embarrassment of Danish ratification, the Senate killed the treaty by inaction. Not until 1916 was Seward's object finally achieved, when the United States paid $25 million for the islands for strategic reasons.

Seward and the Navy Department also looked longingly at Samaná Bay in Santo Domingo. Facing problems of instability and indebtedness, Dominican officials displayed eagerness to sell that potential naval base to the United States and to seek a protectorate status or even annexation. Upon Seward's advice, President Johnson in his annual message in 1868 declared that both the Dominican Republic and Haiti desired annexation to the United States, although Haiti's government had only offered to lease the United States a suitable naval site at the Môle St. Nicholas.

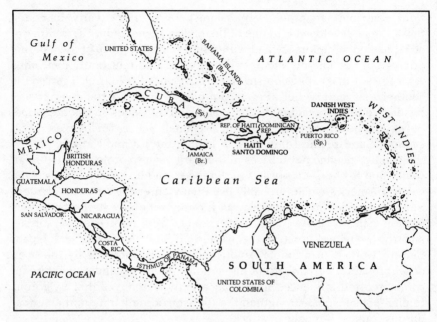

Post–Civil War Expansionism: the Caribbean

Once again Congress and the public were unresponsive to real estate offers.

When Ulysses S. Grant entered the White House in 1869, he too became an enthusiastic convert to Dominican annexation. Profit-seeking speculators apparently influenced the new President and helped engineer an optional agreement in 1869 for annexation of the republic or lease of Samaná Bay. Subsequently treaties were signed providing for either solution and submitted to the Senate for approval. Despite Grant's prestige and influence, however, the Senate declined to accept either treaty. Charles Sumner of Massachusetts, Chairman of the Senate Committee on Foreign Relations, adamantly opposed an acquisition widely regarded as unwise. The country already had enough racial problems, it seemed to many, without compounding them by acquiring additional millions of poverty-stricken and illiterate blacks and mulattoes. As one senator commented, "Such a scheme of empire . . . will destroy our republican system of government." The Senate killed the treaty in June, 1870. Grant could only sulk and obtain personal revenge by having Sumner stripped of his powerful chairmanship.

3. THE PURCHASE OF ALASKA

Most Americans knew little if anything about Russian America prior to Seward's announcement of its purchase. Many historians, therefore, have overdramatized the event to portray the Secretary of State as almost alone in his enthusiasm for the purchase, with a reluctant public and Congress accepting it only because rejection might offend Russia, the Union's great friend during the Civil War. Recent studies, while agreeing that Seward took the initiative, reveal that the public came around to approving the purchase because of America's self-interests as well as friendship with Russia.

Russian claims to what became Russian America dated to the explorations of Vitus Bering, a Dane in the service of Peter the Great of Russia, in the second quarter of the 18th century. For a half century thereafter, hunters and merchants from Siberia pursued their quest for furs in the area. They established settlements at Kodiak Island and elsewhere in 1783, and the Russian-American Company, patterned after the great English trading companies, obtained an imperial charter in 1799 to manage the enterprise. The colony survived but never fulfilled the dreams of its founders. Gradually the Czarist government lost interest and began to consider its sale. Russian America was far away, vulnerable to English seizure, and unprofitable. The Russian-American Company, whose charter expired in 1862, faced bankruptcy.

The United States was a logical purchaser. Russia viewed the sale of this area to the United States as a means to weaken Great Britain and possibly foment additional Anglo-American tensions. In 1866 the Czar's government decided to sell, and early in the following year its minister in Washington, Baron Edouard de Stoeckl, approached Seward. The Secretary eagerly grasped the opportunity. With President Johnson's acquiescence, Seward and Stoeckl hammered out the details. When the Russian minister came by the Secretary's home to announce the Czar's approval and to suggest that a treaty be drawn up the next day, the zealous Seward pushed away the whist table where he had been playing and smilingly said, "Why wait till tomorrow, Mr. Stoeckl? Let us make the treaty tonight." They hastily called clerks from their homes and by four o'clock in the morning completed the work. In the treaty signed on March 30, 1867, Russia conveyed title to nearly 600,000 square miles of land rich in undiscovered or unexploited resources and scenery, in exchange for payment of $7.2 million by the United States. It was a magnificent bargain that in subsequent years paid for itself many times over in wealth and in security during the Cold War with Russia after 1945.

The public initially reacted with surprise and bewilderment to the purchase. Launching a propaganda campaign on the attractions of his purchase, Seward with the aid of Senator Sumner won the support of other influential senators and citizens. Arguments for acquisition emphasized Russia's friendship, the commercial advantages and resources of Russian America, the spread of democratic institutions, and the encirclement of British North America. The Senate granted its approval on April 9, and by October 18 the American flag waved over the capitol at

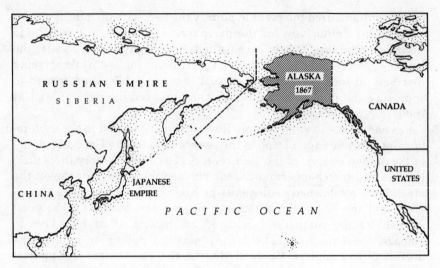

The Alaskan Purchase, 1867

Sitka. The House of Representatives, however, threatened to refuse the necessary appropriations, reflecting both doubts about the wisdom of the purchase and political animosity toward the administration. Seward continued his educational campaign, and Minister Stoeckl freely wined and dined, and apparently even bribed, enough congressmen and influential politicians to float the measure through. The House finally acted favorably on July 23, 1868. By then a majority of Americans had come to approve the purchase. Editors and humorists joked about "Seward's Folly," polar bears, and icebergs, but leading newspapers across the nation endorsed the acquisition. Alaska, most agreed, had vast economic and commercial potential, enhanced the nation's position in the Pacific, and would fulfill the country's Manifest Destiny. Russian friendship supplied only one consideration among many. As the Boston *Daily Evening Traveller* commented, Alaska's "chief value is not its fur trade and its fisheries; but . . . of vastly more importance . . . will be the command it will give us of the western and northwestern territory of this continent."

One reason for Seward's interest in Russian America was his belief that the United States should take advantage of its geographical position to exploit the markets of the Pacific and East Asia. In 1867 the United States occupied tiny uninhabited Midway Island at the suggestion of the China Mail Steamship Company, hoping that the island would provide a convenient coaling station between San Francisco and Yokohama, Japan. It proved too expensive to dredge a harbor, however, and Midway's future awaited the cable and the air age. To bind Hawaii more closely economically to the United States, Seward negotiated a reciprocity treaty in 1867. The Senate rejected it, in part because of the opposition of domestic sugar producers. Seward's successor, Secretary of State Hamilton Fish, managed to get approval for a reciprocity arrangement in 1875. It was subsequently renewed, and the United States acquired the right to build a naval base at what became Pearl Harbor.

Although post–Civil War apathy and politics limited territorial expansion to Alaska and Midway, Seward and Fish laid the basis for an expanded commercial empire in Latin America and the Pacific. The United States experienced an industrial and agricultural revolution during those years, and the State Department helped to open the way for an expansion of markets to absorb the surplus. A "new empire," in the words of one historian, was taking shape, that sought not new agricultural lands as in the past, but markets for American goods. In that sense Seward's expansionism did not simply represent an extension of the older Manifest Destiny but served as a harbinger of the future.

4. THE *ALABAMA* CLAIMS

American relations with Great Britain after the Civil War became deeply troubled. During the war, northern opinion had viewed the British government as distinctly prosouthern. British recognition of Confederate belligerency, southern purchases of arms and the construction of raiders such as the *Alabama* in Britain, the hostile tone of the conservative English press, and rumors of diplomatic intervention rankled the northern public. Americans directed much of this resentment toward Canada, not only because it was a nearby British possession but because it had harbored escaped Confederate prisoners of war and had served as a base for southern nuisance raids into Union territory. The most serious incident came on October 19, 1864 when a small group of armed but nonuniformed Confederate soldiers crossed from the Canadian side of the border to loot and burn the town of St. Albans, Vermont. Although the Canadian government had no foreknowledge of the raid and subsequently imprisoned the raiders, the incident threw northerners living near the international frontier into a near panic. Forgetting their own defective neutrality during the Canadian Rebellion of 1837, Americans harshly criticized Canada for not preventing such violations. In retaliation, Seward threatened to end the Rush-Bagot Convention limiting armaments on the Great Lakes and did terminate the 1854 Reciprocity Treaty with Canada. The latter caused much distress and resentment, since Canadian prosperity increasingly depended upon free access to the American market.

Fenianism brought an additional strain to Canadian-American relations. The Irish Republican Brotherhood, anxious to exploit Anglo-American difficulties in hopes of achieving Irish freedom from British rule, sent James O'Mahony in 1853 to organize the Irish in the United

States. In 1857, the Fenian Brotherhood was established in New York City and pledged to work for Irish independence. Six years later, in Chicago, they proclaimed an "Irish Republic," chose officials, issued bonds and currency, and authorized an army. Canada stood as a tempting target. If it could be conquered, the Brotherhood speculated, perhaps the British would free the Emerald Isle from thralldom for its return. Rumors of Fenian raids during the last years of the Civil War alarmed Canadians, but these incursions did not become serious until 1866. With ranks swollen by Irish-American veterans of the Union armies, and encouraged by American anglophobes, the Fenians launched a series of raids from United States soil into Canada. Radical Republicans, eager to embarrass the Johnson administration, and Democrats, cultivating the Irish vote, encouraged the Fenians. Consequently federal authorities either permitted or failed to prevent the raids. Eight hundred Fenians struck at Fort Erie in June, 1866, and a force of 1,800 raided Lower Canada. Canadians repelled these attacks and captured a number of invaders sentencing them to long prison terms. The American government belatedly called for strict enforcement of the neutrality laws and cooperated with Canadian authorities in ending the incursions. By 1871 peace was restored on the frontier once more, but the raids had left behind a residue of anger and fear in Canada. To the disappointment of many Americans who had long hoped to bring Canada into the Union, the raids also stimulated Canadian nationalism and the establishment in 1867 of the Dominion of Canada.

The most rankling American grievance against Great Britain involved the *Alabama* claims. During the Civil War, the southern Confederacy had tried to improvise a navy to challenge the Union blockade. Since the South lacked adequate shipyards and materials, it turned to the world's leading industrial and maritime power, Great Britain, for naval equipment and ships, and sent Captain James Dunwoody Bulloch to England early in the spring of 1861. After obtaining legal advice, he found a way to circumvent the English law that prohibited the equipping and arming of vessels intended for hostile use against a government with which Great Britain was at peace. He would request the purchase or building of ships ostensibly for peaceful purposes, acquire armament and other military supplies separately, and actually outfit the craft outside British waters. No clear intent of hostile purposes would be revealed, and Bulloch relied upon the benevolent disposition of the British ministry to ignore circumstantial evidence to the contrary. In this way, British shipyards built the *Oreto,* which sailed for the West Indies followed by another vessel carrying its armament and military equipment. There, early in 1862, the transfer was made and the *Oreto* was commissioned as the Confederate cruiser *Florida.* During its career, the *Florida* destroyed 40 Union merchantmen, technically without violating British neutrality law.

The *Alabama* was the most famous of the raiders built in Britain. Lairds Liverpool shipyard constructed the ship known at first as hull "290" and then as the *Enrica*. Despite protests by the Union minister, Charles Francis Adams, the vessel evaded detention and sailed for the Azores where it was armed and commissioned the *Alabama* in the summer of 1862. The *Alabama*, prior to its destruction by the U. S. S. *Kearsarge* off the French coast in mid-1864, took a toll of 67 Union merchant ships. Another English-built commerce raider, the *Shenendoah*, wrecked the North Pacific whaling fleet. These Confederate warships had southern officers but the crews consisted largely of foreign seamen, especially English sailors. Because it was dangerous to attempt to reenter blockaded southern ports, the raiders utilized neutral ports and waters, including the British West Indies, as bases of operations. These cruisers ultimately captured some 250 Union vessels, inflicting heavy cargo losses and driving maritime insurance rates up steeply.

Near desperation, the Union government in 1863 sent John Murray Forbes and William H. Aspinwall on a secret mission to Great Britain. The two men, supplied with large funds, were to gather information about Confederate naval activity and to frustrate Bulloch's building program by preemptive purchasing of the vessels from the shipyards. Although their mission became known and they failed to acquire any major ships, Forbes and Aspinwall succeeded in gathering fuller information on Confederate activity. Adams's increasingly sharp protests and claims for damages ultimately helped persuade the British government to enforce more zealously the neutrality statutes. The government began seizing ships intended for the Confederacy, especially the ironclads being built in the Lairds shipyards.

After the war, the British government began to perceive more clearly the dangerous precedents it had established. What would prevent the United States in some future European war from allowing Britain's enemies to purchase and build warships in American shipyards? The high seas might swarm with *Alabamas*. Congress gave ample warning when the House in 1866 unanimously passed a measure to repeal the laws prohibiting sale of warships to belligerents (the Senate blocked the measure). Moreover, many Britons began to appreciate the depths of northern resentment and the justice of Union complaints. The British in 1866 offered to arbitrate the claims, but Seward's insistence upon including the question of Britain's right to recognize southern belligerency wrecked that opportunity for a settlement. Then in 1868, the first of the Gladstone Liberal ministries renewed the negotiations. Reverdy Johnson, the American minister, signed the Johnson-Clarendon Convention in 1869 for the arbitration by both powers of claims dating back to 1853. The Convention neglected to say anything about an apology for the *Alabama* or about indirect costs such as higher insurance and the loss of shipping from American registry. The treaty obviously seemed unsatisfactory to most Americans. Moreover, many agreed with Senator Sumner that Britain's disregard of neutrality had prolonged the Civil War by two years, which therefore made her liable to damage claims of several billions of dollars. Since even England would find that sum difficult to pay, perhaps she would turn Canada over to the United States in compensation. Of course, it was a gross distortion to contend that Britain's recognition of belligerency and the exploits of the commerce raiders had lengthened the Civil War. The cruisers had been costly annoyances, but they had failed in their primary task of forcing the lifting of the Union blockade and they had not seriously affected northern prosperity. But few voices of reason came forth in 1869, and the Senate rejected the Johnson-Clarendon Convention by an overwhelmingly negative vote.

An apparent deadlock existed when General Grant assumed the presidency in 1869. After first appointing Elihu Washburne as Secretary of State, who held it for only a few days, Grant called from retirement the wealthy Hamilton Fish of New York to assume that post. Although Fish lacked previous diplomatic experience, he proved to be a very able Secretary of State and his tenure marked one of the few redeeming features in the otherwise dismal Grant era. Fish believed that Great Britain owed the United States an apology and reparations for the damages inflicted by the British-built Confederate cruisers, and he too showed interest in the annexation of Canada. On the other hand, he realized that, unwise though it might have been, the British government had acted within its rights in recognizing Confederate belligerency in 1861, and that the United States could not realistically ask her to shoulder half the costs of the Civil War. Fish awaited a cooling of public tempers in both countries before renewing negotiations and, when they did begin, he bypassed Sumner's protégé, John Lothrop Motley, the American minister at London.

Informal exchanges began in mid-1869, when Sir John Rose, Canada's Finance Minister, visited Washington. Rose wanted to renew reciprocity and to discuss other Canadian-American issues. He also indicated a readiness to explore the *Alabama* claims. London's attitude had also become more favorably disposed. The Franco-Prussian War in 1870 raised the possibility of an Anglo-Russian conflict, and the British feared that a hostile United States might permit Russia to build or purchase cruisers in America. The Russian minister suggested to Fish that the opportune time for an Anglo-American settlement of the *Alabama* claims had arrived. After Rose's second mission to America had achieved agreement on procedures, a Joint High Commission concluded the Treaty of Washington on May 8, 1871. Britain agreed to submit to arbitration damage claims based on the activities of the *Alabama* and other raiders built in England. In effect conceding the American case in advance, Britain expressed regret for the construction of the cruisers and specified that new rules, not formerly requirements of international law in 1861–65 but which both powers would accept for the future, would govern the arbitration: "due diligence" by a neutral to prevent the outfitting or arming of ships which it had reasonable grounds to believe were intended for use against a belligerent; the prevention of neutral ports or territory from being used as bases for hostile operations; and due diligence to prevent all persons within a neutral's jurisdiction from violating neutral obligations. The treaty also permitted Americans to exploit Canada's inshore fisheries for ten years, in exchange for similar privileges and money compensations to Canada. Another provision referred a long-pending dispute over the San Juan Islands to arbitration by the Emperor of Germany, who decided in America's favor in 1872. Americans viewed Britain's concessions on the *Alabama* as a victory, and the Senate approved the treaty with little difficulty.

As provided by the treaty, the five-member Arbitral Tribunal met at Geneva, Switzerland, in late 1871. The United States sent Charles Francis Adams, Great Britain named Sir Alexander Cockburn, and the Swiss, Brazilian, and Italian governments provided the other three members. Although it was generally assumed that the indirect claims for allegedly prolonging the Civil War would not come before the tribunal, Secretary Fish had them included in the American case. He apparently hoped by so doing to satisfy the extremists in the United States and to rid Anglo-American relations permanently of the shadow of those exaggerated claims. Unfortunately it caused a great uproar in Britain and led to angry charges of bad faith. The arbitration seemed about to founder, and rumors of war once more agitated both sides of the Atlantic. Fish could not retreat and Britain adamantly refused to allow the claims before the tribunal.

Charles Francis Adams happily arranged a prestige-saving compromise. At his suggestion, the tribunal informally advised that the indirect claims, if they could rightfully come before it, would first have to be ruled invalid. This satisfied each side and the tribunal completed its work in September, 1872. Under the new rules accepted for the arbitration, the tribunal found Great Britain liable for the escape of the Confederate raiders, a foregone conclusion, and assessed her $15.5 million in damages.

Both governments accepted the award. Obviously the settlement was political, not judicial, based on expediency rather than the requirements of international law and practice as they had operated in 1861–65. Great Britain had tried to resolve a major crisis in its relations with the United States and to avoid future embarrassments. She succeeded eminently well. The concessions made in 1871–1872 established precedents that paid off handsomely for Britain during the Boer War and World War I. In these two conflicts, a neutral America felt constrained to observe "due diligence" in enforcing its neutrality.

The Treaty of Washington was hailed at the time as one of the most important treaties in American annals, second only to the epochal treaty of 1783. Many optimistic observers also viewed the treaty and arbitration as notable landmarks in a civilized movement away from war and toward the pacific adjustment of all international disputes. From a later perspective both evaluations seem overdrawn. Yet unquestionably the Treaty of Washington deserved a great deal of credit for ending a serious Anglo-American dispute, averting a possible war, and opening the way for a steady improvement in Anglo-American relations.

Additional Reading

The best study of the evolution of the Monroe Doctrine is Dexter Perkins, *The Monroe Doctrine, 1826–1867* (1933) and his general survey, *A History of the Monroe Doctrine* (rev. ed., 1963). See also J. A. Logan, Jr., *No Transfer* (1961). Frederick Merk, *The Monroe Doctrine and American Expansionism, 1843–1849* (1966) suggests the self-defense doctrine was used to rationalize expansion. American policy toward Napoleon's Mexican adventure is examined by G. G. Van Deusen, *William Henry Seward* (1967); J. F. Rippy, *The United States and Mexico* (rev. ed., 1931); and J. M. Callahan, *American Foreign Policy in Mexican Relations* (1932). L. M. Case, *French Opinion on the United States and Mexico, 1860–1867* (1936) has edited contemporary materials relating both to the Civil War and the Mexican intervention. Also see *A Reappraisal of Franco-American Relations, 1830–1871* (1959) by Henry Blumenthal. Post-Civil War expansionism is covered by T. C. Smith, "Expansion after the Civil War, 1865–1871," *Political Science Quarterly,* XVI (1901), 412–436, and D. M. Dozer, "Anti-Expansionism during the Johnson Administration," *Pacific Historical Quarterly,* XII (1943), 253–275. Charles Vevier analyzes the intellectual aspects of expansionism in "American Continentalism: An Idea of Expansionism, 1845–1910," *American Historical Review,* LXV (1960), 323–335. D. F. Warner, *The Idea of Continental Union* (1960) covers the Canadian aspect of expansionism. *The United States and Santo Domingo, 1798–1873* (1938) by C. C. Tansill examines the Johnson-Grant efforts to annex that area. For the purchase of Alaska, see V. J. Farrar, *The Annexation of Russian America to the United States* (1937) and the general surveys of Russo-American relations by T. A. Bailey, *America Faces Russia* (1950); F. R. Dulles, *The Road to Teheran* (1944); and William Appleman Williams, *American-Russian Relations, 1781–1947* (1952). Also B. P. Thomas, *Russo-American Relations, 1815–1867* (1930) remains valuable. R. E. Welch, Jr., "American Public Opinion and the Purchase of Russian America," *The American Slavic and East European Review,* XVII (1958), 481–494, demonstrates that national interests rather than friendship explain popular approval of the purchase. Walter La Feber, *The New Empire: An Interpretation of American Expansionism, 1860–1898* (1963) emphasizes the quiet growth of the American economy during this so-called era of quiescence in expansionism. For Confederate naval activity in Great Britain during the Civil War consult F. L. Owsley, *King Cotton Diplomacy* (1931) and M. B. Duberman, *Charles Francis Adams* (1961). D. N. Maynard, "The Forbes-Aspinwall Mission," *Mississippi Valley Historical Review*, XLV (1958), 67–89 examines that unorthodox Union effort to frustrate southern activities in England. Also see H. C. Owsley, "Henry Shelton Sanford and Federal Surveillance Abroad, 1861–1865," *Mississippi Valley Historical Review*, XLVIII (1961), 211–228. Fenianism and troubled Canadian-American relations are treated by William D'Arcy, *The Fenian Movement in the United States, 1858–1886* (1947); Brian Jenkins, *Fenians and Anglo-American Relations during Reconstruction* (1969); T. N. Brown, *Irish-American Nationalism, 1870–1890* (1966); and R. W. Winks, *Canada and the United States: The Civil War Years* (1960). The best account of the *Alabama* settlement and of Grant diplomacy in general is by Allan Nevins, *Hamilton Fish: The Inner History of the Grant Administration* (1936). Goldwin Smith, *The Treaty of Washington, 1871* (1941) is good for the English side of the *Alabama* question.

The Samoan rivalry

12

AMERICA LOOKS OUTWARD, 1881–1895

1. THE NEW MANIFEST DESTINY

The decade of the 1890's is often described as a watershed in American history, separating two major periods in the evolution of the United States. On the 19th-century side of the divide stood a predominantly agricultural and rural America, interested largely in its own internal growth and insulated from the currents of international politics. In the phrase of C. Vann Woodward, it was an "age of free security," even if from time to time Americans expressed some apprehension about foreign dangers along their borders. In striking contrast to the European powers, during most of the 19th century the United States found it possible to live in peace and security with a miniscule army and navy. Although most citizens attributed that happy state of affairs to their nation's policy of isolationism or abstention from the wars and politics of the Old World, in fact it resulted from a relatively stable balance of power in Europe and the absence of a general war between 1815 and 1914. On the other side of the 1890's lies modern America. Increasingly industrialized and urbanized, expansionist and outward-looking, the United States in this latter period found itself inextricably involved in world affairs and compelled to pay a vastly higher price for its security.

This method of studying major phases in the history of the United States serves as a convenient and useful aid to understanding if the periodization is not interpreted too rigidly. History rarely falls into neat epochs, clear beginnings, and definite endings. Long before the 1890's, truly revolutionary economic changes began to transform the United States. Increasing surpluses of industrial and agricultural commodities and accumulations of so-called surplus capital had led to a search for markets and investment opportunities abroad many years before 1890.

The basis for what Professor Walter La Feber calls a new empire—the "annexation of trade" rather than of colonial territory—had begun to take shape prior to the Civil War and made great advances during the so-called quiescent period in American foreign relations, 1865 to 1889. These changes and tendencies merely became stronger and more obvious during the 1890's.

A revival of expansionism, the new Manifest Destiny, occurred in the closing years of the 19th century. While it bore many similarities to the old expansionism of the 1840's and 1850's, the new imperialism differed in several significant ways. Largely agricultural and commercial interests acted as the economic impulse behind the old Manifest Destiny, in contrast to the expansionism of the late 19th century, which had an industrial base. By the 1890's, the quickening pace of economic development, the mechanization of industry and agriculture, and the growing concentration of business ownership and control had transformed the American economy. As early as 1876, the balance of foreign trade shifted in America's favor; export trade exceeded the value of imports. By the 1890's, exports of manufactured goods had begun to overtake exports of raw materials and foodstuffs, although these remained important. The United States had become one of the largest and most populous of the western nations, a dynamic country of 70 million people which had already surpassed Europe in the production of many of the essentials of an industrial age.

These economic changes necessarily affected foreign policy. Despite America's great wealth in resources, the country was not entirely self-sufficient. As industry revolutionized itself and spewed forth a flood of products, businessmen became more interested in foreign supplies of raw materials such as rubber, tin, copper, and nickel. Moreover, the nation's farms and factories were producing far more than could be consumed at home. If they could not dispose of the growing surplus abroad, some feared it would inevitably result in a cycle of depressions characterized by overproduction, falling prices and wages, and mass unemployment. The Panic of 1893 triggered a severe economic depression lasting for several years and providing a grim foretaste of the future unless adequate foreign outlets for surplus production could be found. Unemployment bred discontent, strikes and riots, and class conflict. The nation's social as well as economic health seemed to require foreign markets. Finally, the United States also had begun to export capital to underdeveloped areas in Latin America and East Asia, although only on a small scale prior to 1900. American foreign investments increased from about $80 million in 1869 to nearly $700 million by 1897, mostly in Mexico and Canada. Yet at the same time that Americans began to show more interest in the opportunities for foreign trade and investments, European imperialism threatened to preempt all the desirable areas. Africa was being divided into colonies, European economic influence predominated in much of Latin America, and China apparently faced imminent dismemberment. Understandably, the State Department began to reflect the interests and the fears of the American business community. Thus, in contrast to the old, the new expansionism in its economic aspects leaned in an extracontinental direction and sought, with a few exceptions, not to acquire territory but markets.

Heightened nationalism also played an important role in the new Manifest Destiny. Patriotism obviously was not a new sentiment, but it welled to a new intensity in the 1890's. Americans took pride in their nation, its vast territory, its burgeoning population, its apparently inexhaustible storehouse of resources, its almost incredible industrial and agricultural productivity, and its democratic institutions. Despite the youthfulness of the United States, the republic already held the distinction of living under the world's oldest written constitution. Many areas reflected this heightened nationalism. By the end of the century, time had softened or eradicated most of the old hatreds from the Civil War. The thinning ranks of the "Boys in Blue" and the "Boys in Gray" began to hold joint reunions. Painful memories of carnage and destruction dimmed with the years, leaving only the glory of that fratricidal struggle to thrill a new generation unbloodied by war. Patriotic organizations such as the Daughters of the American Revolution and the Society of Colonial Dames, founded in 1890 and 1891, dedicated themselves to preserving the relics of a glorious past and to inculcating patriotism in new generations of native-born Americans and in the annual flood of immigrants. A young American historian, Frederick Jackson Turner, read a paper entitled the "Significance of the Frontier in American History" before a meeting of the American Historical Association in 1893. His very thesis was nationalistic: Americans must look for an explanation of their history and the development of their institutions not so much to the European heritage but to their own frontier experiences—the constant advance of civilization into the wilderness. That process, virtually completed by 1890, largely explained the nature of American society, he believed. In his later writings, Turner foresaw the need for a new frontier, a commercial frontier in the Pacific and elsewhere, that would draw American energies abroad and end the political isolation of the past.

The ideology or rationalizations behind the new Manifest Destiny not only refurbished the old self-justifying arguments of the 1840's and '50's but drew inspiration from the pseudobiological concepts of social Darwinism. In his *Origin of Species* (1859), Charles Darwin hypothesized that all living things had evolved from simpler to more complex forms via a ruthless process of competition and adaptability known as "natural selection." Intellectuals such as Herbert Spencer applied evolutionary concepts to human society; competition, the elimination of the unfit and survival of the fittest, formed the basic law of nature and the means of all human progress. Applied to foreign affairs, social Darwinism postulated the existence of superior and inferior "races" or nations and a ceaseless struggle for survival among them. It seemed obvious to Darwinists that history had demonstrated the greater capacity of the white or Occidental race for the arts of civilization above all other races. Moreover, within the white race itself, certain "sub-races" such as the Teutonic or Nordic, seemed clearly superior to the lesser white breeds. The so-called Anglo-Saxons of England and America branched off from that superior Teutonic race, the creators and bearers of civilization. Darwin himself spoke of the Anglo-Saxon race as the heir of the ages, a theory he felt history had proven.

Popularizers of social Darwinism flourished in the United States in the closing decades of the 19th century. John Fiske, one of the foremost, wrote an article for *Harper's Weekly* in 1885 entitled "Our Manifest Destiny," in which he described the Americans as part of the Anglo-Saxon race, with superior political and economic institutions, and destined by nature to Americanize most of the world. By that he apparently meant that the United States would inspire and influence the world, not conquer or annex large parts of it. The Rev. Josiah Strong, a midwestern Congregationalist minister, combined nationalism, evolutionary concepts, and missionary zeal in a popular book *Our Country*, also published in 1885. In some of his chapters, Strong depicted America as destined by its Anglo-Saxon blood, its vast territory and resources, and its multiplying millions, to assume leadership in civilizing more backward peoples: "This race of unequalled energy, with all the majesty of numbers and wealth behind it—the representative, let us hope, of the largest liberty, the purest Christianity, the highest civilization—having developed peculiarly aggressive traits . . . will spread itself over the earth." Mexico, Central and South American, Africa, and the Pacific would become the beneficiaries of this expansionist tide. Yet Strong, like Fiske, opposed the acquisition of colonies, and favored the carrying of civilization to benighted peoples by American missionaries. Perhaps not all his readers, however, perceived the distinction between spiritual and other forms of expansionism.

Alfred Thayer Mahan was another highly persuasive advocate of expansionism. A professional naval officer whose duties had frequently taken him abroad, Mahan in 1885 joined the faculty of the newly established Naval War College at Newport, Rhode Island, as a lecturer in naval history. Reading widely and reflecting closely on the "lessons" of history, Mahan wrote a series of lectures published in 1890 as *The Influence of Sea Power on History, 1660–1783*. In this and other writings, such as *The Interest of America in Sea Power* (1897), he viewed international relations through the prism of social Darwinism. Mahan saw nation states as locked in a ruthless struggle for survival and expansion, with sea power the key to national power. A nation is like a fort, he said, and since the oceans surrounding a country such as the United States act both as moats and as highways of international communication, control of the sea becomes vital to national power. America's economy required new markets and sources of raw materials, a large merchant fleet to transport its commerce, and a powerful navy with adequate coaling stations and bases abroad to protect those interests. Mahan advocated acquisition of bases in the Caribbean and the Pacific, and the construction of an isthmian interoceanic canal. He has been aptly described not as a neo-mercantilist seeking colonies for their own sake, but as an open-door type of expansionist interested in naval bases and coaling stations to facilitate entry into foreign markets. Not the first to advocate a stronger navy, Mahan did articulate a well-developed theory of the nature and role of sea power.

Gradually the popularizers of navalism and expansionism spread their ideas through an ever-widening circle of politicians and among the masses of Americans. Influenced by the example of contemporary European colonialism and expansionism, some Americans apparently sought national adventure and glory, and found attractive the arguments for a larger destiny for the United States. The press and even the churches by 1898 echoed the exhilarating concepts and mood of the expansionists. How many subscribed to the new Manifest Destiny is impossible to answer. Probably only a minority subscribed fully to the new Manifest Destiny, and then for only a brief time, but the expansionists at least helped set the tone of the decade and influenced America toward a larger role in world affairs. A number of developments and diplomatic episodes both reflected the new mood and contributed to it: the building of a new navy, the launching of Pan-Americanism, the crises over Chile and Samoa, the attempt to annex Hawaii, and the clash with Great Britain over Venezuela.

2. THE NEW NAVY

Except for the Civil War years, prior to the closing years of the 19th century the United States felt little need or desire for a large navy. Unburdened by colonies and overseas bases, and traditionally neutralist, the New World republic seemingly required only a few warships to show the flag abroad. If war came, Americans felt confident that they could improvise a navy and use it along with privateers to raid the enemy's commerce; gunboats or harbor monitors and land fortifications would defend America's own shores.

Jefferson inaugurated the "passive coast defense–commerce raiding" strategy during his two administrations. Yet shortly after Jefferson left office, the War of 1812 demonstrated serious defects in that strategy. The British navy drove American shipping off the high seas, blockaded the American coasts, and carried out landing operations virtually at will. The

Civil War again provided a graphic example of the uses of superior sea power, when the jerry-built Union navy blockaded the Confederacy and denied it substantial access to foreign supplies. In the years after 1865, however, the nation permitted the navy to decay. By 1880, the United States ranked only 13th among naval powers, and it possessed only 40 seaworthy warships, which it scattered across the high seas to show the flag, versus nearly 700 in 1865. The navy also lagged in technology. Most of the world's navies had changed from wooden sailing vessels to iron- or steel-hulled steam-powered craft, heavily armored and firing rifled shells, while in contrast the American navy looked like a veritable floating museum of naval antiquities. Many of its ships were still wooden and relied primarily upon sail power; some still carried smooth-bore cannon firing solid shot or used makeshift rifled pieces.

A number of factors underlay this technological obsolescence. A pinch-penny Congress and politician-Secretaries of the Navy had little understanding or sympathy for naval needs. As humorist Finley Peter Dunne quipped, the first qualification for a head of the Navy Department seemed to be that he should never have seen salt water outside of a pork barrel. The hidebound traditionalism of many naval officers, who preferred clean sail and wind whistling through the rigging to messy steam and smoke, also contributed to this situation. Moreover, since naval vessels remained scattered on station abroad for long periods of time, far from American bases and forced to rely upon expensive foreign supplies of coal, ships were fitted primarily for sail and captains were discouraged from using steam auxiliaries. Naval regulations in 1870 required that captains should not raise steam except when absolutely necessary and that they should enter the reasons for its use in red ink on the ship's log. A disgusted Admiral D. D. Porter compared the nation's decrepit warships to ancient Chinese forts with dragons painted on them to frighten away the enemy. As late as 1889, young Theodore Roosevelt wrote a friend that war with a major power such as Germany would benefit America, for the resultant destruction of our coastal cities would teach the people a badly needed lesson in the value of a navy.

The year 1881 marked a historic milestone in the birth of the new navy. A slow process of reconstruction began, gradually overcoming encrusted traditions and beliefs. By 1881 the Treasury had a surplus, and increasing productivity in industry and agriculture aroused greater interest than before in foreign markets. Responsible political leaders took notice of these changes and registered alarm at the country's naval weaknesses at a time when a foreign company was digging a ship canal across Panama and the American government was involved in an international rivalry over Samoa. President James A. Garfield in 1881 appointed an able and energetic Secretary of the Navy, W. H. Hunt of Louisiana. Surrounding himself with competent naval advisers, Hunt presented Congress with well-planned programs for naval expansion. In

1883 Congress appropriated funds for the first modern vessels of the new navy—three steel-hulled cruisers and a so-called dispatch boat. Although these ships had serious defects in design and still carried masts for sails, they were far superior to the older ships of the navy, and as the famed White Squadron, they became a source of pride to the American people. In succeeding years, Congress appropriated additional funds for new ships. By 1889, 30 vessels had been authorized, including two second-class battleships.

But as yet, American naval strategy showed no important changes. Captain Mahan, as noted before, preached the gospel of the British system of command of the seas. Instead of using warships as commerce raiders, the United States needed a small but compact fleet of capital warships, trained to seek out the enemy fleet and destroy it. In one stroke such a fleet could protect the nation's coast and trade, and effectively bring the war home to the enemy. In 1889 President Benjamin Harrison, a big-navy advocate, appointed the similarly inclined Benjamin F. Tracy of New York to head the Navy Department. Apparently influenced by Mahan's arguments, Secretary Tracy urged Congress to approve a vast program of naval construction, including a capital high seas fleet. Profiting by the timely Samoan crisis, Tracy helped secure passage of the truly epochal Naval Bill of 1890, authorizing three first-class battleships, incongruously labelled "seagoing, coastline battle-ships" by a tradition-minded Congress. These three ships—the *Indiana,* the *Massachusetts,* and the *Oregon*—formidable warships for the time, formed the nucleus of a small but growing capital high seas fleet. The government instituted naval war games by 1894 and, three years later, established the North Atlantic Squadron. The American people took great pride in the new navy, a symbol of their country's newly recognized rank as a great world power. By 1898, the American navy had risen to sixth or seventh among the world's navies and gave a very convincing demonstration of its effectiveness in the war with Spain.

3. PAN-AMERICANISM AND THE CHILEAN CRISIS

Although the phrase "Pan-America" did not become current until the late 19th century, the concept of the New World as a separate sphere apart from Europe and with special interests of its own has a much older history. European philosophers frequently contrasted the purity of the New World with the corruptions of the old, while such statesmen as Jefferson, Simón Bolívar, and Henry Clay dreamed of some kind of union to bind together most of the hemisphere. After the abortive Panama Congress in 1826, however, little progress was made toward that larger goal.

James G. Blaine instigated the modern Pan-American movement. Appointed Secretary of State during the Garfield administration in 1881,

Blaine was dedicated to the advancement of peace and trade in the Western Hemisphere. He was anxious to continue the policy of his predecessors in the State Department—Seward, Fish, and William M. Evarts—who had promoted America's economic expansion in Latin America and in the Pacific. In 1881 Blaine tried to mediate the conflict between Chile and its opponents in the War of the Pacific, Peru and Bolivia. Chile refused to relinquish the valuable guano and nitrate lands she had conquered in the war, and Blaine's interference earned only ill will and mistrust. Blaine hoped that a conference of the states of the Americas could help adjust such disputes and could adopt machinery to prevent future conflict. Moreover, European influence and the possibility of outside political intervention in the Western Hemisphere disturbed him. He also showed great interest in promoting the commerce of the United States. Trade statistics revealed that the United States had an adverse balance of trade with Latin America, taking about 30 percent of its imports from that area but only sending about 12 percent of its exports there. Blaine hoped for a free trade area or customs union between the states of this hemisphere that would reduce European political and economic influence and bind together the United States and Latin America.

Late in 1881, Blaine invited all the independent states of the Western Hemisphere to a "peace congress" in Washington. Unfortunately for his plan, President Chester A. Arthur, who succeeded the assassinated Garfield, decided to replace Blaine in the State Department. The new Secretary, Frederick J. Frelinghuysen, suspected that his predecessor had called the conference primarily to apply pressure against Chile and thereby to serve the interests of a group of American nitrate investors and speculators. Although Blaine actually was blameless, Frelinghuysen cancelled the conference.

The Pan-American idea did not disappear, however. Within a few years, as Blaine's personal sponsorship faded into the background, others perceived the advantages of closer relations with Latin America. At the request of Congress, President Grover Cleveland in 1888 issued another invitation to a conference. The fortunes of politics had returned the Republicans to power by the time the conference met in 1889 and Blaine returned once more to his former position of Secretary of State. Delegates from 17 Latin American states convened with the Americans in Washington. Blaine's welcoming address emphasized the common bonds of political stability and peace that drew together the sovereign states of the hemisphere. The American delegation seemed to highlight the primacy of economic motives, since it contained seven business leaders including Andrew Carnegie. After the delegates took an exhausting 5,400 mile railroad tour intended to display the size and wealth of the United States, the conference reassembled for business.

The conference achieved few concrete results. The group rejected

Blaine's idea of a customs union, although it did recommend reciprocity arrangements. The delegates endorsed arbitration and mediation of disputes, but most of the Latin American governments failed to ratify these arrangements. The problem lay in the fact that Latin America differed profoundly from the United States in culture and language, and in general felt more attracted to Europe culturally and economically than to the Colossus of the North. Even the common bond of republicanism meant little, for most of Latin America honored constitutionalism and democracy more in theory than in practice. The past record of the United States in expansionism and unilateralism also did little to encourage confidence in its aims and leadership among Latin Americans. Yet the conference met and established an International Bureau of the American Republics (later the Pan-American Union) for the exchange of economic, scientific, technical, and other information. Future conferences kept alive the Western Hemisphere idea.

The Chilean crisis of 1891-1892 administered a rude shock to Blaine's Pan-Americanism. During a civil war in Chile between President José Manuel Balmaceda and the rebellious Congress, Blaine and his minister, Patrick Egan, became identified with the presidential faction. The United States detained a rebel steamer, the *Itata,* when it came to San Diego for a cargo of arms. The crew of the Chilean ship overpowered an American deputy marshal placed on board and sailed for Chile. An American warship pursued the *Itata* and compelled it to surrender its cargo of arms. Although this zealous if questionable enforcement of neutrality pleased Balmaceda, it understandably enraged the rebels. Unfortunately for Blaine, they won the civil war. Ironically, after the rebels had triumphed, a United States court ruled that the *Itata* should not have been interfered with in the first place.

In this strained atmosphere the commander of the U. S. S. *Baltimore,* in Chilean waters to protect American interests, gave part of his crew shore leave in Valparaiso. A mob attacked the Americans in the True Blue Saloon, fatally stabbing two sailors and wounding 17 more. The captain of the *Baltimore* blamed the Chilean authorities, while the latter dismissed the riot as a mere drunken brawl. Tempers flared in the United States at what was widely viewed as an insult to the national honor. President Harrison, a proud Civil War veteran, decided that strong measures were required to vindicate the flag and the uniform. Yet the Chilean government acted with agonizing slowness in investigating the incident. Fearful of disrupting the new Pan-Americanism, Blaine was hard pressed to restrain his more bellicose chief and the public. A senator from Iowa expressed the popular mood: "The American Republic will stand no nonsense from any power, big or little."

His patience exhausted by Chile's procrastination, President Harrison sent a threatening message to Congress in December, 1891. The Chilean response proved completely unsatisfactory, compelling Blaine to send an ultimatum on January 21, 1892. A war scare swept the United States. After waiting four days in vain for Chile to reply, Harrison laid the problem before Congress in what was virtually a war message. Meanwhile, the hapless Chilean government had already decided to accept the inevitable humiliation. Chile apologized and subsequently paid $75,000 in reparations for the killed and wounded sailors. The crisis passed, but it left a rankling aftermath. Chileans felt abused and bullied, and most of Latin America agreed that the United States had been guilty of officious interference and gunboat diplomacy. Much of the goodwill that Blaine had so zealously cultivated at the Washington conference dissipated.

4. SAMOA AND HAWAII

American contacts with the Samoan archipelago began in the days of the whalers. In 1839, Lieutenant Charles Wilkes of the U. S. Navy explored the area and made commercial arrangements with the native rulers. Thereafter British missionaries and traders and German copra merchants entered the islands, the latter assuming the predominant economic role. In the late 1860's, American land speculators and shipping interests became involved. Samoa, lying about halfway between Sydney, Australia, and Honolulu, seemed to offer a valuable way station for commerce with the southwest Pacific. Responding to the requests of these American interests, who warned of German and New Zealand schemes to take over the islands, the American government sent Navy Commander Richard W. Meade to survey the harbor of Pago Pago on Tutuila. Meade negotiated a protectorate treaty with the local chief in 1872 that the Senate refused to approve. Six years later, however, and in response to more reports of British and German annexationist schemes, a treaty was concluded whereby the United States obtained a naval base at Pago Pago in return for its good offices in controversies involving Samoa with other powers. Great Britain and Germany negotiated similar treaties with Samoa.

Tripartite rivalry over Samoa became acute in the 1880's. The consuls of the three powers were far more zealous than their governments in trying to dominate the islands. The German consul forced a protectorate treaty upon the Samoan monarch, who promptly appealed to Great Britain and the United States for help. The Cleveland administration warned America's two rivals that it would not permit either to dominate the archipelago. Washington rationalized its stand on the basis of a moral responsibility for the preservation of Samoan independence, but it also admitted that the islands possessed great commercial significance, particularly after the completion of a canal across Central America. As the crisis deepened, Germany appeared particularly aggressive, insisting upon a predominant role in the islands and high-handedly placing a puppet on the Samoan throne. Warships of all three powers gathered at Apia and it seemed that any chance spark might ignite a general conflict.

Fortunately, the German government under the direction of Chancellor Otto von Bismarck appreciated the gravity of the situation and adopted a more moderate course. Bismarck proposed a renewal of negotiations at Berlin. Sobered by a tropical hurricane that devasted Apia in 1889 and destroyed or damaged the German and American ships with much loss of life, the three powers agreed in that year to establish a tripartite protectorate over Samoa and to preserve a facade of Samoan independence. Contrary to its isolationist traditions, the United States thereby became directly involved in an area thousands of miles from its shores. The arrangement worked poorly as rivalry and intrigue among the consuls and nationals of the three powers continued to keep the Samoan kettle boiling. Internal warfare between rival Samoan factions in 1899 threatened armed clashes between the British and Americans, now aligned against the Germans. When Germany suggested partition of the islands as the only practical solution, the United States overcame its earlier objections and agreed. The three powers accepted a convention in 1899 that divided the islands between Germany and the United States, with Germany compensating Great Britain in the Solomon Islands and in Africa. The United States received less than Germany as its share, but it did obtain the badly wanted harbor at Pago Pago. Most Americans accepted the acquisition of this remote colony without question, their consciences already prepared by the territorial spoils gained from Spain in the 1898 war. Yet while the Samoan controversy ended peacefully if imperialistically, it left a residue of anti-German hostility and suspicion in America. The pork controversy of these same years, arising from a German ban against American pork as allegedly infected, was settled in 1891 but it too contributed to a growing American image of the new Germany as aggressive and contemptuous of others.

In the words of President Grover Cleveland, Hawaii served as an "outpost of American commerce and the stepping-stone to the growing trade of the Pacific." The reciprocity treaty that Secretary of State Fish had negotiated in 1875 was renewed in 1887, with a provision guaranteeing that Pearl Harbor should remain an exclusive American naval base. Hawaii's sugar economy, stimulated by reciprocity and completely dependent on the American market, expanded rapidly. To supply cheap labor for the industry, Chinese and Japanese workers were introduced under contract. Yet beneath the prosperous facade, many native Hawaiians resented the influence of the American planters and merchants who dominated the islands' economy and government, and feared the American leviathan would swallow their kingdom whole.

Economic troubles and native anti-Americanism set the stage for annexation in the 1890's. The McKinley Tariff of 1890 dealt Hawaiian prosperity a heavy blow by removing the duty on foreign raw sugar imports and by giving American domestic producers a bounty of two cents per pound, thus eliminating the advantages previously enjoyed by Hawaiian sugar. When the strong-willed and anti-American Queen

Liliuokalani ascended the throne in 1891, she compounded economic and political unrest. An attempt by the Queen early in 1893 to establish an absolute monarchy gave the American planters and merchants in Hawaii their chance. Previously reluctant to push for annexation lest it interfere with the importation of cheap Asiatic labor, many planters now saw no alternative. Encouraged by Washington and by the American Minister, John L. Stevens, who ordered armed American sailors to land in Honolulu, the annexationists overthrew the Queen, established a provisional republic, and requested incorporation within the United States. They hastily concluded a treaty, and Harrison laid it before the Senate on February 15, 1893.

Expansionists advocated annexation to safeguard American economic interests and to ward off British and Japanese influence in the islands. In addition to Hawaii's sugar and rice, the islands offered valuable naval bases and coaling stations for commerce in the Pacific. Opponents of expansionism, however, drawing upon the anticolonial traditions of the past, objected to the political burdens of governing and defending territory remote from the continental United States and inhabited by a racial hodgepodge of native Hawaiians, numerous Chinese, Japanese, and others, and with only 2,000 Americans. Imperialism, many contended, would fatally poison the springs of American democracy. The Democrats won the 1892 presidential election, and Cleveland returned to the White House before the Senate completed action on the treaty. The new chief executive did not necessarily oppose annexation on principle, but he was aware that many native Hawaiians did not want it. He also became convinced that Minister Stevens had played an improper role in the revolution. Consequently Cleveland withdrew the treaty from the Senate. He failed to obtain restoration of the monarchy, which he thought fairness demanded, and the American-controlled republican government remained in power.

The Republic of Hawaii continued to seek incorporation, particularly when attempts to halt the heavy influx of Japanese into the islands caused a crisis with Japan and rumors of war. In 1897 President William McKinley reopened the issue of annexation, but determined Democratic and Republican anticolonialists successfully blocked another treaty. The Spanish-American War in the following year, however, provided a new opportunity. Ostensibly as a war measure, Congress in July, 1898, hastily approved a resolution of annexation and an American territory in the Pacific at last became a reality.

5. THE VENEZUELAN CRISIS OF 1895

The long-smouldering boundary controversy between Venezuela and the British colony of Guiana seemed on the surface remote from American interests. Both powers claimed title to a virtually uninhabited jungle area of 50,000 square miles. Venezuela rejected repeated British offers and insisted on arbitration of the entire dispute. London refused, owing to the well-known tendency of arbitration boards merely to divide a contested area. Tensions increased when gold was discovered in the disputed area. Venezuela broke diplomatic relations with Britain and employed a former American diplomat, William L. Scruggs, to plead its case with the United States. A persuasive propagandist, Scruggs wrote a pamphlet entitled *British Aggressions in Venezuela, or the Monroe Doctrine on Trial.*

The American public was easily aroused. Arrogant Albion seemed once more to be expanding aggressively at the expense of a weak state. Many Americans believed that the British claims represented an attempt at colonization in defiance of the Monroe Doctrine. A temporary British occupation in 1895 of the port of Corinto in Nicaragua, in an effort to force that small republic to pay reparations due some British subjects, further stirred the popular temper.

The Cleveland administration decided to take a vigorous stand in order to warn Europe against further encroachments in the Western Hemisphere. That decision reflected not merely public pressures and Anglophobia, but a growing fear that the major European powers threatened the economic and political interests of the United States in Latin America. In addition to the Corinto incident, Great Britain had occupied a small island off Brazil as a cable station, while France had clashed with Brazil over the boundary between Brazil and French Guiana and had threatened Santo Domingo with force in a dispute over monetary claims. As a State Department official privately commented, Great Britain (and, by implication, other European powers) was playing the old "grab game" in the Western Hemisphere.

At Cleveland's request, Secretary of State Richard Olney prepared a note that the President described as a "twenty-inch gun." Presented to the British government on July 20, 1895, Olney's note had a bombastic and arrogant tone. After reviewing the boundary issue and invoking the sacred Monroe Doctrine, Olney declared: "Today the United States is practically sovereign on this continent, and its fiat is law upon the subjects to which it confines its interposition." He requested that the British agree to submit the dispute to arbitration and asked for a reply prior to Cleveland's next message to Congress.

The British government failed to appreciate the excited nature of American opinion. London tended to dismiss Olney's note as only one more example of "lion's tail twisting" for the sake of domestic politics. Consequently, the Foreign Office very leisurely prepared its reply. It finally arrived, four months after Olney's diplomatic blast, giving a well-reasoned but undiplomatic refusal by Foreign Secretary Lord Salisbury. He bluntly rejected arbitration and tactlessly if correctly denied the validity of the Monroe Doctrine as international law, or its relevance to the present case.

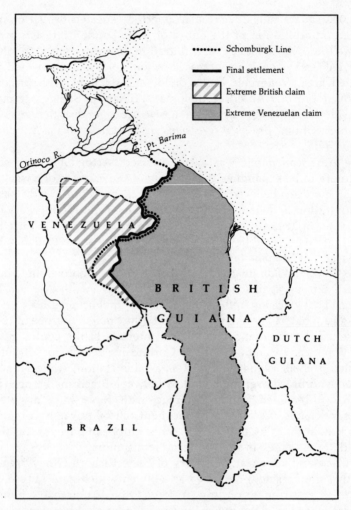

The Venezuelan Boundary Dispute

Public anger ran dangerously high in the United States. Cleveland, "mad clear through," in his words, delivered a fighting message to Congress on December 17, 1895. Reaffirming the Monroe Doctrine, the President declared the United States' intention "to resist by every means in its power" aggression against Venezuela. He asked Congress for authorization to appoint a commission to investigate the merits of the dispute and if necessary to impose a correct boundary. "In making these recommendations," the President emphasized, "I am fully alive to the responsibility incurred and keenly realize all the consequences that may follow." He never even consulted Venezuela before making his decision, indicating that the United States actions represented not only altruistic motives but its own political and economic interests as well. Congress responded enthusiastically and Americans and Europeans predicted war.

Fortunately neither government wanted hostilities. Cleveland merely intended his address to reiterate Olney's warning and to gain time for a solution. In Britain, the Venezuelan controversy aroused little public interest, and the government was anxious to pacify the unpredictable Americans. American friendship was too valuable, and Germany's challenge to British interests caused growing alarm. Moreover, influential economic interests in both nations deplored the possibility of a ruinous war over a relatively insignificant issue. Lord Salisbury agreed to submit the boundary controversy to arbitration, exempting lands that had been settled for 50 years or more. The tribunal rendered a decision in 1899 that gave Britain nearly all the territory in dispute and that closely followed earlier British offers to Venezuela. Venezuela, however, gained control of the Orinoco River. Americans rejoiced that the Monroe Doctrine had triumphed against mighty Britain. The United States put the world on notice that it was the arbiter of the destinies of the entire Western Hemisphere.

The Venezuelan situation serves as an ironic commentary on the customary failure of the United States to associate policy with the means to implement it, because if war had come in 1895, the British fleet had an overwhelming superiority and could have inflicted devastation upon America's commerce and coasts.

Additional Reading

The American Mind (1950), by Henry Steele Commager, contains an excellent discussion of the "watershed" of the 1890's. The ideology and politics of the new Manifest Destiny are examined at length by Richard Hofstadter, *Social Darwinism in American Thought* (1945); and more briefly by A. K. Weinberg, *Manifest Destiny* (1935); Frederick Merk, *Manifest Destiny and Mission in American History* (1963); and Julius W. Pratt, *Expansionists of 1898* (1936). Dorothea R. Muller, "Josiah Strong and American Nationalism: A Reevaluation," *Journal of American History*, LIII (1966), 487–503, exonerates that evangelist of charges of overt imperialism. On the growth of the new navy see Robert Seager, "Ten Years Before Mahan: The Unofficial Case for the New Navy, 1880–1890," *Mississippi Valley Historical Review*, XL (1953), 491–512; William E. Livezey, *Mahan on Sea Power* (1947); and Harold and Margaret Sprout, *The Rise of American Naval Power, 1776–1918* (1944). *Pan-Americanism: Its Beginnings* (1920), by J. B. Lockey is still useful. Recent accounts include A. P. Whitaker, *The Western Hemisphere Idea: Its Rise and Decline* (1954) and J. L. Mecham, *The United States and Inter-American Security, 1889–1960* (1961). Blaine's role is analyzed by

Russell N. Bastert, in "A New Approach to the Origins of Blaine's Pan-American Policy," *Hispanic American Historical Review,* XXXIX (1959), 375–412, and in "Diplomatic Reversal: Frelinghuysen's Opposition to Blaine's Pan-American Policy in 1882," *Mississippi Valley Historical Review,* LII (1956), 653–671. Alice Felt Tyler, *The Foreign Policy of James G. Blaine* (1927) should be supplemented by A. T. Volwiler, "Harrison, Blaine, and American Foreign Policy, 1889–1893," *Proceedings of the American Philosophical Society,* LXXIX (1938), 637–648. An excellent reappraisal is by D. M. Pletcher, *The Awkward Years: American Foreign Relations under Garfield and Arthur* (1961); also see Milton Plesur, *America's Outward Thrust; Approaches To Foreign Affairs, 1865–1890* (1971). F. B. Pike, *Chile and the United States, 1880–1962* (1963) deals with the Chilean crisis. For the Cleveland era, see Allan Nevins, *Grover Cleveland* (1934); C. C. Tansill, *The Foreign Policy of Thomas F. Bayard, 1885–1897* (1940); and G. R. Dulebohn, *Principles of Foreign Policy under the Cleveland Administrations* (1941). Expansionism into the Pacific is examined by G. H. Ryden, *The Foreign Policy of the United States in Relation to Samoa* (1933); S. K. Stevens, *American Expansion in Hawaii, 1842–1898* (1945); W. A. Russ, Jr., *The Hawaiian Revolution, 1893–1894* (1959) and *The Hawaiian Republic, 1894–1898* (1961); and Merze Tate, *Hawaii: Reciprocity or Annexation* (1968). Walter La Feber, *The New Empire: An Interpretation of American Expansion, 1860–1898* (1963) emphasizes the economic factors behind a more vigorous policy, including the Venezuelan crisis. For a very different view, see John A. S. Grenville and G. B. Young, *Politics, Strategy and American Diplomacy: Studies in Foreign Policy, 1873–1917* (1966). The role of the Venezuelan controversy in Anglo-American relations is discussed by A. E. Campbell, *Great Britain and the United States, 1895–1903* (1960) and Bradford Perkins, *The Great Rapprochement: England and the United States, 1895–1914* (1968). Foster Rhea Dulles, *The Imperial Years* (1956) provides a good overview of the entire period covered in this chapter.

The Maine and the Yellow Press

13

IMPERIAL AMERICA, 1898–1901

1. THE CUBAN CRISIS

Cuba, long restive under Spanish rule, naturally captured American sympathy with its desires to cast off Old World rule. Yet during the bloody Ten Years' War, 1868–1878, the American government resisted domestic pressures to recognize the Cuban rebels or to intervene in their struggle. When the revolution revived again in 1895, however, the United States did not escape involvement. In addition to all the former causes of unrest, a collapse in raw sugar prices, precipitated by the American tariff of 1894 and the worldwide depression, rekindled the desire for rebellion. Unable to withstand the Spanish army in regular combat, the rebels resorted to guerrilla warfare. Utilizing scorched-earth tactics, rebels dynamited passenger trains and either destroyed or held for extortion foreign-owned property, including that of Americans. Finding guerrilla warfare extremely hard to suppress—as Americans later realized in Vietnam—Spain fought back with a campaign of counterterror. The Spanish subjected Cubans to arbitrary arrests and executions, constructed a "corral" of blockhouses and wire entanglements across the island to cut off the rebel-infested mountainous eastern sections, and forcibly moved the inhabitants of suspect areas to disease-stricken camps under the *reconcentrado* policy. Cuba seemed a vast charnel house of starvation and violent death, as Captain-General Valeriano Weyler and over 100,000 Spanish troops tried in vain to crush the insurrection.

Americans heard mostly of Weyler's atrocities, although the rebels too were guilty of inhumanities. The rebels established *juntas* or councils in several American cities, with headquarters in New York, to obtain a flow of arms and recruits for the cause and to propagandize for intervention. Despite the efforts of federal authorities to suppress them, expeditions from American waters ferried men and equipment to the insurrectionists in Cuba. Rebel propagandists exaggerated Spanish brutality and atrocities, bad though the situation admittedly was, and depicted the guerrillas as sincere patriots and republicans merely trying to follow the example of the American people by throwing off a rapacious and cruel colonial rule. The *juntas* appealed with particular success to American labor and other groups. *Junta* propaganda probably played a more decisive role in influencing the popular temper toward intervention than did the often criticized yellow press.

Sensational journalism had existed in the United States long before the 1890's. High speed presses, color reproductions, and news-gathering press associations made possible—and, due to their costs, required—mass circulation to justify high advertising rates. While not all editors abandoned ethical professional standards, a number of practitioners of the "new journalism" emerged. Dubbed "Yellow Journalism," apparently because of the garish color of the illustrations and comic strips, the new journalism catered to the tastes of the mass public with sensationalist headlines, human interest stories, special features, and an emphasis upon crime and sex. New York City became the center of the new sensationalism. There in 1895, William Randolph Hearst purchased the failing *Journal*. A free-spending and uninhibited practitioner of the new journalism, Hearst reduced the *Journal's* price to one cent per copy and prepared to fight to the wall Joseph Pulitzer's *World*. Both journals exploited every possibility to increase circulation and to surpass all rivals in a ruthless battle for profits and prestige. Any exciting foreign crisis or controversy, and especially the Cuban revolution, became grist for their mills.

The *World* described "Butcher" Weyler as a modern Genghis Khan who left "the corpses of bound prisoners" in a trail behind his advancing army. Not to be outdone, the *Journal* depicted him as "the prince of all the cruel generals this century has seen," Spain's "most ferocious and bloody soldier . . . [and] fiendish despot. . . ." When Evangelina Cisneros, the daughter of an insurgent leader, was accused of complicity in an attack upon a Spanish official (she claimed that he had attempted to rape her) and was imprisoned in Havana, the *Journal* mounted a campaign against such allegedly cruel treatment of a beautiful and innocent young girl. It actually sent a reporter to Cuba, who sawed through jail bars to rescue the girl and then escaped with her, disguised as a boy, to the United States. The sensational episode aroused enormous interest around the world. Congratulations flooded into the Hearst offices, and the Governor of Missouri suggested that the *Journal* send 500 reporters to Cuba and free the entire island. Yet the impact of the Yellow Press has often been exaggerated. Studies have indicated that the sensationalist New York newspapers had little effect on the press in other sections of the country, which came to advocate interventionism for quite independent reasons. Moreover, sensationalism in any case did little more than mirror the popular mood.

President Cleveland firmly resisted pressures to involve the United States in the Cuban war, although he appreciated the greatly increased American economic stake in the island. Since 1878 large amounts of American capital had flowed into Cuba, mostly into sugar production but also into mining; the United States consumed 75 percent or more of Cuban sugar, and American manufactured goods had found a flourishing market in the island. Estimates indicate that by the 1880's trade with Cuba totaled one-fourth of America's total world trade. Cleveland and Secretary of State Olney apparently had no great sympathy for the rebels, whom they regarded as lawless and unstable, and they feared that an independent Cuba or a Cuba in the hands of another power would jeopardize American interests. The wisest solution seemed to rest in an autonomous Cuba under nominal Spanish authority, but Spain rejected a proposal by Olney along those lines in 1896.

The administration tried to enforce neutrality as efficiently as geography and the sympathy of many federal officials and citizens for the rebel cause permitted. Both the Senate and the House of Representatives passed a resolution advocating recognition of Cuban belligerency, but Cleveland stood fast. At the same time, the President cautioned Spain of the dangerous possibilities if the revolution continued for a long period. In his last annual message, Cleveland called for the end of a situation that threatened to ruin the "industrial value" of the island. Both the Republican and Democratic parties, and the short-lived Populists, adopted platform planks in the 1896 presidential election advocating freedom for Cuba. Cleveland viewed his successor, William McKinley, as a man of peace but frankly admitted leaving him a probable war with Spain.

2. McKINLEY AND CUBAN INTERVENTION

McKinley was a very cautious chief executive. He had spent most of his political career in the House of Representatives, where he became the chief philosopher of the blessings of a protective tariff, and as Governor of Ohio. A fatherly figure, he attended the Methodist church regularly, avoided work on Sundays, and rebuked others for their off-color humorous remarks and stories. He was devoted to his wife Ida, an invalid afflicted with epilepsy. McKinley, who did not keep a diary and felt extremely reticent about recording his views in any form, listened attentively to others and often seemed to agree with them. Because of his pliable and amiable facade and the apparently dominant role of his good friend and adviser, Mark Hanna, McKinley appeared weak to many of his contemporaries and to most historians. Recent reappraisals reveal him as much stronger than previously credited and more of a leader than a follower of public opinion.

McKinley hoped to continue Cleveland's course of neutrality toward the Cuban revolution. To disarm the jingoes or prowar groups in Congress and the nation, and thereby to gain time for patient diplomacy, McKinley openly condemned Weyler's *reconcentrado* policy, supported relief to Cuba's suffering population, and sent the battleship *Maine* to Havana early in 1898, ostensibly to protect American citizens but in fact to pressure Spain into speedily ending the war. McKinley also brought before the Senate in 1897 the question of Hawaiian annexation, which he favored, apparently to divert attention from Cuba.

From the beginning of his term, McKinley hoped for peace, but he concluded that the Cuban bloodletting could not continue indefinitely. He warned the Spanish government that the United States might have to intervene if the struggle dragged on much longer. In a note on June 26, 1897, he reminded Spain of American interests in the restoration of peace in Cuba, because of the disruption of trade and the destruction of property caused by the war, the costs of enforcing neutrality, and the natural sympathy of the American people for the victims of the fighting. McKinley insisted that the fighting be conducted in accordance with the requirements of "civilized" warfare, and that any solution had to be acceptable to the Cuban rebels as well as to Spain.

McKinley earnestly explored several possible solutions to the conflict. One possibility called for the United States to purchase Cuba and then presumably to free the island. Overtures to Madrid fell on deaf ears, however, for the war had aroused Spanish pride and nationalism. Spaniards deeply resented the threatening attitude of the United States, and many still hoped to suppress the revolt. McKinley then tried to promote a truce between the rebels and the Spanish forces, but neither side would settle for less than complete success. It became increasingly obvious that neither opponent could defeat the other, and that because of rebel determination the conflict would continue until either Spain reached exhaustion or the United States intervened.

McKinley took in stride events he could have used to justify war. On February 9, 1898, Hearst's *Journal* created a sensation when it published a private letter (stolen by a rebel sympathizer from the Havana post office) written by the Spanish minister in Washington, Dupuy de Lôme. In the letter, de Lôme bitterly castigated McKinley as a weak political truckler to the jingoes, and he also indicated that recent Spanish moves to institute autonomy and other reforms in Cuba had not been made in good faith. De Lôme resigned before the United States could expel him, but the affair left a bitter aftertaste. While this incident was still the topic of the day, the sinking of the *Maine* aroused the public to a fighting temper. On February 15, that second-class battleship suddenly disintegrated in a mighty explosion in Havana harbor, killing over 266 officers and men. Although the yellow press attributed the explosion to the Spanish—an improbable explanation unless Madrid had abandoned its senses—and the slogan "Remember the Maine" reverberated from the pulpits and the streets of America, McKinley remained calm and awaited a naval inquiry into the tragedy. The causes still remain unclear. The American investigation then, and another one in 1911 when the hulk was raised, concluded that an externally produced explosion had destroyed the vessel, while the Spanish attributed it to an internal cause. Most Americans did not doubt Spain's guilt and became increasingly restless at the President's failure to act. McKinley's calm message to Congress on the findings of the inquiry into the *Maine* disaster caused one newspaper editorialist to comment, "It is hard to find much red, white, and blue in that message, but there is plenty of what looks like yellow."

The President finally despaired of a peaceful solution. Reports indicated that the Spanish government was merely stalling for time, hoping to delay American intervention while making every effort to crush the rebels by the fall of 1898. Therefore, on March 27, 1898, the State Department sent the Spanish government a virtual ultimatum. It requested an immediate armistice to last until October 1, and the complete revocation of the reconcentration policy. It further requested that if a peaceful settlement could not be arranged by October 1, the President of the United States should be permitted to act as the final arbiter between Cuba and Spain, clearly implying mediation based on Cuban independence since the rebels would accept no less.

The Spanish government maneuvered unsuccessfully to escape its dilemma. High Spanish officials realized that hostilities with the United States probably would prove disastrous, but inflamed national pride and the precarious political position of the Spanish monarchy made them prefer defeat in war to capitulation to McKinley's demands. Madrid appealed to the major European powers to bring diplomatic pressure upon the United States to prevent intervention, but met with little success. Except in Great Britain, European opinion sympathized with Spain, but no government cared to risk affronting the American giant on her behalf. Britain's Queen Victoria also sympathized with the plight of the Spanish Queen Regent, but her government prevented any action. On April 7 the ambassadors of six major powers presented McKinley with an inoffensive joint note, urging peace in the name of humanity, but the President suavely evaded any action with a few pious remarks in reply.

Madrid finally acceded reluctantly to McKinley's first two demands but not to the third. Spain put an end to reconcentration and proclaimed an armistice for as long as its commander in Cuba deemed prudent. Washington was naturally sceptical about the value of these concessions. Spain had broken its promises in the past, and the rebels declined to cease fighting until assured of independence. Despite the American minister's optimistic report from Madrid on April 9 that the Spanish government was moving as rapidly as the domestic situation permitted and given more time would meet all of McKinley's demands, the administration concluded that Spain had not and would not agree to the prime essential for peace, mediation on the basis of Cuban freedom. Recent historical inquiry indicates the accuracy of McKinley's analysis. On April 11, McKinley sent a message to Congress requesting authority to take whatever action necessary to settle the Cuban question. While Congress debated, the President still sought a peaceful solution, trying unsuccessfully to persuade Spain to declare its willingness to free Cuba.

McKinley's message threw Congress into an uproar. Sentiment favoring intervention had been mounting in recent weeks across the nation and congressmen responded with an outburst of patriotic jingoism. Politics also clearly played an important role. The dislocations of industrialism and urbanization, compounded by the depression following the Panic of 1893, had sharpened the frustrations of farmers and debtors and had produced deep political cleavages in America. A mood of national confidence and optimism in America's great wealth and power curiously commingled with a protest movement for reform. Populists and Bryan Democrats sympathized with the Cuban rebels, whose plight seemed comparable to their own feelings of being exploited by the newly rich masters of industry and finance within the United States. Rallying from their defeat in the last presidential election, the agrarians saw in Cuba a new cause to supplement the 1896 battle cry of "free silver." Thus advocates of domestic reform united with more conservative nationalists and imperialists in advocating intervention in Cuba. McKinley's cautious policy had made both groups unhappy.

Illustrating the deep divisions and suspicions that existed, a number of Populists and Bryan Democrats succumbed to a conspiracy theory regarding the administration. They suspected that McKinley's peace efforts were part of a plot to enrich alleged American investors in Spanish bonds by keeping Cuba in chains or saddling it with the Spanish debt incurred by fighting the rebellion. The administration had to exert a great deal of pressure to defeat a war resolution limiting executive power and freedom of maneuver by recognizing the rebels as the legitimate government of Cuba. The Teller Amendment was accepted, however, pledging nonannexation of the island. It reflected both America's idealistic and humanitarian motives in intervention, and also the continuing suspicions of some that the McKinley administration was trying to protect investors in Spanish Cuban bonds. On April 19, Congress authorized intervention and on April 25, after a Spanish declaration of war, proclaimed a state of war to have existed since April 21.

Why did the United States finally go to war? One explanation, popular in the 1920's and '30's and recently revived by so-called New Left historians in a more sophisticated way, emphasizes an economic interpretation. According to the older view of historians such as Charles A. Beard in his *Rise of American Civilization,* America intervened because of its investments in Cuban sugar and trade, worth about $150 million, and its desire to exploit further that island's resources. Historian Julius W. Pratt's study in 1936, however, revealed that the big business community generally opposed intervention until almost the eve of war, fearing its destructiveness and a disruption of returning prosperity. Even many of the Cuban investors had anti-intervention leanings. Recent neo-Beardians have again called attention to economic factors. Most business leaders and spokesmen had opposed war, but they finally welcomed it in order to end a situation of intolerable uncertainty disturbing to business confidence and stability. Another interpretation emphasizes the role of a handful of avowed imperialists, such as Mahan, Senator Henry Cabot Lodge of Massachusetts, and Assistant Secretary of the Navy Theodore Roosevelt, in leading America along the path of war and conquest. Still other historians have attributed the war to the influence of the yellow press, or to the "psychic crisis" of the 1890's—the seeking of relief from internal economic and social tensions through a foreign crusade.

Perhaps the most satisfactory answer lies in the idea that 1898 was a people's war, not meaning to imply that the sheer force of public opinion drove McKinley into a conflict that he opposed. The evidence indicates that the President resisted popular pressures as long as he had any hope for a peaceful solution. Yet like most of his fellow citizens, McKinley sympathized deeply with the Cuban rebel cause, on humanitarian grounds and because of an ideological aversion to Old World rule and a belief in the virtues of independence and democracy. Obviously, too, he took into consideration American economic interests in Cuba and the disturbing effects of the civil war upon the business community. But above all, humanitarian sentiments seem to have moved McKinley. Firsthand reports, such as one on March 17 by Senator Redfield Proctor of Vermont, a conservative and respected Republican, described the suffering, starvation, and death in Cuba as almost beyond belief. McKinley and most Americans felt that their country, in their eyes the foremost Christian and civilized power of the New World, could no longer tolerate a charnel house barely off its own coast.

Certainly the President did not lightly choose hostilities. He personally remembered only too vividly the sufferings of the American Civil War and he felt a genuine aversion to going down as a war president. In the days when he wrestled with his final decision, he was so disturbed that he had to take sleeping powders to rest at night. War finally seemed to him the only alternative to the continuation of a situation that was growing more and more intolerable.

3. "A SPLENDID LITTLE WAR"

The brief war with Spain entailed less than four months of actual hostilities. Histrionics, that today seem incredible, blundering and inefficiency, satisfying victories against a badly outmatched foe, and much genuine heroism marked this short conflict. An American people hungry for heroes to worship and glorious exploits to recall, was fully satisfied by the laurels its fighting forces won. John Hay, the ambassador to Britain, called it "a splendid little war." Theodore Roosevelt praised it as "bully for the navy," though he later admitted, "It wasn't much of a war, but it was the best war we had." Yet despite the comic-opera overtones, it goes down in history as a fateful conflict that dramatized America's coming of age as a great world power, added an empire, and immersed the United States as never before in the currents of world politics.

When the war began, most informed observers expected the United States to win, Spain being only a has-been power. The surprise came from the amazing ease with which the United States accomplished Spain's defeat. Victory followed victory in an unbroken succession. To pressure Spain by assaulting her Philippine possessions, Commodore George Dewey sailed the Asiatic Squadron past Corregidor into Manila Bay and there, on May 1, leisurely annihilated the decrepit Spanish fleet. He became a hero overnight. His enthusiastic fellow citizens, in a delirium of joy, named innumerable newborn children in his honor, and several commercial products, one a chewing gum labeled "Dewey's Chewies," tried to capitalize on his fame. Dewey carried on blockade operations the remainder of that hot summer until troops arrived from the United States and captured Manila on August 13. His May Day victory unknowingly, at least for most Americans, opened up an alluring vista of empire in the far Pacific. Ironically, because of naval strategy, a war to free Cuba drew American power virtually to the very shores of East Asia.

The army was less prepared for action than the navy. Numbering only about 28,000 men when the war began, volunteers and the calling up of the National Guard rapidly increased its ranks. Great confusion resulted as an unprepared War Department struggled with unaccustomed problems of supply and transportation. Ironically, disease took far more lives (5,200) than battle casualties (460). After incredible inefficiency and questionable strategic planning, an expeditionary force commanded by General William R. Shafter, a 300-pound officer whose gout sometimes compelled him to confer with his staff while lying on a stretcher, landed in Cuba in late June. Fortunately for the invaders, the more numerous Spanish forces were dispirited and they surrendered Santiago on July 16. In the interval, Spain ordered Admiral Pascual Cervera to Cuban waters on what he and other Spanish leaders viewed as a suicidal gesture to uphold the national honor. Eluding the American navy, Cervera sailed his four cruisers and several lesser craft into Santiago harbor. Ordered to sortie before the city fell, Cervera's ships were destroyed by the more powerful American fleet on July 3. The news reached America the next day and people hailed it as the "July Fourth Victory." Four hundred Spanish sailors and officers were killed or wounded, against the loss of one American. The army also occupied Puerto Rico, without encountering any serious resistance.

Its honor satisfied, the Spanish government sued for peace in late July. Although she expected to lose Cuba, Spain received a jolt when McKinley also demanded the cession of Puerto Rico, one of the Mariana Islands (eventually Guam), and the harbor and city of Manila pending a final decision on the Philippine archipelago. The hapless Spanish authorities signed an armistice on that basis in Washington on August 12.

McKinley exercised firm executive control of foreign policy during the peace negotiations. He did not call Congress into special session to help formulate peace terms, but instead he carefully chose three prominent senators, two Republicans and one Democrat, to serve on a five-man commission, headed by Secretary of State William R. Day. McKinley at first hesitated about whether to ask for more than the main island of Luzon. Yet even after deciding to take all of the Philippines, that skillful politician managed to create the impression of awaiting the mandate of public opinion. On a speaking tour in October, the President uttered resounding platitudes about duty and destiny and carefully gauged the growing public resolve to acquire the entire Philippine archipelago. Later he explained to a group of visiting Methodists that he had not known what to do with this "gift from the gods" won by Dewey's victory, but after much seeking of advice and earnest prayer for heavenly guidance, he finally concluded late one night:

(1) That we could not give them back to Spain—that would be cowardly and dishonorable; (2) that we could not turn them over to France or Germany—our commercial rivals in the Orient—that would be bad business and discreditable; (3) that we could not leave them to themselves—they were unfit for self-government—and they would soon have anarchy and misrule over there worse than Spain's was; and (4) that there was nothing left for us to do but to take them all, and to educate the Filipinos, and uplift and civilize and Christianize them, and by God's grace do the very best we could by them as our fellowmen for whom Christ also died. And then I went to bed, and went to sleep, and slept soundly. . . .

McKinley's pious explanation pithily summarized the mixture of ideals and self-interests underlying the acquisition. Religious groups eagerly sought to Christianize the natives, and many Americans apparently took seriously the old concepts of democratic mission and the "white man's burden" toward "backward" peoples. Nationalists professed reluctance to see Old Glory lowered where it had been raised by brave American fighting men. The Philippines offered attractive economic opportunities, for as McKinley's words indicated, commercial spokesmen had begun to value acquisition of the islands, plus Guam and Hawaii, as desirable way stations to the promising markets of China and East Asia.

The President finally instructed the commissioners in Paris to ask for all of the Philippines. A shocked Spain could only protest, arguing that the United States had not conquered the islands and had occupied Manila only after the signing of the armistice. Their surrender sweetened by McKinley's offer of $20 million in compensation, the Spanish delegates signed the treaty of peace on December 10, 1898.

Opponents of imperialism had begun to voice objections to acquisition of the Philippines soon after Dewey's victory in Manila Bay. An Anti-Imperialist League was formed, backed by a mixed lot of reformers, pacifists, intellectuals, Democrats, Republicans, and a few business and labor leaders. Among others these included Andrew Carnegie, Samuel Gompers of the A. F. of L., David Starr Jordan, the President of Stanford University, and Mark Twain. Carnegie seemed particularly "off his head" to John Hay, Day's replacement as Secretary of State, writing him and others frantic letters against imperialism and threatening McKinley not only with defeat at the polls but "punishment at the hands of the mob." Anti-imperialists argued that acquisition of the islands would be costly, would risk war with other powers, and would violate the letter and spirit of the Constitution. Above all, they protested that a republic could not administer an empire without betraying its own ideals of self-government. Internal political divisions and advocacy of a negative policy so weakened the anti-imperialists that they failed to halt the march toward empire.

McKinley carefully managed the fight for the treaty in the Senate. Although the administration could rely upon the support of virtually all the Republicans in the Senate, several of them plus a number of Populists and Democrats adamantly opposed imperialism and doggedly fought the treaty. Some Populists and Bryan Democrats, however, opposed to imperialism but deeply suspicious of the administration's ties to Wall Street, advocated approving the treaty of peace and then freeing the Philippines without any encumbrances. To the distress of other anti-imperialists, William Jennings Bryan endorsed that strategy. The administration defeated all such attempts to amend the treaty and it finally squeaked through the Senate with one vote more than the required two-thirds majority.

The United States had acquired sovereignty over seven million people, alien in race and language, living in a vast chain of islands only a few hundred miles from the mainland of Asia but over 6,000 miles from continental United States. In addition to the long-term and costly

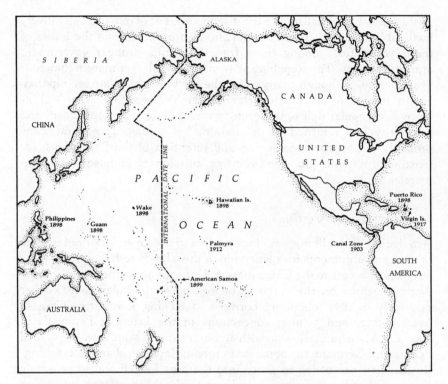

The American Empire, 1898–1917

defense and government commitments that worried so many anti-imperialists, the United States found itself immediately involved in a nasty colonial war. A Filipino insurrection against Spanish rule and the economic stranglehold of large landowners and Roman Catholic religious orders had erupted in 1895 but had been suppressed. Dewey encouraged the insurrectionists, led by Emilio Aguinaldo, to renew their struggle in 1898 and they expected recognition of Philippine independence as their reward. Realizing that Filipinos had merely obtained a new foreign master, Aguinaldo turned his arms against the Americans in 1899. The United States sent 70,000 troops to suppress the revolt, and some of them retaliated in kind to the barbarous rebel tactics. News that their troops resorted to torture to extract information or punish recalcitrants horrified Americans. It required two years of unpleasant guerrilla-type fighting to subdue the insurrection, a fact that helps explain why the current of imperialism burned out so soon after 1898. It seemed ironic that America's civilizing mission had to rely on the bayonet.

In the election of 1900 McKinley again faced the Democratic standard-bearer of 1896, William Jennings Bryan. Bryan campaigned vigorously against imperialism. To the disappointment of more conservatively inclined anti-imperialists, however, he also insisted upon the issues of the 1896 contest, among them free silver and stronger government antitrust actions. The Republicans won and by a larger margin than four years before. Although many called the election a mandate on imperialism, a number of other factors clearly overshadowed that issue: McKinley was a popular figure, the country was traditionally Republican, and prosperity had returned to the nation. Yet a majority of Americans probably did approve acquisition and retention of the Philippines, for reasons of national glory and prestige, missionary impulses, and commercial hopes.

4. AN OPEN DOOR IN CHINA

Acquisition of the Philippines logically led to the Open Door notes. One of the chief arguments for ownership of the islands rested on their value in terms of access to the China market. Unfortunately, the weak Chinese empire seemed on the verge of dismemberment. Japan defeated her decisively in 1895, obtaining Formosa, detaching Korea from Chinese overlordship, and gaining concessions in the Liaotung Peninsula in southern Manchuria. Russia, with ambitions in the same area, persuaded France and Germany to cooperate in forcing Japan to abandon Liaotung. Russia then proceeded to move into the area herself and to penetrate Korea. Other powers acted quickly to establish or enlarge spheres of influence in China and extorted exclusive railroad, mining, and port concessions from the weak Peking government. For example, Germany exploited the murder of two missionaries in 1897 to obtain a leasehold in Shantung province.

British merchants previously dominated the bulk of Chinese trade and naturally felt threatened by these developments. At the same time, the British government realized that the emphasis of the Chinese market was switching from commerce, where competition could prevail, to mining and railroad concessions, which by their very nature were exclusive or monopolistic. British leaders therefore decided that while trying to preserve the Open Door in China—equal opportunity for all—they had to face the prospect of seeking their own sphere in the Yangtze Valley if it proved necessary. As part of that strategy, the British ambassador, Sir Julian Pauncefote, asked the State Department in early 1898 if it would cooperate to prevent Chinese partition or the creation of discriminatory spheres.

President McKinley and the State Department rejected the overture which came amidst troubles with Spain over Cuba. Seeing no immediate threat to American interests, they refused to depart from their country's traditional policy of avoiding foreign alliances and entanglements. The McKinley administration also rebuffed another British bid for joint action in January of 1899. Neither American trade nor power seemed to justify involvement in the morass of China.

Yet the administration was not insensitive to growing American interest in China. In 1895, the American-China Development Company was founded to seek railroad concessions in China. Some of the most influential financial and business leaders of the country numbered among its stockholders. Tobacco and kerosene exporters, and the cotton textile industry, also looked with interest toward China. North China and Manchuria, precisely the areas threatened by German and Russian imperialism, primarily concerned these groups. The Committee on American Interests in China, subsequently renamed the American Asiatic Association, was established in 1898 to interest Americans in China and to warn them of the dangers of partition. A number of influential citizens began to speak optimistically of China's vast potential market, which in itself could absorb, they predicted, our growing agricultural and industrial surpluses. Missionaries, long active in evangelical and educational endeavors in China, and a major influence in shaping our views of the Orient, added their voices to those concerned about the threat of partition.

The Open Door notes of 1899 and 1900 reflected these material and spiritual interests. Far from being a misguided attempt to aid Britain, as older historians have written, the Hay notes aimed at protecting American interests in China while avoiding dangerous entanglements with any other power. Eager to act for some time, Hay deemed mid-1899 propitious because of indications that Great Britain, Japan, and Germany favored commercial equality in China, and he hoped to pressure the other powers into line. Beginning on September 6, 1899, he addressed identical notes to the major powers requesting assurances that within their spheres of influence in China no power would interfere with treaty ports or vested interests or discriminate against the commerce of others. He also asked each power, Britain, France, Russia, Germany, Italy, and Japan, to cooperate with the United States in obtaining the others' support of these principles. Significantly, Hay neither condemned spheres of influence nor referred to the territorial integrity and independence of China. He only requested continued observance of the principle of commercial equality of opportunity for all in China, apparently accepting as inescapable the seeking of exclusive or monopolistic concessions relating to railroads, mining, and other forms of fixed investments.

Hay's note embarrassed several of the great powers and particularly aroused acute resentment in St. Petersburg. All of the replies, except Italy's, evaded the issue and made their commitment dependent upon acceptance by the others. Russia sent the most negative response of all, omitting any references to equal railroad rates within spheres. Yet Hay blandly announced on March 20, 1900 that all the great powers had agreed with the American position.

In 1900 a wave of antiforeign violence known as the Boxer Rebellion engulfed China. Apparently the weak Manchu government encouraged it. The rebels destroyed foreign-owned property, menaced or slaughtered missionaries and foreign businessmen, and beseiged the foreign legations in Peking with an armed horde. They murdered the German minister and the Japanese secretary of legation, and cut off the beseiged legations from communication with the outside world. An allied expeditionary force of 20,000 troops, including 2,500 Americans, was hastily organized and fought its way to the rescue of the foreigners in Peking. Hay and President McKinley were aware that Russia and the other imperialist powers might use the rebellion as an excuse to cut additional slices off the Chinese melon. Moreover, they also realized that some Americans objected to involvement in suppressing the Boxers. Since the next presidential election was imminent, the administration anxiously sought to justify American involvement as merely intended to rescue the legation and to stabilize China. Hay sent a circular to the great powers on July 3, 1900, but this time he avoided requesting a response. His circular stated that United States policy concentrated on finding a solution to China's current troubles that would preserve Chinese integrity and safeguard commercial equality of opportunity in all parts of the Celestial empire.

Americans hailed Hay's bold stroke as a notable diplomatic victory, because it asserted American ideals and principles and protected China from partition, without the United States entering into any alliances or entanglements with others. Although the victorious powers forced China to pay an indemnity of a third of a billion dollars, in which the United States shared, that country was spared further dismemberment. The precarious balance among the competing great powers rather than American diplomacy and power brought about the happy outcome. Yet while Hay's diplomacy was admirably cautious and an apparent success, he seemed to imply in the 1900 circular a commitment by the United States to uphold not only the principle of commercial equality of opportunity in China, but China's territorial and administrative integrity as well. Subsequent administrations felt morally pledged to support China against the imperialist powers and, particularly during the Taft and Wilson eras, greatly enlarged the scope of Hay's policy. The two Open Door notes foreshadowed a dangerous gap between America's available power and her willingness to use it and her actual interests in China, which economically were very small and remained so despite the optimism of the late 19th century.

By 1900, the United States had attained the status of an imperial power with far-flung colonies from the Caribbean Sea across the Pacific to the shores of Asia. These possessions inevitably brought involvements in the rivalries of the great powers, as the Open Door policy in China clearly revealed. The isolationism of the past was over. But while most

Americans rejoiced in their new-found sense of power and destiny, they clung to their isolationist traditions and therefore remained psychologically unprepared for the trials that followed.

Additional Reading

Well-written and well-researched recent studies of the Spanish-American War include: Ernest R. May, *Imperial Democracy: The Emergence of America as a Great Power* (1961) which emphasizes the humanitarian factors; H. Wayne Morgan, *William McKinley and His America* (1963) and *America's Road to Empire: The War with Spain and Overseas Expansion* (1965), which depict McKinley as a stronger leader than usually thought; as does Margaret Leech, *In the Days of McKinley* (1959). Walter Millis, *The Martial Spirit* (1931) illustrates the debunking mood of revisionist writings in the interwar years, as does M. M. Wilkerson, *Public Opinion and the Spanish-American War* (1932). Julius W. Pratt, *Expansionists of 1898* (1936) revealed that big business generally opposed intervention in Cuba, but *The New Empire* (1963) by Walter La Feber argues persuasively that business finally preferred intervention to continued and disturbing uncertainty. For the role of the yellow press and Cuban propagandists, see Jacob E. Wisan, *The Cuban Crisis as Reflected in the New York Press, 1895–1898* (1934) and G. W. Auxier, "The Propaganda Activities of the Cuban *Junta* in Precipitating the Spanish-American War, 1895–1898," *Hispanic American Historical Review,* XIX (1939), 286–305 and "Middle Western Newspapers and the Spanish-American War, 1895–1898," *Mississippi Valley Historical Review,* XXVI (1940), 523–534. Also see the popular biography, *Citizen Hearst* (1961), by W. A. Swanberg. J. C. Appel, "The Unionization of Florida Cigarmakers and the Coming of the War with Spain," *Hispanic American Historical Review,* XXXVI (1956), 38–49 points out the ties between the American and Cuban labor movements. Paul S. Holbo has contributed two articles that strengthen McKinley's claims to leadership and reveal popular suspicions of the administration and Wall Street: "Presidential Leadership in Foreign Affairs: William McKinley and the Turpie-Foraker Amendment," *American Historical Review,* LXXII (1967), 1321–1335 and "The Convergence of Moods and the Cuban-Bond 'Conspiracy' of 1898," *Journal of American History,* LV (1968), 54–72. Lester D. Langley, *The Cuban Policy of the United States* (1968) is an excellent short account. E. R. May, *American Imperialism: A Speculative Essay* (1968) points out the divided attitude of opinion elites toward imperialism. Also see R. E. Osgood, *Ideals and Self-Interest in America's Foreign Relations* (1953) and Frederick Merk, *Manifest Destiny and Mission in American History* (1963). Older but still useful studies of the diplomacy and war of 1898 are by F. E. Chadwick, *The Relations of the*

United States and Spain: Diplomacy (1909) and *The Relations of the United States and Spain: The Spanish-American War* (1911); and Orestes Ferrara, *The Last Spanish War* (1937). Frank Friedel, *The Splendid Little War* (1958) is an interesting illustrated account. On the resistance to imperialism, see F. H. Harrington, "The Anti-Imperialist Movement in the United States, 1898–1900," *Mississippi Valley Historical Review,* XXII (1935), 211–230 and Robert L. Beisner, *Twelve Against Empire: The Anti-Imperialists, 1898–1900* (1968). Bryan's role is analyzed by Paolo E. Coletta, *William Jennings Bryan: Political Evangelist, 1860–1908* (1964). Excellent studies of Anglo-American relations during the war and in regard to the Open Door policy are by Charles S. Campbell, Jr., *Anglo-American Understanding, 1898–1903* (1957) and *Special Business Interests and the Open Door Policy* (1951); and Bradford Perkins, *The Great Rapprochement: England and the United States, 1895–1914* (1968). R. G. Neale, *Great Britain and United States Expansion, 1898–1900* (1966) de-emphasizes the British role in the Open Door notes. For the background of the Open Door notes see the brief account in A. W. Griswold, *The Far Eastern Policy of the United States* (1938); E. H. Zabriskie, *American-Russian Rivalry in the Far East,* 1895–1914 (1946); and Pauline Tompkins, *American-Russian Relations in the Far East* (1949). *China Market: America's Quest for Informal Empire, 1893–1901* (1967) by Thomas McCormick stresses economic expansionism. For correctives see Paul H. Varg, "The Myth of the China Market, 1890–1914," *American Historical Review,* LXXIII (1968), 742–758; Marilyn Blatt Young, "American Expansionism, 1870–1900: The Far East," in B. J. Bernstein, ed., *Towards A New Past: Dissenting Essays in American History* (1968), 176–201 and her *The Rhetoric of Empire: American China Policy, 1895–1901* (1968). Paul S. Holbo, "Economics, Emotion, and Expansion: An Emerging Foreign Policy," in H. Wayne Morgan, ed., *The Gilded Age* (2nd ed., 1970), 199–221, questions the economic interpretation of this era and attributes expansionism to accidental forces. For the role of American policy-makers see Tyler Dennett, *John Hay* (1933) and Paul H. Varg, *Open-Door Diplomat: The Life of W. W. Rockhill* (1952). The latter's *Missionaries, Chinese, and Diplomats* (1958) examines missionary influence on American policy in China. Earl S. Pomeroy, *Pacific Outpost: American Strategy in Guam and Micronesia* (1951) and W. R. Braisted, *The United States Navy in the Pacific, 1897–1909* (1958) deal with strategic factors in America's expansion into the Pacific. An excellent study of America's new great-power role and the "peace movement" is by Calvin D. Davis, *The United States and the First Hague Conference* (1962).

Battleships of the U. S. Atlantic Fleet in San Francisco harbor enroute on their cruise around the world

14

STATESMANSHIP AND DIPLOMACY IN THE EARLY 20TH CENTURY, 1901–1914

1. THEODORE ROOSEVELT: A REALIST IN THE WHITE HOUSE

As a president, Theodore Roosevelt fittingly symbolized an America just emerging as a great world power. Confident and energetic, sometimes boisterous, and trailing clouds of glory from the recent war with Spain, Roosevelt personified a new era in America's foreign relations. During his nearly eight years as President, he achieved a large degree of success in his foreign policies and contributed to the slow process of educating his countrymen to the realities of world power and responsibility.

Born in New York in 1858, Theodore Roosevelt came from a patrician family with roots in colonial America. Overcoming his frail physique as a child by a rigorous course of physical exercise and body building, Roosevelt acquired a lifelong emphasis—perhaps an overemphasis—on the virtues of physical strength and courage for the individual and for the nation. After graduation from Harvard, where he made Phi Beta Kappa, he surprised his family by entering politics. In 1897, President McKinley appointed him Assistant Secretary of the Navy. Roosevelt performed ably, occasionally embarrassing his superiors by his excessive zeal for naval expansion and preparedness. Nurtured on tales of chivalry and combat, and eager for an opportunity for martial glory, Roosevelt resigned his post upon the outbreak of the war with Spain and organized a volunteer outfit known as the Rough Riders. Modestly accepting second command, Roosevelt maneuvered his outfit into Cuba and the immortal charge up San Juan Hill (actually Kettle Hill). Exploiting his well-trumpeted deeds in Cuba (humorist Finley Peter Dunne quipped that Roosevelt should entitle a book on the war, "Alone in Cubia"), Roosevelt gained the Republican nomination for governor of New York and won the election in 1898. Two years later, he accepted the vice presidency under McKinley, and from there McKinley's assassination catapulted him into the presidency on September 14, 1901, six weeks before his 43rd birthday.

Roosevelt brought to the White House a number of characteristics conducive to an effective administration. He was versatile and energetic, knowledgeable in a wide range of topics from science to literature, a historian of some repute (of the West and the navy), and almost incessantly active—boxing, taking jujitsu lessons, playing tennis, walking, and horseback riding—while serving as chief executive. The young President proved particularly trying to ambitious politicans and diplomats. Invited for an apparently innocent day of walking in Washington's Rock Creek Park, an unwary envoy might find himself following the President through streams and thickets or climbing rocks for hours. One diplomat who successfully survived this trial, France's Ambassador Jules Jusserand, afterwards felt thankful that he had been a mountain climber in his youth. Roosevelt had a marked tendency to moralize, speaking and writing in platitudes and seeing political issues as moral crusades.

Prior to entering the White House, Roosevelt had gained a reputation for impetuosity and bellicosity. He admired strength, courage, sacrifice, and daring, and long believed that the country needed a touch of blood and iron in war to purify the materialist dross from its soul and to remind people that there were nobler things than earning a dollar. Yet as President, sobered by the passage of time and his new and awesome responsibilities, Roosevelt usually showed admirable caution and restraint in the conduct of foreign relations. He kept close watch on all major diplomatic developments, and he sometimes conducted delicate exchanges personally and outside the machinery of the State Department. Above all, Roosevelt was a highly intelligent man, and a charismatic leader who was unusually aware of the currents and problems of the times and who tried to delineate a responsible course for the nation at home and abroad.

In foreign policy Roosevelt was a realistic nationalist. He viewed the international arena in Darwinist terms as a struggle for survival and power, where nations pursued their own self-interests and depended in the ultimate analysis on force for their security. Pacifists and advocates of disarmament demonstrated naiveté, he felt, for failing to understand that in this jealous world war was always possible, even probable. Moreover, Roosevelt believed that some wars were morally just, and that the national honor and vital interests demanded power and a willingness to use it when necessary. Nations should be scrupulously fair with each other, he contended, and quick to resent threats to their honor or interests. Yet in general he was a satisfied imperialist by 1901; the country had sufficient territory, colonies, and bases (except for an isthmian canal) for its needs. The nation now required a foreign policy adequate to protect its interests and to help it play a responsible role in the world, necessitated, as he saw it, by America's great power and its geographical position between Europe and East Asia.

Adequate power and no bluffing, in Roosevelt's view, comprised the essentials of foreign policy. He fondly quoted a West African proverb, "Speak softly and carry a big stick, you will go far." Because of the position of the United States, fronting on two vast oceans with far-flung overseas possessions and a growing commerce, adequate power to support its diplomacy meant sea power. For the immediate future, Roosevelt and his advisers no doubt exaggerated the dangers facing the nation. Great Britain did not pose a threat, and imperial Germany, for all the ambition and swashbuckling posturing of its ruler Kaiser Wilhelm II, faced enemies in Europe and lacked bases for operations in the Western Hemisphere. But a general European conflagration or a pronounced shift in the existing distribution of power could have undesirable long-range implications for America. Regarding the Pacific, on the other hand, because of the vulnerability of the Philippines, the United States had a direct interest in the balance of power in East Asia.

As President, Roosevelt took a great interest in the growth of American sea power. Despite mounting opposition from pacifists and from others who feared that a large navy would lead to dangerous involvements abroad, he did not slacken the pace of expansionism until 1905. During those four years, Congress authorized the construction of ten first-class battleships, four armored cruisers, and 17 other craft. In December of 1905, Roosevelt announced a breathing spell. The United States Navy had reached the point where it would soon rank second only to that of Great Britain, and Roosevelt estimated that thereafter Congress would only need to authorize one new battleship annually for the replacement of obsolete units. Yet even then a naval revolution had started. Great Britain completed the H.M.S. *Dreadnought* in 1906, the first all big gun battleship. All previously built battleships immediately became obsolete, and the American Navy prepared to construct its own dreadnoughts. In 1907 and 1908 Roosevelt requested Congress to authorize four of the new type of warship. Although he did not really fear an immediate war with Japan, he did perceive long-range dangers from that quarter and from threatened shifts in the European balance. Therefore he took advantage of controversies with Japan (see Chapter 16), to goad Congress into increased appropriations. Congress used against him his own 1905 pronouncements of the reasons for a lull, and he had to settle for less than he requested. As a result of the naval race between Britain and Germany, and defects in the nature and organization of the American navy, the United States declined from approximately number two in naval power in 1907 to perhaps number three or four by 1914.

A rapprochement in Anglo-American relations, initiated by the British, had begun as early as 1896–1897. Alarmed by the unexpected Venezuelan boundary crisis in 1895, a number of influential Britishers launched a deliberate program to cultivate better relations with the United States. Britain felt isolated from the European continent, where the rival alliances of Germany, Austria-Hungary, and Italy—the Triple Alliance—glowered at the Dual Alliance of France and Russia. Moreover, Great Britain soon became involved in a naval race with Germany, and in clashes over colonies or spheres of influence with France, Russia, and Germany. Under these circumstances, Britain sought to shore up her flanks. Eventually she concluded an alliance with Japan in 1902, and reached colonial understandings or ententes with France in 1904 and with Russia in 1907. Europe was moving perceptibly nearer the threshold of a major world war between the Triple Alliance and what came to be called the Triple Entente.

British wooing of America fared well. The two English-speaking nations had long had close cultural and economic ties, strengthened by many marriages between members of the British and American upper classes. In 1897, as the Venezuelan issue abated, Great Britain and the United States signed a general arbitration treaty intended to prevent a future confrontation. Although the Senate defeated it, jealous of its role in foreign policy, the pact signaled a new spirit of conciliation between the two countries. During the Spanish-American War, the English held distinctly pro-American sentiments, in contrast to the animosity or criticism generally felt on the continent. Prominent men in England founded an Anglo-American League in 1898 to work for closer relations with the United States, and the central float in the annual London Lord Mayor's parade of that year depicted Columbia and Britannia embracing over the label "sea power." Similar groups in the United States worked for hands across the sea. Joseph Chamberlain, Britain's Colonial Secretary, who had an American wife, even proposed an Anglo-American alliance during the war with Spain. Although neither government ever seriously considered an alliance, a number of Americans responded favorably.

Theodore Roosevelt joined the ranks of those influential Americans converted to the cause of closer Anglo-American friendship. Like his friends, A. T. Mahan, Henry and Brooks Adams, and John Hay, he believed that British and American interests in world stability and prosperous commerce paralleled each other, and that friendly cooperation with Great Britain should become the pivot of America's foreign policy. Both countries were great commercial and naval powers, and shared similar political principles. England, he agreed with the two Adamses, might be slowly declining in power, but America's responsibility rested in preparing to take over her civilizing role in the world. While seeking as close an understanding as possible with Great Britain, Roosevelt asked that she recognize the preeminence of the United

States within the Western Hemisphere and that she settle the remaining controversies to America's satisfaction.

The British government consented, particularly after the Boer War underscored her isolated position in Europe. In the second Hay-Pauncefote Treaty in 1901 (discussed in Chapter 15), Britain agreed to discard the Clayton-Bulwer Treaty and to accept American control and fortification of an isthmian canal. Subsequently, to meet the German challenge in Europe, Britain withdrew naval units from the Caribbean Sea and welcomed America's policeman role under the so-called Roosevelt Corollary to the Monroe Doctrine.

In 1903, Britain also settled the Alaska boundary dispute in favor of the United States. The question revolved around whether the boundary of the Alaska panhandle should run approximately 30 miles inland along a straight line drawn parallel to the coast, as Canadians insisted, or should follow the irregularities of the coast, as the United States maintained. The American case seemed stronger, based on the language and intent of the 1825 Russian treaty with Great Britain and the 1867 Alaska purchase treaty, but Canada sought a waterway through the panhandle. A gold strike in the Klondike made the problem more acute. In 1903 the two parties, with Canadian consent, signed a treaty agreeing to submit the controversy to a commission of "impartial jurists." Convinced that righteousness rested on the side of the United States, President Roosevelt appointed two politicians and the Secretary of War as his "impartial jurists" and let the British authorities know of his determination to run the correct boundary unilaterally if the commission decided incorrectly. The British jurist, influenced no doubt by expediency as well as justice, voted with the three Americans against his two Canadian colleagues. Canadians reacted angrily to what they regarded as a sacrifice at their expense, but the event sealed Anglo-American friendship.

Roosevelt had a genuine, if exaggerated, apprehension of Germany and its alleged threat to the Monroe Doctrine. For some time prior to his becoming president, a measure of mutual suspicion had characterized German-American relations. Latecomers to the world scene as major industrial and naval powers, both nations to a degree faced conflicting interests in colonies, bases, and trade. Rivalry had once focused on Samoa until they settled it by partition in 1899. Americans also viewed Germany as one of the main threats to China and the Open Door. During the Spanish-American War, under the mistaken impression that the United States would not retain the Philippines, the German government showed a definite interest in the islands. Moreover, the movements of German naval vessels greatly annoyed Dewey while he blockaded Manila and a legend grew up that Germany had planned to intervene on the Spanish side if a favorable opportunity had arisen. In

Latin America, German immigration and aggressive commercial activities aroused fears of colonization or political control, and suspicions rightly arose that the German navy sought stations in the strategically important Caribbean Sea. The government in Berlin, however, realized that any attempt to acquire bases there inevitably would lead to serious difficulties with the United States.

Kaiser Wilhelm II made several overtures for friendship during Roosevelt's administration. The Kaiser established close contacts with the American President and sent his brother, Prince Henry, on a goodwill visit to the United States. Roosevelt rather liked the German emperor, but regarded him as too "jumpy" and unpredictable. Moreover, his realistic appraisal of the European balance of power and America's interest in it led him to regard Germany as the principal danger to peace and stability. He therefore insisted on keeping the battleship fleet intact in the Atlantic to protect the Western Hemisphere against possible threats from Europe, which in the context of the times could only come from Germany.

Roosevelt foresaw that a major European war would disturb the balance of power and in other ways would affect America's interest. Consequently he used his influence in trying to maintain peace and stability whenever a major war seemed likely to erupt in Europe. He favored arms limitations, not disarmament, at the Second Hague Conference that met in 1907. Although the conference achieved little of concrete value, it at least improved the general diplomatic climate. During the Moroccan crisis of 1905, Roosevelt reluctantly took part in its peaceful resolution. Seeking to disrupt the Anglo-French entente, Germany challenged France's influence in Morocco. In the war crisis that followed, Berlin sought to humiliate France and insisted upon an international conference to settle the issue. Roosevelt reluctantly agreed to use his influence on behalf of a conference, fearing war otherwise and a possible French defeat. He assured France that he would not be a party to her humiliation, and secured what he regarded as the Kaiser's promise to accept any solution proposed by the American President in case of a deadlock.

The Conference met at Algeciras, Spain, in 1906. Germany found herself almost completely isolated because of her overly aggressive tactics and demands. Faced with a deadlock, Roosevelt invoked the Kaiser's "promise" and helped obtain acceptance of a compromise. The Act of Algeciras preserved Moroccan independence in theory while leaving France a predominant economic and political role in the country. The entente remained intact, and Germany had suffered a diplomatic check. The United States signed the Act of Algeciras and the Senate reluctantly approved it after appending a reservation that it in no way signified the country's abandonment of its traditional isolationism. Roosevelt's critics charged reckless meddling in purely European affairs.

He defended himself on the feeble grounds of upholding the commercial open door everywhere (America had little trade with Morocco), and most Americans applauded his role as peacemaker. His primary motive of course had not been to protect the open door in Morocco but to maintain peace and the balance of power in Europe.

In the western Pacific and East Asia, Roosevelt also tried to promote a stable balance of power. Prior to 1905 he viewed Russia as the principal threat to the Open Door in China, and saw Japan as the natural counterweight. After Japan revealed her greater power in the Russo-Japanese War, Roosevelt accepted that fact and relied upon Japanese moderation and friendly Japanese-American relations to safeguard the interests of the United States in the western Pacific. He clearly understood that neither American interests in China nor the attitude of the American people would permit a vigorous defense of the Open Door. In his view, cooperation with Great Britain and above all conciliation with Japan offered the only bases for a viable American policy in that region.

Roosevelt's policies toward Asia and Europe have been criticized as reflecting too much the older diplomacy of imperialism and as ultimately a failure. Such criticism seems unfair. He could hardly be blamed for operating within the context of his times or for failures that followed his administration. When he left office in March, 1909, the United States commanded unusual prestige and influence abroad, its interests seemed adequately secured, and peace reigned in the world. It was hardly his fault that his successors abandoned his realistic course in East Asia and failed to recognize the role that America might play in helping to preserve peace in Europe. Roosevelt's diplomacy revealed great skill and responsibility, and he made some contribution, though perforce limited, in educating his fellow citizens to the world role their nation ought to play.

2. TAFT AND DOLLAR DIPLOMACY

Roosevelt virtually hand-picked his successor, William Howard Taft, in the expectation that he would continue "my policies." The portly Taft, born in 1857 in Ohio, had spent most of his life in governmental service. The law was his first love, and he had served as a federal judge until appointed by McKinley in 1900 to head a five-man commission to organize government in the newly acquired Philippines. Impressed with Taft's administrative talents, Roosevelt named him Secretary of War in 1904. Taft's greatest ambition was to serve on the United States Supreme Court (later Warren G. Harding named him Chief Justice), but his ambitious wife and his brother persuaded him to seek the presidency despite his self-doubts. He won an easy victory over Bryan, once more the Democratic nominee, in 1908.

Taft quickly revealed not only a vastly different presidential style from Roosevelt but he also departed to some degree from the latter's approach to foreign policy. In East Asia, Taft and Secretary of State Philander C. Knox, a corporation lawyer, embarked upon an energetic course designed to advance America's economic interests in China and to challenge the Russian and Japanese spheres of influence in Manchuria. In the Caribbean, the new administration continued the essence of Roosevelt's policy but in a more blundering fashion. In both areas, exaggerated concepts of the nation's interest produced unfortunate results.

Taft relied heavily upon Secretary Knox in foreign policy. Sharing the outlook of the big business community, Knox favored a "spirited foreign commercial policy" and the President agreed with him. The American economy was growing prodigiously, surpassing both Germany and Great Britain in steel production, and doubling in industrial production between 1899 and 1917. The administration resolved, therefore, to use foreign policy and diplomacy not only to protect American economic interests abroad but to advance and encourage those interests. Consequently, the administration reorganized the State Department to increase its efficiency and to give closer attention to economic affairs. The Taft-Knox approach of course went beyond merely economic goals; they sincerely believed that "substituting dollars for bullets," as the President expressed it in 1912, would benefit the foreign countries concerned as well as America. Government concern about overseas markets and the protection of American interests did not represent a new policy; this administration differed chiefly in its rhetoric and all too often in its blundering, unrealistic diplomacy.

Misfortune seemed to plague Taft and Knox even when their foreign goals seemed most praiseworthy. In 1911 the North Pacific Sealing Convention satisfactorily settled the fur seals controversy, dating back to a sharp clash with Canada in the early 1890's over pelagic sealing (indiscriminate killing of seals while swimming), by closely regulating the hunting of seals. And in 1912, an Anglo-American convention also adjusted the perennial fisheries dispute. But an attempt to revive commercial reciprocity with Canada backfired embarrassingly. By the terms of a reciprocity agreement signed in 1911, eagerly desired by Canadian agricultural and timber interests, Canadian farm and forestry products could enter the United States duty-free or at reduced rates, while American manufacturers obtained similar benefits in Canada. Several American advocates of reciprocity unwisely referred to it as a prelude to annexation, while Taft himself undiplomatically spoke of the "peculiar interests" binding the two economies together. This aroused Canadian nationalism, and reciprocity became a burning issue in the general election of 1911. Powerful economic interests in Canada—shipping, railroads, and manufacturers who feared increased competition with American firms—contributed handsomely to opponents of the 1911 agreement. Their efforts resulted in defeat for the party in power and rejection of reciprocity. These developments served to humiliate the Taft administration and to put a strain on Canadian-American relations, but they also exorcised the ghost of annexation once and for all.

Taft also met defeat in his "peace" policy in 1911. The peace movement in America and abroad had gained momentum, encouraged by the Hague Conferences of 1899 and 1907, and the Root Treaties of 1908–1909, in which the parties agreed to submit to arbitration all questions not involving vital interests or honor. Because of this growing sentiment and a desire to take advantage of a provision of the Anglo-Japanese Alliance, renewed in 1911, that precluded its invocation against a power having an arbitration treaty with one of the signatories, Taft negotiated sweeping arbitration treaties with Great Britain and France in 1911. Those pacts made all disputes, including those affecting vital interests and national honor, subject to arbitration. Peace enthusiasts showered Taft with praise and hailed the beginning of a new era of world tranquility, all to no avail. The Senate, fearful that specific issues would go before tribunals without its consent, so mutilated the treaties that Taft disgustedly abandoned them.

The second Moroccan crisis, in 1911, offered a graphic illustration, at least to the perceptive, of the American people's failure to appreciate their country's new role as a world power. Theodore Roosevelt had intervened diplomatically in the first crisis because he foresaw the unpleasant consequences of a general European war to the interests of the United States. When the German gunboat *Panther* arrived at Agadir in 1911, ostensibly to protect German interests in Morocco but actually to coerce France into colonial concessions in the French Congo, it briefly threatened a major international crisis, yet President Taft failed to act. He hoped for peace, of course, but he apparently deemed the issue beyond the scope of America's traditional policy of noninvolvement in European politics. Similarly, neither he nor his successor, President Woodrow Wilson, took any part in the first and second Balkan wars of 1911 and 1913 that helped set the stage for World War I.

3. WILSON AND THE DIPLOMACY OF MORALITY

Woodrow Wilson led the Democratic Party to victory against the splintered Republican ranks in the 1912 presidential election. Born in Virginia in 1856, Wilson adopted from his father, a Presbyterian minister and theologian, the conviction that God called all men to their special vocations. Woodrow Wilson firmly believed that he had a distinct moral duty in the fulfillment of the Divine will in this world, and he approached first academic life and then politics and statecraft as a sort of lay minister charged with spreading moral enlightenment. Educated at Princeton, Wilson, after a brief flirtation with the study of law, earned a doctorate of philosophy in history and political science at Johns Hopkins University and embarked upon a career as a college teacher. A prolific writer of histories that were well-received by his peers, and an inspiring teacher, Wilson mounted the academic ladder and in 1902 gained the distinction of becoming Princeton's first lay president. There, despite two reverses that reflected his reluctance to compromise and his tendency to convert controversies over issues into personal quarrels, Wilson introduced significant academic reforms and acquired the reputation of an outstanding educational leader. Entering politics, he was elected governor of New Jersey in 1910 and during his term won national attention as a progressive reformer. He overcame his rivals to obtain the Democratic presidential nomination in 1912 and then defeated his Republican and Progressive Party adversaries, Taft and Roosevelt.

Woodrow Wilson brought to the presidency surprisingly little knowledge of or interest in foreign affairs. Despite his academic background and travel abroad, he had concentrated his attention on questions of domestic government and progressive reform. The Spanish-American War and its results had convinced Wilson, like most other educated Americans, that the age of isolationism had come to an end; expanding commercially and destined to preeminence in the underdeveloped areas of the world, America thenceforth would have to take a larger part in world affairs. Yet, in contrast to the well-developed view of world politics held by Theodore Roosevelt, Wilson's knowledge and interest in 1913 were superficial. Certain personal characteristics and qualities of the new chief executive, however, eventually made him enormously effective as a leader and elevated him to a commanding world stature: moral zeal, idealism, personal courage, and an eloquence capable of projecting issues and mobilizing the enthusiasms and energies of ordinary men everywhere. Unfortunately, as time also revealed, Wilson had several serious defects. He tended, increasingly with the years, toward rigidity and an inability to compromise. Once Wilson had decided that a given policy or course was morally correct, he tended to reject all criticism and to view his opponents as misguided or worse.

Wilson reluctantly named, for political reasons, William Jennings Bryan, thrice the Democratic presidential candidate, as Secretary of State. Bryan had no more knowledge than his chief about foreign affairs. Little in his previous career prepared him for his new responsibility. He appraised foreign developments not as they actually happened but by the yardstick of American values and practices. Like Wilson, he too was thoroughly imbued with the Protestant ethic and approached foreign politics from a moral point of view. He thoroughly believed, as Wilson eventually did, that the world would inevitably evolve toward universal peace and democracy. After his defeat in the 1904 election, Bryan had undertaken a world tour. He recorded his experiences for his admirers in *The Old World and Its Ways,* an amazing compendium of superficial observations and misleading evidence that corroborated his fondest dreams of world Christianity, disarmament and peace, and universal democracy.

The new President and his Secretary of State intended to use America's power and influence in world affairs to serve not merely the best interests of the United States but those of other peoples as well. It was America's mission to benefit the world by spreading enlightened commerce and political principles. According to Wilson and Bryan the New Freedom diplomacy had to advance not only the legitimate material interests of the nation, but had to accomplish this in keeping with the highest standards of morality and principle. Laudable in theory, if not always in practice, Wilson and Bryan practiced what has been aptly christened "missionary diplomacy"—a sort of purified Manifest Destiny or sense of national mission.

Bryan's "cooling-off" treaties illustrated the naiveté as well as the ideals of "uplift" diplomacy. Inclined toward pacifism and congenitally optimistic, Bryan never wavered in his faith that warfare in a civilized world had become outmoded and increasingly unthinkable. He agreed with other peace advocates that moral law and reason inevitably would triumph over brute force and, as the foremost Christian and democratic state, America had to lead the way toward that goal. President Wilson shared Bryan's hopes. Reared in the Civil War and Reconstruction South, Wilson too had acquired an abiding abhorrence of war and its suffering. He did not harbor the same pacifist ideals as Bryan, however, believing that some wars were just because of the moral issues and principles involved, but he accepted Bryan's plans for a new contribution to the cause of peace.

Bryan designed the "cooling-off" pacts to circumvent the Senate's well-known aversion to binding arbitration treaties. He attempted to accomplish this by negotiating bilateral pacts to submit *all* issues not otherwise solvable to special commissions for investigation. During the time of the investigation and while the commissioners were drawing up their report, both signatory nations would pledge not to resort to arms. After the report, either party could reject it and wage war, but Bryan felt confident that the delay of approximately a year would cool tempers sufficiently to preclude hostilities. Obviously Bryan regarded warfare as a temporary lapse into insanity or irrationality. His simplistic philosophy overlooked the fact that not all countries accepted the status quo as readily as the United States. Peace obviously did not have the same overriding value to all states and many governments still viewed war as a legitimate tool to promote national interests.

Bryan negotiated 30 cooling-off pacts with countries ranging from tiny El Salvador to mighty Britain and France. Germany did not see fit to do so, which it subsequently regretted during World War I, but Bryan took comfort that Berlin professed agreement with the principles involved. Bryan successfully shepherded 22 of the innocuous pacts through the ever-watchful Senate. The French ambassador, Jules Jusserand, reportedly quipped after signing one, "There! At last will end for all time the ceaseless wars between France and the United States. What a happy hour!" And some newspapers sneered at the great relief of being spared wars with El Salvador and Guatemala. Perhaps such criticisms were unfair. Peace advocates praised the treaties as a major contribution to world stability, since they covered even questions of vital national interests and honor. Bryan proudly viewed his treaties as his greatest achievement as Secretary of State, and President Wilson shared his sense of satisfaction.

The more "respectable" classes of society here and in Europe held Bryan in contempt, as the amusement greeting his peace treaties indicated. In many ways, he represented a poor choice for the venerable State Department. He favored the spoils system, believing in replacing Republican officeholders with loyal Democrats. So many hungry job-seekers descended upon him during his first days in office that they clogged the corridors of the State Department and disrupted regular work. He replaced able men in the department and the foreign service with ill-prepared amateurs and an occasional political hack. If not restrained by President Wilson, he probably would have made a clean sweep of all diplomatic and consular posts, though in fairness it must be noted that the President himself was directly responsible for a number of political appointments. Bryan's actions resulted in a greatly lowered morale in the career foreign service that Roosevelt and Taft had begun to build, and decreased efficiency in America's representation abroad.

Less worthy criticism focused on Bryan's personal habits and dress. His substitution of grape juice for alcoholic beverages at state dinners greatly amused his critics. "Grape-juice diplomacy" became a byword, the butt of numerous jokes and sneers. The Secretary's homey habits—he personally shopped for groceries and took a dinner pail to the State Department like an ordinary workingman—and his continued lecturing for pay on the Chautauqua circuit, allegedly sandwiched between programs of magicians and other circus entertainers, provided abundant opportunity for ridicule to the eastern and European presses. He was even accused, incorrectly, of neglecting his official duties for lecturing. In fact, Bryan was hard working, spending far more time at his desk than his Republican predecessor, Philander C. Knox, and performing many useful political tasks for the administration and its legislative program.

Wilson enjoyed one early success—a resolution of the Panama tolls question. Although the Hay-Pauncefote Treaty in 1901 had specified that the shipping of "all nations" using the Panama Canal should pay equal rates, Congress interpreted that as referring only to "all *other* nations." Therefore, in 1912 it exempted American coastal vessels passing through the waterway from payment of tolls. Great Britain naturally protested the exemption as an unfair discrimination and a violation of treaty obligations. Yet the Taft administration refused to submit the issue to arbitration. Many Americans, including President Wilson, considered that an act of bad faith and a stain upon the nation's honor. After a delay due to domestic political factors, Wilson in 1914 requested repeal of the exemption as a matter of national honor. As he told Congress and the people, "we are too big, too powerful, too self-respecting a Nation to interpret with too strained or refined a reading the words of our own promises. . . ." Despite stubborn opposition from agrarians and anglophobes, especially Irish-Americans, Congress passed the repeal measure. Wilson's victory had great significance, vindicating the nation's honor throughout the world, improving the climate of diplomatic relations with Latin America, and removing a serious barrier to Anglo-American cooperation. As the London *Times* editorialized, the President had won "the approbation and respect of all that is best amongst the English-speaking nations of the globe."

Additional Reading

Howard K. Beale, *Theodore Roosevelt and the Rise of America to World Power* (1956) offers a careful and well-researched analysis of Rooseveltian foreign policy. Also see Raymond A. Esthus, *Theodore Roosevelt and the International Rivalries* (1970). An excellent biography is by William H. Harbaugh, *Power and Responsibility, The Life and Times of Theodore Roosevelt* (1961). See also D. H. Burton, *Theodore Roosevelt: Confident Imperialist* (1968) and John M. Blum, *The Republican Roosevelt* (1954). Older but colorful accounts are *Theodore Roosevelt* (1931), by H. F. Pringle, and A. L. P. Dennis, *Adventures in American Diplomacy, 1896–1906* (1928). For Roosevelt's Secretaries of State, see Tyler Dennett, *John Hay: From Poetry to Politics* (1938); Richard W. Leopold, *Elihu Root and the Conservative Tradition* (1954); and the interpretive essays on Hay and Root by F. R. Dulles and Charles W. Toth, respectively, in Norman Graebner, ed., *An Uncertain Tradition: American Secretaries of State in the Twentieth Century* (1961), 22–39, 40–58. Nelson M. Blake, "Ambassadors at the Court of Theodore Roosevelt," *Mississippi Valley Historical Review*, XLII (1955), 179–206, gives an amusing account of T. R.'s strenuous personal diplomacy. Robert E. Osgood, *Ideals and Self-Interest in America's Foreign Relations* (1953) analyzes T. R. as a romantic nationalist in foreign affairs. Anglo-American relations are examined by H. C. Allen, *Great Britain and the United States,* (1955); A. E. Campbell, *Great Britain and the United States, 1895–1903* (1960); Charles S. Campbell, Jr., *Anglo-American Understanding, 1898–1903* (1957); and Bradford Perkins, *The Great Rapprochement: England and the United States, 1895–1914* (1968). The gradual deterioration of German-American relations is traced by C. E. Schieber, *The Transformation of American Sentiment Toward Germany, 1870–1914* (1923). Harold and Margaret Sprout, *The Rise of American Naval Power, 1776–1918* (1944) and William R. Braisted, *The United States Navy in the Pacific, 1897–1909* (1958) examine naval expansion during the Progressive Era. On the Taft era, see W. V. Scholes and M. V. Scholes, *The Foreign Policies of the Taft Administration* (1970) and H. F. Pringle, *The Life and Times of William Howard Taft* (2 vols., 1939). John P. Campbell, "Taft, Roosevelt, and the Arbitration Treaties of 1911," *Journal of American History,* LIII (1966), 279–298, discusses the failure of the pacts. Canadian relations are treated by C. C. Tansill, *Canadian-American Relations, 1875–1911* (1943) and L. Ethan Ellis, *Reciprocity of 1911* (1939). A good account of the foreign and domestic policies of Roosevelt and Taft is by George E. Mowry, *The Era of Theodore Roosevelt and the Birth of Modern America, 1900–1912* (1958). Studies of Woodrow Wilson are numerous. The latest and probably most definitive biography is by Arthur S. Link, *Wilson* (5 vols. to date, 1947–1965). Link's *Wilson the Diplomatist* (1957) is a series of incisive interpretive essays on Wilson's approach to foreign policy and his *Woodrow Wilson and the Progessive Era, 1910–1917* (1954) is very informative. Older but still useful is Harley Notter, *The Origins of the Foreign Policy of Woodrow Wilson* (1937). Excellent short biographies are by John M. Blum, *Woodrow Wilson and the Politics of Morality* (1956) and John A. Garraty, *Woodrow Wilson, a Great Life in Brief* (1956). For psychological studies of Wilson, see A. L. and J. L. George, *Woodrow Wilson and Colonel House* (1956), a well-researched and persuasive study, and the more dogmatic and marred effort by Sigmund Freud and William C. Bullitt, *Thomas Woodrow Wilson* (1967). The best study of Bryan as Secretary of State is by Paolo E. Colletta, *William Jennings Bryan: Progressive Politician and Moral Statesman, 1909–1915* (1969). The essay on Bryan by Richard Challener, in Norman Graebner, ed., *An Uncertain Tradition,* 79–100, is a model of its kind. On the Panama tolls issue, see the recent article by William S. Coker, "The Panama Tolls Controversy: A Different Perspective," *Journal of American History,* LV (1968), 555–564.

The Big Stick in action

15

SECURITY AND BENEVOLENCE
IN LATIN AMERICA,
1901–1921

1. AN ISTHMIAN LIFELINE

The Spanish-American War gave a new urgency to the centuries-old
dream of a canal to bridge the Pacific and Atlantic Oceans through
Central America. The famous voyage of the battleship *Oregon* dramatized the need. Caught on the west coast by the outbreak of hostilities,
the *Oregon* took 68 days to steam at forced draft nearly 13,000 nautical
miles around South America via Magellan Strait to join other naval units
assembled at Key West. After the war, new territories and new defense
responsibilities made a canal imperative. A canal would enable the navy
to move rapidly from one ocean to the other as international crises might
require. Besides aiding defense, a canal would greatly facilitate American
commerce with Latin America and Asia. American policy from 1898,
consequently, had the twofold goal of acquiring a site and constructing a
canal, and obtaining adequate bases to defend it.

First it was necessary to remove the obstacle of the 1850 Clayton-
Bulwer Treaty. That pact with Great Britain had pledged both powers in
effect to exercise joint control over and to maintain the neutrality of any
isthmian canal. Yet as President McKinley told Congress in 1898,
defense considerations required that the United States alone own and
control such a waterway. Although Britain had earlier rebuffed proposals
to modify the 1850 treaty, it seemed willing to yield by the late 1890's. In
the Hay-Pauncefote Treaty of 1900 Britain agreed to permit the United
States to build and operate an unfortified isthmian canal, open on equal
terms to the commercial and war vessels of all nations in peace and in
war. Britons thought they had made a notable concession to the United
States in an area where they had great commercial and strategic

interests. Nevertheless, the treaty met sharp criticism from many Americans. As Theodore Roosevelt pointed out, an unfortified canal would be vulnerable to attack from any strong power and would tie down the American navy in guarding it. Many also denounced the treaty as a violation of the Monroe Doctrine, by involving non-American powers in the control of an isthmian waterway. When the Senate began to amend the treaty to repair these defects, a disgusted Secretary Hay abandoned it and reopened negotiations for a more acceptable pact. Since the British government placed a high value upon America's friendship in this era of rapprochement, the second Hay-Pauncefote Treaty was signed in 1901 and approved by the Senate. The Clayton-Bulwer Treaty was scrapped and, by implication, this permitted the United States to fortify as well as to control an isthmian canal.

A site for the canal posed the next problem. Although the Walker Canal Commission judged the Panama route as preferable, it recommended Nicaragua because of the price asked by the New Panama Canal Company (a French chartered firm) for its Panama concessions. Nelson Cromwell, a New York lawyer, and Philippe Bunau-Varilla, a French stockholder, cooperated effectively as lobbyists for the Panama route. They persuaded the New Panama Canal Company to reduce its price from $109 million to $40 million and, aided by timely volcanic activity in Nicaragua, got Congress to amend a bill for a Nicaraguan canal. Congress authorized the executive to construct a waterway across Panama if the French company would sell its rights for no more than $40 million and if Colombia would agree to the project; if not arranged within "a reasonable time" and upon "reasonable terms," the United States would turn to Nicaragua. President Roosevelt ardently advocated the Panama project, simply because most experts favored it. Although actual construction proved more costly than anticipated, American engineers planning a second canal in the 1960's still chose Panama over Nicaragua.

One of the most questionable episodes in the annals of American diplomacy followed Congress's decision. Exploiting the threat of the Nicaraguan alternative, Secretary Hay persuaded Tomás Herrán, Colombia's chargé in Washington, to sign the Hay-Herrán Treaty in January, 1903, leasing to the United States for 100 years, and renewable at America's option, a canal zone six miles wide across Panama, for which the United States would pay $10 million and an annual rental after the first nine years of $250,000. The American Senate quickly approved the treaty. Colombia reacted adversely, however, because of internal politics, the apparent diminution of Colombian sovereignty, and an understandable resentment at receiving only one-fourth as much money as the new Panama Canal Company. Apparently Colombians hoped to force the United States to raise the offer to $15 million, or to wait until the charter of the French company expired and thereby obtain some or all of its share. Regardless of its motives, the Colombian government obviously had the right to dispose of the nation's assets as it pleased. Yet President Roosevelt, anxious to get construction under way and eager to garland his forthcoming race for the presidency, became outraged at what he regarded as inexcusable obstructionism and blackmail tactics by those "foolish and homicidal corruptionists" in Colombia. He wrote Secretary Hay, " . . . I do not think that the Bogotá lot of jack rabbits should be allowed permanently to bar one of the future highways of civilization." A sharp and threatening note from the State Department failed to prevent the Colombian Senate from rejecting the treaty.

A revolution in Panama "solved" the problem. Prior to that event, Roosevelt had contemplated seizing the canal route under what he called an international right of eminent domain, or by stretching the terms and meaning of the 1846 Bidlack Treaty whereby the United States had guaranteed Colombia the maintenance of free transit across the isthmus. While Roosevelt was drafting a message to Congress justifying such a defiance of Colombia's sovereignty, a small group of conspirators, led by Dr. Manuel Amador, set the stage for revolution in Panama. That province had long resented Colombian rule and had risen in revolt repeatedly in the past. Fear that the United States might turn to the Nicaraguan route and leave Panama to its economic backwardness increased Panamanian discontent. Similarly anxious, representatives of the New Panama Canal Company assured the plotters that Washington would not allow a revolt to fail. Bunau-Varilla had conferred with President Roosevelt and State Department officials. While he had not requested or received any direct assurances, he felt confident that the administration would welcome a revolution. It seems clear that Roosevelt and his advisors were not directly involved, but it is equally obvious that they had a good idea of what was coming and welcomed it.

The rebels unfurled the standard of revolt in Panama City on the evening of November 3, 1903. Utilizing funds supplied by Bunau-Varilla to bribe the detachment of Colombian troops in the city, the rebel leaders mobilized a motley army of railroad section hands and the Panama City fire brigade. American warships, under the guise of enforcing the 1846 treaty, prevented Colombia from landing additional troops to suppress the revolt. Assured of success, the rebels proclaimed the independence of Panama on November 4. Paying off the bribed Colombian officials and troops in Panama City—enlisted men received $50 in gold while the officers got $10,000 or more each—the new republic's leaders publicly hailed President Roosevelt. "The world is astounded at our heroism!" Dr. Amador, the new republic's first President, declaimed, "President Roosevelt has made good. . . ." Roosevelt quickly authorized diplomatic recognition, completed on November 6, and on November 18 Secretary Hay hastily concluded a canal treaty with the republic's first minister to Washington, Bunau-Varilla.

The Hay–Bunau-Varilla Treaty granted the United States a ten-mile wide canal zone in perpetuity, and other rights that made Panama essentially a protectorate, for the same financial terms previously offered Colombia. The Senate granted its approval, and the New Panama Canal Company received its $40 million. Colombia alone emerged empty-handed, shorn of one of its most valuable possessions. Roosevelt vigorously defended his administration against charges of wrongdoing, declaring that the United States had dealt with Colombia on a basis not merely of justice "but of generosity." Later, when he was out of office, he boasted " . . . I took the canal zone and let Congress debate. . . ." The Taft and Wilson administrations subsequently offered financial compensation for the wrong. By that time, Latin American goodwill, possible Yankee oil concessions in Colombia, and American honor, seemed to make some kind of an apology necessary. Yet a treaty could not be pushed through the Senate until 1921, after Roosevelt's death, to pay Colombia $25 million for her loss.

It was unfortunate that Roosevelt had not shown greater willingness to offer Colombia more in 1903, or to adopt the Nicaraguan alternative. Perhaps it is true, as one historian has written, that other great powers facing such a situation in the early 1900's would have acted similarly, but Roosevelt's impatience inflicted a grievous blow to Colombia's sovereignty and pride, tarnished the national image and the reputation of the United States for justice and fairness, and left a heritage of ill will in Colombia and later throughout Latin America.

Securing the canal now became an overriding concern to President Roosevelt. He already had adequate naval bases in hand. American troops had evacuated Cuba in 1902, after it adopted a constitution and held elections. However, the so-called Platt Amendment kept Cuba in leading strings. This amendment originally formed a rider to an Army appropriation bill. Subsequently Washington insisted that Cuba incorporate its provisions into her constitution and accept them as part of a treaty that could be revised only with mutual consent. Its terms prohibited Cuba from alienating territory or control to a foreign power or incurring excessive indebtedness, permitted the United States to intervene to restore order and preserve Cuban independence, and gave the United States the right to buy or lease naval bases in Cuba. Eventually, the navy selected Guantanamo Bay on Cuba's southeast coast as the most suitable base. The Cuban and Panamanian protectorates, together with possible sites in Puerto Rico, satisfied the American navy. The only remaining problems centered not on obtaining more naval bases but on reducing European influence in the zone around the Panama Canal, and on preventing possible naval bases from falling into the hands of a potential enemy. President Roosevelt and his advisors did not feel seriously concerned with Britain or the other European states with possessions in the Caribbean. Their suspicions focused upon Germany, seemingly bent upon expansion almost everywhere. Probably they greatly exaggerated the danger, but it did underlie America's policy in the area around the Panama Canal.

The misnamed Roosevelt Corollary (to the Monroe Doctrine) grew out of the Venezuelan and Dominican debt crises. Cipriano Castro, the Venezuelan dictator, treated foreigners and their property arbitrarily and adamantly refused a settlement or arbitration. In 1902, Great Britain, Germany, and Italy jointly retaliated with a blockade of Venezuela's ports to force Castro to terms. Roosevelt acquiesced in this punitive action, for he did not believe in allowing a small and irresponsible Latin American state to shelter its wrongdoing behind the protection of the Monroe Doctrine. Yet he and the American people soon became alarmed, not at the more circumspect British or Italians, but at Germany's highhandedness in bombarding a fort and destroying a Venezuelan village. According to a version he related years after he left office, which recent historians accept as essentially valid, Roosevelt mobilized the American fleet in the Caribbean for any eventualities and sternly warned Germany to cease its objectionable actions and to accept the arbitration now eagerly desired by Castro. Apparently Roosevelt had begun to fear that Germany indeed sought naval bases in the Caribbean and he decided to put her on warning. In any case, the three powers agreed to arbitrate their claims and the Hague Court of Permanent Arbitration reached a decision in 1904. The decision appeared to encourage further armed intervention to collect debts, for it provided that the three powers which had used force to protect their nationals' claims should have priority in receiving payments from Venezuelan revenues before all other claimants whose governments had not resorted to coercion. If similar interventions should take place against other Latin American debtors, Washington feared that temporary occupation might turn into attempts at permanent control or annexation. Since the small, chronically debt-ridden, and turbulent republics bordering on the Caribbean Sea seemed most susceptible to such attempts, the court's decision appeared to jeopardize the security of the Panama Canal as well as the traditional prohibition of the Monroe Doctrine.

In 1904, the government of the Dominican Republic defaulted on its foreign debt. Rumors that the great powers of Europe planned to use armed intervention in behalf of their citizens with claims against that country alarmed Washington. Roosevelt then decided he had no alternative but to assume a policeman's role in the Caribbean; the United States would forestall European intervention by protecting legitimate foreign interests and averting disorder. As he told Congress in his annual message in December, 1904:

It is not true that the United States feels any land hunger or entertains any projects as regards the other nations of the Western Hemisphere save such as are for their welfare. All that this country desires is to see the neighboring countries

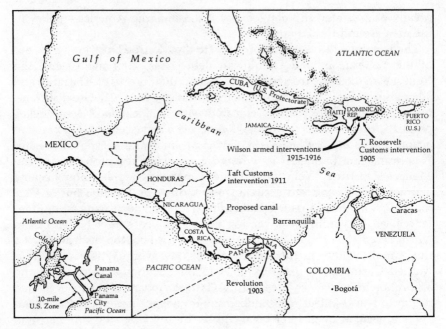

Intervention in the Caribbean, 1903–1917

stable, orderly, and prosperous. . . . [However] chronic wrongdoing, or an impotence which results in a general loosening of the ties of society, may in America, as elsewhere, ultimately require intervention by some civilized nation, and in the Western Hemisphere the adherence of the United States to the Monroe Doctrine may force the United States, however reluctantly, in flagrant cases of such wrongdoing or impotence, to the exercise of an international police power.

Privately he commented that his administration sought to "do nothing but what a policeman has to do. . . . As for annexing the island, I have about the same desire . . . as a gorged boa constrictor might have to swallow a porcupine wrong-end-to." American intervention, he hoped, would "show these Dagos that they will have to behave decently."

A protocol concluded with the Dominican government in 1905 provided that an agent, appointed by the President of the United States, would supervise the collection of Dominican customs and would use 55 percent of the revenues to pay foreign creditors, turning over the remainder to the Dominican government for its needs. Roosevelt had inverted the historic prohibition of the Monroe Doctrine against European intervention to justify American intervention and in fact a financial protectorate. Although large numbers of Americans applauded his action, anti-imperialist Democrats roundly denounced it and prevented

Senate approval of the treaty. Privately Roosevelt criticized the Senate as "such a helpless body when efficient work for good is to be done." Despite the Senate's failure to act, he implemented the financial arrangement anyway until the Senate finally approved it in 1907 with some changes. The financial intervention apparently did not greatly disturb Latin America at the time. Later, however, following other interventions in the name or spirit of the Roosevelt Corollary, denunciations of Yankee highhandedness and imperialism reverberated from the Mexican border to Patagonia. The prevailing moral climate and American suspicions of European intentions make it difficult to criticize Roosevelt's action. Perhaps he might have done better to have acted without formally proclaiming an international police role for the United States.

2. "DOLLAR DIPLOMACY" AND ARMED INTERVENTION IN THE CARIBBEAN

President Taft and Secretary Knox followed the basic course outlined by Roosevelt in the Caribbean, albeit in a more tactless and blundering manner. They too believed that the security interests of the United States required the promotion of more stable governments in the Caribbean to avoid possible European interventions, and they disliked revolutionary disorders in any case. Knox held that the Monroe Doctrine entailed a constant "measure of benevolent supervision over [certain] Latin American countries to meet its logical requirements."

Knox and his chief adviser, Assistant Secretary Francis M. Huntington Wilson, placed greater emphasis both upon protecting American citizens and their property, and upon the establishment of financial protectorates to pay the troublesome debts of these turbulent states. They concluded that the safest way to guard against European interferences was to supplant European capital with American. Moreover, they hoped that financial supervision would promote order by discouraging revolutionaries hoping to feed at the public trough. The State Department encouraged American financiers to provide funds to alleviate the indebtedness of Nicaragua, Honduras, Guatemala, and Haiti, undertakings which of course had to return profits to the bankers. Yet they clearly intended this so-called dollar diplomacy primarily to promote the stability and security of the Caribbean. The State Department closely supervised these financial arrangements to prevent excessive profiteering.

Nicaragua presented the most serious challenge to the Taft-Knox Pax-Americana. General José Santos Zelaya, Nicaragua's ambitious and defiantly anti-Yankee dictator, threatened to disrupt the peace established by Root at the Conference of Central American States in 1907. Zelaya's intrigues and filibustering raids against his neighbors kept the region in an uproar. He also missed no opportunity to flaunt his defiance of Washington, threatening to cancel American-owned mining concessions in Nicaragua and floating a new loan through a London syndicate. As long as Zelaya reigned in Nicaragua, Central America could find no peace or stability. Consequently, when a revolt broke out against him in 1909, the State Department understandably looked with sympathy upon the rebel cause. After Zelaya executed two Americans serving with the rebels, Knox denounced him as "a blot upon the history of Nicaragua" and broke diplomatic relations. Zelaya subsequently resigned and a pro-American government came to power. A financial protectorate, the Knox-Castrillo Convention, was negotiated and put into effect, even though the American Senate rejected it. When a new revolt by Zelaya's followers threatened the pro-American regime, Knox had 2,700 marines landed in 1912 to protect foreigners and help restore order. A small force, ostensibly as a legation guard, remained until 1933 (except for a brief withdrawal in 1925).

Five months prior to the Knox-Castrillo Convention, the State Department concluded a similar agreement with Honduras to refinance its foreign debt through American bankers. Knox intended to negotiate somewhat looser arrangements with Costa Rica, Guatemala, and the other republics of Central America. As Knox explained to the Senate Foreign Relations Committee, he intended his policy "to make American capital the instrumentality to secure financial stability, and hence prosperity and peace, to the more backward Republics in the neighborhood of the Panama Canal." Although Democrats and other Americans, appalled by what they regarded as dollar imperialism, increasingly criticized this policy, the Taft administration's primary motives clearly were to protect the security of the Panama Canal and to end revolutionary disorders in the area. Insofar as the financial arrangements created conditions for peace and progress within these republics, the people of Central America obviously would benefit, the government claimed. Moreover, Knox repeatedly reminded the American financiers involved that the State Department insisted upon equitable terms in the refinancing of the debts of these small republics. He failed to overcome opposition in the Senate, however, that blocked approval of the arrangements with Nicaragua and the other states.

"Dollar diplomacy" on the whole ended up as a failure. As critics have pointed out, armed intervention in Nicaragua was particularly regrettable. It represented the first use of the American military to suppress revolution and to maintain a friendly government in power. The presence of American marines in Nicaragua probably discouraged revolution in other Central American republics, at least for a few years, but it aroused fear and distrust of the United States among the peoples of the region and fed Yankee-phobia throughout Latin America. The Roosevelt Corollary was yielding painful and bitter results, and the end was not in sight.

3. SECURITY AND BENEVOLENCE IN THE CARIBBEAN

The Democratic administration that took office in 1913 hoped to inaugurate a new era in America's relations with its neighbors to the south. The diplomacy of the New Freedom, with its emphasis upon fair dealing, morality, and principle, supplanted the allegedly selfish dollar imperialism of Taft and Knox. President Wilson's policy statement on Latin America, issued on March 11, 1913, disavowed selfish purposes for American diplomacy. Again, in the Mobile Address on October 27, 1913, he condemned selfish economic exploitation of Latin America by American and European financiers as fostering a dangerous domination of weaker states, and he solemnly pledged that the United States would seek friendship with its neighbors on the basis of honor and equality.

Yet the new administration soon came to appreciate the need for order and stability in the strategically important Caribbean. Moreover, Wilson intended to teach constitutionalism and democracy to the disorderly, revolution-prone republics of that region. As he had declared in March, 1913, cooperation with Latin America was possible only when supported "by the orderly processes of just government based on law, not upon arbitrary or irregular force," for, he continued, "We can have no sympathy with those who seek to seize the power of government to advance their own personal interests or ambitions." Wilson's words reflected the belief of most of his countrymen in the superior moral and political virtues of constitutionalism and democracy, in reliance upon free elections as a panacea for political and social ills everywhere, and in America's mission to promote a liberal world order. Despite his Mobile pledge to seek Latin America's friendship on the basis of equality, Wilson obviously valued democracy and stability in the Caribbean more than respect for the sovereignty of those republics. More armed interventions than before resulted. As the *New York Times* commented, Wilson made Taft's dollar diplomacy look like "ten cent diplomacy."

Nicaragua illustrated the paradox of missionary diplomacy. The new administration inherited from its predecessor a financial and military involvement in the government of that country. Secretary of State Bryan quickly perceived that one of the major problems in Nicaragua, and elsewhere in the Caribbean, was a desperate need for capital to repay debts and finance needed improvements. Yet the very weaknesses of these small republics compelled reliance upon foreign capitalists who usually charged very high interest rates because of the risks, and then when defaults occurred, appealed to their governments for protection. Bryan thought such a double standard dangerous as well as unfair. But he had difficulty finding a better alternative. Bryan wanted the American government to extend its credit to these republics, thus reducing the interest rates and eliminating the dangers of exploitation or European intervention, but Wilson rejected the idea as "a novel and radical proposal." That type of enlightened foreign aid had to await the New Deal era of Franklin D. Roosevelt. Instead, Wilson directed the State Department to continue the policy of persuading American financiers to advance needed funds at as low an interest rate as possible. Bryan thus had no choice but to continue Knox's so-called dollar diplomacy with safeguards against exploitation. Consequently, the financial protectorate continued, and the marine legation guard remained in the capital city, Managua, propping up a pro-American regime. Bryan also renegotiated Knox's treaty to purchase the alternate canal route in Nicaragua, which the Senate approved in 1916.

Chaotic Haiti, where a small irresponsible elite ruled two million illiterate and poverty-stricken Negro peasants, possessed a strategically important naval base site at Môle St. Nicholas and lay athwart the main shipping routes into the Caribbean. The Wilson administration repeatedly tried to persuade Haiti to accept a financial protectorate similar to the Dominican and Nicaraguan models. The State Department also sought to lease Môle St. Nicholas in order to prevent it from falling into the hands of a European rival (the American navy already had sufficient bases). A succession of short-lived regimes, each coming to power by revolution and speedily toppled in turn by new rebellions, rebuffed Washington's proposal. Haiti's chronic disorder endangered foreign lives and investments, and encouraged foreign intervention. After one upheaval early in 1914, British, French, and German marines landed to protect foreigners living in Port-au-Prince, and Wilson and Bryan rejected a French and German overture for joint supervision of Haiti's customs revenues. Foreign business interests in Haiti also reportedly were trying to eliminate American investors and to weaken American influence in the republic. Diplomacy having failed to bring order and stability to Haiti, President Wilson reluctantly turned to armed intervention.

The opportunity came in July, 1915. The latest adventurer in power, Guillaume Sam, had slaughtered a number of his political enemies. An enraged mob then dragged Sam from the French Legation, where he had sought refuge, and hacked his body into pieces and displayed them in the streets. His patience exhausted, Wilson approved the landing of American marines, who first occupied the capital and then the entire country. As the President commented to the Secretary of State, "I suppose there is nothing for it but to take the bull by the horns and restore order." Restoring order kept American armed forces there until 1934. The Americans maintained a façade of native government, but marines and naval officials actually ruled Haiti and launched a number of reforms. They began sanitation projects, built roads, and imposed fiscal controls to pay Haiti's foreign debt and to provide funds for internal reforms. They created a small but disciplined native constabulary and hoped it would remain subordinate to civilian control. American officials embodied these long-term reforms into a Haitian-United States treaty in 1915, and into a new Haitian constitution in 1918, solemnly approved at a plebiscite guarded by U.S. marines.

Until 1912, the Dominican Republic seemed fairly stable under the customs receivership. In that year, however, a new wave of political instability and revolutionary disorder began. In a step by step, unplanned process, the Wilson administration became increasingly entangled in this misgoverned and poverty-cursed land. Washington warned would-be rebels that it would not permit any revolutions or increases in the Dominican debt. Unfortunately, the State Department's policy ignored political realities in the republic; because of the power of any group entrenched in office, change could only be brought about by the bullet, not the ballot.

Washington finally resorted to force. Dominican authorities refused to accept a tightening of financial controls, and supervised free elections under the so-called "Wilson Plan" failed to bring the hoped-for constitutional stability. When an insurrection broke out in the spring of 1916, American forces landed at the capital. Washington then decided to occupy the entire country and to disarm the rebels. A new provisional president, chosen by the Dominican Congress, refused to accept more drastic financial supervision. Therefore, the United States withheld funds from him, and his government promptly collapsed. Wilson, with "deepest reluctance," then placed the republic under American military government. The occupation regime suspended the Dominican Congress and administered the country until 1924 through marine detachments and cooperative natives. Ironically, the State Department continued to maintain formal diplomatic relations with the Dominican Republic.

A number of reforms were introduced into the Dominican Republic, similar to those undertaken in Haiti. Armed resistance by "bandits"— they called themselves patriots—led to the imposition of martial law, arbitrary arrests and imprisonment, and censorship of the press. It was not surprising that many sensitive Americans eventually became greatly distressed by these Caribbean ventures in benevolent imperialism. After World War I, a mounting outcry from the liberal or critical press in the United States caused Congress to investigate alleged abuses and atrocities committed by American forces in Haiti and the Dominican Republic and helped quicken the pace of withdrawal in the latter.

In light of subsequent developments in these countries, the interventions fell far short of accomplishing Wilson's idealistic goals, and their undertaking does not seem justified. The American military government achieved some permanent reforms, in sanitation, public health, road building, and perhaps a few other areas, but it made no noticeable progress in promoting orderly constitutionalism and democratic government. To some critics, the principal legacy of the American presence appears to have been even more brutal and efficient military dictatorships imposed by the American-trained constabularies.

By 1917, the Caribbean had become an American-controlled lake. In addition to the five protectorates discussed above, the State Department in 1911 discouraged a Japanese company from operating a concession in Mexico's Magdalena Bay (the so-called Lodge Corollary to the Monroe Doctrine), and for $25 million purchased the Danish West Indies from Denmark in 1916, as a security measure.

4. BENEVOLENT MEDDLING IN MEXICO

The Mexican Revolution presented a far more serious challenge to missionary diplomacy than any encountered in the Caribbean. Mexico underwent an upheaval that endangered foreign lives and investments, and at times affected the security of the American border. The chaos and turbulence in Mexico sorely tried Wilson's patience, and that of the American public. Probably other great powers, facing similar trials and outrages at the hands of a weaker neighbor, would have resorted to force to end a situation deemed intolerable. Yet Wilson firmly rejected intervention to protect mere property interests no matter how large, or to restore order. His principles and a sympathetic perception of the need for reform in Mexico saved him from pursuing that course. On the other hand, his very commitment to constitutionalism and democracy lured him into a dangerous interference that nearly culminated in a large-scale war.

Mexico was experiencing profound political and social changes. Although vast amounts of foreign capital had been invested in Mexico and considerable industrialization was under way, abysmal poverty, illiteracy, and debt-peonage cursed the masses of the Mexican people. These conditions spawned deep bitterness and finally revolution. In 1911 a liberal reformer, Francisco Madero, overthrew Porfirio Díaz, the aging iron-fisted dictator, greatly admired by foreign investors because he had preserved order and stability for so long. Madero proved unequal to the challenge, and a series of armed uprisings began against his government. Early in 1913, Victoriano Huerta, Madero's own general, engineered a conservative coup against him and seized power. Madero subsequently was shot while allegedly trying to escape. A number of European governments promptly gave Huerta diplomatic recognition, and foreigners owning property or having other economic interests in Mexico hailed the new *caudillo* as a strong man who would restore order. The lame duck Taft administration withheld recognition, because it first wanted to negotiate the settlement of certain diplomatic disputes.

President Wilson converted nonrecognition from a bargaining tactic into a firm moral policy. Wilson would not recognize Huerta because he had overthrown a promising constitutional government. Moreover, he viewed Huerta as little more than an ordinary murderer. As he remarked privately, "I will not recognize a government of butchers." He advocated using the power and influence of the United States to encourage constitutional and social reforms in its neighbor to the south. He rejected advice to recognize Huerta, watched hopefully the program of a liberal revolutionary movement—the Constitutionalists led by Venustiano Carranza—and sent special emissaries to Mexico to survey conditions and to urge the dictator to stand aside for democratic elections and the restoration of constitutional government. Wilson, thereby, added moral and ideological criteria to the traditional policy of recognizing de facto regimes. A dangerous confrontation resulted. Huerta, a full-blooded Indian much addicted to alcohol and fully as stubborn as the moralist in the White House, refused to eliminate himself from the presidency or to permit Wilson to mediate among the Mexican factions. Wilson then went before Congress, on August 27, 1913, to proclaim a policy of "watchful waiting" and to impose a total embargo on all arms shipments to Mexico from the United States. Undaunted, Huerta arrested his opponents in the Mexican Congress and established a full-fledged dictatorship. Wilson struck back with a diplomatic offensive. He asked other countries to withhold recognition from Huerta and notified them of Washington's determination to compel the dictator's retirement. The government encouraged Carranza's Constitutionalists in their revolution against Huerta, and early in 1914 it revoked the arms embargo to permit the rebels to obtain military supplies in the United States. Informal exchanges with Carranza indicated, however, that the stiffnecked reformer wanted only recognition from the United States and would not accept Wilsonian tutelage in transforming Mexico.

Still Huerta clung to power until an incident at Tampico offered Wilson the opportunity for a show of force to compel his retirement. On April 9, 1914, during a military confrontation between Huerta forces and his opponents around Tampico, some sailors from an American warship, in the area to protect American nationals, were arrested upon landing a small boat in the city for supplies. Although the local governor quickly released the men and offered an apology, Admiral Henry T. Mayo of the American squadron demanded a formal apology and a 21–gun salute to the American flag. Huerta refused to comply with such humiliating demands. Anxious to avoid a clash, however, he offered either to submit the issue to arbitration or to agree to a face-saving simultaneous exchange of salutes. Brushing aside these offers, Wilson went before Congress and asked for a resolution approving the possible use of force to uphold the nation's honor. Before Congress could complete its favorable response, the President used the scheduled arrival of a German vessel, the *Ypiranga,* at Veracruz with a cargo of arms for Huerta, as an excuse to issue orders on April 21 for American naval forces to seize that port's customs house. By the following day, Veracruz was in American hands, at the cost of 19 American and 126 Mexican lives and a larger number wounded. For a brief period the clash threatened to explode into a full-scale war, which Wilson definitely did not want. Fortunately, the ABC powers—Argentina, Brazil, and Chile—offered their good offices to arrange a Mexican-American peace conference at Niagara Falls. The fighting ended without recognition of Huerta, although Carranza prevented agreement on a new provisional government for Mexico. The "affair of honor" had further weakened Huerta and he fell from power in July, 1914.

Unfortunately, Huerta's fall did not end the Mexican problem. The triumph of the Constitutionalists proved a cruel disappointment to President Wilson. Not only was Carranza intractable and resistent to Wilson's tutelage, he also faced a revolt within his own movement. General Pancho Villa, a colorful but cutthroat adventurer, turned his arms against Carranza and for a while seemed on the verge of success. Wilson and Secretary of State Bryan at first regarded Villa as a noble Galahad who would save Mexico and accept advice from the White House. But Carranza rallied his forces and Villa's strength rapidly declined. Meanwhile, the United States cooperated with the ABC powers, plus Guatemala, Bolivia, and Uruguay, in efforts to persuade the Mexican factional leaders to step aside and permit a broad-based provisional government to take over. Bowing to reality after Carranza refused to be by-passed, the United States and its six Latin American collaborators extended de facto diplomatic recognition to Carranza's provisional government on October 19, 1915.

Recognition failed to end the turbulence in Mexico. Villa, enraged at the recognition of his rival, butchered a number of Americans in northern Mexico and launched pillaging raids across the international border. After the bloody sacking of Columbus, New Mexico, by Villistas on March 9, 1916, Wilson ordered General John Jacob Pershing to lead a punitive expedition into Mexico to harass Villa and his bandit army. That wily Robin Hood eluded his pursuers. As American troops drove hundreds of miles into northern Mexico on their chase, they inflamed Mexican nationalism and Carranza threatened war if the expedition did not withdraw. Armed clashes resulted and large-scale hostilities again seemed almost unavoidable. Fortunately, a Mexican-American joint commission, while failing to resolve the problem of coping with Villa, at least helped avoid further armed clashes. Pershing and his men finally received orders to withdraw, in January, 1917.

Carranza's threat to expropriate American and other foreign-owned oil and mining properties as part of his land reform and nationalist program further roiled Mexican-American relations during these years. Article 27 of the Mexican Constitution, adopted in 1917, provided for public ownership of all subsurface deposits. The question at issue centered on whether its provisions should be applied retroactively against leases and purchases made prior to 1917. Moreover, Carranza's anticlerical policies against the church in Mexico enraged American Roman Catholics. After the United States entered the European war, Carranza provided additional irritants by his unfriendly posture of neutrality. Yet despite these frictions, Wilson resisted interventionist pressures and preserved an uneasy peace. In retrospect, while Wilson's moralistic meddling probably was unwise and obviously left a heritage of virulent anti-Americanism in Mexico, he did successfully avoid all-out intervention and war.

5. WILSON AND PAN AMERICANISM

Despite his troubles with Mexico and in the Caribbean, Wilson made a notable contribution to the cause of Pan Americanism. To be sure, many Latin Americans sharply criticized America's policeman's role proclaimed by Roosevelt in 1904 and continued by Taft and Wilson. Argentina's literary giant, Manuel Ugarte, a bitter critic of United States policy, spoke for many Latin Americans when he recited the litany of American rapacity and advocated a movement for hemispheric unity without the hated Yankee. Latin American intellectuals and students, traditionally attracted to Europe culturally, denounced North American imperialism and called for independence from Washington's tutelage. Yet Woodrow Wilson's liberalism and idealism greatly impressed many thoughtful Latin Americans. That feeling developed particularly after the United States became a belligerent in World War I and President Wilson in a series of lofty addresses proclaimed a new order of liberty and peace for suffering mankind. Wilson's obvious sincerity and statesmanlike vision rallied many Latin Americans to the cause of a just peace and a liberal world order.

In a very real sense, President Wilson served as precursor to the later "Good Neighbor" policy. In 1915, he proposed a Pan American Treaty between all the states of this hemisphere, to guarantee the territorial integrity and independence of each and to promote peace and stability. Although the pact was not adopted, owing to continuing Latin American suspicions of the "Colossus of the North" and to Chile's fear that it might be forced to arbitrate its boundary disputes with Peru and Bolivia, it made a favorable impression and its essential provisions subsequently were incorporated into the Covenant of the League of Nations.

When the United States went to war with Germany in 1917, 13 Latin American states indicated their support of Pan American solidarity by either declaring war against Germany or severing diplomatic relations. Of course, the 13 included several Caribbean countries that were hardly more than puppets or satellites of the United States. Significantly, Brazil was the only large Latin American state to enter the war; unfriendly

Mexico under Carranza, isolated Chile, Colombia with its Panama grievance still unredressed, and Argentina, traditionally a rival of the United States for hemispheric leadership, failed to cooperate. Despite such holdouts, the war quickened hemispheric unity. Finally, in the last year of the Wilson administration, measures were adopted to close the gap between American ideals and practice. The State Department announced that the interventions in Haiti and the Dominican Republic would end as soon as possible, and the United States made determined efforts to avoid any further armed interventions. In late 1920, Bainbridge Colby, Wilson's last Secretary of State, undertook a good will tour of Brazil, Uruguay, and Argentina. Colby eloquently and apparently successfully reaffirmed Wilsonian ideals and good intentions, but the fulfillment of the Wilsonian promise awaited later developments under Presidents Herbert Hoover and, above all, Franklin D. Roosevelt.

Additional Reading

Excellent accounts of the historic interest in a canal across Panama are by D. C. Miner, *The Fight for the Panama Canal* (1940); Gerstle Mack, *The Land Divided* (1944); and Miles P. Du Val, Jr., *Cadiz to Cathay: The Story of the Long Struggle for the Panama Canal* (1947). For the canal treaties with England, see A. E. Campbell, *Great Britain and the United States, 1895–1903* (1960) and Bradford Perkins, *The Great Rapprochement* (1968). Henry F. Pringle, *Theodore Roosevelt* (1931) provides a colorful account of Roosevelt's role in Panama and the Caribbean. A more balanced study is by William H. Harbough, *Power and Responsibility: The Life and Times of Theodore Roosevelt* (1961). C. D. Ameringer, "The Panama Canal Lobby of Philippe Bunau-Varilla and William Nelson Cromwell," *American Historical Review,* LXVIII (1963), 346–363, carefully re-evaluates the role of those two key figures in the drama. Also see J. Fred Rippy, *The Capitalists and Colombia* (1931) and E. T. Parks, *Colombia and the United States, 1765–1934* (1935). *The Latin American Policy of the United States* (1943), by Samuel Flagg Bemis, still provides the best concise survey of Washington's policy in Latin America despite its tendency to present American actions in the best possible light. Julius W. Pratt, *Challenge and Rejection, 1900–1921* (1967) is a brief and interpretive general survey of American foreign policy. Dana G. Munro, *Intervention and Dollar Diplomacy in the Caribbean, 1900–1921* (1964) largely supplants the older accounts by W. H. Callcott, *The Caribbean Policy of the United States, 1890–1920* (1942) and J. Fred Rippy, *The Caribbean Danger Zone* (1940). Still useful is H. C. Hill, *Roosevelt and the Caribbean* (1937). For the various corollaries to the Monroe Doctrine, the authority is Dexter Perkins, *A History of the Monroe Doctrine* (1963). Paul S. Holbo, "Perilous Obscurity: Public Diplomacy and the Press in the Venezuelan

Crisis, 1902–1903," *The Historian*, XXXII (1970), 428–448, questions whether Roosevelt gave Germany an ultimatum. On the Taft era, in addition to the above studies on the Caribbean, see W. V. and M. V. Scholes, *The Foreign Policies of the Taft Administration* (1970) and H. F. Pringle, *The Life and Times of William Howard Taft* (2 vols., 1939). David H. Dinwoodie, "Dollar Diplomacy in the Light of the Guatemalan Loan Project, 1909–1913," *The Americas*, XXVI (1970), 237–253, deemphasizes economic motives. Arthur S. Link, *Wilson: The New Freedom* (1956) and *Wilson: The Struggle for Neutrality, 1914–1915* (1960) closely examine Wilsonian policy in the Caribbean and toward Mexico. See also Link's *Woodrow Wilson and the Progressive Era, 1910–1917* (1954) and Harley Notter's *The Origins of the Foreign Policy of Woodrow Wilson* (1937). William S. Coker, "The Panama Tolls Controversy: A Different Perspective," *Journal of American History*, LV (1968), 555–564, sees a close link between tolls repeal and renewal of the 1908 Anglo-American arbitration treaty. Selig Adler, "Bryan and Wilsonian Caribbean Penetration," *Hispanic American Historical Review*, XX (1940), 198–226 provides a good critique of moral diplomacy in action. Paolo E. Coletta re-evaluates Bryan's role in *William Jennings Bryan: Progressive Politician and Moral Statesman, 1909–1915* (1969). The best study of the Veracruz affair, and a corrective to previous accounts, is *An Affair of Honor: Woodrow Wilson and the Occupation of Veracruz* (1962), by Robert E. Quirk. On Mexican policy generally, see the brief survey by Howard F. Cline, *The United States and Mexico* (1953) and J. Fred Rippy, *The United States and Mexico* (1931). A recent and judicious account of Wilson and Huerta is by Kenneth J. Grieb, *The United States and Huerta* (1969). Britain's role is examined by W. V. and M. V. Scholes, "Wilson, Grey, and Huerta," *Pacific Historical Review*, XXXVII (1968), 151–162. On Wilson and Villa, consult Clarence C. Clendenen, *The United States and Pancho Villa* (1961). Clifford W. Trow, "Woodrow Wilson and the Mexican Interventionist Movement of 1919," *Journal of American History*, LVII (1971), 46–72, examines domestic pressures upon Wilson. Daniel M. Smith, *Aftermath of War: Bainbridge Colby and Wilsonian Diplomacy, 1920–1921* (1970) explores Colby's good will tour of South America and the beginnings of a new policy toward Mexico and the Caribbean.

President Theodore Roosevelt brought the Russo-Japanese War to an end by the signing of the Treaty of Portsmouth

16

IDEALS AND SELF-INTEREST
IN THE FAR EAST,
1901–1921

1. THEODORE ROOSEVELT AND THE BALANCE OF POWER IN EAST ASIA

In 1900 Czarist Russia posed the principal threat to the status quo in the Far East. Russia was building the Chinese Eastern Railway across Manchuria to link with the Trans-Siberian Railway and provide a shorter route to Vladivostok. Moreover, after frustrating Japanese desires in 1895 for a leasehold in the Liaotung peninsula in southern Manchuria, Russia moved in and established warm-water naval bases and ports at Port Arthur and Darien. Then, with the excuse of suppressing the Boxer Rebellion, Russia expanded its influence over other parts of Manchuria. The final straw, in Tokyo's view, came when Russia challenged Japan in Korea, a vital area economically and strategically to the island empire.

Prior to 1904, President Roosevelt gave East Asian problems little attention and left policy largely in the hands of Hay. The Secretary had retreated from the larger implications of his 1900 circular, relative to protecting China's integrity, and concentrated on defending the commercial interests of the United States. Although Americans had cheered his Open Door notes, and Russian expansion into southern Manchuria affected the area where Americans found their most promising market in China, Hay realized that his countrymen were not prepared to support a really vigorous policy in the Far East. Therefore he rebuffed Japanese and British overtures, in 1901 and 1903 respectively, for cooperation to restrain Russian expansionism. He expressed willingness, in fact, to accept Russia's exceptional position in Manchuria, asking only that she observe the principle of commercial equality, but he only encountered empty Russian promises and cynical evasions. Russia seemed determined to make Manchuria an exclusive sphere of influence.

Roosevelt agreed with Hay that Russian imperialism constituted the chief danger to the Far Eastern balance. Both privately fumed at the mendacious replies of the Russian foreign office to American protests and inquiries. They realized, however, that caution and restraint were wisest, given the realities of America's limited interests and power in the area. Japan seemed the obvious counterpoise to Russia. Japanese fighting qualities in the Sino-Japanese War and during the Boxer Rebellion had greatly impressed Roosevelt. He saw Japanese and American interests as generally compatible and he welcomed the Nipponese challenge to the Russian bear.

Buttressed by its alliance with Britain, Tokyo opened direct negotiations with St. Petersburg. Japan appeared prepared to concede south Manchuria as a Russian sphere in exchange for an agreement on Korea. Roosevelt and Hay sympathetically watched Japan's attempts at a diplomatic settlement. Although both hoped to avoid war, they decided it would be futile to get involved in the exchanges. Finally, wearying of Russian refusals and evasions, Japan broke off negotiations and launched a successful surprise attack against the Russian fleet at Port Arthur. War was formally declared two days later.

The American public strongly sympathized with Japan, which they regarded as a protegé since the days of the Perry expedition, and obviously an underdog against the mighty Czarist empire. The press hailed the surprise attack as a brilliant stratagem—there was no talk then of a "stab in the back"—and several American towns were renamed in honor of Japan's stunning victories. Dislike of Czarist tyranny and Russian anti-Semitism and pogroms strengthened pro-Japanese sentiment in the United States. Mob violence against helpless Jews at Kishineff in 1903, for example, had horrified the civilized world. Czarist officials often mistreated or even denied admission to American citizens of the Jewish faith desiring to visit Russia for business or private reasons. It was hardly surprising, therefore, that Jewish-American financiers joined British bankers in underwriting Japanese war loans. As Jacob Schiff of Kuhn, Loeb and Company in New York wrote, Japan's cause had become "not only her own cause, but the cause of the entire civilized world."

Roosevelt and his advisers shared the popular rejoicing at the Japanese victories. He agreed with Elihu Root who wrote, "Was not the way the Japs [sic] began the fight bully?" Roosevelt privately commented that the Japanese were "playing our game" in humbling Russian power and pretensions. Although the administration maintained official neutrality during the conflict, Roosevelt's pro-Japanese sentiments were well known and little liked in St. Petersburg. From time to time he offered friendly advice to Japan, and Tokyo sent Baron Kaneko, an old Harvard classmate of Roosevelt's, as a special liaison agent to the White House.

Though welcoming Japan's success, Roosevelt did not want her to predominate in the Far East. He hoped for enough of a Japanese triumph to establish a genuine balance, no more. Yet an unbroken succession of Japanese victories threatened the complete eclipse of Russian power. Such an outcome, Roosevelt thought, could have unfortunate results for all the countries concerned, including Japan itself. Moreover, some alarming reports soon appeared in the American press about war-stimulated nationalistic arrogance among the Japanese people and the growth of a contemptuous attitude not merely against Russia but toward all westerners. Russian propaganda also effectively exploited the theme of a new "Yellow Peril." The tone of the American press, however, in general remained pro-Japanese throughout the war.

Japan's victories sufficiently disturbed Roosevelt so that he felt compelled to warn her privately against getting a "big head" and embarking upon a course of "insolence and aggression." Even so, he remained convinced that Japan would behave moderately and cooperatively toward the United States. He emphasized to Japanese diplomats his conviction that their nation should take its place among the great powers of the world, with its own sphere of paramount influence in the Yellow Sea comparable to that of the United States in the Caribbean, and with control over Korea and south Manchuria. His remarks that Japan should not again be frustrated by the European powers as it had been in 1895 especially reassured Japanese leaders. Roosevelt later claimed he had warned France and Germany that if they came to Russia's aid the United States would line up with Japan, an assertion doubted by many historians, but in any case Tokyo greatly appreciated his general attitude of friendly support.

After the victory of Tsu-shima Straits, the war-strained Japanese government, near financial exhaustion, requested Roosevelt to propose bringing the belligerents to the peace table. Russia, although its armies remained intact, was in a similar condition. Yet previous peace probes by Washington, aided by France and Germany, had fallen upon deaf ears in the Russian capital. The war party at the court of Czar Nicholas II refused to accept defeat. Writing Hay in April, 1905, the disgusted American President described the Czar as "a preposterous little creature" unable either to make war or peace effectively. Now, after obtaining reassurances from Japan about the Open Door in Manchuria, Roosevelt again approached St. Petersburg. This time, aided by the German Kaiser, he received a favorable response. The formal offer of good offices was issued on June 8, 1905, and the belligerents met at Portsmouth, New Hampshire, in August for the negotiations.

Roosevelt fully deserved the Nobel Peace Prize he was awarded in 1906 for his role in ending the war. Like an anxious midwife, the President encouraged the rival diplomats to persevere and he helped keep the talks afloat despite Russian threats to continue the war rather than concede the island of Sakhalin and a large financial indemnity to Japan. Roosevelt persuaded Japan to mitigate her demands and also put pressure on St. Petersburg to accede. By the Treaty of Portsmouth, signed on September 5, Russia withdrew from Korea and southern Manchuria, which became Japan's sphere of influence, and ceded to her the southern half of Sakhalin. Americans and Europeans fulsomely praised Roosevelt for his successful efforts as peacemaker.

Unfortunately, news of the terms of peace aroused anti-American sentiment in Japan and touched off a riot in Tokyo. The Japanese government knew that Roosevelt's sentiments actually had sided with them during the war and the peace negotiations, and it understood that Japan, despite its victories, desperately needed peace, and peace would not have come if its negotiators had insisted upon an indemnity. Yet the Japanese public had been encouraged to expect more than they obtained—especially an indemnity. Many Japanese believed that the western powers had once again robbed their nation of the full fruits of victory. Japan's leaders apparently dared not reveal the truth to their people and allowed Roosevelt to become the popular whipping boy.

Roosevelt fully appreciated the enormous strides Japan had made during the war. Not only had she become the foremost power in East Asia, but her victories over Russia signalled the beginning of the end of an era of western superiority and predominance. The President realized how essential Japanese moderation and goodwill were if any remnants of the Open Door were to be preserved.

As the war had neared an end, both Washington and Tokyo tried to adjust to changed conditions and to promote Japanese-American harmony. En route to the Philippines on an inspection trip, Roosevelt's trusted lieutenant and Secretary of War, William H. Taft, stopped in Japan for a frank exchange of views with the Prime Minister, Count Taro Katsura. The Taft-Katsura Agreed Memorandum of 1905, long misinterpreted by some scholars as a Rooseveltian bargain conceding Korea as a closed Japanese sphere in exchange for reassurances about the safety of the Philippines, summed up the results of these talks. In fact, Roosevelt had already accepted that Japan would establish a protectorate in Korea. During the exchanges in Tokyo, Taft reiterated America's intention to continue its civilizing role in the Philippines, and he commented that Japanese supervision of the turbulent Koreans would promote stability in the Far East. Within a year, the American Legation in Seoul closed its doors as Japan took full charge in Korea. Katsura reassured Taft that Japan had no designs on the Philippines and fully sympathized with America's presence in the islands. The two also discussed the possibility of an Anglo-American-Japanese alliance. Taft said this was impossible, but he assured Katsura that when the occasion necessitated it, he could confidently expect American cooperation. Cabled the results of the conversations, Roosevelt expressed his complete concurrence. The initialed memorandum of the talks, therefore, represented neither an alliance nor a bargain, but an informal understanding, an effort at preserving good relations and at establishing a community of interests in East Asia.

2. THE IMMIGRATION CRISIS AND FRIENDSHIP RENEWED

During this difficult period of adjustment to Japan's new role as a great world power, the immigration question erupted to plague Japanese-American relations. Japanese immigration to the United States, previously only a trickle, increased sharply during the 1890's. By 1905, about 100,000 Japanese had arrived, the great majority of whom settled in California. Native Americans tended to view these industrious aliens as unassimilable. Anti-Oriental prejudices, directed earlier at the hapless Chinese, now focused upon the Japanese. Since naturalization laws legally barred Orientals from citizenship, many Californians shrilly demanded the exclusion of the Japanese, like the Chinese, to avert a new Yellow Peril to white civilization. San Francisco especially became a hotbed of anti-Japanese sentiment, whipped up by the yellow press and by labor organizations. Responding to such nativist sentiment, the San Francisco School Board in 1906 issued an order segregating Japanese school children because they were allegedly overaged and overcrowding the public schools. Actually, the order involved only 93 Japanese pupils, of whom 25 had been born American citizens and the oldest two were only aged 20.

Such blatant racism greatly disturbed the sensitive Japanese. The moderate Japanese press showed pained restraint, but the political opposition and extremist journals called for vindication of the national honor. The *Hochi Shimbun* threateningly editorialized, "If the United States does not put an end to the anti-Japanese agitation, this country must take some decisive measures for retaliation." Incorrectly assuming at first that the President could easily control the Californians, the Japanese government lodged a strong diplomatic protest and requested revocation of the school segregation order as contrary to the Japanese-American commercial treaty of 1894.

Roosevelt initially failed to take the San Francisco incident very seriously. The shock of the violent reaction in Japan, however, quickly propelled him into action. Aware of Japan's great power, Roosevelt angrily blamed those "infernal fools" in California for recklessly insulting the Japanese and risking a needless war. He asked the Navy Department for a detailed comparison of the Japanese and American fleets, and even after receiving assurance of United States superiority, he used the crisis to obtain larger naval appropriations from Congress, although his real fears of war had then passed. His use of the crisis was not merely opportunistic, because Roosevelt genuinely believed that the most reliable way to peace, with Japan or any other great state, lay in a friendly approach backed by adequate naval power. Public opinion, except on the west coast and in the South, seemed to agree with the President in deploring California's rashness. As the *New York World* commented later, "If somebody has to fight Japan, why not let California bear the whole burden of the war?"

The only politically feasible solution lay in immigration restriction. While President Roosevelt did not regard the Japanese as racially inferior, he believed that nativist prejudices and passions were inescapable as long as immigration continued. After several goodwill gestures to assuage Japan, Roosevelt summoned the San Francisco mayor and school board to the White House early in 1907. Overawed as well as charmed by the President, the San Franciscans gained reassurance from his promise to stop the Japanese influx and they agreed to rescind the segregation order. That obstacle removed, Roosevelt hoped to negotiate a treaty with Japan for mutual exclusion of worker immigration. Japanese officials, however, objected to such a humiliating treaty and requested a less formal arrangement.

The so-called Gentlemen's Agreement of 1907–1908 resulted. In a series of diplomatic notes, the State Department agreed not to bar Japanese immigration by law, in exchange for Japan's promise not to issue passports to workers coming to the United States and to accept American barriers against those trying to enter via Hawaii or Mexico. This assuaged Japan's national honor and pride, but the entire affair left an unpleasant aftertaste.

While negotiations were under way for the Gentlemen's Agreement, renewed anti-Japanese riots and agitation in San Francisco helped touch off a war scare during the spring and summer of 1907. The extremist press in Japan and in California seemed to feed on each others' fears and hatred. A hotbed of war rumors spread through Europe, exploited by the German Kaiser, who was pursuing the mirage of a German-American-Chinese alliance. European military experts not only predicted the inevitability of a Japanese-American war, but rated Japan's chances for a naval victory in the Pacific at five to four over the Americans. Although Roosevelt remained calm and the war scare soon passed, he had been disturbed if not fearful. He decided to send the battleship fleet on a spectacular world tour, to demonstrate the importance of sea power, to reassure nervous west coasters, and to strengthen the Republican party. The tour was widely interpreted at the time as a typical Rooseveltian big stick maneuver to show Japan graphically that Washington acted conciliatorily from strength, not weakness.

Sixteen smoke-belching battleships sailed from Hampton Roads, Virginia, in December of 1907. The Great White Fleet cruised down the coast of South America to the west coast, Hawaii, and Australia, and then, by invitation, visited Japan prior to returning via the Suez Canal and Europe. The fleet arrived back at its home base just prior to the end of Roosevelt's term, in early 1909, to a personal welcome and review ʊy the President. It had been a highly successful and gratifying display. The fleet's reception in Japan was at least outwardly enthusiastic and was unmarred by any unseemly incidents, although some Japanese may well have resented that overawing show of force. The world tour fully revealed to the President and his naval advisers the lack of advanced bases for naval operations in the far Pacific and the vulnerability of the Philippines—"our heel of Achilles," commented Roosevelt—to a determined assault by a major power such as Japan. American strategic thinking consequently centered on Pearl Harbor as the Navy's major base in the Pacific, and on the probable temporary loss of the Philippines in case of war. But Roosevelt thought war with Japan unlikely, and he still viewed Germany with deep suspicion, so he urged his successor to keep the battleship fleet concentrated in the Atlantic.

The air-clearing Root-Takahira Agreement was signed in 1908 at Japan's initiative. While some American diplomats in East Asia suspected Japanese motives and urged a firmer course, Roosevelt and his principal advisers believed that cooperation with Japan was both possible and desirable. Roosevelt had never highly valued America's interests in China and Manchuria nor taken very seriously the preservation of China's integrity and the Open Door. He already had acquiesced to the Japanese control of Korea, and he realistically conceded Japan's special role in south Manchuria, though he hoped to see preserved there at least a remnant of Chinese sovereignty and the commercial Open Door. Thus, the Root-Takahira Agreement, an executive agreement on the part of the United States, tacitly accepted Japan's sphere of influence in Manchuria (Ambassador Baron Kogoro Takahira had wanted to make it explicit, but Root demurred). The two powers pledged to respect each other's possessions and to support the status quo in the region of the Pacific; to uphold by all peaceful means the independence and integrity of China and the Open Door; and to consult jointly in case of a threat to the Open Door. The agreement did not represent a realpolitik bargain to safeguard the Philippines, as often interpreted, but a renewal of friendly assurances and an understanding about the Pacific area and China. It did not give Japan a completely free hand in Manchuria, but it accepted her special position, and also that of Russia to the north, as long as the area remained open to foreign commerce.

Roosevelt viewed his policy toward Japan as a success when he left office in 1909. Realistically adjusting policy to actual interests and available power, he had followed a firm but conciliatory course. Aided by friendly and cooperative elements in Japan, he had helped steer the two nations through a trying period of readjustment in the Far East, which resulted from the increasing tendency of the major European powers to concentrate on their European rivalries, the eclipse of Russian power in Asia, and the emergence of Japan to great-power status. Influential

Japanese leaders genuinely admired Roosevelt, despite the strains of the Portsmouth Treaty and the school board crisis, and most Japanese still looked upon Americans as their traditional friends. Unfortunately for the two nations, this situation changed, and for the worse, under Roosevelt's two successors in office.

3. BLUNDERING IN CHINA: DOLLAR DIPLOMACY

Although Roosevelt's chosen successor, Taft sharply altered his predecessor's course in the Far East. Roosevelt had viewed with contempt the weaknesses and instability of China under the Manchus, and had regarded with some sympathy Japan's moves in that country. As for the Open Door, he wrote Taft in 1910 that it was "an excellent thing" insofar as general agreement among the powers could maintain it, but that they could not defend it against a powerful challenger except at the risk of war. As one of Roosevelt's intimate advisers, Taft might have been expected to concur. Instead, American merchants and diplomats in China, during a visit he made to the Far East in 1908, and his advisers in Washington persuaded him to adopt a firmer course in defense of the Open Door.

Willard Straight and Francis M. Huntington Wilson acted as the chief architects of the Taft-Knox policies toward China. Straight, a young consular official in Korea and Manchuria during the Roosevelt administration, had acquired a deep distrust of Japan's motives. If Chinese integrity and the Open Door were to survive, he felt American capital had to enter the China market in larger quantities to strengthen the diplomatic voice of the United States against both Russian and Japanese expansionism. Straight interpreted the Open Door to mean not only commercial but investment equality of opportunity in China, and vigorous defense of Chinese independence and integrity. He resented Japanese decisions reserving for their own citizens investment opportunities in Manchuria, and he tried to entice American financiers to invest there. Huntington Wilson, First Assistant Secretary of State under Secretary Knox, held similar views. Recalled to the United States to serve as chief of the Far Eastern Division, Straight later resigned and became a private liaison agent between the State Department and American investors. Straight cooperated with Huntington Wilson in persuading Secretary Knox to adopt a new course, using the dollar to buttress American diplomacy in China and to curb both Japan and Russia.

Straight aided in arranging a loan from American bankers for financial reform in China. Serving as the representative of the American group of bankers, he took steps to obtain American participation in the three-power Hukuang Railway Consortium formed by English, French, and German bankers in 1909 to finance railroad construction in central and southern China. The European bankers and governments naturally

greeted the intrusion unenthusiastically, and President Taft had to ma...
a special appeal to the Chinese Regent to obtain the American group's
admission in 1910.

The Knox Neutralization Scheme ended up as an abortive attempt to
halt Russo-Japanese expansionism and to bolster the American role in
China. Secretary Knox and his advisers knew well that Japan was
entrenching herself in south Manchuria, and that she had struck an
agreement with Russia in 1907 recognizing their respective spheres of
influence (Japan in south Manchuria and Inner Mongolia, Russia in
northern Manchuria and Outer Mongolia). Determined, as he privately
remarked, to "smoke Japan out" of Manchuria, Knox in the fall of 1909
proposed that the major powers, through their banking groups, make a
joint loan to enable the Chinese government to purchase all foreign-
owned railroads in Manchuria, or, if that failed, to build competing lines.
Then, no single power would dominate in Manchuria, and China would
find itself in a vastly improved position to preserve its integrity and the
principles of the Open Door. Most unrealistically, Knox had confidently
expected to obtain British support for his proposal. The British government, however, was more concerned about the delicate situation in
Europe, had its alliance with Japan to consider, and was unwilling to
jeopardize the network of understandings between her Russian, French,
and Japanese associates in the Far East. Consequently, Sir Edward Grey,
the British Foreign Secretary, unmistakably rebuffed Knox's overture.
The Secretary's attempt, similar to Hay's in 1899–1900, to claim British
support failed. Russia and Japan rejected the proposal in nearly identical
notes, clearly indicating joint consultation in defense of their spheres of
interest. The two powers also blocked Straight's scheme for an Ameri-
can-built railroad in north China.

Although State Department officials blamed British noncooperation
for Knox's failure, they really had only their own unrealistic optimism to
blame for the fiasco. The net effect of the Taft-Knox dollar offensive was
impairment of the Japanese-American rapprochement so carefully constructed by Theodore Roosevelt. American challenges to Japan's interests merely drove that government closer to Russia, without weakening
the Japanese or Russian spheres in Manchuria or materially strengthening the Open Door. Those two powers reached an agreement in 1910 on
their respective spheres in Manchuria and pledged common action in
their defense. American blunders upset the "balanced antagonisms" that
Roosevelt had sought and forced the two rivals into a defensive cooperation.

Eventually, the State Department under Knox lost some of its previous
interest in defending the Open Door. In 1911, banking groups from
Britain, France, Germany, the United States, Japan, and Russia, formed
a six-power consortium to loan funds to the recently established Chinese
Republic for reorganizational purposes. Its terms in effect accepted the

Japanese and Russian spheres in Manchuria. Ironically, in view of their previous policies, Taft and Knox thereby abandoned the effort to maintain the Open Door in that area. But the legacy of the Straight-Huntington Wilson expanded version of the Open Door policy remained to bedevil future American policy-makers. The gap between American objectives and its capabilities in the Far East grew even wider.

4. THE GREAT WAR AND JAPANESE-AMERICAN ANTAGONISM

President Wilson and Secretary of State Bryan had only a superficial knowledge of the Far East when they took office in 1913. Both believed, however, the missionary-born myth that China was destined to become a Christianized and westernized nation under America's benevolent tutelage, and that it would serve as a valuable market for America's expanding economy. Bryan had made a brief tour of the area after the 1904 elections, and everywhere had perceived signs of the triumph of Christianity over paganism. He hailed the revolution that overthrew the Manchu dynasty in 1911 and established the Republic of China as "a great tribute to America . . . ." He and Wilson determined to adopt a course there, as in other areas, that reflected not only America's material interests but its ideals and principles.

Apparently neither Wilson nor Bryan understood the motives behind the Taft-Knox dollar diplomacy in the Orient. President Wilson issued a statement in March, 1913, withdrawing government support from the six-power consortium on the grounds that the terms of the projected loan impaired China's sovereignty. He and Bryan also viewed the consortium as an undesirable monopoly and as unwisely linking the United States with the policies of other and presumably more selfish nations in East Asia. The administration's decision did not displease the American bankers, already weary of the project. But the President's statement did nothing to resolve China's need for funds; withdrawal of American participation simply deprived China of protection from a relatively disinterested government in the completion of such loans. Yet Wilson viewed withdrawal as the only possible action consistent with what he termed America's "proud position" in China as first asserted by John Hay.

The immigration controversy with Japan flared anew in 1913. The California legislature proposed to prohibit aliens ineligible for citizenship from owning agricultural land. Obviously directed primarily at Japanese aliens, the bill reopened the fissures papered over by the Gentlemen's Agreement, and precipitated another crisis in Japanese-American relations. At first Wilson and Bryan failed to appreciate the serious implications of the California measure. They both believed in a state's right to regulate its own local affairs and they tended to sympathize with the view that Orientals were not assimilable into American society.

The 1911 treaty with Japan provided that Japanese aliens in America could own land for residential and commercial purposes, but it failed to mention agricultural lands. Exploiting that omission, the alien land bill passed the lower house of the California legislature and came before the state senate in April, 1913. Popular protests in Japan quickly convinced the Wilson administration of the necessity for taking some action to assuage Japanese sensitivities. Secretary Bryan made a special trip to California, where he pleaded to no avail with legislators and the governor for a compromise. The law finally adopted contained only slight modifications permitting the leasing of farm lands, a concession primarily to local leasing interests. Nevertheless, Bryan's trip did have a favorable effect upon the Japanese government and people. In subsequent exchanges with the Japanese ambassador in Washington, Bryan tried to drown the crisis in conciliatory words, by letting him "down easy," as he phrased it. Although they arrived at no solution, and eventually ten other states enacted legislation similar to California's alien land law, the crisis gradually subsided. As the *New York Times* commented, "Mr. Bryan's policy of treating every apparently acute disagreement with a prescription of endless conversation has worked well."

The outbreak of the First World War in August, 1914, diverted the attention of the great European powers and eliminated Germany, and later Russia, as major factors in the Far East. Japan and the United States remained the two principal powers on the scene. Japan obviously intended to exploit the European war to increase its influence in China. After a brief hesitation, the United States turned to a more vigorous defense of the Open Door in China and stronger opposition to Japanese encroachments. A new and potentially dangerous epoch had begun.

Japan utilized the Anglo-Japanese Alliance as an excuse to declare war against Germany in August, 1914, and to seize the German leasehold at Kiaochow Bay in Shantung Province on the Chinese mainland. She divided German islands in the Pacific with the British dominions, Japan obtaining those north of the equator, and Australia and New Zealand taking the remainder. The State Department expressed satisfaction at Japanese assurances she would restore the German leasehold to China and that she had no territorial ambitions in Shantung. When it soon became obvious that the restoration was not to happen immediately and that Japan was assuming control of the German railway concession in Shantung, Bryan wrote Wilson that he could not see "anything China can do or that we should do" about it.

Japan's leaders viewed their recent gains as only a beginning. The Japanese government, aware of Japan's inferior position in financial and industrial resources compared to the United States and other major western powers and yet having to compete with them for the China market, resolved to take advantage of the war to alter that situation. In mid-January, 1915, the Japanese minister at Peking presented the

Chinese government with the Twenty-One Demands, printed on paper ominously bearing watermarks of machine guns. These secret demands were divided into five groups. The first four aimed at strengthening Japan's special position in Shantung, southern Manchuria, Inner Mongolia, and Fukien. Group five, the most sweeping of the demands, would have made China a virtual protectorate by forcing her to accept special Japanese military and financial advisers and a degree of Japanese control over the Chinese police forces.

Initially Washington reacted calmly to reports of the demands. Moreover, when the nature of the Twenty-One Demands became fully known, Japan drew a distinction between the first four groups and group five, which she described merely as "wishes" subject to further negotiation. Colonel Edward M. House, the President's adviser, urged great caution to avoid "war with Japan over the 'open door' in China." Some officials in the State Department, led by the Counselor, Robert Lansing, wanted to strike a bargain with Japan by recognizing her special interests in Manchuria and Shantung in exchange for a reaffirmation of the Open Door principles in the rest of China and for a cessation of protests over the alien land law. Though the United States never proposed this bargain, the American note to Japan of March 13, 1915 served as a mild reminder of this nation's interest and rights in China. The note criticized group five demands as contrary to the Open Door, but added that the United States was not presently questioning the Japanese demands relating to Shantung, Manchuria, and Mongolia, for it "frankly recognizes that territorial contiguity creates special relations between Japan and these districts." The note therefore implied that the United States would acquiesce to Japan's gains if she would follow a moderate course in China.

Subsequently reports convinced President Wilson that a firmer policy was mandatory. Contrary to its professions to the United States, Japan threatened to use force to obtain acceptance of all the demands, including group five. Moreover, the Foreign Office in Tokyo apparently interpreted Bryan's mildly phrased note of March 13 as giving Japan a free hand in China. Deciding to champion China's rights, the President warned Japan of America's deep concern.

The American attitude, and British intercessions, persuaded the Japanese government to abandon group five of the Twenty-One Demands, and China accepted the remainder. After the crisis had passed, the State Department formally clarified its position in a caveat to Japan on May 11: the United States would not recognize the validity of any Sino-Japanese agreement that impaired American interests and treaty rights in China or damaged China's integrity and independence. The caveat contained a full statement of American rights to take future action if circumstances warranted. It indicated a hardening of policy toward Japan; a warning not to renew the more extreme demands at a later date. Wilson shifted

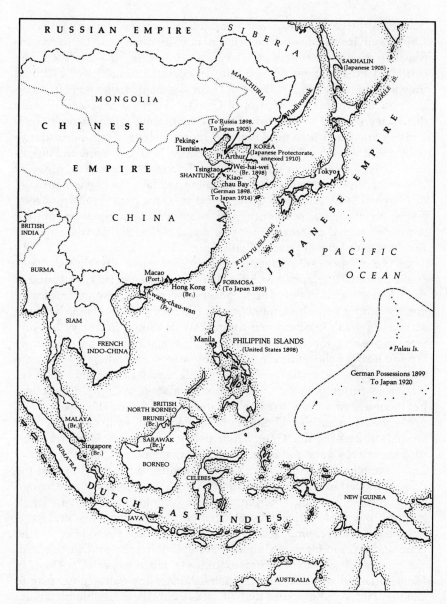

Japanese Expansionism, 1895–1919

from a posture of faith in Japanese moderation toward one of distrust and opposition.

In succeeding months it became obvious that Japan sought nothing less than political and financial predominance in all China. The American minister in Peking warned that the preoccupation of the other great powers with the European war enormously increased Japan's power in China and foreshadowed the elimination of nearly all European influence, to the detriment of America's interests. In late 1915, the disturbed President wrote Secretary of State Lansing that the United States should make Japan aware of "how we should look upon efforts on her part to gain further control of China." A revival of so-called dollar diplomacy seemed to offer one way of countering Japanese ambitions. Lansing tried to stimulate American investments in China in order to reduce that weak republic's dependence upon Japanese loans and investments. For a brief period, American financiers showed a renewed interest in investments and loans to China and launched several projects in 1916 and 1917. Although none of the ventures made much progress, owing to Japanese resistance and more profitable investments for American capital at home, the new dollar diplomacy served notice of Washington's serious concern with China.

Japanese-American antagonism intensified when the United States broke diplomatic relations with Germany in February, 1917, and entered the war two months later. The Japanese government grew anxious for an understanding with the United States, the only power able to challenge seriously Japan's position and aspirations in China. Secretary Lansing was also eager for an understanding. He appreciated Japan's larger economic and political interests on the Asian mainland and he believed that a realistic acceptance of Japan's role could adequately safeguard America's currently more limited commercial stake in China. Ultimately, he thought, America's greater economic and financial power would predominate. Lansing, like Theodore Roosevelt earlier, had a very limited concept of the Open Door policy, focused on America's immediate interests and not upon an idealistic support of Chinese integrity and a completely Open Door. Various reports convinced him that the present moderate Japanese ministry favored a conciliatory course toward the United States and therefore would willingly abandon its larger political and economic claims in Shantung, retaining only the actual investments there, and would pledge scrupulous observance of the commercial Open Door in China proper. If that happened, Lansing held, the United States could afford to concede Japan's special position in Manchuria and its leadership in East Asia. Lansing outlined his plan to Colonel House, who agreed that "if care is not taken, trouble is certain" with Japan. Consequently, the State Department consented to receive a special Japanese war mission to the United States in August, 1917, led by Lansing's old acquaintance, Viscount Kikujiro Ishii.

President Wilson would not agree to a bargain along the lines suggested by Lansing, despite House's warning that "unless we make some concessions in regard to her sphere of influence in the East, trouble is sure, sooner or later, to come" with Japan. The President remained opposed to all spheres of influence in China. Lansing and Ishii had no feasible alternative left but to try to conceal the depths of the Japanese-American divergence with an ambiguously phrased document, the Lansing-Ishii Agreement. Although this "solution" enabled both governments to maintain a façade of wartime cooperation, it did not resolve the underlying animosities and the conflict of interests over China. Whether Lansing's formula would have prevented later Japanese-American rivalry and hostilities cannot be answered, but it seemed a more realistic and promising course than the one Wilson insisted upon following. The President's policy perhaps restrained Japan to some degree, but it did not succeed in abolishing spheres of influence or forcing Japan out of China; instead, it heightened mutual antagonism and helped set the stage for subsequent controversies.

The Lansing-Ishii Agreement, a public exchange of notes on November 2, 1917, reaffirmed mutual respect for the Open Door and the integrity of China. The United States declared its recognition that "territorial propinquity" gave Japan "special interests"—not "paramount interests" as Ishii had wanted—in China and especially in those areas bordering on Japan. A secret protocol in effect pledged Japan not to take advantage of the war to seek additional gains in China at the expense of other powers. The agreement almost immediately elicited divergent interpretations. The American government held it as a victory for the Open Door and Chinese integrity, traded for a virtually meaningless recognition of Japan's special interests on a geographical basis, nothing more. Japan, on the other hand, viewed the exchange of notes as recognizing not only its economic interests in China but its superior political role in that republic. Such were the fruits of a deliberately ambiguous document.

Even as the Lansing-Ishii negotiations began, Wilson approved the State Department's efforts to revive the old six-power consortium to free China from financial dependence upon Japan. Negotiations for the new group consisting of American, Japanese, British, and French bankers, with others possibly being included later, began in 1918. They did not reach an agreement until 1920, after Japan had safeguarded its interests in Manchuria. The new consortium never functioned in any effective way. It once more evidenced, however, Wilsonian opposition to Japanese predominance in China.

By late 1918 Wilson was determined to eradicate all spheres of influence in China. He hoped to compel Japan to restore Shantung to China and to turn over the former German islands in the Pacific, along with other captured dependent territories, to the new League of Nations for administration. But Japan refused to be denied its territorial objectives at the Paris Peace Conference, although it failed to obtain inclusion in the League Covenant of a racial equality clause, important to Japanese leaders, who were seriously disturbed by foreign discrimination against Orientals. It actually possessed Shantung and the north Pacific islands and had treaties and understandings with China and the Allies recognizing its claims. Wilson consented to Japan's retention of the islands as Class C mandates under the League. Theoretically, such mandates could not be fortified. Shantung proved a more explosive issue. The American delegation supported China's contentions that the war had cancelled Germany's leasehold in Shantung and that the treaties Japan had forced upon her were void since they were obtained by coercion. Japan refused to retreat. Finally, the Japanese delegation threatened to leave the peace conference and boycott the League. Correctly convinced that it was not an empty threat and fearful of the effects of a Japanese walkout on the League, Wilson capitulated. The Versailles Treaty formally transferred the Shantung holding to Japan.

Wilson's diplomatic offensive against Japan thus ended on a note of failure. Instead of following Theodore Roosevelt's more conciliatory course, as some State Department officials had recommended, Wilson reverted to Taft's policy. He unsuccessfully challenged Japan's claims to spheres of influence in Shantung and Manchuria. Perhaps his policy to some degree helped prevent even greater Japanese expansion in China, but it caused serious strains in Japanese-American relations. A member of the Japanese Diet summed up the sentiment of many Japanese in 1920: "America appears to think she is divinely appointed to rule the world with a big stick!" By 1921, when Wilson left office, relations between the two countries had reached a nadir, and a costly and dangerous naval arms race seemed inescapable.

Additional Reading

A useful though dated survey is by A. W. Griswold, *The Far Eastern Policy of the United States* (1938). So-called New Left scholars emphasize America's economic motives behind the Open Door policies: William Appleman Williams, *The Tragedy of American Diplomacy* (1959) and *The Roots of the Modern American Empire* (1969); Thomas J. McCormick, *China Market: America's Quest for Informal Empire, 1893–1901* (1967); and Lloyd C. Gardner, "American Foreign Policy, 1900–1921: A Second Look at the Realist Critique of American Diplomacy," in B. J. Bernstein, ed., *Towards a New Past: Dissenting Essays in American History* (1968), 202–231. Gardner denies that American policy was essentially moralistic in the Far East, and elsewhere, and depicts it instead as "the foreign policy of a confident industrial power." Marilyn Blatt Young, *The Rhetoric of Empire: American China Policy, 1895–1901* (1968) and Paul Varg, "The Myth of the China Market, 1890–1914," *American Historical Review*, LXXIII (1968), 742–758, see other factors behind American expansionism. Jerry Israel, "'For God, for China and for Yale'—The Open Door in Action," *American Historical Review*, LXXV (1970),

796–807, describes the interreaction between business, religious, and reform motivations. General studies of Japanese-American relations are by Payson J. Treat, *Diplomatic Relations between the United States and Japan, 1895–1905* (1938); Eleanor Tupper and G. E. McReynolds, *Japan in American Public Opinion* (1937); O. J. Clinard, *Japan's Influence on American Naval Power, 1897–1917* (1947); and W.R. Braisted, *The United States Navy in the Pacific, 1897–1909* (1958). Also see S. W. Livermore, "The American Navy as a Factor in World Politics, 1903–1913," *American Historical Review*, LXIII (1958), 863–879. For the battleship cruise, see Robert A. Hart, *The Great White Fleet* (1965). William L. Neumann, *America Encounters Japan: From Perry to MacArthur* (1963) examines the fluctuating stereotypes of Japan America has held. Russian relations are covered by E. H. Zabriskie, *American-Russian Rivalry in the Far East, 1895–1914* (1946) and by Pauline Tompkins, *American-Russian Relations in the Far East* (1949). The best overall view of Roosevelt's foreign policies is by Howard K. Beale, *Theodore Roosevelt and the Rise of America to World Power* (1956). Tyler Dennett, *Roosevelt and the Russo-Japanese War* (1925) and Thomas A. Bailey, *Theodore Roosevelt and the Japanese-American Crises* (1934) deal with the 1904–05 war and immigration crises. See also Roger Daniels, *The Politics of Prejudice: The Anti-Japanese Movement in California and the Struggle for Japanese Exclusion* (1962). Two excellent and broad-based research studies are by Raymond A. Esthus, *Theodore Roosevelt and Japan* (1966) and Charles E. Neu, *An Uncertain Friendship: Theodore Roosevelt and Japan, 1906–1909* (1967). Eugene P. Trani's *The Treaty of Portsmouth: An Adventure in American Diplomacy* (1969) is a well-written reappraisal of Roosevelt's balance of power concepts. Raymond A. Esthus, "The Changing Concept of the Open Door, 1899–1910," *Mississippi Valley Historical Review*, XLVI (1959), 435–454, is an important study depicting the shift from a narrow to an enlarged view of the Open Door policy. Esthus, "The Taft-Katsura Agreement—Reality or Myth?," *Journal of Modern History*, XXXI (1959), 46–51, denies that the "agreement" was a realpolitik bargain, while Jongsuk Chay, "The Taft-Katsura Memorandum Reconsidered," *Pacific Historical Review*, XXXVII (1968), 321–326, sees it as more than a mere air-clearing discussion. On Taft's reversal, see W. V. and M. V. Scholes, *The Foreign Policies of the Taft Administration* (1970); Charles Vevier, *The United States and China, 1906–1913* (1955); and R. E. Minger, "Taft's Missions to Japan: A Study in Personal Diplomacy," *Pacific Historical Review*, XXX (1961), 279–294. Wilsonian policy is covered by Tien-yi Li, *Woodrow Wilson's China Policy, 1913–1917* (1952); Russell H. Fifield, *Woodrow Wilson and the Far East: The Diplomacy of the Shantung Question* (1952); and Roy Watson Curry, *Woodrow Wilson and Far Eastern Policy, 1913–1921* (1957). A good brief account is contained in Arthur S. Link, *Woodrow Wilson and the Progressive Era, 1910–1917* (1954). Paolo E. Coletta, *William Jennings Bryan: Progressive*

Politician and Moral Statesman, 1909–1915 (1969), presents a careful study of Bryan's role in the alien land law and the Twenty-One Demands crises. See also Spencer C. Olin, Jr., "European Immigrant and Oriental Alien: Acceptance and Rejection by the California Legislature of 1913," *Pacific Historical Review*, XXV (1966), 303–315. A carefully reasoned study by Burton F. Beers, *Vain Endeavor: Robert Lansing's Attempt to End the American-Japanese Rivalry* (1962), examines Lansing's efforts at striking a realistic bargain with Japan. On economic methods of pressuring Japan see Jeffrey I. Safford, "Experiment in Containment: The United States Steel Embargo and Japan, 1917–1918," *Pacific Historical Review*, XXXIX (1970), 439–451. On the final efforts of the Wilson administration to curb Japan, see D. M. Smith, *Aftermath of War: Bainbridge Colby and Wilsonian Diplomacy, 1920–1921* (1970).

The Lusitania *and the U-boat*

OCEAN STEAMSHIPS.

CUNARD

EUROPE VIA LIVERPOOL

LUSITANIA.

Fastest and Largest Steamer
now in Atlantic Service Sails
SATURDAY, MAY 1, 10 A. M.
Transylvania, Fri., May 7, 5 P.M.
Orduna, - - Tues.,May 18, 10 A.M.
Tuscania, - - Fri., May 21, 5 P.M.
LUSITANIA, Sat., May 29, 1C A.M.
Transylvania, Fri., June 4, 5 P.M.

Gibraltar—Genoa—Naples—Piraeus
S.S. Carpathia, Thür., May 13, Noon

ROUND THE WORLD TOURS
Through bookings to all principal Ports
of the World.
Company's Office. 21-24 State St., N. Y.

NOTICE!

TRAVELLERS intending to
embark on the Atlantic voyage
are reminded that a state of
war exists between Germany
and her allies and Great Britain
and her allies; that the zone of
war includes the waters adjacent to the British Isles; that,
in accordance with formal notice given by the Imperial German Government, vessels flying
the flag of Great Britain, or of
any of her allies, are liable to
destruction in those waters and
that travellers sailing in the
war zone on ships of Great
Britain or her allies do so at
their own risk.

IMPERIAL GERMAN EMBASSY

WASHINGTON, D. C., APRIL 22, 1915.

17

THE FAILURE
OF NEUTRALITY,
1914–1917

1. THE IMPACT OF THE GREAT WAR

On June 28, 1914, pistol shots in faraway Sarajevo rudely interrupted the usual midsummer calm in Europe and America. Gavrilo Princip, a youthful member of the Serbian nationalist and terrorist organization—the Black Hand—assassinated Archduke Franz Ferdinand, heir to the Austro-Hungarian throne, and his wife Sophie. While most Americans, after a brief flare of interest, paid little attention to so remote an event—the baseball battle for first place in the American League that summer was far more absorbing to many—the assassinations touched off a crisis that was not to pass quickly. After a month of investigations and military preparations, the Austrian government issued an ultimatum to Serbia, accused of complicity in the killings, and then declared war on July 28. In a chain reaction of violence, one after another of the great European powers came into the war. Within a few incredible days, Austria-Hungary and her mighty ally Germany (the Central Powers) were at war with Serbia, Russia, France, and Great Britain (the Entente or Allied Powers). To knock France out of the war, Germany violated Belgian neutrality, thus bringing Great Britain into the lists. Japan entered the contest as a British ally in the Far East, and in 1915 Italy joined the Allied side. Turkey, Bulgaria, Rumania, and Greece also became entrapped in the conflict, and the United States, parts of Latin America, and China entered in 1917. The war fully deserved the title of the Great War, the first of the titanic struggles of the 20th century that have almost fatally rent the fabric of western civilization.

The outbreak of the war shocked Americans. It seemed unbelievable, in a century of unparalled prosperity and cultural advances, that the most civilized powers of Europe should relapse into a barbaric war. After the initial shock, most Americans rejoiced that geography and their policy of abstention from foreign alliances and entanglements saved their country from such Old World folly. President Wilson voiced their sentiments when he proclaimed official neutrality and urged his fellow citizens to impartiality of thought and speech as well. As one newspaper editor commented, "Peace-loving citizens . . . will now rise up and tender a hearty vote of thanks to Columbus for having discovered America."

Impartiality of sentiment proved easier to request than to obtain. Various ethnic groups in America's melting pot understandably sympathized with their former homelands. In 1914, approximately one-third of the American population of nearly 92 million people fell into the category of "hyphenated Americans," either foreign-born or with immigrants for one or both parents. Eight million German-Americans cheered the cause of the Central Powers. Some four million Irish-Americans, embittered by centuries of English rule of Ireland, tended to concur, as did many of the Russian-hating American Jewry. Most old-stock Americans, on the other hand, at least mildly sympathized with the Entente Powers, reflecting historical, cultural, and economic bonds with England and the traditional Franco-American friendship. Moreover, while Anglo-American relations had been improving steadily in recent years, by 1914 many Americans thought of imperial Germany and its sword-brandishing Kaiser Wilhelm II as the incarnation of militarism and autocracy. The *New York World* reflected the views of probably a majority of Americans when it declared in August, 1914 that "wantonly and deliberately the Kaiser has plunged his sword into the heart of civilization."

Both belligerent camps launched propaganda campaigns to win neutral support for their causes. The German Information Service in New York City released news bulletins, pamphlets, and books to justify the cause of the Central Powers. German spokesmen blamed the war on Russian imperialism and French desires to avenge their defeat in the 1870 Franco-Prussian conflict. The British had a secret and highly organized propaganda machine known to insiders as Wellington House. Sir Gilbert Parker directed its special branch for the United States. The young historian Arnold Toynbee and others numbered among his aides. Parker's staff compiled a carefully selected mailing list of influential Americans who received a stream of propaganda pamphlets, books, and other materials which also went to college libraries and other organizations. The group conducted weekly surveys of the American press and shaped their propaganda to appeal to ethnic, religious, and social groups. British propaganda depicted the Entente as fighting against an enemy who had ruthlessly violated Belgian neutrality (a "scrap of paper"), and in defense of democracy and decency against German autocracy and militarism. Although not ineffective, German propagandists faced a number of serious obstacles in America. They found it difficult to portray the Central Powers as waging a defensive war when their troops stood on Allied soil. Moreover, Germany introduced novel and therefore disturbing new weapons: poison gas, dirigible aerial bombardments of cities, and submarine attacks against noncombatant enemy passenger and merchant vessels. Because of Allied control of the seas and of the trans-Atlantic cables, it was comparatively difficult to get direct news from Germany into the United States. The majority of major American newspapers and magazines, such as the *New York Times,* also tended to adopt a pro-Ally line in editorials and coverage of the war.

Few historians today would attribute America's eventual intervention in the war to belligerent propaganda. Yet the far-reaching British campaign undoubtedly had a considerable cumulative effect on the American public. For example, Britain tellingly used the 1915 German execution of Edith Cavell, a British nurse caught as a spy in occupied Belgium, and alleged German atrocities and war crimes to indict Germany's rulers as barbarous and utterly ruthless. According to the Report of Lord Bryce in 1915, Prussian officers had made war into "a sacred mission, one of the highest functions of the omnipotent State, which is itself as much an Army as a State. . . . The Spirit of War is deified." Shortly after the Bryce Report, the briefcase of Dr. Heinrich Albert, one of the German propaganda officials in America, was found on a New York City elevated train. The American press published its contents and their revelations of propaganda activities touched off a spy scare and discredited the German effort. It should be kept in mind, however, that a majority of Americans held at least mildly pro-Ally sentiments when the war began, before British propaganda and German blunders had any real effect. British efforts undoubtedly strengthened that favorable predisposition, which helps explain why the United States more readily accepted Allied maritime war measures than the German submarine. British propaganda probably also made it easier for the United States eventually to enter the struggle against Germany. Yet until the events of early 1917, the majority of Americans agreed with President Wilson that continued neutrality remained the wisest course for the United States.

A small but influential minority in the United States held "realistic" convictions about the significance of the European War to America's security and economic interests. Since the 1880's and '90's a number of Americans had viewed Germany with growing distrust. They suspected the Kaiser's government of challenging the Monroe Doctrine by seeking coaling stations, naval bases, and perhaps even colonies in the Caribbean and in South America. Army and navy planners concluded on historical and economic grounds that Germany was the one major power most likely to challenge our hegemony in the Western Hemisphere. Theodore Roosevelt, Admiral A. T. Mahan, Henry Cabot Lodge, journalist Walter Lippmann, and a number of academicians, at one time or another shared these views. Thus in a 1909 article in *The Independent,* Professor Amos S. Hershey of Indiana University described Germany as a threat both to American interests and to world peace. He advocated an Anglo-American alliance to meet that danger, and predicted that "the people of the United States could hardly remain neutral in a war between Germany and Great Britain which might possibly end in German naval supremacy. . . ." When the European conflict began in 1914, such citizens concluded that America's own interests, its security, its economic welfare, and the preservation of democratic institutions, required an Entente victory. Conversely, they feared that a German triumph would supplant British with German sea power and would dangerously isolate the United States in the Atlantic and Pacific Oceans. This body of opinion surely made it easier for the nation to enter the contest against Germany.

Several high administration officials and advisers held similar views, including Colonel Edward M. House and Robert Lansing among the most influential. House, an intelligent and wealthy Texan who had taken an interest in politics, attached himself to Wilson's rising political star in 1912. Understanding Wilson's psychology, the soft-spoken Colonel astutely combined flattery, suggestion, and self-effacement in his relations with the new President, and speedily became his most intimate adviser and unofficial executive agent. Since House desired only the role of adviser, Wilson regarded him as selfless in his devotion. House apparently delighted in his "gray eminence" role as a power behind the scenes, and he played a considerable part in shaping Wilson's policies. Lansing, the son-in-law of former Secretary of State John Watson Foster and uncle to a later Secretary, John Foster Dulles, came to the State Department as Counselor or second-in-command in 1914 with an extensive background in international law and arbitration. Formal and reserved, and with a keenly analytical mind, Lansing also wielded much influence in framing neutrality policies. Both Wilson and Secretary Bryan leaned heavily on Lansing's knowledge and experience in international relations.

House thought of foreign affairs essentially in terms of promoting a stable world balance of power. During several trips to Europe on special missions for President Wilson before and during World War I, British leadership impressed him enormously and unrestrained German militarism aroused his fears. Germany, he wrote Wilson in early 1915, "is now controlled almost wholly by the militarists." Late in 1915, House commented to Lansing that the Allies should know that "we considered their cause our cause, and that we had no intention of permitting a military autocracy [to] dominate the world if our strength would prevent it." Yet for a long time House thought that the most preferable outcome of the war would be a limited Allied victory to curb Germany but still leave her strong enough to counterbalance the expansionist tendencies of Czarist Russia. He recommended to Wilson a benevolent policy toward the Allies and eventually, after the failure of attempts to mediate, entry into the struggle against Germany.

Lansing agreed with House, though he thought the Allies should completely shatter German power. In his view, a German victory or even a stalemate in the war would harm America's interests. Not only would Germany then become a more serious rival in Latin America, but Lansing feared ultimately a world-wide "Prussian" menace in the form of a German-Russian-Japanese alliance that would isolate the United States in both the Atlantic and the Pacific Oceans. Moreover, he believed democratic principles and institutions also required a defeat of German autocracy and militarism. Lansing, like House, shared the American faith in the superior virtues of democracy and liberal capitalism, and easily slipped into an ideological view of the war. In that sense, he believed a German victory would force the United States to abandon or modify many of its liberal values in order to arm heavily in defense of the Western Hemisphere. In a private memorandum, recorded in July, 1915 shortly after he succeeded Bryan as Secretary of State, Lansing wrote: "I have come to the conclusion that the German Government is utterly hostile to all nations with democratic institutions because . . . [its leaders] see in democracy a menace to absolutism and the defeat of the German ambitions for world domination." It seemed clear to him that "Germany must not be permitted to win this war and to break even, though to prevent it this country is forced to take an active part." Therefore he advocated a policy of acquiescence toward Allied acts and a strict defense of neutral rights against Germany even at the risk of war.

President Wilson knew and shared to some degree these views of his advisers. His initial reaction to the outbreak of the European war had been one of sympathy for Great Britain and France, whom he viewed as fighting defensively against the aggressive Central Powers. He soon achieved a more balanced and less emotional outlook, which took into account the complex causes of the conflict. Yet, owing to cultural ties and his admiration of the British government and traditions, he had a greater trust in the Allies than in the German leaders. At least until 1916, British war goals appeared far more reasonable to him than those of the Central Powers. From time to time Wilson apparently agreed with House that a German victory was undesirable and that America might have to intervene to prevent it. On one occasion he indicated concurrence with the Colonel's remark that "if Germany won it would change the course of our civilization and make the United States a military nation." Nevertheless the President earnestly believed that continued neutrality remained the correct course for the United States and he made great efforts to stay out of the conflict. America, he thought, should keep itself ready to help mediate the war on the basis of a peace of justice, and thereafter it should play a leading role in achieving a new liberal world order based on an economic Open Door everywhere, especially in the underdeveloped areas of Asia and Africa, and on the peaceful regulation of international relations. Such a new order of course would aid America's trade and assure its prosperity, but it also would benefit the rest of the world.

2. AN UNEVEN NEUTRALITY

Insulating the nation from the effects of the war proved impossible. The immediate economic impact disrupted the flow of trade to Europe, worsening the economic recession already under way in the United States. But soon orders began to flow in from the warring powers for food, raw materials, and munitions. America's economy quickly recovered from the slump and went on to a booming prosperity destined to last until the end of the war. This blessing, however, had some drawbacks, for allied purchases also meant shortages of some materials for home consumption, rising prices, and inflation.

In keeping with its traditional policy and with international practice, the United States opened its markets to all the contending powers and permitted private citizens to export munitions and war materials. In theory the war trade was considered neutral as long as it remained open to all, but, in fact, the Entente countries alone benefited because of their control of the seas. American exports to Europe greatly increased as vast quantities of food, fiber, and metals, and over one billion dollars' worth of munitions were shipped across the Atlantic to the Allies. The State Department brushed aside German and Austrian complaints about the munitions traffic.

In a very practical sense, the one-sided war trade converted America into a silent partner of the Entente. Disillusioned postwar critics and historians concluded that these economic forces eventually drew the United States into the war against Germany. Although the trade no doubt embittered many Germans and adversely affected German-American relations, the evidence does not support that interpretation. The majority of Americans welcomed war-induced prosperity, for why should the New World not profit from the misfortunes of the Old World as it always had in the past? The administration defended the commerce as neutral and desirable for the economy, but it never considered entering the struggle merely to insure continued prosperity. Moreover, most officials and the public assumed that an Allied victory was only a question of time.

Financial ties with the Allies also grew rapidly. At first the administration, upon Secretary Bryan's recommendation in August, 1914, discouraged private loans to the warring powers as inconsistent with "the true spirit of neutrality." The administration also wanted to cushion American finances against any dislocations caused by the European conflict. It soon became apparent, however, that the so-called Bryan loan ban conflicted with the country's interest in the expanding war trade. If the Allies could not obtain sufficient credit and loans to finance their purchases, war orders would diminish and prosperity would vanish. Consequently the administration relaxed its policy in October, 1914, and permitted credit arrangements, quietly abandoning the rest of the ban in the fall of 1915. As Lansing wrote the President, not to rescind the ban would mean "restriction of outputs, industrial depression, idle capital, financial demoralization, and general unrest and suffering among the laboring classes" of America. By early 1917, American bankers and bond purchasers had loaned the Allies nearly $2.3 billion. In contrast, Germany borrowed only $27 million. Securities and other collateral guaranteed the larger portion of the Entente debt against an Allied defeat. Although American neutrality clearly operated in favor of the Entente cause, it was an unplanned and almost inevitable result of the needs of the Allied Powers and their access to the American market. It once again demonstrated that the United States retained a major place in world affairs, and that whether the nation remained passive or active it could not help but exert an enormous influence in the international arena.

Controversies over neutral rights at first arose almost entirely with Great Britain. The United States tried to get the belligerents to abide by the Declaration of London, a liberal charter of neutral rights drawn up in 1909 but not ratified by all the powers, but the British government insisted upon substantial changes to enlarge belligerent rights. The painful reality rested in Britain's determination to use the Royal Navy, as in the Napoleonic Wars, to strangle the enemy by controlling neutral trade. Britain enlarged the contraband lists of goods subject to seizure if intended for the enemy, and effectively blocked direct trade with Germany even in nonmilitary materials. The Royal Navy detained American ships and seized cargoes consigned to neutral European countries, often destined for overland re-exportation to Germany and Austria. Pleading the excuse of retaliation for illegal German naval activities, the British government on March 11, 1915, proclaimed in effect a blockade of the Central Powers and contiguous neutrals.

The State Department vigorously protested Allied interferences as contrary to international law and the rights of neutrals, but it did not press the controversy to the point of a possible diplomatic rupture. The long American note to Britain on October 21, 1915, one of the strongest of Washington's protests to the Allies, contested the legality and effectiveness of the blockade and condemned interferences with neutral cargoes, but ended with the pious hope that Great Britain would govern its actions henceforth by law rather than by mere expediency.

The Allies accounted for the majority of American trade, so it would have proved economically ruinous to permit disputes over neutral rights to disrupt it. Moreover, Wilson and his principal advisers admired the

British and trusted English leaders such as Sir Edward Grey, the Foreign Secretary, who sought to avoid unnecessary interferences with American trade. Indeed Grey, at first, handled relations with the United States with a large degree of understanding, thereby strengthening the moral ties between the two countries. When the British government decided to classify cotton as absolute contraband, it cushioned the effect on southern cotton growers by working out a purchase plan to support the market price of that staple. In the State Department, Lansing particularly tried to prevent acrimonious diplomatic exchanges with Great Britain. He was convinced that American interests required the avoidance of a break, and he was aware of the many precedents created by the Union Navy during the Civil War in extending belligerent controls over neutral commerce. Therefore, as he wrote later, "Everything was submerged in verbosity."

In striking contrast, Washington showed much less tolerance for German submarine warfare. With the German High Seas Fleet virtually bottled up in the Baltic Sea by the British navy, German naval experts turned eagerly to the new underseas weapon as a means of challenging enemy control of the seas and of endangering the very existence of seagirt Great Britain. On February 4, 1915, ostensibly in retaliation for Allied mining of the North Sea, Berlin announced a submarine blockade of the British Isles; within the war zone, all belligerent shipping would be destroyed (that is, would be subject to submarine attacks without warning and without making provisions for the safety of crews and passengers). Germany cautioned neutral vessels to avoid the war zone on the grounds that Allied misuse of neutral flags as a cover, and the ramming of U-boats when they made a surface challenge, precluded the customary procedure of visit and search. Therefore, the Germans claimed, they could not always avoid accidental attacks on neutral ships. Wilson refused to accept such justifications for ruthless underseas warfare. In a note sent February 10, he reminded the government in Berlin of the "grave concern" caused by its proclamation. He warned that if violation of American rights occurred he would find it necessary "to hold the Imperial German Government to a strict accountability for such acts . . . and to take any steps it might be necessary to take to safeguard American lives and property . . . on the high seas. . . ."

The note of February 10 placed the American government in direct opposition to what Germany regarded as the most efficient use of the submarine. The State Department argued that neutral citizens and ships had the right to use the high seas freely, subject only to the customary practice of visit and search by belligerent warships to intercept contraband trade with the enemy. President Wilson and Lansing—Bryan was away from the capital—adopted the strict accountability policy to defend the nation's honor and rights and to protect its economic interests against what they viewed as an illegal and inhumane mode of warfare.

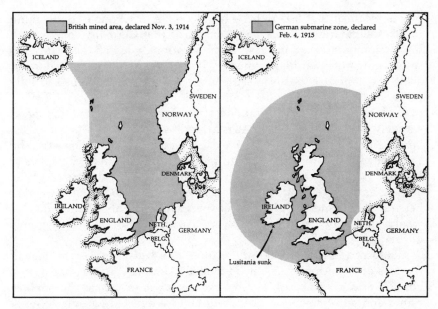

The War Zones at Sea, 1914–1917

They either did not consider or rejected other possible alternatives, such as requesting American ships and citizens to avoid the submarine zone, or filing claims and postponing settlement of issues until after the war.

The first submarine crisis arose when the Germans torpedoed the British steamer *Falaba* on March 28, 1915, with the loss of one American life. While the administration debated what course to adopt, an even more shocking tragedy occurred. On May 7, off the Irish coast, the *U-20* sighted the *Lusitania* in its periscope and fired a torpedo into the starboard side of the great passenger ship. The shot was so effective that the U-boat commander decided to forego firing a second torpedo into the mass of frantic passengers trying to take to the lifeboats. The Cunard liner, the pride of the British trans-Atlantic fleet, sank to the bottom within 18 minutes with the loss of 1,198 noncombatant lives, including 128 American citizens. A feeling of indescribable horror and outrage swept over the American public at an act so wanton and inhumane. War sentiment grew particularly strong in the eastern states, but though outraged, the rest of the country remained more pacifically inclined.

Wilson and Lansing viewed the sinking of the *Lusitania* and the killing of noncombatants and neutrals as an indefensible act contrary to international law, morality, and neutral rights. While the President refused to let emotion sweep him into belligerency—he remarked at Philadelphia on May 10 that, "There is such a thing as a man too proud to fight, . . . a nation being so right that it does not need to convince others by force that it is right"—he adopted a firm course condemning ruthless submarine warfare and demanding that Germany comply with his version of international law. Bryan so strongly feared that war might result, however, that he resigned on June 9 when Wilson refused to put aside the issue for postwar settlement. Apparently he hoped to rally peace sentiment against the administration's course. He failed, for the public approved Wilson's cautious but firm position and the press savagely criticized Bryan for deserting his post in a time of crisis. Lansing replaced him as Secretary of State. Yet while holding firm, the President wanted to avoid a confrontation. When Germany's replies to his first two notes failed to meet his demands for a disavowal of the sinking and for reparations, Wilson in effect retreated from his earlier general condemnation of underseas warfare and only warned that he would view any repetition involving American lives as "deliberately unfriendly."

The torpedoing of another British liner, the *Arabic,* on August 19, with the loss of two Americans, ended the lull. Although House and Lansing advised drastic measures, Wilson again sought to defend the nation's rights and still preserve peace. He therefore directed Lansing to enter into negotiations with the German Ambassador, Count Johann von Bernstorff.

Fortunately, certain factors in Germany favored a truce. The German Chancellor, Theobald von Bethmann-Hollweg, feared that war with the United States, which he expected to follow a break over the submarine issue, would prove fatal to Germany. He foresaw that as an opponent the United States would bring almost unlimited financial strength, industrial resources, and fresh manpower into the struggle, and would greatly boost Allied morale. Although he faced increasing pressure from within Germany for fuller use of the submarine as the best hope for victory, he received temporary support from the military leaders, apprehensive about adding to the country's enemies while the European situation still threatened. Kaiser Wilhelm II, for all his posturing as the Supreme Warlord of Germany, was actually a weak and indecisive ruler increasingly under the control of his own military leaders, to whom he deferred in this crisis. Consequently, the Chancellor made sufficient concessions to the United States to avoid a break, while not entirely renouncing the use of the U-boat. The *Arabic* controversy began to subside with a German pledge on September 1 not to sink passenger liners without warning and without provisions for the safety of those on board. On October 5, Germany announced that she had issued strict orders to U-boat commanders, and promised an indemnity for the losses of American life.

Significantly, however, the *Arabic* pledge applied only to passenger liners and not to all merchant vessels. It was simply a truce; the larger issue remained unresolved. And, as Bryan had feared, President Wilson had so deeply committed American prestige and honor to holding Germany fully accountable for any losses of American lives from U-boat attacks that his policy henceforth grew increasingly rigid.

3. PREPAREDNESS AND POLITICS

The preparedness campaign in 1915 and 1916 reflected the interaction of foreign crises and domestic politics. A growing number of Americans felt apprehensive about the nation's military weaknesses in the face of external dangers. Patriotic organizations such as the National Security League and the American Defense Society demanded increased expenditures for the army and navy. Ex-president Theodore Roosevelt, who had at first supported neutrality, soon advocated both preparedness and a more aggressive foreign policy. He fumed at Wilson's "pussyfooting" and referred contemptuously to the President's note writing to Berlin as typical of a "Byzantine logothete." Believing that both justice and America's own interests required an Allied victory, Roosevelt once sneered that the pacifist song "I Didn't Raise My Boy To Be A Soldier" sounded as nonsensical as would a song entitled "I Didn't Raise My Girl To Be A Mother." Many progressives and peace advocates, however, strongly opposed preparedness; their solution to neutrality problems lay in ending the war, not preparing to enter it.

The U-boat crises and the growing popular appeal of preparedness finally persuaded Wilson to endorse the cause. In the fall of 1915 the administration presented a plan supporting heavy outlays for defensive purposes. The naval program called for construction of ten battleships, six battle cruisers, ten cruisers, and numerous other craft within five years, and aimed at achieving parity with the British by 1925. The plan also provided for substantially enlarging the regular army.

These proposals stirred a furious political debate and split progressive ranks. While many reformers agreed with Wilson on preparedness, others joined the pacifists in opposition. Such organizations as the League to Limit Armament and the Women's Peace Party spearheaded the resistance. A group of Democratic members of Congress, mostly from the South and West, openly rebelled against the President's leadership. Wilson counterattacked by making a speaking tour early in 1916. In a series of addresses he defended preparedness as necessary to safeguard the Western Hemisphere against unnamed threats and to uphold American rights and honor against all challenges—most Americans undoubtedly interpreted such dangers as referring to Germany. America, he told one audience, "must play her part in keeping this conflagration from spreading to the people of the United States; she must also keep this conflagration from spreading on this side of the sea." Although forced to accept a number of compromises, Wilson obtained the approval of Congress for substantial increases in the army and for a large construction program for the navy.

While the preparedness campaign still raged, the Germans torpedoed the *Sussex,* an unarmed French channel steamer, on March 24, 1916. Although no Americans died, the attack clearly violated the *Arabic* pledge and renewed the submarine controversy with Germany. His advisers counseled that the time for mere protests had passed, but Wilson again chose a course of firmness that left room for a German retreat. On April 18, the President solemnly warned the German government that he would break diplomatic relations immediately unless it halted ruthless U-boat warfare against belligerent merchant and passenger ships.

Despite a mounting clamor within Germany for increased use of the underseas weapon, Chancellor Bethmann-Hollweg again succeeded in persuading the Kaiser to avoid a rupture. The *Sussex* pledge of May 4 promised that unresisting belligerent merchant and passenger vessels would not be attacked without warning and without provisions for the safety of those aboard. Ominously, however, the German note declared that if the American government failed to secure Allied observance of "freedom of the seas" for neutrals to trade with either side in the war, Germany reserved the right to alter its policy. The *Sussex* crisis thereby outlined the issue so sharply that any renewal of ruthless submarine warfare would leave the United States no alternative but to break diplomatic relations with Germany.

The presidential campaign of 1916 strengthened Wilson's determination to keep the nation at peace. A sharp deterioration in Anglo-American relations influenced his convictions. The *Sussex* pledge permitted American attention once more to focus squarely on Allied interferences with American commerce. The British government chose that time to tighten its blockade of the enemy and to increase controls over neutral trade. Britain censored neutral mails and publicly blacklisted 85 American firms and individuals suspected of trading with Germany, denying them use of all British-owned insurance, supplies, and other facilities. Reacting sharply to such blatant defiance of American sensibilities, President Wilson obtained retaliatory legislation from Congress authorizing him to withhold clearances and port facilities from foreign ships refusing to transport American goods. The authority was never invoked for the simple reason that it would interfere with America's warborn prosperity.

The popularity of the peace issue in the election of 1916 also strengthened Wilson's desire to preserve neutrality. With the collapse of the Progressive Party, the Republicans gained a good position to win the White House. Charles Evans Hughes resigned from the Supreme Court to accept the Republican presidential nomination. Hughes tried to adopt a middle-of-the-road approach to foreign policy, promising greater executive vigor without alienating the German-American element. Unfortunately Roosevelt's more bellicose support embarrassed Hughes by enabling the Democrats to portray him and the Republicans as prowar.

Wilson appealed to progressive sentiment by supporting a number of advanced reform measures. Moreover, after the dramatic response at the Democratic Convention to the slogan, Wilson "kept us out of the war," the President capitalized on the obvious peace sentiment of most citizens by charging that the election of Hughes would mean war with Mexico and intervention in the European conflict. A Democratic newspaper advertisement exploited the peace theme:

> You are Working—Not Fighting!
> Alive and Happy;—Not Cannon Fodder!
> Wilson and Peace with Honor?
> or
> Hughes with Roosevelt and War?

Even the efforts of certain Irish-American and Roman Catholic spokesmen to vent their wrath at the President's recognition of the anti-clerical Carranza in Mexico, and at his allegedly pro-British attitude on the Irish question and the European war, failed to divert many Irish voters from their traditional Democratic loyalties.

Yet the first returns on election night indicated a Republican triumph. Democratic leaders gathering at the Biltmore Hotel in New York City for a "victory" dinner, felt depressed, and even Wilson retired early that evening, resigned to defeat. Banner headlines in some newspapers hailed Hughes as the victor and next chief executive. Later reports from the western states, however, revealed that Wilson had edged out his opponent by an extremely close margin, receiving 277 electoral votes to 254 for Hughes. The election represented a victory for peace abroad and reform at home.

4. FROM MEDIATION TO BELLIGERENCY

After the election, Wilson made a major effort to end the war before the United States could be pulled in. Earlier, in 1915–1916, Colonel House had developed a scheme for mediation-intervention. Fearing that the submarine issue sooner or later would culminate in war, House had advised the President that "we should do something decisive now— something that would either end the war in a way to abolish militarism or that would bring us in with the Allies to help them do it." The House-Grey Memorandum, an understanding reached with the British Foreign Secretary in January, 1916, provided that the United States, at a time deemed favorable by the Allies, should propose a conference of the belligerents to end the war; if Germany declined or subsequently rejected reasonable terms, the United States would probably enter the war on the Allied side. Apparently House had intervention primarily in mind but Wilson envisaged the plan in terms of mediation. It failed in any case, because the Allied governments opposed a negotiated peace as long as any hope of victory remained. They also probably felt unwilling to bargain for an American entry into the war that appeared increasingly inevitable anyway. Now, after the 1916 election, Wilson undertook two direct moves of his own. On December 18, despite the embarrassment of an ill-timed German peace bid, he requested a statement of war aims from all the belligerents. The Allies reacted adversely, resenting the President's implication that their war aims and those of the enemy stood on the same moral plane. The American ambassador in London, Walter Hines Page, unabashedly pro-Ally, reported that the inquiry had deeply hurt British officials and that the king had "wept." Neither belligerent camp cared to define publicly its war goals or to allow the American President a direct role in peace negotiations. Undaunted, Wilson, on January 22, 1917, addressed the Senate and appealed for a compromise "peace without victory" based on justice and reason. For, he declared, "Only a peace between equals can last. . . ." This effort also failed. Both sides had expended too much blood and money, and passions were too deeply aroused, for either to accept a mere restoration of peace without extensive gains.

Failure of Wilson's peace efforts signalled the approaching end of American neutrality. In Germany the advocates of an all-out U-boat campaign carried the decision. Germany's great military heroes, Field Marshal Paul von Hindenburg and General Erich Ludendorff, had in effect become the nation's wartime dictators. The navy persuaded Hindenburg and Ludendorff that unrestricted submarine warfare offered the best remaining hope for ending the stalemated land war and decisively defeating the Allies by starving Britain into submission. Vociferous elements in the Reichstag and in the public at large, embittered at America and hopeful of victory, also demanded its use. They argued that the United States was already helping the Allies as much as it could, and its entry into the war would be a mere formality. Long before America could play any real role, they claimed, the U-boats could beat Britain to her knees. The Kaiser assented, while Bethmann-Hollweg and a few other officials, still dreading war with America, felt compelled to acquiesce. At the fateful conference at Pless on January 9, 1917, Chancellor Bethmann-Hollweg saw the futility of further resistance. He called the decision the "last card," and added, "But if the military authorities consider the U-boat war essential, I am not in a position to contradict them." Hindenburg replied complacently, "We are ready to meet all eventualities. . . ." On January 31, 1917, the United States was notified that all ships, belligerent and neutral, would be destroyed, obviously without warning and without safety provisions, in the waters around the British Isles. An almost insulting "concession" would permit one American passenger ship clearly marked with the flag to sail each week through the zone to the British Isles.

President Wilson took the only step possible under the circumstances and broke diplomatic relations with Germany on February 3. He still hoped that Germany might yet stay its hand. More than ever, he believed that continued American neutrality offered the only hope for a peace of justice and international stability. The anguished President apparently contemplated several courses short of full belligerency: the arming of American merchant vessels in defense against the U-boat (when a congressional filibuster in the Senate blocked passage of a bill for arming, Wilson armed the vessels on his own authority), or a limited sea war in which the navy would convoy American ships and repel submarine attacks. Gradually he rejected these alternatives as unsatisfactory, since they had all the disadvantages of a formal war without the benefits of clear national purpose and direct military efforts. The destruction of several American ships in mid-March revealed Germany's intention to carry out its threats, while the Zimmermann telegram further clarified Germany's hostile aims. German Foreign Secretary Arthur Zimmermann had proposed to Mexico the conclusion of an alliance against the United States in case of an American-German war—Japan would also be invited to join—and had dangled before Mexican eyes the prospect of recovering former territory lost during the Mexican War of 1846–48. The British intercepted and gave a copy of the decoded telegram to the State Department, which subsequently released it to the American press. An aroused American public needed no additional proof of German duplicity and hostility.

On April 2, ironically during Easter holy week, President Wilson went before Congress and recommended that it declare a state of war with Germany. After reviewing his efforts for peace and Germany's actions, he announced that neutrality was no longer possible. In addition to attacks upon American lives and rights on the high seas, he referred to German espionage within the United States as "One of the things that has served to convince me that the Prussian autocracy was not and could never be our friend. . . ." These and other deeds, such as the Zimmermann Telegram, further evidenced that Germany meant to act "against our peace and security," he explained. The President in moving language then referred to the more lofty goals for which the nation would contend: "The world must be made safe for democracy. . . . we shall fight for the things which we have always carried nearest our hearts—for democracy, for the right of those who submit to authority to have a voice in their own governments, for the rights and liberties of small nations, for a universal dominion of right by such a concert of free peoples as shall bring peace and safety to all nations and make the world itself at last free."

Wilson's message reiterated the themes of his counselors, House and Lansing, that autocracy or "Prussianism" endangered the material and the moral interests of the United States. It was a typically Wilsonian, and American, amalgam of morality and self-interests. Despite rear guard opposition from a minority of progressives and pacifists, such as Senator Robert LaFollette of Wisconsin, Congress approved the war resolution by a vote of 82 to 6 in the Senate and 373 to 50 in the House. Most of the opposition came from certain midwestern areas where large numbers of German-Americans or Scandinavian-Americans lived, and where a type of parochial agrarian progressivism was strongest. The mood in Congress and the nation as a whole reflected a reluctant acceptance of a struggle imposed by Germany. Congress formally declared war on April 6, 1917.

The basic causes of American involvement in the war have aroused much debate among scholars. In the disillusioned aftermath of the war, a wide consensus held that it had been unnecessary and unwise for the United States to abandon neutrality in 1917. So-called revisionist writers and historians charged or intimated that British propaganda and powerful economic and financial forces interested in insuring profits and investments through an Allied victory duped the country into joining the struggle. They further charged that Wilson had used the submarine merely as an excuse, and that at most, patent American disregard of neutrality had prompted its unrestricted use by Germany. Defenders of the official version or the "submarine school," on the other hand, asserted that the United States had followed a genuinely neutral program in its policies, and was forced into the war only because Germany persisted in violating American rights and destroying American lives on the high seas. In recent years, a few other writers have advanced the theory that the United States went to war not for any of these reasons but to defend the national security against the threat of a German victory.

None of these explanations alone seems satisfactory. There can be little doubt that, despite the official position of neutrality, the United States followed a course in 1914–1917 that was benevolent toward the Allies and on the whole uncompromising toward Germany. This reflected the existence of strong bonds of sentiment and trade between the United States and the Allied Powers, especially Great Britain. Yet, while it would be unsound to attribute the eventual entry into the war solely to the submarine issue—other courses besides the policy of strict accountability were available—there probably would have been no involvement without it. The U-boat provided the indispensable point of contact and hence of conflict between the two powers. Wilson's opposition to ruthless use of the underseas weapon reflected concern with America's economic interests as well as a determination to defend neutral rights and the national honor. Moreover, by 1917 he had come to view

Germany as a major threat not merely to the rights of the United States but to the peace and progress of the entire world. The President, and his principal advisers, subscribed to a liberal economic-political world view. They saw that American trade was expanding and was destined to predominate in an Open Door world, benefitting not only the United States but less developed countries such as China, and indeed all mankind. American democratic ideals and principles were spreading their influence over the globe, and if old-fashioned imperialism could be destroyed, a new era of international peace based on law and reason and mutual respect would dawn under American inspiration and leadership. American involvement in the war was necessary, Wilson apparently concluded, not only to safeguard American rights and interests but to eliminate German militarism and to lay the basis for an enduring peace based on justice and reason.

Additional Reading

The causes of American intervention in World War I have been hotly debated by scholars. Two useful guides to the literature are by Richard W. Leopold, "The Problem of American Intervention, 1917: An Historical Retrospect," *World Politics,* II (1950), 405–425, and by Daniel M. Smith, "National Interest and American Intervention, 1917: An Historiographical Appraisal," *Journal of American History,* LII (1965), 5–24. Also see Leopold's *The Growth of American Foreign Policy* (1962) and Smith's *The Great Departure: The United States in World War I, 1914–1920* (1965) for syntheses based upon recent scholarly studies. The submarine or "official" point of view is best represented by Charles Seymour, *American Diplomacy During the World War* (1934) and *American Neutrality, 1914–1917* (1935). In both these works Seymour concludes that the United States tried to be genuinely neutral and would not have gone to war except for the submarine outrages. Others holding that point of view are Harley Notter, *The Origins of the Foreign Policy of Woodrow Wilson* (1937); Samuel R. Spencer, Jr., *Decision for War, 1917* (1953); and Arthur Walworth, *Woodrow Wilson* (2 vols., 1958). Also see Barbara Tuchman, *The Zimmermann Telegram* (1958). Revisionists challenged the submarine explanation and emphasized the pro-Allied sentiment of the American people and government and America's one-sided economic ties with the Allies as unnecessarily and unwisely drawing the country into war. A pioneer revisionist study was *Why We Fought* (1929), by C. Hartley Grattan. *Road to War: America, 1914–1917* (1935), by Walter Millis, is a popularized revisionist work. H. C. Peterson, *Propaganda for War* (1939) attributes great effectiveness to British propaganda in involving the nation in the war, and Charles C. Tansill, *America Goes to War* (1938) is the best-documented study from the revisionist point of view (despite his professed disavowal of any particular thesis). See, too, Edwin Borchard and W. P. Lage, *Neutrality for the United States* (1937) and Alice M. Morrissey, *The American Defense of Neutral Rights, 1914–1917* (1939). An excellent study of the revisionist climate of opinion in the interwar era is Warren I. Cohen's *The American Revisionists: The Lessons of Intervention in World War I* (1967). For studies of public opinion and minority groups, see J. C. Crighton, *Missouri and the World War, 1914–1917* (1947); Cedric Cummings, *Indiana Public Opinion and the World War, 1914–1917* (1945); Edwin Costrell, *How Maine Viewed the War, 1914–1917* (1940); H. C. Syrett, "The Business Press and American Neutrality, 1914–1917," *Mississippi Valley Historical Review*, XXXII (1945), 215–230; C. J. Child, *The German-American in Politics, 1914–1917* (1939); and Carl Wittke, *German-Americans and the World War* (1936). Two recent articles upon German hyphenates and propaganda are by F. H. Bonadio, "The Failure of German Propaganda in the United States, 1914–1917," *Mid-America*, XLI (1959), 40–57, and T. J. Kerr, Jr., "German-Americans and Neutrality in the 1916 Election," *Mid-America*, XLIII (1961), 95–105. Also see James Weinstein, "Anti-War Sentiment and the Socialist Party, 1917–1918," *Political Science Quarterly*, LXXIV (1959), 215–239; Edward Cuddy, "Irish-American Propagandists and American Neutrality, 1914–1917," *Mid-America*, XLIX (1967), 252–275; and William M. Leary, Jr., "Woodrow Wilson, Irish-Americans, and the Election of 1916," *Journal of American History*, LIV (1967), 57–72. An excellent study of British opinion is by Armin Rappaport, *The British Press and Wilsonian Neutrality* (1951). Recent scholarship on the causes of intervention has depicted Wilson as fusing a measure of realism with his moralistic bent, and sees the war entry as reflecting decisions based upon a broad concept of the German threat to America: Edward H. Buehrig, *Woodrow Wilson and the Balance of Power* (1955); Arthur S. Link's biography, *Wilson* (5 vols., 1947–1965), his *Woodrow Wilson and the Progressive Era, 1910–1917* (1954), and *Wilson the Diplomatist* (1957); and Ernest R. May, *The World War and American Isolation, 1914–1917* (1959), the best one-volume study. Karl E. Birnbaum, *Peace Moves and U-Boat Warfare* (1958) examines the problem as seen from Berlin. For the "New Left" approach, emphasizing America's quest for an Open-Door world economic predominancy, see William Appleman Williams, *The Tragedy of American Diplomacy* (1959) and Lloyd C. Gardner, "American Foreign Policy: 1900–1921: A Second Look at the Realist Critique of American Diplomacy," in B. J. Bernstein, ed., *Towards a New Past: Dissenting Essays in American History* (1968), 202–231. N. Gordon Levin, Jr., *Woodrow Wilson and World Politics: America's Response to War and Revolution* (1968) presents a stimulating re-interpretation of Wilsonian policy as the pursuit of a new democratic and liberal capitalist world order. On the role of Wilson's principal advisers, consult Charles Seymour, ed., *The Intimate Papers of Colonel House* (4 vols., 1926–28);

A. L. and J. L. George, *Woodrow Wilson and Colonel House* (1956), a psychological study; Daniel M. Smith, *Robert Lansing and American Neutrality, 1914–1917* (1958); and Paolo E. Coletta, *William Jennings Bryan: Progressive Politician and Moral Statesman, 1909–1915* (1969). John Milton Cooper, Jr., *The Vanity of Power: American Isolationism and the First World War, 1914–1917* (1969) examines Bryan's part in developing isolationist concepts. Ross Gregory, *Walter Hines Page, Ambassador to the Court of St. James's* (1970), a prize-winning study, attributes to the anglophile Page little influence on Wilsonian policy.

The Big Four—Prime Minister David Lloyd George, Premier Vittorio E. Orlando, Premier Georges Clemenceau, and President Woodrow Wilson—at Paris Peace Conference

18

WILSON AND
A NEW WORLD ORDER,
1917–1921

1. AMERICA MOBILIZES FOR WAR

Since Americans had thought the Allies were winning a war of attrition against Germany, most expected their role in the war to be limited largely to economic and financial participation. A series of Allied war missions to the United States quickly dispelled that optimism and made clear to the government and people that victory would require a major military effort.

The British war mission, led by Foreign Secretary Arthur James Balfour, arrived in the spring of 1917. That distinguished British statesman impressed American officials and the public alike, addressing a joint session of Congress with the President applauding from the galleries, and paying homage to George Washington's tomb at Mt. Vernon. Balfour's mission conferred with American officials on problems of procurement and coordination of the war effort. Other missions, among them the French, Italian, Belgian, and Russian, were also received with pomp and ceremony. If the novelty finally began to wear off, at least the visitors aroused popular interest in the war and dramatized the collective nature of the great struggle against autocracy.

With the entry into war, the State Department fell into a partial eclipse. The most pressing problems now involved procurement and military cooperation with the Allies. The State Department played only a nominal role in these affairs, which were handled primarily by the War and Treasury Departments and the newly established American and inter-Allied war agencies. Agencies such as the War Industries Board mobilized the incredibly productive American economy. War materials and foodstuffs poured forth in an ever-growing flood and the United

States became the chief banker and supplier of the coalition fighting the Central Powers. Politics went on as always, of course, but President Wilson beat off critics of his administration and refused to create a coalition war cabinet as Republicans proposed.

The Committee on Public Information rallied public opinion, initially less than universally enthusiastic about the war. The C.P.I. ("Compub" in governmentalese) flooded America and Europe with propaganda materials designed to arouse support for the idealistic goals of the Great Crusade. Lurid movies, such as "The Beast of Berlin" and "The Prussian Cur," pamphlets, books, posters, and photographs inflamed the war emotions of the people. A veritable war hysteria that affected even President Wilson soon swept America. Opponents or critics of the war were silenced, some by imprisonment after Congress passed the Espionage Act in 1917 and the Sabotage and Sedition Acts in 1918. These harsh laws provided heavy fines and prison sentences for anyone obstructing the draft or aiding the enemy, or uttering abuses against the American government, flag, and uniform. Laws suppressed pacifist and radical dissent and the post office banned a number of publications from the mails. German-Americans were particularly suspect, and the anti-German madness even descended to book burning, bans against German music, and renaming popular German foods. Wilson made little effort to counter the hysteria, apparently because it silenced his critics and promoted war unity. Moreover, he felt confident that sanity would eventually return.

Relying primarily upon conscription, the United States raised armed forces numbering about five million men. General John Jacob Pershing commanded the American Expeditionary Force (A.E.F.) sent to France. Although the movement of American manpower to Europe started as only a trickle, it became a flood by the spring and summer of 1918. Pershing eventually commanded over two million troops in France and held about one-fourth of the entire Western Front. The A.E.F. fought courageously and well in the final campaigns that checked the last great German offensive and then drove the enemy into retreat. Thus, while American battle losses were relatively small compared to those of the Allies (50,000 Americans killed to 1.7 million Russians, 1.385 million Frenchmen, and 900,000 Britishers), the fresh American manpower swung the balance decisively against Germany. The navy's role was largely confined to convoying and patrol duty against enemy submarines.

2. A WAR FOR A JUST PEACE

The outbreak of war and its carnage shocked peace societies, active in Europe and America since the early 19th century, into an ever more zealous search for a panacea. They felt that alliances and balances of power, the obvious culprits in 1914, had to be curbed by a world court and law, or supplanted by an international concert of power to achieve peace and promote disarmament. Many earnest peace advocates rationalized the bloody strife as necessary to promote the worldwide triumph of democracy, to abolish secret diplomacy, and to end the war on the basis of an enlightened peace. An organization known as the League to Enforce Peace formed in the United States in 1915 to work for these goals, and a similar society existed in Great Britain.

Even prior to 1917, President Wilson had begun to advocate a liberal peace program. He believed that this country had a special mission to promote a liberal world economic and political system based on democratic institutions and a global Open Door for trade (within which an expanding American economy obviously would take pre-eminence). The new order would respect the rights and interests of backward countries and dependencies, and would supplant the secret diplomacy and alliances of the unhappy past with law, reason, and justice. Within this "new order of the ages," all the great powers could share in the rational development and use of the resources of underdeveloped areas for the benefit of all the world. Wilson thus fused America's own economic, political, and ideological interests with an idealistic concept of global liberalism. He envisioned a collective security organization as the framework for the new order. A universal organization of states pledged to mutual guarantees of the integrity of all states, large and small, would prevent any war contrary to treaty obligations or enlightened world opinion, and would eliminate the necessity for secret diplomacy, alliances, and arms races. In his peace moves in late 1916 and early 1917, and in his war message, Wilson called for a just peace and an international concert of power to insure its preservation.

Wilson knew that the Allied governments had very different war goals. The Allies had made a number of secret treaties and agreements among themselves for a postwar division of spoils—an inevitable and not necessarily objectionable result of a coalition war. The American government had the details of most of these arrangements by the time of the peace conference in 1919. Wilson did not discuss them, however, apparently in order to avoid committing the United States in any way to the Allied plans. Wilson was confident that by the end of the war the Allies would have become so dependent upon American economic and financial power that he could impose his own views of a just peace. To underscore the nation's independent course, the United States did not enter into any formal alliances or ties with the Allies. Even in referring to the coalition, Wilson distinguished the United States from the Allies as an "Associated Power."

Wilson mobilized world opinion to support his new world order. In a series of notable addresses, he drew a distinction between the German people, with whom he declared America had no quarrel, and their leaders, whose imperialistic ambitions had to be defeated. He hoped to weaken German morale and yet to avoid arousing or stimulating extreme anti-German sentiment in America. He depicted the threat of autocracy or "Prussianism" as coming exclusively from "the military masters of Germany." In his Flag Day address on June 14, 1917, the President declared that the German ruling class had driven the United States into the war by its insults and aggressions. If Germany's masters succeeded in their ambitions for conquest, no country would be safe. Thus he again demonstrated his fusion of America's material and moral interests with the good of mankind. Such remarks also revealed that despite his preference for a more idealistic approach, he did try to present the war in more practical terms. He defined autocracy or "Prussianism" as the complete control by an irresponsible minority of the lives and fortunes of their own peoples as well as all others who came under their rule, and as an attempt to "impose its will upon the world by force." That concept of statism—the power of the total state to engulf all aspects of the life of the individual—resembled the stereotype of "totalitarianism" used in the 1930's and 1940's. Moreover, Wilson and some of his advisers, such as Lansing, tended to include Japan and the Russian Bolsheviks in that category.

The President and most Americans thus saw the war as a worldwide ideological struggle of incalculable significance for the future of mankind. When Pope Benedict XV issued an appeal for a negotiated peace in mid-1917, Wilson replied that the free peoples of the world must be delivered from "the menace and the actual power of a vast military establishment controlled by an irresponsible government which, having secretly planned to dominate the world, proceeded to carry the plan out. . . ." Such simplistic and moralistic views distorted the actual situation in Germany and the complex causes of World War I. His own moralistic impulses and his desire to rationalize a war that he found painful swept Wilson into the utterance of historical absurdities.

The President began to prepare for peace in 1917 by establishing a group of scholars, known as the Inquiry, to study war goals and to draft reports on the problems likely to arise at the eventual peace conference. The scholars and experts of the Inquiry—historians, geographers, and others—produced nearly 2,000 reports and gathered or made large numbers of maps. Many of these papers and some of the experts subsequently took part in the peace conference and influenced the nature of the peace.

Wilson delivered the Fourteen Points address, his most famous wartime speech, before Congress on January 8, 1918. He listed the essential provisions of a lasting peace: evacuation of all Allied territory occupied by the enemy; return of Alsace-Lorraine to France; creation of an independent Poland with access to the sea; and autonomous development for the peoples of the Austrian and Turkish empires. He outlined certain general principles that should guide the writing of peace: open diplomacy (no more secret treaties); freedom of the seas in war and in peace; reduction of armaments to a level sufficient for national security; and the adjustment of colonial claims with proper consideration for the interests of colonial peoples as well as the claimant powers. The fourteenth point, in Wilson's view, served as the key to the peace: "A general association of nations must be formed under specific covenants for the purpose of affording mutual guarantees of political independence and territorial integrity to great and small states alike."

In subsequent addresses, Wilson added other points to his prescription for a lasting peace and a liberal world order. Some of the most notable included the idea that the great powers should not treat peoples and territories as mere pawns, and the right of peoples to national self-determination. Rarely in history has a secular leader so touched the conscience and imagination of the western world as Wilson did in 1918. His inspired language and exalted vision not only enormously impressed world liberal opinion, but eventually had some effect in stimulating popular discontent within the Central Powers. Allied leaders, therefore, despite their lack of enthusiasm for the President's noble pronouncements, dared not openly object or criticize. Informally but undeniably, Wilson had become the chief spokesman for the Allied and Associated States.

"Self-determination" of peoples became one of the moving slogans of the war. Yet, it would be incorrect to attribute the emergence of the new states of Poland, Czechoslovakia, Finland, Latvia, Lithuania, Estonia, and Yugoslavia primarily to Wilson's encouragement. Americans, sharing the old liberal belief in the beneficial nature of nationalism, regarded these independence movements with sympathy, and undoubtedly Wilson's words had strengthened these feelings. But the fact remains that nationalism existed in these areas long before 1914 and had helped bring about the war. The emergence of the new states stemmed directly from the war and the disintegration of the Czarist and Hapsburg empires, and not merely from Wilsonian rhetoric.

Russia became a test case for Wilsonian liberalism and a key factor in the development of his thought about the postwar world. America had rejoiced at the overthrow of the Czarist regime in the March revolution of 1917 and at the establishment of a democratic republic. Elihu Root led a special mission to Russia in mid-1917, and the United States extended $324 million and other aid to the new government. Unfortunately, both American officials and private citizens failed to appreciate the depth of war-weariness in Russia, the collapse of military morale, and the growing influence of radical panaceas for social ills. They too easily assumed that such leaders as Prince George Lvov and Alexander Kerensky would keep Russia in the war and follow the pattern of western bourgeois democracies. The Bolshevik Revolution in November, 1917 rudely upset such expectations. The Communist or Bolshevik party imposed a ruthless dictatorial government on Russia and promptly took steps to make peace with the Central Powers. The withdrawal understandably disturbed the Allies, who feared that Germany would shift vast numbers of troops from the Eastern to the Western Front in another effort to accomplish a decisive military breakthrough. Apparently the undemocratic nature of the new regime primarily bothered President Wilson, while Secretary of State Lansing viewed with apprehension Communist ideology and the effort to export revolution and class warfare. The United States, therefore, denied the new regime diplomatic recognition, and Wilson, the messianic leader of the liberal West, soon found himself a rival of the Soviet prophet of world revolution, Vladimir Lenin.

Wilson experienced tremendous Allied pressure for armed intervention against the Bolsheviks and for the restoration of an Eastern Front. He repeatedly refused, despite his anti-Bolshevism and his hope of reabsorbing a liberal Russia into the new world order he planned, arguing that the Russian people should be allowed to determine freely their own form of government, and pointing out the impracticality of the military schemes. Allied pleas and an apparent military necessity finally wore down his resistance. Exaggerated reports arrived that Germany was driving deeper into Russia and threatened complete control of that country. Moreover, the German advance seemed to endanger thousands of tons of war supplies that America and the Allies had shipped to Murmansk and Archangel in northern Russia and to Vladivostok in Siberia. Finally, the Bolshevik withdrawal threatened the safety of the 45,000 to 65,000 Czechoslovak troops, previously allowed by the Russian provisional government to form and fight on the Russian front. While evacuating from Russia, the Czech legion clashed with Soviet forces. Insistent demands to do something to rescue these brave men from the Reds bombarded Wilson.

In mid-1918 the President finally consented to limited armed interventions in Siberia and northern Russia, for the purpose of rescuing the Czechs and preventing German control. By "stabilizing" conditions he hoped also to encourage the emergence of non-Bolshevik and liberal movements in Russia. In that sense, Wilson's decision for limited intervention was anti-Bolshevik. He insisted that these Allied forces should not engage in direct or overt political activity, however, but should confine their role to rescuing the Czechs and guarding the war supplies. Apparently he thought that the Bolshevik regime could not survive long in any case, and that American and Allied troops by their mere presence would encourage the emergence of a more democratic government.

The Allies soon tried to expand intervention in order to overthrow the Bolsheviks and to return Russia to the war. Japan increased her forces in

Siberia to over 70,000 men, far exceeding the American contingent of 9,000 troops. While Wilson did not succeed completely in restraining the Allies, he managed to prevent a much larger intervention than did occur. After the Armistice, he refused to broaden the intervention, and he withdrew American troops from northern Russia in 1919 and from Siberia early in 1920. The President committed himself as fully to preventing the spread of social revolutions as to the destruction of imperialism, and he still hoped Russia would return to liberal democratic paths, but principle as well as practical considerations seemed to rule out attempts to suppress Communism by force. No doubt these interventions helped create a legacy of hatred within the Bolshevik government, but at least they avoided a costly and probably futile all-out intervention.

Allied blows had the Central Powers reeling by the fall of 1918. Turkey, Bulgaria, and Austria-Hungary frantically appealed for peace. Allied armies had checked the last great German offensive on the Western Front and they launched a successful counterdrive that smashed the Hindenburg Line and threatened to invade Germany itself. Facing military disaster, Hindenburg and Ludendorff forced the civilian government to request from President Wilson a peace based on the Fourteen Points. Apparently they hoped for generous terms or at least a breathing spell permitting withdrawal of the German armies to more defensible lines. Despite fears in Europe and America that the wily Germans would dupe him, Wilson skillfully handled the exchanges and probably hastened the end of the war by several months. Although Germany's military leaders soon recovered confidence and preferred to continue the fighting rather than accept drastic military terms, German home morale was rapidly cracking and the civilian officials overruled the army. A full acceptance of Wilson's terms, and the establishment of a republic in Germany, as Wilhelm fled into exile in Holland, resulted. Colonel House went to Europe to obtain Allied approval of Wilson's exchanges with the Germans. Under strong American pressure, the Allied leaders reluctantly acquiesced in the so-called "Pre-Armistice Agreement" to give Germany a peace based on the Fourteen Points, with two qualifications dealing with freedom of the seas and the inclusion of damages to civilians in the clause relating to the restoration of occupied territory.

The day eagerly awaited by a war-exhausted world at last was at hand. On November 8, the delegates of defeated Germany made their way to a railway carriage in Compiègne forest where Marshall Foch and his triumphant staff awaited. The terms presented to the Germans were harsh and designed to insure that Germany could not renew the war. The Germans had to evacuate occupied territory immediately and hand over vast quantities of guns, ammunition, and other supplies to the Allies. The Germans had no choice but to sign the Armistice. The guns fell silent on the shell-pocked Western Front at eleven o'clock on the morning of November 11, 1918, nearly four and a half years and millions of casualties after the war had begun. Americans lighted the Statue of Liberty in celebration, and vast crowds surged joyously through the streets. Stores displayed signs, "Closed for the Kaiser's Funeral," and the deposed emperor was repeatedly burned in effigy. Eight hundred Barnard College girls snake-danced on Morningside Heights in New York City, automobiles blared their horns in the clogged streets, and despite the influenza scare pretty girls kissed every soldier they encountered. The great war for democracy had ended. President Wilson looked forward confidently to the coming peace conference, for the Allied governments had consented to an enlightened peace based on principle and justice, not expediency and vindictiveness.

3. TOWARD A NEW WORLD ORDER

Wilson made two major mistakes on the eve of the conference that cast an ominous shadow over his forthcoming labors at Paris: the 1918 election appeal, and the naming of the American delegation to negotiate the peace. Anxious to retain control of the Congress and to strengthen his hand at the peace conference, Wilson appealed to the electorate to vote Democratic in the 1918 Congressional elections. "The return of a Republican majority," he declared, would ". . . certainly be interpreted on the other side of the water as a repudiation of my leadership." Although his appeal had ample precedent and aided a few Democratic candidates, it proved to be a major political blunder. Republicans charged that the President had violated his own earlier plea that "politics is adjourned" and that he had impugned the loyalty of Republican Congressmen who had cooperated in the war effort. When the Republicans won control of both houses of Congress, it became only too easy to assert that the President had asked for a popular vote of confidence and had lost. This impaired his position at the peace conference and, probably more important, made the new Congress more resentful and rebellious at his leadership.

A far less defensible mistake involved the American commission to negotiate peace at Paris. The President failed to appoint a prominent Republican or any members of the Senate to the commission. Instead he named four individuals who either were closely connected with his administration or who lacked major political stature: Secretary of State Lansing; Colonel House; General Tasker H. Bliss; and Henry White, a diplomat and a minor Republican. Breaking tradition, Wilson decided to lead the commission himself and to take a direct part in the negotiations. Critics raged that he had packed the commission with yes men and charged him with a messiah complex in attending the Paris conference himself. Moreover, Wilson made no effort to consult powerful senators on what terms to seek, despite the obvious fact that the Senate would have to approve any treaty. Apparently Wilson was so convinced of his own rectitude, and so resentful of criticism and opposition, that he ignored the portents of his actions. By so doing he increased the probability that the Senate would challenge his leadership in foreign affairs and that the treaty of peace, regardless of its nature, would become a partisan issue. The embittered ex-President Roosevelt, who had never warmed to Wilson, warned of the coming political battle. "Our allies and our enemies," he declared, "and Mr. Wilson himself should all understand that Mr. Wilson has no authority whatever to speak for the American people. . . ."

Wilson sailed for Europe aboard the S.S. *George Washington* on December 4, 1918, the first American President to visit Europe while in office. Parisians gave him a tumultuous reception, reportedly unequalled since Napoleon's triumphal entries into the city. Wilson passed under one huge banner that expressed the sentiments of the European multitudes, "Honor to Wilson the Just." Prior to the conference, Wilson briefly toured England and Italy. He received a cordial reception in London, but that in Rome almost surpassed belief. Everywhere the Allied peoples hailed him as the deliverer of mankind, the hope of the world. He would ensure peace and justice; but unfortunately, too many of the Allied peoples envisioned justice as crushing Germany into the ground. Equally unfortunately, these wildly enthusiastic receptions apparently strengthened Wilson's assumption that he alone spoke for the best interests of humanity.

Delegates from 32 governments gathered at Paris as the peace conference got under way early in January, 1919. Strictly speaking, this gathering really served as only a preliminary conference among the victors, with the formal peace conference beginning when the delegates of defeated Germany arrived in May to receive the completed treaty. The Big Four dominated the conference: Wilson; British Prime Minister David Lloyd George; French Premier Georges Clemenceau, the "Tiger" of France; and, to a lesser degree, Premier Vittorio Orlando of Italy. Japan constituted a fifth great power on issues directly involving the Far East. The lesser states played only a minor role in the conference, and were reduced to awaiting crumbs from the Big Four. Despite Wilson's slogan of "open diplomacy," the hordes of disgusted newsmen at Paris found everything important cloaked in secrecy.

The Big Four offered an interesting study in contrasts. Unquestionably the moral spokesman of the group, Wilson often pursued highly practical and realistic efforts to obtain a just and workable peace. He expended great energy in mastering the details of the peace making and impressed many observers with the depth of his knowledge. He tended to isolate himself from his fellow American commissioners, however, depriving himself of aid and advice which could have greatly benefited him. Lloyd George, the clever British politician and opportunist, was much less informed about the problems that arose at Paris. In general, however, he joined with the American President in opposing the more selfish schemes of the other powers. Clemenceau, nearly 80 years of age, had one overriding goal—to so weaken Germany by heavy financial reparations and losses of territory that it could never again menace France. Wilson's idealism apparently both puzzled and amused the cynical Clemenceau. On one occasion he supposedly remarked to Colonel House that "talking to Wilson is something like talking to Jesus Christ!" As for the Fourteen Points, he commented, "God gave us the Ten Commandments, and we broke them. Wilson gives us the Fourteen Points. We shall see." Orlando, the last of the Big Four, generally played a smaller role at Paris.

In Wilson's view, the drafting of the Covenant of the League of Nations was the most important task of the conference. The American and British delegations worked together harmoniously, reflecting the fact that the Anglo-Americans agreed on most issues at Paris. France's efforts to convert the League into a military alliance of the great powers met defeat. The essential provisions of the Covenant, which was to form an integral part of the treaty of peace, established an assembly of all members, a council composed of the five great powers as permanent members with elected representatives of the smaller states, and a secretariat for administrative duties. The council was charged with the primary responsibility for preserving or restoring peace, and was empowered to invoke economic and military sanctions and to adopt other substantive measures only by unanimous vote. Article X pledged the signatories to respect and uphold the territorial integrity and political independence of all members of the League. Intended to deter aggression, the Article in effect froze the status quo established at Paris.

Upon completion of the Covenant, the President left Paris in mid-February for a quick return to the United States. Critics, mostly Republicans, were already attacking the League as a world superstate that would seriously curtail American sovereignty. Wilson invited representatives of the House and Senate to a White House dinner and attempted without great success to explain and defend his handiwork. He failed to win over Republican Senator Henry Cabot Lodge of Massachusetts, a cold, reserved man of biting sarcasm, who became chairman of the Committee on Foreign Relations in the new Congress. A bitter personal critic of the President, Lodge hoped to handle the issue in such a way as to humiliate Wilson and to strengthen the Republicans. In a speech two days after the White House conference, the senator urged that the Covenant be separated from the main body of the peace treaty, and he warned against entangling alliances and a departure from America's traditional policy of diplomatic freedom. A Republican "Round Robin," signed by 39 senators or senators-elect, six more than necessary to block approval of a treaty, declared that they found unacceptable the Covenant as drafted. The President had ample warning of the opposition's determination and returned to Paris in a much weakened position.

Swallowing his outrage at such criticisms, most of which he viewed as based on ignorance or blind partisanship, Wilson obtained several modifications in the Covenant that he hoped would satisfy his critics. He had provisions added permitting a member to decline a mandate offered by the League (former enemy territories and colonies were to be administered as League mandates or trusteeships); exempting domestic matters from League jurisdiction; and in effect sanctioning the Monroe Doctrine as a regional understanding permissable under the Covenant. Members also could withdraw from the League after two years' notice and the full performance of their obligations. Wilson was unwilling to ask for additional changes, especially in regard to Article X. He concluded that he had done everything reasonable to answer legitimate criticism; the Senate would either have to accept the revised Covenant or do the unbelievable and reject the entire peace treaty, and he prepared to fight his opponents on that basis.

Wilson resolutely opposed French schemes to dismember Germany by annexing the Saar Valley and establishing an autonomous Rhineland under French control. Such a partition, together with the stringent military terms already agreed upon for Germany—a maximum army of 100,000 men, abolition of the general staff, a small navy, and prohibition of the possession of tanks, poison gas, and military aircraft—would reduce her to impotence and ensure French security and revenge. Lloyd George joined Wilson in opposing France's territorial demands, both on the grounds of principle and because the practical effects would result in inflaming German nationalism and sowing the seeds of a future war. At one stage of the controversy, Clemenceau accused Wilson of being pro-German and angrily stalked out of the conference room. The conference seemed on the verge of disruption as Wilson threatened to return home rather than capitulate to French desires.

The conference finally arrived at a compromise that seemed to provide adequate protection for France without dismantling Germany. France would occupy the Saar Valley, with its valuable coal mines, for 15 years, followed by a League-supervised plebiscite to determine its future allegiance. Germany had to demilitarize the Rhineland to a distance of 50 kilometers east of the river, and France could occupy strategic bridgeheads along the Rhine for 15 years. As an additional guarantee, intended to function only until the League could become operational, Britain and the United States signed bilateral treaties with France promising military assistance in case Germany should launch an aggressive attack on France. These security treaties never took effect, because of the failure of the American Senate to act favorably.

Wilson had less success on reparations. The Americans argued that Germany's responsibility for civilian damages under the Pre-Armistice Agreement should be based on reasonable estimates of Germany's ability to pay over a limited period of time. The Allied peoples, however, expected Germany to assume virtually the entire costs of the war. British voters, for instance, had been promised during the 1918 elections that Germany would be made to "pay to the last farthing." Article 231 of the final treaty held Germany and its allies responsible for the costs of the war (the "war guilt" clause), but Article 232 limited actual reparations to civilian damages. Wilson, however, finally yielded to the inclusion of veterans' pensions in the category of civilian damages, which more than doubled the final bill. Unfortunately the failure of the United States to ratify the peace treaty prevented it from participating in the Reparations Commission that subsequently fixed reparations at $33 billion. A number of unhappy liberals in America and Britain attacked these provisions as unjust and as a violation of promises to Germany, while Germans felt deeply embittered.

In the other territorial settlements at the Conference, Wilson made some compromises but in general stood firmly behind the principle of national self-determination. France sought the creation of a large Poland, Czechoslovakia, and Rumania in order to restrain Germany in the future. Although aware of strategic and security factors, Wilson and Lloyd George resisted the more extreme proposals. Poland received a corridor across German territory to give it access to the Baltic Sea, but the German-inhabited port of Danzig became a free city under League supervision. The conference could not determine the eastern boundaries of Poland, owing to Russia's absence. Strategic factors also made it necessary to include Sudeten Germans within the new Czechoslovakia. Reasonable though these arrangements appeared, they rankled in Germany and later gave Adolf Hitler convenient grievances to exploit. Italy, although it obtained Austrian-inhabited areas in the South Tyrol area and Slavic populations around Trieste on the Adriatic Sea, did not receive the port city of Fiume. The Italian delegation briefly walked out of the conference when Wilson publicly opposed it on Fiume, which he felt the new Yugoslav state should get. The Italian defection and Japan's threat to follow, as noted earlier, also caused Wilson to swallow his objections to giving Japan title to the German holdings in Shantung.

The specter of Bolshevism sweeping across a prostrate and war-impoverished Europe loomed in the background of the deliberations at Paris and underlay many of the strategic concessions and hasty compromises. Statesmen particularly feared that revolutionary communism would take root in the defeated Austrian and German empires, as the abortive Bela Kun regime in Hungary seemed to portend. The Big Four leaders issued a call for a conference of Russian factions at Prinkipo Island, but the anti-Bolshevik groups refused to negotiate with Lenin's regime. A quick peace seemed more and more imperative, therefore, to repair the ravages of war and to curb the appeal of Bolshevism. The Big Four decided to support the anti-Bolshevik movement led by Admiral Alexander Kolchak in Siberia, hoping that he could destroy Lenin's regime and unify Russia. Reactionary elements around the Admiral

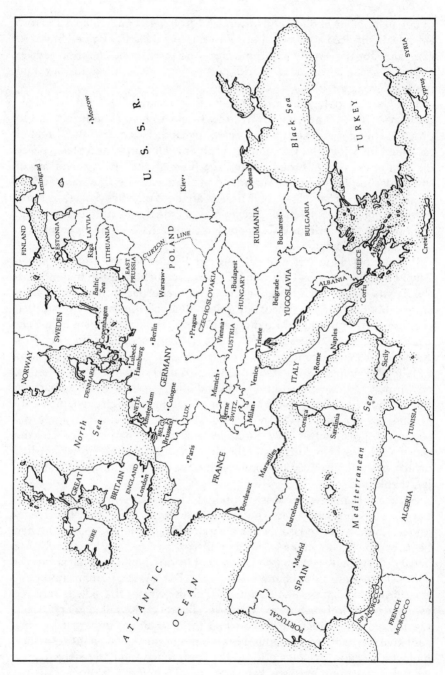

Europe after Versailles

undercut popular support, however, and Kolchak soon collapsed before the advancing Red armies. When Wilson returned to the United States to campaign for the Treaty and the League, he proclaimed that Bolshevism posed a greater threat to world peace than Prussian autocracy and imperialism had.

The German delegates arrived in Paris to receive the Treaty of Peace on May 7, 1919. They had only a few weeks to study the terms and to propose changes, most of which were rejected. Faced with the threat of an Allied invasion, the German government reluctantly accepted a peace dictated at the point of the bayonet. On June 28, the fifth anniversary of the assassination of Franz Ferdinand at Sarajevo, the final tableau was staged in the ornate Hall of Mirrors at the Versailles Palace. There, before the assembled Allied statesmen and crowds of exultant observers, the obscure and unhappy German delegates affixed their signatures to the Treaty of Versailles.

President Wilson left immediately for home, bearing the completed Treaty and its precious Covenant. Critics already had begun to denounce the Treaty, some for giving Germany too generous terms, and disillusioned liberals for its draconian spirit. One of the latter, the British economist John Maynard Keynes, summed up liberal criticism in his *The Economic Consequences of the Peace* (1920), serialized in the *New Republic*. Keynes condemned the treaty for its punitive provisions saddling Germany with extensive losses of territory and all its colonies, and imposing heavy reparations. He and others agreed that the Fourteen Points had been violated and hopes for a liberal peace betrayed, primarily because of President Wilson's personal defects. Keynes savagely depicted the President as slow mentally and easily "bamboozled" by the clever Old World politicians. The New World prophet, he wrote, had turned out to be not a philosopher-king but merely a narrow Presbyterian theologian.

Such criticisms were grossly unfair. Wilson had worked tirelessly at Paris for his principles, and most scholars today agree that the Treaty unquestionably turned out better owing to his efforts. Of course, he had been compelled to make a number of concessions, and no doubt the Treaty of Versailles was harsh in many of its provisions and fell short of a complete realization of liberal peace goals. But it is the human condition, the "irony of history," as Reinhold Niebuhr wrote, that ideals rarely if ever can be entirely achieved. Moreover, liberal critics failed to appreciate the unfavorable situation Wilson had faced at Paris, undercut by conservative elements in the United States and in the Allied countries which had won election victories prior to the conference and had resolved upon a harsh peace in order to weaken their liberal opponents at home. He had met defeat on the reparations and arms issues—Germany alone was disarmed—and on a number of departures from boundaries that were supposed to have been drawn strictly along lines of nationality. On the other hand, he had successfully opposed French schemes to dismember Germany, achieved the mandate system to administer former enemy colonies and dependencies under League supervision, and blocked at least temporarily excessive Italian demands for territorial gain. Above all, he had succeeded in his goal of establishing the League of Nations. Wilson was well aware of many of the defects of the peace treaty, but he hoped that in the course of time, as passions cooled, the League would repair the imperfections.

4. THE DEFEAT OF THE TREATY

On July 10, 1919, President Wilson laid the bulky Treaty of Peace before the Senate. Apparently sensing the hostility of most of his Republican listeners, he delivered his speech in a lack luster fashion until he reached his peroration: "The stage is set, the destiny disclosed. . . . We can only go forward, with lifted eyes and freshened spirit, to follow the vision. . . ."

As the months elapsed after the Armistice, quite a few Americans had begun to lose interest or to become hostile toward membership in the League of Nations. Americans traditionally had shown little concern for foreign affairs, and they tended once again to immerse themselves in private concerns and domestic politics. People had wearied of idealistic exhortations. Moreover, some war-stimulated patriots had begun to fear that the League would endanger America's sovereignty and needlessly entangle the nation abroad. Isolationist sentiment continued to run deep and strong. Large numbers of German-Americans, Italian-Americans, and Irish-Americans, many of whom had supported Wilson in the past, reacted hostilely to the Versailles Treaty because it fell short of the hopes or interests of their former homelands. The defection of many of the President's liberal supporters, alienated by his failure to achieve a more perfect peace, also complicated Wilson's cause. Yet despite growing disillusionment, hostility, and apathy, a majority of Americans in mid-1919 probably still favored membership in the League. Their sentiment did not have much intensity, however, and seemed to diminish as the treaty fight continued. In short, most Americans were only "mild internationalists" and favored limiting their nation's foreign commitments, in contrast to the Wilsonian "strong internationalists" who demanded nothing less than a wholehearted shouldering of world responsibilities. Probably Wilson would have done better to have defended League membership primarily in terms of America's own enlightened self-interests, and to have accepted extensive compromises if necessary, but his temperament precluded that approach.

The Republicans had a narrow majority in the Senate and controlled the influential Committee on Foreign Relations. Republican leaders, looking forward to winning the White House in 1920, wanted to glean maximum gain from the handling of the Versailles Treaty. They would not permit Wilson and the Democrats to claim sole credit for waging war and making peace. Moreover, the issue had divided Republican senatorial ranks. A small group of "Irreconcilables," some of whom were isolationists including such senators as William E. Borah of Idaho and Hiram Johnson of California and others who were anti-war or disillusioned idealists, adamantly opposed participation in any kind of League. They viewed the League as an intolerable diminution of American sovereignty and insisted that the wisest course for America was adherence to its traditional policy of abstention and setting a moral example to the world. Republican "Mild Reservationists" favored membership with only a few changes to clarify the Covenant. The "Strong Reservationists," led by Senator Lodge, advocated more sweeping alterations to make the League safe for American participation. They insisted on safeguarding the Monroe Doctrine, precluding League interference in domestic questions such as the tariff and immigration, and reducing or eliminating the obligations to defend other states under Article X. In addition to their doubts about the Covenant in its present form, many senators of both parties deeply resented Wilson's allegedly dictatorial attitude and apparently saw the debate on the Treaty as a legislative struggle with the executive for control over foreign policy. Senator Lodge particularly personally disliked President Wilson, an emotion warmly reciprocated by Wilson and that had an incalculable effect on the Treaty fight. In fairness, it must also be noted that Lodge, like many others in the United States, believed in advancing world peace through arbitration and law, not collective security.

Lodge shrewdly began to draft a number of amendments (eventually reservations) to the Treaty that would help unify Republican ranks and embarrass the Democrats. If Wilson accepted them, Republicans could claim that they had repaired defects in the League and made it safe for America to belong; if the President rejected them, he and the Democratic party would bear the responsibility for defeat of the Treaty. Lodge probably hoped that Wilson would spurn his changes and thereby doom the Treaty and the League; certainly he expected Wilson to do so. When a Republican colleague, Senator James E. Watson of Indiana, expressed fear that Wilson would swallow the Treaty with the reservations, Lodge replied reassuringly: "But, my dear James, you do not take into consideration the hatred that Woodrow Wilson has for me personally. Never under any set of circumstances in this world could he be induced to accept a treaty with Lodge reservations appended to it."

Deliberately stalling for time to rally the opposition, Senator Lodge took two weeks to read aloud the entire Treaty, 264 pages long, before a nearly empty committee room, despite the fact that senators had printed copies available to them. Hearings took up an additional six weeks, with much of the testimony not only bitterly hostile to the League but sometimes irrelevant as well. Secretary of State Lansing's testimony proved particularly damaging. Embittered by Wilson's neglect of him at Paris, Lansing publicly confessed his ignorance of many of the key decisions made by the Big Four leaders and admitted that he had opposed the Shantung transfer.

In their final form, most of the fourteen Lodge Reservations were petty in nature, designed primarily to reduce the executive's control over foreign policy. The most important reservation bore on Article X of the Covenant and provided that the United States would assume no obligation to defend the integrity of other states or to use its armed forces at the request of the League without the specific approval of Congress in each case. The last reservation, reflecting the Anglophobia still current in the United States, refused to bind the country to any League decision in which any member had cast more than one vote (the British empire and commonwealth had six seats in the League Assembly).

President Wilson decided to take his case directly to the people. He showed willingness to accept mild interpretative reservations, but feared that anything more would force renegotiation of the peace treaty. In any case he viewed most of the proposed changes either as unnecessary or as ruinous to the League. In September, Wilson left on a speaking tour through the midwestern and far-western states. His health, never robust, had been further weakened by the toils and tensions of Paris. After delivering over 30 major addresses in defense of the League, he collapsed at Pueblo, Colorado, and had to cancel the remainder of the tour. Returning to the White House, he suffered a cerebral thrombosis that left him bedridden and partially paralyzed. Despite an apparent disability under the terms of the Constitution, Wilson's wife and aides refused to request the Vice President to assume the executive duties. A virtual conspiracy of silence surrounded the President's sickroom, while members of his cabinet carried on the government as best they could. Mrs. Wilson, putting loyalty to her husband first, carefully controlled the business brought to his attention. Despite the importance of her role, it would be an exaggeration to accuse her of running the government. For a period no one had effective control and the executive branch functioned largely by inertia.

When the President did begin to recover, slowly and never completely, he adamantly refused to compromise with Senator Lodge. Although Wilson's illness left his intellect unimpaired, it apparently left him psychologically more rigid and uncompromising than before. He was warned that the only hope for Senate approval of the Treaty in any form lay in compromise with the Republican leaders. He believed so strongly in the issue, however, that he preferred defeat to a cowardly and hesitant entry into the League under the Lodge Reservations. Undoubtedly he still had confidence that the great majority of the people backed his leadership, when in fact signs indicated that many blamed both Wilson and Lodge for the deadlock and supported a compromise. When the Treaty came up for a vote on November 19, 1919, and again on March 19, 1920, the President requested loyal Democrats to vote against it with the Lodge Reservations. Since the Democrats could not muster enough strength to approve the Treaty without changes, its defeat was insured. The final vote on the Treaty with the Reservations fell seven votes short of the necessary two-thirds for approval, 49 for to 35 against. The Senate then returned the rejected instrument to the White House.

But the fight had not yet ended. Wilson determined to convert the 1920 presidential contest into a national referendum on the League. Apparently he sought a third nomination from the Democratic Party, but his loyal friends, fearful for his life if he tried to campaign, blocked that. The nomination instead went to James M. Cox, Governor of Ohio, with Franklin D. Roosevelt as his running mate. The Republicans nominated Senator Warren G. Harding of Ohio, impressive appearing and politically available; Governor Calvin Coolidge of Massachusetts received the vice presidential nomination. Cox and Roosevelt supported membership in the League, though they agreed to accept moderate reservations that would not impair the Covenant.

Harding's position was more difficult to determine. In his acceptance address, he rejoiced that Republicans in the Senate had rescued America from a "merged government of the world" and preserved American sovereignty and independence. Yet some of his remarks during the campaign indicated that he favored either membership in the League after changing it to conform to American wishes, or the negotiation of a new association of nations. He personally inclined toward an isolationist point of view, however, and after the Irreconcilables brought pressure to bear he finally repudiated Wilson's League as irreparably bad and worthy only of complete rejection. The League, he said, was a "stupendous fraud" and the provisions of Article X endangered America's independence and peace. Even so, pro-League Republicans such as Elihu Root, Charles Evans Hughes, and Herbert Hoover argued in a public declaration that Harding if elected would take the country into the League. Apparently they aimed not at winning more votes for Harding, but at preventing him from turning completely against the idea of a league. The less discerning voter could be pardoned if he remained unclear about the Republican candidate's attitude or intentions.

As Wilson should have known, presidential contests cannot provide a mandate on a single issue. Traditional political loyalties, personalities, and a variety of issues and grievances tended to eclipse or confuse the question of the League in 1920. The Republican Party still commanded the allegiance of a majority of voters, as the 1918 election had indicated. The wartime mobilization policies of the Democratic administration had alienated many farmers, laborers, and consumers; large numbers of German-, Irish-, and Italian-Americans and liberals objected strongly to various provisions of the Versailles Treaty; and highly nationalistic and patriotic groups feared loss of sovereignty through League membership. The progressive coalition that Wilson had created in 1916 had disintegrated by 1920. Moreover Harding was an attractive candidate, and many Americans simply preferred a change in government and a seeming return to the less trying days prior to Progressive crusades at home and abroad.

Harding overwhelmed his opponent by a plurality of over seven million votes. Republicans also swamped the Democrats in races for Congress, winning heavy majorities in both houses. The election was not a mandate on the League or any other single issue, but Wilson's insistence on a "Solemn Referendum" had helped insure that the Republican victors would interpret the results as a decisive popular rejection of the League. Political and personal partisanship, isolationist sentiment, and genuine doubts by many citizens who viewed themselves as at least mild internationalists, all helped explain the defeat of the Treaty and the Covenant. Above all, Wilson, by his insistence on a whole loaf or nothing, had contributed to the final outcome. The United States thus betrayed its own ideals and national interests. Entering the war to defend its interests and rights, the United States had changed the conflict into a struggle for a just peace and a stable postwar world, only to abandon the field when the war had ended. This left a badly weakened France and an impaired Britain to try to uphold the settlement, a task they ultimately failed. Yet, while the Wilsonian internationalists had lost, it proved impossible to ignore the legacy of American intervention and victory in World War I, or to return fully to the 19th-century pattern of isolationism. The First World War marked the beginning of a great departure for the United States from the neutrality and isolationism of the past toward the global responsibilities of the future.

Additional Reading

For a general account of America in World War I, see Charles Seymour, *American Diplomacy during the World War* (1934); Daniel M. Smith, *The Great Departure: The United States and World War I, 1914–1920* (1965); and Julius W. Pratt, *Challenge and Rejection* (1967), which covers American foreign relations from 1900 to 1921. Seward W. Livermore, *Politics is Adjourned: Woodrow Wilson and the War Congress, 1916–1918* (1966) examines wartime political maneuvering. Lawrence E. Gelfand, *The Inquiry: American Preparations for Peace, 1917–1919* (1963) disproves the old charge that Wilson went to Paris unprepared. *Woodrow Wilson and World Politics* (1968), by N. Gordon Levin, Jr., analyzes the Wilsonian goal of a democratic liberal capitalist world order and the measures adopted to achieve it. Also see Lawrence W. Martin, *Peace*

Without Victory: Woodrow Wilson and the British Liberals (1958) and Ruhl J. Bartlett, *The League to Enforce Peace* (1944). Military "diplomacy" is ably handled by David F. Trask, *The United States in the Supreme War Council* (1961). Wartime Anglo-American relations are examined by Arthur Willert, *The Road to Safety, A Study in Anglo-American Relations* (1952) and W. B. Fowler, *British-American Relations, 1917–1918: The Role of Sir William Wiseman* (1969). The best study to date on the Russian question is by George F. Kennan, *Soviet-American Relations, 1917–1920* (2 vols., 1956, 1958) that explains intervention primarily upon military grounds. See also Christopher Lasch, "American Intervention in Siberia: A Reinterpretation," *Political Science Quarterly,* LXXVII (1962), 205–223. Betty Miller Unterberger emphasizes the desire to curb Japan as the principal cause of Siberian intervention in *America's Siberian Expedition* (1956); William Appleman Williams, *American-Russian Relations, 1781–1947* (1952) stresses the anti-Bolshevik motive. See also two articles by C. E. Fike, "The Influence of the Creel Committee and the American Red Cross on Russian-American Relations, 1917–1919," *Journal of Modern History,* XXXI (1959), 93–109 and "The United States and Russian Territorial Problems, 1917–1920," *The Historian,* XXIV (1962), 331–346. On public opinion and the Bolshevik revolution, see Leonid I. Strakhovsky, *American Opinion about Russia, 1917–1920* (1961) and a stimulating interpretive study by Peter G. Filene, *Americans and the Soviet Experiment, 1917–1933* (1967). Louis L. Gerson, *Woodrow Wilson and the Rebirth of Poland* (1953); Victor S. Mamatey, *The United States and East Central Europe, 1914–1918* (1957); and Joseph P. O'Grady, ed., *The Immigrant's Influence on Wilson's Peace Policies* (1967), all deal with Wilson and the several nationality movements. On the Armistice, see H. R. Rudin, *Armistice, 1918,* (1944). A still valuable one-volume study of the Paris Peace Conference is Paul Birdsall's *Versailles Twenty Years After* (1941). A model study of its kind is by Seth P. Tillman, *Anglo-American Relations at the Paris Peace Conference of 1919* (1961) that depicts the essential harmony of British and Wilsonian war aims. The genesis of the Covenant is explored by George Curry, "Woodrow Wilson, Jan Smuts, and the Versailles Settlement," *American Historical Review,* LXVI (1961), 968–986. Warren F. Kuehl, *Seeking World Order: The United States and International Organization to 1920* (1969) concludes that Wilson's views on collective security were out of step with the more legalistic approach of most American internationalists. Also see Sondra R. Herman, *Eleven Against War: Studies in American Internationalist Thought, 1898–1921* (1969). Arno J. Mayer, *Wilson vs. Lenin* (1959) and *Politics and Diplomacy of Peacemaking* (1967) examine the ideological "struggle" between Wilsonianism and Leninism, and the effects of domestic political clashes between right and left in the wartime countries on the peace settlement. See also John M. Thompson, *Russia, Bolshevism, and the Versailles Peace* (1966). Thomas A. Bailey has written two readable and interpretive analyses of Wilson's peace-making: *Woodrow Wilson and the Lost Peace* (1944) and *Woodrow Wilson and the Great Betrayal* (1945), the latter on the defeat of the Treaty in America. David F. Trask, *General Tasker N. Bliss and the "Sessions of the World," 1919* (1966) reveals the role of one frustrated American commissioner. On the defeat of the treaty and the postwar American mood, outstanding studies include Selig Adler, *The Isolationist Impulse* (1957) and John C. Vinson, *Referendum for Isolation* (1961). John A. Garraty, *Henry Cabot Lodge* (1953) and A. L. and J. L. George, *Woodrow Wilson and Colonel House* (1956) analyze the personal interplay between Wilson and Lodge. John B. Duff, "The Versailles Treaty and the Irish-Americans," *Journal of American History*, LV (1968), 582–598, discusses the effects of the Irish defection. Also see Ralph A. Stone, *The Irreconcilables: The Fight Against the League of Nations* (1970). Four articles by Kurt Wimer are indispensable to an understanding of Wilson's thoughts and strategy on the League and Treaty question: "Woodrow Wilson's Plan to Enter the League of Nations through an Executive Agreement," *Western Political Quarterly*, XI (1958), 800–812; "Woodrow Wilson's Plan for a Vote of Confidence," *Pennsylvania History*, XXVII (1961), 279–293; "Woodrow Wilson and a Third Nomination," *Pennsylvania History*, XXIX (1962), 193–211; and "Woodrow Wilson Tries Conciliation; An Effort that Failed," *The Historian*, XXV (1963), 419–438. Arthur S. Link, *Wilson the Diplomatist* (1957) concludes that Wilson preferred nonmembership in the League rather than accept what he deemed injurious reservations. The effects of Wilson's illness are analyzed by E. A. Weinstein, "Woodrow Wilson's Neurological Illness," *Journal of American History*, LVII (1970), 324–351. Daniel M. Smith, "Robert Lansing and the Wilson Interregnum, 1919–1920," *The Historian*, XXI (1959), 135–161 and *Aftermath of War: Bainbridge Colby and Wilsonian Diplomacy, 1920–1921* (1970) examine the last efforts of the Wilson administration to promote a liberal world order. The standard study on the 1920 election is by Wesley Bagby, *The Road to Normalcy* (1962).

French Minister of Foreign Affairs, Aristide Briand (left) and Secretary of State, Frank Billings Kellogg (right) conferring in Paris just before the ratification of the Kellogg-Briand Pact

19

THE DIPLOMACY OF LIMITED RESPONSIBILITY, 1921–1933

1. THE MIDDLE ROAD TO WORLD PEACE

The nature of Republican foreign policy in the Twenties defies easy generalizations. Many historians, perhaps best described as liberal internationalists, have viewed the decade as one of retreat from reform at home and internationalism abroad, a far from creditable interlude between the Progressive Era and the New Deal. Americans sought to enjoy their material prosperity untroubled by foreign obligations and involvements. Ostrich-like, they would have ignored the rest of the world entirely if that had been possible. Other scholars, particularly those of the New Left, have rejected that interpretation. In their view the Twenties were years of active internationalism. The American economy vigorously expanded overseas and, encouraged by Washington, sought a sort of Pax Americana through cooperation with the business interests of the other great powers to establish international cartels and to share the exploitation of markets and resources. The American government hoped thereby to isolate Soviet Russia with its revolutionary doctrines while co-opting the formerly imperialistic Japan and Germany into the new order. This revisionist approach has the virtue of emphasizing the phenomenal expansion of American economic interests abroad and the intimate relationship between business and diplomacy in the Twenties, but to describe these activities as internationalism does not increase our understanding of this decade. Overseas economic expansion had been under way since the second half of the 19th century, and usually with governmental aid and encouragement, yet most historians would hardly describe the intervening years as examples of an internationalist policy on the part of the United States. Historian

Selig Adler has probably suggested the best characterization of the '20's in using the phrase "neo-isolationism" to describe its foreign policies.

Warren Gamaliel Harding, the 28th President of the United States, basically inclined toward isolationism. Born in Ohio in 1865 and raised in a rural community, he had been a journalist and editor of the Marion *Star* prior to entering politics. Long dismissed as lethargic and mediocre, managed by his wife and cronies, recent biographies reveal that the easygoing Harding was a very ambitious and skillful politician. He became a U. S. Senator in 1914, one of the first chosen by popular vote. His nomination by the Republicans in 1920 represented neither an accident nor the work of political bosses behind the scenes. Harding was eminently "available" as a presidential candidate—handsome, appealing, from a key state, and with few political enemies. After his nomination, Senator Lodge lectured him about the new balance to be sought between the executive and legislative branches, and Harding indicated he would defer to the Senate. Inauguration Day 1921 offered the American people a striking contrast between the departing Wilson and the incoming Harding. The recent election indicated that the country had tired of reform at home and crusades abroad, and had become bored with intellectualism and moral exhortations from the White House. Harding offered little to fear on any of those points. The new President had one redeeming quality—he earnestly sought, within his limitations, to be a good chief executive. His private morals and pastimes—mistresses and a fondness for good whisky and poker—and the public scandals of his administration are irrelevant to a study of his foreign policy. He at least had the wisdom to appoint an able man to head the State Department.

Charles Evans Hughes, Secretary of State under Harding and Coolidge (1921–25), was a distinguished political figure. He had served on the United States Supreme Court prior to accepting the Republican presidential nomination in 1916, and he ended his career as Chief Justice. A brilliant man—cautious, legalistic, politically sensitive—and an excellent administrator, he held the respect of Presidents Harding and Coolidge, both of whom deferred to him in foreign policy. Republican Senator Boies Penrose of Pennsylvania remarked, upon Hughes's appointment, "I do not think it matters much who is Secretary of State. Congress—especially the Senate—will blaze the way in connection with our foreign policies." Things did not work out quite that way, but Hughes did have to contend with two strong-willed and personally difficult chairmen of the powerful Senate Committee on Foreign Relations—Henry Cabot Lodge until 1924, and thereafter William E. Borah of Idaho. Unwilling to risk the kind of deadlock Wilson had experienced with the Senate, Harding and Hughes tried to lead it by flattery and co-option. Hughes also tried to shape public support for his policies via frequent public addresses and press conferences, where he performed so impressively that reporters sometimes applauded at the end.

Harding and Hughes marked out a middle-road course between 19th-century isolationism and Wilsonian internationalism. The realities of America's vast economic power, its interests in foreign markets and stability, and the decisive role it had played in the World War, left policy makers little other choice. Limited cooperation with the League of Nations, participation in the movement for arms limitations and peace, and a vigorous expansion of American finance and trade abroad, all without assuming any binding political commitments or positive treaty obligations on the part of the United States, sums up their approach. A course of limited internationalism, it enabled the United States to enjoy the benefits of its commanding economic position without acknowledging many duties to the world. The Senate regularly made that fact clear by attaching reservations or understandings that refused to commit the United States to any kind of obligation to enforce or uphold the treaties it approved.

By the mid-1920's, isolationist currents again ran strongly in the United States, and many people held that the country should not repeat the mistake of intervening as it had in the Great War in 1917. Undoubtedly the booming prosperity that characterized much of the '20's also contributed to the mood of withdrawal and concentration upon domestic and private affairs. Isolationism had particular strength in rural America which was overrepresented in Congress. Most of the great newspaper chains, such as the Hearst and Munsey press groups, and such independents as Colonel Robert McCormick's *Chicago Tribune,* reflected isolationist leanings. The long-maned Borah of Idaho served as congressional watchdog for the isolationists. Sincere but often naive on foreign affairs, Borah viewed the League as a treacherous trap and insisted that America should stand unencumbered as a moral example to the rest of the world.

Internationalists, of course, did not give up the effort to educate their fellow citizens to a broader concept of the nation's duties and interests. Some of the internationalist groups supported the League, while others concentrated upon membership in the World Court or the movement for arms reductions. Millionaire Edward W. Bok gave a Bok Peace Award of $50,000 in 1924 to a contest winner's plan for joining the World Court and for cooperating with the League. The stately *New York Times* and the *New York Herald Tribune* remained staunchly internationalist. The Foreign Policy Association carried on a broad program of educational work in foreign affairs, while the more prestigious Council on Foreign Affairs, established in 1921 in New York and publisher of *Foreign Affairs,* focused on the more influential members of the American public. The cause of internationalism gained strong support from the faculties of the nation's colleges and universities. Many advocates of internationalism tended to concentrate increasingly upon joining the World Court and upon participation in disarmament movements, rather than upon membership in the League, ultimately desirable though they thought that course. Unfortunately for their cause, internationalists did not agree on a program, could not capture control of either major political party during the '20's, and had to contend with a Congress in which rural and small-town isolationist sentiments tended to predominate because of overrepresentation.

2. THE LEAGUE OF NATIONS AND THE WORLD COURT

America's relations with the League of Nations illustrated the postwar middle-of-the-road approach to foreign affairs. Beginning with an initial hostility toward the League and all its works, official policy soon shifted to one of tolerance, and finally to a close though limited form of cooperation with that organization.

Harding quickly disappointed those who had hoped he would take the United States into the League, with reservations of course, or that he would assume the initiative in founding a new global organization. Hughes agreed with other educated and sophisticated citizens that America could no longer feasibly pursue isolationism. He was a conservative or legalistically inclined internationalist, however, and placed his faith for a war-free world in international law and arbitration, rather than in Wilsonian collective security. He hoped to salvage the more worthwhile parts of Wilson's League, particularly by attaching reservations to Article X. But the attitude of Harding and the Senate doomed his plans. Only two days after his victory in November, 1920, the President-elect declared that the League was "now deceased." Senators fearful that Hughes would still try to get the United States into the League warned Harding that any such effort would wreck his administration. The President therefore reassured a cheering Congress, on April 12, 1921, that in the "existing League of Nations, world-governing with its super powers, this Republic will have no part." The administration signed a separate treaty of peace with Germany in 1921 that reserved for the United States all of the privileges but none of the obligations of the Versailles Treaty.

The Harding administration at first even failed to acknowledge the existence of the League of Nations. It simply ignored the League's communications on various matters. When that discourteous attitude became known and aroused protests from the *New York Times*, an embarrassed Hughes had the inquiries bundled up and curtly acknowledged. Officials seemed to feel that since the United States had not joined the League, that organization did not exist. Hostility gradually gave way to tolerance, however, as the League's image as a superstate disappeared and as its performance of a useful peace-keeping function in Europe became clearer. Moreover, the administration realized that the United States had some interest in the nonpolitical work of the League, in such areas, for example, as world health, communications, and supervision of the opium traffic. The American government began to send "unofficial observers" to League-sponsored conferences dealing with such problems, a limited or "bootleg" cooperation without the assumption of any responsibilities.

In August, 1923, Harding died while upon a western tour and the mantle of leadership fell upon his Vice President, Calvin Coolidge. A Vermont-born Yankee (1872), stamped with rural and small-town virtues and outlook, "Silent Cal" was an extraordinarily taciturn and withdrawn chief executive. His dour visage caused Alice Roosevelt Longworth, Theodore Roosevelt's daughter, to quip that he looked as if he had been weaned on a pickle. The new President inclined toward a mild variety of internationalism. Yet, neither he nor his Secretary of State from 1925 to 1929, Frank B. Kellogg, felt disposed toward any daring initiatives or ventured to risk the ire of Borah and his Irreconcilable colleagues in the Senate. Reporters dubbed Kellogg "Nervous Nellie" because of his fear of the isolationist senators. Coolidge assured Congress in 1923 that membership in the League was a closed question; however, he promised to continue to cooperate with other nations in humanitarian endeavors—that is, with the League's nonpolitical activities. Coolidge, a master of ambiguous platitudes, once remarked that "America first is not selfishness; it is the righteous demand for strength to serve."

In the years after 1923, nonpolitical contacts with the League grew swiftly. American delegates attended conferences on such problems as copyrights, pornography, prostitution, health, and the traffic in opium. These delegates soon received the formal designation as official representatives and took part in voting and the financing of such activities. In short, while the United States would not join the League in enforcing peace, it would cooperate in behalf of international improvement and the general welfare. By 1928 the Republican Party platform boasted of this type of cooperation and participation, though it denied any political entanglement or contemplation of membership.

Under President Hoover the United States drew close to membership without formally joining the League. Hoover had been a mild Wilsonian during World War I and he believed in cooperation, without binding commitments of course, to promote world peace and stability. A shy but able man, Hoover had made a fortune as a mining engineer before he achieved fame for his relief activities during and after the World War. As Secretary of Commerce in the Harding and Coolidge administrations, he had ranked among the most influential figures in Washington and had obtained the Republican presidential nomination and electoral victory in 1928. In his inaugural address, Hoover stated that he would make no attempt to join the League of Nations. He took great interest in disarmament and World Court membership, however, and welcomed increasing cooperation with the League's nonpolitical work. During the Manchurian crisis in 1931–32, Hoover even permitted a degree of

American cooperation with the League's Council as it attempted to halt Japan's aggressions in the Far East.

In addition to limited cooperation with the League, the American public seems clearly to have favored membership in the World Court. The Permanent Court of International Justice had been established as a separate organization from the League and its peace-keeping role. Because the United States had long been an advocate of arbitration and conciliation, many Americans believed that it should join what in effect amounted to its own brainchild. Some also saw membership in the Court as a first step toward closer relations with the League, precisely what the arch-isolationists feared. Harding and Hughes endorsed membership in the Court and by the mid-1920's both major political parties went on record as favoring participation. The majority of the American people apparently agreed, but the minority of isolationists in the Senate managed to defeat the project. After years of discussion and maneuvering, the Senate in 1926 finally approved joining the Court, but with reservations that proved unacceptable to other members. Again, in 1935, the Senate voted on entrance to the Court, but it failed by seven votes to obtain the necessary two-thirds majority. Borah participated in the thick of the fight against Court membership, and die-hard isolationists appealed to the chauvinist and nativist prejudices of the American people. Protests poured into Washington in such volume in 1935 that they required wheelbarrows for delivery. One senator exclaimed, "To hell with Europe and the rest of those nations." Yet clearly the internationalists had won a partial victory with the majority of the Americans, even if not in the Senate.

3. ECONOMIC FOREIGN POLICY

In economic foreign policy, the Republican middle-of-the-road approach meant some recognition of America's responsibility and interest in the economic health of Europe and the Far East. But responsible policies intermixed with economic nationalism caused them to fall short of the desired ends.

European debtor nations owed the United States in 1920 about $10.3 billion for wartime and postarmistice loans. The Europeans had spent most of these funds in America to purchase war-inflated goods, thereby contributing to America's booming prosperity in 1917–18. Despite the pleas from war-exhausted Allied governments that the United States consider the money as its contribution to the joint war effort, the American government, starting with the Wilson administration, maintained that the loans represented financial transactions that required repayment in full and with interest. Most Americans believed that morality and business ethics made any other course inconceivable; after all, the American people had asked for no territory or spoils from the war and therefore they should not shoulder most of the costs of that conflict.

When the British government proposed a general cancellation of all intergovernmental debts, in August, 1922—it had served as the Allied creditor prior to 1917—popular indignation swept the United States. President Harding insisted upon the observance of what he termed "the integrity of agreements, the sanctity of covenants, the validity of contracts." As Coolidge later reportedly remarked, "they hired the money, didn't they?" A few Americans—liberals, big businessmen, and financiers with extensive foreign interests—advocated cancelling or reducing the debts on the grounds that Europe could not afford to repay them or that such vast sums if collected would disturb the world's financial system. But the great majority of Americans, regardless of their particular political or foreign policy views, rejected such arguments. Secretary of State Hughes agreed with the necessity of repayment, but he and other responsible officials failed to face the question of how such huge transfers could take place without disrupting the economies of both the debtor and the creditor. Moreover, the United States officially denied European claims that its ability to pay depended upon Germany's meeting its reparations obligations.

Not entirely trustful of the executive, Congress in 1922 authorized creation of the World War Foreign Debt Commission to negotiate settlements with the debtors, subject to congressional approval in each case. The terms provided for full repayment at 4.25 percent interest within a 25-year period. The commission actually departed from these instructions by reducing interest rates, but not the principals, and by lengthening the scheduled repayments to a period of 62 years, presumably reflecting to some degree the differing abilities of the debtors to repay. Despite European resistance and ill will—one French cartoon portrayed the United States as Uncle Shylock seeking his last pound of flesh—funding agreements were forced upon the debtor countries between 1923 and 1926. Great Britain signed an agreement to repay its debt of nearly $4.3 billion at an average interest rate of 3.3 percent, while the Commission reduced the rate on Italy's $1.6 billion to .04 percent in view of her financially strained condition. France balked at signing an agreement for her debt of $3.4 billion. She came to terms in 1926, at an interest rate of 1.6 percent, only after much acrimony and under the pressure of a threatened embargo against private American loans to France. The United States showed not so much greed in its insistence upon repayment of the war debts but shortsightedness in failing to forsee the virtual impossibility of such vast international transfers of payments or their disruptive effects upon everyone's economy if actually made.

The United States emerged from the First World War as the foremost industrial and financial power in the world. In 1920, America produced 40 percent of the world's coal, twice that of its nearest competitor, Great Britain, 70 percent of its petroleum, and about 16 percent of the world's total exports. During the Twenties, the American economy underwent a veritable technological revolution that left even the most advanced foreign economies trailing far behind. By the late 1920's, the United States accounted for 46 percent of the world's total industrial production, and its national income equaled the combined incomes of 23 other leading industrial states, including Britain, Germany, France, and Japan. Unfortunately, such vast power demanded a more enlightened foreign policy than America had in the first postwar decade.

During the World War, some American business and political leaders had recognized that growing production required larger external markets and the creation of an open-door world that would benefit not only the United States but all other nations as well; the goal was a world open to trade and investments and safe from revolutionary disorders. Legislation such as the Webb-Pomerene Act in 1918 and the Edge Act in 1919 relaxed the antitrust laws to permit American exporters, bankers, and industrialists to form cartels to open or to control foreign markets. Little resulted from these efforts, and attempts to supplant the British global fiscal network did not wholly succeed. New York, however, became the leading financial center in the world. American business quickly realized the advantages of establishing branch factories and subsidiaries of their firms within foreign tariff walls. This resulted in a vast expansion of American exports and capital investments overseas. The United States largely replaced Europe as the supplier of capital to Latin America and the Far East, while our imports from Europe declined sharply.

The State Department attempted to guide overseas loans and investments, with no great success, in the hopes of protecting America's own best interests, of aiding European recovery, of stabilizing the world, and of discouraging arms races. The State Department requested financial firms handling foreign bond issues to allow it to express its opinion on projected loans, but the firms involved often ignored or circumvented the Department's recommendations. Thus, despite the State Department's warning, American banks and investors, attracted by high interest rates, poured some $2 billion into postwar Germany, much of it into unsound projects. Herbert Hoover, Secretary of Commerce in the Harding and Coolidge administrations, built his previously obscure department into a major instrument of government. An economic nationalist, Hoover encouraged business to gain control of important foreign raw material sources and to increase exports. At the same time, in a form of economic idiocy, the Commerce Department discouraged imports by seeking American self-sufficiency in those areas still dependent upon foreign manufacturers.

Conflicts inevitably arose between the State and Commerce Departments, which the latter usually won. Both cooperated, however, in forcing admission of American interests into oil production in the Middle East. The World War had demonstrated the military importance of petroleum, and America's industrial development in the 1920's involved a vastly increased consumption of oil products. Fearing that domestic supplies might soon be exhausted, American oil companies began a vigorous search for foreign sources of supply. The Middle East already had a reputation as an area of vast resources, and during the Wilson Administration the State Department challenged an Anglo-French attempt to monopolize the petroleum of the mandated territories in Palestine and Mesopotamia. Diplomatic and economic pressures finally succeeded in breaking down British resistance. In 1925, seven American oil companies obtained a 25 percent share in the exploitation of Iraq's oil resources, Standard Oil Company of California secured a concession in Bahrain in 1928, and in 1934 the Arabian-American Oil Company formed to develop the resources of Saudi Arabia.

Despite the fact that the United States had now become a creditor nation on both the governmental and private levels, Republicans insisted upon returning to a high protective tariff. As President Harding put it in one of his muddled comments, "We should adopt a protective tariff of such a character as will help the struggling industries of Europe to get on their feet." In 1922 Congress passed the Fordney-McCumber Tariff that sharply raised duties on numerous imports. Although it viewed the rates as too high, the administration welcomed the tariff as a major weapon to promote an open-door world, because of its provisions to obtain equality of treatment for American goods entering foreign markets with those of other countries. The 1922 act caused protests abroad and threats of retaliation against American goods, but the heavy export of private American capital to Europe cushioned temporarily the impact upon trade. Thus, in a very real sense the outflow of American loans and investments financed Europe's purchases in the United States. With the coming of the Great Depression, Congress passed the Hawley-Smoot Tariff in 1930, hiking the rates from the previous average of 25.9 percent to 50.2 percent on dutiable imports. Bankers and industrialists involved in foreign trade feared the effects of the tariff upon world trade, and over a thousand economists denounced the measure. Nevertheless President Hoover signed it into law as a means of trying to cope with the Depression. The results were as feared. European countries, already running an adverse balance of trade with the United States and also beginning to feel the effects of the Depression, retaliated by striking at American exports. By 1932, 25 governments had adopted retaliatory measures. France imposed quotas on American imports, Great Britain raised duties on imports and adopted an empire preference system, and Nazi Germany soon turned to barter arrangements. The combined effects of tariff wars and the Depression by 1932 had reduced America's foreign trade to the levels of 1905. Free trade appeared on the verge of disappearing as country after country turned to economic nationalism.

American policy on the war debts and the tariff thus made Europe's postwar recovery more difficult and heightened the effects of the subsequent world depression. Yet the nation did recognize some of her responsibility to promote European readjustment. Despite its refusal to acknowledge any connection between war debts and reparations, the State Department was disturbed when Germany defaulted on reparations in 1922–23 and France retaliated by occupying the Ruhr. An American plan in effect resolved the crisis. With the State Department's blessings, Charles G. Dawes headed a group of bankers that formulated the 1924 Dawes Plan for private loans to Germany to enable it to reorganize its fiscal system and to resume reparations payments. France withdrew her troops from the Ruhr and Germany seemed well on the road to economic and political stability. Beneath the surface, however, Germany's financial system did not have a sound base. Not permitted to pay reparations in goods and services to the Allies, which their own economies made undesirable, and lacking a large supply of gold, Germany's ability to pay in fact depended largely upon the influx of American capital. When the Great Depression began to spread from America to Europe, Germany felt it severely and soon defaulted on the bonds that she had so freely sold to American investors. Meanwhile Germany had persuaded the Allies to agree to a new commission to readjust reparations. In 1930, American financiers participated in the formulation of the Young Plan, named after Owen D. Young, the commission's chairman. They reduced German reparations from the original $33 billion to approximately $9 billion plus interest.

In 1931, as the world depression deepened, President Hoover obtained a one-year moratorium or suspension in the payment of all intergovernmental debts. He hoped to promote world economic recovery, and not least to shore up American investments in Germany. The only long-term result of his statesmanlike act, however, was to end virtually all payments on the war debts. The Allies and Germany met at Lausanne and offered to cancel practically all reparations if the United States would cancel or sharply reduce the war debts. Hoover had to decline, because the American people would have found cancellation or reductions highly unpopular.

After expiration of the moratorium, all of the debtors except Finland soon defaulted on payments of the principles, and after a short time even stopped payments of interest. The defaults deeply angered Americans and some proposed novel schemes to resolve the problem, such as accepting British warships or British and French colonies in the New World in lieu of money. President Hoover even suggested such a solution to British Prime Minister Ramsay McDonald when the latter visited America. A *Chicago Tribune* ditty, parodying the stirring "Over There" of World War I, summed up the mood of many disgusted Americans: "They owe us there, they owe us there, and we'll never get it back What they owe us over there!" Resentment of the defaulters surfaced as late as

1967–68 when France's President Charles DeGaulle attacked the stability of the American dollar and its gold reserve and some Americans suggested that instead of redeeming French-held dollars in gold, they would credit them against the unpaid and almost forgotten French war debt to the United States.

Ironically, the United States received payments on the war debts approximating the amount of private American loans to Germany and Germany's payment of reparations to the Allies. This curious and unsound chain broke down with the Depression and the cessation of the flow of American capital to Europe.

4. THE WASHINGTON CONFERENCE AND NAVAL LIMITATIONS

The calling of the Washington Conference in 1921–1922 offered a graphic illustration of the United States's inability simply to retire into an isolationist cocoon. The World War had brought a major change in the structure of power in the Far East; Japan obviously had emerged as a great power of the first rank, while Britain and France had been weakened and Russia and Germany eliminated as competitors. Japan and the United States emerged as the chief rivals in the Pacific area. The Washington Conference represented a statesmanlike effort to adjust peacefully to these changes.

When the war ended, the United States, Great Britain, and Japan found themselves on the threshold of a great naval arms race. The American government planned construction of a vast fleet of 39 battleships and 12 battle cruisers. Britain and Japan would either have to expend vast sums in counterbuilding or fall behind in the race. The United States's intention to seek naval supremacy puzzled and distressed the British since Britain already had accepted the concept of parity. The reason, apart from national pride and resentment of Britain's wartime blockade, lay in a growing American sense of uneasiness about the Anglo-Japanese Alliance. The State Department informed London in 1920 that it hoped the British would not renew the alliance when it expired in 1921, or at least that they would change it to make clear that it did not apply against the United States. The British government gave reassurances on the latter, but Washington still preferred the alliance be scrapped.

The public and Congress revealed increasing resistance to heavy naval expenditures after the Great War had ended. Pacifists and peace advocates, very vocal after 1918, warned of a dangerous arms race and urged the calling of an international conference to avert it. Congress felt the need to reassert its power after the war and applied pressure via the Borah resolution for a slowdown in naval building. Although Harding and his advisers resented congressional intrusion into foreign policy making, and would have preferred to continue naval construction until they actually reached parity with England before discussing reduction, public pressures proved too great to resist. The administration decided to call a conference of naval powers in Washington, and to include China and related Far Eastern issues on the agenda. Harding and Hughes then wisely lavished attention upon the Senate to insure that it would approve whatever treaties emerged from the conference. They appointed senators from both major political parties to the delegation to assist Hughes in the negotiations, although they bypassed the unpredictable Borah. As another concession to the Senate and the public, Harding and Hughes took great care to present the conference as "open" in contrast to the secrecy that had prevailed at the recent Paris Peace Conference.

The Washington Conference was the first major international conference held in the American capital. Secretary of State Hughes dominated its deliberations from the opening day, November 12, 1921. On the previous day, the conference delegates had attended a solemn ceremony at Arlington Cemetery—the interment of America's Unknown Soldier. President Harding opened the session in Constitution Hall with one of his typically banal addresses. Then the audience settled down to hear Secretary Hughes. Instead of the expected generalities, however, Hughes boldly seized the initiative. "The time has come," he declared, " . . . not for general resolutions or mutual advice, but for action." The Secretary proceeded to stun the assembled diplomats and observers with detailed proposals for the halting of naval construction and the scrapping of vast quantities of existing naval tonnage. Specifically he called for the United States to scrap 15 capital vessels under construction (some 80 percent or more completed) and 15 older battleships, for a total of 845,740 tons; Britain to junk 19 older capital warships and four planned battleships, for a total of 583,375 tons; and Japan, the third-ranking naval power, to abandon 15 vessels planned or being built and ten older ships, for a total of 448,928 tons. Diplomats and navalists listened glumly to the Secretary's words, but the galleries cheered. Bryan, that ardent advocate of peace, listened to Hughes with tears running down his face. All over America, and indeed throughout the world, Hughes' proposals received similarly favorable reactions. As one American reverend declared, Hughes' speech was "one of the greatest events in history."

Hughes had rallied world public opinion to his cause. Moreover, the fact that neither the British nor the Japanese had any enthusiasm for a costly arms competition with rich America aided his cause. Working closely with Lord Balfour of Great Britain and Tomasaburo Kato of Japan, Hughes subordinated the naval experts to the diplomats and achieved an essentially political, rather than technical, naval agreement. Through hard bargaining, where each power sought the maximum security at the minimum cost, they hammered out a series of treaties.

The Five Power Pact proclaimed a ten-year naval holiday in the construction of capital vessels, except for replacements of obsolete units, set limitations for each ship of 35,000 tons and 16-inch guns, and established a 5:5:3 ratio in battleships and aircraft carriers for the United States, Great Britain, and Japan respectively, with smaller ratios of about 1.75 each for France and Italy. Because of France's insistence upon a large tonnage in smaller naval craft and submarines, and Britain's desire for more destroyers, lesser craft remained unregulated. Japan received compensation for its smaller ratio and for the scrapping of the Anglo-Japanese Alliance, by pledges that the United States would not increase fortifications in the Pacific west of Hawaii and Great Britain would not increase them east of Singapore and north of Australia. The Four Power Pact, between the Naval Big Three and France, supplanted the Anglo-Japanese Alliance with an agreement declaring mutual respect for each other's possessions in the Pacific and providing for consultation if problems arose endangering the peace and stability of the area. The Nine Power Pact solemnly pledged its signatories to uphold the independence and integrity of China and to observe the Open Door. The Lansing-Ishii Agreement was terminated, but Japan regarded the Nine Power Pact as in effect conceding her special interests in China and a free hand in Manchuria-Mongolia. In related agreements, by-products of the conference, Japan promised to restore Shantung to China and to evacuate Siberia, and granted the United States cable rights on the Japanese mandated island of Yap.

When the Senate received the Washington treaties, critics such as Borah attacked the toothless Four Power Pact as a dangerous entanglement and a kind of alliance with Great Britain. Administrative spokesmen vigorously denied such charges and defended the pacts, buttressed by the tide of popular support sweeping the American press and pulpit. The Senate approved the treaties, although it attached a reservation to the Four Power Pact stating that the United States assumed no obligation to uphold its provisions by force or by alliance. This helped make the treaties virtually worthless when subsequently challenged by aggressors.

Although Republican spokesmen hailed the Washington pacts as the "greatest peace document[s] ever drawn," the treaties obviously did not compensate for nonmembership in the League of Nations and full participation in its labors for peace. From a long-range point of view, the Washington Conference was only an ephemeral success. Yet, perhaps in a world where men are unable to foresee the future with any notable degree of accuracy, that judgment is too harsh. It did end the capital ship arms race and promoted stability in the Pacific for a decade. It also ended talk of a possible Japanese-American war, as Japan turned to a more moderate and cooperative course. Owing to the factors of distance, lack of advanced bases, and other naval responsibilities for the United States and Great Britain, the settlement actually did concede Japan naval predominancy in the far Pacific. The Navy General Board warned that the effects would "greatly . . . lessen the power of the United States to . . . defend its interests or unaided to enforce its policies in the western Pacific. . . ." But in fact, even if the Navy had fulfilled its pre-Washington construction plans, the American Navy might still have fallen short of the desired supremacy over the Japanese Navy. Moreover, American public opinion probably would have compelled reductions in naval outlays in any case, and if Japan had built according to schedule, the naval ratio between the two countries might have become even less desirable to the American admirals. In short, the United States had given up not an actual naval superiority but only a doubtful potential superiority. In return it achieved realistic goals of stabilizing the Far East and protecting its relative naval position without any great costs or commitments.

The failure at Washington to fix limits for lesser naval vessels still left the possibility of an arms race in cruisers, destroyers, and submarines. A conference called in Geneva in 1927 to try to avert a race in these categories foundered. Great Britain and the United States could not agree upon either the size or total tonnage limits for cruisers; the British, with an empire to guard, wanted more and smaller cruisers, versus American desires for parity and larger-sized vessels, and Japan insisted upon an increased ratio. Armed with a congressional authorization in 1929 for the building of fifteen 10,000 ton cruisers and an aircraft carrier, President Hoover obtained a new conference. It met at London in 1930, and this time the effort succeeded. Anglo-American differences were resolved by an approximately equal overall tonnage limitation; Britain obtained a larger number and tonnage in light cruisers, while the United States gained a roughly similar advantage in heavier cruisers. Japan had asked for a 10:10:7 ratio in all categories below capital warships, but accepted about 10:10:5 in cruisers, 10:10:7 in destroyers, and parity in submarines. Because Italy and France refused to agree to most of the limitations, an escalator clause permitted a signatory power to ignore the limitations in case it felt endangered by the building of a nonsigning power. The Senate approved the London agreement by a heavy margin, despite some criticism that it would weaken America in the Pacific and strengthen Japan. Conversely, the agreement made many Britishers unhappy, and supernationalists in Japan severely castigated their returning delegation. Yet scholars generally agree that Japan gained the most at the conference.

The entire structure of naval limitations collapsed in the Thirties as Japan embarked upon an aggressive expansionist course. In contrast, a frugal Congress had failed to build the American Navy to treaty limits until the full significance of the limitation treaties at last became painfully clear. But these developments could not be attributed to the statesmen who had negotiated the agreements. Judged within the climate of the Twenties, naval limitations and the Nine Power Pact must be viewed as a realistic success in reducing international tensions.

The United States also took part in the League-sponsored World Disarmament Conference. American delegates attended the Preparatory Commission from its initial sessions in 1926 until the completion of its work and the convening of a general conference early in 1932. The Preparatory Commission bogged down in long and inconclusive exchanges, with France demanding adequate provisions for security before it would consider military reductions on the continent, and Great Britain and the United States taking the opposite tack. When the World Disarmament Conference met, neither Hoover's nor Franklin D. Roosevelt's proposals for sweeping reductions could resolve the dilemma of security versus disarmament. Neither chief executive could offer France the kind of reassurances she demanded. The conference collapsed after the Nazi revolution in Germany and the German rearmament that soon followed.

5. THE OUTLAWRY OF WAR

An even simpler panacea for international conflict than arms limitations attracted many Americans. Why not merely outlaw war? Many internationalists supported the movement to ban aggressive war, seeing it as a means to link the United States indirectly to the cause of collective security, and pacifists and isolationists found it attractive because of its simplicity and lack of entangling obligations. Presumably the enforcement of such a general prohibition of war would require no alliances or pacts, only the force of world moral opinion and international law. A Chicago lawyer, Salmon O. Levinson, became one of the most ardent crusaders for the outlawry of war and he managed to interest Senator Borah. Although Borah's support was invaluable, and later he described the pact concluded in 1928 as "the only kind of a treaty the United States could sign" with the rest of the world, he failed to throw his energies into the project as vigorously as its proponents desired. Two other individuals also played an important part in the drama that unfolded—Professor James T. Shotwell of Columbia University and its president, Nicholas Murray Butler. They apparently viewed outlawry as a way to associate America more closely with the League of Nations and its peace-keeping functions, while most Americans only saw it as *the* simple and universal solution in itself.

In 1927, Shotwell called upon the French Foreign Minister, Aristide Briand, and urged France to support the movement for the outlawry of war. Apparently hoping to link a security-hungry France more closely to the United States even in an indirect manner, Briand in a speech on April 6, 1927, the tenth anniversary of America's entry into World War I, proposed a Franco-American treaty outlawing war between the two countries. President Coolidge and Secretary of State Kellogg resentfully ignored Briand's unorthodox overture. Public enthusiasm for outlawry, however, finally forced the reluctant administration into action. Once he had thrown himself into the project, Kellogg became an enthusiastic advocate of outlawry, although most diplomats were skeptical of its value.

Kellogg turned the tables on France by proposing not a bilateral but a multilateral treaty prohibiting war as an instrument of national policy. France yielded without enthusiasm, and representatives of 15 nations gathered in Paris in August, 1928 to sign the Kellogg-Briand Pact or Pact of Paris. Ultimately, 64 nations ratified that instrument. The treaty solemnly pledged signatories to "condemn recourse to war for the solution of international controversies, and [to] renounce it as an instrument of national policy. . . ." Signatories further agreed that solutions for "all disputes or conflicts of whatever nature . . . shall never be sought except by pacific means," but they made no provisions for the enforcement of these self-denying pledges.

The Kellogg-Briand Pact captured the world's imagination and appealed to its hopes for a simple and clear-cut solution to the problems of war. For his contributions to the cause of peace, Kellogg received the Nobel Peace Prize in 1930, one of the few Americans so honored. The pact easily obtained the Senate's approval, by a vote of 85 to one, although some senators agreed with more cynical observers about the worthlessness of the treaty. The Senate added its customary interpretation reserving to the United States the right to self-defense and to the preservation of the Monroe Doctrine, and disavowing any obligation to uphold the treaty against violators. In retrospect, the Pact of Paris at best was an innocuous international kiss of peace. Unfortunately it further encouraged Americans, and many Europeans, in the false but comforting assumption that peace and security could be easily obtained without costs or obligations on the part of anyone. The pact did have one important positive effect—it helped make it close to impossible for most Americans in the future to preserve moral neutrality in the face of foreign aggressions and wars of conquest.

Republican neo-isolationist policies seemed to have succeeded as the decade of the 1920's neared an end: the war-debts question apparently had been settled satisfactorily; a naval arms race had been avoided; and the Pacific area and the Far East were more stable and peaceful than before, while most of the world's states had solemnly renounced war as an instrument of policy. Europe had recovered from the effects of the World War, and the American economy flourished at home and overseas, all without membership in the League of Nations or any other form of entangling foreign commitment. This illusion of prosperity and a relatively cost-free security speedily disappeared into the dustbins of history with the two great cataclysms of the next decade: worldwide economic depression, and the rise of totalitarian and aggressive dictatorships. In the face of new foreign perils in the 1930's the United States slowly and painfully abandoned neo-isolationism for a return to Wilsonian internationalism.

Additional Reading

A useful survey of postwar diplomacy is by L. Ethan Ellis, *Republican Foreign Policy, 1921–1933* (1968). John D. Hicks, *Republican Ascendancy, 1921–1933* (1960) depicts Republican foreign policy as essentially isolationist; in contrast, William Appleman Williams, "The Legend of Isolationism in the 1920's," *Science and Society,* XVIII (1954), 1–20, finds the traditional interpretation invalid and labels the decade as one of vigorous economic internationalism and diplomacy. See also Williams, *The Tragedy of American Diplomacy* (1959). The 'New Left' or revisionist viewpoint is also expressed by Robert Freeman Smith, "American Foreign Relations, 1920–1942," in B. J. Bernstein, ed., *Towards a New Past: Dissenting Essays in American History* (1968), 232–262. Carl P. Parrini, *Heir to Empire: United States Economic Diplomacy, 1916–1923* (1969) sees a basic continuity between Wilson's and Harding's economic policies. Selig Adler, in *The Isolationist Impulse* (1957) and *The Uncertain Giant* (1965), an excellent survey of American foreign relations from 1921 to 1941, uses the label "neo-isolationism" to describe Republican middle-of-the-road foreign policies. Details on economic foreign policy are provided by H. G. Moulton and Leo Pasvolsky, *War Debts and World Prosperity* (1938); Herbert Feis, *The Diplomacy of the Dollar* (1950); Joseph Brandes, *Herbert Hoover and Economic Diplomacy* (1962); and Benjamin Rhodes, "Reassessing 'Uncle Shylock': The United States and the French War Debt, 1917–1929," *Journal of American History,* LV (1969), 787–803. D. F. Fleming, *The United States and World Organization, 1920–1933* (1938) treats relations with the League of Nations. See also Kurt and Sarah Wimer, "The Harding Administration, the League of Nations, and the Separate Peace Treaty," *Review of Politics,* XXIX (1967), 13–24. The disarmament movement is examined by Merze Tate, *The United States and Armaments* (1948) and by B. H. Williams, *The United States and Disarmament* (1931). *The United States and the Washington Conference, 1921–1922* (1970), by Thomas H. Buckley, is the most recent study of that conference. Also see Y. Ichihashi, *The Washington Conference and After* (1928); Harold and Margaret Sprout, *Toward a New Order of Sea Power* (1940); and Ernest Andrade, Jr., "The United States Navy and the Washington Conference," *The Historian,* XXXI (1969), 345–363. John Chalmers Vinson, *The Parchment Peace* (1956) examines the role of the Senate in the Washington Conference. For the Japanese version of the Nine Power Pact, see Sadao Asada, "Japan's 'Special Interests' and the Washington Conference, 1921–22," *American Historical Review,* LXVII (1961), 62–70. The navy and subsequent conferences are treated by Raymond G. O'Connor, *Perilous Equilibrium: The United States and the London Naval Conference of 1930* (1962) and Gerald E. Wheeler, *Prelude to Pearl Harbor: The United States Navy and the Far East, 1921–1931* (1963). The movement for the outlawry of war is ably handled by John Chalmers Vinson, *William E. Borah and the Outlawry of War* (1957) and by Robert H. Ferrell, *Peace in Their Time* (1952). Also useful is M. C. McKenna's *Borah* (1961). Robert James Maddox, *William E. Borah and American Foreign Policy* (1969) views Borah as more practical and cynical in foreign policy than usually thought. The most recent biographies of President Harding are *The Available Man: The Life behind the Masks of Warren Gamaliel Harding* (1965), by Andrew Sinclair, which partially rehabilitates the image of that chief executive, and *The Shadow of Blooming Grove: Warren G. Harding and His Times* (1968), by Francis Russell. Coolidge also has been the subject of a recent re-evaluation by Donald R. McCoy, *Calvin Coolidge: The Quiet President* (1967). The best biography of Hoover is by H. G. Warren, *Herbert Hoover and the Great Depression* (1959). On Secretaries of State, consult M. J. Pusey, *Charles Evans Hughes* (2 vols., 1951); Betty Glad, *Charles Evans Hughes and the Illusions of Innocence* (1967), a thoughtful analysis of American thought about foreign affairs; L. E. Ellis, *Frank B. Kellogg and American Foreign Relations, 1925–1929* (1961), which views Kellogg as a mediocre Secretary of State; and the more favorable account by Robert H. Ferrell, *The American Secretaries of State and Their Diplomacy,* Vol. XI (1963). Stimson is also covered by Ferrell in the same volume. The standard study on East Asian relations is still A. W. Griswold, *The Far Eastern Policy of the United States* (1938). An interpretive study concentrating upon recent American diplomacy is by Richard W. Leopold, *The Growth of American Foreign Policy* (1962).

"All he wants is elbow room"

20

DEPRESSION DIPLOMACY, 1931-1936

1. THE GREAT DEPRESSION AND THE COLLAPSE OF THE POSTWAR ORDER

The year 1931, in Arnold Toynbee's apt phrase, was the *annus terribilis* of the postwar world. The Great Depression spread across the globe, inflicting economic collapse and mass unemployment virtually everywhere and undermining the international structure erected at Versailles and Washington.

The collapse of the postwar order unleashed a wave of political extremism and war. Irrationalism and violence within nations and on the international level seemed to threaten the extinction of civilization itself. Both the Left and the Right attacked democratic societies. In their despair, millions of people turned to demogogic spellbinders and soothsayers peddling strange wares of salvation. In Italy, democracy collapsed in the early 1920's as jut-jawed Benito Mussolini and his Fascist blackshirts wielded dictatorial power and sought to build a corporate society. For all his emphasis upon physical fitness and military prowess, the new Caesar remained relatively pacific, however, until the 1930's. Many American liberals admired the Duce and observed his Fascist experiment with some sympathy in its earlier phases. Russia since the Bolshevik revolution had been in the grips of a dictatorship that also aroused some sympathetic interest among American liberals as an experiment aimed at the ultimate betterment of society, however deplorable the means being utilized. In Germany, the frail Weimar Republic collapsed under the double onus of the depression and national resentment of the Versailles settlement. Adolf Hitler and his National Socialist (Nazi) party grasped dictatorial power in January, 1933 and soon began to transform Germany into a police and militaristic state. He proclaimed totalitarianism as a whole new way of life that would transform the individual and society. Fascist movements proliferated in Europe, even to some degree in the old democracies of Great Britain and France, while the United States also experienced some stirrings in that direction. In East Asia, superpatriotic and militaristic groups surged to the fore in Japan with their plans for solving Japan's problems by militarism and conquests.

In the face of these new perils, a strange paralysis of will seemed to afflict the western democracies. Great Britain and France, with the United States on the sidelines, supinely observed the rise to power of totalitarian dictators who made no secret of their contempt for democracy and their determination to destroy the Versailles settlement in order to gain *lebensraum* (living room) for their peoples by intimidation and violence. The comparatively milder mood of the American people in the 1920's for withdrawal from world obligations became more intensely isolationist during the Great Depression. Preoccupied with problems of economic recovery at home and alarmed by ominous signs of another great wave of wars, Americans seemed all the more determined to insulate their country within this hemisphere. Only belatedly did they begin to perceive that the threat of totalitarianism left no nation secure, no matter how devoutly it might desire to remain at peace.

2. THE MANCHURIAN CRISIS

Manchuria became the scene for the opening round of crises and violence that finally culminated in World War II. Japan was the first major power to challenge the postwar order, a challenge that ten years later reached a fiery climax at Pearl Harbor. The crisis appeared all the more startling following the bright promise of the Twenties. After the Washington Conference had stabilized the Pacific area, Japan seemed to make substantial progress along democratic lines. Moderates curbed military expenditures and initiated social measures at home, and in foreign policy adopted a conciliatory course toward China and the West. The Nationalist movement in China, led by Chiang Kai-shek, broke with its Communist left wing and by 1929 apparently had reunited that vast country.

Yet beneath the surface, powerful nationalistic and social currents threatened to disrupt the Pacific treaty system. China determined to throw off the unequal treaties forced upon her by the great powers in the past and to expel Russia and Japan from Manchuria. Popular boycotts and riots broke out repeatedly against western and Japanese business interests in China. An attempt to force Russia to abandon the Chinese Eastern Railway in Manchuria erupted into a brief and relatively bloodless border war in 1929. Rebuffed by Soviet power, the Nationalists then tried to harass the Japanese from south Manchuria. The Nationalists refused to recognize the validity of past Sino-Japanese treaties regarding Manchuria, carried on anti-Japanese propaganda and boycotts, and planned to construct a railroad and port to undermine the Japanese-owned South Manchurian Railway. These activities alarmed many

Japanese, who feared that the Foreign Office was following too mild a course in protecting Japan's interests. Manchuria had obvious strategic and economic importance to the island empire. Moreover, many Japanese looked apprehensively at Communist Russia to the north.

Japanese militarists and superpatriots eagerly plotted a new course for the empire, and Manchuria provided the occasion to put it into action. These militaristic and chauvinistic elements, such as the Black Dragon Society, the Cherry Blossom Society, the Blood Brotherhood, and the junior officer class of the army, resolved to reform Japan by sweeping away the alien trappings of democracy, by evicting allegedly corrupt big businessmen from control of the government, and by restoring the ancient values and virtues. They envisioned Japan under the code of Bushido and led by the army as one great national family united under the divine emperor and aggressively asserting her leadership over all East Asia. Unfortunately certain western actions helped weaken the moderates in Japan. Many Japanese bitterly resented the inferior naval ratios allotted their country at the Washington and London conferences, and the tariff barriers that America and Europe had erected against Japanese goods. The American Immigration Act of 1924, excluding Japanese and other Orientals, especially offended sensitive Japanese. If assigned a quota under that restrictive act, only about 246 Japanese a year could have entered the United States and this would have satisfied Japanese pride, but prejudiced Americans insisted upon complete legal exclusion. The worldwide depression of the 1930's hit Japan hard and increased the social turmoil already under way as a result of rapid industrialization and urbanization. The militarists took advantage of western preoccupation with the depression to strike in Manchuria.

On the night of September 18, 1931, a small explosion went off along the lines of the South Manchurian Railway near Mukden. Charging Chinese sabotage, the Japanese Kwantung army moved out of the railway zone and leased bases to seize the major cities and to evict Chinese soldiers and officials from the area. By early 1932 the Japanese army controlled most of Manchuria, and had proclaimed the puppet state of Manchukuo. The attack shocked Emperor Hirohito and the civilian authorities in Tokyo, both of whom opposed the conquest but were unable to control the army.

The conquest of Manchuria enormously stimulated Japanese nationalism and greatly strengthened the militaristic faction. Fanatics launched a campaign of intimidation and assassination to silence critics of the army and to bend the government to its control. In 1930, a prime minister had been assassinated for consenting to the London Naval Agreement, two years later another prime minister and a cabinet minister met a similar fate, and in 1936 an attack missed the prime minister but killed his brother-in-law by mistake, along with several other officials. Gradually the campaign of patriotic propaganda and intimidation enabled the militarists and superpatriots to control Japan's destinies and to embark upon an aggressive policy to achieve Japanese hegemony in the Far East. The military began to subvert the rule of Chiang Kai-shek in northern China, withdrew Japan from the League of Nations, and denounced the naval limitations treaties in 1934 after failing to obtain naval parity for Japan with Great Britain and the United States.

Despite the loss of Manchuria, Chiang Kai-shek at first adopted a conciliatory attitude toward Japan and conceded her special economic privileges in North China and Inner Mongolia. Growing anti-Japanese sentiment among the Chinese people, however, forced him to begin to oppose further Japanese encroachments. The Japanese army decided to break Chiang Kai-shek by force. A clash in Peiping in July, 1937, the so-called "China Incident" (because of the Pact of Paris declaring war was no longer fashionable), broadened into an all-out war to reduce China to a protectorate status. Japan had embarked upon a course that eventually bogged down her armies in the land mass of China and led to a fateful collision with the United States.

3. THE HOOVER-STIMSON DOCTRINE

Henry L. Stimson, Secretary of State under President Hoover, differed greatly in temperament and policies from his chief. Hoover had not known Stimson very well and decided on him for the State Department only after three others had declined that post. Stimson, an old follower of Theodore Roosevelt, had a much bolder approach. Assured, moralistic, and with a stern sense of duty to the republic, Stimson believed that strict moral principles and mutual respect should govern international relations. He felt confident in his knowledge of the "Oriental mind" and believed that a firm policy would compel Japan to respect its treaty obligations. In contrast, although Hoover was not an isolationist in the traditional sense, he had a deep aversion to war and was determined to limit America's foreign commitments and to keep the nation at peace. The two officials also differed in petty but mutually annoying ways. Hoover regularly rose early in the morning and put in extremely long days at his presidential duties. Stimson's more relaxed pace and shorter working day frequently irritated Hoover; he viewed it as slackness but charitably attributed it to the Secretary's poor health.

The American government reacted to Japanese aggressions in China with moral resistance only. Stimson at first inclined toward trusting the Japanese moderates to curb the army in Manchuria. He rebuffed a Chinese appeal to invoke the Kellogg-Briand pact; Great Britain and France, the major powers in the League Council, also hesitated to rebuke Japan. Perhaps a more vigorous opposition to Japanese aggression might have proved quite effective at that early stage. As the Japanese army continued its conquests, despite the promises of the government in

Tokyo, Stimson and the leaders of the major League powers realized that they had greatly underestimated the will and power of the Japanese military. Washington agreed to allow Prentiss Gilbert to represent the United States when the League Council met to consider the Manchurian problem. The Council invoked the Pact of Paris in notes to Japan and China, and the State Department followed with similar action a few days later. Hoover and Stimson, fearing the isolationists and not wanting to unduly antagonize Japan, planned to withdraw Gilbert from the Council's sessions but the pressure of opinion in America and Europe dissuaded them. The Council fixed a deadline for the withdrawal of the Japanese forces to their original zones in Manchuria but to no avail. Subsequently the United States had an unofficial representative on the League's Lytton Commission that investigated the causes of the Sino-Japanese clash. The commission reported in 1933 that Japan bore the primary responsibility, although China also had acted provocatively. Japan then showed its contempt for world moral opinion by walking out of the League.

President Hoover recoiled in alarm at the prospect of sanctions against Japan. He refused to consider cooperating with any such measures taken by the League. Yet the American attitude was not alone to blame for the failure to back up moral condemnation with more practical measures. Neither the British nor the French government felt great alarm at Japan's actions, particularly as long as they remained confined to areas remote from Anglo-French interests in China. Moreover, important elements in both countries inclined to look upon Japan as a salutary check to the disorderly Chinese and to the designs of Communist Russia in Asia.

The so-called Stimson Doctrine underscored America's policy of moral condemnation. In identical notes to Japan and China on January 7, 1932 the State Department refused to recognize any changes in China brought about by force and in violation of the Pact of Paris. Although the British and French governments failed to issue a similar warning at the same time, the pressure of the smaller nations in the League eventually persuaded those two governments to follow the American lead in refusing to recognize Manchukuo. When Japanese forces brutally bombed and attacked Shanghai, in retaliation against anti-Japanese boycotts and riots, Stimson tried to obtain British cooperation for a show of naval force and the invocation of the Nine Power Pact against Japan. Decisive Anglo-American cooperation at that point might have compelled a halt to Japanese aggression, but Britain left the responsibility primarily to the United States. Stimson interpreted the cautious response of the British Foreign Secretary, Sir John Simon, as a refusal, and with President Hoover's approval he decided to act alone.

Stimson wrote a public letter to Senator Borah, the chairman of the Senate Foreign Relations Committee, on February 23, 1932. His letter reaffirmed the principles of the Open Door in China, and the bearing of the Nine Power Pact and the Pact of Paris upon recent events in Manchuria. He intimated that since the Five Power Pact on naval limitations was closely linked to the Nine Power Pact, the United States might regard the violation of one as nullifying the other. Stimson invited other powers to join in refusing to recognize any changes in China that violated these treaties. Stimson's threat of a new naval arms race apparently had some effect upon Tokyo, for the Japanese arranged a truce in Shanghai. Japan's leaders felt only a momentary alarm, however, for they soon realized that the United States was too isolationist and too preoccupied with the depression to follow words with deeds.

Stimson wanted to adopt a tougher policy toward Japan, persuaded by his advisers in the State Department of the necessity for economic sanctions against Japan to halt her aggressions and to avert an eventual war. Japan's large export trade with the United States and its dependence upon America for much of its oil and other imports made it particularly vulnerable to economic pressures. Although Stimson had some doubts about actually using the economic weapon, he wanted at least to brandish it at Japan. President Hoover, on the other hand, feared that economic coercion would lead to war rather than to peace. Unquestionably the President fell more in step with American public opinion on this point than did Stimson. Most Americans heartily approved nonrecognition of Japan's conquests and sympathized with the Chinese as victims of aggression, but they did not want the United States to risk war with the island empire. Their mood reflected the peculiar ambivalence long prevalent among the American people—the desire to set a moral example to the world while remaining detached from it.

The Hoover-Stimson policy of nonrecognition and moral condemnation reflected essentially a legalistic and sentimental reaction against Japanese aggression. In realistic terms, the United States lacked both will and adequate naval strength to restrain Japan, and attempts to obtain British cooperation had not received noticeable success. Economically, the United States was affronting one of its best customers. American trade with China, despite the myth of a vast market, had never reached significant proportions. Japan, on the other hand, had become the third largest purchaser of American exports, valued at about one-half billion dollars per year, and annually exported to the United States goods worth about a quarter of a billion dollars. Despite that favorable balance of trade with Japan, many Americans believed grossly exaggerated charges that the country was being flooded with cheap Japanese textiles and other goods threatening our domestic industry and workers. Although a tariff study in 1934 revealed that only 8 percent of imported Japanese goods seriously competed with American products, agitation mounted for higher tariffs to exclude Japanese exports. America's pro-Chinese sentiment, therefore, reflected less material interests in China and more popular sympathy for the underdog and the old missionary-born myth that

America had a special role in Christianizing and westernizing China. Chiang Kai-shek's conversion to Christianity, for example, favorably impressed many Americans.

The United States's moralistic policy failed to appreciate Japan's vital stake in Manchuria, threatened both by the Nationalists and by Soviet Russia. Manchuria long had been Chinese mainly in theory, while in fact Japan and Russia had competed for predominance in that relatively underdeveloped area. In hindsight, perhaps the western powers would have been wiser to have accepted Japan's conquest. In any case, if the American government had decided to oppose the conquest of Manchuria, and perhaps it could be argued that Japan was endangering the entire Pacific structure and had to be curbed sooner rather than later, deeds should have followed words. Mere moral pronouncements only enraged the Japanese without restraining their expansionism. Hoover and Stimson only provided the militarists and chauvinists with additional arguments to convince the Japanese people that the United States was their great opponent, while encouraging the expansionists in the conviction that actions would not follow moral wrist-slapping. Moreover, many Japanese viewed western criticism of their imperialism as hypocritical. As the later Japanese Foreign Minister, Yosuke Matsuoka, once cynically remarked, "The Western Powers taught Japan the game of poker but after acquiring most of the chips they pronounced the game immoral and took up contract bridge."

4. EARLY NEW DEAL FOREIGN POLICY

Franklin D. Roosevelt, the Democratic winner in the 1932 election, became one of the most charismatic presidents in American history. Born in 1882 into the aristocratic Roosevelt family, Franklin attended Harvard and subsequently emulated his famous cousin, Theodore Roosevelt, by entering New York state politics. During the Wilson administration, FDR served ably as Assistant Secretary of the Navy under Josephus Daniels of North Carolina. An ardent navalist, Roosevelt gained far more popularity with the admirals than did Daniels, but the latter, who had a great fondness for Roosevelt, kindly overlooked the indiscretions of his snobbish young assistant. After his losing race as the vice presidential nominee in 1920, young Roosevelt in the following year suffered an attack of infantile paralysis, from which he never fully recovered. Even so he continued to take an active interest in politics. In 1928, when Governor Al Smith of New York finally won the Democratic presidential prize, Roosevelt reluctantly agreed to run for the governorship and won. He then was in a good position to obtain the Democratic presidential nomination in 1932 and to defeat the depression-burdened Hoover. Exuding confidence and optimism, FDR became one of the most dynamic chief executives in our history as he led the nation into battle first against the Depression and subsequently against Japan and the European dictators. This gay and charming man may have been several intellectual notches below the level of Theodore Roosevelt and Woodrow Wilson, but the quality of his temperament cannot be questioned.

Early New Deal foreign policy long has puzzled scholars. Did it essentially represent a continuation of the neo-isolationism of the Twenties, or a return to Wilsonian internationalism? Roosevelt's personal and official correspondence from 1933 through 1936 clearly reveal that he became increasingly interested in foreign affairs and paid close attention to ominous developments in Europe and Asia. Yet he was not entirely immune to some of the isolationist illusions of the times, and in his speeches he repeatedly declared that the United States should avoid involvement in foreign wars. As the threat of totalitarian imperialism increased, therefore, his isolationist tendencies conflicted with his dislike of aggressors and his belief that the United States should take a responsible part in promoting world peace. Consequently, his foreign policies during his first term did not differ greatly from those of Hoover. Moreover, Roosevelt concerned himself first necessarily with the domestic depression, and he was aware of the growing isolationist mood of the American public. A practical statesman, FDR realized the need for caution in foreign affairs if he wanted to obtain the domestic support of influential isolationists in Congress. He once remarked, "It's a terrible thing to look over your shoulder when you are trying to lead—and to find no one there." His first administration, therefore, revealed no clear and consistent pattern in foreign policy.

Cordell Hull was 61 years old when he was sworn in as Secretary of State. He held that position for nearly 12 years, longer than any other occupant. A Tennessee politician and dedicated Wilsonian, Hull had little experience in foreign affairs. He based his solution for the world's ills on a simple prescription of freer trade (the open door), a revival of international morality, and the sanctity of international law and treaties. Hull resembled the great leader he so revered; like Wilson, he had a pronounced penchant for expressing moral indignation, often in language well salted from his Tennessee hills background. Hull made his most notable contributions to New Deal foreign policy in the fields of trade and the Good Neighbor Policy toward Latin America; some New Leftists, fond of economic emphases, consequently tend to depict him as more realistic and effective than usually thought. Never an intimate of the President's and highly suspicious of FDR's very able and sophisticated friend, Undersecretary of State Sumner Welles, Hull found himself increasingly bypassed in diplomacy as the United States entered World War II. Like Wilson, Roosevelt in his second and third terms used personal agents and immersed himself increasingly in the business of foreign affairs.

The Roosevelt administration continued the neo-isolationist policies of the Twenties toward the League of Nations and the war debts question. During the 1932 campaign, Roosevelt had reassured die-hard isolationists that the present League had strayed far from Wilson's ideal and that the United States had no place in it. He soon saw only too clearly the many weaknesses of the League. He also continued to insist upon full repayment of the war debts, declining to discuss reductions that he obviously thought most Americans would oppose. When all the debtors except Finland defaulted, Roosevelt signed the Johnson Act in 1934 prohibiting private or governmental loans to defaulting governments. Subsequently he regretted that measure as tying his hands in foreign policy.

Historians have often cited the London Economic Conference in 1933 as an example of early New Deal isolationism. It really indicated, however, that most major powers chose to follow narrowly nationalistic economic policies and that Roosevelt was not a particularly efficient administrator. The conference had intended to restore an effective international system of monetary exchange and to stimulate an increase in international trade. Hoover had hoped to speed recovery by stabilizing world currencies or exchange rates and persuading countries such as Great Britain and Germany to return to the gold standard. Roosevelt apparently did not know what he wanted from the conference. Prior to his inauguration, he had already ruled out Hoover's suggestion of parallel negotiations on war debts and reparations, so eagerly sought by the European debtors. Then before and during the conference he decided to experiment with the currency in the hopes of generating a domestic rise in wages and prices, taking the nation off the gold standard and varying the so-called gold content of the dollar. He named a strangely mixed lot of free traders and protectionists to represent the United States at the London conference. One of the delegates, Senator Key Pittman of Nevada, the chairman of the Senate Foreign Relations Committee, scandalized London with his drunken sprees, while an adviser, William C. Bullitt, apparently viewed himself as an early-day James Bond and went around trying to detect hidden microphones and to pry secrets out of the female secretary of the British Prime Minister. Hull, devoted to the panacea of freer trade and lower tariffs, was deeply disappointed when the President ruled out any tariff reductions for the present.

While the London conference was under way and after it had hammered out a temporary stabilization of currency exchanges, Roosevelt decided it would interfere with his inflationary experiments with the dollar. On July 2, he sent the famous "bombshell" message torpedoing even a temporary stabilization agreement. In the message, Roosevelt expressed satisfaction that the "old fetishes" of the financiers were being supplanted by planned national currencies, and he piously rebuked the European nations for not balancing their budgets and living within their means. Blame for the failure of the conference fell upon the "bombshell" message, but in fact it never had much prospect of taking effective measures for world recovery owing to a general lack of agreement among the powers and selfish maneuvering for advantage in any currency stabilization. Roosevelt's chief mistakes lay in not defining policy clearly and early enough, and in not selecting a more experienced and cohesive delegation.

Roosevelt's record in other areas during his first term proved more constructive. The World Disarmament Conference, convened in 1932, was still limping along when FDR took office. Hoover had proposed the abolition of all "offensive" weapons and a one-third across-the-board reduction in armaments. Roosevelt edged as close as he apparently dared to collective security by proposing a package plan for a pledge of nonaggression, an overall arms reduction, and an American promise to consult with other powers in case of a crisis. The United States, he added, would also not interfere with any sanctions the League might impose against an aggressor. Hitler quickly sealed the fate of the conference by ordering Germany's delegates to walk out and announcing Germany's withdrawal from the League. Obviously that dictator had his own ideas about the best means to achieve security. In 1934, Hull obtained the lower tariff approach he had long desired via the Reciprocal Trades Agreement Act. By 1940, the United States had completed 22 reciprocal agreements with other countries, but while earning some good will and quickening some trade, especially with Latin America, the results fell far short of Hull's idealistic goals of a peaceful free-trade world.

Recognition of the Soviet Union represented a long overdue step. During the '20's, the Republicans had continued Wilson's policy on nonrecognition of Communist Russia. We could have no dealings, Americans believed, with a dictatorial regime that advocated class warfare and world revolution and repudiated its foreign debts. The Great Red Scare of 1919–20, when many Americans reacted hysterically to the alleged threat of radicalism within the United States, froze nonrecognition into a fixed policy. In the following years, however, public hostility and suspicion of Soviet Russia gradually diminished. A number of Americans, many of them influential businessmen and politicians, began to urge diplomatic recognition of the Soviets on the grounds that it would open a large market for American exports. The economic argument became more persuasive during the Great Depression, when Joseph Stalin, Lenin's successor, launched a five-year plan to speed up Russia's industrialization. American industries eagerly wanted to do business with the Communist dictator. Other Americans argued that the establishment of diplomatic relations would enable Russia and the United States to cooperate in restraining Japanese imperialism. Moreover, it seemed manifestly absurd to refuse to recognize a government that clearly held power and that had received recognition from the major

European states. Conversely, opponents of recognition, such as the American Legion, the American Federation of Labor, and many Protestant and Roman Catholic clergymen, condemned any rapprochement with such an atheistic and brutal police state. Yet a poll of American newspapers in the early 1930's revealed that 60 percent of the editors favored recognizing the Soviet government.

Roosevelt's decision to end 16 years of nonrecognition apparently arose out of a realistic acceptance of Soviet existence and the hope that recognition would bolster the status quo in the Far East against Japan and would strengthen nonaggressive forces in Europe. After preliminary explorations, Soviet Foreign Commissar Maxim Litvinov came to Washington for negotiations. Roosevelt personally took a direct part in shaping the recognition agreements of November 16, 1933. The accord, in the form of a group of letters and agreements, established diplomatic relations between the two countries, provided freedom of religious worship for Americans in Russia, and promised to halt Russian propaganda and subversion in the United States. Roosevelt and his advisers insisted upon the religious provision, it seems, for its effect upon the American public. As for the reciprocal promise that neither government would interfere "in any manner" in the internal affairs of the other, that too was deemed necessary because of American public opinion, though perhaps some of the American negotiators took it seriously. Russia dropped its claims for damages suffered during the 1918 interventions, and the two governments agreed upon further negotiations about the American claims against the Soviet Union. Under recognized international practice, a government still takes responsibility for the foreign debts of its predecessors. American claims amounted to over $630 million, including about $187 million owed to the United States by the former provisional government of Russia, private loans to the Czarist and provisional governments, and claims for property confiscated by the Bolsheviks. In their "gentlemen's agreement," Litvinov mentioned a possible settlement of $100 million while Roosevelt referred to the sum of $150 million.

Most Americans approved Roosevelt's action. Litvinov was given a farewell luncheon at the Waldorf-Astoria Hotel in New York City, attended by the officials of such giant capitalistic firms as J. P. Morgan and the Pennsylvania Railroad. The President of International Business Machines even urged his fellow citizens to promote better relations with that Communist country by refraining "from any criticism of the present form of Government adopted by Russia." Unfortunately for such enthusiasts, recognition soon proved disappointing: trade remained small, because Russia could not obtain long-term credits; no significant collaboration ensued in regard to restraining Japan; and negotiations over the debt claims soon broke down. Russia tied the debts issue to a long-term credit or loan from the United States, which the administration refused to grant. And Communist propaganda did not cease in the United States. When Hull protested the continuation of revolutionary propaganda, trumpeted at the seventh congress of the Comintern held at Moscow in 1935, the Soviet government blandly disavowed any connection with what it called a purely unofficial gathering on Russian soil. An increasing number of Americans had come to view recognition as a grievous mistake by the late '30's.

5. THE GOOD NEIGHBOR POLICY

A new era in American relations with its southern neighbors began during the Wilson administration. Despite armed interventions in the Caribbean and clashes with Mexico, Wilson's idealism and Pan Americanism had favorably impressed many Latin Americans. His successors in the '20's continued his efforts to cultivate better relations with Latin America. American businessmen, eager for new markets and resources, urged a conciliatory course, as did other citizens who were appalled by the often exaggerated stories of our harsh military rule in Haiti and the Dominican Republic. Such imperialism seemed obviously contradictory to the democratic ideals which America had proclaimed in the Great War. For these reasons and because after 1918 the United States felt more secure than earlier, the government began to liquidate its interventionist policies.

American marines withdrew from the Dominican Republic in 1924, although financial controls remained until 1941. The Senate finally approved a treaty in 1921 compensating Colombia by $25 million for the 1903 Panama affair, and clearing the way for eager Yankee oilmen to operate in that country. American troops left Nicaragua in 1925, only to return the following year when new revolutionary disorders broke out. A truce patched up by Colonel Henry L. Stimson soon broke down and American forces remained in Nicaragua until 1933, financial controls continuing until 1944. The Clark Memorandum, released by the State Department in 1930, disclaimed any valid connection between the hated Roosevelt Corollary and the Monroe Doctrine, although it did not repudiate interventionism on other grounds. The United States carefully avoided any appearance of dominating the Fifth Pan American Conference held in 1923 at Santiago, Chile. President Coolidge personally opened the Sixth Pan American Conference, at Havana in 1928. These conferences made progress in strengthening hemispheric harmony and adopting agreements for the pacific settlement of disputes.

Mexico posed a more difficult problem, but there, too, relations briefly improved. In the Bucareli settlement of 1923, President Álvaro Obregón agreed not to apply Article 27 of the 1917 Constitution, which provided for public ownership of subsurface oil and mineral deposits, retroactively to foreign-owned oil concessions obtained prior to 1917 and on which development had begun. He also agreed to pay compensation for all foreign-owned properties expropriated under Mexico's agrarian reform program. Unfortunately the next Mexican administration, under Plutarco Elías Calles, reversed Obregón's course and imposed severe restrictions upon foreign-owned oil properties and land holdings. Calles's anticlerical program further alienated many Americans, when he closed convents and religious schools, and required priests to register with the state. President Coolidge and Secretary of State Kellogg at first reacted sharply, implying Communist influence in Mexico and the supplying of Mexican arms to Nicaraguan rebels against the American-backed regime. The two officials quickly adopted a more conciliatory course, however, after the Senate revealed its opposition to any armed intervention or threat of force. Calles intimated his willingness to arbitrate the economic issues. Coolidge sent his old friend Dwight Morrow on a special peace mission to Mexico City. The *simpatico* Morrow speedily established rapport with the Mexican government and people. He arranged a goodwill visit by humorist Will Rogers and a special flight to Mexico City by America's young air idol and Morrow's son-in-law Charles A. Lindbergh. Morrow paved the way for a face-saving arrangement reviving the Bucareli understanding. It resulted in only a temporary solution to the oil problem, but it restored a degree of harmony to Mexican-American relations.

Hoover's contributions to Pan Americanism were so notable that some scholars have credited him with originating the Good Neighbor Policy. The President-elect toured Latin America in 1928 and made several speeches using the phrase "good neighbor." As chief executive he avoided further armed interventions, as in the case of the Panamanian disorders, recalled the troops from Nicaragua in 1933, and promised withdrawal from Haiti (accomplished in 1934). Hoover also abandoned Wilson's moralistic nonrecognition policy, returning to the traditional practice of recognizing de facto regimes without questioning how they had come to power. But Hoover showed no more readiness than his predecessors to renounce the possible use of intervention in the future, fearing that events might sometimes compel action to protect foreign lives and property within the less stable Caribbean countries.

FDR in his inaugural address pledged a policy of a Good Neighbor attitude toward all nations. The phrase caught on as a folksy summary of his policy toward Latin America. Roosevelt wanted to promote greater hemispheric harmony and solidarity as desirable in themselves, and to quicken trade and recovery from the Depression. Subsequently, the need to protect the hemisphere against the totalitarian dictators of Europe added another powerful motive. Latin Americans hailed FDR as "el gran democrata," and many saw his New Deal as a model for social and economic reforms in their own countries. Ultimately FDR—the Good Neighbor, and the inspired spokesman for common people everywhere—took on a nearly deified stature to Latin Americans.

The essence of the Good Neighbor Policy, as it developed over a period

of years, can be summarized as noninterventionism, the multilateralization of the Monroe Doctrine, diplomatic noninterference in the affairs of
Latin American states, the lowering of tariff barriers, and the sacrificing
of private American economic interests in Latin America when necessary
to promote larger political goals. At the Seventh Pan American Conference at Montevideo in 1933, Cordell Hull greatly pleased Latin Americans when he voted for a resolution of noninterference by armed force in
the internal affairs of any state in the Western Hemisphere, except as
sanctioned by international law. At the next conference, a special session
held at Buenos Aires in 1936 and personally opened by President
Roosevelt, Hull reiterated that pledge without any reservations. At last it
seemed that the shadow of American interventionism had disappeared.
A Mexican delegate at the Montevideo Conference expressed the sentiment of most Latin Americans, "I wish to submit my profound conviction that there is in the White House an admirable, noble, and good
man—a courageous man who knows the errors of the past but who feels
that the errors really belong to the past."

The marines left Haiti, as Hoover previously had promised, and in
1934 the United States abrogated the Platt Amendment with Cuba
(Guantanamo remained an American base). The latter action occurred
only after the United States had intervened diplomatically and had come
close to armed intervention during the overthrow of the Gerardo
Machado dictatorship and its successor. Roosevelt and Hull saw from
this experience that even diplomatic intervention had its dangers. They
handled the difficulties with Bolivia and Mexico over the expropriation of
American-owned oil properties successfully by in effect sacrificing the
private interests involved to the political interests of the United States.
Thus, they settled Mexican expropriation of American-owned oil properties in 1938, during the presidency of Lázaro Cárdenas, for a compensation of $24 million on holdings valued by the American companies at half
a billion dollars, and a subsequent Import-Export Bank loan from the
United States helped Mexico pay even that small amount. Clearly the
State Department, while very concerned with the legitimate economic
interests of American citizens in Latin America, no longer acted as a
bond-collector for Wall Street.

The multilateralization of the Monroe Doctrine in effect began at
Montevideo and Buenos Aires, when Hull pledged the United States to
nonintervention in the affairs of its neighbors. Alarmed by the rising tide
of aggression in Asia and Europe, the administration sought to create
machinery for the collective defense of the Western Hemisphere. It did
not wholly succeed, however, as Argentina, long a rival of the United
States for hemispheric leadership, repeatedly forced the watering-down
of American proposals for joint action to repel aggressors. Hull did
obtain a loose declaration at the Eighth Pan American Conference at
Lima in 1938, the Declaration of Lima, that proclaimed the solidarity of

the Western Hemisphere and promised consultation and cooperation against subversion or external threats to the peace of the hemisphere. Canada, a self-governing dominion within the British Empire and Commonwealth, remained apart from the Pan American movement in order to preserve its nationality and its ties to England. In effect, however, FDR brought it within the scope of the inter-American system by declaring, at Kingston, Ontario, in 1938, that the United States could not see Canada threatened by invasion. The Good Neighbor Policy succeeded in promoting a large degree of hemispheric solidarity prior to the outbreak of the Second World War.

Additional Reading

A general account of the Hoover era is by H. G. Warren, *Herbert Hoover and the Great Depression* (1959). Biographies and general accounts of the New Deal era are numerous. Among the most valuable are the multivolume study by Arthur M. Schlesinger, Jr., *The Age of Roosevelt* (3 vols. to date, 1957–60); James MacGregor Burns, *Roosevelt: The Lion and the Fox* (1956), an excellent political study; Dexter Perkins's briefer sketch, *The New Age of Franklin D. Roosevelt, 1932–1945* (1957); and the superb account by William E. Leuchtenburg, *Franklin D. Roosevelt and the New Deal, 1932–1940* (1963). Robert A. Divine, *Roosevelt and World War II* (1969) views Roosevelt in the early years of his first term as essentially an isolationist. Interpretive essays on Stimson and Hull are by Richard N. Current and Donald F. Drummond, respectively, in Norman Graebner, ed., *An Uncertain Tradition: American Secretaries of State in the Twentieth Century* (1961), 168–183, 184–209. The Bemis series is continued by Robert H. Ferrell's essay on Stimson in *The American Secretaries of State and Their Diplomacy,* Vol. XI (1963), and by Julius W. Pratt's two-volume study, *Cordell Hull* (1964). Also see Richard N. Current, *Secretary Stimson* (1954) and Elting Morison, *Turmoil and Tradition: A Study of the Life and Times of Henry L. Stimson* (1960). *American Diplomacy in the Great Depression* (1957), by Robert H. Ferrell, is a solid account of Hoover–early New Deal diplomacy. On the Far Eastern crises, the best studies are by Armin Rappaport, *Henry L. Stimson and Japan, 1931–1933* (1963) and Dorothy Borg, *The United States and the Far Eastern Crisis, 1933–1938* (1964). Herbert Feis, *The Road to Pearl Harbor* (1950) touches briefly on the early '30's. William L. Neumann, *America Encounters Japan* (1963) presents a stimulating analysis of Japanese-American relations. A. W. Griswold, *The Far Eastern Policy of the United States* (1938) is useful through the early New Deal years. For economics and foreign policy, see Lloyd Gardner, *Economic Aspects of New Deal Diplomacy* (1964). General accounts of relations with Soviet Russia are found in Thomas A. Bailey's well-written

America Faces Russia (1950) and the critical account by William Appleman Williams, *American-Russian Relations, 1781–1947* (1952). Also see the broader survey by the diplomat-historian George F. Kennan *Russia and the West under Lenin and Stalin* (1960). For the establishment of official relations, consult Robert P. Browder, *The Origins of Soviet-American Relations* (1953) and Donald G. Bishop, *The Roosevelt-Litvinov Agreements* (1965). Robert E. Bowers, "Hull, Russian Subversion in Cuba, and Recognition of the U.S.S.R.," *Journal of American History,* LIII (1966), 542–554 reveals the State Department's lack of enthusiasm for recognition. Latin American relations are traced by Samuel Flagg Bemis in *The Latin American Policy of the United States* (1943) and by Graham H. Stuart in *Latin America and the United States* (1938). The interreactions between Pan Americanism and security requirements are handled by A. P. Whitaker, *The Western Hemisphere Idea* (1954) and by Dexter Perkins, *A History of the Monroe Doctrine* (1955). Wilsonian beginnings of the Good Neighbor are examined by Daniel M. Smith, *Aftermath of War: Bainbridge Colby and Wilsonian Diplomacy* (1970). Alexander De Conde, *Herbert Hoover's Latin American Policy* (1951) gives Hoover much credit for the Good Neighbor, while Edward Guerrant, *Roosevelt's Good Neighbor Policy* (1950) credits Roosevelt primarily, as does the excellent interpretive study by Bryce Wood, *The Making of the Good Neighbor Policy* (1961). On Mexico, see E. David Cronon, *Josephus Daniels in Mexico* (1960).

The battleship USS Arizona *burning furiously following the Japanese attack on Pearl Harbor*

21

THE CHALLENGE
OF TOTALITARIANISM,
1935–1941

1. THE SURGE OF ISOLATIONISM

A tidal wave of isolationist sentiment swept the United States in the mid-1930's. The persisting blight of the Great Depression, growing disillusionment with World War I, and multiplying signs of another great cycle of wars caused many Americans to resolve that their country should never again get entangled in a foreign war. Isolationism seemed to be strongest in the midwestern states, though by no means was it limited to that section. Ethnic factors played some role in the midwestern reaction, because of the large numbers of German and Scandinavian-Americans living there. Agrarian radicalism, however, seems to have exerted even more influence. Radical farm spokesmen viewed the recent war as benefitting eastern industry and bankers at the expense of agriculture, and blamed the farmers' plight in the 1920's and '30's upon intervention in 1917. Isolationism at first cut across political party lines and frequently went hand in hand with liberalism and reform. Eventually, it became more identified with domestic conservatism as liberal reformers and intellectuals converted to the cause of internationalism.

Antiwar novels, motion pictures, and revisionist histories both reflected and contributed to the popular mood of pacifism, disillusionment, and withdrawal. Peace movements flourished, and students paraded against war and urged the eviction of R.O.T.C. units from campuses. Novels by Erich Remarque, Ernest Hemingway, and John Dos Passos, among others, portrayed war as senseless and dehumanizing. Books such as *Merchants of Death,* by H. C. Englebrecht and F. C. Hanighan, and George Selde's *Iron, Blood and Profits,* strengthened the popular belief that common men fought and died so that bankers and arms makers might profit. Scholars joined the hunt for villains and scapegoats. Revisionist historians such as Harry Elmer Barnes and Walter Millis tried to prove that Germany had neither borne the major guilt of World War I nor driven the United States into that great conflict. Liberal revisionists sought not merely the truth about 1914 and 1917 but to influence the current debate upon foreign policy. Resembling currents in the early 1970's, they strongly believed that America should not again divert its attention from domestic reform to needless foreign crusades; war should not destroy the New Deal, as the First World War had allegedly slain Progressivism. To a large extent, the revisionists won the liberal intellectual community to their views and helped create that climate of opinion that explains passage of the neutrality acts in the mid-1930's. A Gallup poll in 1937, for example, revealed that 64 percent of the public viewed intervention in World War I as a mistake. And in that same year, the Emergency Peace Crusade observed the 20th anniversary of the 1917 intervention with a "no foreign war crusade," and extolled those members of Congress who had voted against war in 1917.

The significance of the Nye Committee hearings probably has been exaggerated, but they were symptomatic of popular disillusionment and isolationism. Responding to the demands from such groups as the Women's International League for Peace and Freedom for regulation of the arms industry, the Senate in 1934 authorized a special inquiry. The administration was caught off guard when the Senate selected Senator Gerald P. Nye of North Dakota, a rough-hewn arch-isolationist and agrarian spokesman, to head the inquiry. FDR probably could have tempered the hearings by reminding the public that the nation had fought for more than profits in the recent war, but he failed to do so, apparently because, to some extent, he shared the popular aversion to foreign involvements and war profiteering. Nye staged a public carnival of sensational testimony and committee releases revealing vast profits made by arms manufacturers and financiers during the World War. As he summed it up, "When Americans went into the fray, they little thought that they were . . . fighting to save the skins of American bankers who . . . had two billions of dollars of loans to the Allies in jeopardy." The investigation seemed almost as anti–big business in bias as antiwar, and reflected the widespread view that greedy bankers and industrialists encouraged or instigated international strife. Americans seem particularly prone to periodic public hysterias and devil-seeking. The "merchants of death" theme has a later counterpart in the thesis of a "military-industrial complex" of the 1960's and '70's, as simple explanations for painful events.

Ironically Roosevelt himself suggested neutrality legislation in 1935 to bar American citizens from travel aboard belligerent ships. Apparently he hoped to avoid being dragged into a future war by issues of neutral rights and war profiteering, and then he could base American policy more clearly on fundamental national interests. Roosevelt wanted a flexible arms embargo to permit him to distinguish between aggressive and defensive states, but a threatened filibuster by the pacifist and isolationist bloc in Congress forced him to retreat. A substitute measure, prepared by Senators Pittman and Borah, provided for a mandatory embargo; upon a presidential proclamation of the existence of a foreign war, the sale or transportation of munitions to belligerent countries would be prohibited, and at the executive's discretion citizens might be warned not to take passage on belligerent vessels. Although he had hoped for a better act, FDR signed the measure into law because it would expire in six months. He also thought its application to a threatened Italo-Ethiopian War might help restrain Italy.

At the time of the adoption of the Neutrality Act, Europe seemed once more on the threshold of a major war. Although Mussolini had headed a Fascist regime in Italy since 1922, he refrained on the whole from an aggressive foreign policy until Hitler began to assault the Versailles settlement. Hitler fastened a brutal dictatorship upon the German people and began to rearm Germany in defiance of the Versailles Treaty. The Third Reich's violent anti-Jewish persecutions appalled the peoples of the western democracies and the United States. The American Ambassador in Berlin, William E. Dodd, warned the President and the State Department about Nazi militarism and plans for conquest. A growing number of German Jewish refugees came to America, among them physicist Albert Einstein. Unfortunately, owing to apathy and prejudice, neither the executive nor Congress made any significant effort to relax the immigration laws to provide a haven for the still larger numbers of Jews seeking to escape Nazi persecutions.

Hungry for conquests to garland his new Roman empire, Mussolini invaded Ethiopia in the fall of 1935. The League Council condemned the attack and invoked economic sanctions prohibiting loans and the exportation of arms and certain other materials to Italy. The alarmed British and French governments, however, fearful of the spread of war and anxious not to drive Italy into Hitler's arms, carefully excluded oil, vital to Mussolini's war machine, from the list of sanctions. The Duce's legions, armed with advanced weapons and poison gas, rapidly overran primitive Ethiopia, the first sacrificial victim to appeasement.

Roosevelt invoked the Neutrality Act in this undeclared war, falsely thinking that it would hurt Italy more than Ethiopia. The administration then went well beyond the feeble sanctions imposed by Britain and France to apply a moral embargo against oil shipments to Italy. The embargo proved difficult to enforce and it failed to encourage the League to adopt sterner measures. Britain and France thereby missed a possible opportunity to involve the United States in collective security. Moreover, their failure encouraged Hitler to reoccupy and fortify the Rhineland in 1936, to restore conscription, and to build a large military air force, all in defiance of the Versailles Treaty. The Rome-Berlin Axis in 1936 created a totalitarian front against the western democracies, and extended into the Far East that same year by the conclusion of German and Italian anti-Comintern pacts with Japan.

American isolationism seemed to deepen as crisis followed crisis abroad. The Second Neutrality Act, adopted in 1936, banned private loans as well as arms sales to belligerents and extended its application even to states enforcing League sanctions. When the Spanish Civil War broke out in 1936, between the republican "Loyalists" and the Fascist-tinged conservative rebels led by General Francisco Franco, the administration supported the attempt of Britain and France to isolate the conflict. Germany and Italy cynically violated the nonintervention agreement to aid the rebels, while Russia gave some help to the Loyalists. The administration proclaimed a moral embargo against arms sales to both sides and Congress extended the Neutrality Act to cover the civil war. Conservative Americans and some Roman Catholics hailed Franco as a bulwark against communism but most Americans tended to sympathize with the Loyalists. Several thousand Americans volunteered to fight for the republic in the Abraham Lincoln Battalion. Roosevelt eventually considered raising the arms embargo against the republican government but desisted because of domestic opposition and the hopelessness of the Loyalist cause.

The Third Neutrality Act, in 1937, still denied the President flexibility to distinguish between aggressors and their victims in imposing an arms embargo. The new act prohibited travel on belligerent ships as well as loans and arms sales. The chief executive could also use his discretion to ban export of nonmilitary strategic materials during the next two years, unless done on a "cash and carry" basis. Underlying this act, as the earlier ones, were highly debatable assumptions that no basic moral issues were involved in the struggles taking place abroad and that no fundamental American interests were at stake. For the sake of isolation and peace, Congress had drastically altered the nation's traditional policy of neutral trading rights on the high seas. As several commentators quipped, the neutrality acts appeared as an attempt to legislate the United States post facto out of World War I. The whole episode revealed not that people fail to learn from history but that often they learn the wrong lessons.

2. APPEASEMENT AT FLOOD TIDE

Events moved inexorably toward a second world war. In July, 1937, Japan initiated the "China Incident," an armed attack in north China that broadened into a war to control all China. In March, 1938, Hitler entered Vienna in triumph and annexed Austria to the Third Reich, in violation of the Versailles Treaty. Flushed with easy triumphs, the

Fuehrer threatened Czechoslovakia with war if it did not return its Sudeten Germans to the Reich. Great Britain and France seemed to lack the will to defend the Versailles settlement. The Italo-Ethiopian War had discredited the League. Moreover, British Prime Minister Neville Chamberlain, under the delusion that he was dealing with rational men, hoped to appease the dictators. Important groups in England and France deluded themselves that concessions to the "legitimate" grievances of Germany would satisfy the Nazis and avert a new war. Chamberlain and the French Premier, Edouard Daladier, journeyed to Munich in the fall of 1938 and there bought "peace in our time" by sacrificing Czechoslovakia. The Nazi dictator quickly broke his promises. After digesting the Sudetenland, he seized the remainder of Czechoslovakia early in 1939. Not to be outdone, Mussolini invaded tiny Albania in April of 1939. Only then, as Hitler turned his attention to the German population in the Polish Corridor and Danzig, did Britain and France resolve to resist even at the price of war.

The "China Incident" marked a turning point in American policy. Prior to 1937, Roosevelt and Hull had by no means followed a consistently internationalist policy. The administration not only had accepted crippling neutrality legislation without putting up prolonged resistance, but FDR himself sometimes sounded an ambiguous or isolationist note in public. After the China war began, however, Roosevelt turned to a more clearly internationalist course. He hoped somehow to prevent war, but, if that failed, to strengthen peace-loving states against their assailants. He had agreed with Stimson earlier that the United States had to oppose Japanese expansion by more than moral censure. Yet the conquest of Manchuria was a fait accompli. After Japan renewed its conquests in 1937, however, Roosevelt slowly resumed where Stimson had been compelled to halt, but he did not invoke the neutrality law in Japan's undeclared war, in order to give China whatever aid possible. Unfortunately, nonapplication probably initially benefited Japan more than China.

In the "Quarantine Speech" in Chicago, on October 5, 1937, President Roosevelt tried to alert the American people and to prepare them for a more responsible foreign policy. In the heartland of isolationist America, he indicated that the nation's security depended on cooperation with other peaceful states: "Let no one imagine that America will escape, that America may expect mercy, that this hemisphere will not be attacked. . . ." After suggesting that international gangsters should be segregated as society quarantines the carriers of dangerous diseases, Roosevelt cautiously declared, "We are determined to stay out of war . . . but we cannot *insure* ourselves against the disastrous effects of war and the danger of involvement; we cannot have complete protection in a world of disorder in which confidence and security have broken down."

The Chicago address aroused favorable response across the country, but it also ignited a firestorm of isolationist criticism and charges of war mongering. It soon became apparent, moreover, that the President had no clear policy changes in mind and that he himself, still torn between isolationist and internationalist tendencies, felt ambivalent. Apparently he had only intended some kind of collective neutrality that would morally condemn aggression. In any case, he beat a hasty retreat from whatever his address had indicated and denied even the intention of passing moral condemnation on the aggressors. Prime Minister Chamberlain's observation, apropos of the Quarantine Speech, seemed painfully true: "It is always best and safest to count on nothing from the Americans but words." FDR had burnt his fingers at Chicago and thereafter perhaps felt more apprehensive than he should have about the strength of isolationism in America.

In due time, the League of Nations condemned Japan's aggression in China and suggested a conference of signatories of the Nine Power Pact. Shortly before the United States and the other signers met at Brussels in November, 1937, Roosevelt made it clear that he would not take any vigorous measures; all he had in mind for the conference was to exert moral pressure upon Japan. Japan declined to attend, and only Russia advocated strong action. Britain and France left the initiative to America, while Roosevelt and Hull recoiled from economic sanctions against Japan. They achieved nothing beyond a pious reaffirmation of treaty principles. The Brussels Conference turned out not only as a fiasco but a disaster, for which the United States must bear much of the blame. China continued resistance in the vain hope of substantial aid, while the conference's failure emboldened Japan's leaders to persist in their course.

The *Panay* incident in December, 1937 underscored American reluctance to risk conflict with Japan. Japanese warplanes attacked the United States gunboat *Panay* and three Standard Oil Company tankers on the Yangtze River and strafed survivors in the water. Unlike 1898, no mass shouts like "Remember the *Maine*" resulted; most Americans merely wanted to get out of China. The government accepted Japanese apologies and reparations. The incident also sped congressional action on the so-called Ludlow Amendment to the Constitution, prohibiting war except in case of actual invasion or with majority approval in a national referendum. The administration had to exert strong pressure to defeat the bill, in January, 1938.

Gradually, as public support for a stronger course slowly developed in America, the State Department indicated to Japan that a line was being drawn. The Two-Ocean Naval Act of 1938 vastly increased naval construction. Meanwhile Japan, previously apologetic for many of her acts, openly proclaimed in late 1938 a "New Order" for East Asia, claiming she would no longer pay lip service to the Open Door in China.

Hull objected vigorously to the "New Order" and reasserted American rights in China and the Far East. Chiang Kai-shek received a small loan in 1938 to bolster China's currency, and the United States imposed a moral embargo against the sale and shipment of aircraft to Japan. The Pacific Fleet was moved temporarily to Pearl Harbor, a graphic reminder to Tokyo of American power and will to resist. Finally, the administration in mid-1939 gave the required notice to terminate the Japanese-American commercial treaty of 1911, thereby opening the way for economic sanctions against Japan.

War with Japan was not yet inevitable, although diplomatic options had been greatly narrowed. American opposition to Japanese expansionism in Asia had a highly moralistic tone, since the United States actually had only a small economic stake in China as opposed to a much greater one in Japan. Would America, therefore, have shown greater wisdom by choosing another course, perhaps one of mere protest while patiently striving for moderation by Japan's leaders? From the perspective of the Cold War and the Japanese-American Security Treaty, our policy in the '30's has seemed highly questionable to some scholars. Policy-makers, however, are not gifted with our hindsight. Roosevelt and Hull feared to condone aggression lest it breed more aggression, and they were convinced that they had to defend America's interests in the Pacific. Moreover, they saw firmness as the only promising means to avert an eventual war.

Roosevelt played only a minor role in the Czechoslovakian crisis. He cabled Hitler twice on behalf of peace and approved Prime Minister Chamberlain's request that Mussolini use his influence to avert hostilities. Thus America's role, feeble though it was, must be described as favoring appeasement of the voracious Nazi Fuehrer. Here as elsewhere people greeted the Munich settlement with a profound sense of relief that war had been avoided. As Hitler violated his pledges and anti-Jewish outrages multiplied in Germany, Roosevelt publicly voiced disapproval. He pointedly recalled the American Ambassador for consultation after a particularly violent anti-Jewish outbreak in Germany, the so-called *Kristallnacht,* and he never returned to Germany.

Hitler fully reciprocated American dislike and recalled his ambassador. In his contemptuous view, the United States comprised a racially mongrelized society that could not even cope with the economic depression. He saw no need to take America seriously, for as he remarked in 1938, it was impotent and would not go beyond meaningless moral gestures in international affairs. The German military shared his opinion and the neutrality laws merely increased his contempt.

By 1939 President Roosevelt clearly recognized the bankruptcy of isolationism, even though many of his countrymen did not feel the same way. He warned Congress and the nation of the serious crisis facing the world and advocated measures short of war to restrain aggression.

Earlier he had considered calling a special Armistice Day conference to try to prevent aggression and war, but had encountered opposition from Hull and a lack of enthusiasm on the part of Prime Minister Chamberlain. Now in mid-April, 1939 he appealed to Hitler and Mussolini to reassure 31 nations by name that they would not be attacked. Hitler rebuffed him in a satirical speech to the Reichstag, his puppet legislature, while Mussolini ignored the appeal. FDR and Hull also attempted, without success, to persuade Congress to repeal the Neutrality Law or at least to modify it so that the executive would not have to apply an arms embargo against countries attacked by the dictators. The administration implied that in case of war between the western democracies and the totalitarian states, America's interests and its sympathies required a victory by the democracies. The isolationists refused to relent, however, and Senator Borah confidently predicted that no war would take place in Europe in 1939.

Contrary to Senator Borah's prediction, Hitler prepared to unleash the *Wehrmacht* against Poland and the western democracies. On August 23, 1939, a shocked world learned of the signing of the Nazi-Soviet Pact in Moscow, a perfidious deal made during Anglo-French military talks with Russia for a common resistance to aggression. Apparently Stalin had despaired of any meaningful agreement with the Anglo-French and the Poles, and cynically decided to drive a bargain with the Nazis. With the danger of a major two-front war eliminated, Hitler had greater freedom to pursue his Polish venture. On September 1, the Luftwaffe rained destruction from the skies over Poland; two days later, Great Britain and France fulfilled their promises to the Poles and declared war on Nazi Germany. World War II had begun.

Isolationism seemingly still remained powerful in America, but events already had weakened it badly. Various polls dating from 1937 had indicated that most Americans viewed Nazi Germany as morally wrong, and that in case of a major war they favored supplying arms to the western democracies despite the neutrality laws. Now as Germany fired the first shots, another Gallup poll indicated that 84 percent of the American people desired an Allied victory and 76 percent, despite an overwhelming desire to remain at peace, expected America to become involved sooner or later. After Hitler had crushed Poland, a poll revealed that 63 percent of Americans believed Germany would attack the United States eventually if it won the war in Europe.

3. FROM NEUTRALITY TO NONBELLIGERENCY

On September 3, 1939, President Roosevelt assured the American people that the United States would remain neutral. Unlike President Wilson in 1914, however, FDR pointedly did not ask the public to avoid moral judgments about the belligerents. Two weeks after Hitler began his attack upon Poland, the President called Congress into special session to repeal the arms embargo in order to return to the rules of "true neutrality." Americans generally recognized that repeal would aid Great Britain and France against Hitler. Opponents attacked repeal as a step toward voiding neutrality and getting involved in the war, but a majority supported the administration's recommendation. After impassioned debate, Congress passed the Fourth Neutrality Act, and Roosevelt signed it into law on November 4, 1939. Belligerents now could purchase arms and other war goods provided they paid cash and transported their purchases in their own ships. The act still banned loans to belligerent governments and prohibited American ships from entering the war zones. "Cash and Carry" obviously would primarily benefit the Allies while giving Americans profits without any risk of involvement. The administration and a majority of Americans felt confident that, assured of American supplies, England and France could defeat Hitler in a war of attrition without American intervention.

After the fall of Poland, the war in Europe entered the "phony war" or "sitzkrieg" phase. Allied and German troops glared at each other almost bloodlessly across their fortified lines. Meanwhile the Roosevelt administration tightened the bonds of hemispheric solidarity. A foreign ministers conference at Panama in October, 1939 prohibited belligerent operations within a "hemispheric safety belt" around the Western Hemisphere (excluding Canada). Both belligerent sides ignored that novel ban. Subsequently, after the Nazi conquest of the Netherlands and France, another foreign ministers conference met at Havana in July, 1940, and agreed upon collective intervention if necessary to prevent the Dutch and French colonies in this hemisphere from passing under Hitler's control. The conference also declared that an outside attack upon one hemispheric state should be treated as an attack upon all. The Monroe Doctrine was rapidly being multilateralized.

The phony war ended abruptly in the spring of 1940. Hitler's seemingly invincible legions overran Denmark and Norway in April, 1940 and in May struck at the Netherlands, Belgium, and Luxemburg. The Germans trapped the Allied forces in Belgium and forced them to evacuate from the continent at Dunkirk. The Nazi hordes then flooded into France, smashing its armies and forcing a humiliating French capitulation on June 22, 1940. The successes of the German *blitzkrieg* (lightning war) stunned Americans. It seemed incredible that France, which had held out so heroically in World War I, could be utterly defeated in a campaign of a few weeks duration. Many feared that beleaguered Britain also would soon fall, leaving no one to stand between the Nazi juggernaut and an unprepared America.

Roosevelt sounded the alarm on June 10, 1940. Speaking at Charlottesville, Virginia, on the day that Mussolini entered the war against an already beaten France, the President warned that democratic institutions

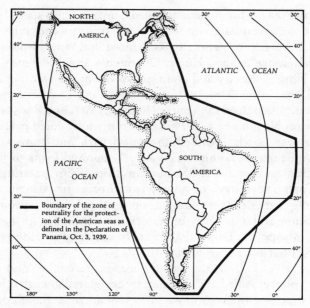

The Hemispheric Safety Belt

and the safety of the Western Hemisphere were in jeopardy. He called for measures to strengthen America's defenses and to aid those countries resisting the Axis aggressors. Obviously, genuine neutrality had become a thing of the past. While still hoping that the country could remain at peace, the administration realized that defeat of the dictators demanded more than mere access to American markets. In this crisis, FDR also decided to seek an unprecedented third term in the presidency. He strengthened his cabinet by bringing in two Republican internationalists, Frank Knox as Secretary of the Navy and Henry L. Stimson as Secretary of War. Congress was galvanized into appropriating over $10 billion for military defense and passing the first peacetime military conscription law in American history.

A desperate Britain, now led by the indomitable Winston S. Churchill, pleaded with FDR for more arms, particularly some old World War I American destroyers needed to cope with German U-boat attacks. Roosevelt had full knowledge of Britain's plight and resolved to do all he could to help her survive. As he remarked to Secretary of the Treasury Henry Morgenthau, "If we want to keep out of this war, the longer we keep them [Allies] going, that much longer we stay out of this war." Yet he feared isolationist criticism and did not quite know how he could legally transfer the destroyers to a belligerent power. Finally his advisers worked out a deal to trade them for defensive bases upon British territory in the Western Hemisphere. Churchill would have preferred merely a free exchange of gifts to demonstrate Anglo-American friendship, but Roosevelt feared a public outcry unless the transaction could be presented as an advantageous "horse trade." Formal approval of the exchange took place on September 2. Britain granted the United States long-term leases to six bases, and gave two others for free, in exchange for 50 American destroyers. London also announced that the British fleet would never fall into German hands. The eight bases, from Newfoundland to British Guiana, greatly strengthened the ability of the United States to defend the Western Hemisphere. Roosevelt publicly defended the swap as the most important contribution to American security since the Louisiana Purchase. He had acted solely upon his executive authority, which enraged the isolationists, but a poll revealed that 70 percent of the public approved. The destroyers-for-bases deal marked the end of neutrality for the United States; henceforth it assumed the role of a nonbelligerent aiding one side in the war against the other.

The impact of the war polarized public opinion. William Allen White, liberal Republican editor of the Emporia (Kansas) *Gazette,* backed FDR's policy by forming in May, 1940 the Committee to Defend America by Aiding the Allies. The White Committee established over 600 local chapters and mounted a massive campaign to convince Americans that the United States could protect its interests and remain at peace only by providing all-out aid to the Allies. White and many of his followers, however, showed reluctance to face the underlying question: if America's interests demanded Hitler's defeat, did not honor as well as self-interest require the nation actively to enter the war? Yet polls bore out White's position, revealing that while four of every five Americans supported aid to England, 82 percent opposed entering the war. The America First Committee formed in September, 1940 to oppose the position of the administration-backers. Drawing upon the talents of such isolationists and noninterventionists as Henry Ford, Lindbergh, and Nye, America First argued that Hitler posed no real threat to the United States and warned that aid to Britain would drag the nation needlessly into war. America First drew much of its strength and funds from wealthy conservative Republicans, particularly in the midwest. Increasingly, as most of the liberals and intellectuals went over to the side of the administration, it found itself identified with anti–New Deal reactionaries.

In the presidential election of 1940, Republicans bypassed well-known conservatives and isolationists to nominate Wendell L. Willkie, a wealthy liberal businessman, for the presidency. Willkie approved of aid short of war to the Allies and at first muted foreign policy issues in the campaign against Roosevelt. In late September, however, fearful that FDR was exploiting the sentiment of most Americans for peace and aid to Britain, Willkie questioned the sincerity of the administration's policy. "If his [FDR's] promise to keep our boys out of foreign wars," Wilkie declared, "is no better than his promise to balance the budget, they're already almost on the transports" for Europe. Apprehensive of the effectiveness of that attack, Roosevelt at Boston assured Americans that, "Your boys are not going to be sent into any foreign wars." Of course, he meant unless in case of attack, as the Democratic platform and his other statements carefully specified, but his unfortunate omission of that qualification at Boston left him open to charges of deliberately deceiving the American public. When the November returns came in, Roosevelt had won a third term in the White House, though by a closer margin than in 1932 and 1936.

4. THE UNDECLARED WAR

Many thoughtful observers realized that defeating the Axis powers would require a much greater national effort, but President Roosevelt postponed grappling with the problem for several months. Apart from his tendency toward improvisation and half measures, FDR naturally feared any new departure during the election. England survived the Luftwaffe's bombing in the Battle of Britain and the feared invasion did not occur, but the island nation faced intensified U-boat warfare and had nearly exhausted its funds for the purchase of war supplies in America. The presidential election out of the way, Roosevelt finally decided that piecemeal aid would not suffice. He had to ask Congress to approve a massive aid program if Britain were to survive, much less triumph over the Axis.

In a fireside chat to the nation, late in December, 1940, FDR declared that the United States must become "the great arsenal of democracy." The United States had to make vast quantities of arms and military aid available to those countries whose defense was vital to American security. To avoid the painful experience of war debts, the President proposed that he receive authorization to transfer or lease defense materials to those nations resisting aggression, for payment in kind "or any other direct or indirect benefit" of value to the United States. Isolationists and noninterventionists attacked lend-lease as unneutral, which it manifestly was, and as likely to provoke war with Germany, also a reasonable assumption. Proponents argued that it represented the best means of insuring both America's peace and its security. While the administration underplayed the dangerous implications of lend-lease, Roosevelt apparently believed sincerely that the measure would enable the country to stay out of the war while insuring the defeat of the aggressors. Most Americans concurred. Lend-lease also contained, in Clause VII, a blueprint for a postwar open-door world designed to break down such barriers to trade as the British imperial preference system. Congress passed the bill by a vote of 260 to 161 in the House and 60 to 31 in the Senate. On March 11, 1941, Roosevelt signed the Lend-Lease Act into law.

Lend-lease marked a major turning point in America's involvement in the war. Hitler could have used it as a justification for a declaration of war. He chose to turn the other cheek, however, in order not to increase Germany's enemies at that time. Passage and support of lend-lease indicated the decline of the isolationist appeal. Americans still wanted to stay out of the war, but they were beginning to desire even more the defeat of Hitler. Congress appropriated $7 billion to inaugurate lend-lease. Ultimately the country expended around $50 billion under the act.

During this period, American relations with the Soviets became progressively less than harmonious. One Soviet act after another indicating Joseph Stalin's fitness to become a partner in a league of totalitarian dictators brought relations almost to the breaking point. The cynical Nazi-Soviet pact in August, 1939 even shocked American Communists and sympathizers, many of whom fell away from the faith. Soviet partition of Poland with Germany deepened American disgust and hostility. Then came the Soviet attack upon little Finland, in the winter of 1939–1940, and the seizure of the Baltic states, Latvia, Lithuania, and Estonia, in the spring and summer of 1940. The United States could do little except express its sympathy with the victims. The nadir was reached when Russia concluded a five-year neutrality pact with Japan in April, 1941, freeing the Japanese militarists for new armed ventures. The administration then froze Soviet assets in the United States and virtually halted Russian purchases of tools and machinery. Yet Roosevelt, sharing a view similar to Churchill's, refused to invoke the neutrality laws or to be pushed to a diplomatic break, hopeful that ultimately the Nazi-Soviet marriage of convenience would end in divorce.

Hitler's sudden attack upon the Soviet Union, on June 22, 1941, revolutionized the war. Churchill urged the United States to extend aid to Russia, in the belief that her addition to the anti-Hitler coalition assured an ultimate Axis defeat. Left to itself, the State Department would merely have removed restrictions on trade with the Soviet Union. Roosevelt, however, agreed with Churchill that Russia's entry into the war at least promised a breathing spell for Britain, and if Russia survived, its enormous territory and population would contribute greatly to Axis defeat. FDR had never taken ideology very seriously, and apparently he expected time to humanize and democratize to some degree the communist system in Russia. Hence he decided to extend aid to the Soviet Union. As he wrote Pope Pius XII, in defense of that decision, "Russia is governed by a dictatorship, as rigid . . . as is the dictatorship in Germany. I believe, however, that this Russian dictatorship is less dangerous to the safety of other nations than is the German form. . . ." Roosevelt also naively thought that Britain and America could restrain Russia after the defeat of the Axis. Most Americans approved his decision to extend lend-lease to Russia as one more means of promoting American security while remaining at peace.

The United States rapidly drifted into a limited and undeclared war with Germany after the passage of lend-lease. Roosevelt acted primarily upon his own executive authority in taking these measures, despite the fact that Congress alone possesses the power to declare war. That only underscored a fact long realized by scholars: under the American system, and particularly in the 20th century, the President necessarily makes war by his policies and Congress only declares it post facto, if then. Apparently Roosevelt felt the perils too great to wait upon Congress, especially after the House of Representatives extended the length of service of draftees by only a one-vote margin. He still feared the isolationists, and he was aware of popular ambivalence toward the war—desiring to aid the Allies but also to remain at peace. Moreover, although by mid-1941 FDR must have realized that the United States probably would have to enter the war, he could feel that Congress and the people had approved his general course and that it was up to him to fill in the details whatever the consequences. The United States seized Axis shipping in American ports, the navy patrolled Atlantic shipping routes, and American troops occupied Greenland in April, 1941 and Iceland in July, to prevent an Axis seizure. As the isolationists had feared, Roosevelt ordered the American navy to convoy American and Icelandic shipping, loaded with lend-lease goods, through submarine-infested zones as far as Iceland. In August, Roosevelt met Churchill off Newfoundland to plan further measures in the war, and in the Atlantic Charter the two issued a Wilsonian-type declaration of war goals.

Patrolling and convoying inevitably led to clashes with German submarines. In September, a U-boat attacked the destroyer *Greer* while en route to Iceland. Less than candidly, Roosevelt publicly branded the attack as unprovoked and issued orders to the navy to shoot on sight at those "rattlesnakes of the sea." Germany, he declared, sought to control the Atlantic as a prelude to an attack upon the Western Hemisphere, so he added British shipping to American-escorted convoys. Only later did it come out that the *Greer* actually had been cooperating with a British patrol plane attacking the U-boat when the latter fired at the American destroyer. In October, the Germans attacked the destroyer *Kearney* and sank the *Reuben James,* both of which were engaged in convoying. These incidents outraged the public, and Congress in November revised the Neutrality Act to permit the arming of American merchantmen and their sailing into the war zones. Polls revealed that a majority of Americans still desired peace, but that they wanted Hitler defeated even at the price of active involvement in the war.

An undeclared limited naval war existed between the United States and Germany by the fall of 1941. Hitler still refrained from a declaration of war. Yet the President correctly believed that the Nazi dictator had designs upon the Western Hemisphere. Postwar study of captured Nazi documents revealed that while the Fuehrer had not developed a plan for the conquest of this hemisphere, he viewed it with interest and had

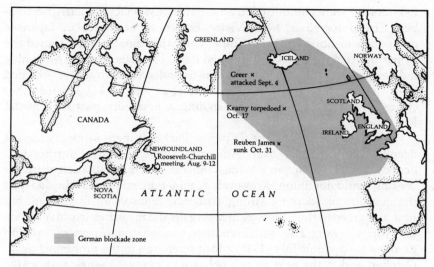

GREENLAND

ICELAND

NORWAY

Greer ×
attacked Sept. 4

Kearny torpedoed ×
Oct. 17

SCOTLAND

CANADA

IRELAND   ENGLAND

Reuben James ×
sunk Oct. 31

NEWFOUNDLAND
Roosevelt-Churchill
meeting, Aug. 9-12

NOVA
SCOTIA   *ATLANTIC   OCEAN*

German blockade zone

The North Atlantic, 1941

spoken privately of colonizing Brazil and Mexico and eventually using the German element in the United States as the dynamic "racial" force to regenerate a "degenerate Yankeedom." Even if such talk is dismissed as the idle daydreams of an egomaniac, Nazi Germany had an extensive network of agents and spies in Latin America, busily engaged in trying to counter the influence of the United States. Quite probably, once free in Europe, Germany would have seriously threatened the United States within the Western Hemisphere. Historically expansionism has proved to have its own dynamics and rarely seems to recognize self-imposed limits.

5. WAR VIA THE PACIFIC

For a brief period Roosevelt's policy of putting Japan on her good behavior, signalled by the abrogation of the commercial treaty in mid-1939, seemed effective. American public opinion strongly favored the embargo of war materials to Japan, but the administration acted cautiously as Japanese leaders began to show signs of restraint. Hitler's dazzling victories in the spring of 1940, however, emboldened the expansionist militarist element within the Japanese government to carve out the "Greater East Asia Co-Prosperity Sphere." A new ministry formed in Tokyo, headed by Prince Konoye, the Prime Minister, and with General Hideki Tojo, the War Minister, and Yosuke Matsuoka, the Foreign Minister, as the dominant influences. Tojo, known as the "Razor" because of his intellectual abilities, and the violently Yankee-phobe Matsuoka, whom Hull described as "crooked as a basket of fishhooks," were committed to an expansionist policy. In early September, Tokyo forced a weak Vichy France to acquiesce in Japanese occupation of northern Indo-China. Later that month Japan signed the Tripartite Alliance with Germany and Italy. The Axis pact was ostensibly a defensive pact, but obviously it was intended to neutralize the United States by the threat of a two-ocean war. In April, 1941 Japan further cleared the decks for action by signing a neutrality pact with Soviet Russia.

Washington dismissed the Tripartite Pact as a mere formality but felt deeply disturbed. Moreover, American public sentiment further hardened against Japan, an obvious consort of the totalitarian dictators seeking world dominion. Roosevelt's cabinet previously had divided over the question of adopting strong economic reprisals against Japan, but now all agreed to the necessity of taking drastic measures in order to stop her without war. The administration banned the export of aviation gasoline to Japan in July, 1940, added scrap iron to the prohibited list in October, and in the next month bolstered Chiang Kai-shek with a $100 million loan and promises of military aid. Roosevelt also stationed the Pacific Fleet permanently at Pearl Harbor. During this period, American intelligence officers managed to decipher the secret Japanese diplomatic code, known as "Magic" intercepts, and Washington learned more clearly than before Japan's diplomatic aims (though not its military plans). FDR and Hull carefully reserved crude petroleum exports as a last desperate weapon, however, aware that Japan derived 80 percent of its oil needs from western-controlled sources and might react violently if they were closed.

Japanese-American relations had reached a deadlock by mid-1940. Neither government wanted war but neither would retreat. The American government believed that reasons of morality and security dictated the support of China and the curbing of Japanese expansionism. Yet it viewed Hitler as the main peril and hoped to avoid war with Japan. FDR and his advisers saw economic coercion as the only alternative to war. Japan's leaders also preferred to avoid hostilities with America, but they refused to abandon their gains in China. They had spent too much blood and money, and committed too much national pride and prestige to back down under Washington's pressure. Moreover, Japanese military leaders, proud, nationalistic, and largely ignorant of the western world, determined to end what they regarded as a dangerous and humiliating economic dependence upon the United States. Neither side, consequently, felt in a position to make any important concessions to the other.

Apparently endless but futile diplomatic exchanges continued. Admiral Kichisaburo Nomura came to Washington as ambassador early in 1941 but he had no more success than his predecessor. Hull wanted Japan to withdraw from the Axis pact, to pull back in China, and to refrain from further adventures. Japan sought a restoration of trade and the cessation of America's moral and material encouragement of Chinese resistance, and refused to give any guarantees about the Tripartite Alliance. Late in July, 1941, after Hitler's invasion of Russia, Japanese troops moved into southern Indo-China, obviously preparing for a military drive to gain control of the oil in the Dutch East Indies and other targets. Roosevelt now saw no alternative but to embargo oil exports to Japan. On July 26, 1941, he froze all Japanese assets in America and trade in effect ceased. The British and Netherlands governments also took similar action.

The oil embargo apparently stunned Japan's masters and in a sense threw them onto the defensive. With only about a year's supply of petroleum on hand, Japan would either have to come to terms with the United States or strike for an independent supply. The military prepared to strike southwards, while Tokyo continued negotiations with Washington for a resumption of trade. American policy, backed overwhelmingly by the public, had become more moralistic and rigid than before; Japan must not only be halted, she must also be forced out of China. FDR, Hull, and other advisers felt certain that a less resolute course would weaken China, impair America's world position, and encourage further Japanese expansion. The American public, particularly its liberal spokesmen, seriously underrated Japanese power and loudly opposed any discussion of relaxing the embargo as an immoral appeasement of an aggressor.

The Japanese militarists decided to fight rather than accept what they regarded as a demand for a humiliating surrender. They reluctantly agreed to allow Prince Konoye to propose a personal conference with President Roosevelt, but only on the condition that war would follow if he failed. Roosevelt found the idea of a "summit" meeting appealing, but his advisers dissuaded him on the grounds that it would damage America's moral posture and that it was foredoomed to failure. Probably they judged correctly. Meanwhile, the Japanese high command prepared to seize the Dutch East Indies and to attack the Anglo-Americans by late November if an agreement had not been reached. The Japanese navy began to practice a raid on Pearl Harbor to tie up the American fleet and gain time for the southward lunge. Its commander, Admiral Isoroku Yamamoto, had no illusions about the meaning of war with America, but he went along with the army generals. Other Japanese officials also recognized that Japan would face great odds in a war against an opponent with a ten to one advantage in industrial power and nearly a two to one margin in manpower. The Japanese military brushed such considerations aside, confident that Japan's national spirit would prevail and hoping that America would fight only halfheartedly before accepting Japan's gains. In any case, they preferred national suicide to what they viewed as an ignoble capitulation to American demands.

Japan made her final diplomatic bids to Washington in November.

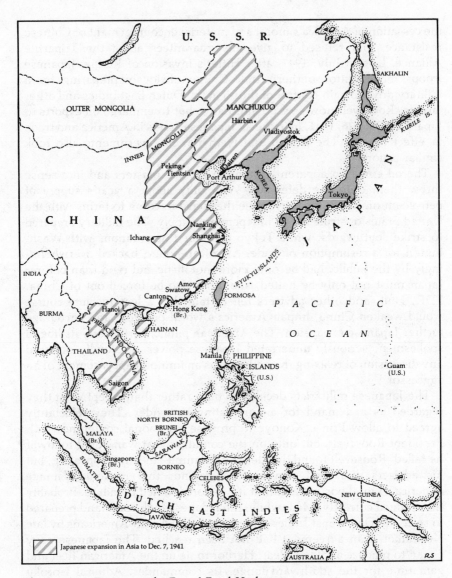

The Japanese Empire on the Eve of Pearl Harbor

Hull rejected the first proposal, Plan A, as completely unsatisfactory. Japan's diplomats submitted the second, Plan B, on November 20. It provided that the United States should lift the embargo and cease to encourage Chiang Kai-shek's resistance to Japanese demands, in exchange for Japan's removal of its troops in south Indo-China and a promise not to launch any new military drives elsewhere. The American authorities also found Plan B unacceptable, since it would have given

Japan a free hand in China. But Hull knew, through the code intercepts, that Plan B was Japan's final offer, and he was aware of American unpreparedness in the Pacific, so he briefly thought of proposing a 90-day truce in the Far East. After discussions with China, Great Britain, and the Netherlands, Hull and the President abandoned the idea. Chiang Kai-shek adamantly opposed what he viewed as an appeasement that would weaken Chinese morale. Consequently Hull and FDR decided to reject Plan B in a note, presented on November 26, fully stating America's demands for a complete Japanese withdrawal from Indo-China and China. Some revisionist historians have called Hull's note an "ultimatum." Not that in any sense, it was merely a formal summary of the American position for the historical record. It did not end negotiations with Japan; her leaders, as Washington knew, had done that earlier when they decided upon Plan B as the final offer.

The American government anxiously awaited Japan's next move, and it did not have to wait long. Washington knew that Japan would strike but it did not know where. All signs pointed to an imminent attack upon the Anglo-Dutch territories in Southeast Asia, but would Japan also strike at American territory? If she bypassed the Philippines, the administration could not tell how Congress and the public would react to a request for a declaration of war. The surprise attack upon Pearl Harbor on the morning of December 7 removed these uncertainties. In a masterfully executed raid, a Japanese task force of aircraft carriers slipped undetected across the Pacific to unleash a devastating aerial attack against the Pacific Fleet in Pearl Harbor and nearby naval and military installations. As the smoke cleared, five battleships, three cruisers, and lesser warships rested on the bottom or showed heavy damage. The Japanese destroyed large numbers of aircraft and killed approximately 3,000 men. Japan lost only 27 aircraft and six submarines. Fortunately, the American aircraft carriers were away from the base when the raid occurred, and carriers became the principal weapons in the Pacific naval war. Even so, Japan had severely crippled American naval power in the Pacific and thereby gained time to overrun her targets in Southeast Asia.

The surprise attack upon Pearl Harbor aroused impassioned debate both then and later. How could the United States have been caught so unprepared? Some revisionist historians have charged a deliberate plot by the administration to provoke Japan into striking and thus to get into the European war via the "back door" of the Pacific. The evidence does not support so monstrous an accusation. FDR and his advisers did not want war with Japan and appreciated our military and naval weaknesses in the Pacific. They viewed Germany, not Japan, as the greatest menace to the United States and its friends. Yet the administration rejected buying peace with Japan at the price of abandoning China. Undoubtedly a sense of moral outrage at Japan's behavior underlay the American position; a more realistic appraisal of American interests in the Pacific and of Japanese power might have dictated an acquiescent attitude. To criticize FDR's policy, however, means arraigning American sentiment and policy since 1898, and especially since 1931. Most Americans in 1941 heartily endorsed a firm stand against Japan and would have condemned any move that suggested appeasement. As for the disaster at Pearl Harbor, the evidence reveals no single culprit to blame; the government and the military simply were unready for war. The administration and its military advisers had expected the main Japanese attack to come in Southeast Asia, as it did. They had dismissed a possible diversionary raid against Pearl Harbor as too risky for even Japan to undertake. Only in retrospect can one conclude that the American government should have suspected more strongly a possible surprise attack at Pearl Harbor than it did. No secret breakings of codes nor zealous intelligence agencies can insure a government against errors of interpretation and expectation.

A brilliant tactical victory for Japan, the Pearl Harbor raid in the long run proved her undoing. Enraged by what they saw as a perfidious "sneak" attack, Americans united into an all-out war effort. Isolationism and the America First movement died in the shock waves of the attack upon Pearl Harbor. Congress on December 8 declared a state of war against Japan, with only one dissenting vote. Three days later, Hitler and Mussolini removed all remaining ambiguities by declaring war against the United States. At last the American nation fully engaged in the Second World War.

Additional Reading

Two excellent studies on isolationism are by Manfred Jonas, *Isolationism in America, 1935–1941* (1966) and Selig Adler, *The Isolationist Impulse* (1957). Also see Adler's *The Uncertain Giant* (1965), an account of American foreign relations from 1921 through 1941. Arnold A. Offner, *American Appeasement: United States Foreign Policy and Germany, 1933–1938* (1969) holds the United States partly responsible for the appeasement of the dictators in the Thirties. Francis L. Loewenheim, "An Illusion That Shaped History: New Light on the History and Historiography of American Peace Efforts before Munich," in Daniel R. Beaver, ed., *Some Pathways in Twentieth-Century History* (1969), 177–220 agrees. On the prologue to the Second World War, see Brice Harris, Jr., *The United States and the Italo-Ethiopian Crisis* (1964); Richard P. Traina, *American Diplomacy and the Spanish Civil War* (1968); F. Jay Taylor, *The United States and the Spanish Civil War* (1956); and Allen Guttman, *The Wound in the Heart: America and the Spanish Civil War* (1962). Two articles of interest are by J. David Valaik, "Catholics, Neutrality, and the Spanish Embargo, 1937–1939," *Journal of American History*, LIV (1967), 73–85, and Robert H. Rosenstone, "The Men of the

Abraham Lincoln Battalion," *Journal of American History,* LIV (1967), 327–338. Different views of Hitler's attitudes toward the United States are examined by H. L. Trefousse, *Germany and American Neutrality, 1939–1941* (1951); James V. Compton, *The Swastika and the Eagle* (1967); Saul Friedlander, *Prelude to Downfall: Hitler and the United States, 1931–1941* (1967); Alton Frye, *Nazi Germany and the American Hemisphere, 1933–1941* (1967); and Gerald L. Weinberg, "Hitler's Image of the United States," *American Historical Review,* LXIX (1964), 1006–1021. For a recent account of the White committee, see William P. Tuttle, Jr., "Aid-to-the-Allies Short-of-War versus American Intervention, 1940: A Reappraisal of William Allen White's Leadership," *Journal of American History,* LVI (1970), 840–858. On lend-lease to Russia, consult R. H. Dawson, *The Decision to Aid Russia, 1941* (1959); Robert H. Jones, *The Roads to Russia: United States Lend-Lease to the Soviet Union* (1969); and W. F. Kimball, *The Most Unsordid Act* (1969). Arthur D. Morse's *While Six Million Died* (1967) is a trenchant criticism of American inaction during Nazi persecution of the Jews. Neutrality legislation is covered by Robert A. Divine, *The Illusion of Neutrality* (1962) and *The Reluctant Belligerent: American Entry into World War II* (1965); and Donald Drummond, *The Passing of American Neutrality, 1937–1941* (1955). Also see Divine's *Roosevelt and World War II* (1969), a collection of interpretive essays on the major New Deal foreign policies. John E. Wiltz, *In Search of Peace: The Senate Munitions Inquiry* (1963) concludes that the Nye hearings had no direct influence upon the 1935 neutrality legislation. On agrarian isolationism, see Wayne S. Cole, "Senator Key Pittman and American Neutrality Policies, 1933–1940," *Mississippi Valley Historical Review,* XLVI (1960), 644–662 and *Senator Gerald P. Nye, and American Foreign Relations* (1962); and F. I. Israel, *Nevada's Key Pittman* (1963).

For the "revisionist" or nonintervention critique of Roosevelt's foreign policy, see Harry Elmer Barnes, ed., *Perpetual War for Perpetual Peace* (1953); Charles A. Beard, *American Foreign Policy in the Making, 1932–1940* (1946) and *President Roosevelt and the Coming of the War, 1941* (1948); and Charles C. Tansill, *Backdoor to War* (1952), a well-documented but biased account. For the New Left, see the essay by Robert Freeman Smith, "American Foreign Policy, 1920–1942," in B. J. Bernstein, ed., *Towards a New Past* (1968), 232–262. The "interventionist" school is represented by Basil Rauch, *Roosevelt from Munich to Pearl Harbor* (1950), and William L. Langer and S. Everett Gleason, *The Challenge to Isolation, 1937–1940* (1952) and *The Undeclared War, 1940–1941* (1953). An excellent guide to the literature on American involvement is by Wayne S. Cole, "American Entry into World War II: A Historiographical Appraisal," *Mississippi Valley Historical Review,* XLIII (1957), 595–617. For Hull's role, see Julius W. Pratt, *Cordell Hull* in S. F. Bemis and R. H. Ferrell, eds., *The American Secretaries of State and Their*

Diplomacy, Vols. XII and XIII (1964). Also see John M. Blum, *From the Morgenthau Diaries* (2 vols., 1959, 1965); Robert Dallek, *Democrat and Diplomat: The Life of William E. Dodd* (1968); and W. H. Heinrichs, Jr., *American Ambassador: Joseph C. Grew and the Development of the United States Diplomatic Tradition* (1966).

An excellent and balanced account of Japanese-American relations is by Herbert Feis, *The Road to Pearl Harbor* (1950). Paul W. Schroeder, *The Axis Alliance and Japanese-American Relations, 1941* (1958) emphasizes that Hull exaggerated the danger from the Axis pact. See also S. E. Morison's *The Rising Sun in the Pacific* (1948). A critical study of *Secretary Stimson* (1954) is by Richard N. Current; more detailed and balanced is the account by E. E. Morison, *Turmoil and Tradition: A Study of the Life and Times of Henry L. Stimson* (1960). R. J. C. Butow has written two excellent studies on Japanese-American relations: "The Hull-Nomura Conversations: A Fundamental Misconception," *American Historical Review,* LXV (1960), 822–836; and *Tojo and the Coming of the War* (1961). See, too, John H. Boyle, "The Drought-Walsh Mission to Japan," *Pacific Historical Review,* XXXIV (1965), 141–161. Manny T. Koginos, *The Panay Incident: Prelude to War* (1967) examines American public reaction to that affair; see also Frederick C. Adams, "The Road to Pearl Harbor: A Reexamination of American Far Eastern Policy, July 1937–December 1938," *Journal of American History,* LVIII (1971), 73–92. The best analysis of the Pearl Harbor attack is Roberta Wohlstetter's detailed *Pearl Harbor, Warning and Decision* (1962).

The Big Three at Yalta—Churchill, Roosevelt, and Stalin

22

THE GRAND ALLIANCE,
1941–1945

1. THE CHALLENGE OF COALITION WARFARE

During the Second World War, America basically aimed to establish unity and cooperation between Great Britain, the Soviet Union, and the United States in order both to win the war and the peace. President Roosevelt and his chief advisers never lost sight of those larger goals. While the public and many historians have viewed FDR as essentially a Wilsonian internationalist, he was far more realistic and readier to make practical compromises than his great predecessor in World War I.

As Winston Churchill once remarked, the only thing worse than fighting a war with allies is to fight it without them. Although the course of Anglo-American relations usually ran smoothly, some frictions developed about military strategy. Moreover, while Churchill established a very warm personal relationship with President Roosevelt, he could not help feeling troubled by the increasingly obvious fact that he represented a declining great power while FDR spoke for a nation of growing wealth and energies. Sometimes it seemed to Churchill and his advisers that the Americans with their anticolonial bias and their dislike of the semiclosed imperial trading system looked upon the British more suspiciously than they did the Russians. Yet Churchill and Roosevelt essentially agreed upon the broad goals of the war. Soon after Pearl Harbor, the Prime Minister hurried to Washington and the President reassured him that the United States still viewed powerful Germany as the main enemy. The two leaders agreed that Japan would follow in short order after the defeat of Germany. They created an Anglo-American Combined Chiefs of Staff and other coordinating bodies in Washington to cope with global problems of strategy, supplies, and production. The Declaration of the United Nations, signed on January 1, 1942 by representatives of 26 nations, pledged to observe the principles embodied in the Atlantic

Charter and to wage a joint war–joint peace against the enemy. In effect the United States allied itself to the other countries fighting the Axis.

Soviet relations with the two great English-speaking powers developed into a much more difficult problem. Stalin's Russia harbored too many resentments and suspicions from the past, buttressed by Communist ideology, to enter easily into harmonious relations with the western democracies. Roosevelt hoped that a policy of conciliation would create the basis for an enduring collaboration. Some writers have charged Roosevelt with naively trying to charm Stalin into amiability and have accused the President of being blind to the dangers of Soviet expansionism. According to one disillusioned adviser, William C. Bullitt, FDR told him in 1943 that he believed the Soviet dictator would not try to dominate postwar Europe: "I think if I give him everything I possibly can [aid] and ask for nothing in return . . . he won't try to annex anything and will work with me for a world of democracy and peace." In Roosevelt's view, which Churchill shared, they could not afford to spare any effort in establishing a Grand Alliance not only to achieve victory but to promote a more stable and harmonious postwar world order. Undoubtedly Roosevelt, like Charles de Gaulle and Churchill, took ideology very lightly and regarded Russia essentially as pursuing traditional national goals. Moreover, it seemed to the American President that Wilson's rigidly anti-Communist attitude in World War I had achieved little except mutual animosity and suspicions. Since Soviet Russia would inevitably emerge from the war with large gains, unless the Allies were prepared to do the unthinkable and deal with the Nazis, a flexible cooperative course offered the only hope for a more promising future.

In grim 1942, an overwhelming majority of Americans agreed with the President that the Grand Alliance had to welcome the Soviet Union as a partner. Former President Hoover and some other prominent persons continued to look upon Russia with marked distaste and suspicion, but most people readily perceived the need for Russia as an ally. Moreover, the Russian bear seemed to be changing for the better as the Soviet government signed the Declaration of the United Nations, spoke of the need to liberate Europe, concluded an alliance with Britain, and in 1943 dissolved the Comintern, that dread instrument of world revolution. A poll revealed that 30 percent of the American public thought Russia was improving, while 46 percent viewed Russia's government as merely reflecting Russian history and conditions. A speaker assured the Daughters of the American Revolution in 1942 that Stalin was an educated gentleman who knew how to admit his mistakes and that communism in Russia was practically nonexistent! Popular journals such as *Time, Life,* and *Collier's* presented Russia in a far more favorable light than prior to Pearl Harbor. In short, most Americans were in a mood to overlook past difficulties and to hope for an enduring cooperation with Russia.

2. THE SECOND FRONT DILEMMA

With Nazi legions at its throat, Russia desperately sought relief through a second front in western Europe. Moreover, no doubt recalling his own Machiavellian past, Stalin harbored suspicions that Britain and America might make a sudden deal with Hitler or at least welcome the spectacle of Germany and Russia bleeding each other to death. Roosevelt, aware of Soviet anxiety and eager to bolster Russian resistance, told Foreign Minister Vyacheslav Molotov in Washington in May, 1942, that he hoped to launch a second front in Europe that year. The President's well-intentioned gesture proved a serious error, for the Russians wrongly interpreted it as definite promise for a second front in 1942. The subsequent inability of the United States and Great Britain to strike across the channel in 1942 and in 1943 deeply disappointed the Soviets and heightened their suspicions of the western Allies. The issue of a second front began to sow the seeds of the later Cold War.

FDR's "promise" to Molotov foundered on the harsh realities of 1942. As Churchill pointed out, the western Allies were woefully unprepared to challenge Hitler's vaunted west wall in Europe. Although this displeased American military planners, Roosevelt went along with Churchill's recommendations for peripheral operations to wear down the Nazis before invading their heartland. It fell to Churchill's painful lot to journey to Moscow in late 1942 to explain to a bitterly disappointed Stalin that no invasion of western Europe would take place in the near future. As he described his mission to this "sullen, sinister Bolshevik State," it was like "carrying a large lump of ice to the North Pole."

The North African invasion in November, 1942—"Torch"—was designed to throw Mussolini and Hitler on the defensive in the Mediterranean and, hopefully, to relieve some of the pressure on the Russian front. Politically it would strengthen western influence in the area after the war, a consideration always in the forefront of Churchill's thought. Since the Vichy French regime, which collaborated with the Nazi conquerors, controlled North Africa, the Allies opportunistically struck an arrangement with Vichy's number two man, Admiral Jean François Darlan, who was in Africa when the invasion started. American and British liberals denounced this deal with a Vichyite "fascist," but it undoubtedly saved many Allied and French lives and facilitated the success of the invasion. Darlan's subsequent assassination removed that embarrassment.

Charles de Gaulle's Free French movement further complicated the North African situation. De Gaulle, then a virtually unknown French general, had fled to Britain as France collapsed in 1940. With British support, he had organized a resistance movement—the French National Committee—recognized by Britain but not by the United States. Roosevelt and Hull found the prickly general a pretentious and difficult

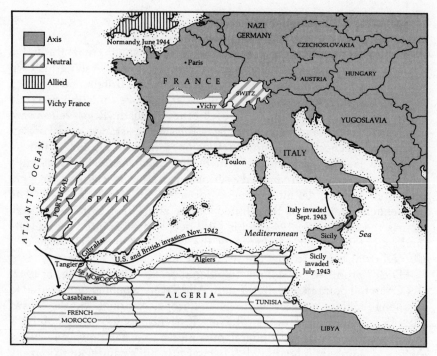

North African and Italian Campaigns

protagonist. Moreover, they questioned the extent to which he genuinely represented the French people and had no desire to impose him upon that nation after its eventual liberation. For his part, de Gaulle suspected the Americans, and the British too, of trying to deny the restoration of France to its rightful position as a great power. In any case, by mid-1944 de Gaulle held such a commanding position that even Washington found it necessary to recognize his committee as the provisional government of France.

3. UNCONDITIONAL SURRENDER

As the North African campaign neared an end, Roosevelt journeyed to Casablanca to confer with Churchill on January 14, 1943. Stalin had declined to attend, pleading the urgency of the military situation in Russia, but no doubt still piqued over the failure to establish a second front in Europe. Roosevelt and Churchill again disappointed him as they agreed that the Allies were still not ready for a cross-channel invasion. They decided instead to follow up the North African operation by invading Sicily. Roosevelt in May, 1943 agreed to an invasion of Italy after Sicily fell, postponing the date of the cross-channel operation to

May, 1944. Stalin sharply warned that Soviet confidence in its allies was being "subjected to severe stress," and word got out that Moscow had made a peace feeler to the Nazis. Stalin probably had intended the overture merely for its effects upon the western Allies; in any event, Hitler spurned it.

Roosevelt announced the formula of "unconditional surrender" during a press conference at Casablanca and Churchill heartily concurred; the enemy must lay down his arms without any conditions when defeat finally arrived. Although FDR gave the impression that unconditional surrender occurred to him on the spur of the moment, he and the State Department actually had given it much thought beforehand. It offered a means of reassuring Russia that the Allies would press the war to a final conclusion, despite the delay in a second front, and it tended to postpone potentially disruptive boundary questions and related issues until after the enemy had laid down his arms. Moreover, unconditional surrender reflected the mood of the British and American peoples and Russia's as well. General opinion held that the great mistake of World War I lay in not having physically occupied Germany and thereby compelling the German people to realize the full implications of their defeat. Any dealing with the Nazi or Japanese regimes short of full surrender seemed immoral and almost inconceivable in the climate of 1943. Polls in America revealed that 65 percent of the people opposed negotiations with the German military leaders in case they overthrew Hitler. Although some historians have charged that unconditional surrender weakened potential resistance to Hitler within Germany and thereby helped prolong the war, no substantial evidence supports that view. Nazi propaganda distorted unconditional surrender to mean the enslavement of enemy peoples, despite repeated Allied clarifications that it meant military disarmament only. The nature of a modern police state such as that of the Nazis makes a popular uprising almost impossible. As for the German military, even after defeat in the war became obvious, its leaders bungled an attempt upon Hitler's life in mid-1944.

The tide of war slowly began to turn in favor of the Grand Alliance in 1943. The Allies invaded Sicily on July 10, and on July 25 Mussolini fell from power and was placed under arrest. On September 3, as Allied armies landed in southern Italy, the new government under Marshal Pietro Badoglio signed an armistice. Fighting continued, however, as Hitler ordered German troops to hold this southern bastion of Fortress Europa, and rescued Mussolini to head a puppet Italian republic. Because of tenacious German resistance and Anglo-American concentration upon the planned invasion of France, the Allied armies advanced slowly up the Italian peninsula. Meanwhile the British and American governments permitted the Badoglio regime to declare war upon Germany and thus become a cobelligerent on the Allied side. Churchill took a particularly active role in preserving a conservative monarchical government in Italy as a bulwark against radicals and Communists, while Roosevelt reluctantly acquiesced. The Allies did not really consult Soviet Russia on the Italian surrender, despite its token role in an advisory council and control commission for Italy. Clearly the power that occupied an area would control it. This situation exemplified the western unilateralism within its military "sphere" that Stalin would not forget when Russia's turn came in eastern Europe.

A Conference of Foreign Ministers at Moscow in October, 1943 greatly facilitated Soviet-Western collaboration. Cordell Hull, 72 years of age and in declining health, joined the dapper English Foreign Secretary, Anthony Eden, in three-power talks in the Kremlin with the morose Molotov, while a genial "Uncle Joe" Stalin observed from the background. An ardent Wilsonian, Hull hoped to avoid a disruptive debate over the details of a postwar settlement by obtaining Big Three consent to a new international peace organization. The Secretary of State assured the Russians that plans for the cross-channel invasion had advanced considerably, and an elated Stalin orally promised that after Germany's defeat the Soviet Union would throw its armed weight against Japan. The three foreign ministers agreed to establish a European Advisory Commission to discuss problems relating to the Axis defeat, promised Italy a nonfascist government, and assured Austria of the restoration of its independence. The Four Power Declaration, most important of all the agreements in the American view, provided for a new global security organization, the future United Nations. The conference ended on a note of cordiality. At a farewell dinner in the Kremlin, Stalin was in a jocular and congenial mood, impressing Hull with his sincere desire for cooperation with the West. The idealistic Secretary returned overjoyed to inform a joint session of Congress of the progress made in Moscow and his hopes that the projected United Nations would guarantee future world security without the alliances and spheres of influence of the unhappy past.

4. TEHRAN AND YALTA

The Moscow conference cleared the way for the meeting that Roosevelt had eagerly sought with Stalin. It was to take place at Tehran. Enroute to the Iranian capital in November, Roosevelt and Churchill discussed military plans with Chiang Kai-shek at Cairo and warned Japan that it would be stripped of its conquests. A few days later the Big Three chieftains gathered in Tehran. An atmosphere of cordiality and even exhilaration quickly appeared, and Roosevelt at last had an opportunity to apply his famous charm to the pipe-smoking Soviet dictator. Stalin smiled at the witticisms between FDR and Churchill, and the Grand Alliance seemed firmly rooted in the personal rapport between the three leaders. Stalin promised to coordinate Russian military plans with the

Allied cross-channel invasion, and he repeated his pledge to enter the war against Japan after the defeat of Germany.

Stalin began to sketch his postwar demands at Tehran. Roosevelt listened sympathetically as the Soviet dictator spoke of an ice-free port for Russia in Manchuria and the possibility of acquiring the Kurile Islands and the southern half of Sakhalin. Both Roosevelt and Churchill indicated agreement that Russia should obtain that part of prewar Poland east of the Curzon Line, with Poland receiving compensation in German territory up to the Oder River. Although they made no firm decision on the question of dismembering Germany into several states after the war, the three leaders agreed that the three powers would occupy the Reich with an inter-allied zone in Berlin. Tehran clearly foreshadowed the Yalta decisions. Roosevelt, in good health in contrast to Yalta, and Churchill indicated a willingness to make concessions to Russia that the Crimean conference merely formalized later. On the whole, the progress made at Tehran pleased the President, and Stalin impressed him as a realist with whom cooperation was possible. As he reported to the American people upon his return, "We are going to get along very well with him [Stalin] and the Russian people—very well indeed."

Roosevelt's own thoughts for the postwar world ran along realistic lines. He knew of the weaknesses of the League of Nations and believed that only the great powers could insure peace in the postwar era. In his view, the "Four Policemen"—the United States, Great Britain, Russia, and China—should assume the responsibility of preventing aggression after subduing the Axis. The movement to found a new league based upon the concepts of the equality of all states and collective security gathered strength, however, especially in Congress, and the President had little choice but to embrace the scheme. He did succeed in incorporating some of his views in it: the five great powers would become permanent members of the Security Council of the United Nations, its principal executive organ, and they would possess a veto over its actions. The U.N. Charter, hammered out at the Dumbarton Oaks Conference in 1944 and at the San Francisco Conference in the spring of 1945, with its General Assembly representing all states, large and small, superficially resembled Wilson's ideas of collective security. But the Security Council in fact embodied Roosevelt's concept of the primacy of the great powers. Russia caused some difficulty by its demands for multiple seats in the General Assembly and an absolute veto power in the Security Council, but these were resolved at Yalta and after. Russia received three seats in the assembly—the United States also if it so chose—and the veto was limited only to substantive issues involving actions and not to mere discussions. The Senate of the United States approved membership in the United Nations on July 28, 1945, by the overwhelming vote of 89 to 2.

In 1944 the momentum of the war in Europe dramatically quickened. Supreme Commander General Dwight D. Eisenhower directed the invasion of Normandy on June 6, 1944. After heavy fighting, his armies broke through the German defenses and speedily liberated most of France. Although the very rapidity of his offensive and the daring German counterattack in the Battle of the Bulge delayed the crossing of the Rhine until March, 1945, the advancing western and Russian armies sealed Germany's doom. Russia meanwhile had rallied at Stalingrad in 1943 and mounted a series of offensives that by early 1945 had evicted the Germans from much of the Balkans, had overrun Poland, and had opened the road to Berlin.

As victory neared, the leaders of the Big Three met at Yalta in the Crimea, February 4–11, 1945, to plan the final military campaigns and to begin to deal with postwar issues. Roosevelt, victor over Republican Thomas E. Dewey in the 1944 election, had just begun his fourth term in the presidency. Although he showed some of the strains of his age and burdens, and he tired more quickly than before, the 62-year-old President seemed as mentally alert as ever. The atmosphere as the three aging chiefs gathered around the conference table was again a cordial one. And again, as at Tehran, FDR exerted his personal charm to the utmost to win Stalin to a lasting cooperation, making sallies at Churchill's expense and almost creating the impression of a Soviet-American entente against British colonialism. Yet despite subsequent criticism of his concessions to Stalin, he based most of them not upon a naive wishfulness but upon a practical recognition of the enormous increases in Soviet power and influence that inevitably resulted from the defeat of the Axis states. Moreover, the main outlines of these concessions had already been settled at Tehran.

Germany obviously presented the most immediate problem at Yalta. The three leaders generally agreed to denazify and demilitarize postwar Germany but not about how to achieve these laudable goals. Should the Reich be left as one state or partitioned? How much should its people pay in reparations for the damages they had caused, and what level of economic life should be set for them in the future? Disagreement existed not only between the Allies but even within the American government. Planners in the State Department and Secretary Stimson in the War Department believed that while Germany deserved rather drastic treatment, the Allies should not reduce its sixty-odd millions of talented and industrialized people to a semi-starvation level. They felt Germany should have a sufficient economic base to feed itself and to play a constructive role in the revival of the European economy. The Secretary of the Treasury, Henry Morgenthau, Jr., however, regarded the State and War Departments as soft. He believed that the only wise and safe course was to partition Germany and reduce her as close as possible to a pastoral agricultural economy, depriving her of the industrial sinews of war and hopefully transforming her allegedly warlike national psychology into a peaceful one through a life lived near the soil.

Roosevelt's own thoughts about Germany at first ran along similar lines to Morgenthau's. As he remarked in 1944, "We have got to be tough with Germany and I mean the German people and not just the Nazis." Their living standard should be kept low after the war, he thought, and their people might have to line up before army soup kitchens thrice daily. Such an approach had the difficulty, as the State Department realized, that it would impede Europe's postwar recovery and might well sow the seeds of another war. Thus, although the Treasury Secretary temporarily won Roosevelt's and Churchill's assent at Quebec in September, 1944, to his "Morgenthau Plan" for a deindustrialized and dismembered Germany, Hull and Stimson persuaded the President to back away from it. Churchill's cabinet colleagues also dissuaded him. Consequently while Roosevelt at Yalta still spoke of Germany in Morgenthau-like terms, his actual course kept open the possibility of a more rational treatment.

Stalin favored a drastic policy toward Germany. He particularly wanted heavy reparations in capital equipment, goods, and labor, to rebuild his devastated country, and he referred to a total of $20 billion as reasonable, with one-half going to Russia. While FDR and Churchill agreed to the payment of reasonable reparations, they doubted the feasibility of such a vast sum, and they resolved not to reduce Germany to such a level that the western Allies would have to feed it. The Big Three finally decided to leave the amount to a reparations commission, with $20 billion as a discussion point and with the payments to consist of capital goods, annual production, and forced labor. They also left the question of Germany's dismemberment to the future. Meanwhile they agreed to divide it into occupation zones with Berlin jointly occupied, and a joint control commission to set policies for Germany as a whole. At British wishes primarily, France received an occupation zone carved from the British and American zones. Churchill, unsure of future American involvement on the continent, thus sought French help in curbing Germany and in watching closely the Soviet Union. To the West's subsequent great regret, the conference did not formalize the access routes between the main zones of the western powers and their zones in Berlin, but left this to future determination. If that proved a grievous error, it should be remembered that Russia too has regretted giving the western powers a share in the occupation of Berlin, deep within her eastern zone. Clearly neither the West nor the Soviets then foresaw the struggle over Germany that followed the end of the war. Neither side gained a victory at Yalta. It merely reflected the prevailing realities of military power, and, from the western point of view, it left open the possibility of a reasonable settlement of the German problem.

The three leaders spent a disproportionate amount of time at Yalta in debate about the future of Poland. Its significance lay not so much in its intrinsic importance but as a symbol or test of Big Three unity and Soviet intentions. Great Britain had gone to war in 1939 over Hitler's threat to Poland, while many Americans recalled Wilson's role in the creation of that state during World War I and millions of Polish-Americans had an intense interest in its fate. Unfortunately for the West, geography and military realities meant that only the advancing Soviet armies could free Poland of Nazi control. A Polish government in exile existed in London, and Russia had recognized it after Hitler's attack upon the Soviet Union. Stalin insisted, however, that the portion of prewar Poland east of the Curzon Line, drawn by the Paris Peace Conference in 1920 to separate ethnic Poland from areas inhabited by other nationalities, go to the Soviet Union. Poland had obtained the area originally by military force from a weak Soviet government in 1921. Churchill and FDR felt inclined toward admitting the justice of Stalin's demand. They urged the suspicious, nationalistic Polish government in vain to recognize the realities of Soviet power and the imperative necessity of quickly striking an agreement with Moscow. Their warnings proved realistic when Moscow broke relations with the exile government in 1943 and subsequently installed in Warsaw a Communist-dominated Polish group, originally known as the Lublin Committee, as the provisional government of Poland.

Churchill bore the main burden of defending Poland's interests at Yalta. Roosevelt gave him support, however, as both principle and the Polish-American voting block seemed to require. Since the Anglo-American leaders at Tehran had indicated their acceptance of a revised boundary along the Curzon Line, at Yalta they conceded that point and only asked for some variations in Poland's favor. Stalin resisted any adjustments. All agreed that Poland should receive compensation with German territory, but Churchill questioned the wisdom of Soviet proposals to extend the boundary to the Western Neisse River, fearing that Poland could not digest so huge and populous an area. Consequently no definite boundaries were fixed at Yalta, as the question was held open for future decision. Roosevelt and Churchill made a determined effort to assure Poland of a genuinely free and democratic government, although they appreciated Russia's understandable desire for "friendly governments" along its borders. What they did not perceive, or at least not clearly, was that in Moscow's vocabulary "friendly governments" meant Soviet-controlled ones. They urged the creation of a new and broadly based provisional Polish government, and the holding of supervised free elections as soon as possible. Stalin adamantly rejected a supervised election and refused to discard the Lublin regime. Churchill and Roosevelt therefore decided to accept a compromise rather than deadlock the conference. The compromise included reorganization of the Lublin government on a wider democratic basis, and the holding of free elections as soon as possible. A face-saving Declaration on Liberated Europe also called for Big Three cooperation in the establishment of

The New Poland, 1945

democratic governments and free elections in the Balkan countries freed from Nazi rule.

The Polish terms at Yalta have met severe criticism. Some critics have charged that the West deliberately sacrificed Poland as a pawn for Soviet cooperation, others that the terms revealed the naiveté of the Anglo-American negotiators. There can be no question that the Yalta terms on Poland were ambiguous, as Roosevelt himself acknowledged. Yet it seemed to him and to Churchill as the best obtainable, and the terms, if observed, seemed to promise a viable and free Poland. No agreement at all, they felt, would leave Russia free to do as it chose. The painful fact of 1945 was that the western powers could do little directly to help Poland. The military map favored Russia and any attempt to coerce her would have endangered collaboration in the war and hopes for postwar harmony. Yalta at least offered the hope of a reasonable settlement in Poland. Finally, it should be noted that if Yalta left the way open for Soviet dominance of eastern Europe, the outcome of the war gave the western Allies a far more valuable "sphere" in the industrially advanced countries of western and northern Europe.

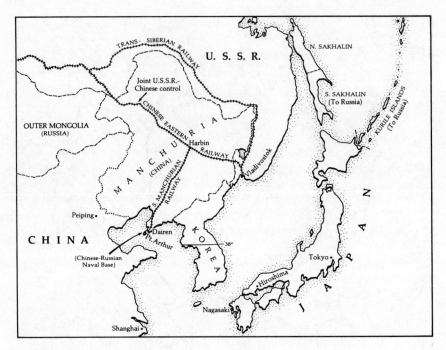

Yalta: the Far East

Stalin at Yalta renewed his pledge to enter the war against Japan,
within two to three months after the defeat of Germany. He asked and
obtained in return recognition of Soviet ambitions in the Far East. Russia
would acquire possession of the Kuriles and southern Sakhalin, a naval
base at Port Arthur in Manchuria, an internationalized port at Darien,
joint ownership and management with China of the Manchurian rail-
ways, and recognition of Outer Mongolia as a Soviet-controlled area.
Roosevelt conducted these negotiations with Stalin, although Churchill
at Tehran had agreed upon the main outline and at Yalta he subsequently
approved the results. FDR, without consulting China, promised to obtain
Chiang Kai-shek's acceptance of these terms. Meanwhile, because
Russia needed time to prepare for violating her pact with Japan, and
because Chiang's capital, Chungking, had become a sieve of information
to the Japanese, they decided to keep the terms secret even from China.

Roosevelt based these concessions in the Far East on essentially
realistic motives. Not only did he view Stalin's requests as merely asking
for what Japan earlier had seized from Russia, which was largely correct,
but he was told by his military advisers that while Russia's entry into the
Far Eastern war was not essential for victory it was highly desirable.
Russia's participation would further weaken Japanese resistance and pin
down her troops in Manchuria and North China. Russia's cooperation

also seemed necessary to strengthen Nationalist China and prevent any attempt at a seizure of Manchuria. Stalin had indicated that he would support only the Nationalist regime, and not the rival Chinese Communists who threatened Chiang's control. Finally, and in answer to later critics, it was clear that Russia would enter the war when her interests made it desirable. The question, therefore, was not if Russia should enter the war but when and under what circumstances. Certainly Yalta gave the Russians nothing that they could not have and probably would not have taken anyhow, except possibly the Kuriles. Yalta in that sense was an attempt to ensure that Russia came into the war at a time most advantageous to the Americans, and to limit her subsequent expansion.

These were the main terms, public and secret, reached at Yalta. On the whole, they reflected the realities of the existing military situation in Europe and Asia. Above all, they testified to Roosevelt's and Churchill's search for a lasting accord with Soviet Russia, both in order to finish the war and to insure the peace and harmony of the postwar world. Perhaps more "realism" on Roosevelt's part would have been desirable, but it probably would not have greatly changed the final results. Roosevelt returned home and reported optimistically to the nation that Big Three cooperation was continuing. Churchill made a similar report to his people, though in less buoyant phrases.

5. POTSDAM AND THE END OF THE WAR

Germany by 1945 reeled under the blows from the advancing western and Soviet armies. Allied bombers rained death and destruction upon Germany's cities, 1,000 airplanes causing 25,000 deaths in Berlin on February 3, followed by 14 hours of continuous bombing of Dresden that blasted out the heart of the city and took an estimated 135,000 lives. Eisenhower's forces crossed the Rhine and Soviet armies opened a great offensive only 35 miles east of Berlin. Churchill and his military advisers wanted to launch a quick thrust to beat the Russians to Berlin. Eisenhower, with Washington's support, overruled the plan on military grounds—Allied armies then were about 200 miles west of Berlin, and he deemed nearby military objectives more imperative. Probably the Supreme Commander was correct, although critics since have charged that Berlin was within the West's reach and that Eisenhower and the administration underrated the psychological gains of entering the enemy capital first. As it turned out, Russia paid over 100,000 casualties for the dubious honor of taking Berlin, while the West obtained its zones there painlessly. Less defensible, perhaps, was the American failure to take Prague, allowing Russia the prestige of liberating all three of the capital cities of Central Europe—Vienna, Berlin, and Prague.

As the Allies overran Germany, Hitler conducted a last-ditch resistance from his bunker beneath war-wracked Berlin. Finally, as Russian shells exploded overhead, the Fuehrer and his bride committed suicide, and loyal adherents cremated their bodies. On May 7, the remnants of Germany surrendered at Rheims, followed by a similar ceremony at Berlin on May 8. The most bloody war in Europe's modern history was over, leaving behind a vast pall of death and destruction in the very heart of western civilization.

Even before Hitler's Wagnerian *Götterdämmerung* in Berlin, a rift had begun to emerge within the Grand Alliance. The approaching end of the war reduced the military reasons for cooperation and allowed old suspicions and ambitions to surface. Russia accused Britain and the United States of duplicity in the Nazi surrender in Italy, and failed to carry out what the West regarded as Soviet pledges at Yalta in regard to Poland and the Balkans. Stalin's suspicious and uncooperative attitude dismayed FDR and Churchill. Yet to the last, Roosevelt strove to preserve the wartime coalition. As he wrote the Soviet dictator, "it would be one of the great tragedies of history if at the very moment of the victory now within our grasp, such distrust, such lack of faith, should prejudice the entire undertaking after the colossal losses of life, material, and treasures involved." His last message to Stalin, prior to the President's sudden death at Warm Springs, Georgia, on April 12, 1945, indicated that despite a growing disillusionment he saw no alternative but to continue efforts at Big Three collaboration.

FDR had woefully neglected to keep his Vice President, Harry S. Truman, informed of his diplomacy and the secret engagements at Yalta. The new President, an ex-haberdasher and a product of Missouri machine politics, had an unpretentious appearance and manner. He seemed greatly in need of the divine support he requested as he succeeded FDR. He was intelligent and hard-working, however, and he responded remarkably well to the challenges of the presidency. Choosing excellent advisers and unafraid to make difficult decisions, Truman ultimately merited high marks, primarily for his statesmanlike record in foreign affairs.

Truman continued Roosevelt's policy of seeking harmonious relations with the Soviet Union. He soon had to recognize that past efforts at conciliation had proved far from successful, however, and that in fact Moscow had seen those gestures more as evidences of softness than of goodwill. Like his predecessor, Truman considered Poland the acid test of relations with Stalin. Yet reports from Eastern Europe revealed that Russia ruthlessly was organizing Poland and the Balkans in her own interests. The Soviets did not reconstitute the Polish government, in accordance with the western views of Yalta, as only a handful of non-Communist Poles received ministerial posts. When Molotov came to Washington, an angry Truman tongue-lashed him in words more suitable to Missouri ward politics than formal diplomacy. Some revisionist writers, therefore, have accused Truman of reversing Roosevelt's acceptance of a Soviet sphere of influence in Eastern Europe. In their view America, not Russia, first violated the spirit of Yalta and initiated the Cold War. Roosevelt and Churchill in a sense had conceded a type of Soviet sphere in Eastern Europe, but they understood thereby only the creation of friendly governments and not the fastening of a harsh Communist control over those countries.

On May 11, after the Nazi surrender, Truman ordered a drastic curtailment in lend-lease aid to Russia. Subordinates interpreted his order more narrowly than he had intended and even recalled ships already enroute with cargoes of aid for Russia. Heretofore, the Soviets received lend-lease without the restrictions imposed upon other recipients. Truman agreed with his advisers that Russia interpreted such generosity as a sign of weakness rather than of friendship, and that future aid should be placed squarely on a quid pro quo basis. Moreover the legal requirements of lend-lease and the mood in Congress seemed to rule out aid to Russia until it should enter the Pacific war. Truman had intended his directive, therefore, not to cut off aid to Russia but to reduce it to the requirements of the Pacific war and to place it upon the same basis as for other countries. This reduction affected Great Britain as well as the Soviet Union. This alleged example of American bad faith and attempted coercion deeply offended Stalin. Revisionist historians now in effect echo the Russian charge that it all formed part of Truman's turn from conciliation to toughness, an attempt to use America's vast economic power to force the Soviet Union to retreat from its newly won sphere in Eastern Europe. The evidence seems to most historians to indicate only an undue abruptness in the cutoff order and a shift to a more realistic policy by the United States.

American policy, in Republican Senator Arthur H. Vandenberg's words, remained one of "give and take" with Russia, but with more emphasis than before upon a genuine equality in that relationship. Under Truman the State Department recovered its primacy in formulating foreign policy, and it began to shape a firm but reasonable occupation program for Germany. Yet Truman declined Churchill's advice to leave western troops deep within the projected Soviet zone of Germany, where they had driven during the final days of the war in Europe. Churchill hoped to use their position as a bargaining device with Stalin, but Truman wanted to avoid unnecessary disputes with the Soviet government and to insure its cooperation against Japan. In May, 1945, Truman sent Harry Hopkins to Moscow to try to smooth over recent difficulties. His talks with Stalin were very frank and seemed to hold out hope of renewed collaboration. The United States resumed lend-lease aid to Russia and Truman prepared for his first conference with Stalin.

The Big Three selected Potsdam, near war-ruined Berlin, for their final wartime meeting. The sessions began on July 17 and ended on August 2. Despite a recent heart attack, Stalin appeared calm and patient, deferential to Truman but rather scornful toward Churchill. The latter was in a gloomy mood, depressed by the signs of Soviet expansionism in Europe and worried about the outcome of a general election in Britain—his party lost and Laborite Clement Attlee replaced Churchill midway through the conference. Still struggling to master his new office, Truman had not felt eager for the summit conference. He assumed a brisk, no-nonsense attitude, obviously anxious to get the conference over with and irritated by Churchill's long remarks for the record, and Soviet maneuverings. Partly for these reasons, but more importantly because the war was nearly over and discussion of disruptive issues could no longer be avoided, the atmosphere at Potsdam was more formal and less cordial than at Yalta.

Potsdam postponed more important issues than it settled. A conference of Foreign Ministers (including France but not China on European matters) had the task of drafting peace treaties for the lesser Axis states before trying to frame one for Germany. Poland again became a bone of contention. Churchill strongly objected to the fact that Russia had already turned over to Poland that section of Germany east of the Oder-Neisse line. He had to accept that fait accompli, however, disguised as a temporary administrative adjustment pending a final peace treaty. The nature of Poland's government continued to disturb the western Allies. The Soviets finally allotted six of 20 ministerial posts to non-Lublin Poles, but that still left the Communists in control and fell far short of the broadly based and reconstructed regime spoken of at Yalta. On the positive side, the Big Three affirmed the occupation zones in Germany and the administration of the country as an economic entity by the Four Power Control Council. Reparations proved a thornier problem. Stalin insisted upon the figure of $20 billion mentioned at Yalta, which the Anglo-Americans viewed as excessive and likely to reduce Germany to chronic semistarvation. A compromise formula papered over the rift: each power would obtain its reparations from within its own occupation zone, provided that they left Germany enough resources with which to function. Because the western zones contained the bulk of Germany's industries, and in view of Russia's enormous sacrifices in the war, the western Allies agreed to give her 15 percent of the capital equipment within their zones in exchange for food and raw materials from the Soviet zone and another 10 percent as a free gift.

Potsdam ended on a note of outward harmony. Truman reported to the American people the continuation of the cooperation established at Tehran and Yalta. But privately he and his advisers viewed the future much less optimistically. Soviet Russia had revealed only too clearly, from his viewpoint, the shape of its postwar ambitions and intentions. Appropriately christened "Terminal," the Potsdam Conference became not only the last of the Big Three wartime conferences, but it marked the ebb of that unity and cooperation sought so eagerly by FDR and apparently achieved at Yalta.

The Far Eastern war drew rapidly to an end after the Nazi collapse freed the United States to concentrate upon Japan. Even before then, American aircraft carrier task forces had smashed through the protective screen of fortified islands surrounding Japan. General Douglas Mac-Arthur's forces leapfrogged northward from Australia, invading Leyte in the Philippines in October, 1944. The capture of Okinawa in the spring of 1945, after a bloody suicidal defense, opened the Japanese home islands to invasion. By mid-1945, Japan was a shambles, subjected to daily bombing by carrier-based airplanes and by huge long-range B-29 bombers operating from the Marianas, her navy and merchant marine largely destroyed, her cities and factories devastated by high explosive and fire-bombing raids, and an estimated eight million people homeless. Although the more moderate elements within the Japanese government recognized that they had lost the war and should seek peace, the military determined to fight on. Japan had within the home islands about a million and a half troops and over 5,000 airplanes useful in kamikaze or suicide attacks against the Americans. Military leaders spoke hopefully of meeting the invader on the beaches and hurling him back into the sea, and thereby snatching victory from the very jaws of defeat. They believed that Japan then could obtain peace and retain much of its empire and certainly escape occupation. Even more moderate Japanese officials hoped for a while to obtain terms much better than unconditional surrender, and in vain they made repeated overtures to persuade Russia to mediate the war.

Washington was aware of the Japanese peace bids, but it judged their terms as unacceptable. In the light of Japan's suicidal defense of its island outposts, American authorities concluded that an early end of the war on the basis of unconditional surrender would require an invasion of the home islands. Truman approved plans to invade Kyushi in late 1945 and Honshu, the main island, early in 1946. A second method, the atomic bomb, promised at least to speed up Japan's collapse. The United States had spent over $2 billion in the highly secret development of this new weapon, whose full potential not even the scientists involved yet foresaw. Finally, some members of the State Department and Stimson in the War Department wanted to ease Japan's surrender by permitting her to retain the imperial system. This ultimately was done, but only after use of the A-bombs. Initially, Truman and other high officials had opposed any special concessions to Japan. At Potsdam, where he learned of the successful test in New Mexico of the atomic bomb, Truman joined Churchill in issuing the Potsdam Declaration warning Japan to surrender her armed forces and assuring her people that Japan would eventually gain readmission to world society. The Japanese government's reply was interpreted as a rejection of this final warning.

The United States dropped the first A-bomb over Hiroshima on August 6. An estimated 80,000 people died in the holocaust unleashed by this terrifying new weapon. Events now moved rapidly toward ending the war. Russia came into the conflict on August 8, and on the following day the second atomic bomb fell on Nagasaki with devastating effects. At a special meeting of the Supreme War Council, Japanese generals attempted to minimize the effectiveness of the new weapon and talked of continuing the war. Emperor Hirohito finally broke the deadlock. He ordered a capitulation on the best terms obtainable from the Allies. On August 14, Japan accepted the Allied terms for surrender, with the proviso that the imperial system would remain. The formal ceremony of surrender took place on September 2 aboard the battleship *Missouri* in Tokyo Bay.

Few people in America at the time questioned the use of the atomic bombs against Japan. Later many conscience-stricken Americans, awed by the new weapon and fearful for the future of mankind, asked if the United States was justified in its course. Some argued that the destruction of Hiroshima and Nagasaki were unnecessary because Japan already was beaten, and some critics claimed to detect a racial bias in the use of a dread new weapon deemed fit for Orientals but not for Europeans. One recent revisionist study by Gar Alperovitz even asserts that America did not use the two A-bombs to defeat Japan, a feat already accomplished, but to strengthen its hand against Russia in order to force her out of her Eastern European sphere of influence. To fairly appraise these charges, one must retain a sense of historical perspective. The United States had developed the atomic weapon in a "race" to beat the Germans and she surely would have used it first in Europe if the war there had lasted long enough. As for Japan, there never was any debate about whether to use the new weapon but only about how to exploit it. A small group of scientists, the Franck group, did protest its use against an unwarned civilian target, but the United States then had in readiness materials for only three bombs, it had no certainty that the triggering device would work, and it had difficulty in discovering how to use the bomb effectively against an uninhabited target. Moreover, wartime passions and the momentum of weapons development virtually insured the use of the A-bomb against a live target. Its side effects were not then known, and in many ways it seemed to represent merely a new advance in weaponry. Fire bomb raids over Tokyo already had killed nearly a quarter of a million people, more than the toll at Hiroshima. Most importantly, the American government saw the atomic bomb as a method of avoiding a costly invasion of the Japanese home islands, an operation that undoubtedly would have multiplied the casualties of Hiroshima and Nagasaki many times over. And in fact its use did have that result, aiding the Emperor and his moderate advisers to overcome the stubborn Japanese military and to seek surrender terms from the Allies. The revisionist charges thus fall wide of the mark, although as a secondary gain American officials no doubt welcomed the new weapons as enhancing their nation's position vis-à-vis the Russians. From our perspective today, at least one advantage in this spectacular if terrible way of terminating the war seems to emerge: the mushroom clouds that rose above the two doomed Japanese cities dramatized to the world, as probably nothing else could have, the new era of possible total annihilation into which mankind was entering.

Additional Reading

Herbert Feis has written three excellent studies that provide the most satisfactory detailed account yet of the diplomacy of the Second World War: *Churchill, Roosevelt, Stalin* (1957); *Between War and Peace: The Potsdam Conference* (1960); and *Japan Subdued: The Atomic Bomb and the End of the War in the Pacific* (1961; revised ed., 1966). Also see William L. Neumann, *After Victory: Churchill, Roosevelt, Stalin and the Making of the Peace* (1967). Willard Range, *Franklin D. Roosevelt's World Order* (1959) and Robert A. Divine, *Roosevelt and World War II* (1969) are generally favorable accounts of FDR's diplomacy. More critical is a recent study by James MacGregor Burns, *Roosevelt: The Soldier of Freedom* (1970). An excellent brief account that criticizes Roosevelt for lack of realism and a certain flightiness is *American Diplomacy During the Second World War* (1965) by Gaddis Smith. More favorable is a short study by John L. Snell, *Illusion and Necessity: The Diplomacy of Global War* (1963). A stimulating brief comparison of the Tehran and Yalta conferences is by William M. Franklin, "Yalta Viewed From Tehran," in Daniel R. Beaver, ed., *Some Pathways in Twentieth-Century History* (1969), 253–261. On the difficulties of coalition warfare, see R. M. Leighton, "Overlord Revisited: An Interpretation of American Strategy in the European War, 1942–1944," *American Historical Review*, LXVIII (1963), 919–937, and Kent R. Greenfield, *American Strategy in World War II* (1963). Charles de Gaulle's *War Memoirs* (1955–60, 3 vols.) and Milton Viorst's *Hostile Allies: F.D.R. and Charles de Gaulle* (1965) are revealing accounts of that difficult relationship. The British point of view is presented by Chester Wilmot, *The Struggle for Europe* (1952), very critical of American policy; Winston Churchill, *The Second World War* (1948–1953, 6 vols.); and Lord Moran, *Churchill* (1966). Arthur D. Morse, *While Six Million Died* (1967) sharply criticizes Washington for ineffective measures to aid the victims of Hitler's policy of genocide. John M. Blum, *From the Morgenthau Diaries: Years of War, 1941–1945* (1967) treats the foreign policy intrusions of the Secretary of the Treasury. On Stimson, see E. E. Morison, *Turmoil and Tradition* (1960). On the influence of the State Department, consult the sketches of Hull, Stettinius, and Byrnes by Donald F. Drummond, Walter Johnson, and Richard D. Burns in N. Graebner, ed., *An Uncertain Tradition: American Secretaries of State in the Twentieth Century* (1961); and Julius W. Pratt,

Cordell Hull, 1933–1944, vols. XII and XIII of *The American Secretaries of State and Their Diplomacy* (1964). For a lengthier account of Stettinius's brief tenure, see Richard L. Walker, *E. R. Stettinius, Jr.,* vol. XIV of *The American Secretaries of State and Their Diplomacy* (1967). On the movement within America for the United Nations consult Robert A. Divine's *Second Chance* (1967). The policy of unconditional surrender is sharply criticized by Anne Armstrong, *Unconditional Surrender* (1961) and by George F. Kennan, *Russia and the West under Lenin and Stalin* (1960). Edward J. Rozek attacks Anglo-American compromises at Poland's expense in his *Allied Wartime Diplomacy: A Pattern in Poland* (1958). The German problem is handled by John L. Snell, *Dilemma Over Germany* (1959) crediting Anglo-American policy at Yalta and elsewhere as realistic and reasonable. For the military decision not to race Russia for Berlin, see Stephen E. Ambrose, *Eisenhower and Berlin, 1945: The Decision to Halt at the Elbe* (1967). An excellent treatment of Japan's surrender, that credits the decisive influence of the A-bomb and Russia's war entry, is by Robert J. C. Butow, *Japan's Decision to Surrender* (1954).

Recent revisionist accounts of World War II diplomacy, many by the so-called New Left, are increasing. Gar Alperovitz, *Atomic Diplomacy: Hiroshima and Potsdam* (1965) argues that the A-bomb was used in the hopes of forcing Russia to abandon its sphere in Eastern Europe. He also sees the abrupt halt in lend-lease to Russia as part of that strategy of coercion. For a contrary view, see the carefully written article by George C. Herring, Jr., "Lend-lease to Russia and the Origins of the Cold War," *Journal of American History,* LVI (1969), 93–114. Thomas G. Paterson, "The Abortive Loan to Russia and the Origins of the Cold War, 1943–1946," *Journal of American History,* LVI (1969), 70–92, attributes much responsibility for the deterioration in Soviet-American relations to Washington's refusal to extend a loan to Russia for postwar rehabilitation. Gabriel Kolko, *The Politics of War: The World and United States Foreign Policy, 1943–1945* (1968) depicts American policy as neither idealistic nor naive; he vastly over simplifies American policy as a sustained and consistent quest for an open-door world congenial to America's economic interests.

Hiroshima

23

THE COLD WAR, 1945–1953

1. ORIGINS OF THE COLD WAR

The breakdown of Big Three cooperation after the war seems to have been virtually inevitable. At the time, millions of Americans and Europeans were cruelly disappointed as their hopes for the postwar world faded. Their dismay turned quickly to anger and fear, as most western observers attributed sole responsibility to Soviet Russia for a new cycle of international rivalries and conflicts that we know as the Cold War.

Neither antagonist deliberately planned nor sought the Cold War, nor was either alone responsible for its eruption. The old world balance of power lay in ruins in 1945, with Germany and Japan prostrate, Italy defeated and powerless, France humiliated in the war and obviously not a first-rate power, and Great Britain so severely weakened by the cumulative effects of two world wars that it no longer could play the role of a great world power. With old checks and restraints removed, "power vacuums" appeared in Europe and Asia. Two great "super-powers" had emerged from the maelstrom of the war—the United States and Soviet Russia—each towering above its allies and client states, and each unavoidably drawn by its own interests and fears into a rivalry and struggle for preeminence.

Soviet Russia sought to organize and to dominate the areas along its periphery. In Eastern and Central Europe this meant a sphere of influence in territories "liberated" by Soviet armies: Poland, Czechoslovakia, Rumania, Hungary, Bulgaria, Yugoslavia (actually freed by Josip Broz Tito's Communist-led partisans), part of Austria, and East Germany. Probably Russia under czarist, Communist, or any other form of government would have pursued rather similar goals after 1945. Czarist Russia prior to 1917 had exercised considerable influence over much of the same area that Stalin coveted in 1945. Ideology no doubt played a part in Soviet expansionism, but security and traditional national goals became even more important.

Scholars now widely agree that Stalin was a realist rather than a fanatical ideologist or communist world revolutionary. Stalin revealed his sense of the realities and the limitations of power in his wartime comment about the Nazi dictator. Hitler "doesn't know where to stop," said Stalin, but "I know where to stop." As a kind of "illegitimate czar," Stalin sought to secure his personal power in Russia and to advance the national interests of his country. Probably at no time, therefore, did Stalin seriously plan a communist take-over of all Europe, much less the whole world. Apparently he viewed foreign communist movements with much scepticism and distrust, fearful that they might escape his control, and he was cynically prepared to use them and to sacrifice their interests for goals of his own. He looked askance upon Tito's Yugoslavia and Mao Tse-tung's communist movement in China. Unfortunately, an expansionist tone characterized the rhetoric and dynamics of communist ideology, and the social and economic disintegration of postwar Europe inevitably drew Russian power westward and spawned strong communist movements in Italy, France, Greece, and other countries.

Stalin apparently was ready to accept the existence of western spheres of influence in return for the acceptance of his own. He probably believed that the negotiations at Tehran and Yalta had arrived at an agreement or understanding about the Soviet sphere in Eastern Europe. President Roosevelt and Prime Minister Churchill had conceded the desirability of "friendly governments" along Russia's borders, but they had not understood thereby complete Soviet dominance and communization of the countries of Eastern and Central Europe. The American people and government ascribed to the ideal of a democratic and economically open postwar world. Most believed that dictatorship and economic nationalism had caused the Second World War. The remedy, they felt, lay in establishing genuinely self-governing and democratic states and in removing artificial barriers to the flow of world commerce. In truth, as New Left historians recently have asserted, an open-door world would have benefited America's economic interests, exorcizing the spectre of another great depression by opening world markets to American investments and trade. But most Americans sincerely thought that an open-door system also would benefit other peoples. Consequently, Soviet Russia's brutal exploitation of its sphere and the forcing of undemocratic communist-dominated governments upon Poland and Rumania came as a shock to Americans and began to shatter their hopes for a harmonious postwar world.

Seen in this light, as Hans Morgenthau has pointed out, two basic causes of the Cold War become evident. First, insecurity and historic interests drove Russia to impose its rule upon the nations and peoples of

Eastern and Central Europe, including harsh police methods, one-party government, and economic exploitation. Conversely, the American people and the democracies of Western Europe understandably reacted to these developments with feelings of moral outrage and policies of opposition. The western reaction now seems unrealistic, since the West could not really challenge Russia except at the risk of a major world war. Moreover, the United States did not have vital economic or security interests at stake in Eastern Europe. Furthermore, the western powers also had spheres of influence of their own, though they acted more benevolently in their spheres than Soviet Russia did in its. But asking the western powers to remain silent about Russia's behavior would have been asking them to abandon their moral convictions. If they had reacted more mildly, might Stalin have adopted a more moderate course? As it was, he responded to western criticism and challenges by taking more ruthless measures to establish complete control over Eastern Europe.

The second cause of the Cold War came from the very real danger that Soviet power and influence might move westward into the heart of Europe. The war had greatly weakened the economic and social fabric of the continent and left Western Europe vulnerable to Soviet penetration and the growth of native communist movements closely tied to Kremlin control. The seeming danger of a general collapse in Western Europe and the consequent expansion of Soviet power alarmed the Americans and the British. This became the principal Soviet threat to the western position, one that fully merited realistic concern. Aided by hindsight, that danger now appears largely economic and political, rather than military. That was not so clear in 1946–47, however, in view of the recent war against expansionist dictators and the vast military machine of Soviet Russia. The expansionist rhetoric of communism and the theoretical ability of Soviet armies to overrun all Europe in a short time tended to overly impress western leaders. They did not give enough weight to such counterbalancing factors as the ravages that Russia had suffered in the war and the restraints imposed on her by the nuclear weapons and vast economic power of the United States.

Soviet leaders, especially Stalin's successors, no doubt have retained to some degree a messianic belief in the inevitability of a communist world. However, they have shown unwillingness to risk a major world war to attain that goal. Unfortunately, communist rhetoric aroused an overreaction in the West, particularly in the United States where an almost hysterical fear of Russia and communism affected the popular mind in the late 1940's and early 1950's. By then Americans saw Soviet communism as "red fascism," another variety of totalitarian ideology and dictatorship that threatened human decency and freedom. As President Truman himself remarked in 1947, "There isn't any difference in totalitarian states. I don't care what you call them, Nazi, Communist, or

Fascist. . . ." Most American liberals and intellectuals came to a similar conclusion about the nature of Soviet communism. Analogy with the prewar dictatorial states seemed to indicate what the West could expect from Stalin's Russia: aggression, demands for appeasement, subversion, conquests, and war. The atmosphere had become so fevered on both sides of the "Iron Curtain" by 1949 and after, that a major world war seemed imminent. Probably only the possession of nuclear weapons by both sides, eventually creating a "balance of terror," has prevented its occurrence.

2. 1946, A YEAR OF TRANSITION

As World War II drew to an end, increasing signs indicated to the West that the Soviet government was abandoning cooperation and turning to a unilateral expansionist course. In September, 1945, the month of the Japanese surrender formally ending the war, the Conference of Foreign Ministers met in London to draft peace treaties for Italy and the lesser Axis states. The conference ended in complete deadlock. Molotov, the Soviet Foreign Minister, rebuffed proposals by the West for reorganization of the governments of Rumania and Bulgaria along more democratic lines. Postwar attempts by the United States to internationalize control of nuclear weapons—the Baruch Plan—failed because the United States insisted upon retention of its advantage in A-bombs until such time as foolproof international controls could be established, while the Soviet Union proposed the immediate outlawry of such weapons. In effect, Russia refused to permit effective inspection on its territory and would not concede a temporary American superiority. Although the Allies eventually hammered out peace treaties for Italy and the lesser Axis countries by 1947, they made no progress on a final settlement for Austria and Germany.

In the months following the conclusion of the Second World War, the Soviet government tried to pressure Turkey into sharing the defense of the Straits, delayed withdrawal of her troops from northern Iran beyond the deadline set earlier, and fastened a harsh communist rule upon Poland and Rumania. Finland remained independent but necessarily subservient to the Soviet Union. Czechoslovakia tried to build a bridge between East and West with a coalition government containing strong communist representation, while Soviet authorities permitted a measure of political freedom in Hungary. In Greece civil war raged between the British-supported conservative monarchy and the Communist-led rebels. Although Stalin apparently sought to discourage the Greek Communists, the communist regimes in Yugoslavia and the other Balkan countries aided them. The western powers did not know of Stalin's views and attributed the Greek civil war to his machinations.

In this climate of growing tensions and suspicions, the American

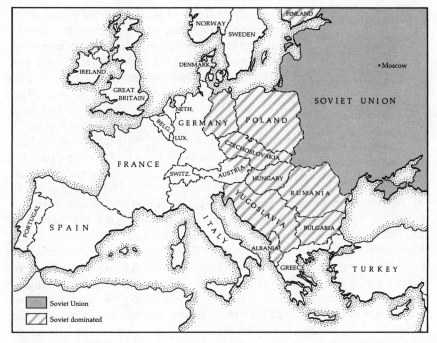

Europe in the Cold War

government loaned Great Britain nearly $4 billion and France $1 billion for recovery measures, but failed to respond similarly to Russian requests. Perhaps a large and unencumbered postwar loan to the Soviet Union, for desperately needed reconstruction of its economy, might have significantly improved Soviet-American relations. On the other hand, Russia might have interpreted such a loan as one more sign of western weakness and gullibility. In any case, it would have been difficult to obtain congressional approval of such a loan without attaching various restrictions, if any kind of loan at all would have been possible in the months after the war.

Germany posed the most immediate problem to western relations with the Soviets. Russia, facing staggering problems of postwar reconstruction, ruthlessly stripped its zone in Germany of industry and even current production. At the same time, the Soviet government tried to insure its control of East Germany, and perhaps ultimately of all Germany, by resurrecting the almost moribund German Communist Party and installing its members in political positions. The American and British governments feared that they might face feeding a starving populace, while Russia drained Germany of resources and blocked agreement upon a common economic policy for all four occupation zones. Attributing Russian behavior to deep-seated fear of a German resurgence, James F. Byrnes, whom Truman had appointed Secretary of State in 1945, suggested a four-power alliance for a term of 25 years to guarantee German demilitarization. Subsequently he offered to extend such a pact to 40 years, but the Soviet Union did not wish to see the United States involved in Europe for so long a time.

The American people felt growing disillusionment in the year 1946. On February 9, Stalin issued what the West widely regarded as a declaration of cold war. He reasserted the validity of Leninist teachings about the virtual inevitability of war between the capitalist and communist systems, and he called for a series of five-year plans to prepare for such an eventuality. His words, perhaps mere rhetoric to justify his iron rule, had a chilling effect upon those westerners who had clung to hopes of postwar cooperation. On March 5, in Fulton, Missouri, Winston Churchill, with President Truman present, warned that from "Stettin in the Baltic to Trieste in the Adriatic, an iron curtain has descended across the continent." East of that line Soviet Russia exercised a brutal rule and cut off ancient countries from their historic ties with Western Europe. Since the Soviets respected strength, Churchill urged an Anglo-American alliance to preserve the free world. Many Americans praised Churchill's speech as a call for timely action, but others still clung to the possibility of collaboration with the Soviets and denounced him as an aged anticommunist and warmonger.

Truman already had decided that he was "tired of babying the Soviets." At Stuttgart in West Germany, Secretary Byrnes on September 6 called for a renewed effort at a common policy for all Germany, and he warned that the United States would not withdraw its forces from Europe until a settlement had been achieved. This shift toward a tougher policy alarmed some New Deal liberals in the United States, who viewed the Truman administration as abandoning FDR's goals at home and abroad. Henry A. Wallace, FDR's Secretary of Agriculture and Vice President who currently headed the Commerce Department, became their chief spokesman. An expert on the problems of agriculture but always something of a naive visionary and mystic, Wallace regarded himself as the true heir of the New Deal. In an address at Madison Square Garden in New York City, on September 12, Wallace challenged Byrnes's approach. Russia naturally sought to organize its sphere of influence in its own interests, he asserted, and therefore it did not present any immediate threat to the West. A policy of toughness would merely call forth more toughness on Russia's part, he added. At Byrnes's urging, Truman fired Wallace from his post. Subsequently Wallace rallied those of similar views and ran as the "Progressive" candidate against Truman in the 1948 presidential election. The great majority of New Deal liberals, however, came to the support of the administration's domestic and foreign policies.

3. CONTAINMENT

The existence of a "cold war" between the western democracies and the Soviet empire became painfully obvious in 1947. Despairing of Soviet cooperation in an economic policy for all Germany, Great Britain and the United States merged their zones into "Bizonia" as the new year began. France held out for a while, but the de facto partition of the former Third Reich into a West and an East Germany was taking place, and by 1949 rival governments were installed in each half. But the Truman Doctrine most dramatically signalled the new era.

Early in 1947 the nearly bankrupt British government informed Washington that it could no longer prop up Greece and Turkey against internal communist subversion and external Soviet threats. Fearful for the security of the entire Mediterranean area, President Truman concluded that the United States had to assume Britain's burden. He decided to go before Congress and, in the words of Senator Arthur Vandenberg, "scare hell out of the country." On March 12, before a joint session of Congress, the President sketched a depressing picture of a Europe struggling to overcome the effects of the war while confronting subversion stimulated from without. He did not mention Russia but clearly implied it as the chief source of these disturbances. He requested an appropriation of $400 million for economic and political aid to Greece and Turkey, but warned of totalitarian dangers around the world and called upon America "to support free peoples who are resisting attempted subjugation by armed minorities or by outside pressures."

Most Americans agreed with their President that the nation had no other choice. Senator Vandenberg, the Republican leader in the Senate, helped guide the Greek-Turkish aid bill successfully through Congress. On the other hand, the "Truman Doctrine" of support for "free peoples" everywhere stunned or dismayed some observers. Would not such a policy bankrupt the United States and undercut the United Nations? Others questioned the allegedly undemocratic nature of the Greek and Turkish regimes, while the columnist and political pundit, Walter Lippmann, warned against an ideological crusade against communism, a new holy war without any clearly defined goals or limitations. Yet most citizens could see no alternative to costly measures to check communist expansion. Paralyzed by the veto, the U.N. obviously could not live up to its founders' hopes of insuring peace and security for all nations. Only the United States, among the democracies, had sufficient wealth and power to assume the task that the U.N. could not perform. Thus, the Truman Doctrine marked a revolution in American foreign policy, the assumption of extensive obligations in Europe, and by implication elsewhere, in a time of nominal peace. Despite the ideological overtones of Truman's address, the new policy in practice offered aid to even communist governments, such as Tito's Yugoslavia after his break with Stalin in 1948. The "free world" came to mean merely free from Moscow's control, as the United States extended support during the next decade and a half to a variety of regimes that were far from democratic. Security, therefore, and not ideology, guided the application of the Truman Doctrine.

George F. Kennan of the State Department elaborated the philosophy of containment. In an article signed "X" in *Foreign Affairs,* in July, 1947, Kennan urged firm resistance to Soviet expansionism: "the main element of any United States policy toward the Soviet Union must be that of a long-term, patient but firm and vigilant containment of Russian expansive tendencies." If the United States contained Soviet pressures "by the adroit and vigilant application of counter-force," Kennan predicted that eventually the Soviet system might disintegrate because of internal weaknesses or it might undergo a gradual mellowing process. Kennan's article—his authorship soon became known—aroused great interest in America and Europe and made "containment" a popular phrase. It was generally regarded as a realistic exegesis of American policy. A few critics of his contentions, such as Lippmann, feared that the Truman-Kennan approach would dangerously overcommit American power around the globe and that it placed too much emphasis upon containing a Soviet military threat. Kennan himself subsequently regretted what he described as imprecise language, for he, too, believed that containment should emphasize economic and political measures rather than military ones, and should be limited to areas most vital to western interests.

As the Marshall Plan demonstrated, containment as yet essentially relied upon economic and political measures. In January, 1947, Byrnes resigned as Secretary of State and George C. Marshall replaced him. The distinguished wartime Army Chief of Staff, Marshall placed duty to the republic above personal wishes and at the President's request left his retirement, first to head a mission to China in 1946 and then to serve as Secretary of State. A disciplined and reserved person, Marshall surrounded himself with a team of able advisers and established the Policy Planning Staff to try to formulate long-term foreign policies for the United States. Returning in March, 1947 from another frustrating foreign ministers' conference held in Moscow, General Marshall expressed concern over the obvious signs of social and economic decay in Europe which communism could easily exploit. In Churchill's phrase, Europe resembled "a charnel house, a breeding ground of pestilence and hate." Germany remained in ruins, a crop-destroying drought afflicted France, and Great Britain despite frantic efforts failed to boost production sufficiently to cover the costs of its imports. Then an unusually severe winter in 1946–47 lashed western and northern Europe with violent storms and heavy snows, followed by destructive floods. Mines and factories closed and an acute fuel shortage left homes and buildings heatless for hours each day. Production in Great Britain dropped by 50 percent; other countries also experienced declines and Europe's unfavorable dollar balance with the United States grew worse. It seemed quite possible that native communist parties, which already polled one-third of the popular vote in Italy and one-fourth in France, might capitalize upon the general misery to capture political power by peaceful parliamentary means.

Secretary Marshall called upon his advisers for a long-range plan to cope with Europe's crisis. His advisers responded with the Marshall Plan, an enlightened and bold proposal to help rebuild Europe's shattered economy. Under this program the European nations would plan collectively for their own needs, thus promoting continental unity, and Russia was to be invited to participate. The American government then would undertake to supply Europe's requests. Marshall announced the proposal at a commencement address at Harvard University on June 5, 1947. "Our policy," he declared, "is directed not against any country or doctrine but against hunger, poverty, desperation and chaos."

Europe responded immediately and joyously. The British and French governments quickly called for a conference at Paris to frame a reply. Even the Soviet Union displayed an initial interest, apparently hoping for an American handout or postwar lend-lease aid without any restrictive conditions. Molotov arrived in Paris accompanied by 80 Soviet economic advisers. When the British and French rejected his proposal that each country draft a separate estimate of its needs, the Foreign Minister and his delegation abruptly left Paris. Subsequently, as 16 nations gathered at Paris to complete a general plan for systematic American aid, the Soviet government barred its satellites from participating and denounced the Marshall Plan as a Yankee trick to exploit and dominate the European economy. It seems obvious that Stalin feared the growth of American influence in Europe and that he felt particularly anxious about his authority in Eastern Europe. Perhaps, too, a Europe on the verge of economic collapse favored his designs.

Most Americans approved wholeheartedly of the Marshall Plan. The policy appealed to their humanitarian instincts as well as to their desire to halt the inroads of communism, nicely harmonizing ideals and enlightened self-interest. If Western Europe collapsed and fell under communist domination, the United States would find itself cut off from traditional markets and dangerously isolated in an increasingly Soviet-ruled world. Moreover, a generous program of aid to Europe would shore up the free enterprise system everywhere, and would stimulate the American economy. Republican Senator Vandenberg again helped obtain the approval of Congress for a policy originating from a Democratic administration. The public's horrified reaction to the brutal Soviet coup in Czechoslovakia in February, 1948 greatly helped him. Soviet pressures toppled the coalition

Czech government and replaced it with a communist regime. The suicide or murder of Jan Masaryk, the Czech Foreign Minister and son of the great founder of the republic, particularly appalled the western world.

In April, 1948, Congress appropriated over $5 billion to get the Marshall Plan under way. By 1952, when military aid began to supplant economic assistance, the United States had expended nearly $14 billion to promote European recovery. On the whole, the venture proved eminently successful, checking the growth of communism and laying the basis for the remarkable affluence enjoyed by Western Europe in the 1960's. Europe's productivity by 1952 already exceeded that of 1948 by nearly 200 percent. The explanation for this remarkable success, in contrast to the meager results obtained from later programs in the so-called underdeveloped world, rests in the fact that Europe could benefit so effectively from American aid primarily because it already possessed the skills and basic industry essential to its constructive utilization.

4. INTO THE DEPTHS OF THE COLD WAR

Soviet countermoves quickly followed the Marshall Plan. The intensity of the Cold War and the sharp division of Europe into an "East" and a "West" resulted largely from the nature of the Russian reaction to the European recovery program. The paranoid Soviet dictator struck back harshly in the Czechoslovakian coup and in drastic measures to eliminate all possibility of resistance to his rule in Eastern and Central Europe. Molotov proclaimed a bogus aid plan to offset the Marshall Plan. In September, 1947, the Kremlin created the Communist Information Bureau—the Cominform—to tighten its authority over the satellite nations and over foreign communist movements. Waves of communist-inspired strikes and sabotage swept Western Europe. The Soviet government also adopted a harsher line in opposition to Bizonia and western plans to revive Germany economically and politically. Soviet propaganda expressed an irrational fear of attack from a United States still possessing an atomic bomb monopoly. Even diplomatic communications between Russia and the West began to break down into the soon all-too-familiar litany of Soviet invective, fear, and hatred.

The Berlin blockade in June, 1948 seemed to threaten a major world war. Russia apparently sought to wreck western plans to create a West German republic, or at least to force the West to abandon its zones in Berlin and thereby strengthen Soviet rule in East Germany. The Soviets severed land and water routes between the western zones and Berlin, some 200 miles within East Germany. At first, an anguished Washington and its allies saw no feasible alternative but to withdraw from Berlin. Russia obviously had far greater military strength to exert in Germany than did the western powers, who were in a general state of demobilization and unpreparedness, and the atomic bomb did not seem particularly appropriate to the situation. While President Truman and Secretary Marshall contemplated withdrawal, the American commander in Germany, General Lucius D. Clay, advised challenging what he interpreted as a Soviet bluff by sending an armed convoy through the blockade. The situation posed a painful dilemma, between the terrors of war and a humiliating retreat, but fortunately for the West, the airlift offered a happy compromise. It proved possible to supply the people of Berlin with enough food and raw materials to insure survival by around-the-clock shuttling of planes between the western zones in Germany and Berlin. Russia dared not molest the air traffic and thereby precipitate a war. Moreover the spectacular airlift gave the peoples of Europe a great psychological lift and graphically demonstrated American technological superiority over the Soviets. By May, 1949, Stalin agreed to call off the blockade. Berlin resulted in an obvious defeat for Russia and a victory, defensive though it was, for the West.

The verbal onslaught unleashed by the Soviet Union and the Berlin blockade aroused increasing fear in the western world of Soviet aggression and war. Many feared that Russia might strike while time remained in her favor, before the Marshall Plan could revitalize Europe's economy. In March, 1948, Great Britain, France, the Netherlands, Belgium, and Luxembourg formed a defensive alliance in the Brussels Pact. In the United States, the Senate, by the Vandenberg Resolution, endorsed membership in such a defensive grouping. Assured of support at home, the State Department began negotiations for the first formal peacetime alliance in American history. The 12 signatories of the North Atlantic Treaty (the United States, Canada, Iceland, Norway, Denmark, Great Britain, France, the Benelux countries, Portugal, and Italy), on April 4, 1949, solemnly pledged that "an armed attack against one or more of them in Europe or North America shall be considered an attack against them all. . . ." The allies agreed to consult and plan for the common defense. The pact warned Soviet Russia in effect that it could not isolate its victims one by one, as Hitler had done before the Second World War; an armed Soviet attack anywhere in Western Europe would ignite a third world war. The Senate granted approval of the treaty on July 21, by a vote of 82 to 13.

How necessary and wise was the North Atlantic Treaty? There can be little doubt that conclusion of the pact greatly deepened the Cold War. The Soviet Union and the international communist apparatus reacted with an almost unbelievable fury, reflecting both genuine fear and frustration at effective western measures to halt the growth of communism. The rift between East and West widened and the tempo of the Cold War, at least in the sense of mutual suspicions and invective, increased. Russia further tightened its control over its sphere and later formed a rival armed alliance, the Warsaw Pact bloc. From the perspective of the

1970's some scholars have argued that the North Atlantic Treaty was a mistake, because Russia actually did not pose a serious military threat to Western Europe and the alliance further poisoned western relations with the Soviets. From their point of view, America was too powerful and Russia too weak internally for the ever-practical Stalin to launch an armed attack against the western position. Yet western leaders making decisions during a time of great crisis could not be positive of Russia's intentions. They believed that the Soviet Union was aggressive, unpredictable, and reckless, and that a western defensive alliance represented only prudent common sense.

The western powers had not at first intended to create an actual allied army-in-being in Europe. However the shock when Russia broke the American atomic bomb monopoly in the late summer of 1949, by exploding a nuclear device of her own, caused the United States and its allies to fear that the Soviets might soon subject Europe to atomic blackmail. They decided therefore to build up a conventional military force in Western Europe. Such a joint force would serve as a shield capable of fending off or delaying a Russian attack while the United States drew its nuclear sword for a devastating counter blow against the aggressor. Such a forewarning, they hoped, would deter the Soviet Union from armed adventures. President Truman also brushed aside the moral objections of some American scientists and others and ordered development of the hydrogen or superbomb. The North Atlantic Treaty Organization (NATO) established a permanent council and secretariat and a supreme headquarters for the command of naval, air, and land forces committed by the allies to the defense of Western Europe. General Eisenhower was called from retirement in 1950 to become the first Supreme Commander of the NATO forces, and President Truman moved four divisions of American troops to Europe to join the American occupation forces in Germany as part of this nation's commitment to the common defense.

Although NATO furthered the unity of Western Europe, it never achieved the level of conventional forces deemed necessary by the American government. At first the European allies feared that heavy expenditures would sap their economic recovery; later, it seems clear, the allies contentedly accepted a more or less "free ride" behind the American nuclear deterrent. As NATO fell short of its goal in conventional land forces, the United States increasingly contemplated rearming West Germany. Europeans, particularly the French, did not find that prospect very alluring. Moreover French leaders began to resent what they regarded as an undue American preponderance in European affairs. The American government persisted, however, and accepted a French-proposed compromise: the European Defense Community, patterned after the Schuman Plan's successful integration of the German coal and steel industry with that of the rest of Western Europe, sought to rearm

West Germany and yet guard against any future revival of German militarism by integrating its military units with those of the NATO allies. Although EDC followed a French plan, it never gained much popularity in France and finally the French parliament rejected it in 1954. The British salvaged the project with a new compromise. West Germany would be allowed to recover full sovereignty and to raise 12 divisions of troops, provided that it joined NATO and placed its divisions under the command of that alliance, promised not to manufacture atomic or chemical-bacteriological weapons, and came into the Western European Union. Completed by 1955, these arrangements increased the membership of the North Atlantic Treaty to 15 (Greece and Turkey had been admitted earlier). Yet the struggle over the question of rearming West Germany increased French resentment of American leadership, with unfortunate results that became clearer in the 1960's.

5. THE CHINA TANGLE AND THE KOREAN WAR

The first four years following World War II showed creditable progress in American foreign policy. The United States responsibly and constructively met the challenges of postwar reconstruction in Europe and the Cold War with Soviet Russia. President Truman, a peppery and sometimes crude Missouri politician, had more than measured up to the burdens of his great office. His continuation of liberal New Deal programs at home and his record in foreign policy enabled him to pull off one of the great political upsets in American history. Most informed observers in the 1948 election gave Truman little chance against the confident Republican nominee, Thomas E. Dewey, especially with the Democratic party splintered into a leftist Wallace Progressive faction and a conservative anti–civil rights Southern Dixiecrat revolt. But Truman gave his opponents "hell" in a whistle stop, old style political campaign and to the surprise of almost everybody except himself emerged the winner. In his inaugural address in January, 1949, the victorious President promised to continue his previous foreign policies and called for a new approach, the Point Four Program, to provide technical assistance to the underdeveloped areas of the world. American policy at this point in time aimed at building an adequate military force to deter Soviet aggression, at promoting the unity of Western Europe, and at aiding the more backward countries of the world in achieving a peaceful and orderly transformation of their societies.

But the confident mood of 1949 did not last. An unfortunate series of events threatened to undermine America's confidence in its policies and even in itself. The collapse of Nationalist China by 1949 and its replacement by a hostile communist regime shocked Americans. A second and almost simultaneous traumatic blow came when Russia broke America's nuclear monopoly in 1949, three to five years earlier than even the experts had anticipated. The frustrating Korean War that began in June, 1950 tended to divide the American public. Finally, a number of sensational communist espionage cases, such as former State Department official Alger Hiss's trial and conviction for perjury in 1950 and the Rosenberg atom bomb spy trial, persuaded many fearful citizens that native communists and Soviet agents had extensively penetrated their government. How else, Americans asked, could Russia so quickly have constructed nuclear weapons of her own?

These shocks resulted in a domestic anticommunist hysteria and the launching of a witch hunt to unearth suspected "Reds" in American government, industry, and higher education. Quite a few Republican politicians, such as the demogogic junior senator from Wisconsin, Joseph R. McCarthy, and some Democrats, too, eagerly exploited the public's fears and anxieties, stirring a hysteria that came to be known as "McCarthyism." The Democratic administration and especially the State Department, symbol of America's costly and unwanted responsibilities abroad, became the target of the redbaiters. McCarthy and others of his ilk singled out Secretary of State Acheson, a cultivated and intellectual gentleman who did not always suffer fools and poltroons gladly, for unbelievable personal abuse. The morale of the State Department and Foreign Service understandably declined under these assaults. Domestic politics, a growing public mood of weariness and frustration, and the typical American penchant for searching out scapegoats to blame for national failures or disappointments, rocked Europe's confidence in the United States and seemed to endanger the entire structure of American postwar foreign policy.

From 1941 to early 1945 the war with Japan had severely restricted America's ability to provide military aid to Nationalist China. Moreover, to the Nationalists' great disappointment, American strategy against Japan shifted from an emphasis upon the China mainland to an island and sea approach. In part, the change resulted from increased American awareness that Chiang Kai-shek's armies were being used primarily to oppose the Chinese Communists, rather than in fighting the Japanese. American officials viewed a truce in China's persistent civil war as absolutely necessary if China were to play a more vigorous role against Japan and if it were to protect itself against possible Soviet designs against Manchuria. The corruption and inefficiency within the Nationalist armies and government appalled American military advisers and diplomats in China, such as General Joseph W. "Vinegar Joe" Stilwell, while the zeal and efficiency of Mao Tse-tung's Red Chinese impressed some much more favorably. Mao's forces fought hard against the Japanese and by early 1945 controlled a vast slice of China with perhaps 116 million people. American attempts failed to persuade or to coerce Chiang into adopting reforms to clean up his regime and to reach an understanding with the Chinese Communists. In the words of one historian, the Nationalists practiced the "blackmail of weakness," alternately playing upon American hopes for a strong unified China and American fears of China's collapse or a sudden deal with the Japanese.

The war ended before the United States could do much to strengthen Chiang's forces. Yet after Japan's surrender, the American government supplied the Nationalists with over $2 billion in aid. The civil war continued, however, and the Red Chinese aggressively occupied formerly held Japanese areas and received from the Russians in Manchuria vast quantities of captured Japanese arms. Yet most authorities agree that the chief cause of the Nationalists' failure came not from the Red Chinese and the Russians but from within Chiang's own regime. Widespread corruption, the autocratic nature of Chiang's rule, the lack of agrarian reform, runaway postwar inflation, and orgies of looting and raping as Nationalist armies "liberated" cities formerly held by the Japanese, alienated much of the Chinese peasantry, middle class, and intellectuals.

The American government gave what additional support it could to Chiang by transporting his troops to key areas to receive the Japanese surrender before the Red Chinese could get there. Although Washington refused to become directly involved in the civil war, it still earned the deep enmity of the Chinese Communists. General Marshall went to China in 1946 on a futile special mission to work for a compromise between the Nationalists and the Communists. He failed as both sides maneuvered for advantage, and conservative elements within the Nationalist movement blocked meaningful reforms. Against American military advice, Chiang overextended his forces in an effort to drive the Red Chinese from Manchuria and to crush Mao's movement. The drive swiftly turned into disaster. Chiang's armies reeled back from Manchuria and then lost to the advancing Red armies one important Chinese city after another. The swiftness of the Nationalist disintegration surprised even the Chinese Communists. Chiang's armies surrendered or deserted en masse, and 75 to 80 percent of American military aid fell into the hands of the Reds. By the end of 1949, Mao Tse-tung reigned supreme over the mainland of China, while the remnants of Chiang Kai-shek's forces sought refuge on the island of Formosa. Russia promptly recognized the new People's Republic of China and signed an alliance with it, while other countries prepared to establish diplomatic relations with the new government.

During the final stages of the Nationalist debacle, the Truman administration dissociated itself from further involvement in China. Aid was virtually ended, and in mid-1949 the State Department issued a China White Paper that recited America's past efforts and denied that it could do any more to save the Nationalists. Probably only a massive military intervention by the United States could have saved Chiang—an intervention for which the United States was unprepared and which its public might not have favored. Yet the Truman administration made a serious mistake in not earlier presenting Congress and the public with the painful alternatives in China. If it had done so, perhaps fewer irresponsible charges would have cropped up later that the administration had betrayed Chiang and allowed him to collapse.

While America was still trying to adjust to the emergence of an unfriendly Red China, Korea erupted into war. After Japan's surrender Russian armies had occupied north Korea and Americans the south, with the 38th parallel as the dividing line. The two powers evacuated Korea in 1948 and 1949 respectively. Russia left behind a communist regime in the north that refused to permit a U.N. supervised election to unify Korea, while the Americans left a more or less democratic government in the south headed by Syngman Rhee. American military and civilian officials did not regard Korea as having any great strategic importance, as Acheson disclosed in a famous press conference in January, 1950. Suddenly on June 25, 1950 North Korean armies invaded South Korea. Apparently Russia and Red China deliberately planned the attack to coincide with an invasion of Formosa (Taiwan). Also apparently the Communists did not expect American resistance, since the Soviet delegate to the United Nations had recently walked out of the Security Council. But President Truman decided to resist force with force rather than witness the undermining of America's position in Japan and East Asia and the further impairment of collective security. Acting solely upon his own authority, he committed American forces for the first time in history to fight in large numbers on the mainland of Asia. Fortunately, because of the Soviet walkout, Truman obtained U.N. endorsement as well as the support of America's allies in Europe. Sixteen nations fought under the U.N. banner, though America bore most of the burden. Air and naval forces were rushed to Korea, the Seventh Fleet was ordered to neutralize the Formosa Straits, and General Douglas MacArthur, in command of the occupation forces in Japan, was given charge of American and U.N. forces in Korea. The war also led to a massive rearmament program in the United States, the defense budget rising from $13.5 billion in 1949 to $50 billion in 1951.

The war in Korea oscillated violently. American and South Korean forces built up within the Pusan perimeter and in September launched a daring landing behind enemy lines at Inchon. They trapped and almost annihilated the North Korean armies, liberated Seoul, and drove the enemy north of the 38th parallel. Truman then made a fateful decision, sanctioned by a U.N. Assembly resolution, to drive into the north and unify all Korea, despite Red Chinese warnings of intervention. He concurred with the dashing MacArthur, who exuded confidence that Communist China would not intervene; if it did, American air power would destroy its troops as they tried to enter Korea. As U.N. forces neared the Yalu in November, 1950, vast numbers of Red Chinese "volunteers" entered the conflict and for a while threatened to crush

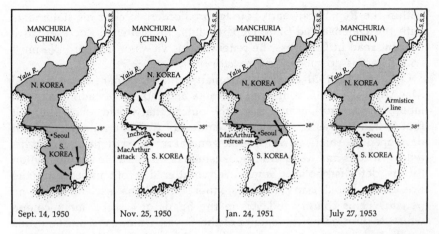

The Korean War

MacArthur's forces. American and allied troops rallied after a hasty retreat from North Korea, however, and by early 1951 had fought their way back to approximately the 38th parallel.

The "Great Debate" of 1950–51 took place within this atmosphere of stalemate and frustration. Truman and his advisers, with the encouragement of the British government and other European allies, decided to keep the war in Korea limited. They judged a full victory in Korea not worth the cost of large-scale war with Red China and possibly Russia, particularly since Europe still remained the Communists' main target in the Cold War. That approach seemed defeatist to General MacArthur and to many other Americans. MacArthur, a brilliant if histrionic general, who had directed a constructive and successful campaign to democratize occupied Japan, smarted from his defeat at Red China's hands. Moreover he genuinely felt convinced that time was fast expiring for an effective challenge to international communism and that Korea provided the best and perhaps the last chance. Therefore, he urged bombing of the Chinese "sanctuary" in Manchuria, blockading its coast, and unleashing Chiang Kai-shek to threaten an invasion of the China mainland. The administration rejected his advice as likely to lead to a hopeless war in Asia, thereby freeing Russia for new ventures in Europe and perhaps igniting a third world war. A number of Republican politicians, angered by defeat in 1948 and hoping to discredit the Democrats, rallied to MacArthur's cause. Joseph W. Martin, the Republican leader in the House of Representatives, called for an all-out drive for victory in Korea: "If we are not in Korea to win, then this Administration should be indicted for the murder of thousands of American boys. . . ." Failing to win his case within the government, General MacArthur began to appeal to the American public and particularly to elements within the Republican party. He ignored orders to clear his statements with the Defense and State Departments. In a letter to Representative Martin, read in Congress, he reiterated his views on Korea: "We must win. There is no substitute for victory."

On April 11, 1951 President Truman announced that he had recalled MacArthur from his command in Korea and Japan. The administration labored under no illusions about the outcry that would follow, but felt that it had to reassert presidential authority over the military. A furor developed in America as the heroic general returned to the cheers of his fellow citizens and Republican spokesmen denounced the administration for its defeatist policy. Some even muttered about impeaching the President. Republican William Jenner of Indiana exclaimed in the Senate, "This country today is in the hands of a secret inner coterie which is directed by the agents of the Soviet Union. We must cut this whole cancerous conspiracy out of our Government at once. Our only course is to impeach President Truman and find out who is the secret invisible government which has so cleverly led our country down the road to destruction." Senator Richard M. Nixon of California branded MacArthur's recall an appeasement of communism and asked the Senate to censure the President and demand the General's reinstatement. Senator McCarthy joined the fray with wild and unsubstantiated charges of communist infiltration of the government. A congressional committee held hearings on MacArthur's recall and the Far Eastern situation, during which shrill charges arose that Chiang Kai-shek had collapsed in China because of American betrayal or undercutting. A veritable witch hunt for traitors and suspects took place, in which a number of reputable citizens were smeared for alleged softness on communism. Even the conservative and respected Republican spokesman, Senator Robert A. Taft of Ohio, son of a former chief executive, found it possible to remark, "The Korean War and the problems which arise from it are the final result of the continuous sympathy toward Communism which [has] inspired American policy."

The Great Debate, therefore, not only centered on whether American foreign policy should emphasize Asia first or Europe, but manifested much latent isolationist sentiment in America and a search for convenient scapegoats to blame for undesirable foreign events. It finally died away, leaving American policy much as before: an emphasis upon Europe as the prime Soviet target and a rational preference for limited hot wars over greatly expanded conflicts. In Korea itself, a successful Allied campaign of attrition persuaded the enemy to agree to truce talks in mid-1951. Unfortunately, with the military pressure reduced, the Communists stalled the negotiations until mid-1953 when an armistice was finally agreed upon. The war had remained limited, a victory for common sense and a rational policy of containment, but at a great cost to the American national psyche. American policy in the Far East froze into a rigid and increasingly unrealistic refusal to recognize Red China or to see it admitted to the United Nations.

Additional Reading

The most recent and balanced accounts of the origins of the Cold War and the containment policy are by Louis J. Halle, *The Cold War as History* (1967); the revisionist account by Walter La Feber, *America, Russia, and the Cold War, 1945–1966* (1967); and Robert Sellen, "Origins of the Cold War: An Historiographical Survey," *West Georgia College Studies in the Social Sciences,* IX (1970), 57–98. *The Cold War . . . And After* (1965), by Charles O. Lerche, Jr., is a carefully reasoned brief analysis. See also the third edition of John Lukacs, *A New History of the Cold War* (1966); David F. Trask, *Victory Without Peace* (1968); Jules David, *America and the World of Our Time* (3rd ed., 1970); and John Spanier, *American Foreign Policy Since World War II* (rev. ed., 1962). For New Left interpretations that blame the United States in part or in whole, consult the following: William Appleman Williams, *The Tragedy of American Diplomacy* (rev. ed., 1962); D. F. Fleming, *The Cold War and Its Origins* (2 vols., 1961); Christopher Lasch, "The Cold War, Revisited and Re-Visioned," *New York Times Magazine,* January 14, 1968; and the more dogmatic and unconvincing treatments by David Horowitz, *Empire and Revolution: A Radical Interpretation of Contemporary History* (1969) and Gabriel Kolko, *The Roots of American Foreign Policy* (1969). Lloyd C. Gardner, *Architects of Illusion: Men and Ideas in American Foreign Policy, 1941–1949* (1970) stresses American ideology in causing the Cold War. Excellent historiographical essays on the New Left are by Irwin Unger, "The 'New Left' and American History—Some Recent Trends in United States Historiography," *American Historical Review,* LXXII (1967), 1237–1263 and William W. MacDonald, "The Revisionist Cold War Historians," *Midwest Quarterly,* XI (1969), 37–49. Also see Daniel M. Smith's review essay, "The New Left and the Cold War," *Denver Quarterly,* IV (1970), 78–88. Gar Alperovitz's revisionist study, *Atomic Diplomacy: Hiroshima and Potsdam* (1965) asserts that the A-bombs were used to coerce Russia. Arthur M. Schlesinger, Jr., "Origins of the Cold War," *Foreign Affairs,* Vol. 46 (1967), 22–49, refutes such interpretations. Les K. Adler and Thomas G. Paterson, "Red Fascism: The Merger of Nazi Germany and Soviet Russia in the American Image of Totalitarianism, 1930's–1950's," *American Historical Review,* LXXV (1970), 1046–1064 sharply criticizes America's Cold War rhetoric. Paterson's essay in B. J. Bernstein, ed., *Politics and Policies of the Truman Administration* (1970), 97–101, concludes that the Marshall Plan furthered Europe's division. A penetrating account of America's postwar divisions over foreign policy is by Alonzo L. Hamby, "The Liberals,

Truman, and FDR as Symbol and Myth," *Journal of American History,* LVI (1970), 859–867. See also Selig Adler's study, *The Isolationist Impulse* (1957). John L. Snell handles the German problem in *Wartime Origins of the East-West Dilemma over Germany* (1959). On the containment policy, see Herbert Druks, *Harry S. Truman and the Russians, 1945–1953* (1967); George Curry, "James F. Byrnes," in S. F. Bemis and Robert H. Ferrell, eds., *The American Secretaries of State and Their Diplomacy,* vol. XIV (1965); R. H. Ferrell, "George C. Marshall," *The American Secretaries of State and Their Diplomacy,* vol. XV (1966); and George F. Kennan, *Memoirs, 1925–1950* (1967). Also the *Memoirs of Harry S. Truman* (2 vols., 1956) and *Present at the Creation* (1969) by Dean Acheson are important. Tang Tsou, *America's Failure in China, 1941–1950* (1963) concludes that Chiang Kai-shek and his regime alone were to blame for their failure. G. P. Paige, *The Korean Decision* (1968) examines the American decision to intervene. David Rees, *Korea: The Limited War* (1964) sees that war as a victory for a rational policy of containment. There are several good studies of MacArthur's role in the war: John W. Spanier, *The Truman-MacArthur Controversy and the Korean War* (1959); Trumbull Higgins, *Korea and the Fall of MacArthur* (1960); and R. N. Rovere and A. M. Schlesinger, Jr., *The MacArthur Controversy and American Foreign Policy* (rev. ed., 1965). An excellent account of Red China's intervention is by Allen S. Whiting, *China Crosses the Yalu* (1960). A recent study by Ronald J. Caridi examines the politics of the Cold War in *The Korean War and American Politics: The Republican Party as a Case Study* (1968).

CHERRY PICKER
LAUNCH PAD WITH ERECTOR
LAUNCH PAD WITH ERECTOR
MISSILE READY BLDGS
OXIDIZER VEHICLES
FUELING VEHICLES

Top: Before View of Missile Base.
Bottom: Surveillance in the Caribbean.

24

THE BALANCE OF TERROR,
1953–1962

1. THE EISENHOWER ERA: RHETORIC VERSUS REALITIES

The death of Joseph Stalin, the ruthless architect of the Soviet empire, in March, 1953, marked a new and more hopeful era in the history of the modern world. A cloud seemed to lift as Stalin's obscure heirs officiated at his enshrinement in Lenin's tomb in Moscow's Red Square. In the United States, John Foster Dulles, the new Secretary of State, hailed the event as the end of the dread Stalin epoch and the dawn of the brighter and more hopeful Eisenhower era. Dulles presumably had in mind the disintegration of the communist tyranny and the forthcoming triumph of western democracy. Events soon revealed that he was a poor prophet; not victory but an age of mutual coexistence between East and West, founded upon a balance of terror between the two superpowers, was about to begin.

The 1952 presidential election in the United States took place in an atmosphere seething with anxieties, fears, and uncertainties. A revival or resurgence of isolationist sentiment had resulted from the frustrations of the Cold War, and particularly from the indecisive and apparently endless conflict in Korea. Many citizens questioned the reliability of America's allies in Europe and their small contribution to the Korean War, and some urged that the United States must "go it alone" in its bid for victory over communism. Senator Taft, a leading candidate for the Republican presidential nomination, advocated what his critics described as "bargain-basement" containment. A prewar isolationist, Taft genuinely feared that America might tax and spend itself into bankruptcy and socialism. He called for a less expensive policy of containment that would reduce foreign aid and rely upon less costly naval and air power for defense, and for a propaganda campaign to put Russia on the defensive within its satellite empire. Taft's appeal gained greatest strength within traditionally conservative and isolationist midwestern states. More moderate and European-oriented Republicans, especially strong in the eastern states, rallied behind the candidacy of General Eisenhower, who was persuaded to resign his NATO post to seek the nomination. "Ike" enjoyed a genuine and vast popularity, and large numbers of Americans confidently expected him to lead the nation successfully to security and peace. He obtained the Republican nomination and won a smashing electoral victory over his Democratic opponent, Illinois Governor Adlai E. Stevenson. Stevenson impressed the electorate as too much of an intellectual, in contrast to the man from Abilene, Kansas with the famous grin and the laurels of a wartime hero. Moreover, Republicans successfully exploited popular unhappiness with Democratic corruption in office, alleged large-scale communist infiltration of government, and the costly and inconclusive war in Korea. Eisenhower spoke during the campaign of Democratic blunders or worse that had "allowed the Godless Red Tide [to] engulf millions" and had failed to see "the Red Stain" seeping into the government itself. His promise if elected to visit Korea and seek an honorable termination of the conflict undoubtedly accounted in large part for his triumph over Stevenson.

Eisenhower named John Foster Dulles to serve as his Secretary of State and to plan a more dynamic policy for America. The grandson of one Secretary of State (John Watson Foster) and the nephew of another (Robert Lansing), Dulles was an enormously able man with an extensive background in foreign affairs. He also was a deeply religious Presbyterian, who viewed the Cold War as a titanic struggle between the forces of good and evil. He was convinced that American foreign policy had to be placed on the highest moral plane in order to command support at home and respect abroad. If that were done, he believed in the inevitability of victory over the Soviet system, for western moral force and superior resources would expose the weaknesses and contradictions that he saw as inherent within communism. Yet his very penchant for moralizing and the rigidities of his policies alienated many in America and in Western Europe. The Secretary often baffled and irritated foreign diplomats and observers. A British diplomat aptly described him as a "Reformation Character" who saw the world in simple dualistic terms. At first, too, he alienated many officials in the State Department and Foreign Service by his anxiety not to find another Alger Hiss on his hands; he urged departmental and diplomatic officials not merely to loyalty but to "positive loyalty" and for a while allowed the McCarthyites to tyrannize the State Department with loyalty and security probes. Yet Dulles throughout his tenure retained the confidence and affections of President Eisenhower and exerted an enormous influence over the foreign policy of the administration.

The Republicans came into the executive offices with a platform and campaign rhetoric that alarmed many close observers of American foreign policy. Not only had the Republicans unleashed much loose talk during the 1952 election campaign of blunders and near treason by the Democrats, but Dulles and others had called for a dynamic new policy that would roll back the Iron Curtain and liberate the enslaved peoples living within the satellite empire of Russia. They denounced containment as immoral because it left millions of hopeless people under communist tyranny. A policy of liberation, they believed, would change that unhappy situation by bringing the superior moral and material resources of the Free World to bear upon the Soviet empire. Therefore Dulles as Secretary of State shunned agreements with Russia that in any way seemed to imply acquiescence to its system. The Dulles-Eisenhower approach to foreign policy in 1953 supported the liberation of the satellite peoples, encouraged America's allies to bear more of the burden of their own defense, and extended a network of alliances and bases virtually to encircle the Soviet Union and draw a line against further communist aggression in any direction.

In practice, however, Republican foreign policies did not differ greatly from those of Truman. They reduced financial outlays for defense and foreign aid and placed greater emphasis upon the conclusion of additional alliances and pacts. One apparent departure involved the so-called "new look" in defense and foreign policy—the doctrine of instant and massive retaliation. As Dulles explained it in 1954, henceforth the United States would refuse to allow Russia to divert and to bleed her by local wars waged through proxies, as in Korea; instead, if such aggressions occurred, the government would "respond vigorously at places and with means of its own choosing." In accordance with this so-called policy, the Eisenhower administration curtailed conventional forces and emphasized the development of nuclear weapons. As one administration supporter reportedly said, America would get "more bang for the buck." In practice, massive retaliation would have meant a third world war, increasingly unthinkable as Russia caught up with the United States in nuclear weapons and delivery systems. Instead, America soon found itself relatively less able to wage limited conventional wars, the type of challenge most likely to occur, while prepared for a thermonuclear war that few rational individuals dared contemplate. Russia's cruel suppression of the Hungarian Revolution in 1956 graphically demonstrated the bankruptcy of "liberation." Americans and their government deeply sympathized with the brave Hungarian patriots but dared not intervene lest it trigger a major and mutually destructive war.

Other Eisenhower decisions also revealed that he basically continued the containment policy in its essentials. The Korean War, as noted before, ended with a truce in July, 1953 that left that war-devastated country divided approximately along the 38th parallel. American troops remained to help guard the armistice line, and the United States signed a security pact with the government of South Korea. As for Taiwan,

Truman had already begun to protect the Nationalist Chinese against attack from Red China. Eisenhower continued that protection and "unleashed" Chiang Kai-shek to invade the mainland if he chose. When Red China subsequently threatened to seize the Nationalist-held off-shore islands of Quemoy, Matsu, and the Pescadores, however, Dulles concluded a mutual security treaty with the Nationalist regime in 1954 that in effect released Chiang. The Formosa Resolution, adopted by Congress in 1955, authorized the executive to use force to protect Taiwan and other territories vital to its defense. Twice, in crises in 1955 and in 1958, American support of Chiang forced Red China to abandon its invasion plans. In the French colonial war in Indo-China, covered in the following chapter, Eisenhower overruled his advisers and decided not to risk involvement to prevent a communist triumph. Instead, after the Geneva conference in 1954 temporarily ended the civil war, Dulles negotiated a new defensive pact intended to halt further communist advances. The Southeast Asia Treaty Organization (SEATO) included the United States, Great Britain, France, Australia, New Zealand, the Philippines, Thailand, and Pakistan, but it never became a really effective alliance. The Baghdad Pact of 1955 was another weak defensive system, designed to deter Russia. The United States did not become a formal member of this alignment of Great Britain, Iraq, Iran, Turkey, and Pakistan, because of its concern over Arab sensibilities, but it encouraged its formation. From our perspective today, SEATO and the Baghdad Pact seem to represent misguided attempts to transplant the kind of contain-ment that had succeeded in Europe to areas that were most unsuitable.

2. THE ROAD TO COEXISTENCE

A thaw in Soviet relations with the western powers followed Stalin's death. The new collective leadership, first led by Georgi Malenkov and subsequently by Nikita Khrushchev, began to relax the Stalinist system at home, and to profess a course of peaceful competition and coexistence abroad. The domestic changes reflected pressures from within Russia for a less frenzied pace of industrialization, less police terror, and more consumer goods. Khrushchev's denunciation of the crimes of the Stalin era, before the 20th Congress of the Communist Party in 1956, seemed to insure that the regime would not return to the harsh tyranny of the past. In foreign policy, the new leadership perceived the dangers of mutual destruction in a nuclear age and decided that a smiling visage might make for greater success abroad than a threatening scowl.

The Soviet "smiling offensive" proved a mixed blessing in western eyes. On the one hand, the post-Stalin leadership seemed to take ideology more seriously than had the old dictator as Khrushchev earnestly pursued the old dream of world communism. Rotund, exuber-ant, garrulous, and often crude, that shrewd peasant in the seat of the czars encouraged the growth of neutralism in Western Europe and competed effectively with America for influence in the underdeveloped "third world" of Asia and Africa. He confidently predicted to the capitalist world that "we will bury you," peacefully of course, and smiled benignly upon so-called wars of national liberation against the remnants of European colonial empires and neocolonial influence. The United States soon found it had a serious rival in foreign aid, as the Soviet Union directed economic assistance to those areas where it could gain most in influence and western embarrassment.

Yet the West could only welcome changes in the Soviet regime that seemed to promise a better life for the Russian people and the possibility of reasonable adjustments with the noncommunist world. Moreover, these changes unintentionally encouraged a desire for greater freedom from Moscow's control among the satellite nations of Eastern Europe. The new rulers in the Kremlin reluctantly tolerated national communism in such countries as Poland in the 1950's and Rumania in the 1960's. When the movement seemed to threaten complete independence, however, the Soviet authorities acted ruthlessly to suppress it, in Hungary in 1956 and Czechoslovakia in 1968. Another seemingly hopeful development, long ill understood by American policy-makers, sprang from the emergence of "poly-centrism" or rival centers of power within the formerly monolithic communist world. Yugoslavia had asserted its independence in 1948, while the important rift between Peking and Moscow emerged by the early 1960's. In addition, the large communist parties in Western Europe followed the Moscow line less slavishly than in the past.

The first of the postwar "thaws" in Soviet relations with the western powers lasted from 1953 through 1955. The receding danger of a major world war encouraged hope for mutual reductions in armaments and control of nuclear weapons. Although no real progress in arms reductions resulted, our European allies urged a big power conference on the principal issues dividing that continent. Khrushchev in effect "bought" a summit conference by recognizing West Germany, concluding a peace treaty with Japan, and agreeing to end the occupation of Austria, henceforth recognized as a neutralized country. President Eisenhower joined Britain's Anthony Eden and France's premier of the moment, Edgar Faure, in a conference with Khrushchev at Geneva in July, 1955. The atmosphere was very cordial, but little more took place beyond an exchange of views. Eisenhower tried to break the deadlock on armaments limitations by an "open sky" proposal for mutual aerial surveys to reduce fears of surprise attacks. Russia instead proposed a mutual withdrawal of forces stationed on foreign soil in Europe and the dismantling of the NATO and Warsaw Pact alliances. Although mutual disengagement aroused some interest in the West, it would have meant a complete American withdrawal from the continent while Soviet troops merely pulled back to the Russian border where they could readily re-enter the disengaged zones. Therefore the western allies declined to accept this plan. Even so, many hailed the "spirit of Geneva" as presaging the end of the Cold War.

3. CRISIS IN THE MIDDLE EAST

Neither the United States nor the Soviet Union played much of a role in the seething Middle East prior to the mid-1950's. Washington left responsibility largely in British and French hands, while Russia apparently contentedly observed the gradual erosion of western influence in the region. The situation changed drastically in 1955, however, as the Cold War engulfed this turbulent area.

Great Britain and France had supplanted Turkey after World War I as the new overlords of the Middle East. Disappointing Arab nationalist hopes that they had encouraged during the war, the British added the mandates of Iraq, Transjordan, and Palestine to their protectorate in Egypt, while France obtained mandates in Syria and Lebanon. Arab nationalists thereafter viewed the Anglo-French as the "new Turks" or oppressors. Nazi propaganda skillfully exploited Arab nationalism during the Second World War to undermine the western position. After 1945, France released its hold on Syria and Lebanon, but Great Britain clung to its position because of the great strategic and economic importance of the region. The Suez Canal formed an essential link between Great Britain and its overseas territories, and the Middle East contained an estimated two-thirds of the world's proven oil reserves upon which Europe increasingly depended for heat and fuel.

The emergence of the Jewish state of Israel further complicated the western position in the Middle East. The modern Zionist movement to found a Jewish national state began in the late 19th century, a product of age-old Jewish hopes, western liberal nationalism, and the anti-Semitism so widely prevalent in Eastern and Central Europe. While the Allies attempted to exploit Arab nationalism against the Turks in World War I, the British government also appealed to Jews for support by the Balfour Declaration in 1917, promising them a "national home" in Palestine, with due consideration for the rights of the Arabs already living there. The Jewish population in the British mandate, increasing slowly at first and then much more rapidly as the result of the Nazi persecutions, rose from 55,000 in 1918 to 528,000 by 1944. The ratio of Jew to Arab in Palestine thus changed from one to eight in 1922 to one to two in 1944. Naturally the Arabs resented these "alien intruders," and criticized Britain as their sponsor. An Arab rebellion broke out in Palestine in 1937, inaugurating an era of growing tensions and terror within the mandate. The British government capitulated to Arab pressures in 1939 by promising to limit drastically further Jewish immigration

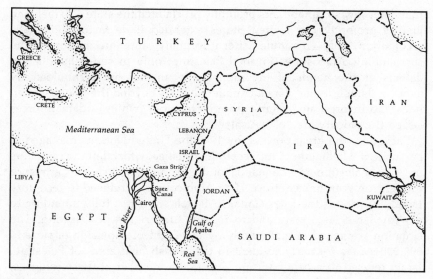

The Middle East

and to create what in fact would have been an Arab-ruled independent state of Palestine. Dismayed Zionists called for an independent Jewish state.

President Wilson had endorsed the Balfour Declaration and his successors had manifested some concern with the Palestine mandate. During World War II, Washington endorsed the Zionist cause. Democratic and Republican platforms in 1944 advocated unrestricted Jewish immigration to Palestine and the creation of a Jewish state. President Truman in 1945 urged the harried British to permit 100,000 Jewish refugees to enter the mandate immediately, leading to the quip that obviously few Arab voters lived in the United States. When Britain dumped the troublesome issue in the lap of the United Nations in 1947, and prepared to surrender its mandate, the United States and the Soviet Union found themselves in rare agreement. Both endorsed a plan approved by the U.N. to partition Palestine into separate Arab and Jewish states and to internationalize Jerusalem, a city sacred to Jews, Christians, and Moslems.

The partition plan enraged the Arab world. Their spokesmen blamed it upon the United States, then the home of the largest single Jewish population in the world and the headquarters of the world Zionist movement. The partition favored the Jews, who were to gain the largest slice of the more desirable agricultural lands in Palestine, containing also most of the mandate's cities and railroads. Arabs warned that they would resist creation of a Jewish state, and armed bands began to attack Jewish settlements. On May 14, 1948, Great Britain formally terminated her mandate. Jewish inhabitants promptly proclaimed the state of Israel, and just as promptly the United States extended it de facto diplomatic recognition, only 11 minutes after it formally came into existence. The surrounding Arab states invaded Palestine, only to suffer humiliating defeats at the hands of the numerically smaller but technologically superior Israeli forces. Israel conquered areas beyond the 1947 partition lines and incorporated them within its territory, while Jordanian forces seized the old city area of Jerusalem.

Backed by the great powers, by 1949 the United Nations managed to persuade the belligerents to accept an armistice, which left the remnants of Arab Palestine in the hands of Egypt and Jordan. The armistice brought only an uneasy truce. The Arab countries refused to recognize Israel and closed the Suez Canal to Israeli shipping, fully intending to destroy Israel as a state and to restore Arab rights in Palestine. The situation worsened immeasurably by the flight or expulsion of close to 800,000 Arabs formerly resident in the Jewish-held areas of Palestine. Israel refused to accept back any substantial number of these refugees, whom it contended had fled voluntarily, while the Arab countries blocked their resettlement elsewhere. Unfortunately, this resulted in the establishment of poverty-wracked refugee camps around the borders of Israel, within which the miserable inhabitants were kept alive by U.N. handouts, largely paid for by the United States, and by a festering hatred of Israel.

The successful Egyptian Revolution in 1952 presaged a new wave of troubles for the western powers in the Middle East. The previous year, Mohammed Mossadegh, an ardent if hysterical nationalist, had come to power in Iran and nationalized the British-owned Anglo-Iranian Oil Company. British and American pressure brought about Mossadegh's fall in 1953, with American oil firms thereafter sharing in Iranian oil and Washington supplanting London as sponsor of the Shah's regime. The Egyptian Revolution at first seemed more promising than the short-lived one in Iran. A group of army officers, led by Colonel Gamal Abdul Nasser, overthrew the monarchy of the corrupt and pornography-loving King Farouk and promised to bring an era of economic development and social reform to Egypt's impoverished masses. Nasser was an intelligent and charismatic leader who also aspired to unite the Arab world behind his leadership; the destruction of Israel became the chief means to that end. Initially, however, Nasser seemed to western observers a moderate with whom cooperation was possible. Great Britain for some years had fended off Egyptian nationalist demands that it withdraw its forces from bases along the Suez Canal. With American encouragement it agreed to do so in 1954, and both powers promised financial assistance for Nasser's developmental program. One of these projects was the Aswan High Dam, designed to increase Egypt's supply of irrigated land and electric power and intended by Nasser to become the chief showpiece of the new Egypt.

Two events upset western hopes for a peaceful and stable Middle East: the launching of the Baghdad Pact in 1955, and the Czech arms deal. Ironically, the first was primarily intended to bar Russian penetration into the region and to shore up Britain's position in uneasy Iraq. A weak alliance of Great Britain, Iran, Iraq, Turkey, and Pakistan, the Baghdad Pact polarized the Middle East by alienating Egypt and other Arab states. It also alarmed the Soviet Union and caused it to undertake a more active role in the Middle East. The second and closely related development arose from continuing Arab-Israeli tensions. Over 2,000 border incidents and raids occurred along the Israeli frontiers between 1949 and 1956, instigated by the Arab governments and frequently involving the Palestinian refugees. Israeli strategy called for periodic large-scale counter raids in retaliation. One crushing Israeli reprisal in February, 1955 caught the Egyptian army unprepared and inflicted heavy damages and casualties in the Gaza Strip. Humiliated and enraged, Nasser demanded more arms from the western powers. When they refused, hoping to avoid an arms race, he turned to the communist world. In an arms deal with Czechoslovakia in September, 1955, Egypt pledged cotton exports in payment for arms and military equipment valued at over $200 million. Although the United States and Great Britain declined an Israeli request for large amounts of arms in compensation, Israel secretly obtained much of what she desired from France. Nasser's pro-Soviet leanings and above all the aid and encouragement that he gave to the Algerian rebels against French rule disturbed Paris.

As the Egyptian dictator continued to edge closer to the Soviet orbit, recognizing Red China and expressing sympathy for the rebels on British-held Cyprus, Washington and London began to reconsider their policies. Secretary of State Dulles regarded Nasser's attempts to play off Russia against the United States in financing the Aswan Dam as crude blackmail. Underestimating Russia's capacity for selected foreign aid and misreading Nasser's determination, the British and Americans decided to withdraw their promises of aid for the dam and other projects. Dulles announced the withdrawal in a calculatedly humiliating manner on July 22, 1956.

Nasser struck back by nationalizing the Suez Canal and pledging the revenues to build the Aswan Dam. He also later obtained large Soviet assistance. Britain and France then prepared for war, unwilling to tolerate any longer what they regarded as a pint-sized Hitler arrogantly twitting the West and threatening to cut off its vital oil imports via the Suez Canal. Although Nasser acted within his rights to break a contract with a private company (the Suez Canal Company was largely British-French owned), London and Paris charged that he had violated international law by impeding the flow of commerce through the canal. Britain asked canal pilots to walk off their jobs, but Nasser managed to keep ships moving through the waterway.

Although the Americans had ample warning of how seriously Great

Britain and France viewed the issue, Eisenhower and Dulles opposed the use of force as totally unjustified. The crisis caught Eisenhower in the midst of his campaign for re-election, and Dulles hoped to calm the situation in an apparently unending round of discussions and conferences. The two American leaders woefully failed to appreciate the desperation and recklessness of the Anglo-French mood. Prime Minister Anthony Eden, in poor health and like many of his countrymen still clinging to the shreds of empire, was convinced that Nasser had to be crushed, not appeased; French officials agreed. Britain and France failed to understand Eisenhower's opposition to the use of force and too confidently expected him to "take care of the Bear" while they surgically excised the "cancer" of Nasserism.

The stage was set for a comic-opera tragedy of mutual misunderstandings and recriminations. Prime Minister David Ben-Gurion, a white-maned elderly man of scholarly interests and steel-willed nationalism, decided that Israel had to eliminate Nasser in a preventive war before the Czech arms upset the balance of military power in the Middle East. France, apparently eager to pursue a course independent of American tutelage, encouraged Israeli plans and Eden finally went along. Hence, on October 29 the Israeli army suddenly invaded the Gaza Strip and overran most of the Sinai Peninsula. In a brilliantly executed operation the Israelis captured most of the Czech equipment that Nasser recently had obtained and some 6,000 Egyptian prisoners, the latter subsequently exchanged for four Israeli captives. By prearrangement, Great Britain and France issued an ultimatum to both sides for withdrawal from the vicinity of the Suez Canal and on November 4–5 they launched an invasion of the canal zone.

Before the Anglo-French forces could seize the entire canal, however, world condemnation forced them to halt. What looked like great power bullying of a weak Arab nation shocked world opinion, and the Soviet Union exploited the situation to the hilt to embarrass and discredit the West. Khrushchev rattled his rockets, spoke of sending "volunteers" to aid Egypt, and even had the temerity to suggest a joint Soviet-American use of force to evict the Anglo-French "aggressors." Although Washington rejected that suggestion and made clear its opposition to forcible Soviet intervention, the crisis deeply worried the administration. Western prestige and influence in the Middle East were jeopardized and vital oil supplies endangered. Moreover, Eisenhower and Dulles felt personally betrayed by their allies, who had carefully concealed their military plans from them. Eisenhower talked in blunt barracks-room language to Eden in a trans-Atlantic telephone conversation and reportedly reduced the distraught Prime Minister to tears. The world then saw a novel picture of Russia and the United States in effect censuring the Anglo-French action and cooperating in the passage of a U.N. resolution for a cease-fire and withdrawal. As an additional irony, the

Suez War distracted world attention from Russia's bloody suppression of the Hungarian Revolution in early November, 1956.

The First Suez War ended in withdrawal of the invading forces and a U.N.-supervised cease-fire. A real peace, however, seemed more remote than before. The only gainers were Israel, which at least captured large quantities of arms and preserved its military superiority in the region, and Nasser, who managed to attribute his defeat to British-French intervention. Nasser emerged as an even more towering Arab leader, whipping up hatred for Israel and making preparations, with Soviet aid, for another round with the hated enemy. The outcome of the affair deeply humiliated America's two principal allies. While Britain, if anything, thereafter clung more closely to its ties with the United States, France increasingly moved away from Washington's leadership.

In 1957 Congress passed the administration-requested "Eisenhower Doctrine." Designed to enable the United States to take over the western role from the discredited British and French in the Middle East, the resolution authorized the executive to provide military and economic aid to protect the integrity and independence of Middle Eastern states that requested it in resisting communist aggression. Although hailed by Dulles as a milestone in curbing communist expansionism, the doctrine obviously was not designed to deal with the most likely menace in the area, internal subversion. It did score a limited success, however, in shoring up Jordan's King Hussein and the Lebanese government against Nasser-inspired coups and threats in 1957 and 1958. In succeeding years, especially after the failure in 1961 of Nasser's union of Egypt and Syria (United Arab Republic), the Middle East seemed to become less of a tinderbox. That proved illusory, however, as a renewed arms race and the Second Suez War in 1967 attested.

4. FERMENT IN LATIN AMERICA

Washington's ardent prewar courtship of Latin America had paid handsome dividends during the Second World War. In the postwar era, however, American attention focused more upon Cold War challenges in Europe and Asia and policy-makers became oblivious to growing resentment in Latin America. In addition to feeling neglected, many Latin Americans resented the lavishing of American aid upon Europe while their countries received in comparison mere paltry handouts. After all, Latin America had even more staggering economic and social problems worthy of Yankee attention. The region as a whole suffered from a rapidly increasing population, vast illiteracy and poverty, and under-industrialized economies overly dependent upon agricultural and raw material exports. Fifteen Latin American countries sent from 40 to 80 percent of their total exports to the United States, yet American officials were loath to discuss marketing agreements to stabilize the prices of such staples as coffee on the world market. Moreover, our trade quotas and tariff rates in effect discouraged economic diversification in Latin America. Both the Truman and Eisenhower administrations in effect told Latin America not to expect much in the way of foreign aid and to rely instead for increased economic growth upon attracting foreign investors.

The Cold War became another irritant in the relations between the Yankee Colossus and Latin America. Interventionism long had aroused unpleasant reactions from most Latin Americans, but in the era of the Cold War Washington feared that a communist movement might come to power in some Latin American country. Guatemala seemed to present that danger in the early 1950's, when the communist-tinged regime of Jacobo Arbenz nationalized American-owned property and purchased arms from Communist Poland. At the Tenth Inter-American Conference at Caracas in 1954, Secretary of State Dulles vainly sought approval of a resolution for strong collective action in case of a communist threat in the hemisphere. The Latin American delegates reacted unenthusiastically, apparently because they disliked interventionism in any guise and feared the communist menace less than Washington. Dulles had to profess satisfaction with a weaker resolution that provided for consultation in the event of a communist threat within the hemisphere. Shortly thereafter the Central Intelligence Agency helped a Guatemalan exile group topple Arbenz from power. Clearly the American government no longer felt as secure as before World War II and began to revert to interventionism, which grew much more pronounced during the Kennedy and Johnson administrations.

A somewhat contradictory Latin American complaint charged Washington with coddling dictators within the hemisphere. Liberals within the United States and Latin America accused the United States not only of failing to encourage democracy but of buttressing conservative militarists in Latin America through its policy of arms aid and military missions. Washington in fact did tend to regard the military as the most stable element in many countries of Latin America. Yet *caudillismo*—strongman rule—in Latin America long antedated arms aid from the United States. Moreover, Washington correctly reasoned that if the Latin American military establishments could not obtain arms from the United States they would merely turn to other foreign sources, with all the dangers of outside influence and meddling that would entail. Hence from 1938 on, the American government sought to replace European governments (in particular, Nazi Germany) as the source of arms for Latin America. During and after the Second World War, the United States supplied Latin America with arms and special military missions to train troops in the use of the equipment. Furthermore, as the fear of communism mounted, the Eisenhower administration particularly seemed to smile benignly upon the military dictatorships chronically afflicting much of Latin America.

Until Vice President Richard Nixon's ill-starred tour of South America in the spring of 1958, Washington seemed blissfully unaware of mounting anti-American sentiment within the hemisphere. Instead of the goodwill that he had hoped to promote, the Vice President found himself the target of anti-Yankee demonstrations and abuse. He was heckled in Buenos Aires, spat upon in Lima, and trapped in his car by a rock-throwing and howling mob in Caracas. For a brief moment even his life seemed seriously endangered. Nixon revealed much personal courage during his ordeal and returned to the United States resolved that the administration had to adopt new policies to reduce Latin American discontent and hostility. Thereafter, the Eisenhower administration displayed greater reserve in relations with Latin American dictators and more sympathy for the cause of democracy and liberal reforms within the hemisphere.

The Cuban Revolution confronted the American government with a far more serious challenge. Rebel leader Fidel Castro overthrew the brutal dictatorship of Fulgencio Batista in January, 1959. Although Washington once had close ties with Batista, it cut them before his final collapse and promptly recognized the Castro regime. Castro seemed to offer great promise of building a democratic and progressive Cuba, and most Americans sympathized with his apparent goals. American friendship and hopes soon turned to bewilderment and hostility, however, as Castro veered to a shrilly anti-Yankee and pro-Marxist course. It now seems clear that Castro probably inclined toward a crude Marxism for some years before coming to power and that he never genuinely sought aid and cooperation from the American government. Apparently he regarded the United States as controlled by big business and unalterably hostile to social revolutions. Moreover strident anti-Americanism, by no means new to Cubans, served as a useful device to rally Cuban nationalism behind his regime. Probably nothing that the American government did or failed to do could have substantially altered the situation.

During 1960 Castro's Cuba became more apparently a Marxist dictatorship. Thousands of upper- and middle-class Cubans fled or were driven into exile, large numbers seeking haven in the United States. Castro recognized Red China and entered into barter arrangements with the Soviet Union to exchange sugar for economic and military aid. He confiscated American-owned property in Cuba, valued at $1.5 billion, without provisions for adequate compensation. In retaliation, Eisenhower suspended the Cuban sugar quota, whereby the United States had purchased Cuban sugar at a two cent per pound rate above the world price. Khrushchev welcomed his new ally and chortled at American discomfiture. He mocked the Monroe Doctrine as dead and needing burial, while threatening to use his rocket missiles if the United States intervened against Castro. The State Department failed to obtain any effective hemispheric action against the menace of Castroism, although a meeting of foreign ministers did adopt a resolution condemning extracontinental intervention in the affairs of the Western Hemisphere. Washington began to clamp an economic blockade on Cuba, while promising more economic assistance to the rest of Latin America. Finally, on January 3, 1961, President Eisenhower reacted to Castro's drastic limitation of American embassy personnel by severing diplomatic relations with Cuba.

5. THE BRINK OF ARMAGEDDON

Dulles had viewed the Geneva conference in 1955 as a victory for his policy of patient force to obtain Soviet concessions. He felt confident that if America continued on that course, eventually it could dictate the terms of a general settlement. Yet even then Russia was making such enormous strides in the development of rockets and nuclear weapons as to upset his calculations. In August, 1957, Russia announced the successful testing of an intercontinental ballistic missile, and in September it became the first power to launch a man-made satellite, Sputnik I, into orbit around the earth. Sputnik not only indicated that the Soviet Union had made great scientific and technological progress, but that it surpassed the United States in developing large rockets capable of carrying thermonuclear warheads across thousands of miles to their targets. President Eisenhower and his advisers dismissed Sputnik as a mere game of cosmic basketball, but the Soviet achievement greatly impressed the world. Many Americans began to question not only their government's lagging space program but also the quality of American education and the nation's slow rate of economic growth in comparison with that of Russia. It also seemed obvious to observers that the Soviet Union had caught up with the Americans in nuclear weapons, and that it might even soon forge ahead.

Khrushchev seemed to believe that Russia had already surpassed America in the arms race. A number of influential Americans began to fear the development of a dangerous "missile gap" in Russia's favor. If the Soviet Union should acquire a three to one advantage over the United States in intercontinental ballistic missiles (ICBM's), as one Defense Department official predicted, it might tempt Khrushchev to try to knock out America's Strategic Air Force in a surprise attack and leave the nation helpless. Eisenhower refused to succumb to pressure to increase defense spending, however, maintaining that the nation's deterrent forces were adequate. Yet it seemed to many critics here and in Western Europe that the United States under Eisenhower's lackluster leadership had fallen behind the Soviet Union in national power and prestige. Unquestionably America's reputation as the foremost scientific, industrial, and nuclear power had declined around the world. As one consequence, a growing sentiment toward neutralism and greater independence began to emerge among America's NATO allies in Europe. France despite Washington's discouragement began to build its own nuclear force. Under President Charles de Gaulle, who returned to power in 1958, France first sought an equal voice with America and Britain in NATO's councils and when refused began to follow a more independent foreign policy.

Khrushchev tried to exploit his country's apparent gains in power to extort western concessions in Germany. In 1958 the Soviet leader threatened to sign a peace treaty with East Germany and to turn over to that puppet regime control of Berlin and its access routes, unless the western powers within the next six months would agree to his version of a satisfactory German settlement. He hoped thereby either to obtain western recognition of East Germany or to strengthen the unpopular communist regime of Walter Ulbricht by forcing a western withdrawal from Berlin. Either objective, if obtained, would discredit American leadership and weaken NATO. President Eisenhower refused to fall into either trap and made clear America's commitment to NATO and the defense of West Berlin. Khrushchev then accepted an invitation to tour America in 1959 and he agreed to another summit conference for mid-1960. Obviously Khrushchev was not prepared to risk an all-out war, yet his "conciliation" by Eisenhower represented a reversal of the Dulles policy of forcing the opponent to make concessions for peace.

Eisenhower's foreign policy problems mounted during his last two years in office. Not only did he face Castro in Cuba, unrest in Latin America, and growing neutralism in Europe, but reasons of health compelled his trusted adviser, John Foster Dulles, to resign as Secretary of State in April, 1959. In May, 1960, virtually on the eve of the summit conference scheduled the next month in Paris, the Soviets shot down a high-flying American U-2 airplane engaged in aerial espionage over the Soviet Union. Although all great powers engage in espionage, and the United States justifiably had been using the U-2 for four years to keep informed about Soviet missile and nuclear developments, the overflight technically represented a violation of Soviet airspace. It would have been wiser if at least this particular flight, so near the time of an important international conference, had been postponed. Compounding the blunder, Washington first issued a transparent "cover" story, and then admitted responsibility for the flight. Most foreign observers, horrified by such bungling, simply could not understand why Eisenhower had not remained silent or blandly denied any knowledge of the incident. Moreover, Eisenhower at first implied that the U-2 flights over Russia would continue. Russian propaganda exploited all this to the maximum. An apparently enraged Khrushchev berated Eisenhower personally at Paris and then walked out of the meeting. The Soviet leader cancelled Eisenhower's projected visit to the Soviet Union and announced that he would not resume negotiations until the general's successor took office.

Subsequently Khrushchev attended the session of the U.N. Assembly in New York where he rattled Soviet rockets and staged a crude desk-thumping shoe-waving personal display of truculence. Leftist anti-American riots in Tokyo further embarrassed the unfortunate Eisenhower by compelling him to cancel a planned visit to Japan. He left office deeply disappointed that he had not been able to accomplish more for peace. Yet though American prestige and leadership apparently had fallen into disarray by 1960, Khrushchev for all his boasting dared not touch his primary target, West Berlin.

Foreign policy became an overriding issue in the 1960 presidential election. How could the United States cope with growing Soviet power and yet advance the cause of peace? Senator John F. Kennedy of Massachusetts, wealthy, relatively young, handsome, and with a glamorous wife, outspent and outmaneuvered his rivals to emerge with the Democratic nomination. He chose Lyndon B. Johnson of Texas, majority leader in the Senate, as his running mate. The Republicans nominated Vice President Nixon, also relatively young and obviously well-versed in public affairs, as their candidate. Eight years of identification with Eisenhower "stand-pattism" at home and declining prestige abroad handicapped Nixon. Kennedy hammered away at the sluggish economy, Cuba, the missile gap, and Russia's lead in space. "I think it's time America started moving again," he declared at the end of his first televised debate with the Vice President. And apparently a majority of Americans agreed with him, although the election results were extremely close. Kennedy edged Nixon by less than 120,000 votes out of nearly 69 million votes cast.

A few days after he took office, at age 43 the youngest chief executive in American history, President Kennedy outlined a vigorous program to Congress. After briefly reviewing domestic issues, the new President noted that "all these problems pale when placed beside those which confront us all around the world. . . . the tide of events has been running out and time has not been our friend." With the support of Congress, the administration moved quickly to upgrade the nation's nuclear deterrent, increasing its land-based ICBM's and Polaris missile-firing submarines, and launching a massive effort to surpass Russia in the so-called space race. Kennedy adopted the advice of General Maxwell Taylor, who favored a graduated or flexible military response to any conceivable communist armed challenge. He advocated strengthening conventional as well as nuclear forces to permit the nation, in case of a challenge, to select any option from counterinsurgency methods in coping with "wars of national liberation" to conventional warfare, the use of tactical nuclear weapons, and, as the ultimate resort, the unleashing of the Strategic Air Command and land- and sea-based ICBM's. Defense spending rose sharply by $6 billion during Kennedy's first year in office.

It soon developed that no real missile gap had existed. Russia, perhaps because it was awaiting development of more advanced models, had built fewer than expected of the first generation liquid-fueled ICBM's. Sharply reversing earlier predictions, by 1963 the American crash program gave the United States an estimated three to one superiority in ICBM's over the Soviet Union. By 1965, the margin had increased to about four to one; thereafter, as the American program tapered off and Russia began a massive and costly effort to catch up, the margin of superiority declined until a rough parity existed by 1970 (because of the large size of its rockets, the Soviet Union long has held a decided lead in deliverable nuclear megatonnage). The American space program also paid off in remarkable progress in launching manned space craft and in exploring the solar system. The crowning achievement came in 1969, after Kennedy's death, when two Americans became the first men to land on the moon.

Two bold Kennedy innovations—the Peace Corps and the Alliance for Progress—captured the imagination of much of the world in the early 1960's. The Peace Corps sent abroad thousands of Americans, the majority of them filled with youthful energy and idealism, to assist underdeveloped countries in achieving modern skills and to give a practical demonstration of democracy at work. President Kennedy announced the Alliance for Progress early in 1961 and a hemispheric conference at Punta Del Este gave it formal approval in August of that year. The Alliance, obviously intended as a preventive to the spread of Castroism within the hemisphere, was designed as a broad-gauged assault upon the economic and social problems of Latin America. The United States pledged to make available over a billion dollars a year for the next decade, combined with public and private capital in Latin America and foreign private funds, in a massive program of industrial development and economic-social reforms within the region. Kennedy hoped Latin America as a whole would shortly achieve a sustained growth rate of five percent annually. Nineteen states—Cuba excluded—pledged appropriate land and tax reforms and increased expenditures for housing, health, and education.

Yet by the late 1960's the Alliance for Progress had fallen lamentably short of its goals. As critics complained, there was no alliance and very little progress. Productivity rose a feeble two percent, less than the population explosion sweeping much of Latin America. The conservative propertied classes opposed meaningful social and economic reforms. It proved impossible to raise investments to the desired level, because foreign capital was reluctant to risk future expropriations, while domestic capital too often flowed outside to safety in European and American bank vaults. Even the initial hopes for the emergence of a new era of democracy in Latin America proved a cruel disappointment as another wave of military coups and dictatorships swept the hemisphere in the mid-1960's. Some observers began to suspect that perhaps the goals sought by the Alliance could never be achieved by peaceful evolutionary and democratic means. By the mid-1960's Washington had lost interest in foreign aid programs and once more viewed Latin America with a degree of complacency. Castro had not yet succeeded in exporting his brand of revolution, while a Soviet Union, burdened for years with his costly support, apparently was not eager for any new client states in the Western Hemisphere. Yet resentment of the United States again has increased in Latin America and the rise to power in Chile of an elected Marxist chief executive in 1970 may portend a new era of crises within this hemisphere.

American relations with the so-called Third World, or states newly emerging from colonialism, with the exception of Vietnam, have experienced only moderate trouble. Japan, in a sense in this category because of American military occupation, recovered its sovereignty by the peace treaty signed at San Francisco in 1951. It has remained relatively disarmed since then, shielded by a security treaty with the United States that permitted the latter to retain military bases in Japan. Official relations have remained close, despite anti-Americanism among leftist students in Japan and economic competition. The two countries renegotiated the defense treaty in 1960, and in 1969 Washington temporarily satisfied renascent Japanese nationalism by agreeing to restore Okinawa to Japan. Americans had sympathized with India's struggle for independence, finally granted by the British in 1947. Yet under Prime Minister Jawaharlal Nehru and his successors, India often manifested dislike of America's Cold War policies and particularly its arming of India's rival, Pakistan. Clashes with that state and with its giant neighbor, China, led India to seek arms and aid from the Soviet Union. Nevertheless Washington by 1961 had granted or loaned India nearly $4 billion in economic assistance. The United States also played a role in the emergence of Indonesia, helping persuade the Dutch to grant its independence in 1948. Indonesia under the leadership of the charismatic but woefully impractical Achmed Sukarno, like Nehru, pursued a neutralist and even more clearly anti-American policy. His antics and his disputes with the Dutch, the Philippines, and Malaya over island territory kept the region in turmoil, while Russia and Red China generously financed his pet projects. His extravagances led to his overthrow in 1965 attended by a massacre of Indonesian Communists, and his successors have pursued a much more moderate policy toward the United States and its friends.

Thirty-nine states have emerged from colonial status in Africa since the end of World War II. The United States has never had a large economic interest in Black Africa nor much political contact with it until very recently. The Eisenhower and Kennedy administrations made modest amounts of American assistance available to these new nations, although the primary burden of foreign aid has fallen to the former colonial masters. Black African resentment of Portuguese colonialism in Angola, and of white supremacy in South Africa and the breakaway regime in Rhodesia, have caused Washington policy-makers some distress. The most acute difficulty came in the former Belgian Congo, given independence without adequate preparations in 1960 and immediately plunged into tribal warfare and secessionist plots. For a brief period it seemed that Soviet-American rivalry would extend the Cold War to that area, but both powers apparently decided that the game would not reap much profit or reward. A U.N. peace force helped end the incipient civil war in the Congo and fostered the re-absorption in 1963 of Katanga province, which had tried to secede.

The crisis over Berlin continued into the Kennedy era. Khrushchev reiterated his threat to sign a separate peace treaty with East Germany and to liquidate western rights in Berlin. Kennedy journeyed to Vienna in June, 1961 for a two-power discussion of this and related issues with the Soviet leader. Unfortunately the preceding fiasco at the Bay of Pigs had seriously weakened his prestige. Viewing Castroism as a serious danger to the security and tranquility of the Western Hemisphere, Kennedy had approved a plan begun by the previous administration for an invasion of Cuba by an American-trained and equipped force of Cuban exiles. He decided, however, that the American military would have no direct part in the operation nor provide air cover for the invaders. The result was a disaster. The exiles landed at the Bay of Pigs in April, only to be surrounded and forced to surrender by Castro's army. America's reputation suffered greatly, both because of its role in the operation and the abysmal failure. Khrushchev evidently concluded from the affair that Kennedy was indecisive and weak. Hence, he repeated his determination at the Vienna meeting to get the West Berlin "bone out of my throat," and he set a six-month time limit for a settlement. Russia, the Soviet Premier informed Kennedy, had "grown up" and in his heart he felt it was now superior in power to the United States. Although Kennedy did not flinch, the conference became a grim confrontation. Upon his return home, the President warned his countrymen of the grave crisis and called up military reserves to strengthen the defense of Western Europe and West Berlin. For a few days the world watched with horrified fascination as Allied and Soviet tank crews glared at each other across their leveled guns in Berlin. The crisis ebbed when the East Germans erected the Berlin Wall in August, 1961 to halt the flood of refugees from East to West Germany. The western powers condemned the wall as both cruel and a violation of a wartime agreement but they prudently refrained from trying to demolish it. Ulbricht at least had stopped the hemorrhaging of his state, and Khrushchev made no move to carry out his threats about Berlin.

Kennedy is reported to have remarked after the Bay of Pigs that the substance of power, not prestige, really counted in world affairs. In the following year he received a painful lesson to the contrary. Emboldened by the Cuban invasion fiasco, Khrushchev decided to challenge the United States within its own Caribbean sphere of influence by installing medium range ballistic missiles and bombers in Cuba. Apparently he expected Kennedy to bend before Russia's presumed missile superiority, and thus to bolster what in fact was a weaker force and to damage American prestige around the globe. Such a victory, he hoped, might yet wreck NATO and evict the West from Berlin. All during the summer and early fall of 1962 rumors circulated that Soviet offensive weapons and military personnel were being moved to Cuba. Washington maintained a careful scrutiny of the island but not until early October did a U-2 overflight gather clear evidence of the rapid construction of missile bases. Yet Soviet Foreign Minister Gromyko, on a visit to Washington shortly before the crisis broke, blandly denied to President Kennedy that Russia was installing offensive weapons in Cuba.

Kennedy decided to take decisive measures to prevent the successful installation of missiles in Cuba. He had to act at once to prevent the completion of the Soviet challenge, thereby disturbing the balance of power and laying much of the Western Hemisphere open to Soviet nuclear blackmail or attacks; later estimates showed that the Cuban missiles would have doubled the available megatonnage that Russia could use against the United States. Khrushchev was directing the kind of challenge toward the United States that it had wisely refrained from making toward Russia during the Berlin riots of 1953, the Hungarian Revolution in 1956, and later on, the Czechoslovakian invasion of 1968. After considering a quick air strike or an invasion, Kennedy decided upon a naval blockade to prevent the importation of additional rockets or bombers into Cuba. If Russia refused to remove those already on the island, Kennedy threatened that the United States would knock them out by force. On October 22, 1962, the President somberly warned the American people and the Russians of the dangerous crisis at hand. "The path we have chosen . . . is full of hazards. . . . ," he acknowledged, but there is "one path we shall never choose, and that is the path of surrender or submission." Khrushchev thus found himself facing a painful choice of retreat or risking an escalation of the crisis to a major war. He chose to retreat. In his first letter to Kennedy, an emotional and rambling epistle, he offered to recall the weapons if Kennedy would promise not to invade Cuba. A second, calmer letter asked in addition for the dismantling of American missiles in Turkey. Kennedy shrewdly chose to act upon the first letter and the Russians acquiesced. In effect, he promised not to invade Cuba if the weapons were withdrawn and removal verified by on-the-spot inspection; Castro refused to permit the latter. As Dean Rusk, the Secretary of State, aptly remarked, the two leaders had stood "eyeball to eyeball" and "the other fellow just blinked." Kennedy had displayed great courage and statesmanship in solving what was probably the most serious confrontation of the Cold War era. And equally important, leaders of both countries seem to have learned from the episode the necessity for greater caution in order to avoid another such dangerous confrontation. Yet the entire crisis probably would never have arisen if the United States had not needlessly risked its prestige at the Bay of Pigs.

Additional Reading

A good overview is provided by previously cited studies of the Cold War: John Spanier, *American Foreign Policy Since World War II* (rev. ed., 1971); Charles O. Lerche, Jr., *The Cold War . . . And After* (1965); John Lukacs, *A New History of the Cold War* (1966); Walter La Feber, *America, Russia, and the Cold War, 1945–1966* (1967); and Louis J. Halle, *The Cold War As History* (1967). Jules Davids, *America and the World of Our Time* (3rd ed., 1970) is an excellent general account. Apart from his not very informative memoirs, the best studies of Eisenhower are journalistic accounts: Marquis Childs' critical *Eisenhower: Captive Hero* (1958) and R. J. Donovan, *Eisenhower: The Inside Story* (1956). A scholarly study of the Dulles era is by Louis L. Gerson, "John Foster Dulles," vol. XVII (1967) in *The American Secretaries of State and Their Diplomacy,* edited by S. F. Bemis and R. H. Ferrell. His successor is covered by G. Bernard Noble, *Christian A. Herter* (1970). *Duel at the Brink* (1960) is a worthwhile journalistic version by Roscoe Drummond and Gaston Coblentz. The best account of the First Suez War is by an English historian, Hugh Tomas, *Suez* (1966). Herman Finer's *Dulles over Suez* (1964) is sharply critical of American policy, as is *The Suez Crisis of 1956* (1960), reprinted from the *Memoirs* of Anthony Eden. A useful contemporary summary is by Guy Wint and Peter Calvacoressi, *Middle East Crisis* (1957). American policy and Castro's revolution are examined by R. F. Smith, *The United States and Cuba: Business and Diplomacy, 1917–1960* (1960); Theodore Draper, *Castro's Revolution* (1962); and a more critical version by H. L. Matthews, *The Cuban Story* (1961). C. Wright Mills, *Listen Yankee!* (1960) is the forerunner of New Left critiques of American policy toward Castro. The best study is by Ramón Eduardo Ruiz, *Cuba, The Making of a Revolution* (1968). An excellent study of American arms policy in Latin America is by Edwin Lieuwen, *Arms and Politics in Latin America* (1960). A general account of the Kennedy era is *To Move a Nation* (1967), by Roger Hilsman, an official in the State Department during that administration. Two other accounts by participants are by Arthur M. Schlesinger, Jr., *A Thousand Days: John F. Kennedy in the White House* (1965) and Theodore C. Sorenson, *Kennedy* (1965). On the Alliance for Progress, see Karl M. Schmitt's "Contradictions and Conflicts in U.S. Foreign Policy: The Case of Latin America,"

No. 7, *Offprint Series* (1969) of the Institute of Latin American Studies, and Abraham F. Lowenthal's "Alliance Rhetoric versus Latin American Reality," *Foreign Affairs,* Vol. 48 (1970), 494–508. Robert F. Kennedy provides an inside report on the Cuban missile crisis, *Thirteen Days* (1969). See too Elie Abel, *The Missile Crisis* (1966). On African relations, see Rupert Emerson, *Africa and United States Policy* (1967). A short interpretive account emphasizing recent Chinese-American relations is by Paul S. Holbo, *United States Policies Toward China* (1969).

President Kennedy signs the Test Ban Treaty

25

THE WANING OF THE COLD WAR, 1960'S AND 1970'S

1. AN ERA OF DETENTE?

Some observers have argued that by the 1970's the Cold War either has come to an end or has changed into a less dangerous form of great power competition. Since 1962 the United States and the Soviet Union have indicated in words and in actions their realization that both countries possess more than enough nuclear weapons to destroy each other and render much of the world uninhabitable. Yet the "balance of terror" remains unstable and only time will tell whether or not the two powers have really perceived the incredible danger of continuing the nuclear arms race in search of what can only be an illusion of superiority.

Paradoxically the Cuban missile crisis fathered a detente or period of improved relations and a search for a measure of agreement between the two superpowers. In the aftermath of that nerve-wracking crisis, both powers seem to have resolved to avoid such dangerous confrontations in the future. The growing Soviet–Red China rift also seems to have spurred Russia to seek better relations with the West. One sign of this more sober climate came with the creation of the Moscow-Washington "hot line" or communication link to facilitate a quick exchange of views in case of major crisis. The conclusion of the Nuclear Test Ban Treaty in mid-1963, effective on October 10 of that year, represented another harbinger of detente. An earlier informal suspension of nuclear testing had lasted from 1958 to 1961, after which the Soviet Union and then the United States resumed test firing. The formal ban applied only to surface, atmospheric, and outer space testing, because of Russia's refusal to agree to an effective inspection system, but at least it halted pollution of the atmosphere by nuclear fallout. The world hailed the treaty as a milestone pointing toward significant arms limitations, although both Red China and France refused to impede their nuclear development programs by signing the ban. Kennedy contributed further to the improving climate by agreeing to help Russia cope with recent crop failures by selling her American wheat valued at one-fourth of a billion dollars. Despite the strain of Vietnam, the detente has continued during both the Johnson and Nixon administrations. After Red China exploded a nuclear device in 1964, Khrushchev revealed a sudden interest in an agreement to retard the dispersion of nuclear weapons. Negotiations led to the conclusion of the Nuclear Nonproliferation Treaty in June, 1968, signed by the two super powers and over 78 other nations. The United States delayed formal ratification until March, 1970, owing to western resentment of the Soviet invasion of Czechoslovakia. France and Red China also refused to recognize this treaty, raising serious questions about its long-term value.

Khrushchev fell from power in October, 1964. His demotion apparently reflected the unhappiness of his colleagues in the Kremlin with his foreign policy failures in Cuba, his public displays of boorishness in diplomacy, and his inability to repair the rift with Red China. Mao Tse-tung had objected strongly to Khrushchev's de-Stalinization policy, and he denounced the Soviet leader's warm smiles toward the West as revisionism or deviationism from the true gospel of Marxist-Leninism. It seems that the breaking point between Peking and Moscow came when Khrushchev declined to provide Red China with nuclear and other modern weapons during the 1958 crisis in the Formosa Straits. The rift became so sharp that in 1960 Khrushchev withdrew Soviet military and economic advisers from China and halted Soviet economic assistance to its communist ally. Yet his repeated attempts to rally the rest of the communist world to Russia's side in the ideological dispute with Mao failed. National communism or polycentrism had by then become too strong in Communist Rumania and within the communist movements elsewhere for any return to monolithic control by Moscow. Khrushchev's successors, Aleksei Kosygin and Leonid Brezhnev, had no more success in restoring a semblance of unity to world communism.

The ideological cold war between the two rival citadels of communism flared into armed border clashes and territorial disputes along the long Sino-Soviet frontier during the mid-1960's. Kosygin and Brezhnev meanwhile continued the detente with Washington. In 1966 they reached an agreement for direct air service to link Moscow and New York City. The following year they signed a consular treaty and concluded a multilateral pact banning nuclear weapons from outer space. Despite a threatened arms race in MIRV's (multiple independently targeted re-entry vehicles—i.e., several nuclear warheads on a single rocket) and ABM's (antiballistic missiles), the United States and the Soviet Union greatly encouraged world hopes for peace by undertaking the SALT talks in 1969–72. These aimed at achieving a Strategic Arms Limitation Treaty.

Obviously the road to any such agreement will be extremely difficult, involving questions of mutual trust and an effective inspection system.

2. THE TORCH IS PASSED

Americans, and indeed people all over the world, were deeply shocked and saddened by President Kennedy's assassination in Dallas, Texas, on November 22, 1963. The senseless slaying of the young and promising President plunged the nation into deep mourning. Although in office for too short a period to accomplish many of the goals of his "New Frontier," Kennedy's sense of style and the intelligence he brought to bear upon problems, and his tragic death, have earned him a high place in the affection and memories of the American people and of countless millions abroad. Perhaps the most important contributions of his short presidency were his firm, wise handling of the Cuban missile crisis and the subsequent beginnings of a detente with Soviet Russia.

Lyndon B. Johnson, an able politician and former Democratic leader of the Senate, succeeded Kennedy in office. Intelligent and deeply patriotic, the tall and lugubrious-appearing Texan sincerely sought to create a post–New Dealish "Great Society" for America and even for the world. His fatal flaw arose from his excessive sensitivity to criticism and his stubborn pride that made him unduly rigid in his policies and extremely reluctant to admit error or to alter course. His secretiveness and his reputation as an arch–congressional manipulator soon earned him the distrust of the press and a so-called "credibility gap" with the public. Signs of this existed even before Vietnam became a burning issue, and he ended his term as one of the least trusted and least admired chief executives in our history. Yet already it seems safe to say that his record in achieving notable domestic social legislation will rank him high among our outstanding presidents. Even in foreign policy, where he faced the most intense criticism, his record may seem much better in the eyes of future historians than his own generation would admit.

Johnson was a strong chief executive in foreign policy. He wielded to the maximum the immense powers and prestige of that office built up during the hot and cold wars of this century. He believed in the necessity of taking to heart the "lessons" of Munich and the Cold War—foreign bullies had to be forewarned and checked, not appeased. Johnson detested weakness and was thoroughly imbued with the psychology of the Cold War. Communism remained a global menace, he thought, and the United States had to contain it wherever it threatened aggression against peaceful states and peoples. Johnson's toughness was rooted in his conviction of the morality and soundness of America's role as a world policeman. He supported the idea that great power had to be used responsibly. As he reportedly remarked to a journalist, "The real danger is that the other side is going to underestimate us—it's happened before. The danger is that they'll think we are fat and fifty—just the country-club crowd."

American intervention in the Dominican Republic in April, 1965 revealed Johnson's resolve not to tolerate another potential Castro in the Caribbean. The Dominican Republic had suffered under one of the oldest and most repressive dictatorships in Latin America until the assassination in 1961 of its aging and egoistic caudillo, General Rafael Leonidas Trujillo. For a brief period the republic at last seemed ready for democracy when Dr. Juan Bosch, a liberal reformer but inept politician, was elected President. Conservative elements rallied around the military, however, which soon overthrew Bosch's disintegrating regime and drove him into exile. The military junta failed to cope satisfactorily with the republic's economic problems, and it, too, was overthrown in April of 1965. The triumphant rebels then split into a conservative faction and a pro-Boschist group that contained some Communists and admirers of Castro's revolution. Heavy fighting broke out in Santo Domingo, the capital city, between these two factions. Washington, apparently exaggerating the dangers of a Castro-like government if Bosch returned to power, decided on April 28 to intervene by armed force to prevent that possibility. The immediately announced reason for intervention, no doubt genuine so far as it went, was to protect American lives endangered by the civil war raging in Santo Domingo. Again overreacting in the view of many critics, President Johnson sent over 30,000 marines, soldiers, and sailors to restore order and in effect to prevent a Bosch victory.

The Dominican affair shocked and infuriated much of Latin America. The United States appeared to be returning to the hated interventionism of the past. Moreover, the so-called Johnson Doctrine, intimated though not formally proclaimed by the administration, held forth the prospect of further interventions if necessary to ward off the spread of Castroism within the hemisphere. Johnson had not consulted the Organization of American States before he acted. Only after the fact did the United States persuade the O.A.S., by a vote of 14 to five with one abstention, to provide the mantle of a hemispheric peace force to cover the naked American intervention in the republic. Johnson's critics in the United States, including the Chairman of the Senate Committee on Foreign Relations, J. William Fulbright, sharply questioned the danger of a communist coup in the Dominican Republic. Although the O.A.S. sanctioned the intervention, the most ardent endorsements came from the military dictatorships in Argentina and Brazil, while such countries as Mexico and Chile refused to cooperate. Moreover, Washington failed in its efforts to create an interhemispheric force for use against any future threats of communist revolutions in Latin America. From a short-term point of view, however, the Dominican intervention succeeded. A truce was established between the factions within the republic, free elections were held, and an apparently stable government safely installed before the O.A.S. peace-keeping force withdrew in September, 1966.

3. THE DECLINE OF NATO

In striking contrast to Soviet attempts to impose its rule upon Eastern Europe, the United States followed a constructive course toward Western Europe during the years of the Cold War. One of Washington's major goals was to encourage the evolution of Western Europe toward a greater degree of economic, political, and military unity. The Marshall Plan and the creation of NATO contributed greatly to that end. For a while a United States of Europe, allied to America but able to stand upon its own feet, seemed a very real possibility. In 1957, the formation of the European Common Market capped previous measures to integrate the coal and steel industries of Western Europe. France, Italy, West Germany, and the Benelux countries banded together to integrate their entire economies and to remove all tariff barriers over a period of years. To its subsequent regret, Great Britain chose not to join, preferring instead to remain outside and thus preserve its special relations with the United States and the Commonwealth nations. Britain then took the lead in forming a looser trading bloc, known as the Outer Seven, but it proved a poor substitute for membership in the thriving Common Market. Therefore, in 1963 Britain knocked on the door of the Common Market and requested admission, only to meet repeated rebuffs.

The principal cause of Britain's rejection, and indeed the spoiler of the movement for greater European unification, was Charles de Gaulle of France. De Gaulle had retired from the presidency shortly after the war, in disgust at divisive French politics. Recalled by popular demand during the Algerian crisis in 1958, de Gaulle saved France from revolution and obtained popular approval for a system of strong presidential leadership. He planned to rebuild French power and greatness, determined to end what he regarded as Europe's supine dependence upon the United States. Initially he sought an agreement with Washington and London for a tripartite directorship of NATO. Rebuffed and resentful of American attempts to discourage France's nuclear program, he concentrated upon building an independent nuclear force that would restore a measure of great-power prestige to his country. De Gaulle objected to the preponderant American influence in Western Europe and to its plans for unification of the continent. In his periodic Delphic utterances, de Gaulle indicated his grand design for a Europe led by France, that would stand free both of America and the Soviet Union, and that eventually might also bring the Russian east within its folds. In short, while retaining the North Atlantic Alliance, and behind the shield of the American strategic deterrent (de Gaulle's nuclear force could hardly be more than a pinprick in an all-out war) the French leader sought to exclude the United States from the affairs of Europe. Hence, he turned a deaf ear to President Kennedy's July Fourth call in 1962 for a declaration of interdependence between North America and Western Europe, a closer partnership between the NATO allies. Since in his view Great Britain was slavishly dependent upon the United States and refused to sever its ties with that non-European state, he also vetoed the British application in 1963 for membership in the Common Market. He made clear what Britain would have to do before he would permit its admittance, and he effectively blocked her subsequent applications; not until 1971, after de Gaulle's resignation, did the Common Market at last agree to admit the British. For the same reason, de Gaulle cultivated closer relations with West Germany, and he rejected Kennedy's plans for a Multilateral Nuclear Force or a form of nuclear sharing with NATO because it left control in American hands.

De Gaulle dealt a major blow to the movement for European unity and partnership with the United States. He began to respond warmly to Soviet overtures, spoke of a possible all-European settlement of Cold War issues (without American participation), and demonstrated his independence from Washington's foreign policy by recognizing Red China in 1964. In that year he also began a gradual process of dissociation from NATO. By 1966, he announced France's complete withdrawal of its military forces from NATO's integrated command structure, although not from the alliance itself. He compelled NATO headquarters, bases, and personnel to evacuate French soil by April, 1967. Prior to his resignation in 1969, de Gaulle acted as a frequent and astringent critic of American foreign policy, especially in Vietnam.

It would be an oversimplification, however, to attribute the atrophy of NATO and the waning of the movement for European unity solely to Charles de Gaulle. He more symbolized than caused that trend. The basic cause arose from the success of American policies to rebuild and to revitalize Western Europe. American actions had pumped new life into Europe's almost moribund economic and social systems after World War II and had provided security for the continent by checking Soviet expansionism. This laid the groundwork for the economic and national revival of Europe. By 1970, a quarter of a century after the ending of Europe's most destructive modern war, the nations of Western Europe enjoyed more prosperity and affluence than ever before, and began to rival their great benefactor and patron in the blessings, and the curses, of a high standard of living. Fears of Soviet aggression largely faded away, and a new mood of security and prosperity reigned on the continent, which not even the Soviet invasion of Czechoslovakia in 1968 could long discourage. Even the long-smouldering Berlin crisis seemed to lift as Russia in 1971 agreed with the West on assured access routes to that city. It was inevitable under these changed circumstances that Western

Europe should begin to end its abnormal dependence upon the United States.

4. THE VIETNAM MORASS

No one person or administration can be blamed for the Vietnam entrapment. If blame must be fixed, it might be better placed upon the American people themselves and upon their historic beliefs, values, and attitudes. Although the United States long has ranked among the great powers of the world, it really matured as a responsible world power only during the era of the Cold War. Far too many illusions of innocence and morality have carried over into this era from a long-gone Age of Free Security, from outdated concepts of America's unique mission to spread its democratic, political, and economic institutions throughout the world, and from assumptions of America's moral superiority and omnipotence. The American people and their elected leaders developed a common set of Cold War beliefs and attitudes: communism was an evil political-social system and a worldwide menace centered in Moscow, and in Peking to a degree; it was inherently aggressive and expansionist; and it must be resisted wherever it reared its head, with the United States necessarily assuming the primary burden of its containment and ultimate defeat. Accurate enough during the Stalin era, this Cold War syndrome there-after became increasingly unrealistic as the communist monolith cracked and splintered, and the focus of American concern shifted from Europe to Asia and Africa. Americans too readily saw the evil of communism behind the anticolonial and nationalist revolutions that swept much of the underdeveloped "Third World," and they failed to realize that as great as their power was it had definite limitations in coping with such upheavals.

The involvement of the United States in Vietnam began in a serious way during France's attempt to suppress the communist-led movement for national independence in that colony. Vietnamese nationalism and anti-French sentiment long antedated World War II, but the Japanese occupation and the subsequent French effort to reestablish their colonial rule greatly quickened it. Ho Chi Minh, a Moscow-trained communist, had established the Vietnamese Communist Party in 1930. During the Japanese occupation, he captured the nationalist movement through a broad-front organization known as the Vietminh. By the time France tried to restore its authority in 1946, Ho's so-called democratic republic already controlled much of the country. For a brief period an acceptable compromise seemed possible, with Vietnam becoming a free state within the French Union. Mutual distrust and charges of bad faith, however, led to the outbreak of a full-scale colonial war in late 1946. Destined to last for seven and a half years, the war cost France the lives of 74,000 soldiers before the French people demanded an end.

France established Bao Dai as the nominal ruler of the "free state" of Vietnam within the French Union, and both the British and the Americans recognized his government in 1950. It was virtually inevitable, in the aftermath of the Korean War, that the American government and people would view the war in Vietnam as instigated by Moscow and Peking. They considered Ho Chi Minh and the Vietminh as puppets or agents of aggressive communism, whose victory would upset the balance of power and encourage further aggression in Southeast Asia. They saw France's colonial war, therefore, as a vital part of the worldwide struggle to contain communism. For these reasons, both the Truman and Eisenhower administrations underwrote much of the costs of the French war effort, paying for over 78 percent by 1954, or a total of about $3 billion in arms aid. Secretary of State Dulles declared that "At the moment, Indochina is the area where international communism most vigorously seeks expansion. . . . ," while President Eisenhower warned that the entire area resembled a row of dominoes, of which the fall of one would lead inevitably to the fall of the others. Yet, when the French fortress of Dienbienphu was about to fall to the Vietminh besiegers in 1954, Eisenhower overruled his advisers and refused to authorize the use of American air strikes or ground troops to aid the French. Eisenhower obviously was loath to become entangled in the ground war in Indochina, particularly without British cooperation, which was not forthcoming. A poll revealed that a majority of Americans agreed with his decision, favoring military aid to France but opposing the sending of American troops to Vietnam.

The first phase of the Indochina War terminated at the Geneva conference in mid-1954. Nineteen nations, including Red China and the Soviet Union, but not South Vietnam, sent representatives to this conference, called to deal with the problems of Korea and Indochina. France accepted a settlement that provided for a cease-fire in Indochina, the division of Vietnam along the 17th parallel, and the evacuation of French troops to the south, and of Vietminh forces to the north of that parallel. The settlement permitted a mutual exchange of those Vietnamese desiring to move to either area and subsequently nearly a million people, mostly Catholic Vietnamese, left North Vietnam for the South, versus less than a hundred thousand who chose to leave for the North. Laos and Cambodia gained recognition as independent states. Canada, India, and Poland formed an International Joint Commission to supervise the carrying-out of these agreements. The Final Declaration at Geneva termed the partition a temporary one and called for free elections in 1956 in both halves to determine the future of Vietnam. The American representative at Geneva refused to sign the agreement, because President Eisenhower and Secretary Dulles still viewed Russia and Red China as the instigators of the Vietnamese movement led by Ho Chi Minh and objected to becoming a party to a settlement that abandoned some 13

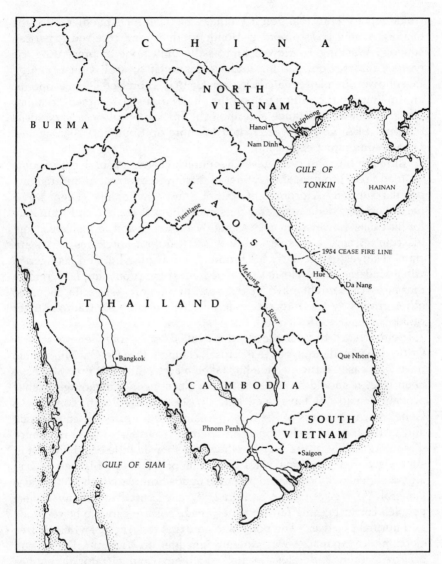

Southeast Asia, 1954

million people to Red rule. The United States, however, independently promised to refrain from disturbing the settlement, warned against further aggression, and said that it favored reunification of Vietnam if supervised free elections were held. Ho Chi Minh accepted less than he desired, or even held, because he expected France to carry out the pledges and felt confident that he would win the 1956 election.

The North Vietnamese dictator failed to foresee that the United States would replace France in South Vietnam. Ngo Dinh Diem emerged as the head of a new government in South Vietnam and received American support. Washington viewed him as the only hope of preventing the entire country from passing under communist control. Consequently, Eisenhower, in a letter dated October 23, 1954, promised Diem economic and military aid conditional upon the ability of his government to utilize effectively such assistance and upon the institution of necessary social reforms. SEATO also was created to shore up Southeast Asia against further communist expansion.

Although few observers gave Diem much chance to survive, for a time he made real progress in creating an effective government and rallying popular support. A prominent Catholic and a nationalist, Diem was a hard working, dedicated, and personally honest leader. Unfortunately for his cause, however, he proved highly autocratic and self-isolated from his countrymen. Moreover, he was saddled with ambitious and avaricious relatives, particularly his brother, Ngo Dinh Nhu, and his tigerish wife, Madame Nhu. He never carried out some promising land reform measures that might have rallied peasant support, while he alienated other groups by his autocratic rule and his partiality for Catholics over Buddhists.

Diem refused to hold the elections called for by the Geneva accord. Critics have made much of that refusal, claiming that Ho Chi Minh could have won easily if the election had taken place. While that may well have been true, it should be noted that free elections in a meaningful sense probably could not have been held in 1956. In the South, contrary to Geneva, armed cadres of Vietminh remained to terrorize the countryside and to frustrate free elections and Diem of course also tried to silence dissenters; while in the North, where Ho showed little or no interest in supervised free elections within his half of Vietnam, his agents had already liquidated or silenced potential opposition. As North Vietnamese General Vo Nguyen Giap admitted, "We executed too many honest people. Terror became far too widespread. Torture came to be regarded as a normal practice." The point is to note that the American faith in free elections as a panacea was woefully unsuited to Vietnam. Repression occurred, then and later, in both Vietnams and dictatorial regimes developed in both halves of the country.

The second phase of the Indochina War began in mid-1958. This time the United States did not escape direct involvement. Violations of the Geneva agreements occurred on both sides of the border. In withdrawing from the South, the Vietminh left behind hidden stores of arms and trained cadres that subsequently tried to organize village cells against Diem. For his part, Diem harassed opposition groups and refused to consult with the North on the holding of free elections. The Vietminh criticized the Saigon regime as an American puppet and by 1958 launched a campaign of guerrilla attacks and assassinations to wreck the government's reform programs and to deprive Diem of local support. From 1956 on, several hundred American military advisers, eventually exceeding the Geneva limits, arrived to help train the Vietnamese army, usually concentrating upon conventional military rather than antiguerrilla tactics. By the end of 1958, the Vietcong (Vietnamese Communist) controlled large areas of the countryside, and southerners who had gone North in 1954 and had been retrained were recalled to the South to terrorize civilians and attack the Saigon government. The Vietcong frequently assassinated hamlet and village chiefs, local security officials, and teachers in order to paralyze Saigon and establish Vietcong authority in the villages and countryside. By 1960, the Vietcong controlled an estimated one-third to one-half of South Vietnam and put Diem's forces, though numerically stronger, on the defensive. Until mid-1964, southerners apparently constituted most of the Vietcong; after that time, problems of recruitment required an increasing infusion of North Vietnamese into Vietcong ranks.

Kennedy as President faced the prospect of the anticommunist government in South Vietnam losing the war against the Vietcong. Both he and Vice President Johnson shared the opinion of the outgoing Eisenhower administration that the interests of America and the non-communist world required the suppression of the Vietcong. From a later perspective, it seems that they exaggerated both the dangers of a communist triumph in South Vietnam for the rest of Southeast Asia and the degree of American interest in that region. Yet they merely reflected the prevailing national state of mind. Kennedy saw the problem in the South as more political than military and he tried to develop an effective counter to the guerrillas based upon social reform and counterinsurgency techniques. He stepped up American aid to the Saigon government and sent larger numbers of American military advisers—16,000 by late 1963—to help implement the new approach. After an initially optimistic period, by 1963 it became painfully clear that the Vietcong were growing stronger rather than weaker. Diem's rule became increasingly unpopular, and he encountered severe difficulties with the Buddhists. A number of Buddhist monks dramatized their unhappiness with Diem by grisly self-immolation, and while Madame Nhu sneered at "barbecued monks" such demonstrations deeply impressed a horrified world.

On November 1, 1963, apparently with American encouragement or at least acquiescence, South Vietnamese generals overthrew Diem. Whether Kennedy, if he had lived, would have thrown additional troops into South Vietnam to save it from collapse of course cannot be answered. We do know that he had sent troops to Thailand when communist forces threatened to overwhelm Laos in 1962, until a fourteen-nation conference at Geneva in July agreed upon the neutralization of that kingdom. And shortly before his death, the President reaffirmed America's stake in South Vietnam: " . . . for us to withdraw from that effort would mean a collapse not only of South Vietnam but Southeast Asia. So we are going to stay there."

During the first months after he succeeded the murdered Kennedy, Johnson opposed taking a direct role in the Vietnamese conflict. Yet each week made clearer the insufficiency of Kennedy's methods to thwart a Vietcong victory. Not until after he defeated Barry Goldwater, the hawkish Republican nominee for the presidency in 1964, did Johnson decide to send large numbers of American ground forces to South Vietnam. By then the choice was painfully obvious: either direct American involvement or the loss of South Vietnam to the Vietcong and Ho Chi Minh. Johnson and his key advisers, carry-overs from the Kennedy years such as McGeorge Bundy, Walt W. Rostow, Secretary of Defense Robert McNamara, and Secretary of State Dean Rusk, had no doubt that Red China sought to dominate all Southeast Asia and supported North Vietnam's "aggression" against the South.

In early August, 1964, several North Vietnamese torpedo boats attacked or threatened some American naval vessels in the Gulf of Tonkin. Firmly believing in the use of force as the only way to deal with aggressors, President Johnson ordered retaliatory strikes against North Vietnamese naval bases. Congress at his request passed the Gulf of Tonkin Resolution on August 7, by heavy majorities, authorizing the executive to take "all necessary measures" to prevent future aggression against American forces and to aid the countries of Southeast Asia in their struggle to preserve their freedom. Although many members of Congress later regretted this "blank check" to the chief executive, the Tonkin Resolution clearly defined Southeast Asia as vital to America's national interests. Early in 1965 the President ordered massive aerial assaults against North Vietnam, initially in retaliation for Vietcong terror raids against American forces in South Vietnam and subsequently as part of a campaign to isolate the Vietcong from outside support and manpower. In a steady process of escalation, Johnson sent ground combat forces to South Vietnam, always in the hope that a few thousand more men and a few more months of intensified fighting would bring a decisive victory over the Vietcong. As Johnson remarked to a group of soldiers, he wanted the Vietcong "coonskin" brought home and nailed to our door.

But the wily opponent fought on. By early 1966, over 200,000 American troops were in South Vietnam and by mid-1968 the total rose to over a half-million men. Financial costs of the war increased to approximately $30 billion a year, retarding expenditures for needed domestic social reforms and eventually resulting in a spiral of inflation and rising prices. The number of Americans killed in this cruel and ugly war grew steadily. By June, 1970, more Americans had lost their lives in South Vietnam than in the Korean War, 42,265 to 33,629. During the same period an estimated 107,579 South Vietnamese soldiers had lost their lives and 643,209 Vietcong–North Vietnamese. No one knows how many Vietnamese civilians died from Allied sweeps and bombings and from enemy raids and assassinations, but the total is surely vast.

Johnson's escalation of the war saved the South Vietnamese regime from defeat, but at the price of Americanizing the conflict. As more American troops entered into the fray, more North Vietnamese forces infiltrated into the South via the so-called Demilitarized Zone along the 17th parallel and the "Ho Chi Minh Trail" through Laos and Cambodia. Opposition to the apparently endless involvement began to mount within the United States, and the spectacle of a mighty super power raining devastation upon both Vietnams appalled much of the world. Many critics saw a gross and hence immoral disparity between American ends and the means being utilized—concentrated artillery fire, saturation bombing, napalm and flame throwers, and tear gas and chemical defoliants. With a mounting feeling of moral outrage came serious questioning of the reasons for American involvement. Was Vietnam, and for that matter all Southeast Asia, really that vital to the security of the United States and its friends? Was not the Vietnamese War in origin essentially a civil war, in which the United States should not have intervened? As intellectuals and liberals began to question the war, a wave of protest "teach-ins" swept American college campuses during the spring of 1965 and after.

Many critics of Vietnam voiced fears that Red China might be provoked into entering the war—significantly, it did not—and charged Johnson with waging an unconstitutional war because undeclared by Congress. The latter charge overlooked that Johnson had adequate precedent for waging an undeclared war and that Congress had approved it in a sense by appropriating money for that struggle and by passing the Tonkin Resolution. Moreover, while it is embarrassing to declare war against an unrecognized government, Johnson probably could have obtained such a declaration if he had sought it in 1965–1967. The country tended to divide into "hawks" who approved the war, "hard-liners" who urged even more drastic measures to win the conflict, and "doves" who advocated a de-escalation or a pullout. President Johnson personally became the target of a rising tide of criticism and charges of a "credibility gap" between his professions of a desire for an honorable peace and his steady escalation of the war. Until March, 1968, however, polls revealed that a majority of Americans approved the intervention in Vietnam.

The Tet offensive marked the turning point both in the war and in popular support for the war. In January and February of 1968, Vietcong and North Vietnamese units launched a furious and suicidal wave of attacks upon the principal cities in South Vietnam. These assaults were repulsed and with heavy losses to the enemy, but their very occurrence in the presence of over half a million American troops shook the confidence of the American people and fatally undermined Johnson's war policies. The American military leaders claimed that the Tet offensive resulted in a major defeat for the enemy, which apparently was true, but psychologically it served as a victory for their cause. Similar to the French people a decade and a half earlier, the American public after Tet revealed a growing disgust with limited action or weariness with the endless war in the jungles and rice paddies of Vietnam. More and more people perceived that while American intervention had denied victory to the Vietcong, we failed to win an essentially guerrilla war in a country where the masses of the people seemed either pro–Viet Cong or apathetic. Harassed at every turn and unable to make a public appearance without being heckled, President Johnson decided to bow out of office as gracefully as possible. He announced in late March, 1968, that he had ordered a restriction in the bombing of North Vietnam and that he would not seek re-election in 1968. Subsequently, exploratory conversations began in Paris with North Vietnamese representatives. A complete halt in the bombing of the North, announced in late October, cleared the path for a four-way conference that included the Saigon regime and the Vietcong.

5. TOWARD A MORE REALISTIC INTERNATIONALISM?

Vietnam became the overriding issue in the 1968 presidential race. Hubert H. Humphrey, Johnson's Vice President and political heir, rallied Democratic party regulars behind his candidacy and tried to stake out, insofar as his delicate position would permit, a moderate policy on Vietnam. Senator Eugene McCarthy of Minnesota, and more belatedly the late President's brother, Senator Robert F. Kennedy of New York mobilized Democratic "doves." Antiwar youths enthusiastically launched what wits called a "children's crusade" for the poetry-writing McCarthy. The faction-ridden Democrats also faced the defection of Alabama's Governor George C. Wallace and his running mate, General Curtis Le May, who spoke of bombing North Vietnam back into the stone age. The assassination of Senator Kennedy in Los Angeles during the primary cast a pall over the nation and heightened fears that the country was entering a new era of domestic violence.

Republicans anticipated victory with growing confidence as signs of Democratic factionalism multiplied. That essentially hawkish old standard-bearer, Richard Nixon, won the G.O.P. nomination. Nixon and his vice presidential running mate, Governor Spiro Agnew of Maryland, tried to capitalize on public unease by emphasizing the need for "law and order" at home and an honorable peace in Vietnam. Nixon thus softened his earlier position on the Vietnam War, promising in an Eisenhowerish gesture that if elected he would "end the war and win the peace." The Democratic convention in Chicago left the party in shambles. Humphrey won the nomination but at the price of deep divisions within the party. Moreover, during the convention, Chicago police subdued a near-riotous antiwar demonstration. Youthful militants flaunted the Vietcong flag and screamed obscenities or hurled objects at the police, who retaliated with what many television and press observers described as excessive force and brutality. The "battle of Chicago" polarized the nation and increased Humphrey's woes. Nixon thus emerged the winner on election day by an extremely close margin, receiving 43.4 percent of the popular vote to 42.7 percent for Humphrey and 13.5 percent for Wallace.

The new administration began slowly to wind down the American role in the Vietnam War. As the deadlock continued in the Paris talks, President Nixon unveiled his strategy to "Vietnamize" the conflict, combining reductions in American troops with an intensive effort to prepare the South Vietnamese army to take over the burden of the fighting. The President and his White House adviser on foreign affairs, Harvard professor Henry A. Kissinger, thereby hoped to assuage domestic critics of the war and at the same time to pressure North Vietnam into meaningful negotiations. As a warning to Hanoi of American power, Nixon, in April, 1970, sent American forces into Cambodia to prevent the Communists from overrunning that strategic country. A storm of protest again erupted on American college campuses and redoubled the efforts of congressional doves to clip the executive's war-making powers. The Cambodian operation seems to have been a tactical success, and by June, American forces had retired to South Vietnam. Meanwhile the pace of American withdrawal from South Vietnam continued, until by May, 1971 300,000 troops had left. The Paris talks, however, droned on in an endless round of charge and countercharge and propagandistic appeals. Not even Nixon's offer of a standstill cease fire could resolve the deadlock. Although the North Vietnamese forces appeared seriously weakened they fought on, insisting as the price of peace upon a complete American withdrawal and the formation of a coalition government in Saigon that would exclude the leaders of the present Thieu-Ky regime. On its part, the Nixon administration obviously refused to accept what it regarded as a defeat and in effect insisted the other side settle for far less than it sought.

Periods of vigorous presidential leadership in America have often been followed by renewed attempts by Congress to reassert legislative powers against what it views as an overgrown executive. The Vietnam War particularly heightened this traditional rivalry between the two branches of the federal government. Congressmen hurled charges at President Johnson that he was waging an undeclared and therefore unconstitutional war and that administrative foreign aid commitments might also bring about armed involvements in Laos and Cambodia. Nixon inescapably fell heir to such criticism, as "Johnson's War" became "Nixon's War." In June, 1969 the Senate adopted a nonbinding resolution advising the President that any future national commitments abroad involving the use of American forces must have congressional approval. The administration itself asked Congress to rescind the Gulf of Tonkin Resolution (completed in January, 1971). Even the House of Representatives, more conservative and more hawkish in the Vietnam War than the Senate, adopted a resolution in November, 1970 that recognized the emergency war powers of the President but requested advance consultation with Congress whenever possible before he invoked them. The publication of the "Pentagon Papers" in mid-1971, secret documents on the Viet-namese War illegally released by a former official, heightened criticism of executive secrecy and war-making in the Johnson era and redoubled critics' efforts to compel withdrawal from Vietnam. The administration, however, prevented Senate passage of the McGovern-Hatfield amend-ment to cut off all spending in the Vietnam War by a specified date. Of course these resolutions did not and could not curtail the chief executive's constitutional powers to use the armed forces as he deemed necessary nor his primary responsibility in formulating foreign policy. They did have the practical effect, no doubt, of causing Nixon and probably his immediate successors to act more cautiously in foreign affairs in the future.

The troubled national mood in the 1960's led to a searching re-examination of American foreign policy. An increasingly vocal number of citizens began to conclude that the Cold War at last had ended and that the nation should revise its policies to fit the new realities of the international scene. Some spokesmen, such as President Nixon, have admitted that an updating is clearly necessary but have expressed great fear that emotional reactions to Vietnam may result in a revival of isolationism. That formed the essence of Nixon's speech at the Air Force Academy on June 4, 1969. The simple formulas of the new isolationists, he warned, "would be disastrous for our nation and the world. . . . There is no advancement for Americans at home in a retreat from the problems of the world," he declared. "I say that America has a vital national interest in world stability, and no other nation can uphold that interest for us." Subsequently during his Asian tour in the summer of 1969, the President enumerated a "Nixon Doctrine" for that area. The United States would honor its treaty commitments and would stand ready to cope with any communist nuclear threats or attacks upon a country deemed vital to the security of the United States and of Asia. For other kinds of aggression, by which Nixon apparently meant internal subversion and border clashes, the United States would supply aid while relying upon the governments directly concerned to assume the main responsibility for coping with those dangers. In other words, no more Vietnams.

Nixon summed up his general approach in a lengthy report to Congress on February 18, 1970, on the state of the nation's foreign policy. In essence he called for a lowered profile for the United States in world affairs, a greater emhasis upon partnership and self-help in dealing with America's allies and friends, and continued efforts at detente with the Soviet Union. Despite his earlier reputation as an anti-communist hardliner, Nixon apparently accepted a real balance of terror with the Soviet Union in the number of ICBM's possessed by each country. By 1971, Russia had an estimated 1,440 land-based ICBM's to America's 1,054, while trailing in submarine Polaris-type missiles by 350 to 656. A twenty-year-period of clear American superiority in nuclear weapons thus was practically over, although the United States retained a lead in deliverable warheads, 4,600 to 2,000, and in manned strategic bombers. The SALT talks did go on in a hopeful climate, while both mighty antagonists continued to develop improved multiple warheads for their missiles and ABM systems. Nixon announced plans to reduce the manpower level of American forces fairly sharply after the war in Vietnam ended. The President's highly successful visit to Communist Rumania in 1969 also indicated a more flexible foreign policy in an age of resurgent nationalism within the "free" and communist worlds. Finally, the Nixon administration indicated a readiness to improve relations with Red China and to let it into the U.N. The celebrated "ping-pong" diplomatic gambit—China invited an American table tennis group to tour its country in 1971—seemed to indicate that China also desired to "normalize" relations. The stage was set for a dramatic rapprochement between the two powers, to Russia's obvious distress. After a secret flight to Peking by Henry Kissinger, the President's foreign policy adviser, Nixon announced in July, 1971 that he would visit the People's Republic of China sometime before May, 1972. Subsequently the United States openly advocated Peking's admission to the U.N. General Assembly and a place on the Security Council, while retaining an Assembly seat for the Taiwan regime. In October, 1917 the General Assembly admitted China but expelled Taiwan. An era of confrontation seems over and one of negotiation about to begin.

While seeking detente with the Soviet Union, and negotiations with Red China, Nixon anxiously sought to avoid weakening America's national prestige or credibility in world affairs by a hasty withdrawal from Vietnam and domestic debates over foreign policy. He feared that such actions might encourage Russia or Red China to dangerous adventurism abroad. The Middle East seemed to present precisely that kind of danger.

In 1967, an Egypt emboldened with Soviet arms forced withdrawal of the U.N. truce team and made threatening gestures toward Israel. Fearful of a concerted Arab attack, Israel launched the lightning Six Days War, June 5–10, 1967, inflicting devastating defeats upon Egypt, Jordan, and Syria. Israeli forces drove across Sinai to the bank of the Suez Canal and occupied parts of Jordan and Syria. Yet though Israel triumphed more decisively than in 1956, she still failed to obtain a formal peace and Arab recognition. Fearing a direct confrontation, both the United States and the Soviet Union carefully refrained from threats or direct involvement in the fighting. After a U.N. truce, Russia again rearmed Egypt and

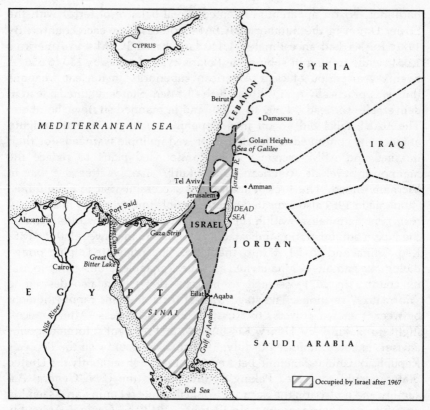

The Middle East and the Six Days' War, 1967

this time sent comparatively large numbers of Russian military personnel to aid Nasser. This expansion of Soviet power and influence into the Mediterranean disturbed the American government. Apparently Moscow also perceived the dangers of a new confrontation. The situation resulted in four-power talks to try to find some route to a Middle Eastern settlement. The resumption of shelling along the Suez front and Israeli air raids deep into Egypt, with reports that Soviet pilots were flying Egyptian fighters, spurred the development of a new peace bid. Secretary of State William Rogers obtained Soviet cooperation in a proposed cease-fire and Arab-Israeli talks through a U.N. mediator. In August of 1970, the two superpowers persuaded their "client" states to agree to a three-month truce. During that truce, a threatened collapse of King Hussein of Jordan, locked in battle with Palestinian refugee guerrilla organizations, caused Nixon to put on a display of American naval power in the Mediterranean in order to warn the Soviets to restrain Nasser. Hussein survived, and Nasser's death in September seemed to have a sobering effect in the region.

A flare-up of the Cuban crisis also threatened Soviet-American relations, but the Nixon administration handled it successfully. In the fall of 1970, indications that the Soviets might construct a naval base in Cuba for missile-firing submarines alarmed Washington authorities. A major crisis similar to that in 1962 seemed in the offing. Stern warnings from the White House, however, obtained Soviet reassurances that no bases were being constructed and that no other activities would be undertaken to contravene the Kennedy-Khrushchev agreement in 1962.

6. AFTER THE COLD WAR?

What can be forecast for the decade of the 1970's? Three tentative conclusions perhaps can be offered with some degree of assurance. First, the Soviet Union and the United States appear to have found new means of approaching problems, or at least to have adopted new forms of competition between communist and noncommunist worlds. Regardless of any temporary advantage that the United States or the Soviet Union may achieve over the other in the number or types of nuclear weapons, each possesses more than enough to destroy its opponent. Since 1962 both powers have indicated by words and actions that they recognize this balance of terror and want to avoid a direct confrontation. A degree of detente thus seems a fact of international life for the future, barring some unusual development by one side or the other. Second, America's policy of global containment reached its highwater mark during the Johnson presidency and has receded since. The Vietnam War and its divisive effects within the United States seem to insure that the Nixon administration and its successors will hesitate about future armed intervention abroad. Moreover, American officials and the public now perceive more clearly than before that the communist world is no longer a Moscow-ruled monolith, and that nationalist and socialist revolutions within the underdeveloped world do not necessarily represent threats to America's vital interests. Third and finally, the abnormal situation of a bipolar world that prevailed since 1945 seems near an end. Indications of this change abound: nationalism and polycentrism have weakened or destroyed the Soviet Union's former dominance of the communist world; an affluent Europe shows less inclination than in the past to defer to American leadership; Red China is emerging as a great nuclear power; and Japan, while relatively disarmed at present, has become one of the economic giants of the modern world. By the early 1970's, although still the world's leading economic power, the United States suffered from an adverse balance of trade, resulting largely from war inflation, heavy overseas investments, and foreign aid. President Nixon responded by halting the redemption of foreign-held dollars in gold, thus abandoning the international system established at Bretton Woods in 1944, and by imposing a temporary surtax on imports to reduce the outward flow of dollars. New states in Africa and Europe now comprise a large majority within the U.N. General Assembly, and India conceivably may join the ranks of the great powers. Undoubtedly the United States and the Soviet Union long will remain the two most powerful states in the world, but within an international system containing a number of other very strong states independent of their influence. A two-power world, created by the Second World War, is giving way to what might be viewed as a multipower world. Whether these developments auger for good or ill remains a question for the future to answer.

Additional Reading

On the Kennedy foreign policy, see the works listed at the end of the last chapter. An excellent account of the Johnson years as seen from inside the White House is by Eric F. Goldman, *The Tragedy of Lyndon Johnson* (1968, 1969). Goldman depicts Johnson as an immensely able and ambitious chief executive undone by his own hubris. Also good is another "inside" account, *The Limits of Intervention* (1969), by Townsend Hoopes, that concentrates upon the Vietnam entanglement. The literature on Vietnam is voluminous and mostly highly partisan. Joseph Buttinger, *Vietnam: A Dragon Embattled* (2 vols., 1967) is a good detailed account, as is *The United States in Vietnam* (1967), by George M. Kahin and J. W. Lewis. Robert Scalapino, "We Cannot Accept a Communist Seizure in Vietnam," *New York Times Magazine*, December 11, 1966 argues the case for intervention. Critics include Arthur M. Schlesinger, Jr., *The Bitter Heritage* (1966) and R. N. Goodwin, *Triumph or Tragedy: Reflections on Vietnam* (1966). Other accounts of value are by journalist Bernard Fall, *The Two Viet Nams* (2nd rev. ed., 1967) and by Robert Shaplen, *The Lost Revolution: The U.S. in Vietnam* (1966) and *Time Out of Hand* (1970). Gabriel Kolko, *The Roots of American Foreign Policy: An Analysis of Power and Purpose* (1969) has written a New Left radical critique of the causes of American interventionism that few scholars will find convincing. For two perceptive analyses of the recent past and proposals for future policy, see Edmund Stillman and William Pfaff, *Power and Impotence: the Failure of America's Foreign Policy* (1966) and Hans Morgenthau, *A New Foreign Policy for the United States* (1967).

Appendix

President	Party	Secretary of State
George Washington (1789–1797)	Fed.	Thomas Jefferson, 1790–Dec., 1793 Edmund Randolph, 1794–Aug., 1795 Timothy Pickering, 1795–
John Adams (1797–1801)	Fed.	Timothy Pickering, –May, 1800 John Marshall, 1800–1801
Thomas Jefferson (1801–1809)	Rep.	James Madison, 1801–1809
James Madison (1809–1817)	Rep.	Robert Smith, 1809–April, 1811 James Monroe, 1811–1817
James Monroe (1817–1825)	Rep.	John Quincy Adams, 1817–1825
John Quincy Adams (1825–1829)	Rep.	Henry Clay, 1825–1829
Andrew Jackson (1829–1837)	Dem.	Martin Van Buren, 1829–May, 1831 Edward Livingston, 1831–May, 1833 Louis McLane, 1833–June, 1834 John Forsyth, 1834–

Martin Van Buren (1837–1841)	Dem.	John Forsyth, –1841
William Henry Harrison (March 4–Apr. 4, 1841)	Whig	Daniel Webster, 1841–
John Tyler (1841–1845)	Whig	Daniel Webster, –May, 1843 Abel P. Upshur, 1843–Feb., 1844 John C. Calhoun, 1844–1845
James K. Polk (1845–1849)	Dem.	James Buchanan, 1845–1849
Zachary Taylor (1849–1850)	Whig	John M. Clayton, 1849–July, 1850
Millard Fillmore (1850–1853)	Whig	Daniel Webster, 1850–Oct., 1852 Edward Everett, 1852–1853
Franklin Pierce (1853–1857)	Dem.	William L. Marcy, 1853–1857
James Buchanan (1857–1861)	Dem.	Lewis Cass, 1857–Dec. 14, 1860 Jeremiah S. Black, 1860–1861
Abraham Lincoln (1861–1865)	Rep.	William H. Seward, 1861–
Andrew Johnson (1865–1869)	Rep.	William H. Seward, –1869
Ulysses S. Grant (1869–1877)	Rep.	Elihu B. Washburne, March 5–16, 1869 Hamilton Fish, 1869–1877
Rutherford B. Hayes (1877–1881)	Rep.	William M. Evarts, 1877–1881
James A. Garfield (Mar. 4–Sept. 19, 1881)	Rep.	James G. Blaine, 1881–
Chester A. Arthur (1881–1885)	Rep.	James G. Blaine –Dec., 1881 Frederick T. Frelinghuysen, 1881–1885
Grover Cleveland (1885–1889)	Dem.	Thomas F. Bayard, 1885–1889

Benjamin Harrison (1889–1893)	Rep.	James G. Blaine, 1889–June, 1892 John W. Foster, 1892–1893
Grover Cleveland (1893–1897)	Dem.	Walter Q. Gresham, 1893–May, 1895 Richard Olney, 1895–1897
William McKinley (1897–1901)	Rep.	John Sherman, 1897–April, 1898 William R. Day, Apr. 28–Sept. 16, 1898 John Hay, 1898–
Theodore Roosevelt (1901–1909)	Rep.	John Hay, –July, 1905 Elihu Root, 1905–1909 Robert Bacon, Jan. 27–Mar. 5, 1909
William H. Taft (1909–1913)	Rep.	Philander C. Knox, 1909–1913
Woodrow Wilson (1913–1921)	Dem.	William Jennings Bryan, 1913–June, 1915 Robert Lansing, 1915–Feb., 1920 Bainbridge Colby, 1920–1921
Warren G. Harding (1921–1923)	Rep.	Charles Evans Hughes, 1921–
Calvin Coolidge (1923–1929)	Rep.	Charles Evans Hughes, –1925 Frank B. Kellogg, 1925–1929
Herbert C. Hoover (1929–1933)	Rep.	Henry L. Stimson, 1929–1933
Franklin D. Roosevelt (1933–1945)	Dem.	Cordell Hull, 1933–Nov., 1944 Edward R. Stettinius, 1944–
Harry S. Truman (1945–1953)	Dem.	Edward R. Stettinius, –June, 1945 James F. Byrnes, 1945–Jan., 1947 George C. Marshall, 1947–Jan., 1949 Dean Acheson, 1949–1953

Dwight David Eisenhower (1953–1961)	Rep.	John Foster Dulles, 1953–Apr., 1959 Christian A. Herter, 1959–1961
John F. Kennedy (1961–1963)	Dem.	Dean Rusk, 1961–
Lyndon B. Johnson (1963–1969)	Dem.	Dean Rusk, –1969
Richard M. Nixon (1969–	Rep.	William Rogers, 1969–

Index

tion, 203; and Reciprocal Trades Agreement Act, 346; treaty, between Japan and western powers (1866), 148; U.S., and postwar Latin American trade, 433–434; U.S. protective policy, 325–326

Taylor, Gen. Maxwell, 438

Taylor, Zachary, 12th U.S. President, 124, 128, 137

Tea Act of 1773, 3

Tecumseh, Chief, 67

Tehran Conference (1943), 384–385

Teller Amendment (1898), 208

Tenth Inter-American Conference, Caracas, 1954, 434

Ten Years' War (Spain-Cuba, 1868–1878), 203

Tet Offensive (Vietnam War), 459–460

Texas, 84, 88; action by J.Q. Adams on, 107; declaration of independence by, 116; emigration to, 114, 116; entry into Union, 118–120; expansion of U.S. into, 80; Jefferson's attempted inclusion in Louisiana Purchase of, 80; Mexican control of, 115–118; Polk on, 108; U.S. exchange for East Florida of, 83

Texas Republic: foreign recognition of, 117–118; U.S. recognition of, 117

Thailand: member of SEATO, 426; U.S. troops in, 457

Thames, Battle of the, 67

Thoreau, Henry, 127

Tientsin, Treaty of (1858), 145

Tigre Island, 137

Tippecanoe, 62

Tito, Josip Broz, liberator of Yugoslavia, 401, 402

Tojo, Gen. Hideki, 369

Tonkin Resolution, Gulf of (1964), 458, 459, 461

totalitarianism, 298; rise in Europe of, 337–338

Townshend Duty Act of 1767, 3

Toynbee, Arnold, 276

Tracy, Benjamin F., 191

Trafalgar, battle at, 50

Trans-Continental Treaty (1819), 81–84, 105

Transjordan, 428

Trans-Siberian Railway, 255

travelers, British, effect on Anglo-American relations of, 99–101

treaties and agreements, U.S., (for page numbers of references, find each entry as listed alphabetically throughout index): Adams-Onís Treaty; Alaska purchase treaty; Algericas, Act of; Alliance, Treaty of (1778); Alliance for Progress; Amity and Commerce, Treaty of (1778); Atlantic Charter; Baghdad Pact; Bidlack Treaty; Brussels Pact; Bucareli agree-

ment; Burlingame Treaty; Casablanca conference; Clayton-Bulwer Treaty; commercial treaty (U.S.-Great Britain, 1815); Convention of 1800; Convention of 1818; Dumbarton Oaks Conference; Erskine Agreement; European Defense Community; Final Declaration at Geneva; Four Power Declaration; Four Power Pact; Gadsden Purchase; Gentlemen's Agreement; Ghent, Peace of; Guadalupe Hidalgo, Treaty of; Haitian-U.S. treaty; Harris Treaty; Hay–Bunua-Varilla Treaty; Hay-Herran Treaty; Hay-Pauncefote Treaty (1900, 1901); House-Grey Memorandum; Japanese-American commerical treaty (1894, 1911); Japanese-American Security Treaty; Jay's Treaty; Johnson-Clarendon Convention; Kellogg-Briand Pact; Knox-Castrillo Convention; Lansing-Ishii Agreement; League of Nations, Covenant of; London, Declaration of; Monroe-Pinckney Treaty; Môrtefontaine, Convention of; New Granada Treaty; Nine Power Pact; North Atlantic Treaty; Nuclear Nonproliferation Treaty; Nuclear Test Ban Treaty; Organization of American States; Oregon Treaty; Pan American Treaty; Peace Treaty of 1783; Perry Treaty; Pinckney's Treaty; Platt Amendment; Potsdam conference; Pre-Armistice Agreement; Progress, Alliance for; Reciprocity, Treaty of (U.S.–Hawaii); Reciprocity Treaty (Canada–U.S.); Root-Takahira Agreement; Root Treaties; Rush-Bagot Convention; San Ildefonso, Treaty of; San Lorenzo, Treaty of; Southeast Asia Treaty Organization; Spain, U.S. 1819 treaty with; Strategic Arms Limitation Treaty; Taft-Katsura Agreed Memorandum; Tientsin, Treaty of; Trans-Continental Treaty; Utrecht, Treaty of; Versailles Treaty; Wanghia, Treaty of; Washington, Treaty of; Webster-Ashburton Treaty

Trent affair, 157–158

Tripartite Alliance (1940), 370, 371

Triple Alliance (1882–1915), 224

Triple Entente (1904–1907), 224

Tripolitan War (1801–1805), 52–53

Trist, Nicholas P., 128, 129–130

Trollope, Frances, 100

Trujillo, Gen. Rafael Leonides, 450

Truman, Harry S., 33d U.S. President, 392, 413; decision to unify Korea, 416; and Great Debate, 417–419; and Indochina War, 454; on leaving western troops in Soviet Zone, 393; at Potsdam Conference, 394; reaction to totalitarianism by, 403; Soviet Union policy of, 392; and